AMERICAN PHILOSOPHY

AMERICAN PHILOSOPHY

THE EARLY SCHOOLS

BY

I. WOODBRIDGE RILEY, Ph. D.

Johnston Research Scholar in Johns Hopkins
University. Some Time Professor in the
University of New Brunswick

NEW YORK / RUSSELL & RUSSELL

FIRST PUBLISHED IN 1907
REISSUED, 1958, BY RUSSELL & RUSSELL
A DIVISION OF ATHENEUM PUBLISHERS, INC.
L. C. CATALOG CARD NO: 58-13298
PRINTED IN THE UNITED STATES OF AMERICA

To
JAMES MARK BALDWIN

PREFACE

THIS volume is the result of a three years' tenure as Henry E. Johnston, Jr., scholar in Johns Hopkins University. Written almost wholly from first hand sources, a large part of which exists only in manuscript, it attempts to reconstruct a period of philosophy but little studied and imperfectly understood. Its aim being both historical and biographical, the work seeks to present tendencies and movements through their personal channels. Hence there are given, in order, the psychological characteristics and intellectual development of each of the more important thinkers, an exposition of his system under the proper metaphysical captions, a summary of his doctrines, and the transitional relations to predecessors and successors, both at home and abroad. Here it is necessary to quote copiously the writers discussed, to let each man speak for himself, for, in the absence of any source book of American philosophy, it has been found necessary to present, in their original form, materials scattered, inaccessible, or almost unknown.

In writing this preliminary study, to be followed by others in an historical series, I have been especially indebted to Professor J. Mark Baldwin of Johns Hopkins University, to whom I have the honour of dedicating this volume; to Professor George T. Ladd of Yale University, my chief instructor in philosophy; to Professor Josiah Royce of Harvard University, for his generosity in founding the Royce Collection of philosophic Americana; and to Dr. Henry W. Rankin, of Brooklyn, New York, for the use of his valuable materials on American speculation. In addition to the library authorities in the older universities and historical societies, I beg to acknowledge kindly assistance of various sorts furnished by Professor F. J. E. Woodbridge, of Columbia University; Professor A. Campbell Fraser, of Edinburgh University; Dr. Benjamin Rand, of Harvard University; Professor E. H. Griffin and Dr. W. D. Furry, of Johns Hopkins University; Dr.

V. L. Collins, and Professors A. L. Jones and John DeWitt, of Princeton University; Professor W. R. Newbold, of the University of Pennsylvania; Professor H. N. Gardiner of Smith College; Professor F. B. Dexter, of Yale University; Professor A. C. Armstrong, of Wesleyan University; Professor M. M. Curtis, of Western Reserve University.

I. W. R.

CONTENTS

ix

x CONTENTS

BOOK V—REALISM

INTRODUCTION

I

HISTORICAL SURVEY

I THINK that in no country in the civilised world is less attention paid to philosophy than in the United States. The
Americans have no philosophical school of their own; and
they care but little for all the schools into which Europe
is divided, the very names of which are scarcely known to
them.'[1] With this statement the French traveller, Alexis de
Tocqueville, began his chapter on philosophical methods among the
Americans. Uttered in 1835, at the close of the period of the early
schools, this sweeping generalisation was based on the assumption
that in a political democracy there could be no intellectual aris-
tocracy, that in a rule of the most there could survive little of
the thought of the best, and that an entire country, two hundred
years after its settlement, could offer scarcely anything beyond
backwoods philosophies, or speculations from log cabins.

Hence it was by a kind of historical paradox that it remained
for a modern Frenchman to qualify his compatriot's remarks, to
show that while the early Americans may have had no distinctive
philosophical schools of their own, they still paid some attention
to philosophy, and cared considerably for the speculative schools
of Europe. Father F. L. van Becelaere, like a modern Diogenes
Laertius, was the first to go through the country in the philosopher's cloak, to glean the scattered traditions of the past, to discover that there was scarcely a metaphysical movement in the old
world which was not reflected in the new. In his invaluable
brochure,[2] the Thomistic scholar has shown that the American
spirit was receptive of speculative thought, that the men of the
first settlement, despite their struggle for existence against climate
and soil, aborigines and foreign enemies, often took the high

[1] *Democracy in America,* New York, 1898, Part II., Book I., Chapter I.
[2] *La Philosophie en Amérique, depuis les Origines jusqu'à nos Jours,*
New York, 1904. (With an introduction by Josiah Royce.)

a priori road; that the men of the colonial period, despite the preponderance of orthodox clerical influences, were not without liberty
in philosophising; and that the men of the succeeding era, despite
the mischances of war and the levelling tendencies of the philosophy
of common sense, did not suffer from entire metaphysical depres-
sion. All these subjects, together with chapters on the influence
of German transcendentalism, the doctrine of evolution, and the
present idealism, form the most valuable work on the development
of philosophy in America which has yet appeared. Nevertheless,
much is left to be done in presenting a connected story of the
growth of opinion in the land. The account of the French scholar
is expository rather than critical; it suggests, but does not evaluate
the different tendencies of speculation in their reciprocal influences
and complicated interrelations. It gives a great number of interesting personal details and local traditions, but it fails to present,
in its larger aspects, a history of the most important movements
as they crossed from Europe to America, developed during two
centuries, and slowly grew into the more typical native philosophy
of Emerson.

For such deficiencies there are adequate excuses: what was said
of Cousin in his relation to the Scottish, may be said of Père van
Becelaere in his relation to the American thinking; it could not
be expected of a foreigner that he should thoroughly comprehend
the state of the country when its peculiar philosophy arose, nor
be able to estimate its relation to the national character.[1] And
so, to take an obvious example, there arises the French Catholic's
air of bewilderment at the vagaries of Calvinism, his astonishment at what has been called the refined New England school
through whose veins slowly coursed a mixture of ink and ice-
water. And since the author, even with his scholastic training,
stands apart from the frigid philosophy of Puritanism, he is unable
to comprehend the succeeding movements of recoil, to perceive
how the intensity of subjective introspection, in a movement like
idealism, naturally led to an empirical study of objective phenomena, in a movement like materialism.

In neglecting this principle of action and reaction, whereby

[1] James McCosh, *The Scottish Philosophy*, New York, 1874, p. 1.

satiety in one course of intellectual diet prepares the palate to relish the next, it has likewise escaped the notice of the French writer how the early schools fall into the scheme of his compatriot, Auguste Comte,—Puritanism representing the theological stage, in which all events, all causes are referred to the action of super-human beings; idealism and deism representing the metaphysical period, in which causative power is ascribed to metaphysical entities like supersensible archetypes, and eternal laws of nature; and materialism and natural realism representing the so-called stage of positive science, in which metaphysical principles are recognised as mere abstractions or fictions, and both science and philosophy are restricted to the observation, classification and prevision of phenomena.[1] But the Comtean generalisation, though highly suggestive, is not wholly sound—being justifiable in a relative, not an absolute way, holding true not so much in a dynamic as a static sense. In a word, it furnishes not a necessary programme of successive stages in the development of thought, but rather a convenient classification of modes of thinking, which, as Francis Bowen has pointed out, may coexist in many, perhaps in most, thoughtful and inquiring minds.[2]

Therefore, in giving an historical summary of the progress of philosophical thought in America, further guiding principles are to be sought. Here native writers have studied the subject both from the point of view of directive tendencies and ultimate sources, considering the matter both as *Kultur-Geschichte* and as *Quellen-Suche*. Thus Professor Sanborn, referring to the colonial and early national periods, has used the term philosophy as indicating the guide of life, the exponent and directress of national existence, rather than a certain metaphysical insight, fruitful of speculation, even when barren of results. Again, in describing the phases of thought in America, he has in part traced their sources. He attributes the Puritanic philosophy, represented by Edwards, to Calvinism with English modifications; the philanthropic philosophy, represented by Franklin, to realism; the ideal or vital philosophy, represented by Emerson, to German transcendentalism. For the

[1] Francis Bowen, *Modern Philosophy*, New York, 1877, p. 264.
[2] *Ib.*, p. 265.

intermediate phase, the negation of philosophy between 1820 and 1850, no sufficient representative has been found.[1] This classification is suggestive but inadequate. The intermediate period, as Professor Curtis has shown, was important for the rise of a type of French eclecticism, moving on the lines of Cousin, Jouffroy and Constant, significant as a protest against the realism of the Scotch school, so dominant in the ordinary American college.[2]

Another outline of speculative movements has been given in an essay of John Fiske. He traces the rise of liberal thought in America to two sources: First, the secularised Gallio spirit that deems it folly to interpose obstacles in the way of the natural workings of reason and common sense; this deadens into the worldliness typified in Franklin. Second, the intense devotion to spiritual ideals which, in spite of all inherited encumbrances of bigotry and superstition, never casts off its allegiance to reason as the final arbiter. This may commit many an error, but its drift is toward the light and stimulus and exaltation of life typified by Emerson.[3] Here is a general characterisation of two divergent rationalistic tendencies, utilitarianism and transcendentalism; it is followed by a more particular classification and the introduction of two philosophic movements not previously mentioned. In addition to a transplanted Elizabethan Puritanism, Fiske introduces Quakerism as a phase of Puritanism more liberal than Independency, and as a more notable advance in the direction of individualism. Further in the course of the eighteenth century came deism from England. Here 'Tom' Paine had some influence, but no appreciable effect was produced by the atheism of the French encyclopedists, which was a reaction mainly emotional and aided by the shallowest of metaphysics against the effete ecclesiastical system of France.[4] This statement as to the Anglo-French deism is valid as to its importation but not as to its influence. The definition of deism as a quiet religion of humanity, which sets little store by miracles or abstruse doctrines, or the divine authority

---

[1] F. B. Sanborn, *Journal of Speculative Philosophy,* Vol. 17, p. 401, ff.
[2] M. M. Curtis, *Western Reserve University Bulletin,* April, 1896.
[3] *Liberal Thought in America,* Buffalo, 1897.
[4] *Ibid.*

of scripture, would apply to Franklin but not to Jefferson. The former had the strong, prosaic common sense of the British deist, the latter was practically gallicised in temperament and belief. Jefferson's deism, before his chance acquaintance with Dugald Stewart, was akin to the creed of his friends, the *idéologues,* while his naturalism, borrowed from the encyclopedists, was reflected in his political tractates, from the measure for religious freedom in Virginia, to the Declaration of Independence itself.[1] Passing beyond the colonial period, Fiske's description of New England transcendentalism is better than his resolution of the forces back of it. He says that early in the nineteenth century the most advanced phase of liberal thought was represented by the Massachusetts Unitarians, who were trying to hold an intermediate position, half way between narrow orthodoxy and untrammelled free thinking. The ground was cut from under them by the transcendentalists, whose native temperaments, akin to Edwards, were stimulated by a brief contact with Kantian and post-Kantian speculation in Germany. In accounting for transcendentalism Fiske has gone back to Puritanism as represented by Edwards. The latter's practical negation of free will, he contends, resulted in a reaction toward Arminianism and Methodism, his doctrine of predestination toward Universalism, his doctrine of original sin and atonement against Trinitarianism and towards Unitarianism.[2] In this emphasis of the theological at the expense of the philosophical Fiske has given the remote and neglected the immediate causes of the New England idealism. As will be observed later, the negations of the deists immediately preceding Emerson furnished the positive points of departure for the Concord school. As against Voltairean atheists and Lockean sensationalists, Frothingham, the historian of transcendentalism, declared that man has by his spiritual nature an intuitive knowledge of God, as a being infinite and absolute in power, wisdom, and goodness, a direct perception like to that which the senses have of material objects.[3]

Beside these three interrelated movements—Puritanism, deism and transcendentalism—a fourth has been recently recognised.

[1] See below, Book III., Chapters V. and VI.

[2] Fiske, *Liberal Thought.*

[3] *Transcendentalism in New England,* New York, 1876, p. 189.

Professor Adam Leroy Jones has given a valuable exposition of the idealism of the Yale scholars, Samuel Johnson and Jonathan Edwards,—the former as taken directly from Berkeley, the latter as derived independently from Locke.[1] It is further stated that the philosophy of these men was not an outgrowth of the theology they were taught, despite the influence upon the colonial Puritans of the Cambridge Platonists, of Malebranche, and of his follower Norris. It is moreover asserted that Edwards worked out his idealism early in life, before he was wholly dominated by the received dogmas, but it has not been suggested whence these peculiar notions of external reality were derived. Edwards' mystic experiences, his youthful trances and apparent ravishments of soul out of body, furnish perhaps a new, at any rate, a probable psychological explanation of his early convincement of the unreality of the material world. Edwards' mysticism gave way to the exigencies of his Puritanism, just as the Berkeleian idealism, which gained a foothold at Yale and Princeton, was pushed aside by the Scottish realism. But mysticism as a doctrine of the inner light, as a means of secret knowledge, had elsewhere a development strangely at variance with the prevalent objective assurance of the age of reason. President Noah Porter has maintained that philosophy in America, as in England, has been prosecuted chiefly as an applied science and in its special relations to morals, politics and theology. Not a few of the early planters were men of decided speculative tastes, who were familiar with the abstract philosophy of their times; but their interest being chiefly practical, they fell back upon the fundamental principles of political and ethical science, because of their desire for political independence.[2] But thus to reduce colonial thinking to mere empiricism is to shut the eyes to a curiously antithetical movement which was prevalent at this time among certain peaceful and obscure men. During the very period when the revolutionary leaders were gathering paper ammunition from the political notions of Locke and Hobbes, and the social contract theories of Montesquieu and the conti-

[1] *Early American Philosophers*, New York, 1898, pp. 23, 47.
[2] Appendix to Ueberweg, *History of Philosophy*, New York, 1874, Vol. 2, p. 442.

nental jurists, colonial mysticism reached its bloom. In the year previous to the Address to the King was published the *Journal* of the New Jersey Quaker, John Woolman, a book which Charles Lamb has pronounced a classic of the inner life. In the year of the adoption of the Constitution, the Ephrata brotherhood of Pennsylvania pietists issued their *Göttliche Wunderschrift,* the culmination of a long series of publications based on mediæval theosophists like Tauler and Ruysbroeck. Of the sources, meaning and tendencies of this movement only a little can be said in a formal history of philosophy, for this current of occultism was lost in a broader stream of thought which flowed through these regions.

It was in Pennsylvania that the important and hitherto neglected movement of materialism took its rise and spread over the whole South. To this fact Northern writers have been blind, for New Englanders, whether from a certain spirit of condescension, or from a habit of self-satisfied introspection, have failed to take much notice of what lay beyond their borders. This movement will be described in its proper place; but it may here be remarked that its amplification is of great importance, since it tends to give a right proportion, to restore a proper balance in the estimate of the speculative forces in the land. In previous studies the sections north of Mason and Dixon's line have been considered to have had the preponderance of authority on their side; rightly considered, materialism was cherished by as weighty minds as was the conventional spiritualism, in the old and respectable sense of that term. The clerical heads of the colonial colleges were in the numerical majority,[1] yet there was a large class of scientists like Doctor Rush of Philadelphia, and of free-thinkers like President Jefferson of Virginia, who welcomed the objective solidities offered by a study of the body as well as of the mind, of the physiological as well as the psychological.

With this preliminary notice of materialism, it is in order to proceed to a brief summary of the various philosophical movements as they arose and developed along the Atlantic seaboard. These

[1] Cf. A. C. Armstrong, *Philosophy in American Colleges, Educational Review,* January, 1897, p. 11.

movements were five in number: First, Puritanism as it sprang from English sources; second, deism, or free-thinking, as it began in reaction against a narrow Calvinism and ended with the revolutionary French scepticism; third, idealism, as it arose spontaneously with Jonathan Edwards and was fostered by the Irish Bishop Berkeley, through his adherent Samuel Johnson; fourth, Anglo-French materialism, as it came over with Joseph Priestley and developed in Philadelphia and the South; fifth, realism, or the philosophy of common sense, as it was imported directly from Scotland, and came to dominate the country until the advent of the German transcendentalism. These five movements, extending over the two hundred years between 1620 and 1820, constitute the early schools. Primarily, they are to be studied in and of themselves as they reciprocally attracted or mutually repelled one another; but secondarily, they have a further interest in their affiliations and connections with an older civilisation. Traced to their sources, they may all be said to have organic relations with a parent stock, to be but the transatlantic offshoots of the European tree of knowledge. Yet these manifold dependencies do not rightly deprive the early schools of the right to be counted as independent entities. Again and again has American philosophy been declared a thing of no moment, because lacking in originality. But, as has been well observed, it must be remembered that originality is a highly relative term in speculative philosophy, and that there is no modern system that has not its roots and antecedents in the past.[1] Or, to employ the words of Milton, ' as wine and oil are imported to us from abroad, so must ripe understanding be imported into our minds from foreign writings.' Granting, then, that a philosophy may be indigenous, though it receive its stimulus from outside, one may go on to consider whence the nation obtained its materials, and how it went on to develop its own constructive work. As has been intimated, among the foreign influences in American philosophy the British was predominant: first in the English sensationalism of Locke, then in the Irish idealism of Berkeley, and lastly in the Scotch realism of Reid and his followers. Succeeding the British came the French influence: first a trace of the naturalism of Montesquieu, then the materialism

[1] Curtis, *Outline*, p. 1.

of La Mettrie, lastly the eclecticism of the positivists. Finally came the German influence: first in the distorted form of mystic illumination, then as indirectly embodied in New England transcendentalism, lastly as directly known in the works of the Kantian and post-Kantian idealists.

In recognising this dependence upon foreign ways of thinking, a dependence so steady and constant as to furnish an almost chronological reduplication of the European cycles, it is only fair to insist that American philosophy, as a whole, is not a mere incoherent eclecticism. Until the coming of the monism of New England, the country may not have offered a single consistent and predominant system, but the various phases of belief, through which the men of the seventeenth and eighteenth centuries passed, formed essential stages in the development of a national self-conciousness. Men did not pick up whatever happened to be within reach, they selected and chose what best suited the real cravings of their nature. For example, the universal demand for life, liberty and the pursuit of happiness was no chance grasping of a revolutionary bauble, it was a positive substitute, by means of the deistic conceptions of activity, freedom and optimism, for the unsatisfying negations of the Calvinistic doctrines of passivity, determinism and pessimism. Therefore, while it may be acknowledged that American philosophy has had but little direct influence on the main currents of the world's speculative thought,[1] those larger currents have been turned, directed and utilised in America in a way which betokens no small originality. In the colonial period, as fitted a state of political dependency, the country may have been more imitative than creative; but after the second war with England, and especially with the coming of transcendentalism, there arose a form of thought which though derivative was yet new, old materials being presented in a novel combination. Rejecting the Puritanic determinism and deistic transcendence, accepting the idealistic immanence and the materialistic naturalism, Emerson contributed to his country a unique and welcome type of eclecticsm, a pantheism which was as filled with optimism as its author was filled with the joy of living. Believing in an Absolute One and All, which through countless transformations maintains itself in un-

[1] H. N. Gardiner, *Philosophical Review*, Vol. 9, p. 573.

impaired splendour and strength, the Concord philosopher, not
with an air of professional cheerfulness, but of profound trust in
nature as the embodiment of an invisible archetype, called on his
countrymen to 'come forth into the azure and worship the day.'
Here was a form of belief which though derivative as to its raw
materials was yet novel as a finished product, a system rooted and
grounded in the past, but still possessing a fresh and native air of
originality. New England transcendentalism was a pantheism, a
belief that the universe, nature and God are all one and the same
thing, yet it was no dark philosophy of the unconscious, leading
to the world-weariness of the continental fatalism. With the latter
doctrine Emerson was familiar because of his Calvinistic antecedents, but from that doctrine he was at the same time free.
Descendant of Puritans, the age of reason lay like a golden veil
between him and the age of inscrutable decrees. Hence it came
about that in place of the strange and overwhelming mischances
of this world, he would substitute the orderly and comprehensive
course of nature, and, extending that spirit of optimistic rationalism
to human nature, in place of the depravity of man and special
providences for the elect, he would substitute the dignity of
humanity, the rights of the individual, the excellence of self-
reliance.

In these teachings there are of course to be recognised the echoes
of foreign thought, the rational elements being suggestive of Leibniz and his theodicy, the ethical of Kant and his categorical im-
perative. But this does not mean that New England transcendentalism was more imitative than indigenous. Those who grew
up with the movement have inclined to the latter view, contending
that, although Emerson used an imported veneer of technical terms,
the solid framework of his system was already in existence; later
critics, more skilled in tracing historical sources, have inclined to
the imitative view, contending that without the foreign phraseology, such as was furnished by Coleridge's *Aids to Reflection,*
Emerson would have been inarticulate, if not ineffective. These
views are discrepant, but not irreconcilable; the compromise between the traditional and the academic points of view lies in this,
that the transcendental movements at home and abroad possessed

numberless common elements, were, each in its place, the resultants of similar causes. To instance but a few of these historic parallels,—the insistence on pure intuitions was a protest against the Hobbite materialism; the assertion of subjective principles of reason a protest against the Lockean negation of innate ideas; the avowal of synthetic judgments *a priori* a protest against the disintegrating Humean scepticism.

In this discovery that philosophical history repeats itself on both sides of the water lies the answer to the question, not only as to the originality of transcendentalism, but of American philosophy as a whole; it can now be said that, while there was no important intellectual movement of Europe which was not reflected in some measure among thoughtful minds in America, there was also no important movement which did not receive either local colour or a local habitation. This is conspicuously evident in what might be called the sectional distribution of the different types of speculation throughout the country. In its broader aspects the North stood for idealism, the South for materialism, and the Middle States for the mediating philosophy of common sense. In addition to this broader distribution there was a more precise localisation of the philosophical schools, since the places where they originated also depended upon the periods in which they originated. Here the larger colonial colleges, almost in the order of their founding, constituted so many radiating centres of speculation, Harvard being identified with deism, Yale with idealism, and Princeton with realism. This peculiar coincidence between the locality and chronology of the various schools tends to simplify the problem of the development of American philosophy: nevertheless such a treatment has its disadvantages. It tends to disregard Puritanism as a mere dark background, a primeval twilight from which the movements of illuminism emerged; it also confuses the relations between deism and the other rationalistic schools, for deism was more a mode of thinking than a system of thought, and as such affected the minds of idealists, materialists and realists alike. But though such a classification of schools leads to some overlapping of epochs, and some repetition of principles, it has the advantage of recognising both the dynamic and static aspects of the case. Taking account of temporalities, it recognises the growth, development and historical setting of the problems; taking account of environment, it recognises the dependence of one mind upon another, the quickening interaction between the various schools in their various localities.

Of these schools a brief summary may now be given in their more external aspects, and especially in their academic significance. It is noteworthy that in its earliest phases, the history of American philosophy is in great measure the history of the American colleges; not only did that philosophy grow with their growth and strengthen with their strength, but also through them it spread in ever widening circles over the land, and thereby gradually filtered down among the masses. In short, as was said well nigh a century ago, if one seeks for those of our ancestors who contributed most largely toward forming and rearing up the intellectual character of the nation, neglected and almost forgotten as their labours now are, and that amidst all the difficulties of a new and half-peopled country, one must look for instructors in provincial colleges, since it is now only from hasty and occasional publications, from hoarded manuscripts, or scanty tradition, that we are enabled to estimate the powers and acquirements of the Coldens, the Cutlers and the Edwards of the last century.[1] In this passage the relative importance of the ancient worthies is somewhat misrepresented, yet the suggested method of investigating their works is perfectly valid. So although it may be objected that the study of early American philosophy affords but a scanty contribution to knowledge, still its restoration furnishes a true opportunity for reconstruction from actual materials. To piece together, bit by bit, the most casual intellectual remains, is to discover that even in a mosaic of small minds there is a pattern common to the rest of the world.

Of all the systems that call for this process of reconstruction, the first is the most dry and the most forbidding. Puritanism has come down to us marked by the incoherences of a cult, rather than the sanities of culture. This tradition is misleading; Puritanism is a mighty maze but not without a plan, for the leaders in the

[1] *American Medical and Philosophical Journal,* October, 1812, p. 137.

New England way were not blind guides; indeed, those leaders who were responsible for the fundamental creeds and platforms of American Calvinism can scarcely be accused of lack of definite expression and clearness of vision. Applying the scholastic method learned at Oxford and Cambridge, their fault was rather seeing too much; minute philosophers, they perceived the most infinitesimal lines of difference, and applied them with a pitiless rigidity. Abstract distinctions between good and evil, for example, they turned into concrete distinctions between saint and sinner, saved and lost. But the matter did not stop with a logical libel on humanity; it was carried with an academic thoroughness from things human to things divine. Here the doctrine of the depravity of man, of hard and fast division between a chosen people and the unhappy remainder of mankind, was rendered possible by its attachment to the religious belief in the doctrine of predestination, and this in turn to the larger metaphysical conception of transcendence and determinism, or the conception of a deity who lives apart from the world, and still guides and governs that world in the smallest details.

Such, in brief, was Calvinism, the earliest phase of speculative thought in America. Being an imported system, the practical concern does not so much lie with its origin and analysis, as with the vicissitudes it underwent through the assaults of academic rationalism. As containing the substance of New England theology, the Boston platform of 1680 was originally made in England under the form of the Savoy Confession; but while relics of this platform were long cherished among the people, its workmanship was as little that of the popular artisan, as its demolition was that of the commonalty. Representatives of the people like Tom Paine and Ethan Allen may have given the hardest knocks to the structure, but its foundations were undermined by quieter and more insidious forces. It was the slow encroachment of rationalism, by way of the colleges, that brought about the disintegration of Calvinism. Here the most potent solvent was deism, or that view of the deity which represents him not merely as transcendent above the world and distinct from it, but also separate, that is, having once created the world he is not immanent in it as its providential ruler and guide, but allows it to pursue an independent course.[1] This is the classic definition of deism in its developed form: being of recent date, it does not wholly apply to the beginnings of the movement in question. Deism in America, during the first half of the eighteenth century, was of the constructive, not the destructive sort. Its earliest colonial representatives, like the father of English deism, argued from natural reason for the existence of God, the immortality of the soul, the certainty of rewards and punishments, and the life to come. The system was at first hardly distinguishable from theism; it was more akin to Butler's *Analogy* than to Hume's *Enquiry;* it took two generations to develop into the revolutionary systems of the doubting Thomases, Paine and Jefferson. Such deism was imbued with optimism and receptive of evidences of design; it was not as yet that thorough-going rationalism which would reduce religion to ethics, and revelation to a spiritual law in the natural world. Genetically, this deism arose in a partial reaction against high Calvinism; it taught the transcendence and benevolence of the deity, but not the depravity of man or the determinism of his moral actions. American deism, in its inceptive stages, thus marked a change from a theology to a theodicy; from the assumption of decrees inscrutable to the human mind, to an attempt to justify the ways of God to man. The movement began in a conservative way; its first defenders did not argue for natural religion in opposition to revealed, but for revealed religion as a necessary supplement to natural. How this movement developed through the aid of the colleges can be but suggested here. Veritable deistic principles were promulgated by Cotton Mather in 1702, reappeared in the teachings of Rector Clap of Yale, were carried by President Samuel Johnson to New York and thence to the College of Philadelphia. In a word, the unwritten history of deism in America is a fine illustration of the reversal of human judgment, for as another has observed, in going from the age of Edwards to the age of Franklin, one goes from the puritanic philosophy, where God is everything and man nothing, to the philanthropic

[1] G. v. Lechler's definition in Schaff-Herzog, *Encyclopedia,* New York, 1882, Vol. 1, p. 621.

philosophy, where man's welfare is everything and God's glory little or nothing.[1]

When Calvinism had suffered a complete inversion, deism also had its day. As if in fulfilment of the Comtean formula, the metaphysical, as well as the theological stage, was giving way to a more positivistic, or psychological. In America, as in Europe, the systematic impulse, repressed in the metaphysical field, took up the analysis of the human mind as a substitute.[2] Deism carried to extreme had become unimaginative and mechanical. The system as a cosmology, or world-plan, exhibited as much red tape as the foreign office of the British Government; as a teleology, or theory of design, it fulfilled ends as monotonously prearranged as a Sabbath in New England. And so, tired of a system which reigned, but did not govern, which was as inflexible as it was impersonal, tired of the workings of the heavens above, men began to look within themselves and found that the wonders of the celestial spheres were less interesting than the wonders of the human sensorium, the law of gravitation than the law of the association of ideas. Expressed superficially, there is nevertheless to be seen in all this a profound change going on. Putting one's self back in the latter part of the eighteenth century, it is evident that the age of objective thinking is being succeeded by the age of subjective thinking. As a theology has given way to a theodicy, so is a theodicy giving way to an anthropology,—the deductive study of the attributes of nature to an inductive study of the faculties of human nature. On all sides it is coming to be held that the proper study of mankind is man. So the old evidences of cosmic design are now relegated to the back shelves; in the place of Paley and Watts and Butler and the Bridgewater treatises are to be found books dealing with the mental processes of the individual. From England come Locke's *Inquiry on Human Understanding,* and Hartley's *Observations on Man;* from France Condorcet's *Progress of the Human Spirit* and La Mettrie's *Man a Machine;* from Scotland come the similar humanistic treatises of Hume, Reid and Stewart.

[1] F. B. Sanborn, *Journal of Speculative Philosophy,* Vol. 17, p. 403.
[2] Windelband, *History of Philosophy,* p. 457.

These are casual citations; they however indicate the course which the new empiricism was to take in the western world. Which of the three foreign schools became dominant may be easily imagined. Owing to the excesses of the Revolution in France, the Gallic philosophy, whether of the materialists or of the idealists, received an unmerited stigma. But while the English empiricism was considered safe in Locke, it was counted dubious, if not dangerous, in Hartley. This was the chance of the Scotch school in America. As Hutcheson and Beattie were early looked upon with approval, so Reid and Brown were endlessly edited, Dugald Stewart's works received their first complete publication, and the philosophy of Hamilton, purged of its Kantian elements, was declared by one of his pupils to be pre-eminently *the* American philosophy. To these general statements certain qualifications must necessarily be made. The Scottish realism was the most widely spread of any of the empirical influences, yet its influence varied greatly in different localities. New England, imbued with the idealistic traditions of Cudworth, Norris and Berkeley, was of too fine a spirit to be satisfied with the coarser methods of common sense: the South had too much of the Anglican indifference, too much of the Gallic scepticism, to accept as final the dogmatism of a small group of North British philosophers. Hume's *Essays,* indeed, were published in the Old Dominion, but the other Scottish books did not cross the Potomac until they were forced across. Consequently it remained for the Middle States, like the middle classes, to accept a way of thinking which was plain, practical, and easily applied to the affairs of life, to welcome what had been anciently called ' a summary knowledge of urgent truths suitable for people who are in a hurry.' In the propaganda of this common sense philosophy, as an antidote to the Voltairean infidelity and Humean pyrrhonism, the College of New Jersey was the chief agent. Natural realism, officially introduced into the country by President Witherspoon of Princeton, formed an entering wedge of thought which was destined to push aside the resisting masses of Southern materialism, and to deflect even the more intangible forces of Northern idealism. Of this idealism unfortunately but a brief account can ever be given. It is a very

regrettable thing in the history of speculation in America that the
movement which had the most promising inception and produced
the only writings which merit the name of philosophical classics,
had, in its final issues, the most meagre and unsatisfactory results.
The movement formally began under the auspices of the only
European philosopher of the first rank who visited the colonies; it
was fostered by the only early American philosopher whose fame
reached across the waters. When Berkeley visited Newport and
there wrote his *Minute Philosopher,* Jonathan Edwards had
already composed his youthful but remarkable *Notes on the Mind.*
Besides these two men there was another early idealist who has
been aptly described as ' the grand vicar of the immaterialistic faith
in America.' [1] Samuel Johnson of Yale College, after his personal intimacy with the Irish idealist, has been characterised as
' without doubt an acute and even profound thinker who entered
fully into the spirit of Berkeley's sense-symbolism and spiritual
causation.' [2] Cognisant of the Berkeleian phraseology and freed
from the rigidities of the Edwardean scheme, Johnson wrote his
Elementa Philosophica, consisting of *Noetica, or Things relating
to the mind or Understanding,* and *Ethica, or Things relating to
Moral Behaviour.* This little work was dedicated to the Bishop
of Cloyne and printed by Benjamin Franklin, yet it failed to receive much attention in the College at New York of which its
author was the first head.[3] In truth, even at King's College the
use of this work was thwarted by commercialism, just as it was
at Princeton by common sense, and at Philadelphia by the utilitarian
spirit. But it was in the New England institutions that Johnson's idealistic efforts received scantiest recognition. The oldest
of these institutions, with its prescription of Henry More,[4] might
have been expected to recognise the merits of Johnson's work,
which was based in part on Cudworth's conception of the mind as
a notional or representative world, a crystalline globe reflecting

[1] Georges Lyon, *Idéalisme en Angleterre,* Paris, 1888, p. 376.

[2] So Professor A. Campbell Fraser, in a letter to the writer, 9th July,
1906.

[3] *History of Columbia University,* New York, 1904, p. 450.

[4] Benjamin Rand, *Philosophical Instruction at Harvard,* (MS.).

the true and real world of being; for all that the American Neo-
Platonist seems never to have been mentioned at Harvard. But
if Johnson fared ill at New Cambridge, he fared worse at New
Haven. In his own institution, to which Berkeley himself had
donated his Newport library, the ' New Principle ' was considered
to be naught but a revival of the scholastic obscurantism, or as
it was expressed in some casual verse of the period:

> Substantial forms grown old are chang'd away
> A new substratum next is brought in play—
> Each scheme alike involves th' inquiring mind,
> In ten-fold darkness and a horrid gloom.[1]

This betrays a strangely narrow point of view, but it has its explanation; it is indicative of the panic fear that fell upon the Con-
gregational College when it was suspected that Johnson's idealism
was connected with his defection to Anglicanism.[2] Without entering into the validity of that suspicion, one cannot but regret that
through sectarian blindness Yale College lost a splendid opportunity to found a splendid school of thought.

This lack of appreciation shown towards immaterialism was
only equalled by that shown towards its metaphysical opposite.
Materialism in America has been hitherto considered but a casual
and episodic thing, whereas it was an orderly reproduction of the
European movement—deriving its mechanical notions from Newton, its psychological from Hobbes, its physical from Hartley and
Darwin, and, as the last step in this historic succession, approaching the sensualistic philosophy of the French schools. Nevertheless,
besides these larger historical connections, American materialism
had a double national significance, first, as a form of naturalism,
and in marked contrast to the austere idealism of the North, it
prevailed in sections other than New England, Philadelphia being
its radiating centre and the South the chief sphere of influence;
secondly, as a scientific movement, it was not the clergy but the
medical profession which sought to reduce mental activities to a

[1] John Hubbard, *The Benefactors of Yale College*, Boston, 1733, p. 9.
[2] Cf. letter of Jeremiah Dummer to Timothy Woodbridge, 3d July,
1743. (Col. Socy. of Mass. Trans., Vol. 6, p. 195.)

physiology of the nerves and to combine therewith the study of pathology and of the psychology of infants and of animals. Since practically nothing has been written of this early group of thinkers, who were in large measure forerunners of the modern age, a brief summary of their doctrines may here be given. Earliest of the colonial materialists was Cadwallader Colden of Philadelphia and New York; this graduate of Edinburgh University, combining the Newtonian mechanics with the ancient hylozoistic doctrine of a cosmic substance as itself intelligence, ultimately reached a kind of dynamic panpsychism, substance being conceived as a self-acting and universally diffused principle, whose essence is power and force. Of the native materialists the most original was Joseph Buchanan of Kentucky; following the Hobbite principles to the extreme, he denied to the soul an independent and immaterial existence, and asserted that mind is merely an organic state of matter. Next, with the advent of the celebrated chemist, Joseph Priestley, there was introduced into the country the modified Hartleian principle of the homogeneity of human nature, it being contended, against the anthropological dualists, that one substance may admit all the properties of man. Priestley's ideas were amplified by his colleague, Thomas Cooper of South Carolina, who, influenced not only by Hartley and Darwin, but by the French physiologists, reduced ideas of whatever kind to notions excited in the brain and there felt or perceived—judgment, reasoning, and reflection being not distinct entities, but particular states or functions of the cerebral mass. The last of the materialists was Benjamin Rush, who from his Princeton training was likewise precursory to the Scottish realism. Rush has been denominated the father of American psychiatry; he was, at least, the first American to combine lectures on abnormal psychology and psycho-therapeutics with a regular medical course, and the first to show the relations of those subjects to jurisprudence, for he appears to have recognised the existence of the criminal insane, the moral imbecile, whose morbid operations are to be considered not as vices, but as symptoms of disease. Rush and the Philadelphia school represent the most modern type of thought in the early period; but in addition to these veritable anticipators of present day views, there was a smaller group of thinkers who popularised, and thereby rendered somewhat ineffective, the more scientific views of their colleagues. These were the minor materialists, the dogmatic no-soul psychologists, whose insistence on a crass objectivism led in part to the subsequent recoil toward subjectivism and the belief in the Emersonian over-soul.

Here ends the historical survey of the early schools, those five chief movements, the resolution of whose forces alone furnishes a proper understanding of the coming transcendentalism. Meanwhile, without anticipating the results of this preliminary volume, one must consider another indication of the various historical elements which came to be bound together in a genetic development, and therein constituted an approach to the absolute principle of the later monism. This indication is furnished by the study of the interrelations of philosophy and politics. Here, as has been shown elsewhere,[1] the higher criticism plays its part; taking, for example, the preamble of the Declaration of Independence as a sort of reservoir of ideas, it strives to follow up the contributing streams of thought to those altitudes whence they sprang. Herein it is led to somewhat lofty heights—theories regarding the rights of revolution and the laws of nature put forth by Locke and Harrington, Grotius and Puffendorf, Ulpian and Aristotle. Next, it strives to show how these *a priori* speculations, from the classic age to the Georgian era, sifted down into the lower air of practical politics and at last found expression in the writings and speeches of the American patriots from John Wise to Patrick Henry. Finally, employing the figure of speech used by one of the Signers, concerning the Declaration as a ' fabricated machine,' its task is to show how the various parts were tentatively conceived, slowly forged, and at last laboriously assembled in the American ideal of the state.

[1] Cf. my review of Friedenwald's *Declaration of Independence,* in the *Bookman,* May, 1906.

II

PHILOSOPHY AND POLITICS

THE conception of the absolute in America assumes three forms in three successive centuries, namely, monistic in the seventeenth, dualistic in the eighteenth, pantheistic in the nineteenth. Under Puritanism, there is a belief in one, supreme, self-sufficient being, the sole ruler and disposer of all things. Under deism, there is a belief in a deity whose powers and functions are limited by a law outside himself, —the law of nature which is inviolable and immutable. Under transcendentalism, the deity, becoming immanent, is submerged in nature, can scarcely be distinguished from the cosmic processes. As with Spinoza so with Emerson, the concept of God and the concept of the world-ground are identical, the absolute is one with the ordering and creative power of the universe. Assuming these philosophical conceptions to be true in their broad and general sense, the present problem is to show how they were influenced in their shaping by the current theories of government. The latter, broadly speaking, were three: under absolute monarchy, sovereignty is conceived to be given by God to the King, who thus rules by divine right. Under limited monarchy, sovereignty is conceived to be shared between ruler and subject. There is a dual control, for even the absolutists in the contractual origin of government had to concede an original sovereign power of the people.[1] Under representative democracy, sovereignty is conceived to be vested in the people through the inalienable right of the law of nature, nature here, as *natura naturans,* being viewed as an active legislative principle and as itself by its own will, and as a living entity, dictating the manner in which its operations shall proceed.[2]

In showing how these conceptions in philosophy fluctuated with

[1] W. W. Willoughby, *The Nature of the State,* p. 61, New York, 1896.
[2] *Ib.,* p. 91.

23

the varying conceptions in politics, it is scarcely necessary to suggest that the latter conceptions were part of the great movement from absolutism to democracy, the period when, for example, in France the monarch's dictum *L'état c'est moi* was supplanted by Montesquieu's *Esprit des lois,* and in England Hobbes and his *Leviathan* by Locke and his *Treatises on Government.* In America the movement began later than in Europe, but was accelerated by special causes; small bodies move quickly and petty colonies, as has been pointed out, applied the law of nature and practised the rights of man long before Rousseau wrote his *Social Contract.*[1] Without anticipating, one may now consider the consonant origin and reflex action of those two sets of conceptions,—from the Puritan theocracy, through the period of colonial revolt, to the final location of sovereignty in the body politic. Here ample sources are to be found in the covenants, creeds and platforms of the state-church;[2] in the colonial charters, declarations and bills of right,[3] in the Declaration of Independence,[4] the Federal Constitution and the various State constitutions evincing a desire for a more perfect union. With the addition of the revolutionary orators and pamphleteers, these are the authorities commonly given in tracing the development of the spirit of nationality. Yet herein one should pay less attention to these publicists than to obscurer speculators such as John Wise, Jonathan Mayhew and William Livingston, who, relying on the continental jurists, constituted a genuine background to the whole picture.[5]

Turning to the seventeenth century, the close connection between the two sets of conceptions is attested by the fact that the

[1] Charles Borgeaud, *The Adoption and Amendment of Constitutions,* p. 19, New York, 1895.

[2] Cf. Williston Walker, *The Creeds and Platforms of Congregationalism,* New York, 1893.

[3] Cf. C. Jellinek, *The Declaration of the Rights of Man,* New York, 1901.

[4] Cf. H. Friedenwald, *The Declaration of Independence,* New York, 1904.

[5] Cf. W. A. Dunning, *A History of Political Theories from Luther to Montesquieu,* New York, 1905; G. L. Scherger, *The Evolution of Modern Liberty,* New York, 1904.

one may be expressed in the terms of the other. If in Europe this was an age of absolute sovereignty in both politics and philosophy,[1] so was it in America. Under Puritanism, as set forth by the Boston Platform of 1680, the deity is represented as a dread monarch, a sovereign ruler of inscrutable decrees, a being ' almighty, absolute, working all things according to the counsel of his own immutable will, for his own glory.' [2] This is the Calvinistic description of the immortal God; with it may be compared the description of the chief exponent of English autocracy, Hobbes' definition of Leviathan,—' that mortal god, who hath the use of so much power and strength conferred on him, that by terror thereof he is enabled to perform the wills of them all.' [3] Such language had perhaps not come under the eyes of the Pilgrim fathers, yet echoes of it were ringing in their ears. Thus, John Robinson and William Brewster, in the articles of the Plymouth Church of 1617, saw fit to write: the King's majesty we acknowledge for supreme governour.[4] And the subscribers to the Mayflower compact of 1620 signed themselves the loyal subjects of our dread sovereign Lord King James.[5] These resemblances are not to be dismissed as the superficial marks of custom and convention, for there was an intimate connection between the two; the doctrines of English monarchy and New England theocracy were essentially similar, because each possessed the underlying principles of transcendence and determinism, or as Tom Paine bluntly expressed it in his *Common Sense,*—the state of a King shuts him off from the world, yet the business of a King requires him to know it thoroughly.[6] To carry the parallel out: if with the advocates of divine right the King was high above his people and at the same time determined the most minute affairs in the outmost bounds of a world empire, so with

[1] Cf. Harald Höffding, *Modern Philosophy,* Vol. 1, p. 243, New York, 1900.

[2] Cotton Mather, *Magnalia,* Vol 2, p. 182, Boston Platform, Chapter 2, § 1.

[3] Hobbes, *Leviathan,* (Morley ed.), p. 84.

[4] Walker, *Creeds,* p. 90.

[5] Charles Borgeaud, *The Rise of Modern Democracy,* p. 108, New York, 1894.

[6] *Political Works,* (Conway ed.), p. 70.

the Calvinists of Massachusetts 'the most high doth direct, dispose and govern all creatures, actions and things, from the greatest even to the least.' [1]

Here existed side by side two kindred theories, the one derived from practical experience, the other from actual speculation, and both received with outward submission and loyalty. However, neither King nor Calvin was to reign forever. Therefore, as the system of one contained elements hostile to civil, and of the other to religious liberty, their direct application led to similar results: in affairs of state to political, in affairs of the church to philosophical revolt. The former is a commonplace of history, the latter has not been made sufficiently prominent. The Puritan divinity was too much like the Stuart dynasty to be long acceptable to Anglo-American Independence. Special providences, exerted in behalf of the elect, bore too striking a resemblance to his Majesty's partiality to a favoured few. Moreover, the Calvinistic doctrines of the necessity of God's determination of men's actions, and of the creature's entire dependence upon God, seemed naught but the court doctrine which invested the sovereign with the unconditional right of command, the subject with the unconditional duty of obedience.[2] The Calvinistical principles last quoted were set forth in 1703 by Samuel Willard, president of Harvard College. In addition came the warning that the faithful 'were bound to withstand those who seek to overthrow the doctrine of an absolute decree, that so they may establish an uncontrolled sovereignty in the will of man.' [3] This admonition was ineffectual, for both the political notion of the indefeasible sovereignty of the people indicated how men might revolt in turn against the philosophical doctrine of an absolute decree, and this consummation was in fact realised in the spiritual as well as in the civil system. For example, at the time when Jonathan Edwards was expounding the sovereignty of God—absolute and unchallenged in will, power and decree [4]—the political equivalents were already under fire. In

---

[1] *Boston Platform, Chapter* 5, § 1.
[2] J. E. Erdmann, *History of Philosophy*, Vol. 2, p. 717.
[3] Samuel Willard, *Body of Divinity*, p. 8, Boston, 1726.
[4] G. E. Ellis, *The Puritan Age*, p. 140, Boston, 1888.

1746 Jonathan Mayhew, a graduate of Harvard, a colleague of James Otis and an extreme Whig, delivered his *Discourses* ' Concerning Unlimited Submission and Non-Resistance to the Higher Powers—with some Reflections on the Resistance made to King Charles I.' Familiar with the teaching of Sidney, Milton and Locke, and referring to Grotius on the *Law of War and Peace,* Mayhew held that rebellion is justifiable in vindicating natural and legal rights, and that the hereditary, indefeasible divine right of Kings is not fetched from human reason, but is fabulous and chimerical. ' The right reverend drones,' he exclaims, ' who preach the divine right of titles and the equity of sinecures, are not ministers of God but pirates and highwaymen.' He concludes that the essence of government is the making and executing good laws, attempered to the common felicity of the good.[1]

Seven years later, views similar to these were expressed by William Livingston, a graduate of Yale and a patron of King's College, New York. Treating of ' Passive Obedience and Non-Resistance,' Livingston picturesquely writes:

The tyrant used to club with the clergy and set them a-roaring for the divine rights of royal roguery. 'Twas a damnable sin to resist the cutting of throats and no virtue more Christian and refulgent than of a passive submission to butchery and slaughter. To propagate such fustian in America argues a disposition prone to senility. And yet 'tis not above four years ago, that in this very province I heard a dapper young gentleman, attired in his canonicals, contend as strenuously for nonresistance as if he had been animated with the very soul of Sacheverel.[2]

After this outbreak Livingston proceeds to discuss more calmly the right of rebellion against the arbitrary will of a superior, as justified by the different effects of the two species of monarchy:

In absolute monarchies a vindication of the natural rights of mankind is treason; every generous spirit is broke and depressed: human nature is degraded, insulted, spurn'd and outraged; the lovely image of God is defaced and disfigured, the tyrant's sword is reason and law. *Stet pro Ratione voluntas.* . . . But in

[1] Mayhew, *Sermons,* pp. 9, 12, 14, Boston, 1749.
[2] *New York Independent Reflector,* p. 121.

limited governments there are inherent rights and fundamental reserves. The resisting therefore the person or will of the ruler, when he resists those rights and reservations, is not resisting the ordinance of God (which is the frame and constitution of the government not the person or will of the prince) but plainly defending it against the powerless, unauthoritative, and illegal attempts of the superior. . . . The right of self defence is not a donation of law but a primitive right prior to all political institution, resulting from the nature of man and inhering in the people till expressly alienated and transferred, if it be not in its nature inalienable. . . . Nor is the defence of our lives and properties in such cases an act of judgment or the object of law; it is a privilege of nature, not an act of jurisdiction. Hence these indisputable maxims: *Vim vi repellere omnia jura permittunt; defendere se est juris Naturae; defensio vitae necessaria est, et a jure naturale profluit.*[1]

In quoting the opinion of that learned civilian, the incomparable Grotius, the writing of Livingston, like that of Mayhew, marks the change from the Calvinistic or Puritan to the deistic or rational point of view. What has been said of this change in England holds true of the colonies,—the theological conception of politics is giving way before what may be termed the naturalistic; instead of the constructive theory of divine rights there is a transition to the theory of natural rights, vested not only in the king but in the people as well. The latter, as propounded by Locke, was merely the former in disguise, for the doctrine of divine rights not only was transformed by imperceptible degrees into the theory of natural rights, but left behind it a legacy, in the sense that, because it is natural, government in general is divine.[2]

An American book which earliest marks the exact point of departure from the biblical and theological to the historical and utilitarian standpoint, is John Wise's *Vindication of the Government of New England Churches.* Coming from a Harvard graduate, the work was printed in Boston first in 1717, and twice later in 1772 for use as a revolutionary treatise. The *Vindication,* as the sub-title reads, is ' Drawn from Antiquity; the Light of Na-

[1] *New York Independent Reflector,* p. 153.

[2] J. N. Figgis, *The Theory of the Divine Right of Kings,* pp. 150, 174, Cambridge, 1896.

ture; Holy Scripture; Its Holy Nature; and from the Dignity Divine Providence has put upon it.' The general significance of this transitional work is that the functions of human reason and of natural rights, so tentatively expressed in the ecclesiastical standards, had come to their own. In the opening section of the Boston Platform it was declared that the light of nature simply left men inexcusable; by this time that light was looked upon as a helpful beacon. Nevertheless the views presented in Wise's book were not entirely original. Of the author's predecessors at least three groups had offered concrete instances of this changed belief. The subscribers of the Mayflower compact did covenant and combine themselves into a civil body politic ' to frame such just laws as shall be thought most meet and convenient for the general good of the colony.' Likewise the signers of the Friendly Orders of Connecticut of 1638 did associate and conjoin themselves to be as one public state or commonwealth ' to be guided and governed by such laws, rules, orders and decrees as shall be made.' So the general assembly of Rhode Island in 1641 defined their body politic as a democracy or popular government, and added that it was ' in the power of the body of freemen orderly assembled to make and constitute just laws by which they will be regulated.'[1] In these and other plantation covenants there is more of practical assertion than of speculative interest. The same is true of the works of the native writers of the seventeenth century. Richard Mather in his *Apologie,* 1639, and John Cotton in his *Way of the Churches,* 1645, use arguments more scriptural than metaphysical. Thomas Hooker in his *Summe of Church Discipline,* 1648, may have partially anticipated Locke,[2] but the Connecticut divine, like his English namesake, is writing from the standpoint of ecclesiastical polity. With John Wise it is different. He is as much interested in the origin of political as of religious society, and in addition cites such writers as put him in the legitimate line of philosophical succession. He belongs by right to the school of Locke, for he uses the same authority that influenced the latter in his *Two Treatises of Government.* Therefore, after vindicating

[1] Borgeaud, *Adoption,* pp. 10, 12, 13.
[2] C. E. Merriam, *American Political Theories,* p. 20, New York, 1903.

the constitution of the New England Churches from the voice of antiquity, he turns to his second demonstration from the light of nature. Treating of man in both his natural and civil state, he takes Baron Puffendorf for his chief guide and spokesman and argues as follows:

I shall consider man in a state of natural being, as a free-born subject under the crown of heaven, and owing homage to none but God himself. It is certain civil government in general is a very admirable result of providence, and an incomparable benefit to mankind, yet must needs be acknowledged to be the effect of human free-compacts and not of divine institution; it is the produce of man's reason, of human and rational combinations, and not from any direct orders of infinite wisdom, in any positive law wherein is drawn up this or that scheme of civil government. Government (says Lord Warrington) is necessary—in that no society of man can subsist without it; and that particular form of government is necessary which best suits the temper and inclination of a people. . . . But to proceed under the head of a state of natural being . . . the prime immunity in man's state, is that he is most properly the subject of the law of nature. He is the favourite animal on earth; in that this part of God's image, namely, reason, is congenate with his nature, wherein by a law immutable, enstamped upon his frame, God has provided a rule for men in all their actions, obliging each one to the performance of that which is right, not only as to justice, but likewise as to all other moral virtues, the which is nothing but the dictate of right reason founded in the soul of man. (Molloy, De Mao. Praef.) . . . The second great immunity of man is an original liberty enstamped upon his rational nature. He that intrudes upon this liberty, violates the law of nature. . . . The native liberty of man's nature implies a faculty of doing or omitting things according to the direction of his judgment. . . . Therefore, as Plutarch says: Those persons only who live in obedience to reason, are worthy to be accounted free: they alone live as they will, who have learned what they ought to will. . . . The third capital immunity belonging to man's nature, is an equality amongst men; which is not to be denied by the law of nature, till man has resigned himself with all his rights for the sake of a civil state, and then his personal liberty and equality is to be cherished and preserved to the highest degree, as will consist with all just distinctions amongst men of honour, and shall be agreeable with the public good.[1]

[1] Wise, *Vindication*, pp. 29-34, Boston, 1860.

The treatise of the Ipswich pastor shows that theocracy, however monistic in principle, contained within itself a dualism. Nevertheless, the complete deistic distinction between God and nature had not as yet been reached; that was left for the revolutionary separatists. In spite of his appeal to antiquity and his citations from Plutarch, Ulpian and Boethius, Wise does not hold to the Stoic notion of the law of nature as a thing standing by itself; with him it is derivative, not independent, a bare immunity, not a real entity. Herein, contrary to the statement of an English interpreter,[1] Wise is not an exact forerunner of Samuel Adams, for the latter, in his *Boston Declaration* of 1772, refers to a double source of legislative principles—'the eternal and immutable laws of God and nature.'[2] Like the distinction of James Otis in his *Rights of the British Colonies*, 1764, between 'the law of nature and the grant of God Almighty,' this dualism is drawn from the principle of Grotius concerning natural law as absolutely immutable, incapable of change even by God himself.[3] With this severance of divine and natural laws, the dualism, from the standpoint of philosophic progression, becomes complete. John Adams in his *Dissertation on the Canon and Federal Law*, 1765, had appealed to natural law as 'derived from the great legislator of the universe.' But now that law is considered more original than derivative, and is put over against the deity as a separate entity.

This process was destined to be carried further: under the constant appeals to an absolute law and absolute right, there was a tendency to substitute *lex* for *legislator,* the principle for the person, and thus to run from the dualistic to the pantheistic stage. Consequently, that law of nature which under Puritanism was a subordinate source of authority, and under deism a co-ordinate, under transcendentalism became in itself an ultimate source of authority—a veritable absolute. Or, put in terms of political history: that sovereignty which first appertained to the King by divine right, and was then shared by the people by natural right,

---

[1] J. A. Doyle, *English Colonies in America,* Vol. 1, p. 378, New York, 1887.

[2] *Works* (W. V. Wells, ed.), Vol. 1, p. 501, Boston, 1865.

[3] Dunning, *Political Theories,* p. 165.

was at last lodged inalienably in the democracy. With this supersession of the *vox dei* by the *vox populi,* there resulted a curious analogy between the pantheism of Emerson and the doctrine of popular sovereignty. As on the one side the universe governs itself, is sufficient to itself and is itself its own end, so, on the other, the federal government is declared of the people, by the people and for the people.

A brief reference may here be made to certain intermediate political writings which prepared for this developed doctrine. According to Thomas Paine, 1786, in republics, such as those established in America, the sovereign power remains where nature has placed it,—in the people.[1] According to Thomas Jefferson, 1787, the new constitution proposes to melt all down into one general government.[2] Earlier than either of these writers there appeared an unexpected forerunner of the Concord philosopher. In 1784, Ethan Allen published his *Reason the Only Oracle of Man, or a Compenduous System of the Universe.* In this rare work, sometimes entitled *Allen's Theology,* there is a decided approach to an identification of divine and cosmic activities. It is not entirely accurate to say that Allen's conception of the absolute is that of a constitutional deity, whose powers and functions are limited by a law outside himself.[3] Rather, in his attempt to identify the essence of God and of the world in general, there is an anticipation of the later spiritualistic monism. Allen first refers the laws of nature to a superior, superintending, ruling power, and then makes those operations of nature eternal and infinite. Treating in his first chapter ' Of the Being of God,' and in a final chapter of the ' distinction between the immediate and mediate act of God,' he says:

The laws of nature having subjected mankind to a state of absolute dependence on something out of it, and manifestly beyond themselves, or the compound exertion of their natural powers, gave them the first conception of a superior principle existing; otherwise they could have had no possible conception of a super-

[1] *Writings,* (Conway ed.), Vol. 2, p. 133, New York, 1894.
[2] *Writings,* (P. L. Ford ed.), Vol. 4, p. 470, New York, 1894.
[3] Cf. Moncure D. Conway in *Open Court,* January 28, 1892.

intending power. . . . This first glimpse of a deity powerfully attracts the rational mind to make further discoveries.
. . . The mediate act of God is the same as the eternal series
of the exertions of the various parts of nature on each other, which
properly speaking act intermediately or between the external cause
and the succeeding or final event of things. The immediate act
of God is the mere operations of nature which act by succession
and are the complicated exertions of created beings. But the
eternal cause cannot act by succession, but is one eternal, infinite
and uncompounded exertion of God, giving being, order and support to the universe.[1]

These two elements,—the rational principle and the natural
effect,—are harmonised by Emerson under a form of idealistic pantheism, which, be it finally noted, is couched in terms of political
sovereignty. Philosophically considered, run the Essays on *Nature* and on the *Method of Nature,* the universe is composed of
nature and the soul. . . . That which once existed in intellect
as pure law, has now taken body as nature. . . . Nature is
not only the material, but is also the process and the result.
. . . The dread universal essence is that for which all things
exist and that by which they are.[2] Finally, in conjunction with
the philosophical is presented the political interpretation. Against
those reformers who would fill the land with cries of No-govern-
ment the descendant of Puritan divines asserts that ' conscious
law is King of Kings.' And he concludes: the Revolution, sequent
to the coming of the Pilgrims, was not begun in Concord, or
Lexington, or Virginia, but was the overflowing of the sense of
natural right in every clear and active spirit of the period.[8]

[1] Allen, *Oracles,* pp. 25, 323, Bennington, Vt., 1784.
[2] R. W. Emerson, *Works.* (Riverside ed.), pp. 10, 19, 48, 67, 188.
[3] *Ib.,* pp. 204, 209, 246. Cf. further, H. L. Osgood, *The Political Ideas
of the Puritans, in Political Science Quarterly,* Vol. 6, p. 1, ff.; Vol. 2,
p. 202, ff.

BOOK I—PURITANISM

CHAPTER I

PURITANISM

THE history of Puritanism in America has suffered considerably at the hands of the literary expositor, who delights to present the more picturesque works of the Calvinistic worthies, the *Curiosa Americana,* to use a phrase of Cotton Mather. Thus, a sulphurous poem like the *Day of Doom* is taken as a fair example of the distressing illusions once inflicted upon themselves, in the name of religion, by the best of men, and its author declared to have attributed to the Divine Being the most execrable and loathsome character to be met with in any literature, Christian or pagan. This is said to be his narrow and ferocious creed: all men are totally depraved, all of them caught from the farthest eternity in the adamantine meshes of God's decrees; the most of them, also, being doomed in advance by those decrees, to an endless existence of ineffable torment, and the whole world, when the Judge of all the earth appears, to an universal conflagration.[1] Such, in brief, is the exposition of the Dies Irae of New England at the hands of the historian of colonial literature. Yet besides this explicit and unshrinking rhymer of the five points of Calvinism even their greatest advocate is held up to odium. Disregarding Edwards' mystical writings with their sweetness and light, emphasis is laid on such controversial treatises as his *Doctrine of Original Sin Defended.* Upon this the reviewer now passes his strictures, declaring that to teach that man is born in a state of moral inability, is to teach a kind of spiritual hemiplegia; and to believe that every infant of the human race is entitled to one undivided share of guilt, is to believe that the little albuminous automaton is not sent into the world without an inheritance of depravity.[2] While from the literary point of

[1] M. C. Tyler, *A History of American Literature,* New York, 1878, Vol. 2, Chapter XI., § V., Michael Wigglesworth.

[2] Oliver Wendell Holmes, *International Review,* Vol. 9, pp. 1-28.

view it may be held that this particular work of the New England divine was one of the most revolting books that ever proceeded from the pen of man,[1] that does not prevent the system which it represents from having great philosophical significance. One may deplore the mental sufferings caused by the workings of such a speculative rack, and still admire the structure of the machine from which these torturing doctors proceeded.

To look at the matter directly, Calvinism as a system stands four-square, for it may be viewed from the four philosophic standpoints of ontology, cosmology, epistemology and psychology. First, as a theory of being, Calvinism teaches that the deity lives outside the framework of the universe; that he interferes as he sees fit according to an absolute and arbitrary will; that he works through inscrutable decrees; that he foreordains whatsoever comes to pass. Second, as a theory of the cosmos, Calvinism teaches that the world is under the curse of the divine displeasure; that it conceals rather than displays its creator; that it is created from nothing and destined for nothingness; that its evil is a permissive act of God. Third, as a theory of knowing, Calvinism teaches that true knowledge comes more through revelation than through reason, being a gift of the divine pleasure rather than a result of human endeavour; that the decretive will of God is involved in deep mystery, which is for us little better than a learned ignorance; that man has only a dim revelation of a hidden God communicated from without; that the human has no natural capacity for understanding the divine nature. Fourth, as a theory of personality, Calvinism teaches that God is alien in essence from man; that human progress comes through arbitrary grace, man being by nature corrupt; that our liberty is not self-determined, but works only within the limitations of our foreordained nature; that the last dictate of the understanding determines the will,—and yet, that within the will are included the inclinations.

Such, in brief compass, was the system of high Calvinism as it was expressed in official standards, like the Boston platform of 1680, and in the utterances of its expositors from the Mathers to Jonathan Edwards. In point of local distribution the system,

[1] W. E. H. Lecky, *Rationalism in Europe*, London, 1875, Vol. 1, p. 368.

in its extreme form, obtained chiefly in New England, for like an Arctic current of thought, it grew slowly warmer and was gradually dissipated as it flowed south into the more genial regions of Anglican belief. Although the system was local in its distribution, it was not limited in point of time. Recent investigations have shown that the theology of New England was a world phenomenon, and that, in spite of its apparent isolation, the same great periods of thought historically appeared in this obscure corner of civilisation as in Europe. In other words, as the continental cycles of scholastic orthodoxy were repeated in England, so were the English cycles repeated in New England. The Puritans and Pilgrims had shared in the constructive period of English Protestantism at home; they planted their settlements just as Puritanism was on the eve of triumph in the mother-country; they shared in its victory and appropriated its results when, in 1648, they adopted the Westminster standards as their own. Then when the period of great systematic divines was succeeded by that of Latitudinarianism, 1680-1700, they too had their period of theological corruption, promoted by influences communicated from the debased England of the Restoration. While from 1720 to 1750 the Arminian tendencies of the old country powerfully affected the life of the colonies, yet in New England there was a more immediate reaction against theological corruption than in either Germany or England, for the Arminian movement was met almost at its beginning by the youthful Jonathan Edwards in his sermons on Justification in 1734, and by his *Freedom of the Will* in 1754.[1]

This is the story of early American Puritanism as it traces the natural results of the defective theories of the original Calvinism, which united with the universal tendencies of frontier life to produce degeneration and decay, and as it shows how the influence of theological degeneration in Britain, with its deism and Arminianism, contributed to accelerate the downward movement.[2] This history of the dominating school of thought in New England has

[1] F. H. Foster, *A Genetic History of the New England Theology,* Chicago, 1907, Introduction.
[2] *Ib.,* p. 10.

at last been adequately told from the theological, but not from the philosophical standpoint; its author employs the genetic method, recognises the action and reaction of mind upon mind, of idea upon idea, but he does little but name the influences of the larger speculative forces in the overthrow of Calvinism. He mentions the influence of Des Cartes' appeal to consciousness, of Francis Bacon's method of induction, of Locke's new doctrine of freedom, and the powerful impulse from the work of Sir Isaac Newton. In these pertinent references the critic mentions great names, he does not fully correlate them with greater movements. He indeed allows the influence of Arminianism as an ethical protest against the five points of Calvinism, but he has little to say regarding the disintegrating influence of deism.

So it is held that Arminianism was an appeal to consciousness against a system of abstract logic. Here, on the one hand, Calvinism had emphasised the Godward side of theology, and turned the divine government into an inexorable determinism, by deriving the whole system from the sole causality of God, through logical deduction. Arminianism, on the contrary, emphasised the manward side of theology, and regarded the activity of human agency as a necessary condition for the maintenance of moral responsibility.[1] Yet in this also, as another has pointed out, the Arminians did not go so far as they might; anxious to guard against overmuch liberty of action, they grew cautious and fell back on the Scotist idea of the absolute supremacy of the divine will, teaching that a thing is good because God has commanded it, not that God commanded it because it was good.[2] This contradiction of the Thomistic view, that the good exists in and of itself, was now taken up by the deists, who said that there are natural rules of morality which do not depend on the arbitrary fiat of the creator, but have an absolute and independent existence, whose character is to be discovered by the study of human nature.[3]

---

[1] *A Genetic History of the New England Theology*, pp. 77, 80.

[2] Cf. G. P. Fisher, *History of Christian Doctrine*, New York, 1896, p. 339.

[3] Cf. J. E. Erdmann, *History of Philosophy*, New York, 1890, Vol. 2, p. 210.

In fine, the theological attempt to harmonise the antithesis between transcendence and determinism being unsuccessful, philosophy essayed the task of reconciliation. Deism by postulating a third term, the natural law, partially succeeded in bringing back liberty of action within the limits of reason. But in emphasising the importance of that law, in making its bounds more and more extensive, deism tended to push the Creator entirely away from his world. Hence by the time the law of nature was made universal, the deity was brought to an infinite remove, and while counted the maker, was no longer considered the ruler of the universe. Here was the absentee landlord theory carried to extreme; for with this banishment of the master the servant grew boldly arrogant. Man, looking within himself, was becoming a law unto himself; hence that air of moral conceit and self-sufficiency assumed in increasing measure towards the end of the eighteenth century, as seen in such typical productions as Thomas Paine's *Age of Reason,* and Ethan Allen's *Oracles of Reason.*

Without anticipating the entire scheme of contrast between the old and the new, it may now be shown what were some of the solvent processes in the disintegration of Calvinism. In general these processes were four in number: first, there was a gradual degradation or lowering of the doctrine of transcendence, through the belief in miraculous intervention; here the deity is brought into the world, not by immanence, but by interference, and general providence is turned into special providences. Thus, in place of the noble definition of ' the living and true God, infinite in being and perfection, a most pure spirit, immutable, immense, eternal, incomprehensible,' [1] there comes a conception of a being who manifests himself in ' remarkable sea-deliverances, remarkables about thunder and lightning, remarkable judgments upon Quakers, drunkards and enemies of the church.' [2] Second, there was a gradual integration or hardening of the doctrine of determinism; here the freedom of the will verbally allowed in the West-

[1] Cotton Mather, *Magnalia Christi Americana,* Vol. 2, p. 182, Boston Confession of Faith, Chapter II., § I.
[2] Cotton Mather, *Essay for the Recording of Illustrious Providences,* Boston, 1684.

minster standards is practically denied by the later consistent Calvinists. Thus, instead of the provision whereby ' no violence is
offered unto the will of the creature, nor is the liberty or contingency of second causes taken away,' [1] there comes Samuel Willard's avowal that there is in man a ' miserable impotency and
malignity of will with respect to holy choices.' [2]   Third, there
was a gradual elimination or softening of the doctrine of the
necessary depravity of human nature; here the new world being
perforce a better world than the corrupt society Calvin had in view,
men began somewhat egotistically to plume themselves on their
virtues.   Thus, in place of the ancient saying that ' all noisome
lusts abound in the soul like snakes in an old hedge,' [3] even Cotton
Mather could say that the Puritan ' flying from the depravity of
Europe to the American strand, *emollit mores nec sinit esse feros.*[4]
Fourth, there was a gradual elevation or heightening of the humane and philanthropic elements in the character of the Absolute;
here there was no longer a sovereign will at an immeasurable
distance from man, but a more kindly leader, commander and
ruler of nature.   Thus, in place of the outpourings of the divine
fury,[5] there comes the infiltration of the quality of mercy, until
one of the Boston divines can dwell with a high enthusiasm upon
the essential benevolence of the deity.[6]

In tracing these four processes at work in the amelioration of
Calvinism, it is clear that the last two were more powerful factors
for good than the first, for the best minds preferred the positive
factors to the negative, the progressive to the reactionary.   Hence,
in contrast to the old defenders of the faith these men showed
that, within the very first century after the settlement, they had
advanced into a new age of thought.   That age was the age of
reason, when, by the importation of the optimism of Leibniz and
the empiricism of Locke, a new complexion was put upon the
world.   How great was the change that had come over men's

[1] *Confession,* Chapter III., § 1.
[2] *Body of Divinity,* Boston, 1726.
[3] Thomas Hooker, *Soul's Humiliation,* London, 1638.
[4] *Magnalia,* Vol. 1, p. 25; Vol. 2, p. 8.
[5] Samuel Willard, *The Best Privilege,* Boston, 1701, p. 10.
[6] Charles Chauncy; see below, Book II., Chapter II.

spirits may be seen in a contrast between the old Calvinism and the new deism, as given under the former philosophic captions. Here, as to ontology, the one tended to determinism, the other to voluntarism; as to cosmology, the one to pessimism, the other to optimism; as to epistemology, the one to agnosticism, the other to rationalism; as to psychology, the one to a doctrine of inability, the other to that of ability. That this contrast between Calvinism and deism, although schematic, is not artificial, is proven by the fact that there is scarcely one minor tenet in the one which is not contradicted or at least contravened in the other. Again, employing the usual divisions, it may be shown that, while in causative transcendence there is agreement between the two systems, there is in little else, for point by point the two are antithetical. First, as a theory of being, deism teaches that the deity is the self-sufficient and efficient cause of all things; that, being immutable, he makes no interference in the movements of nature; that he works entirely through second causes, the laws of nature; that he cannot control the actions of free and accountable agents. Second, as a theory of the cosmos, deism teaches that the divine munificence designed the good of being in general; that external nature displays the divine nature, is the medium for the divine benignity; that the world, whether temporal or eternal, exhibits evidences of supreme design; and that, nothing being made in vain, evil is but a foil for the good, the means to a better end. Third, as a theory of knowledge, deism teaches that the outward universe is a real book of revelation; that by the universal light of nature every man is capable of understanding the workings of the world-machine; that the being and the attributes of the deity are as demonstrable as the laws of science, for the almighty lecturer displays the principles of science in the structure of the universe; that from our own rational nature we gain an idea of God's moral perfection. Fourth, as a theory of personality, deism teaches that God and man are akin in their essential rationality; that humanity is perfectible in and by itself; that the law of nature intuitively evinces the certainty of human liberty; that the body is subject to mechanism, but the mind is free; that the powers of man are competent to all the great purposes of human existence.

Here, in the very language of their authors, is American deism as conceived by such writers as Thomas Paine and Ethan Allen. Since of this pair the former stands for deism in its decline, and the latter for deism as preparatory to transcendentalism, it is necessary to return and consider the prime causes back of the disintegration of Calvinism. In this a most interesting parallel may be drawn between the mother-country and the colonies, for in both similar forces were at work. Among these Anglo-American correspondences the first phase appears as a struggle against dogma. The decay of the Christian religion, which Principal Cairns notes in old England,[1] is also to be found in New England. The period from the father of English deism, Herbert of Cherbury, to the great sceptic, David Hume, is of equal length with the period from the half-way Covenant of 1662 to the Unitarian manifesto of 1815. But though the colonies lagged a full generation behind the mother country, nevertheless, during these one hundred and fifty years there was a similar shifting of emphasis from revelation to reason. To follow the parallel further, the second phase appears as the rise of naturalism. Here the drift of the English mind away from the supernatural, as evinced in the success of natural philosophy through the impulse given by Bacon and the Royal Society, is paralleled in America by the popularity of Newton and by the foundation in 1743 of the American Philosophical Society for the Promotion of Useful Knowledge. This change from the magical to the scientific standpoint is further seen in the change from an interest in wonder-working providences to an interest in the observation of external nature, and even to an appreciation of the beauties of natural scenery; the one being illustrated by Franklin's experiments in electricity, and the other by Cotton Mather's half-scientific, half-æsthetic work, the *Christian Philosopher*. To conclude the matter, the third phase appears in the struggle against the union of Church and State and in behalf of freedom of conscience. In England, says Principal Cairns, the institution of the established church made men ambitious to defy the ecclesiastical dignitaries. In America, this is

[1] John Cairns, *Unbelief in the Eighteenth Century*, p. 63, Edinburgh, 1881.

matched by the assaults on clerical authority among such politicians as Thomas Jefferson, and by the common practice of inveighing against the power and tyranny of priests, among such deists of the baser sort as Thomas Paine. This was not without its evil effects. In the North, indeed, the attempts of the conservative clergy to preserve a state-supported church tended, in the figurative language of Jefferson, to exclude the advances of information, by making the clergy follow the barque of liberty only by the help of a tow rope.[1] But in the South, conditions were different. There not only were the prescriptive rights of the Anglican Church opposed by various legislative measures, but after the revolutionary war that church, as the Church of England, became unpopular and thereby a certain humanistic trend towards liberalism was lost to the country.

How potent were these three phases of thought,—rationalistic, naturalistic, and political—is fully to be seen only in the eventual changes wrought upon Puritanism by the opposition of the rival schools. In the meantime, as a popular representative of that opposition, there may be presented the speculations of one who, while half-deist and half-transcendentalist, was yet wholly anti-Puritanical.

[1] To Pierrepont Edwards, July 21, 1801, *Works,* Vol. 7, p. 84 (Ford ed.).

CHAPTER II

ANTI-PURITANISM

ETHAN ALLEN of Vermont has been previously known for his military exploits, but quite ignored for his speculative ventures. In the preface to his *Oracles of Reason,* 1784, the captor of Ticonderoga confesses that he has been denominated a deist; whether he is, he does not know, but this he does know, that he is no Calvinist. In a pungent letter to one who inquired concerning his philosophy, he says that he expects that the clergy, and their devotees, will proclaim war upon him, in the name of the Lord, having put on the armour of faith, the sword of the Spirit and the artillery of hell fire. 'But,' he concludes, ' I am a hardy Mounttaineer and have been accustomed to the ravages and horrors of War and Captivity, and scorn to be intimidated by threats; if they fright me, they must absolutely produce some of their tremendous fire, and give me a sensative scorching.' [1]

For Allen's roughness of manners and coarseness of speech Jared Sparks gives as mitigating circumstances the rude and uncultivated society in which the author lived. It might be added that the ' Green Mountain Boy ' was one of those backwoods thinkers who claim to be largely independent of outside ideas. Some rival asserted that he stole his title from Blount's *Oracles of Reason,*[2] but the author of this ' Compenduous System of Natural Religion ' throws no direct light on its sources. He maintained that the bible and the dictionary were his only authorities, but while he might have made a better use of both, it is hard to learn of what other means of information he availed himself.[3] He tells

[1] From a holograph letter in the possession of Mr. E. D. Church of New York City; for a reprint see Cothren, *History of Woodbury, Connecticut,* Vol. 1, pp. 444-5.

[2] M. D. Conway, *Life of Thomas Paine,* New York, 1892, Vol. 2, p. 192.

[3] Allen gives nothing by name but much by implication; there are apparent references to Jonathan Edwards,—p. 232; to Pope's *Essay on Man,*—p. 278; to Warburton's *Divine Legation of Moses,*—p. 269.

46

how in his youth, being educated in what were commonly called 'Armenian,' principles, he was much disposed to contemplation, and at his commencement in manhood being in the habit of committing to manuscript such sentiments or aguments as appeared most consonant to reason, he practised this method of scribbling for many years.[1] So claiming to have something of a smattering of philosophy, he recounts that while in an English prison-ship in 1775 and meeting two clergymen,—We· discoursed on several parts of moral philosophy and Christianity, and they seemed to be surprised that I should be acquainted with such topics, or that I should understand a syllogism or regular mode of argumentation.[1]

Elsewhere Allen narrates that his affections being Frenchified, he began to learn the French tongue, but this was evidently too early for his book to be affected by the revolutionary principles of 1789. Therefore in the absence of specific information, one is left to the mere conjectures that in the war of independence the Vermont philosopher may have picked up some of the sceptical opinions brought in by Lafayette's followers, or that in the earlier French and Indian war he may have absorbed certain loose ideas from those British officers who were charged with bringing in deistical sentiments, and with added force and authority because they were from the mother country.[2]

Whatever the impulses that affected Ethan Allen, whatever the value of his claims as a self-made thinker, his work furnishes a good example of the popular recoil from Puritanism on the part of one who wished to pursue the 'natural road of ratiocination.' This negative side of the *Oracles* is couched in a lively and aggressive style, for the writer is appealing to readers who despise the progressive and wearisome reasonings of philosophers and are prepossessed with principles opposed to the religion of reason. In these parts of America, he explains, men are most generally taught that they are born into the world in a state of enmity to God and moral good and are under his wrath and curse; that the way to heaven and future blessedness is out of their power to pursue, and that it is encumbered with mysteries which none but the

---

[1] Preface to *Oracles*.　　[2] *Narrative*, pp. 25, 46.　　[3] *Ib.*, p. 126.

priests can unfold; that we must ' be born again,' have a special kind of faith and be regenerated.[1]

Upon the priests and their so-called scheme of mysteries, Allen now proceeds to make his onslaught. This is the substance of his tirade: the spiritualists, who pretend to be as familiar with the supernatural world as with their own home-lot, talk as if the creator and governor of the universe had erected a particular academy of arts and sciences in which they, the tutors, were alone intellectually qualified to carry on the business of teaching. With their special revelations they talk as if they only were rational creatures, and the rest of mankind a pack of clodhoppers, as ignorant as a stable of horses; but that is no revelation to me which is above my comprehension, or which from any natural sagacity I knew before. They may keep their alleged manuscript copy of God's eternal law, it is sufficient for me to possess the deistical bible, reason, by which I judge that even the commandments of the decalogue would not be binding upon any rational being, unless they coincided with the law of nature.[1] Moreover to insist upon the depravity of reason is derogatory to the nature of man, inasmuch as reason, depraved or spoiled, would cease to be reason. There are, of course, degrees in the knowledge of rational being, unless they coincided with the law of nature.[2] Moreover down to the lowest exercise of it among the species,—still it is reason and not depraved, for a less degree of reason by no means implies a depravity of it. It is thus at least that the Arminian clergymen in the circle of my acquaintance have exploded the doctrine.[3]

With this long-winded defence of reason, Allen proceeds to attack the Calvinistical system with all the homely wit of which he was master. Against the cardinal belief in magical interferences in the course of nature he argues that such intervention would turn nature into a supernatural whirligig, an inconstant and erring piece of mechanism; would reduce all nature to the level of fanaticism; would lead men to abandon the great discoveries of Newton for awful apprehensions of God's providence, whereby world would crush upon world, or the tail of the next comet

[1] *Oracles*, p. 467.   [2] *Ib.*, pp. 190-199.   [3] *Ib.*, pp. 182-185.

would set this world on fire. But such apprehensions are unwarranted and lead to a logical fallacy; either the great architect of nature has so constructed its machinery that it never needs to be altered, or, admitting miracles, we must admit this syllogism: the laws of nature have been altered, the alteration has been for the better, therefore, the eternal establishment thereof was imperfect.[1] In fine, to demonstrate such a scarecrow belief, one need but quote the anecdote attributed to his Most Christian Majesty, the King of France: ' By the command of the King, God is forbidden to work any more miracles in this place.' [2]

As with intervention, continues Allen, so with inspiration: In the early days of my manhood I did not dare dispute the infallibility of that activity, but now its extravagances should lead my countrymen to examine strictly into the claims of reality of ghostly intelligence in general. A case in point is the local celebrity, Mother Ann Lee, the Elect Lady of Conestaguna, who professes to give in unknown tongues communications from the damned since the Apostolic age. This whole belief in instantaneous illuminations or infusions of wisdom is based on another fallacy: should we admit that the divine mind thinks and reflects in our minds, this would be confounding the divine and human essences together, and such a mental correspondence would form a revelation like Nebuchadnezzar's idol, partly iron and partly clay. The whole bustle is mere enthusiasm; were a revelation to be made known to us, it would be accommodated to our external senses and also to our reason; we must perceive by our senses before we can reflect in our mind, hence our sensorium is the essential medium between the divine and human mind, through which God reveals to man the knowledge of nature.[3]

Based on the Newtonian physics and the Lockean psychology, these are fair examples of Allen's anti-Calvinistic bias. Against other connected doctrines of the old systems he argues in a like short and easy manner, asserting for example, that original sin had as little to do with the premised Adam as with the man in the moon; that the doctrine of imputation, or the transfer of the personal demerit of sin, is contradicted by the old proverb

[1] *Oracles*, pp. 235, 237, 258.   [2] *Ib.*, p. 261.   [3] *Ib.*, pp. 223-226, 326.

that every tub stands upon its own bottom; and that instead of insisting upon the gloomy doctrine of predestination, the teachers of this doctrine should spend their salaries in good wine to make the heart glad.[1]

With this vigorous but coarse attack upon the five points of Calvinism, there is little wonder that Allen's miscalled theology should have been cordially detested by the orthodox, and that it should have been considered an evidence of the workings of a beneficent providence, when most of the edition was accidentally burned.   Nevertheless the Vermont free-thinker had something else to do but startle the natives with his rustic wit; besides the negative part of his work, in which he attempted to lop off the excrescences, there was the positive, in which he feels confident that he has struck the outlines of a consistent system.   Briefly, in place of the conception of a transcendent being, occasionally active in the affairs of the world, quite incomprehensible within the mere limits of reason, he would substitute the conception of an immanent power, continually active in the world, knowable in his nature from man's own rational nature.   Here, as the matter has been previously summarised, the origin of the conception of a superintending power is traced to the sense of dependence on the laws of nature; from studies of those laws reason discovers the perfections of that power; order implies an orderer, harmony a regulator, motion a mover and benefits goodness; chaos would prove a creator, but order and beneficent design are necessary to prove a providence.[2]   Or, as Allen himself expanded his scheme:

The globe with its productions, the planets in their motions, and the starry heavens in their magnitudes make us truly sensible that their being and preservation is from God. . . . We cannot trace the order of the succession of causes back to that self-existent cause, inasmuch as it is eternal and infinite, yet we may conclude that the system of nature, or natural cause, is as much dependent on a self-existent cause as an individual of the species on its progenitors. . . . So certain as God is, we cannot comprehend his essence, eternity or manner of existence, yet as far as we understand nature, we are become acquainted with the char-

[1] *Oracles,* pp. 96, 396.

[2] M. D. Conway in *Open Court,* January 28, 1892.

acter of God; for the knowledge of nature is the revelation of God. . . . If we form in our imagination an idea of the harmony of the universe it is the same as calling God by the name of harmony. If from the composition, texture and tendency of the universe in general, we form a complex idea of general good resulting therefrom to mankind, we implicitly admit a God by the name of good. . . . Furthermore there could be no proportion, figure or motion without wisdom or power. That wisdom, order and design should be the production of non-entity, or of chaos, confusion and old night is as absurd as to suppose effects without a cause.[1]

Allen has now taken the first forward step in his system and that step is optimism; as he expressed the matter in a line obviously drawn from the *Essay on Man:* of all possible systems, infinite wisdom must have eternally discerned the best. This, it is explained, implies the essential benevolence of the deity and thereby we discover the prime requisite of moral perfection. But great difficulties arise in attempting to discover God's natural attributes, especially his eternity and infinity:

To ask how God came to be, implies a contradiction to his being as God, inasmuch as it supposes him to come from, and to be dependent on some pre-existing cause. If we extend our minds retrospectively on the chain of pre-existing causes, we are at as great a remove from God as when we first attempted the order of pre-existing causes, for a mere succession of causes cannot extend themselves ad infinitum. . . . The conception, often expressed from the desk, that God exists from eternity to eternity implies that God existed in time, and that in time he will cease to be. Considered separately eternity may be divided into the preceding and succeeding; considered complexly it is but one entire eternity without beginning or end. The idea of existence without beginning or end contains in it the idea of self-existence which is the highest appellation we can ascribe to God. . . . It is not good sense when we are speaking of God, to say that he is the first cause of all things, for that would imply a beginning to the succession and consequently to the being of God. But succession, which can operate no other way but according to the order of time or numerical calculations of the successions of causes, cannot eternally extend itself. Suppose a mathematical eternal or endless line upon which is discharged in either direction a cannon ball with unabated rapidity forever, it would

[1] *Oracles,* pp. 26-33.

never reach the endless extension of that line: for which reason it is in nature impossible to trace the series of natural causes up to the self-existent and eternal cause. . . . These arguments at first sight appear to clash. A mathematical eternal line, an infinite circle, an eternal series or succession of causes exceed all our mathematics and swallow up all our thoughts and comparisons. Nevertheless an eternal series or succession in nature is as reconcilable to our understandings, as the eternal existence of nature, or of a God. For if one may be, the other is possible, whether we can comprehend them or not. The manner of these infinite calculations are to us incomprehensible but not contradictory: for we cannot understand that to be a contradiction which to us is incomprehensible.[1]

Starting with the categories of time and space and meeting the inevitable paralogisms of reason, Allen is now forced to postulate two absolutes: God, the efficient cause, eternal and infinite, and nature the eternal and infinite effect; eternal here being defined as without end or duration, infinite as without degree or measure; hence, on the one side, is a cause uncaused and eternally self-existent who gave being and order to nature coeval with his own existence; on the other, is nature coextensive and coexistent with the divine nature, eternal because of an eternal and immense fulness, infinite because infinitely complete and independent of any particular form.[2]

This is an astonishing metaphysical scheme for one with scanty education and scantier authorities. Starting to argue against the current cosmology, the Mosaic account of creation, the mountain philosopher has reached an almost Spinozistic description of the universe.[3] However, Allen is not yet a speculative monist, has not yet succeeded in abolishing the theological dualism between God and the world; this he himself early recognises when he says that it is mysterious how there can be, on the one hand, a being self-existent and eternally independent, and, on the other, a creator likewise infinite and as eternal as God.[4] To harmonise this antithesis a distinction is now made between creation and formation:

[1] *Oracles*, pp. 31-41, 67.   [2] *Ib.*, pp. 41, 71, 111.
[3] Cf. Höffding, *Modern Philosophy*, Vol. 1, p. 311.
[4] *Oracles*, pp. 43, 53.

Formation belongs to that which we call the eternal series of causes and effects; it is in the eternal order of nature dependent on creation; and creation is eternally dependent on the eternal self-existent cause. Creation affords the materials of formation or modification; having been eternal and without succession, it could not be repeated, inasmuch as there was an eternal and immense fulness. Yet acts of natural production by formation have been carried on in an eternal series. Creation affording that power of nature called production gives birth to the vast variety of animal and vegetable life. Death and decay are nothing else but a dissolution of forms and not annihilation or a dissolution of creation, for this is infinitely complete and independent of any particular form. Yet creation must exist in some form or other and is necessarily united with all possible forms, and thus it is that all forms in general are indebted to creation for their existence. . . . The immense creation, consisting of elements, possesses its various forms and is endowed with all necessary properties, qualities, dispositions and aptitudes that we denominate by the name nature. This must have been coeval with the eternity of God, and must necessarily remain to all duration coextensive and coexistent with the divine nature.[1]

In promulgating the foregoing theory of creation, the writer confesses that it will probably be rejected by most people in this country, inasmuch as they are prepossessed with the theory of Moses which represents creation to have had a beginning. And yet Moses' theory of creation, he adds, the theory of a laborious working by the day, is better calculated for the servile Israelitish brick-makers than for men of learning and science in these modern times; it is trifling to suppose that an eternal being worked by the day or rested from labour, or carried on the work of creation according to our notions of time.[2] This is the popular cosmology, easy to demolish according to the religion of nature and reason; but to put a better one in its place Allen is driven to a peculiar form of pantheism. Arguing in turn against a creation in time, a successive creation, and a creation with a beginning, he proceeds as follows:

Creation being eternal, and not in time, is nothing short of an infinite exertion of God, who being eternally omnipresent, the operation or exertion of the act of creation was eter-

[1] *Oracles*, pp. 70-71.   [2] *Ib.*, pp. 65, 72, 244.

nally everywhere; as omniscient it was perfectly consistent and best; as omnipotent it was perfected without succession of time; and being eternally and infinitely complete, the almighty act of creation could never be repeated. . . . A successive creation, or a progressive one consisting of local parts, which collectively considered could make but a local whole, could not be of the creation and providence of God, for by our mathematical calculations we could comprise it, and therefore it could be but finite. This would be infinitely inadequate for the territorial providence of an absolutely perfect and infinite being. . . . If creation had a beginning, there was a beginning to the moral government and display of the divine perfections, and it follows there was also a beginning to the being and existence of God. Creation and dependent creatures on such a position would, as to their eternity, be co-eval with God, how then could they be dependent on him? I answer as well as the act of God, which may be eternal and yet dependent on the being or essence of God, or as there may be eternal emanations eternally flowing from an eternal cause.[1]

Allen has, in truth, reached a peculiar form of pantheism in his theory of emanations; still he fears to apply to the extreme the correlated doctrine of the plenum, or as he had previously described it, an eternal and universal fulness. God may be infinitely capacious, the creation eternally replenished, yet one must distinguish between God's essence and the creation itself, since the infinity of the divine nature does not include all things, for if so, it would include all imperfections; nor does it include the actions of free and accountable agents, for God cannot control the vicious agency of man, which has been the destruction of individuals, families, republics, kingdoms and empires.[2]

Evidently realising that his compendious system is going to pieces upon the problem of the free will, Allen proceeds to attack the doctrine of determinism by denying the fatality of the actions of mankind. Freedom, he continues, may be blended with mechanism, the universe may be subject to the laws of fate, our bodily sensorium not excepted; nevertheless the action of intelligence is not analogous to that of matter, for moral beings are by nature free, and by intuition we know them to be so; it is only for want of skill to distinguish liberty from compulsion that we involve it with the operation of mechanical laws; man's freedom is not like

[1] *Oracles*, pp. 55-70.   [2] *Ib.*, pp. 58-86.

tne freedom of running water, nor is his conscience like scales or steelyards, mechanically moved. In fine, if God made moral agents act necessarily, they would have been only mechanically happy, and if he predetermined the conduct of mankind, it would make him the author of moral evil.[1] How are we then to escape this dilemma between the diametrical opposites, necessity and freedom? While the author purposes to write a future volume on free will, because the problem is so intricate, his present purpose is merely to exclude human agency from the providence of God, by showing that omniscience is neither foreknowledge nor foreordination.[2] Here he boldly proceeds:

We suppose an eternal series of causes, in which there could not be a first cause, though there must have been an eternal one, so that God cannot be the first cause of all things. And as the eternal cause was not a first cause, so there can be no first or last knowledge to an omniscient eternal mind. Eternal and infinite knowledge being always the same, always one eternal now, necessarily precludes the notion of before or after, and consequently the supposed prescience of God. Therefore, instead of the actions of mankind being necessitated by the eternal knowledge of God, they necessitate the knowledge of God. God cannot know that a free agent acts necessarily or that a necessary agent acts freely, but he knows things or facts to be in truth as they are; so that provided we act freely, God knows we act freely, but if necessarily he knows we act necessarily. Upon the whole we may rationally conclude that, instead of our actions being necessitated by the divine prescience, they necessitate it. Inasmuch as the knowledge of God or man must be predicated on truth, and truth cannot fail of being predicated on nature, nature is therefore our polar star to direct us relative to the question of the liberty or destiny of our actions in life.[3]

In his return to nature, the Vermont philosopher thinks he has settled the conflict between liberty and necessity, whereas he has but stultified his former principles. Seeking to avoid the exigencies of transcendence, he had formerly postulated a doctrine of emanations. At present, since this threatens to turn into a doctrine of immanence, he is forced to make a distinction between a

[1] *Oracles,* pp. 89-92.   [2] *Ib.,* p. 101.   [3] *Ib.,* pp. 85,99.

first and an eternal cause. But such distinction does not at all harmonise with the previous summary of the infinity of the deity, when it was said that, as infinite nature comprehends all things, so an infinite mind is not included in any place, or excluded from any place, but fills immensity with cogitation, perfectly understands all things, and is possessed of all possible powers, perfections and excellencies without addition or diminution.[1] In other words, Allen has now two absolutes on his hands, and yet each of them is held to be limited. How is this discrepancy to be reconciled? It is by recourse to a crass dualism, a separation between those two parts or aspects of the cosmos which once seemed on the verge of being identified. In this, as will be seen, Allen admits a fatal rift in his system. There is, he continues, in God's infinite plenitude, creation and providence, an infinite display of reason, yet every part of the universe of which we have any conception is exterior from the essence of God; for as in nature there is no annihilation of matter, but only change of forms and fluxilities, much more mind, being immaterial, is excepted from physical evils.[2] As if fearing from this diremption between universe and creator, that his system will no longer preserve its boasted consistency, Allen tries to mend the break by expanding his previous hypothesis of nature as being in a constant state of flux:

All forms are indebted to creation for their existence. The dissolution of forms animate or inanimate neither adds to nor diminishes from creation; reduced to their original elements they are changed into new and diverse forms in never ceasing rounds. The particles of matter which compose my body may have existed in more millions of different forms than I am able to enumerate, and be still liable to fluctuations equally numerous. This elementary fluxility of matter, which is mere creation, is as eternal as God, yet the particular productions, arising from natural causes, have a beginning and an end.[3]

With this reference to the ancient doctrine of nature as a plastic principle one may leave the *Oracles of Reason*. This work the elder President Dwight of Yale called the first formal publication in the United States openly directed against the Christian

[1] *Oracles*, p. 44.   [2] *Ib.*, pp. 171, 183, 211.   [3] *Ib.*, p. 253.

religion;[1] President Jared Sparks of Harvard described it as a crude and worthless performance, in which truth and error, reason and sophistry, knowledge and ignorance, ingenuity and presumption are mingled together in a chaos which the author denominates a system.[2]   These academic strictures were perhaps deserved from the standpoint of the orthodox, yet the author received some praise, for as his friend General Washington said: There is an original something about Allen that commands attention.[3]   This word of commendation was not unmerited.   Allen's book had at least two points of originality: in its destructive side, it voiced the popular protest against high Calvinism; in its constructive, it essayed to be an home-spun substitute for the prevalent cosmology.   In the latter respect the work, with all its faults, has a peculiar interest; in the absence of specific information, one is unable to specify the author's historical sources, yet there is in this neglected volume much to remind one of the great system builders.   In its first conjectures, the book suggests Newton's hypothesis of space as the divine sensorium; in its theological way of arguing, concerning benignity to being in general as God's ultimate end in creation, it suggests Edwards' treatise on the latter topic; in its doctrine of the infinitude and divinity of nature alongside of God as the one, infinite being, it suggests Spinoza.   Of these three thinkers Allen mentions the first, was evidently cognizant of the second, but of the last he presumably knew nothing directly.   In his beliefs that without temporal relations God is always perfect; that nature as matter or extension persists through all changes; that things produced immediately by God are identical with infinite modes,—in these three respects Allen reminds one of Spinoza; nevertheless, in its final issues, the ' compendious system ' lacks the keystone, the binding conception of the unitary substance, the all-embracing world order.[4]   Nevertheless, in this very failure to identify the two conceptions, to make creator and creation the

---

[1] *Travels,* Vol. 2, p. 406.

[2] *Life of Ethan Allen,* p. 350, New York, 1839.

[3] *Proceedings of the Vermont Historical Society,* p. 69, 1902.

[4] Cf. Höffding, *Modern Philosophy,* Vol. 1, p. 308, ff., and my review of Ritchie on the *Finite in Spinoza, Journal of Philosophy,* May, 1904.

same One and All, permanent and infinite, the Vermont philosopher did but leave a speculative task to be undertaken by a greater mind in a neighbouring State, for it was Emerson who, struggling with the apparent dualism between God and nature, had the boldness to announce that the Absolute is one with the ordering and creative power of the universe.

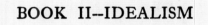

BOOK II--IDEALISM

CHAPTER I

IDEALISM

EARLY American idealism had but two representatives, yet both were notable, the one, Samuel Johnson, being declared as the first in the Berkeleian roll of honour,[1] the other, Jonathan Edwards, as the ablest metaphysician of the period between Leibniz and Kant.[2] But as neither of these colonial thinkers left formal definitions of the movement for which they stood, recourse must be had to the native writers of a later age. Here idealism has been described as ancestrally familiar to a race of Puritan origin. That life is a fleeting manifestation of unfathomable realities which lie beyond it, that all we see and all we do and all we know are mere symbols of things unseen, unactable, unknowable, had been preached to New England from the beginning. Believing that there is ever something beyond, you may call it God, you may call it Nature, you may call it Over-Soul, the philosophical thinkers of renascent New England were idealists. They became aware that our senses perceive only the phenomena of life, and that behind these phenomena, beyond the range of human senses, lurk things not phenomenal.[3] This is the account of an historian of American literature; a more exact philosophical description of idealism makes it the doctrine that the perceptions of sense have no existence independently of the mind; that, though they are not originated by us, but by a power without, that power is not a material substance or substratum, but the will of God acting in a uniform method. Sensations are the divine ideas, communicated to created minds by the will of him in whom these ideas inhere, and by whom they all consist.[4]

[1] C. P. Krauth, *Berkeley's Principles*, p. 36, Philadelphia, 1887.

[2] F. B. Dexter, *Yale Biographies and Annals*, Vol. 1, p. 218, New York, 1885.

[3] Barrett Wendell, *A Literary History of America*, pp. 293, 319, New York, 1905.

[4] G. P. Fisher, *Discussions in History and Theology*, p. 229, New York, 1880.

It was to the elucidation and defence of the above doctrine that Jonathan Edwards was devoted from his earliest years. Samuel Johnson, less of a recluse and more of a scholar, had somewhat wider interests, for as an avowed disciple of Berkeley his was a conscious defence of immaterialism. And this belief of his, also, may be put in the terms of subsequent thought, since what he uttered against materialism may be said to be re-echoed in the following explication of idealism. That hypothesis, said a member of the Concord school of philosophy, is that the material phenomena are but the thought and imagery of the mind of God immediately impressed upon us. It is more simple than materialism, because it makes creative attributes more nearly in accord with the powers which we are conscious of exercising. If matter could be imbued with motive power it could have no inducement, no tendency, no means to determine its motion in one direction more than another, and a tendency or power of self movement which is equally in all directions is a nullity. Moreover, of the existence of matter or of its properties we are not directly conscious. We know nothing of it except by the sensations which we impute to its agency. All our sensations which we attribute to matter are as fully accounted for by the hypothesis that they are the thought, the imagery of the mind of God directly imparted or made palpable to our finite minds, as by that of a distinct external substance in which he has embodied this thought and imagery. In either case it is but the expression of his thoughts and conceptions. In either case, too, it is to us equally real, the sensations by which alone we apprehend these, to us external phenomena, being the same. In either case, too, matter and spirit are still antithetically distinguished, the one having the properties of knowledge, feeling and volition, while the other is unintelligent, senseless and inert.[1]

With these native definitions of idealism it is time to take up the consideration of the two sole representatives of that movement in the American colonies, both of the same province and both of the same college.

[1] R. G. Hazard, *Man a Creative First Cause,* in *Journal of Speculative Philosophy,* July, 1883, Vol. 17, pp. 285-286.

CHAPTER II

SAMUEL JOHNSON

SAMUEL JOHNSON, of Connecticut (1696-1772), was the earliest of native idealists, and the most direct in the formal line of philosophic succession, for it was he who became the close disciple and able expositor of Bishop George Berkeley on the latter's visit to Rhode Island. By his admirers this philosopher of the town of Stratford was considered one of the most learned scholars and acute thinkers of his time in America,[1] while even by his critics it was granted that he loved to see what was going forward in the learned world, and that in conversation he was very social, instructive, agreeable, and much of the gentleman.[2] But whether profound or superficial, Johnson was agreed on all sides to be one who always loved learning and colleges, since he persuaded his idealistic master to donate money and books to Yale College, and was himself the first choice as head of the Philadelphia Academy, and first president of Kings College, New York.

Reputed a very considerable reader all his days, the education of the future neophyte of Berkeleism was gained under difficulties. Among his earliest recollections he mentions finding in a book of his grandfather's several Hebrew words which excited his curiosity, but no one could tell him their meaning. Ultimately this led to his writing an Hebrew grammar, the earliest to appear in the country; immediately it so whetted his desire for learning that he was marked out in the minds of the household as a candidate for instruction in the collegiate school, then being started at Saybrook. But in this infant seminary, destined to be the future Yale College, the New England learning was, at that time, at its lowest ebb. According to an old chronicler, the first generation of learned Puritans having died off, their immediate successors were encum-

[1] A. Campbell Fraser, Berkeley's *Works,* Oxford, 1871, Vol. 4, p. 174.
[2] *Literary Diary of Ezra Stiles,* ed. F. B. Dexter, New York, 1901, Vol. I, p. 268.

bered with all that was useless and pedantic in the academic course of study. The logic and philosophy, in the worst form into which they had been tortured by the Dutch and German compilers of these ponderous scholastic systems of universal knowledge, were the studies of the highest classes.[1] How low was the state of education at Yale is expressed in the summary statement of Johnson's earliest biographer, that the metaphysics taught there was not fit for worms.[2]

Connecticut as yet knew nothing of Descartes, Locke, and Newton, but such dry tomes as Ames' *Medulla Theologiæ* and Wollebius were the established standards of orthodoxy. Johnson early acquired a reputation for skill in making synopses of these foreign systems, and reducing to some method all parts of learning then known,—a curious cobweb of distinctions and definitions, which, as he expressed it, only seemed to blow him up with a great conceit that he was now an adept. But his pride of opinion was to be thoroughly humbled. Accidentally falling in with a rare copy of Lord Bacon's *Advancement of Learning,* there was opened to him a new world of thought, where he found himself like one at once emerging out of the glimmer of twilight into the full light of open day.[3]

As a guide for others who might attempt to grope through the ' palpable obscure ' of scholasticism, Johnson wrote, some years later, what President Ezra Stiles of Yale called a technological system of universal literature.[4] As an intellectual bill of fare for young and hungry minds this was not such an appetising production, but as a basis for his subsequent *Introduction to Philosophy,* written for young men at college, there may be here presented what was a very early draft of

A GENERAL IDEA OF PHILOSOPHY.

PHILOSOPHY is the study of Truth & Wisdom, i. e. of the Objects & Rules conducing to true Happiness.

[1] *American Medical and Philosophical Journal,* New York, October, 1812, p. 136.

[2] T. B. Chandler, *Life of Samuel Johnson,* London, 1824, p. 5.

[3] E. E. Beardsley, *Life of Samuel Johnson,* New York, 1874, p. 6.

[4] Stiles, *Literary Diary,* Vol. 2, p. 340.

For to be Happy being our Great Aim & chief Good this is the Chief End of Philosophy.

And this is the End pursued in all the Arts & Sciences which are only so many means of our Happiness.

For that we may be compleatly happy, both our understandings & Wills must be united with their proper Objects Truth & Goodness, & directed in their exertions in order hereunto.

To this purpose, Philosophy 1st Teaches us to cultivate our Rational powers of Thinking & Speaking, that in the Right Use of them we may know the Truth &, (being Sociable Creatures) may communicate our knowledge one to another: this may thfore be called Rational Philosophy.

2. Philosophy instructs us in the knowledge of things. i. e. all the Truths that concern us, as being the Objects in the Knowledge of which a great part of our happiness consists:—this is called Natural Philosophy.

3. Philosophy teaches us from this Knowledge of things, the rules of behaving ourselves. i.e. chusing & Acting in such a manner as will make us compleatly Happy: & this is called Moral Philosophy.

The two first of these beatifies the Understanding & the third the Wills & Affections.

I. Rational Philosophy teaches us to cultivate our rational powers of thinking & speaking, in Logic, Grammar & Critic—

1. In Logic, by leading us into our own Minds & giving us a Survey of the several powers & objects, & prescribing such general Rules as may happily secure us from error & lead us to the Knowledge of Truth.

2. In Grammar & Critic by teaching us, according to the several Languages, how to express the Truth we know, & communicate intelligibly the sense of our own Minds to others.

But because Speech is various according as it serves several different purposes, there are several other Arts relating to it, as

1. Rhetoric & Oratory which teach us to cultivate & adorn our Speech for the purposes of Instruction & persuasion.

2. History which teaches us to compose a just & true Narration of Matters of Fact, for examples to Posterity.

3. Poetry which teaches us to make a lively description of other things & Facts whither real or imaginary, with the Advantages of numbers & Harmony, for the better conveying & more strongly fixing in our Minds, the most profitable Instructions with the utmost Delight & Pleasure.

II. Natural Philosophy influences us in the Knowledge of

Things, whither Ideas or Spirits, for to these two Heads all things may be referred, hence Physics & Metaphysics.

1. Certain Combinations of Ideas we call Bodies, & that part of Natural philosophy which explains the Nature of Bodies is called Physics.

1. In Mathematics teaches us to number & Measure

2. In Mechanics—explaining the Laws of Motion, Gravitation &c.

3. In Geology (if I may make a New Word) it takes a survey of & explains all the phenomena of Nature in the Several Tribes of Beings in this Globe of Earth & lastly

4. In Astronomy it passes off from this Globe & contemplates the System of the Universe, describing & accounting for the phenomena of the Heavens.

2. Intelligent & Active Beings are called Spirits, & that part of Natural Philosophy which treats of the Nature of Spirit is called Metaphysics or pneumatology, which

1. Treats of the Nature & powers of our own Souls. & then

2. Inquires concerning other Tribes of Intelligence, &

3. Of the Nature Attributes & Operations of GOD, the Supreme & Almighty Spirit, who made preserves & Governs all, in whom are the Architypes of all our Ideas, & who is Father & Original of all Created Spirits. (This is called Theology).

III. Moral Philosophy, from this knowledge of Things, & especially that of Spirits, teaches us how to behave & Conduct our Selves, to chuse & act in every relation, so as to be truely Happy.

particularly It teaches us the Rules of our Behavior

1. Towards God: our Maker preserver & Governour, who is our Chief Good.

2. Towards our Neibours, Other Spirits of the same Nature with our Selves.

3. In the Government of our Selves, our Reasons, Appetites, & Affections, & this is called—

Ethics, to which belongs Politics.

But because some parts (especially the second part) of Natural Philosophy, & the whole of Moral Philosophy, are of the greatest concern to us, God has of his special Kindness to us, given us, relating to them a particular and express revelation of his Mind & Will, & how we, (having offended Him) may yet secure his Favour, thro' the Mediation of his Son.

Here therefore belongs the Christian Philosophy which is only Theology & Morality more clearly & perfectly revealed to us, & improved by positive Intimations of the Divine Will in those things wherein Natural Reason did not suffice to instruct us. This

Divine Revelation, therefore must be called in to our Assistance in all those parts of philosophy whither Natural or Moral, wherein God is pleased to hold forth any Light unto us.[1]

In this primitive draught of his *Cyclopædia of Learning* there is noticeable the first phase of the future idealist's speculative beliefs. Both student and teacher in a strictly Puritan institution, Johnson has nevertheless gained two characteristics of a more liberal form of thought, inasmuch as the beginning of this scheme exhibits him as imbued with optimism, while the aim of the whole is to reach evidences of cosmic design. In a word, the author is already of one mind with those milder British deists from whom he had derived views which he had been obliged hitherto to conceal with caution. As a further expression of the rationalism of his first period there came the *Introduction to Philosophy* of the year 1731. The purpose of this small tract, ' by a gentleman educated at Yale College,' was declared to be: the setting before young gentlemen a general view of the whole system of learning in miniature, as geography exhibits a general map of the whole terraqueous globe. As in the natural world, so in the intellectual, young students must have a prospect of the whole compass of their business and the general end pursued through the whole.[2]

As a work for juveniles, Johnson's first publication cannot be considered profound; yet by its very simplicity and directness it the more clearly discloses the writer's earlier beliefs. Adopting the Lockean divisions of philosophy into rational, natural, and moral, as the three great provinces of the intellectual world *toto coelo* different and distinct from one another, the writer gives as his three disciplines: first, ontology, which treats of things intellectual and abstracted from every particular nature; next, somatology, which concerns the world of bodies, from this earth with its furniture, to our sun with his noble and splendid chorus of planets, satellites and comets; lastly, pneumatology, which inquires after the true efficient cause of all these phenomena, and evidently

---

[1] MS. in the possession of the Columbia University Library, New York.

[2] Advertisement from second edition, New London, 1743; for full title see Notes.

demonstrates it to be an omnipresent, omnipotent and infinitely wise and benevolent spirit.[1]

Such is the author's brief preface to his *Introduction to Philosophy*. Further examination thereof discloses its initial emphasis on practical ethics, since it presents an easy utilitarianism, which rises into an intellectual hedonism, and, at the same time, is given an altruistic rather than an egoistic turn by including in its scope the public welfare. However, this little work is more than a manual for practical living; it contains the elements of an interesting system of speculation,—a deistic framework sufficiently loose and flexible to receive a later idealistic covering. As a cosmology, that system is optimistic; it considers all nature to be directed by a supreme mind outside itself, and man's chief end to be the study of the works of an infinitely wise and benevolent spirit, in the knowledge of whom the greater part of our happiness consists.[2] As a psychology, the system is only partially empirical; it holds to the twofold Lockean division of mind into sensitive and rational, but instead of emphasising the former at the expense of the latter, it insists that spirits only can properly be said to be efficient causes, as having alone an internal principle of activity or of variously exerting or determining themselves, according to design, counsel and free choice.[3] As an ontology, the system postulates a Cartesian conception of matter as inert and passive, and mind as unextended and active, and thus leaves an opening for an idealistic doctrine of occasionalism, whereby not only is the corporeal world subsisted, acted and adjusted by an infinitely wise and powerful mind, but that mind has constituted fixed and established laws, according to which sensible objects are constantly connected one with another.[4] It is here that Johnson runs over into an epistemology akin to the Berkeleian divine language of signs, for he makes the deity to be the immediate efficient and author of all the phenomena of nature in whose eternal, all comprehending mind are the archetypes of our ideas.[5] All these matters are more fully expanded in the following simple but dignified passages from the *Introduction*.

[1] *Introduction to Philosophy*, pp. 15, 17.   [2] *Ib.*, pp. 5, 6.
[3] *Ib.*, p. 20.   [4] *Ib.*, pp. 5, 14.   [5] *Ib.*, p. 20.

The great end that above all things concerns us is that we be truly happy in the whole of our nature and duration; our true happiness consists in the pleasure which attends the contemplation of all things that come within the compass of our knowledge. In order that we may be completely happy all the powers of our souls, our understandings, wills and reflections, must be united with their proper objects which are truth and good. In order to accomplish this, the whole business of philosophy, truth must be distinguished into natural and intellectual, good into natural and practical. Natural or real truth or the truth of things is the reality of their existence; intellectual truth is the knowledge of things as being what they really are, in their existence together with all their related connections and dependencies with regard to the whole. . . . Natural good is either of things or persons. The natural good of things is their fitness or suitableness to answer the harmony, beauty and usefulness of the whole, so as to render it subservient to the pleasure and happiness of the sensitive and rational nature. The natural good of persons is their pleasure or happiness, and the means, whether things or actions, necessary to promote it. . . It is necessary to the character of a true philosopher that he thoroughly understands not only his own personal good, but also wherein the publick good or the good of the whole consists, and that in all his conduct he firmly and steadily adheres to it and ever acts with a sincere, zealous and disinterested view at promoting it. . . . The great system of the universe consists of bodies and spirits. By bodies we mean the extended, solid beings that we perceive by our sense; as such they are merely passive and inert, i. e. utterly destitute even of the least degree of perception and activity. Such are all sensible things, as consisting of certain fixed combinations of sensible qualities, such as extension, figure, solidity, motion or rest, colours, sounds, tastes, smells, heat or cold, hardness or softness,—in short whatsoever we perceive by our senses. As our spirits or minds are liable to error in contemplation as well as to irregularity and viciousness in practice (in both which consists our greatest depravity and misery) we must first cultivate our intellectual or rational powers. Furnished with these faculties we go forth and contemplate the natural world and thereby demonstrate the being, wisdom, power and goodness of God who is our chief good. . . .

Concluding his *Introduction* with the observation that philosophy, to obtain the whole draught in one view, is the study of truth and knowledge in the pursuit of true wisdom, Johnson discloses the second step of importance in his intellectual career. Before his memorable meeting with Dean Berkeley, from whose very lips he derived those notions of idealism which are as yet but faintly portrayed, Johnson had emerged from the chrysalis state of spinning out inherited systems of thought into the freer state of acting for himself. Thus he was led to abandon his tutorship at Yale College, and the faith in which he had been bred, from the belief that there was less of truth in Puritanism than in Anglicanism. At the least, the reading of such writers as the Archbishop of Cambray, of Leland, Stillingfleet, Tillotson and Wollaston showed that he preferred a religion appealing to reason to a religion appealing to inscrutable decrees. At this juncture there arises a striking contrast between the Anglican and Puritan types of mind as represented by the two Yalensian idealists. Johnson's system was much less profound than that of his casual pupil Edwards, but far better fitted to be human nature's daily food, the one being founded on the strictest metaphysical reasoning, the other designedly accommodated to the general rate and bulk of mankind.

In achieving this easier way of thinking, Johnson had no light task. As he himself wrote, it was only after many scruples and intolerable uneasiness of mind and after a public avowal of the same, that he was enabled to leave the collegiate church and to cross the ocean for the sake of that excellent church, the Church of England.[1] Voyaging across the Atlantic for the purpose of being ordained, the Anglo-American's errand served as an introduction to notable places and persons. Among the former he visited Oxford and Cambridge Universities, from which in due course he was to receive honourary degrees; among the latter he met Alexander Pope at his villa, the English Samuel Johnson in London, and many others of a rationalistic turn. Returning from these larger interests to the narrow bigotry of the British provinces, possibly by reason of the very irritation of that contrast, Johnson was now led into the only controversey of his life which did not harmonise with his reputation for possessing such a sweetness and benevolence of character, and such an affection for everything that God made, that he would have had every creature completely

[1] Beardsley, *Life*, p. 23.

happy. Settling in Stratford, Connecticut, so early as 1725, Johnson was drawn into an acrimonious debate with the Calvinistic Jonathan Dickinson, who was subsequently to become the first head of Princeton College. As published in later years, this debate took the form of *A Letter from Aristocles to Authades concerning the Sovereignty and Promises of God*.[1] Herein the anonymous pamphleteer confesses that he is not insensible that the odious name of Arminian will be the cry against these papers for those little minds that are affected with sounds more than sense. Still he is obliged to argue as follows:

The Doctrine of Divine sovereignty as implying God's eternal, arbitrary and absolute determination of the everlasting fate of his creatures from his meer inner motion and without any consideration of their good and ill behaviour, is contrary to the nature and attributes of God because inconsistent with the very notion of his being a moral governor of the world. For it represents him as laying his creatures under a necessity of being what they are, whether good or bad, and so leaves no room for either virtue or vice, praise or blame, reward or punishment, properly speaking . . . I cannot think it consistent with the divine attributes, God's wisdom, holiness, justice, etc., to give Being to any of his intelligent creatures without putting them into a condition that would render being desirable to them; nor to put them eternally into a condition that is worse than not to be. . . . Strictly and philosophically speaking, there can be no propriety in attributing prescience or foreknowledge to God, because there's neither past nor to come, neither fore or after in him; for these expressions imply succession, which implies limitation, which cannot be in an infinitely perfect and immutable being. With strict propriety we must not say God foreknows or foreordains, but that he knows or ordains, that is, by one single act, one infinite, all-comprehending view, (to which all things, that with respect to our narrow, limited minds, are past, present or to come, are equally and at once present), he sees and knows, approves or disapproves his creatures as being what they really are, and appoints, orders and conducts them according, his great end to his creatures being that they might be happy.[2]

Having attacked Calvinism with the deistic argument from optimism and the scholastic argument from the nature of time,

[1] Boston, 1745.

[2] *Letter from Aristocles*, written September 10th, 1744, pp. 2-12.

Johnson is not yet satisfied. His is also the practical concern of securing the minds of poor, mistaken people from entertaining such impious ideas, as that everything we do is under a fatal necessity, and we can do no otherwise than we do.[1] Hence in a second *Letter,* Aristocles of Connecticut thus proceeds against Authades of New Jersey:

Your notion of the Divine Sovereignty represents God as laying his creatures under a necessity of being what they are whether good or bad. Necessity is a state or condition of Being in which as man is so placed that however freely he may be supposed to act, it is absolutely out of his power by any means that are allowed him, to think or act otherwise than he does. Suppose some unhappy wretch entirely in the power of some arbitrary sovereign prince. Suppose the sovereign had beforehand absolutely resolved he should be hanged, but for the fancy of the thing, or purely to please himself, and gratify a capricious humour of his, commands him to lift a weight of ten thousand pounds and heave it to the distance of a mile, and tells him if he will do this he will give him an estate of ten thousand a year, and if he will not do it he shall certainly be hanged. At the same time he promises and designs him no manner of help or means whereby he might be enabled to accomplish it. It is true he speaks very kindly to him, and gives him several great encouragements expressed just like promises. He tells him if he will be up and doing he will be with him, and that if he will try and strive and pray for help, his labour shall not be in vain. However, the truth of the matter at the bottom is that he never intends to help him, having beforehand absolutely resolved he shall be hanged, and without help he can no more stir the weight than create a world. Now I humbly conceive that this unhappy wretch is under a necessity of disobeying and being hanged.[2]

These polemical letters of the Stratford controversialist have little philosophic worth, yet they serve to illustrate the most important transition in their author's intellectual life, namely, the transition

---

[1] 'A letter to Mr. Jonathan Dickinson in defence of Aristocles against Authades concerning the Sovereignty and Promises of God,' Boston, 1747, p. 22.

[2] 'Letter . . . in defence of Aristocles,' pp. 14-20. Cf. also Johnson's sermon 'Against absolute predestination, with its horror, despair, and gloomy apprehension.' (Columbia MS., n.p., n.d.).

from a popular deism to a high idealism. That change was indicated in a casual reference to the author of the *Minute Philosopher* as supplying him with his strongest arguments against the doctrine of necessity. It was the Reverend George Berkeley, the dean of Londonderry, who in 1729 took up his residence in Newport, Rhode Island. According to the account of Berkeley's chief biographer it was then that Johnson became a convert to the New Principle, which he regarded, when rightly understood, as the true philosophical support of faith. The denial of the absolute existence of Matter, a whimsical paradox to the superficial thinker, he found to mean nothing more than a denial of an inconceivable substratum of sensible phenomena. The affirmation of the merely relative existence of sensible things was to him the affirmation of orderly combinations of sensible phenomena, in which our corporeal pains and pleasures were determined by Divine Ideas that are the archetypes of physical existence. This conception of the Universe, habitually kept before him, seemed to Johnson more apt than any other system to harmonise with our individual dependence on the Supreme Mind or Will, perpetually present and perpetually active. In his own works he adopted and applied this philosophy, with a force and clearness which entitle him to an eminent place among the thinkers of America.[1] The date of the first interview between the Irish idealist and his American follower has not been discovered, but so early as June 25th, 1729, Berkeley wrote to Johnson at much length in answer to objections and inquiries which had been made in reference to the immaterialistic philosophy. It is said that this first letter explained or defended under eleven heads the speculative ideas which Berkeley had already published; at the least it contains a reference to the *Principles of Human Knowledge* and the tract, *De Motu,* which the Dean offers to send to his disciple.[2] Except for a reference to Johnson as a man of parts and a philosophic genius, there is little of interest in the published portions of this epistle, but such is not the case in regard to the lost portions. Here it is declared that it is a great pity that most of Berkeley's many letters to Johnson have been lost, as some fragments which have been preserved are of more interest

[1] A. Campbell Fraser, Berkeley's *Works,* Vol. 4, p. 175.
[2] Beardsley, *Life,* p. 71.

to the metaphysician than any others in his correspondence.[1] Fortunately there is offered, at this late day, an indirect way of reconstructing by inference the contents of this lost correspondence, and that is through Johnson's answers to the problems originally raised by the idealist from over seas. To the eleven points raised in the first letter Johnson makes specific rejoinder in this hitherto unpublished

Letter to the Rev.d Dr. Berkeley Dean, of London Derry, upon reading His Books of the Principles of Human Knowledge & Dialogues

Stratford Sept. 10. 1729

Rev.d S^r.

The Kind Invitation you gave me in Reading those Excellent Books which you was pleased to order into my Hands, is all the Apology I shall offer for the Trouble I now presume to give you: But nothing could encourage me to expose to your views my low and mean way of Thinking & writing, but my hopes of an Interest in that Candor & Tenderness which are so conspicuous both in your writings & Conversation.

These Books, (for which I stand humbly obliged to you) contain Speculations the most surprisingly ingenious I have ever met with: & I must confess that the Reading of them has almost convinced me, That Matter as it has been commonly defined for an unknown Quiddity is but a meer non-Entity. That it is a strong presumption against the Existence of it, that there never could be conceived any manner of connexion between it & our Ideas: That the *esse* of Things is only their *percipi*: & that the Rescuing us from the Absurdities of Abstract Ideas & the Gross Notion of Matter that have so much obtained, deserves well of the Learned World, in that it clears away very many difficulties & Perplexities in the Sciences.

And I am of Opinion that this way of Thinking can't fail of prevailing in the World, because it is likely to prevail very much among us in these parts, Several Ingenious Men having intirely come in to it: But there are many others on the other hand Tt cannot be reconciled to it; tho' of these there are Some who have a very good Opinion of it & plainly see many happy Consequences attending it, on account of which they are well inclined to embrace it, but think they find Some Difficulties in their way which they can't get over, & some Objections not sufficiently answered to their Satisfaction: And since you have condescended

[1] Fraser, Berkeley's *Works*, Vol. 4, p. 176.

to give me leave to do so, I will make bold to lay before you Sundry Things, which yet remain in the Dark either to my self or to others, & which I can't account for either to my own, or at least to y^r Satisfaction.

1 The great prejudice that lies against it with some is its Repugnancy to & Subversion of Sr I. Newton's philosophy in Sundry points: to which they have been so much attached, T^t. they can't Suffer themselves in the least to call it in Question in any Instance, But indeed it does not appear to me so inconsistent therewith as at first blush it did, for the Laws of Nature th [it] so happily explains are the same whither Matter be supposed or not. how ever, let S^r. *Isaac Newton,* or any other man be heard, only so far as his opinion is supported by Reason:— But after all I confess I have so great a Regard for the Philosophy of that Great Man, That I would gladly see as much of it as may be, to obtain in this Ideal Scheme.

2 The Objection, That it takes away all Subordinate Natural Causes, & accounts for all Appearances meerly by the immediate will of the Supreme Spirit, does not seem to many to be answered to their Satisfaction: It is readily granted that our Ideas are inert & can't cause one another, & are truly only Signs one of Another. For Instance my Idea of Fire is not the Cause of my Idea of burning & of ashes. But inasmuch as these Ideas are so connected as that they seem necessarily to point out to us the Relations of Cause & Effect, we can't help thinking our Ideas are Pictures of Things without our Minds at least, tho' not without the Great Mind, & which are their Archetypes, between which these Relations do obtain. I kindle a Fire & leave it, no created Mind beholds it: I return again & find a great alteration in the Feuel: has there not been in my absence all the while that gradual alteration making in the Archetype of my Idea of Wood which I should have had the Idea of if I had been present? & is there not some Archetype of my Idea of Fire, which under the Agency of the Divine Will has gradually caused this Alteration? & so in all other Instances, our Ideas are so connected, that they seem necessarily to refer our Minds to, some Originals which are properly (tho' subordinate) causes & effects one of another; insomuch that unless they be so, we can't help thinking our Selves under a perpetual Delusion.

3. That all the Phenomena of Nature must ultimately be refered to the Will of the Infinite Spirit, is what must be allowed; But to suppose his immediate Energy in the production of every Effect, does not seem to impress so lively & great a Sense of his Power & wisdom upon our Minds, as to Suppose a Subordination

of Causes & Effects among the Archetypes of our Ideas as he that should make a watch or clock of ever so beautiful an appearance, & that should measure the Time ever so exactly, yet if he should be obliged to stand by it & influence & direct all its motions, he would seem but very deficient in both his ability & skill, in comparison with him who should be able to make one that would regularly keep on its motion & measure the time for a considerable time, without the Intervention of any immediate force of its Author or any one else, impressed upon it.

4. And as this Tenet seems thus to abate our Sense of the Wisdom & Power of God, so there are some that cannot be persuaded that it is sufficiently cleared from bearing hard on his Holiness: Those who suppose that the Corrupt affections of our Souls & Evil Practices consequent to them, are occasioned by certain irregular mechanical motions of our Bodies, and that these motions, come to have an habitual irregular Byass and Tendency by means of our own voluntary indulgence to them, which we might have governed to better purpose, do in this way of thinking, sufficiently bring the guilt of those ill habits & actions upon our Selves; but if in an habitual sinner, every object & Motion be but an Idea, & every wicked Appetite the Effect of such a Sett of Ideas, & these Ideas, the immediate effort of the Almighty upon his Mind; it seems to follow, That the Immediate Cause of such Ideas must be the cause of those Immoral Appetites & Actions; because, he is born down before them seemingly, even in spight of himself. At first indeed they were only Occasions, which might be withstood, & so, proper means of Tryal, but now they become causes of his Immoralities: When therefore a person is under the power of a vicious habit, & it can't but be foreseen that the suggestion of such & such Ideas will unavoidably produce those Immoralities, how can it consist with the Holiness of God to suggest them?

5. It is after all that has been said on that Head, Still something shocking to many to think that there should be nothing but a meer show in all the art & contrivance appearing in the Structure, (for Instance) of a Human Body, particularly of the Organs of Sense: The Curious Structure of the Eye, what can it be more then meerly a fine show, if there be no connexion more than you Admit of, between that & vision? It Seems from the make of it to be designed for an Instrument or means of conveying the Images of External Things to the perceptive Faculty within; & if it be not so if it be really of no use in conveying visible objects to our minds, & if our visible Ideas are immediately cre-

ated in them by the Will of the Almighty, why should it be made to seem to be an Instrument or medium as much as if indeed it really were so? It is evident from the Conveying of Images into a dark room thro' a Lens, that the Eye is a Lens, & that the Images of Things are painted on the Bottom of it: But to what purpose is all this, if there be no connexion between this fine apparatus, & the Act of Vision: can it be tho't a sufficient Argument that there is no connexion between them because we can't discover it, or conceive how it should be?

6. There are some who say, That if our Sensations don't depend on any Bodily organs—they dont see how Death can be supposed to make any Alteration in the Manner of our Perception, or indeed how there should be, (properly speaking) any Separate State of the Soul at all: For if our Bodies are nothing but Ideas, & if our having Ideas in this Present State does not depend upon, what are tho't to be the Organs of Sense, & lastly if we are supposed (as doubtless we must,) to have Ideas in that State; It should seem that immediately upon our Remove from our present Situation, we should still be attended with the same Ideas of Bodies as we have now, & consequently with the same Bodies, or at least with Bodies however different: & if so what Room is there left for any Resurrection, properly so called? So that while this Tenet delivers us from the embarrassments that attend the Doctrine of a material Resurrection, it seems to have no place for any Resurrection at all, at least in the Sense that word seems to bear in St Jn. 5.20/29.

7. Some of us are at a loss to understand your meaning when you speak of Archetypes. You say the being of Things consists in their being perceived. & that things are nothing but Ideas, That our Ideas have no unperceived Archetypes, but yet you allow Archetypes to our Ideas when things are not perceived by our Minds they exist in i. e. are perceived by some other mind. Now I understand you, That there is a two fold Existence of things or Ideas, one in the Divine Mind, & the Other in Created Minds the one archetypal & the other Ectypal: That therefore the Real original & permanent Existence of Things is Archetypal, being Ideas in *mente Divinâ,* & that our Ideas are Copies of them, & so far forth Real Things, as they are correspondent to their Archetypes & exhibited to us, or begotten in us by the Will of the Almighty, in such Measure & Degrees & by such stated Laws & Rules as he is pleased to observe: that therefore there is no unperceived Substance intervening between the Divine Ideas & ours as a medium occasion or Instrument by which to G [muti-

lated] to our Ideas in us, but that which was tho't to be the
Material Existence of things, is in Truth only Ideal in the Divine
Mind. Do I understand you right? Is it not therefore your
meaning, That tho' Existence of our Ideas, (i. e the Ectypal
Things) depends upon our perceiving them, yet There are External to any Created Mind, in the All-Comprehending Spirit, Real
& permanent Archetypes, (as stable & permanent as ever matter
was thought to be,) to which these Ideas of ours are correspondent, & so that, (tho' the visible & tangible Ideas are *toto cœlo*
different & distinct Things, yet) there may be said to be External
to my mind, in the Divine Mind, an Archetype, (for Instance of
the Candle that is before me) in which, the Originals of both my
visible & tangible Ideas, Light, Heat, Whiteness, Softness, &c
under such a particular cylindrical Figure, are united, so that it
may be properly said to be the Same Thing that I both see &
feel?

8. If this, or something like it might be understood to be
your meaning, it would seem less shocking to say that we dont
see & feel the same thing, because we cant dispossess our Minds
of the Notion of an External World, & would be allowed to conceive That, tho' there were no Intelligent Creature before *Adam*
to be a spectator of it, yet the World was really six days, *in
archetypo,* gradually proceeding from an informal chaotic State,
into that beautiful Show wherein it first appeared to his mind, &
that the Comet that appeared in 1680 (for instance) has now, tho'
no created Mind, beholds it, a real Existence in the All-comprehending Spirit, & is making its prodigious Tour, thro' the vast
Fields of Ether, and lastly that the whole vast Congeries of
Heaven and Earth, the mighty Systems of Worlds, with all their
Furniture, have a Real Being in the Eternal Mind, antecedent
to, & Independent on, the perception of Created Spirit, & that
when we see & feel, &c. That that Almighty Mind, by his Immediate Fiat, begets in our Minds, *(pro nostro modulo)* Ideas Correspondent to them, & which may be imagined, in some degree Resemblances of them.

9. But if there be Archetypes to our Ideas, will it not follow
that there is External Space, Extention Figure & motion, as being
Archetypes of our Ideas, to which we give those names? And
indeed for my part I cannot disengage my mind from the persuasion that that is external space: when I have been trying ever
so much, to conceive of space as being nothing but an Idea in my
Mind, it will return upon me even in spight of my utmost Efforts,
certainly there must be, there can't but be, External Space. The

Length, Breadth & Thickness of any Idea, its true, are but Ideas: The Distance between two Trees in my mind, is but an Idea, but if there are archetypes to the Ideas of the Trees, there must be an Archetype to the Idea of the Distance between them. Nor can I see how it follows, that there is no external Absolute height bigness or Distance of Things, because they appear greater or less to us, according as we are nearer or remote from them, or see them with our naked Eyes or with Glasses; any more than it follows that a Man, for instance, is not really absolutely six foot high measured by a two foot rule apply'd to his Body, because divers pictures of him may be drawn some 6. some 4. some two foot long according to the Same measure. Nobody ever Imagined that the Idea of Distance is without the Mind, but does it therefore follow that there is no External Distance, to which the Idea is correspondent, for Instance, between Rhode Island & Stratford: Truly I wish it were not so great, that I might be so happy as to have a more easy access to you, & more nearly Enjoy the Advantages of your Instructions.

10. You allow Spirits to have a Real Existence external to one another: Methinks, if so, there must be Distance between them, & Space wherein they exist, or else they must all exist in one Individual Spot or point, & as it were coincide one with another: I cant see how external Space & Duration are any more Abstract Ideas, than Spirits: As we have, (properly speaking,) no Ideas of Spirits, so indeed, neither have we of External Space & Duration: But it seems to me that the Existence of these must unavoidably follow—from the Existence of those Insomuch, that I can no more conceive of their not being, than I can conceive of the non-Existence of the Infinite & Eternal Mind: They seem as necessarily existent independent of any Created Mind as the DEITY Himself. Or must we say there is nothing in Dr. Clarkes Argument *a priori, in his Demonstration of the Being & Attributes of God,* or in what S.ʳ Isaac Newton says about the Infinity & Eternity of God in His *Scholium Generale* to his *Principia?* I should be glad to know your sense of what those two Authors say upon this Subject.

11. You will forgive the Confusedness of my Tho'ts & not wonder at my writing like a Man something bewildered, since I am as it were got into a new world amazed at every thing about me: These Ideas of ours, What are they? Is the Substance of the Mind the Sub*stratum* to its Ideas? Is it proper to call them Modifications of our Minds? or Impressions upon them? or what? Truly I can't tell what to make of them,

any more than of matter it self. What is the *Esse* of Spirits? — you seem to think it impossible to abstract their Existence from their Thinking. Princ. p. 143. sec. 98. Is then the *Esse* of Minds nothing else but *percipere,* as the *Esse* of Ideas is *percipi?* — Certainly, methinks, there must be an unknown Somewhat, that thinks & Acts, as difficult to be conceived of as Matter, & the Creation of which, as much beyond us, as the Creation of Matter. Can Actions be the *Esse* of Any thing? Can they exist or be exerted without some Being who is the Agent? And may not that Being be easily imagined to exist without acting, e. g. without Thinking? And Consequently, (for you are there speaking of Duration,) May he not be said *Durare, etsi non cogitet,* to persist in Being, tho' Thinking were intermitted for a while? & is not this sometimes fact? The Duration of the Eternal Mind, must certainly imply some thing besides an Eternal Succession of Ideas; May I not then conceive that tho' I get my Idea of Duration, by observing the Succession of Ideas in my Mind; yet there is a *perseverarin existendo,* a Duration of my Being, & of the Being of other Spirits distinct from, & independent of this Succession of Ideas.

But S^r. I doubt I have more than tired your patience with so many, (& I fear you will think them impertinent,) Questions: for tho' they are Difficulties with me, or at least with some in my neighbourhood, for whose sake, in part, I write, yet I dont imagine they can appear such to you, who have so perfectly digested your tho'ts upon this Subject. & perhaps they may vanish before me upon a more mature Consideration of it: However, I should be very thankful for your Assistance, if it were not a pitty you should wast your Time, (which would be employed to much better purpose,) in writing to a person so obscure, & so unworthy of such a Labour as I am. But I shall live with some Impatience, till I see the second part of your design accomplished, wherein I hope to see these, (If they can be tho't such) or any other objections, that may have occurred to you, since your writing the first part, obviated; & the usefulness of this Doctrine more particularly displayed in the further Application of it to the Arts and Sciences May we not hope to see Logic, Mathematics, & Natural Philosophy, Pneumatology Theology & Morality all in their Order, appearing with a new Lustre, under the Advantages they may receive from it? You have, at least given us to hope for a Geometry cleared of many perplexities that render that Sort of Study troublesome, which I shall be very glad of, who have found that Science more irksome to me than any other, tho' indeed, I am but very little versed in any of them. but I will not trespass any further upon your Patience: My very humble Service to M^r. James & M^r. Dalton, & I am with the greatest veneration,

Rev^d. S^r.

your Most obliged
& most obedient
humble servant
Samuel Johnson

For the Rev^d. D^r. George Berkeley
Dean of London Derry
at Rhode Island [1]

To this ingenious and interesting document of Johnson, Berkeley made reply in what was presumably the third letter in the series, for it is specifically called an answer, and takes up in order at least six out of the eleven topics originally set forth. Says the Dean:

. . . It is a common fault for men to hate opposition, and to be too much wedded to their own opinions. I am so sensible of this in others that I could not pardon it in myself, if I considered mine any further than they seem to me to be true; which I shall be the better able to judge of, when they have passed the scrutiny of persons so well qualified to examine them as you and your friends appear to be; to whom my illness must be an apology for not sending this answer sooner.

1. The true use and end of Natural Philosophy is to explain the phenomena of nature, which is done by discovering the laws of Nature, and reducing particular appearances to them. This is Sir Isaac Newton's method; and such method or design is not in the least inconsistent with the principles I lay down. This mechanical philosophy doth not assign or suppose any one natural efficient cause in the strict and proper sense; nor is it, as to its use, concerned about *matter;* nor is matter connected therewith; nor doth it infer the being of matter. It must be owned, indeed, that the mechanical philosophers do suppose (though unnecessarily) the being of matter. They do even pretend to demonstrate that matter is proportional to gravity, which, if they could, this indeed would furnish an unanswerable objection. But let us examine their demonstration—It is laid down in the first place, that the momentum of any body is the product of its quantity by its velocity, *moles in celeritatem ducta.* If, therefore, the velocity

---

[1] Holograph letter in possession of Columbia University Library.

is given, the momentum will be as its quantity. But it is observed that bodies of all kinds descend in vacuo with the same velocity; therefore the momentum of descending bodies is as the quantity or moles *i. e.* gravity is as matter. But this argument concludes nothing, and is a mere circle. For, I ask, when it is premised that the momentum is equal to the *moles in celeritatem ducta,* how the moles or quantity of matter is estimated. If you say, by extent, the proposition is not true; if by weight, then you suppose that the quantity of matter is proportional to matter: i. e. the conclusion is taken for granted in one of the premises. As for absolute space and motion, which are also supposed without any necessity or use, I refer you to what I have already published; particularly in a Latin treatise, *De Motu,* which I shall take care to send you.

2. Cause is taken in different senses. A proper active efficient cause I can conceive none but Spirit; nor any action, strictly speaking, but where there is Will. But this doth not hinder the allowing occasional causes (which are in truth but signs), and more is not requisite in the best physics, *i. e.* the mechanical philosophy. Neither doth it hinder the admitting other causes besides God; such as spirits of different orders, which may be termed active causes, as acting indeed, though by limited and derivative powers. But as for an unthinking agent, no point of physics is explained by it, nor is it conceivable.

3. Those who have all along contended for a material world have yet acknowledged that *natura naturans* (to use the language of the Schoolmen) is God; and that the divine conservation of things is equipollent to, and, in fact, the same thing with a continued repeated creation: in a word, that conservation and creation differ only in the *terminus a quo.* These are the common opinions of the Schoolmen; and Durandus, who held the world to be a machine like a clock, made and put in motion by God, but afterwards continuing to go of itself, was therein particular, and had few followers. The very poets teach a doctrine not unlike the schools,—*Mens agitat molem.* (Virg. Ænid VI.) The Stoics and Platonists are everywhere full of the same notion. I am not therefore singular in this point itself, so much as in my way of proving it—Further, it seems to me that the power and wisdom of God are as worthily set forth by supposing him to act immediately as an omnipresent infinitely active spirit, as by supposing him to act by the mediation of subordinate causes, in preserving and governing the natural world. A clock may indeed go independent of its maker or artificer, inasmuch as the gravitation of its pendulum proceeds from another cause, and that the

artificer is not the adequate cause of the clock; so that the analogy would not be just to suppose a clock is in respect of its artist what the world is in respect of its Creator. For aught I can see, it is no disparagement to the perfection of God to say that all things necessarily depend on him as their Conservator as well as Creator, and that all nature would shrink to nothing, if not upheld and preserved in being by the same force that first created it. This I am sure is agreeable to Holy Scripture, as well as to the writings of the most esteemed philosophers; and if it is to be considered that men make use of tools and machines to supply defect of power in themselves, we shall think it no honour to the divinity to attribute such things to him.

4. As to guilt, it is the same thing whether I kill a man with my hands or an instrument; whether I do it myself or make use of a ruffian. The imputation therefore upon the sanctity of God is equal, whether we suppose, our sensations to be produced immediately by God, or by the mediation of instruments and subordinate causes, all which are his creatures, and moved by his laws. This theological consideration, therefore, may be waived, as leading besides the question; for such I hold are points to be which bear equally hard on both sides of it. Difficulties about the principle of moral actions will cease, if we consider that all guilt is in the will, and that our ideas, from whatever cause they are produced, are alike inert.

5. As to the art and contrivance in the parts of animals, &c., I have considered that matter in the *Principles of Human Knowledge,* and, if I mistake not, sufficiently shown the wisdom and use thereof, considered as signs and means of information. I do not indeed wonder that on first reading what I have written, men are not thoroughly convinced. On the contrary, I should very much wonder if prejudices, which have been many years taking root, should be extirpated in a few hours' reading. I had no inclination to trouble the world with large volumes. What I have done was rather with a view of giving hints to thinking men, who have leisure and curiosity to go to the bottom of things, and pursue them in their own minds. Two or three times reading these small tracts, and making what is read the occasion of thinking, would, I believe, render the whole familiar and easy to the mind, and take off that shocking appearance which hath often been observed to attend speculative truths.

6. I see no difficulty in conceiving a change of state, such as is vulgarly called Death, as well without as with material substance. It is sufficient for that purpose that we allow sensible bodies, *i. e.* such as are immediately perceived by sight and touch;

the existence of which I am so far from questioning (as philosophers are used to do,) that I establish it, I think, upon evident principles. Now, it seems very easy to conceive the soul to exist in a separate state (*i. e.* divested from those limits and laws of motion and perception with which she is embarrassed here), and to exercise herself on new ideas, without the intervention of these tangible things we call bodies. It is even very possible to apprehend how the soul may have ideas of colour without an eye, or of sounds without an ear.[1] . . .

Berkeley's fragmentary letter of answer, breaking off at the sixth point of metaphysical investigation, probably considered in its latter portion the questions of archetypes, ectypes, space, spirits, and substance,[2] for such, in order, are the topics principally discussed by Johnson in another unpublished document:

Second Letter to the Rev^d. D^r. Berkeley in Answer to His Reply to the foregoing Letter

Rev^d. S^r.

Yours of Nov^e. 25th, I received not till Jan^{ry}. 17th. & this being the first convenient Opportunity I now return you my humblest Thanks for it.

I am very sorry to understand that you have laboured under the Illness you mention; but am exceeding Glad & thankful for your Recovery: I pray God preserve your Life & Health, that you may have Opportunity to perfect these Great & Good Designs for the Advancement of Learning & Religion wherewith your mind Labours.

I am very much obliged to you for the favourable opinion you are pleased to express at what I made bold to write to you & that you have so kindly vouchsafed so large & particular an Answer to it: But you have done me too great an Hon^r., in putting any vallue on my Judgment; for it is impossible my Thots on this subject should be of any consequence, who have been bred up under the Greatest Disadvantages, & have had so little Ability & opportunity to be instructed in things of T^s Nature. & therefore I should be very vain to pretend any thing else but to be a learner: 'tis meerly with this view that I give you this trouble.

I am sensible that the Greatest part of what I wrote was owing

[1] Fraser, Berkeley's *Works*, Vol. 4, 179-181; also in Chandler, *Life*, pp. 155-160.

[2] Johnson puts these five topics under three heads, to the latter of which Berkeley replies in his letter of March 24th, 1729-30.

to not sufficiently attending to those three important Considerations you suggest at the End of your letter: & I hope a Little more time & a more careful Attention to & Application of them, will clear up what Difficulties yet lie in the way of our intirely coming into y^r Sentiments. Indeed I had not had opportunity sufficiently to digest your Books; for no sooner had I just read them Over, but they were greedily demanded by my Friends, who live much Scattered up & Down, & who expected I would bring them home with me, because I had told them before that if the Books were to be had in Boston, I intended to purchase a Sett of them: and indeed they have not yet quite finished their Tour: The Theory of vision is still at New York & the Dialogues just gone to Long Island. but I am the better content to want them because I know they are doing Good.

For my part I am content to give up the Cause of Matter, glad to get rid of the absurdities thereon depending: if it be defensible, I am sure, at least, it is not in my power to defend it. & being Spoiled of that Sandy foundation, I only want now to be more thro'ly taught how, & where to set down my Foot again, & make out a clear & consistent Scheme without it. And of all the particulars I troubled you with before, there remain only these that I have any Difficulty about. viz. Archetypes Space & Duration & the *Esse* of Spirits: And indeed these were the chief of my Difficulties before: Most of the rest were such Objections, as I found by conversation among my Acquaintance, did not appear to them sufficiently answered. But I believe upon a more mature Consideration of the matter, & especially of this kind Reply, they will see reason to be better satisfied: They that have seen it, (especially my Friend M^r. Wetmore) join with me in thankfully acknowledging your kindness, & return their very humble Service to you.

1. As to those Difficulties that yet remain with me, I believe all my Hesitation about the first of them, (& very likely the rest,) is owing to my Dullness & want of Attention so as not lightly [rightly ?] to apprehend your meaning: I believe I expressed myself unworthly about Archetypes in my 7th & 8th articles, but upon looking back upon your Dialogues, & comparing again 3 or 4 passages, I can't think I meant any thing different from what you intended.

You allow, Dial. p. 74. ' That things have an Existence different from being perceived by us,' (i. e. any Created Spirits) '& that they exist in, i. e. are perceived by the Infinite & omnipotent Mind who contains & Supports this sensible World as being perceived by Him.' & p. 109. ' That Things have an Existence exterior to our Minds, & that during the Intervals of their being perceived by us, they exist in another, (i. e. the Infinite) Mind '; from whence you justify & excellently infer the Certainty of His Existence, ' who knows & comprehends all Things & exhibits them to our view in such manner & according to such Rules as he himself has ordained.' & p. 103. ' That, e. g. a Tree, when we don't perceive it exists without our Minds in the Infinite Mind of God.' And this Exterior Existence of Things, (if I understand you right) is what you call the Archetypal State of Things. p. 150.

From these & the like Expressions I gathered what I said about the Archetypes of our Ideas, & thence Inferred That there is exterior to us, in the Divine Mind a Substance of universal Nature, whereof the Ideas we have, are in such a Degree Resemblances, as the Almighty is pleased to communicate to us. And I cannot yet see but my Inference was just: because according to you, the Idea we see is not in the Divine Mind, but in our own; When therefore you say Sensible Things exist in as being perceived by the Infinite Mind I humbly conceive you must be understood That the Originals or Archetypes of our Simple things or Ideas exist independent of us in the Infinite Mind, or that Simple things exist in Archetype in the Divine Mind: The Divine Idea of a Tree suppose (or a tree in the Divine Mind), must be the Original or Archetype of ours, & ours a Copy or Image of his (Our Ideas Images of His, in the same sense as our Souls are Images of Him.) of which there may be several, in Several Created Minds, like so many several pictures of the same Original to which they are all to be referred.

When therefore several people are said to see the same Tree or Star &c whither at the same, or at so many Several Distances from it, it is, if I understand you) *unum & idem in Archetypo,* tho' *multiplex & diversum in Etypo* for it is as evident that your Idea is not mine nor mine yours when we say we both look on the same Tree, as that you are not I nor I you; But in having each our Idea we being dependent upon & impressed upon by the Same Almighty Mind, wherein you say this Tree exists, while we shut our Eyes; (& doubtless you mean the same also, while they are open,). Our Several Trees must, I think be so many pictures, (If I may so call them,) of the One Original, the Tree in the Infinite Mind, & so of all other Things. Thus I understand you not indeed that our Ideas are in any measure Adequate Resemblances of the System in the Divine Mind, but however that they are just & true Resemblances or copies of it, so far as he is pleased to communicate his mind to us:

2. As to Space & Duration, I do not pretend to have any other notion of their Exterior Existence than what is necessarily implied in the notion we have of God; I do not Suppose they are any thing distinct from, or exterior to the Infinite & External Mind; for I conclude with you that there is nothing exterior to my Mind but God & other Spirits with the Attributes or properties belonging to them & Ideas contained in them.

External Space & Duration therefore I take to be those properties or Attributes in God, to which our Ideas which we signifie by those names, are correspondent, & of which they are the faint Shaddows: This I take to be S^r. Isaac Newton's meaning when he says. *Schol. General. Deus—durat Semper & adest ubique & existendo semper & ubique, Durationem & Spacium, Eternitatem & Infinitatem constituit.* & in His Optics calls Space *as it were Gods boundless* Sensorium nor can I think you have a different Notion of these attributes from the Great Philosopher, tho' you may differ in your ways of Expressing or Explaining your Selves. However it be, when you call the Deity Infinite & Eternal, & in that most beautiful & charming Description, Dial. p. 71. &c. when you Speak of the *Abyss of Space & boundless Extent* beyond *Thought* & Imagination, I dont know how to understand you any otherwise, than I understand S^r. Isaac, when he uses the like expressions. The Truth [is] we have no proper Ideas of God or His Attributes & conceive of them only by Analogy from what we find in our Selves: & so, I think we conceive his Immensity & Eternity to be what in Him are correspondent to Space & Duration.

As for the *punctum stans* of the Schools, & the *to nun* of the platonists, They are Notions too fine for my Gross Tho'ts: I can't tell what to make of those Words, they don't seem to convey any Ideas or Notions to my mind, & whatever the matter is, the longer I think of them, the more they disappear, & seem to dwindle away into nothing: Indeed they seem to me very much like Abstract Ideas, but I doubt the Reason is, because I never rightly understood them. I don't see why the Term *punctum Stans,* may not as well, at least, be applied to the Immortality, as the Eternity of God; for the word *punctum* is more commonly used in relation to Extension or Space, than Duration: & to say that a Being is immense, & yet that it is but a point, & that its Duration is perpetual without beginning or End, & yet that it is but a *to nun,* look to me like a contradiction.

I can't therefore understand the Term *to nun* unless it be designed to adumbrate the Divine Omnisciency or the perfection of the Divine Knowledge, by the more perfect notion we have of things present than of things past: & in this sense it would imply that all things past present & to come are always, at every point of Duration equally perpetually known or present to Gods Mind, (tho' in a manner infinitely more perfect) as the Things that are known to us, are present to our Minds at any point of our Duration which we call *Now*. So that with respect to his equally perfect knowledge of Things past present or to come, it is in effect always now with Him. to this purpose it seems well applied & intelligible enough, but His Duration I take to be a different Thing from this, as that point of our Duration which we call *Now,* is a different thing from our Actual Knowledge of Things, as distinguished from our Remembrance. And it may as well be said that Gods Immensity consists in His knowing at once what is, & is transacted in all places, (e. g. *China, Jupiter, Saturn,* all the Systems of the *Fix't Stars,* &c) everywhere, however so remote from us, (tho' in a manner infinitely more perfect,) as we know what is, & is transacted in us & about us just at hand; as that His Eternity consists in this *to nun* as above explained, i. e. in His knowing Things present, past & to come however so remote, all at once or equally perfectly as we know the Things that are present to us *Now*.

In Short our Ideas exposed by the Terms Immensity & Eternity are only Space & Duration considered as boundless or with the Negation of any limits, & I can't help thinking There is something Analogous to them without us, being in & belonging to, or Attributes of, that Glorious Mind whom for that Reason we call Immortal & Eternal, in whom we & all other Spirits *Live move & have T^r Being,* not all in a point, but in so many different points places or *alicubis*. & variously situated with respect one to another, or else as I said before, it seems as if we should all coincide one with another.

I conclude, if I am wrong in my Notion of Eternal Space & Duration, it is owing to the rivetted prejudices of abstract Ideas; but really when I have thought it over & over again in my feeble way of thinking, I can't see any connexion between them, (as I understand them) & that Doctrine: They don't seem to be any more Abstract Ideas then Spirits, for, as I said, I take them to be Attributes of the necessarily existing Spirits: & consequently T^e same reasons that convince me of his Existence, bring with them the Existence of these Attributes: So that of the ways of coming to the Knowledge of Things that you mention, it is that of Inference or Distinction by which I seem to know that there is External Infinite Space & Duration because there is without me a Mind Infinite & Eternal.

3. As to the *Esse* of Spirits, I know *DesCartes* held the Soul always Thinks, but I tho't Mr. *Locke* had sufficiently confuted this Notion, which he seems to have entertained only to serve an Hypothesis: The Schoolmen It is true call the Soul *Actus* & God *Actus purus:* But I confess I could never well understand their meaning perhaps because I never had opportunity to be much versed in their writings. I should have tho't the schoolmen to be of all sorts of writers the most unlikely to have had recourse to for the understanding of your sentiments, because they of all others, deal the most in Abstract Ideas: tho' to place the very being of Spirits in the meer Act of Thinking, seems to me very much like making Abstract Ideas of them.

There is certainly something passive in our souls, we are purely passive in the reception of our Ideas: And Reasoning & willing are Actions of Something that Reasons & wills, & therefore must be only modalities of that Something: Nor does it seem to me that when I say (something) I mean an abstract Idea: It is true I have no Idea of it, but I feel it; I feel that it is, because I feel or am conscious of the Exertions of it: But the Exertions of it are not the Thing but the Modalities of it, distinguished from it as actions from an Agent, which seem to me distinguishable without having recourse to Abstract Ideas.

And therefore when I suppose the Existence of a Spirit while It does not actually think, it does not appear to me that I do it by supposing an Abstract Idea of Existence, & another of absolute Time: The Existence of *John* asleep by me, without so much as a Dream is not an Abstract Idea. They are only partial Considerations of him: *Perseverare in existendo* in General [1] I take to be what is called an Abstract Idea of Time or Duration; but the *Perseverare in existendo* of John is if I mistake not a partial Consideration of him.

[2] Has a Child no Soul till it actually perceives? & is there not such a thing as Sleeping without dreaming, or being in a *Deliquium* without a Tho't? If there be, & yet at the same time the *Esse* of a Spirit be nothing else but its actual Thinking, the Soul must be dead during those Intervals: & if ceasing or intermitting to think be the ceasing to be, or Death of the Soul, it is many times & easily put to death. According to this Tenet, it seems to me the Soul may sleep on to the Resurrection, or rather may wake up in the Resurrection State, the next moment after Death: Nay I don't see upon what we can build any natural Argument for the Souls Immortality.—I think I once heard you allow a principle of perception & Spontaneous motion in Beasts: Now if their *Esse* as well as ours consists in perceiv-

[1] Note illegible.   [2] Note illegible.

ing, upon what is the natural Immortality of our Souls founded that will not equally conclude in favour of them? I mention this last consideration because I am at a loss to understand how you State the Argument for the Souls Natural Immortality: for the Argument from Thinking to Immeterial, & from thence to Indivisible, & from thence to Immortal dont seem to obtain in your way of thinking.

If *Esse* be only *percipere,* upon what is our consciousness founded? I perceived yesterday, & I perceive now, but last night between my yesterdays & todays perception there has been an intermission when I perceived nothing. It seems to me there must be some principle common to these perceptions, whose eye don't depend on them, but on which they are as it were connected, & on which they depend, whereby I am & continue conscious of them.

Lastly, Mr. Locke's Argument B. 2. ch. 19 sec. 4. from the intention & remission of Thought, appears to me very considerable; according to which, upon this supposition the Soul must exist more or have a greater degree of Being at one time than at another, according as it thinks more intensely.

I own I said very wrong when I said I did not know what to make of Ideas more than of matter; My meaning was, in effect, the same as I expressed afterwards about the Substance of the Soul's being a somewhat as unknown as Matter: & what I intended by those Questions was whither our Ideas are not the Substance of the Soul itself, under so many various modifications, according to that saying (if I understand it right) *Intellectus intelligendo fit omnia?* It is true, those Expressions, (Modifications, Impressions, &c.) are metaphorical, & it seems to me to be no less so, to say that Ideas exist in the Mind, & I am under some doubt whither this last way of Speaking don't carry us further from the thing, than to say Ideas are the Mind variously modified: but as you observe, it is scarce possible to speak of the Mind without a metaphor.

Thus S^r your goodness has Tempted me to presume again to trouble you once more: & I submit the whole to your Correction: but I can't conclude without saying that I am so persuaded that your *Books teach Truth* indeed the most Excellent Truths, & that in the most excellent manner, that I can't but express my Self again very Solicitously desirous that the noble design you have begun may be yet further persued in the second part. & every body that has seen the first is earnestly with me in this Request. In hopes of which I will not desire you to wast your Time in writing to me, (tho' otherwise I should esteem it the greatest Favour) at least till I have endeavoured further to gain Satisfaction by another perusal of the Books I have, with the other peices you are so kind as to offer, which I will thankfully accept, for I had not principles of my own, it was a borrowed one I used.

The Bearer hereof Capt Gorham is a Coaster bound now to Boston, which Trade he constantly uses. (except that it has been now long interrupted by the winter) But he always touches at Newport, & will wait on the Rev^d. Mr. Honyman both Going & returning, by whom you will have Opportunity to send those books

I am Rev^d. S^r.
with the greatest

Stratf^d Feb. 5. 1729/30   Gratitude

Y^r most devoted

To T^e R^d. Dr Berkeley [1]   humbl Servt.

S. Johnson

Here ends the last of Johnson's known letters to Berkeley. They have been found valuable, not so much in fixing the order of question and answer, as in serving indirectly and in part to restore the contents of the lost correspondence of the great idealist. But as further exhibiting the pains to which the master went in forming the opinions of his pupil, there should be added the last epistle in this speculative series, that of March 24th, 1729-1730:

Rev. Sir—Yours of Feb. 5th came not to my hands before yesterday; and this afternoon being informed that a sloop is ready to sail towards your town, I would not let slip the opportunity of returning you an answer, though wrote in a hurry. I have no objection against calling the ideas in the mind of God, archetypes of ours. But I object against those archetypes by philosophers supposed to be real things, and to have an absolute rational existence distinct from their being perceived by any mind whatsoever, it being the opinion of all materialists that an ideal existence in the divine Mind is one thing, and the real existence of material things another.

1. As to space, I have no notion of any but that which is relative. I know some late philosophers have attributed extension to God, particularly mathematicians; one of whom, in a treatise *de Spacio reali,* pretends to find out fifteen of the incommunicable attributes of God in space. But it seems to me that, they being all negative, he might as well have found them in nothing;

[1] Holograph letter in possession of Columbia University Library.

and that it would have been as justly inferred from space being impassive, uncreated, indivisible, etc., that it was nothing, as that it was God.

Sir Isaac Newton supposeth an absolute space different from relative, and consequent thereto, absolute motion different from relative motion; and with all other mathematicians, he supposeth the infinite divisibility of the finite parts of this absolute space; he also supposeth material bodies to drift therein. Now, though I do acknowledge Sir Isaac to have been an extraordinary man, and most profound mathematician, yet I cannot agree with him in these particulars. I make no scruple to use the word Space, as well as other words in common use, but I do not mean thereby a distinct absolute being. For my meaning I refer you to what I have published.

By the *to nun* I suppose to be implied that all things past and to come are actually present to the mind of God, and that there is in Him no change, variation, or succession—A succession of ideas I take to constitute time and not to be only the sensible measure thereof, as Mr. Locke and others think. But in these matters every man is to think for himself, and speak as he finds— One of my earliest inquiries was about time, which led me into several paradoxes that I did not think fit or necessary to publish, particularly into the notion that the resurrection follows next moment to death. We are confounded and perplexed about time. (1.) Supposing a succession in God. (2.) Conceiving that we have an abstract idea of time. (3.) Supposing that the time in one mind is to be measured by the succession of ideas in another. (4.) Not considering the true use and end of words, which as often terminate in the will as the understanding, being employed rather to excite influence, and direct action than to produce clear & distinct ideas.

3. That the soul of man is passive as well as active I make no doubt. Abstract general ideas was a notion that Mr. Locke held in common with the Schoolmen, and I think all other philosophers; it runs through his whole book of Human Understanding. He holds an abstract idea of existence exclusive of perceiving and being perceived. I cannot find I have any such idea, and this is my reason against it. Descartes proceeds upon other principles. One square foot of snow is as white as one thousand yards; one single perception is as truly a perception as one hundred. Now any degree of perception being sufficient to existence, it will not follow that we should say one existed more at one time than another, any more than we should say one thousand yards of snow are whiter than one yard. But after all, this comes to a verbal

dispute. I think it might prevent a good deal of obscurity and dispute to examine well what I have said about abstraction, and about the true use of sense and significancy of words, in several parts of these things that I have published, though much remains to be said on that subject.

You say you agree with me that there is nothing within your mind but God and other spirits, with the attributes or properties belonging to them, and the ideas contained in them. This is a principle or main point from which, and from what I had laid down about abstract ideas, much may be deduced. But if in every inference we should not agree, so long as the main points are settled and well understood, I should be less solicitous about particular conjectures. I could wish that all the things I have published on these philosophical subjects were read in the order wherein I published them, once to take the design and connection of them, and a second time with a critical eye, adding your own thought and observation upon every part as you went along. I send you herewith ten bound books and one unbound. You will take yourself what you have not already. You will give the principles, the theory, the dialogue, one of each, with my service to the gentleman who is Fellow of New Haven College, whose compliments you brought me. What remains you will give as you please.

If at any time your affairs should draw you into these parts, you shall be very welcome to pass as many days as you can spend at my house. Four or five days' conversation would set several things in a fuller and clearer light than writing could do in as many months. In the meantime I shall be glad to hear from you or your friends when ever you please to favour, Rev. Sir.

Your very humble serv't,
Geor. Berkeley.[1]

Taken as a whole here was the most notable philosophic correspondence that had taken place in the early American schools, yet in its final issue that correspondence was without wide results. The effect of Berkeley's thinking upon Johnson was notable, but the latter's efforts to extend the doctrines of immaterialism beyond the confines of New England were impalpable to a degree. As to the first of these matters, so early as May 27th, 1730,[2] John-

[1] Beardsley, *Life*, pp. 73-75.

[2] Cf. the *Concio ad Clerum*, a sermon preached before Dean Berkeley at Newport, wherein Johnson gracefully refers to Berkeley. (MS. in Columbia University Library.)

son had visited Berkeley at Whitehall, the latter's country place near Newport, and within another year Berkeley had finished his *Alciphron; or, the Minute Philosopher,* which formed a most pleasing set of idealistic dialogues, wherein, from their many allusions and touches of local colour, Berkeley may be said to stand for Euphranor, the philosophic farmer, and Johnson for his friend Crito. So it was about this time that the neophyte expressed his conversion to the ideal theory, since, as he himself acknowledges, he found the Dean's way of thinking and explaining things, utterly precluded scepticism, and left no room for endless doubts and uncertainties. His denying matter at first seemed shocking; but it was only for want of giving a thorough attention to his meaning. It was only the unintelligible scholastic notion of matter he disputed, and not anything either sensible, imaginable, or intelligible; and it was attended with this vast advantage, that it not only gave new incontestible proofs of a Deity, but moreover, the most striking apprehensions of his constant presence with us and inspection over us, and of our entire dependence on Him and infinite obligations to his most wise and almighty benevolence.[1]

With his own mind made up in favour of Berkeleism, Johnson now sought to gain other converts to the cause. From the tenor of his first letter to the Dean there seems to have been in existence a little circle of New Englanders inclined to the ideal way of thinking, but where this circle was it is difficult to say. It was not located in Rhode Island, because it was the Quaker mysticism, rather than the Anglican idealism, that left as a residue that strain of immaterialism which was to reappear from time to time,[2] for those of the Dean's books, which he left to the literary

[1] Beardsley, *Life,* p. 82.

[2] Cf. Ezra Stiles upon certain aspects of Newport Quakerism: ' He that has access to the human mind and can touch its most secret springs unperceived by us, or rather undistinguished, is it not possible for him to do it in such manner as that mind certainly perceives Deity shining in and operating upon it. We probably live under the constant Impressions and Irradiations of the Father of Lights, the universal mind, but he is generally unperceived in them.' (Stiles MSS., Folio, p. 464, Yale University Library.) Traces of a later idealism are to be found in Job

and philosophical society founded by him, had no direct or immediate influence.[1] Nor in Connecticut itself, outside of Johnson's unnamed friends, was there ever more than a problematical interest expressed in Berkeleism. This was particularly true in Yale College after Johnson's taking up with the Anglican belief, and that despite the Dean's bounty to that institution. Some part of the benefactions, originally intended for the chimerical college of Bermuda, Berkeley bestowed upon the institution in New Haven to promote human learning and the improvement of reason.[2] As a result of these benefactions, which are perpetuated in what are known as the Berkeley scholarships, Rector Clap said that this college would always retain a most grateful sense of the donor's generosity and merits; and probably a favourable opinion of his idea of material substance; as not consisting in an unknown and inconceivable substratum, but in a stated union and combination of sensible ideas, excited from without, by some Intelligent Being.[3] The reason for this half-hearted praise of the idealistic system was given by Johnson as the fear of the trustees of Yale to accept the noble donation, from their suspicion that there was behind it a proselyting design.[4] All this brought about a painful disillusionment in the mind of the foreign visitor. In that land for which he had prophesied another golden age when ' men shall not impose for truth and sense the pedantry of

Durfee's *The Panidea; or, An Omnipresent Reason considered as the Creative and Sustaining Logos* (*Works*, Providence, 1849), and in Rowland G. Hazard's *Man a Creative First Cause*, Boston, 1883; here Durfee was more considerably influenced by Swedenborg, and Hazard by Hegel. (Information from Professor W. G. Everett, of Brown University.)

[1] Cf. Edward Field, *Rhode Island and Providence Plantations*, Boston, 1902, Vol. 1, p. 178; W. E. Foster, *Some Rhode Island Contributions to the Intellectual Life of the Last Century*, Worcester, 1892, p. 32; *Proceedings American Antiquarian Society*, April 27th, 1872; Winsor, *Narrative and Critical History of America*, Vol. 5, p. 141.

[2] Beardsley, *Life*, pp. 79-80.

[3] Quoted by G. P. Fisher, *An Unpublished Essay of Edwards on the Trinity*, p. 20.

[4] Cf. below Book III, Chapter III. Also D. C. Gilman, ' Bishop Berkeley's gifts to Yale College,' (*New Haven Colony Historical Society*, Vol. 1, pp. 147-170.)

courts and schools,'[1] he found the discordance and pettiness of sectarian divisions, the incipient stage of that reaction from believing too much to believing too little.

If the author of the *Minute Philosopher* found it hard to break new ground in the rocky soil of New England, the same was eminently true in the regions to the south. Johnson had been enjoying a correspondence with William Burnet, governor of New York, and by reputation a bookish man and much of a scholar; yet even by this means he was unable to introduce idealism into the neighbouring province. He had already penned a letter to the publisher of the *New York Gazette,* but the brief defence of Berkeley's immaterialism contained in the original draught was never printed.[2] So, too, in the founding of King's College, Johnson, as its first head, had scarcely time, in the face of sectarian difficulties, to expound that system of which he was proudest. However, there was one person connected with the institution whom the idealist strove to use as an agent to spread his favourite theories. Cadwallader Colden, lieutenant-governor of New York, was counted one of the few academics of the province; an avowed materialist, he was, nevertheless, open to the arguments of his immaterialistic friend, for, in his attempt to identify the Coldenian system with the Berkeleian, Johnson confessed that he was little more than jocular, being not dogmatically tenacious of his peculiar sentiments, much less zealous of making Colden a proselyte to them.[3] For all that, the latter did approach the ideal theory in respect to the inferential nature of our knowledge of external reality, but in other respects he did not. In general the correspondence between materialist and immaterialist has been summed up as relating to active causation, which Johnson confines to spirit, while Colden considers matter as well as spirit a centre of power. Johnson sees in all so-called material causation only sense-symbolism, interpretable in natural science. The question goes to the root of Berkeley's

---

[1] Cf. Berkeley's 'Verses on the Prospect of Planting Arts and Learning in America,' in Duyckinck, *Cyclopædia of American Literature,* Vol. 1, p. 179.

[2] See below Book III, Chapter IV.

[3] Beardsley, *Life,* p. 142.

philosophy, but Colden, who was exercised more in natural science than in metaphysical philosophy, hardly sees the point of the question, or the grounds on which it is settled by Johnson.[1] As an example of the idealist's persuasive methods may be given the following letter, the last part of which has not hitherto been published:

Stratford, June 23. 1746.

S[r]

I now return you my hearty Thanks for yours of the 2d Instant, & especially for your kind present that accompanied it— It is my sincere Opinion that it is a very ingenious peice & the Result of much & deep Thought— There is one thing that I am much pleased with, which is, That you make the *Resistence* of what you call Matter to be an *Action* deriving from a Self exerting principle.— This I take to be a point of very great Importance & use both in physics & metaphysics as well as Religion.— All the odds between you and me is that you make Matter a Self Exerting Active principle, whereas I give that Denomination only to what is meerly passive & inert & give the name of *Spirit* to that which is the principle of Activity, pervading & agitating all things, according to *Virgil's* philosophy, *mens agitat Molem* &c which tho' it be the most ancient, I take to be nevertheless the most true & undoubted System; and that Elasticity, Attraction or pulsion & Repulsion as well as Resistance or what S[r] Isaac calls *Vis Inertiae,* & perhaps some other Forces, are so many Exertions of the One universal Intelligent Self exerting Active principle who pervades all things & in *whom we live & move & have our Being.*— Your Attempt to assign the Cause of Gravitation appears to me a curious Dissertation—but I have hardly furniture & force of Mind enough to comprehend it, having for many years discontinued those kind of Studies, & indeed never turned my thoughts that way so closely as I find you have done, nor had proper means to enable me for it: your System seems to me pretty near of kin to M[r] Hutchinson's, as far as I have had opportunity to be acquainted with his from my Lord Forbes, but I beleive you have much outdone him in the exactness of your Range of Thoughts & mathematical Reasoning —but I think his notion of pulsion or protrusion is something like yours; however, I dare not pronounce.

And now in Answer to your candid Inquiries. You ask, *How consciousness & Intelligence become essential to all Agents that act from a power within themselves?* Where by a *Power within*

[1] Professor A. Campbell Fraser, in a letter to the writer, 9th July, 1906.

themselves I apprehend you mean a *principle of Activity* belonging to their own proper Essence, & not either arbitrarily annexed to them or exerting it self in & by them.— To which I answer; A power [of] Action without a principle of Self-Exertion & activity in which it resides I can have no Notion of; & a blind senseless power or principle of Activity appears to me repugnant & if it were possible, it would be [so] far from being of any use in nature that it would be mischievous without a Mind to direct and over rule it.— In fact we find that all the motions & consequently Actions in nature are comformable to the wisest Laws and Rules ever aiming at some useful End which evidently discovers design & Contrivance & must therefore be under the active management of a most wise & designing principle or cause; so that it seems to me repugnant to place Intelligence & Activity in or derive them from different principles;[1] for if you suppose a blind principle of Action in Matter, you must still suppose it under the over ruling Force of an intelligent & designing principle. And, as it is not the part of a philosopher to multiply Beings & Causes without necessity, it seems plain to me that we ought not to imagine any other principle of Action than the principle of Intelligence, which we know from our own Soul has, & in Nature must have, a power of Self Exertion & activity. We must come to it eventually in our Inquiries & I see not how we can avoid admitting it immediately as soon as ever we begin to inquire after efficient causes. For my part I can find nothing but what is meerly passive in any immediate object either of Sense or imagination & must therefore conceive of what is called matter to be no more than a meer passive instrument or Medium acted by the One principle of Intelligence & activity.—Thus I say Things appear to me; nor can I with the utmost Force of Mind that my Capacity will admit of, conceive of things any otherwise.— After all I do not see that my way of Defining Things affects your ingenious performance considered as a physical Essay. If there be any difference in our Thoughts divested of all words as perhaps there is none, it is, as I apprehend, not of physical, but rather of metaphysical Consideration,— But be it how it will, I am not tenacious, & submit the whole to your better Judgment, & remain,

S^r. y^r most obliged Friend
& very humble Servt.
Samuel Johnson.

P.S. I have a little peice of Morals in the press of which I will send you a copy as soon as I receive any, & with it D^r. Berkeley's Tract de motu, which will explain what I take to be

---

[1] I can have no notion of action without volition.

the justest way of Speaking of these Subjects, better than I can do.—[1]

In the midst of his active and extended intercourse with his friend in New York, the Connecticut scholar had not neglected to advance his own learning and to produce certain speculations which exhibit a further progress toward the thought of his maturity. These speculations are contained in two neglected discourses delivered in the village of Stratford in the years 1746 and 1747; from these the following extracts may be given:

This is certain, That light being a positive Being pervading and filling everything where it would come insomuch that there is not the minutest part of any temporal body that does not appear full of it, & by it all visible things become visible, does very fitly represent GOD, who is absolutely positive and fullness of Being itself, & by whom all other things exist.— All that is real in them or that can be called truly Being of Perfection, they derive from him, portioning out such degrees and measures as He thinks fit with an endless variety, & they entirely depend upon him for it & for every moment of the continuance of it; They might not have been at all or in fact such a Degree of Being as they are if he had not been pleased of his own meer Notion to give it them, & they must of course cease to be, or to be what they are when he ceases to will their existence or subsistence in their present state: so that they are wholly precarious and dependent Beings;— Whereas He exists absolutely by an intrinsic necessity of his Nature, & cant but be & be what he is, because all other things depend upon Him, without whom they could never have been, but He upon nothing & would have existed & been just what he is if they had never been. They therefore are wholly in his power & are limited as pleaseth Him, but He is absolutely out of the power of any being to limit or controul Him.— So that He being of Himself an independent, necessarily existent Being, must have all being, reality and absolute perfection in & of himself, & being out of the power of any Being to limit him can have no limitation or Imperfection at all & consequently must be *All in All,* & existence must necessarily be implied in his existence, which can be the case of no other Being; so that the very notion or conception of his existence must necessarily infer *that He is.*

[1] Holograph letter of Samuel Johnson, D. D., First President of Kings (now Columbia) College, New York City, in the possession of Charles William Johnson, his great-great-great-grandson, of Baltimore, Md.

God is therefore rightly called TO ON; *The BEING* by way of Eminency, as containing in Him all that truly is, or exists absolutely; for we and all creatures exist only conditionally, or on condition of his willing our Existence, but He exists independent of the Will of any Being, nay independent of any act of his own Will; for every act of his Will supposes his Existence. . . . He hath given and preserves to us our Reason & understanding which renders us capable of knowledge, & it is by a perpetual intercourse of our minds with Him who is the great parent mind that we are enabled from the moment that we begin to exist to understand any thing at all that occurs to us. For there are certain universal Maxims of Truth which are Necessary & Eternal, that are the tests and Standards by which we judge of every thing that comes within the compass of our Thoughts: Such as these, That it *is impossible for the same Thing to be & not to be:*— *Nothing can act that is not:*— *There can be no Effect without a Cause:*—*The Whole is bigger than either of its parts,*—*and equal to all of them taken together:*— *Things equal to another must be equal among themselves:*— *What is right or wrong in me towards another, must be equally right or wrong in him towards me.*— These and many others are principles of Eternal & unchangeable Truth, that would have existed if we had never had a Being: do exist independent of any created mind, & are the principles of Truth that enlighten every Created mind, antecedent to its judging of any particular thing, & do as it were stand by & are ready at hand to our minds, enabling us to think & judge rightly of every thing to which we apply them & by his eternal mind they are one pure Light of Truth, but are diversified in our narrow conception according as we are able to apprehend.

Now where are these Eternal Truths, & how come we by them?— Truth cannot exist without a Mind. As sure therefore as there are Eternal Truths independent of our minds, there must be an eternal Mind necessarily existing independent of our Minds, which on the one hand must by the necessity of their Nature depend on that both for the existence and intelligence.— Thus these Truths must originally exist in Gods eternal Mind and consequently demonstrate his existence. But then how come we by them?— we find we are meerly passive in the reception of them, —passive with regard to them as we are with regard to sensible light. They shine upon our minds just as the light of the Sun does upon our eyes, & enable us to understand God & all other things, just as the Sun enables us to see himself & all other things. It is there fore plain that all intellectual Light is from

God affecting our eyes: i. e. God by these Eternal Truths impressed upon our minds inlightens our understandings, as the Sun through his Influence by sensible light impressed on our minds enlightens our sight.—So that it is by a perpetual intercourse of our minds or Understanding with the Deity that we are enabled to understand & know everything that comes within the compass of our knowledge.[1]

These immortal Souls of ours being not objects of sense any more than the Deity, the *Father & Former of them,* we scarce know how to reckon them, as well as Him, & real beings; they seem to our weak minds just airy fugacious Beings that we are sometime almost tempted to doubt of their existence independent of these gross tangible Bodies:—whereas if we would accustom ourselves to withdraw our thoughts from the *things that are seen* & raise them as much as we can above them, we might soon be convinced that their existence is so far from depending on the existence of the Body, that on the other hand, the Existence of Body depends intirely on the Existence of Mind, & that its existence can have no sense or meaning in it separate from its being perceived & acted by mind: & consequently that it is these Bodies that are really the empty uncertain, unstable fugacious things, & that it is mind Soul or Spirit, that is the real stable & certain thing. Bodies are *the things seen* which are temporal & minds are *the things unseen which are eternal.* What are all the objects & Pleasures of Sense but meer fleeting fugacious, unstable & uncertain things: I had almost said, but meer imaginary things & but little better than dreams.[2]

In his sermon on *God is Light,* Johnson presents a doctrine similar to Malebranche's vision of all things in God, and in that on the *Intellectual World* a phenomenalism akin to that of Berkeley. In these analogies there is a consistent progress in the author's mental life and that much after the design of his approaching work, wherein he essays to trace out the several steps of the mind of man, from the first impressions of sense, through the several improvements it gradually makes, till it arrives to that perfection and enjoyment of itself, which is the great end of its being.[3] Before taking

[1] Extract from a sermon on ' God is Light,' July 6, 1746. (MS. in Columbia University Library.)

[2] Extract from a sermon on the 'Intellectual World,' Advent, 1747. (MS. in Columbia University Library.)

[3] *Noetica,* p. 1.

up the exposition of this most significant work, one may utilise this outline of a veritable genetic method, and thereby trace the successive stages in the author's intellectual career. As his biographer expresses it, daring to think for himself, and careful to accept no new views until he had fairly examined the opposing arguments, he had gradually exchanged the principles of the old philosophy for those of the Newtonian system, and had relinquished the rigid predestinarian tenets for what appeared to be the more rational doctrines of Anglicanism.[1] So just as he had once emerged from a provincial standard of orthodoxy into a moderate deism, so now he is emerging from an unsatisfactory dualism into a more consistent monism. His correspondence discloses this. He writes to Cadwallader Colden that, although he has a profound veneration for Mr. Locke and Sir Isaac Newton, yet he will not be determined by their authority, nor by their reasons, any farther than he can see for himself. Sir Isaac was doubtless very exact; but no wonder if even he, in matters very abstruse, should sometimes be mistaken; nor is it less to be wondered at, if this should be the case now with Bishop Berkeley.[2] In these remarks upon his chief authorities, Johnson exhibits a noteworthy independence of thought, and thereby disposes of the captious criticism of President Stiles of Yale College, that he was reputed to be always of the opinion of the last author he read.[3] He had just been reading a copy of the *Siris*, lent him by Benjamin Franklin, but whether he was successful in amending the pantheistic tendencies of that work, is to be judged only from the last of his own speculations. For the present, at any rate, Johnson had not gone beyond Berkeley, but was engaged in disentangling himself from the perplexities of Newtonism. That system, philosophically considered, was a crude dualism, portraying a creation apart from its creator, a world set in motion like a vast machine, yet liable to be stopped at intervals for repairs. Against such a possibility, which Leibniz himself had satirised, Johnson revolted, attempting, in the manner of Malebranche, to

---

[1] Beardsley, *Life*, p. 354.

[2] Beardsley, *Life*, pp. 131-132.

[3] *The Literary Diary of Ezra Stiles*, ed. F. B. Dexter, Vol. 1, p. 206.

introduce a pure occasionalism in the place of a haphazard interference, a permanent in the stead of a partial miracle. He would
not have the deity interpose at times to alter the workings of the
established order, but adopting the phrase of Berkeley, he would
look upon the deity as a conservator as much as a creator; in his
own words he would represent the ruler of the universe as absolutely positive, the fulness of being itself, by whom all other things
exist.

This emergence out of a mechanical dualism into a more
idealistic sphere of thought was doubtless brought about by Johnson's sense of the insufficiency of his previous thinking. In his
Introduction to Philosophy of fifteen years before, he had left
certain problems in an undeveloped condition. In his cosmology
he had reasoned that the world was, on the whole, a happy
system, yet he had left it subject to irregularity; in his psychology
he had made human minds active, intelligent creatures, able
freely to choose, yet he had allowed defects and imperfections
in both perception and volition; in his epistemology he had remained content with a crass realism, thinking the knowledge of
things within the reach of our understandings as being what they
really are; finally, in his ontology, he had presented all sensible
things as consisting of certain fixed combinations of sensible qualities, but he had not intimated wherein their stability consists.
These are the faults of Johnson's philosophical tract of 1731;
by 1746 he had essayed to mend these faults in his *System of
Morality,* published in Boston under the old pseudonym of Aristocles, and intended for the use of his sons in Yale College. At
that time the students in New Haven were using as their text-
book in ethics President Thomas Clap's *Foundation of Moral
Virtue and Obligation,* a work described as a meagre and juiceless
compend of familiar commonplaces of theological doctrine, with
nothing of the sprightliness and philosophical ingenuity of Johnson's work.[1] Except as a comparison this high praise was not

---

[1] F. B. Dexter, *Thomas Clap and his Writings, New Haven Colony
Historical Society Papers,* Vol. 5, p. 264 (November, 1889.) There is in
the Yale University Library a copy of Norris' *Ideal World,* 1704, read
by Clap.

altogether deserved. Johnson's *Ethica,* being utilitarian at its base and theological at its summit,[1] did not possess the full idealistic significance of the later *Noetica.* Its point of departure was that of Berkeley's *Discourse on Passive Obedience,* yet its aim was not single, but manifestly diverse. In fact, an early criticism made the Johnsonian morality an eclecticism, different systems, each imperfect by itself, coinciding in their general effects. Like many writers of that day, Johnson is said to have founded moral obligation on the will of God; yet, like Clarke, to have considered it as resulting from the truth and nature of things, and like Hutcheson to have viewed it as arising purely from the suggestions of the moral sense. However, concludes the critic, the author was justified in all this diversity, for three different excitements are needed for the practice of virtue, namely, something that will hit men's palate, something that will satisfy their reason, and something that will subdue their will.[2]

Johnson has indeed put forth an eclectic system of morality, yet over it all he has cast an idealistic tinge. Avowedly following Shaftesbury, Hutcheson and Turnbull, he admits the reality of a moral sense, which, exhibited in man, whether as the law of reason or of conscience, is still, in its last resort, naught but the perpetual presence and irradiation of the deity in our spirits. But to this high point Johnson does not mount without the help of others. To prove the existence of the creator he employs three arguments derived from three foreign philosophers: one, celebrated since Descartes, consists in finding above each one of ourselves and other imperfect beings a supreme cause of our existence; a second proof, frequently invoked by Malebranche, reasons for the existence of eternal truths to the existence of a necessary spirit; the third reason, employed by Berkeley and here carried out in a wholly Platonic way, is based on the certainty which possesses each one of us not being the cause of our different sensible impressions.[3] Employing the first of these arguments, Johnson reasons *ex analogia hominis* and takes as his specific authori-

---

[1] Lyon, *Idéalisme,* p. 400.
[2] *Medical and Philosophical Journal,* 1812, p. 146.
[3] Lyon, *Idéalisme,* p. 397.

ties Clarke's and Burnet's *Boyle's Lectures;* in the second he
refers to Norris's *Ideal World* and the Archbishop of Cambray's
Demonstration; in the third he seems but to paraphrase the
aphorisms from the *Minute Philosopher,* and yet is declared to
have improved on the work, by transposing to morality the arguments advanced in the physics and psychology of Berkeley.[1]
These more idealistic passages are as follows:

Since, therefore, there are eternal Truths necessarily existing,
independent of any created Mind, or any Thing existing in
Nature, it is evident there must be an eternal, necessarily existing,
independent Mind, in which they originally exist, as one eternal
Light of Truth, and by whom they are exhibited to all other
Minds in various Measures, according to their several Capacities
and Application, enabling them to Judge of every particular Thing
that comes within their Notice.   He is therefore the great *Parent
Mind*, from whom derives all Light and Knowledge to every
Created Intelligence, being, as it were, the intellectual Sun
enlightening our Minds, as the sensible Sun by his incessant Activity, enlighteneth our Eyes.

What I have thus argued from my own Existence, Powers and
Faculties, and those of every other intelligent and active Creature,
and from the Existence of eternal Truth, may be also demonstrated
from the Existence of every Sensible Thing that I see, hear and
feel, from without me.   I know that I am not the Cause of any
of those Impressions that are made upon my Senses.   Light,
Colours, Sounds, tangible Qualities, &c.   I am sure they do not
depend upon my Will and Activity; for I am intirely passive in
the Reception of them.   Nor can they be without a Cause, nor
yet from any Senseless, inert or inactive Cause, for that is a
Contradiction in Terms.

They must therefore be the constant Effects of an intelligent
Cause, intimately present with me, and incessantly active upon
me, who continually produceth all these Sensations in my Mind,
correspondent to the Archetypes in his all-comprehending Intellect, according to certain stated Laws, or fixed Rules, which He
hath established to Himself, and which are commonly called
the Laws of Nature.   When therefore I consider the whole
System of these sensible, as well as the intelligible, Objects that
surround me, and under the Impression of which I continually
live, I must conclude, that I *live, and move, and have my Being,*
in Him, who is the perpetual and *Almighty* Author of them. . . .
I find these sensible Objects are all firmly connected together,

[1] Lyon, *Idéalisme*, p. 398.

Things visible with Things tangible. . . I do not, indeed, find, upon a close Examination, that there is any necessary Connection between them; for Instance, between the Objects of *Sight and Feeling;* the one appears to have only the *Nature* of a Sign with *Regard* to the other, being all alike, meer passive Perceptions in our Minds, between which there can be no Relation of Causality: So that the Connection between them, tho' stable, is entirely arbitrary; as is that between the Sound, *Man,* and the Thing signified by it: From whence I gather, that I must unavoidably consider the one with regard to the other, to have the Nature of a wonderful Language, whereby the great Author of Nature appears to be continually present with me, discovering his Mind and Will to me (and that in a stable and invariable Manner, which I find I can always depend upon) and, as it were, speaking to me, and directing me how to act, and conduct myself in all the Affairs of Life; whereby he manifestly discovereth a constant watchful *Providence* over me in all my Ways. From whence it is evident, not only that He is, but that He must be, both a Being of infinite *Goodness, Wisdom* and *Power,* and of the most stable *Truth,* and invariable *Integrity.* . . . I say, we both *see and feel his Universal Presence;* for it is manifest, that He may as truly be said to be an Object of Sense as any human Person; for, what do I see when I behold a King? Not the Spirit or Soul, which is properly the Person, and which in the Nature of it, can not be an Object of Sense; I see only the Shape and Colour of a Man cloathed with gorgeous Robes. In like Manner, I cannot see GOD, as He is a Spirit, and as such, is invisible; but I as truly see Him, as I see a Man like myself; nay, indeed, more manifestly than I can behold any mortal Man; for I see Him in every visible Shape and Form in all Nature; I behold Him in all the infinitely various Modifications of *Light* and Colours throughout the whole Creation; in all which, He is every where present, being, as it were *Cloathed with Light, as with a garment;* which Expression is rightly observed to be of like Import with that Saying of the ancient Eastern Sages That GOD *hath Light for his Body and Truth for his Soul.* In the same Manner, I may truly say, I feel Him in the *Heat* and Wind, and in every tangible Figure and Motion, &c. I hear Him in every Sound and taste Him in every Morsel, &c. In a Word, I must again say, it is He who is *All in All.*[1]

Here end the idealistic portions of the first or speculative part of Johnson's ethics; the second or practical part rises to no such eloquence; fashioned more in accordance with the original pur-

[1] *Ethica,* Part I, Chapter II, §§ 10, 13, 15.

pose of being chiefly for the use of young beginners, it descends into a sort of moral catechism, ranging from the question of truth—What am I?—to the question of duty—What ought I to do, as a means, in order to do what I ought, and in order finally to answer the end of my being?[1] In attempting this short system of ethics, which has, of late, been called the religion of nature, the author returns to his old deistic way of reasoning, employing for his sources such dry authorities as Hutchinson, Lord Forbes, and Bishop Butler. This is the least original piece of work that Johnson had done for thirty years, and merely recalls his salad days, when he had learned to draw up abridgements of some of those old English or Dutch systems which the country afforded. But soon there was to be a change.

On quitting the American strand, Berkeley has been most vividly described as leaving behind him a metaphysical double, another self, sharing his faith, speaking his language; viewing all things from the same angle; reasoning, discussing, concluding as he himself had done or would have done.[2] In dedicating his principal work, from the deepest sense of gratitude, to George, Lord Bishop of Cloyne, Johnson indeed fitted this description, for he confessed that he was in a particular manner beholden to that excellent philosopher for several thoughts that occur in the following tract. This was the *Elementa Philosophica: Containing chiefly, Noetica, or Things Relating to the Mind or Understanding; and Ethica, or Things Relating to the Moral Behaviour.* To the second part of this work, which here appeared in its second edition,[3] consideration has been already given. The first part, the *Noetica,* was the most clear and consistent presentation of idealism that had as yet appeared in the colonies. Unfortunately that book was too late to be seen by him who had inspired its issue, it being published in 1752, the very year of the good bishop's death. However, the philosophy of Berkeley suffered no harm at the hands of his ardent disciple, for the

---

[1] *Ethica,* p. 12.

[2] *Lyon, Idéalisme,* p. 404.

[3] Philadelphia, 1752, printed by Benjamin Franklin. For second title see below, Notes.

latter was able enough to give it a fair elucidation, and skilful enough to correlate and harmonise many of its principles with the kindred thought of other idealists. In one respect, also, Johnson seems to have advanced, in a measure, upon his master's principles, for that portion of the *Noetica* which deals with the pure intellect and its notions and with intuitive intellectual light has been pronounced more akin to Plato and Malebranche, and even to Kant, than to Berkeley's early philosophical works.[1]

Taking, then, for its motto a selection from the *Siris,* Johnson's treatise opens by defining mind from the standpoint of dynamism, body from that of occasionalism, and ideas from that of Platonism. Mind or spirit in general, says the American, signifies any intelligent active being, which notion we take from what we are conscious of in ourselves who know that we have within us a principle of conscious perception, intelligence, activity and self-exertion. By reasoning and analogy we apply this to all other minds besides or superior to us, and, removing all limitations and imperfections, to that great supreme intelligence, an infinite mind or spirit, or a being infinitely intelligent and active. . . . Our spirits or minds are connected with gross, tangible bodies by a mere arbitrary constitution or establishment. The union between our souls and bodies consists in this law of our nature, which is the will and perpetual fiat of that infinite parent mind, that our bodies should be thus acted by our minds and that our minds should thus perceive and act by the organs of our bodies. . . . An idea as understood by Plato was the original exemplar of things, whether sensible or intellectual, in the external mind, conformable to which all things exist; or the abstract essences of things as being originals or archetypes in that infinite intellect of which our ideas or conceptions are a kind of copies. Here we confine the word idea to the immediate objects of sense and imagination, and notion or conception to the objects of consciousness and pure intellect, though both may be expressed by the general word thought.[2]

In drawing this sharp distinction between ideas and notions

---

[1] Fraser, Berkeley's *Works,* Vol. I, p. 176 note.
[2] *Noetica*, Chapter I, §§ 2-4.

Johnson has performed a double service, having amended that confusion in the use of the word idea of which Locke was guilty, and also advanced beyond the distinction made by Berkeley in his later writings. So, too, in the succeeding sections, he avoids the further Lockean confusion attaching to the denial of innate ideas, yet leaves himself free to ascribe to the mind certain inherent activities a posteriori, after the manner of the *Siris*. Our minds, he continues, may be said to be created mere *tabulae rasae;* that is, they have no notices of any objects of any kind properly created in them, or concreted with them. Yet I apprehend that in all the notices they have of any kind of objects they have an immediate dependence upon the deity, as really as they depend upon him for their existence: i. e. they are no more authors to themselves of the objects of their senses, or of the light by which they perceive them, than of the power of perceiving itself; but that they perceive them by a perpetual intercourse with that great parent mind, to whose incessant agency they are entirely passive, both in all the perceptions of sense, and in all that intellectual light by which they perceive the objects of the pure intellect. Notwithstanding which, it is plain from experience that in consequence of these perceptions they are entirely at liberty to act or not to act, and all their actions flow from a principle of self-exertion. . . . The notices which the mind has, derive originally from (or rather by means of) the two fountains of sense and consciousness. By means of the senses we receive simple ideas. These are sorted out into a vast variety of fixed combinations or compound ideas distinct from each other, in which the simple ideas are always found to co-exist; of these compounded ideas consists every individual body in nature, such as we call horse, tree, etc. These various distinct combinations, connected together in such a manner as to constitute one most beautiful and harmonious whole, make up what we call universal nature or the entire sensible or natural world. In the perception of these ideas or objects of sense we find our minds are merely passive, it not being in our power (supposing our organs rightly disposed and situated) whether we will see light and colours, hear sounds, &c. We are not causes to ourselves of these perceptions, nor can they be produced in our minds without a cause, or (which is the same thing) by any imagined, unintelligent, inert or inactive cause. Hence they must derive from an almighty, intelligent, active cause, exhibiting them to us, impressing our minds with them, or producing them in us. Consequently it must be by a perpetual intercourse of our minds with the deity, the great author of our beings, or by his perpetual influence or activity upon them, that they are possessed of all these objects of sense and the light by which we perceive them.[1]

In making our ideas or objects of sense dependent upon the perpetual intercourse of the deity, Johnson has given a consistent, but withal an extreme explanation of our knowledge of the sensible or natural world. To consider divine archetypes to be the only ultimate realities, to make a supreme mind alone to validate the thinking of many finite minds, is to make a double subjective reference. Here, being less prudent than Berkeley, who left in suspense the problem of the formation of ideas, Johnson has gone back to the excessive occasionalism of Cudworth, who held that all understandings are constantly furnished with forms and ideas to conceive all things by, through the agency of an infinite, eternal mind, necessarily existing.[2]   In such affinities the colonial idealist is declared to have been unsatisfied with the vague Platonism of the *Siris,* and to have approached the more precise views of the Cambridge scholars and more especially of his later authority, Norris.[3] Hence, in further explication of the original of our ideas, he says: Thus much for sense; by consciousness is meant our perception of objects *ab intra,* or from reflecting or turning the eye of our mind inward and observing what passeth within itself; whereby we know that we perceive all those sensible objects and their connections, and all the pleasures and pains attending them, and all the powers or faculties of our minds employed about them. Thus I am conscious that I perceive light and colours, sounds,

[1] *Noetica,* Chapter I, §§ 5-7.
[2] Ralph Cudworth, *The True Intellectual System of the Universe,* Andover (Mass.), 1839, pp. 475-476.
[3] Lyon, *Idéalisme,* p. 390.

odours, sapors, and tangible qualities, with all the various combinations of them; and that of these, some give me, or rather are attended with pain or uneasiness, others with pleasure or ease, and the complete enjoyment of myself—I find, moreover, that when I have had any perception or impression of sense, I retain a faint image of it in my mind afterwards, or have a kind of internal sense or remembrance of it; as having seen the sun, a flower, a horse, or a man, I retain the image of their figure, shape, colour, &c. afterwards. Thus I have now a faint idea of the sun at midnight, and of a rose in winter: I know how such a tree, such a horse, or such a man looks, tho' I have neither of them before my eyes. This power of the mind is called imagination and memory, which implies a consciousness of the original impression.[1]

In his distinction of the pure intellect from sensation, Johnson has been esteemed for having made a real contribution to the psychology of the eighteenth century, and in his explication of the intellectual light or intuitive evidence, to have left Berkeley's guidance and adopted a principle which was not yet furnished by the empirical psychology. Here he does not propose innate ideas or principles in the sense in which they were understood by Locke; he does not assert that we can have knowledge without experience; but experience once given, there are certain truths of intuition as certainly known as are those of sensation. In short, there are for him certain synthetic a priori propositions, though he does not call them by that name.[2] As to how he believed these possible, this is his statement: No sooner does any object strike the senses, or is received in our imagination, or apprehended by our understanding, but we are immediately conscious of a kind of intellectual light within us (if I may so call it), whereby we not only know that we perceive the object but directly apply ourselves to the consideration of it both in itself, its properties and powers and as it stands related to all other things, and we find that we are enabled by this intellectual light to perceive these objects and their relations in like manner as by

[1] *Noetica,* Chapter I, § 11.
[2] Jones, *Early American Philosophers,* p. 28.

sensible light we are enabled to perceive the objects of sense and
their various situations; so our minds are passive in this intellectual light as they are to sensible light and can no more withstand the evidence of it than they can withstand the evidence of
sense.   Thus I am under the same necessity to assent to this—
that I am or have a being and that I perceive and freely exert
myself, as I am of assenting to this—that I see colours or hear
sounds   I am as perfectly sure that $2+2=4$, or that the
whole is equal to all its parts, as that I feel heat or cold,
or that I see the sun. I am intuitively certain of both.
This intellectual light I conceive of, as if it were a medium
of knowledge just as sensible light is of sight. In both
these is the power of perceiving and the object perceived; and
this is the medium by which I am enabled to know it. This light
is also one, and common to all intelligent beings, a Chinese or
Japanese, as well as an European or American. By it, all at
once see things to be true or right, in all places at the same
time, and alike invariably at all time, past, present and to come.
If it be asked, whence does this light derive whereby all created
minds at once perceive as by a common standard the same thing
to be true and right, I answer, I have no other way to conceive how I come to be affected with this intuitive intellectual
light whereof I am conscious, than by deriving it from the universal presence and action of Deity, or a perpetual communication with the great Father of lights, or rather his eternal Word
and Spirit. For I know I am not the author of it to myself,
being passive and not active with regard to it, though I am
active in consequence of it. Therefore though I cannot explain
the manner how I am impressed with it (as neither can I that of
sense), I humbly conceive that God does as truly and immediately enlighten my mind internally to know these intellectual
objects as he does by the light of the sun (his sensible representative) enable me to perceive sensible objects. So that those expressions are indeed no less philosophical than devout, that God
is light, and in his light we see light. And this intuitive knowledge, as far as it goes, must be the first principle, from which
the mind takes its rise, and upon which it proceeds in all its

subsequent improvements in reasoning, and discovering both
truth in speculation and right in action; so that this intellectual
light must be primarily and carefully attended to, if we would
avoid and be secure from either error or vice. . . . Nor must
this manner of thinking be suspected to savour of enthusiasm, it
being the settled course or law of nature, according to which the
great parent mind enlighteneth us; and that in things, in their
own nature capable of clear evidence; whereas either reason implies an imaginary, as revelation is a real and well-attested adventitious light, above and beyond the settled law or course of
nature, discovering truths not otherwise knowable—and giving
directions, or enjoining rules of action in things arbitrary or
matters of mere institution. . . . And from this intuitive
intellectual light it is (as I conceive) that we derive what we
call taste and judgment, and, with respect to morals, what some
call the moral sense or the conscience, which are only a sort of
quick intuitive sense or apprehension of the decent and amiable,
of beauty and deformity, of true and false, and of right and
wrong, or duty and sin: And it is the chief business of culture,
art and instruction, to awaken and turn our attention to it, and
assist us in making deductions from it.[1]

Here ends the first and most important chapter of the *Noetica*.
For his defence of the doctrine of intellectual light or intuitive
evidence the writer gives as his sources Berkeley's earlier works,
his own favourites, Malebranche and Norris, the Archbishop of
Cambray and Plato in the *Epinomis*. Yet how far he was in
advance of his authorities is a mooted question. One expositor
claims that not only did his familiarity with the sensationalistic
psychology lead him to an explanation of intellectual perception
somewhat analogous to sense-perception, but the most important
fact was his recognition of the intuitive principles thus known.
Mathematical principles, for instance, are here, as with Kant,
universal and necessary for all rational beings, or, as he states it,
for all created minds. Locke and Berkeley had not denied these
principles from Johnson's point of view; they had not taken his
point of view. What Locke opposed was the belief that these
ideas could be in the mind without experience. Whether they

[1] *Noetica,* Chapter I, § 14.

could be innate, in another sense, was a question which he did not try to answer.¹ This opinion of an American interpreter that Johnson advanced so far beyond the idealism of his day as to approach the modern idealism, has been partially contravened by a French critic. By the latter it is allowed that the apparent contradictions of Berkeley in the last phase of his philosophy are reconciled by Johnson's belief that notions comprise ideas which we have of our own states and operations, as well as of general principles. But this very belief, common to both Johnson and his master, that minds are passive in the reception of intellectual light, itself overthrows any tentative adaptation of the Berkeleian to the Kantian rationalism.

If Johnson did not anticipate the thought of a later age, he was nevertheless able to reconcile the systems of an earlier period, for he now makes it clear that, in spite of their superficial differences, the universal immaterialism of Berkeley, and the vision of all things in God of Malebranche, are hypotheses of the closest kin.² So, coming, in his second chapter, to a consideration of the mind as simply apprehending, he discusses such topics as being in general, the first being, and universal truth after this manner: As soon as the mind is possessed of any variety of objects, being assisted with that inward intellectual light above mentioned, deriving, and, as it were, perpetually beaming forth from the great fountain of all light, both sensible and intellectual, it immediately falls to contemplating its ideas and conceptions, and comparing them one with another. And here, the first thing it is enlightened to know or be conscious of, is, its own existence from the existence of its perceptions and exertions and their objects, which it conceives of as real beings or things, whence it gets the notion of being in general. But even this first object of its knowledge it is made to know from that first principle of intellectual light, flowing from the parent mind. That perception and action, and being perceived or acted upon, implies existence, of which principle, it has an inward intuitive sense and certainty. Hence it immediately infers, I perceive and act, therefore I am; I per-

¹ Jones, *Early American Philosophers*, p. 30.
² Lyon, *Idéalisme*, p. 394.

ceive such an object, therefore it is. Not that its existence depends
on my mind, but on that mind by whom I am enabled to perceive it. . . . In this necessarily existent and eternal being
or mind must originally exist all those necessary and eternal
truths with which our minds are furnished, either by intuition
or demonstration; such as these: that perception and action imply
existence; that what begins to be, must have a cause; that the
whole is equal to all its parts; that all the rays of a circle are
equal; that what is right or wrong in another towards me, must
be equally right or wrong in me towards him. We know that
these and the like eternal truths do not depend on our minds, or
the actual existence of things, but must have an eternal and
necessary existence, antecedent to our knowledge of them, and
independent of it, or of any particular existence. And as we
can have no notion of truth without a mind perceiving it, their
necessary and eternal existence must infer the necessary existence of an eternal mind; and consequently, it must be in that
eternal mind that we behold them, or rather by our communication with him that we are enlightened with the knowledge of
them. In him they must exist as one archetypal and eternal
light of truth; but as they are from him reflected on the various
objects in our finite minds, they appear various and manifold, as
sensible light is one in the sun, though it becomes various colours
and other sensible qualities in different objects.[1]

As Johnson had succeeded in harmonising the views of Berkeley and Malebranche in this, his theory of perception, so does
he perform a like service in his doctrine of causality, since, in
his identification of secondary causes in nature with both ' signs '
and ' occasions,' he again shows the two philosophers to be of
kindred origin.[2] Discussing real and apparent causes, he proceeds: By the word Cause, we mean, that being by whose cause
and activity, force or exertion, another being exists; and that
being which exists by the design, force, action, or exertion of
another, is called effect; what is called an effect therefore must
be supposed not to have existed, and consequently to have had
a beginning of existence, or at least a dependent existence, and

---

[1] *Noetica,* Chapter II, §§ 2, 3.   [2] Lyon, *Idéalisme,* p. 395 note.

must therefore have had a cause, by the force or activity of which it came into existence, and without which it would not have been. And this must be the case of everything that is, till you come to a first cause, *i. e.* to a being that never had a beginning or any dependent existence but exists by the absolute necessity of his own nature, having an original perfect fulness of being in and of itself without depending on any other being. Such a being there must be, otherwise nothing could ever have been, unless you can suppose a thing to be its own cause, *i. e.* to act before it is, which is impossible; or unless you suppose an infinite succession of causes and effects, which, in effect, would be an infinite effect without any cause at all. But an effect without a cause is a contradiction in terms; for, by the definition, to everything that is produced, there must be a correspondent power adequate to the production of it or an active force sufficient to produce it. . . . There are indeed many things that occur to our senses and thoughts that appear at first sight to be agents or causes, which, strictly speaking, are not so, as we find upon a more exact scrutiny, though they are vulgarly so called. Thus we say, the sun warms, enlivens, ripens the fruits; whereas we find upon a more strict enquiry that it is by no means the adequate cause; the sun and (what we call) other natural causes, are in themselves but mere passive, inert beings, connected with one another, according to the established laws of nature; so that, being things merely passive and inert, they cannot, properly speaking, be the causes of the effects vulgarly ascribed to them; they must therefore be called only signs, occasions, means or instruments, and we must look for some other being in whom resides, and by whom must be exerted, that adequate power or force by which the effect is truly produced which, therefore, is the true and real cause; as the others can only be called the apparent causes, having no real efficiency or activity in the production of the effect. . . . Certain activities of our bodies, like breathing and the circulation of the blood, take place without any design or activity of ours. These may be called, with regard to us, necessary effects. On the other hand, we walk, speak, write, etc., from a principle of conscious, designed self-exertion and voluntary activity; these, therefore, are called free or voluntary effects with regard to us, which we produce or not as we please: in doing which we are voluntary causes, and produce voluntary effects. By voluntary effects we mean such as are produced by a free voluntary cause acting from a principle of conscious design and self-exertion, exciting a force of its own, or from within itself, which it chooseth to exert and might do otherwise. This is properly called a cause, an efficient cause or agent, unlike these natural effects above mentioned, of which the apparent is not the real cause, having neither design nor force in itself, as the water in turning a mill. Whence it appears that only intelligent, active beings or spirits can be truly efficient causes, which alone are properly called causes.[1] This theory of causation was further expounded in the idealist's correspondence with his friend Colden. Here, against the contention of the latter that bodies are active, as well as spirits, Johnson argued that a blind principle, or power of action, was repugnant and useless, consciousness, intelligence, or self-active cause, being the only real cause. The significance of this conception has been described as not only foreign to the English philosophy of the times, but as carrying the colonial thinker into the nineteenth century, and even to that doctrine of self-activity which owed its importance to the German philosophy, and especially Hegel.[2]

With his discussion of causality Johnson completes the idealistic portions of the *Noetica.* The rest of that work is taken up with the explication of general notions and with a presentation of the ordinary formal logic of the day. There is, however, one chapter which merits consideration, since it presents the fruits of the author's practical services to education. The *Noetica,* according to its title-page, was to end with an account of the gradual progress of the human mind, from the first dawnings of sense to the highest perfection, both intellectual and moral, of which it is capable. Though this account is but arbitrarily connected with the author's idealism, and presents pedagogical rather than philosophical results, it is nevertheless such a treasure of

[1] *Noetica,* Chapter II, §§ 4-7.
[2] Jones, *Early American Philosophers,* p. 31.

the natural history of the mind [1] as to deserve generous quotation. At a time when another New England idealist could publicly assert that children were 'like little vipers,' and almost an half century before the first hints of the Pestalozzian system had reached the country, Johnson thus presented his educational theory: The first notices of the mind are doubtless those of sense, but directly joined with a consciousness of its perception. Warmth and hunger, and probably some pains, are, perhaps, all the sensations the infant hath before its birth; and when it comes into the light of this world, it is directly impressed with the sense of light and colours, as well as sounds, tastes, odours, and frequent uneasy and painful sensations, all of which still more and more awaken its consciousness; and every fresh notice of sense and consciousness still goes on to excite its admiration, and engage its attention. And being a perfect stranger to every thing about it, it hath every thing to learn; to which it diligently applies itself, as its consciousness more and more awakens, upon the repetition, every moment, of fresh impressions of sense, until by degrees, having a great number of feelings, tastes, odours, sounds and visible objects, frequently repeating their several impressions, its conscious memory still enlarging, it begins, by means of the intellectual light with which it finds its consciousness attended, gradually to collect and recollect the several relations and connections it observes to obtain among its various ideas. And at length, when it is in ease, it discovereth a wonderful curiosity and delight in observing these connections, as well as being impressed with new ideas. Now it hath been made very evident, both by reasoning and experiment, that, as Bishop Berkeley shows in his *Theory of Vision,* the objects of sight and touch are entirely different and distinct things, and that there is no necessary connection between them. It must, therefore, be a matter of great exercise of thought in an infant mind to learn this connection, and particularly, to learn the notion of the vari-

[1] Such a natural history of the child mind was desired by Thomas Reid, who is here anticipated by Johnson just as he is said to be surpassed in his classification of the sciences. Cf. A. E. B. Woodward, *A System of Universal Science,* Philadelphia, 1816, p. 234.

ous distances and situations of things tangible, by its observations on the various degrees of strength or weakness, of vividness or faintness of the light reflected from them, in the things visible constantly connected with them. And, at the same time that it hath these things to learn, which must be a laborious work, as being the same thing with learning a language, it is also learning the names of things, and the connection and use of words, which is another language. And, as if all these were not task enough, it hath all this while to be learning how to use its limbs, its hand in handling, its tongue, and other organs of speech, in making and imitating sounds, and its whole body in all its exertions, and particularly, at length, the poise of its centre of gravity and the use of its feet in walking. All these things require a great deal of application, and the exercise of much thought and exertion. So that it seems evident that these little creatures, from the beginning, do consider, reflect and think a prodigious deal more than we are commonly apt to imagine. . . . The reason why so many little, low, weak and childish things appear in them, which we are apt to despise and think beneath our notice, is not for want of good sense and capacity, but merely for want of experience and opportunity for intellectual improvement. Hence also it appears that we ought to think little children to be persons of much more importance than we usually apprehend them to be; and how indulgent we should be to their inquisitive curiosity, as being strangers; with how much candour, patience and care we ought to bear with them, and instruct them; with how much decency, honour and integrity we ought to treat them; and how careful it concerns us to be, not to say or do anything to them or before them that savours of falsehood or deceit, or that is in any kind indecent or vicious. *Pueris maxima debetur reverentia* is a good trite old saying.[1]

This remarkable sketch of the progress of the mind concludes the *Noetica*. This, together with the *Ethica,* made up the *Elementa Philosophica* which was used in both King's College during Johnson's presidency and also in the philosophy school of the Academy of Philadelphia. And yet the use of this idealistic text-

[1] *Noetica,* Chapter VI, §§ 1-3.

book was without palpable effect upon either institution, and that because of an unfavourable environment; in the one case, there was such a spirit of commercialism as to stifle pure speculation, in the other such a tendency towards materialism that, as Franklin wrote to Johnson, those parts of the *Elements of Philosophy* that savour of what is called Berkeleism are not well understood here.[1]

But while Johnson was much disappointed that his work was not more generally appreciated, he received some crumbs of comfort. Benjamin Franklin generously assumed the expense of printing the American edition of the *Elements;* William Smith, provost of the College of Philadelphia, wrote a laudatory introduction to the London edition, and Cadwallader Colden of New York was so stimulated by the perusal of the latter, that he renewed the amicable controversy regarding the material universe as a dynamic whole. Although there were these gratifying results for the Connecticut idealist in Pennsylvania and New York, in other provinces there was a different condition of affairs. During Berkeley's sojourn in Rhode Island, Edwards was living in Massachusetts, yet here there were no sure signs of the Irish idealism to be found. Even the college at Cambridge was so satisfied with its own speculations, so wrapped up in its peculiar ecclesiasticism, that it paid no attention to the distinguished foreign visitor of another faith. The same result obtained in New Jersey, but for somewhat different causes. Harvard was rationalistic to a degree, but Princeton was so imbued with the common sense philosophy that the Berkeleian idealism, which had somehow stolen into that abode of orthodoxy, was denominated a mere philosophical day-dream.[2]

Besides these special causes there were general causes for the American indifference to Berkeleism. It has been declared the fault of circumstances that Johnson's book fell on a time when the new world was more engaged in conquests in the material than in the immaterial sphere.[3] As uttered by a Gallic critic, this is a polite but shrewd way of saying that Anglo-Americans of the

[1] Letter of July 2nd, 1752, Beardsley, *Life,* p. 173.
[2] See below Book VI, Chapters II, III, IV.
[3] Lyon, *Idéalisme,* p. 403.

late eighteenth century were unfit to receive or to develop a true idealism, for what was true in the British colonies was much the more true in the mother country. The indifference with which Johnson's work was received in England was owing to its appearance at a moment the most inopportune; the spiritualistic philosophy was then losing ground, a crass sensualism or a radical scepticism was taking its place. If only Johnson had presented his immaterialism to an entirely new age, he might perhaps have arrested the general attention; but it was not to be so.[1] Consequently the most that can be said of Johnson's endeavours was that he was the metaphysical double, the ideal image of the good Bishop of Cloyne, but withal unsuccessful in spreading, to any great extent, that form of idealism for which the latter stood.

Hence, as a sort of anti-climax to the work of the earliest American idealist, as a proof of the cruel indifference with which his countrymen treated his utterances, there may be given in conclusion a neglected document, wherein Johnson's highest speculations are so set forth as to afford both a summary and a conclusion of his philosophy: [2]

. . . Our nature properly consists in this, that we are perceptive or thinking & active creatures, or have a principle or power of perceiving, thinking, understanding & reasoning & of exerting ourselves in an endless variety of actions of all which we are evidently conscious to ourselves: & in this consists our Being & Existence: for the moment we begun to perceive & act we begun to be, & if we should utterly cease to think & act we should cease to be & be no more.—But whence is it that we think & act? Did we give ourselves these powers & faculties? —No, by no means; for this would imply that we should act before we had a Being. i. e., that we should be & not be at the same time.—Do we continue our selves in being, or (which is the same thing) in the exercise of these powers?—No, by no means:—we find it is utterly out of our power to continue ourselves in being or Health a moment, or in the exercise of any of our Faculties: this is evident from daily experience: So that

[1] Lyon, *Idéalisme,* pp. 403-404.

[2] Extract from a sermon, "On the Intire Dependence of the Creature upon God.' MS. in possession of Columbia University Library.

we are wholly dependent Beings, both for our Existence & continuance & all our sufficiency for either is intirely of God.— The meaning of which must be this: That it was from the Exertion of the Almighty will & power of God that we at first came into Being. & that it is from the continued exertion of the same Almighty will & power of God every moment that we continue to exist, to think & act. So that the moment God should cease to will our continuance in being, we should utterly cease to be no more: for as the Psalmist says, *It is He that holdeth our Soul in Life & perpetually replenisheth us with his Loving & tender mercy.*—Not but that the Being he gave us & continueth to us is of such a kind that it is we ourselves that do truly think & act, & our thoughts & actions are properly our own exertions, & not the Exertions of any other Being: of this we are intuitively certain, otherwise we could not blame our selves if we think or act amiss: nevertheless that we do at all think & act depends intirely on the Will & Power of that Almighty Being, *in* & by whom alone it is that we do all of us *live & move & have our Being.*—So that *all our sufficiency is of him.*

Furthermore let it be considered that besides these powers of thinking & acting which are the properties of our spiritual nature which is properly our selves, we have an Animal & corporeal Nature to which we are confined in this our present state, which also depends on the constant exertion of the Will & Power of Almighty God.—The very Law of Union between our Souls & Bodies, as far as we can understand, is a meer arbitrary Law or Establishment of the Divine Will, there being no other imaginable connexion [between] Natures so intirely different from each other: So that the moment he should let go his hold of us or cease to will their union, they must immediately fall asunder.—Nay the union & consistence of the parts of these Bodies of ours, & indeed of all other Bodies depends upon a Law of Nature, which can be no other than an arbitrary constitution which God hath made according to which he perpetually wills & acts *all in all,* & without which we & everything about us should immediately dissolve into dust & atomes.—Our Health & Ease as well as our Existence in this present State does in the nature of it depend on the good order not only of all the minute parts of our Bodies, but also of all Nature around us, with which, by the same arbitrary Law of Nature, they are connected: particularly with the air in which we breath, with the food we eat & the water we drink: & who sees not that our supplies of food & drink depend on *rain & fruitful seasons,* & the universal good order of all Nature. So that if God should suspend the Laws of Nature, or cease to exert his Almighty power conformable to them we are immediately deprived of all the means of our subsistence. Upon this Account also, it is evident that *all our sufficiency is of God.*

Moreover, As we thus depend upon God intirely for the being & continuance of our powers of perceiving & acting, & our Subsistence in this present State; so we do no less depend on him, for the Objects on which these Faculties of ours are constantly employed.—Thus it is particularly in the first place as to our powers of perceiving & thinking.—We have no *sufficiency to think* anything, *as of ourselves, but all our sufficiency is of God.*—If we have ever so good eyes to see with, yet if there were no objects to be seen whereby we could behold them, or if we have ever so good ears, yet if there were no sound to be heard, our faculties of Seeing & hearing could turn to no account. So if we are ever so well furnished with the powers of Feeling, tasting & smelling, yet if there were nothing to be either felt, tasted or smelt, we should be ne'er the better for them.—Now it is God's Allsufficiency that constantly supplies us with all these objects of sense.—We have no power of our selves to furnish our selves with any one of them & are meerly passive to every one of them for they are all Impressions made upon our senses or perceptions constantly produced in us by that Almighty Being who is the Father of our Spirits, who knows our frame & continually affects us with the perception of these endlessly various Objects, & with respect to every one of them, *All our Sufficiency is of Him.* He is the Great Light that perpetually shines in upon both our Eyes & our minds, & continually furnishes them with all their Objects.—Particularly as to our Sight.—Be it so that we have from him Eyes & a Power of Seeing, yet none of the Objects of Light depend on our Power:—This beautiful Earth & Sea; this endless variety of plants & animals; this splendid & glorious System of Sun moon & stars; are they our creatures? Did we make them, or do we perceive them? No; it is God that continually subsists & exhibits them to our view, & it is he that conveys to us thro' them all the pleasure & advantage which we imagine they give us; they flow to us from his boundless Allsufficiency.—But suppose them to exist, yet if there was no light wherewith to behold them, they would be to us as tho' they were not: we see every night how darkness draws a vail over all the objects of Light & prints an universal blot upon the whole Creation; now what is this light by which we see visible objects?—Is it our Creature?—No we are meerly passive to it, & find it is a constant impression on our eyes reflected to us from the various Objects deriving from the Sun whom we find to be the Fountain of Light.—But is the Sun the proper Cause of it?—No, from all we can learn or guess of Him, he is only a vast senseless inert Body of himself & has no principle of Thought or power in himself & is therefore only the Tool or Instrument that it pleases God to make use of in this affair, & that it is He, even the Almighty *Father of Light* who is the true Cause & Author, the true Original & Fountain of all that Light wherewith our minds are impressed, & by which we are enabled to be hold all the objects of Light; so that all *our sufficiency is still of Him.*

And as you see the Case is evidently thus with regard to sensible Objects & sensible Light, so it is no less so with regard to intellectual objects & intellectual Light; or the Objects & light of our Reason & understanding.—The Objects of our Understanding, as distinguished from Sense, are Spiritual beings, just as our own Souls; of whose Existence & power or Faculties we are intuitively certain by our own Consciousness, & other intelligent Creatures of whose Existence we are sure by the exercise of our Reason, & above all God the *Father of Spirits,* of whose existence we are sure both by Intuition & Demonstration, and all those necessary & eternal Relations & Connexions of Cause & Effect, Whole & parts, Equality & Inequality, Likeness & Unlikeness, Proportion, Agreements & Disagreements, &c. And all those necessary, Eternal & unchangeable Truths that result from them.—All these objects we know are not the Creatures of our Minds: They depend not on our Will & power, & especially these Eternal Truths: they were just the same before we had being, & would invariably be the same they are if we were reduced to our original nothing, & all the power we have with regard to them is only to perceive & know them which we could never do if they had not an Existence. But how do we perceive them or think of them & know them?—Is it by any Light of our own originally in ourselves?—No, we have indeed a power of perceiving them given us of God, but we have no Light of Our Selves wherewith to behold them; It is He that perpetually irradiates our minds, it is *in his Light that we see Light,* for it is his Eternal Word & Wisdom that *enlighteneth every man that commeth into the World,* who is that glorious Intellectual Sun, the *Sun of Righteousness* who inlighteneth all minds, as the Sensible Sun in the Firmament inlighteneth all our eyes.—How it is as to the manner of it, we are not able to explain the manner of his inlightening us with sensible light, but we find that we are alike passive to this as well as that, & must therefore conclude that it is by the perpetual Action of Deity upon our Minds that we are enlightened to behold those necessary & eternal Truths which are originall in him, in this eternal Mind, & are therefore indeed one with him; without whose perpetual beaming upon us, or irradiating our minds, there would be all darkness or Ignorance, just as we see the moon has no light in herself, but derives all her Light from the Sun; in like manner you see *we have no Sufficiency of our selves but all our Sufficiency is of God.*

CHAPTER III

JONATHAN EDWARDS

JONATHAN EDWARDS (1703-1758), the most subtle of New England idealists, was the quintessence of Puritan culture. Of mingled English and Welsh blood, the Saxon and Celtic strains appeared in his dual nature, with its conflicting logical and imaginative powers. Outwardly Edwards was an advocate of cold ratiocination, of the strict metaphysical way of reasoning; inwardly, a philosopher of the feelings, a fervent exponent of the dialectic of the heart; traditionally he has been known as the preacher of the cold austerities of Puritanism; in reality he was an advocate of the interior or hidden life which results in an intimate union between the individual and the absolute. To judge from his private journal, which presents a series of exquisite miniatures, this saint of New England may be fitly described in the words upon his memorial window: *Dei cultor mystice amantissimus.*

As in the case of the *Confessions* of Saint Augustine, to whom the Puritan divine has been often compared, these early experiences were significant in setting the tone and colour of his subsequent intellectual life. In this life three phases have been recognised, for Edwards has been entitled a mystic because of his wonderful sense of the immediateness of the Divine Presence and agency; an idealist, because of his agreement with Plato's conception of God as the idea of the good; a pantheist, because of his approximation to Spinoza's doctrine of the one substance, of which the universe is the manifestation.[1] All these comparisons have been made, but not all have been correlated. In presenting these as the progressive stages in the philosopher's thinking, it is reasonable to hold that the first is the most fundamental, inasmuch as it goes far to explain both that precocious postulate that ' the material universe exists nowhere but in the mind,' and the final

[1] V. G. Allen, *Jonathan Edwards,* Boston, 1889, p. 12.

126

conclusion that 'existence is constantly proceeding from God.' And so, broadly considered, Edwards' philosophical career may be distributed into three phases of belief: first, the idealism of his youth and early manhood, when a student at Yale College; second, the determinism of his middle period, when the professional exigencies of his ministry kept him within the rigid bounds of Calvinism; third, the tentative pantheism of his maturity, when a recrudescence of certain primary convictions led to such a view of God's last end in creation as to constitute an almost monistic doctrine of immanence.

How may these varying phases of belief be harmonized? Between Edwards the philosopher and Edwards the theologian there may be granted a certain intellectual duality, yet in Edwards the ecstatic there is little variableness, since there is a common element which, like a subterranean stream, flows steadily beneath the entire field of his speculations. This common element is Edwards' mysticism, for his idealism appears to be based upon a mystic form of phenomenalism, his determinism upon a mystic doctrine of passivity, his pantheism upon a mystic absorption of the individual into the absolute. This interpretation of the course of the thinker's internal life is in close accord with the account of his external career.[1] Edwards' father, a graduate of Harvard in 1691, and minister in the East Parish of Windsor, Connecticut, was reputed a man of superior ability and polished manners. As a preacher, it is said that his people gave him the credit of learning and animation, while for his son Jonathan they reserved the epithet profound. But it was to his mother that Edwards was chiefly indebted for his intellectual inheritance. Educated in Boston, she possessed an amount of mental independence which no amount of precedent or prestige could intimidate. Brought up the only son in a family of ten daughters, apart from all distracting influences, in

[1] The following account is compiled chiefly from Allen's *Edwards;* H. N. Gardiner's *Selected Sermons of Jonathan Edwards*, New York, 1904, and from the biography by Sereno Dwight in the tenth edition of Edwards' *Works*, London, 1865, the first volume of which contains all the references in this chapter.

an atmosphere of religion and serious study in the home, the
boy is described as having developed that absorbing interest in
the things of the spirit and that astonishing acuteness of intellect
which are the most prominent characteristics of his genius. Spending much of his time in religious exercises in a retired spot in
the woods, his mind dwelt much on the doctrines he was taught,
especially on the doctrine of God's sovereignty in election, against
which for a time he violently rebelled. Trained by his father to
read with pen in hand, and being a keen observer of the mysteries
of the outward world and eager to discover its laws, when not
more than twelve years old he wrote a letter in a bantering style
refuting the idea of the materiality of the soul, and at about
the same time he sent to an European correspondent of his father
a remarkably accurate and ingenious paper on the habits of the
flying spider. He .was not quite thirteen when he entered Yale
College, where in his sophomore year he made the acquaintance
of Locke's *Essay on the Human Understanding,* reading it, as
he says, with a far higher pleasure ' than the most greedy miser
finds when gathering up handfuls of silver and gold from some
newly discovered treasure.' Under its influence he began a series
of *Notes on the Mind,* with a view to a comprehensive treatise
on mental phenomena. He also began, possibly somewhat later,
a series of *Notes on Natural Science,* with reference to a similar
work on natural philosophy. It is in these early writings that
we find the outlines of an idealistic theory which resembles that
of Berkeley, and which seems to have remained a determining
factor in his speculations to the last.

Of the facts of Edwards' professional life only a brief account
need be given. Residing for two years after graduation in his
college studying for the ministry, he supplied the pulpit of a
small Presbyterian church in New York, whence he ' used frequently to retire into a solitary place on the banks of the Hudson's
River for contemplation on divine things and secret converse
with God.' Returning in 1723 to New Haven to receive the
master's degree, Edwards was retained as a tutor in the college
until 1726, when he resigned his tutorship to become colleague-
pastor in the church of Northampton, Massachusetts, with his

grandfather, the Reverend Solomon Stoddard, whom he succeeded in 1729. Carrying his church through those two great periods of revival, which were the occasion of his treatise on the *Religious Affections,* Edwards was at last, after three and twenty years, unhappily estranged from his people by his extreme demands for conversion against the loose terms of the Halfway Covenant. Declining an offer of assistance from his friends in Scotland, where his ability as a theologian was more appreciated than at home, he now received a call from the little church in Stockbridge, in the Berkshires, where at the same time he became a missionary to the Housatonic Indians. It was in this retired spot that the scholar found time and opportunity for the writing of those great treatises on the *Freedom of the Will,* on *God's End in the Creation of the World,* on the *Nature of True Virtue* and on the *Christian Doctrine of Original Sin,* which were the principal foundations of his theological reputation and which occasioned a matter of some public importance—his election to the presidency of Princeton College. Here, in 1758, the Puritan divine was suddenly carried off, before he could perform the duties of his office, and before he could complete his last projected work, the *History of Redemption,* which, like Saint Augustine's *City of God,* was to be summed up in the latter's mystical words: *Omne bonum aut Deus aut ex Deo.*

With this account of Edwards' professional career, it is in order to take up the speculative interests with which his name stands identified. The problem of Edwards' idealism is the most difficult in the history of American philosophy. Was it his own, or borrowed, or both? Was it the product of precocious genius, or an adaptation of the Berkeleian system, or a blending of the idealistic hints and suggestions then in the air? In the absence of a definitive edition of Edwards' works, no final answer can be given to these questions. Nevertheless one may present the materials already published, review the history of the case, and suggest a principle which may throw a little new light on this vexed controversy. For a full understanding of the completed Edwardean scheme there are four sets of records to be examined: first, the early theoretical presentation of his idealism; then his account of his youthful ecstasies and mystic raptures; next, his maturer treatises, such as the *Inquiry on the Freedom of the Will;* finally, his posthumous publications, such as that on *God's Chief End in the Creation.*

While in his entire system there was a fourfold root, it was in the undeveloped essays of Edwards' youth that the real ground of his idealism is to be sought.[1] Of this the earliest expression is to be found in certain remarkable undergraduate papers, for Edwards, entering Yale College when not quite thirteen, began to arrange his reflections in a series of note books under the title of *Mind, Natural Science, the Scriptures* and *Miscellanies.* This entire series has been hitherto accepted as authoritative and has been pronounced as astonishingly precocious as the *Thoughts* of Pascal. But nowadays the contention that discussions so independent and original in conception, acute in distinction, sequacious and persistent in reasoning, and embracing so great a variety of subjects, often complex and difficult, should emanate from a youth from fourteen to sixteen years of age has been questioned by the more critical spirit of the present day.[2] Nevertheless, a renewed examination of some of the original manuscripts, with their absence of punctuation, bad spelling, misuse of small letters and capitals, has recently shown that the claims of Sereno Dwight, Edwards' great-grandson and careful biographer, are valid, for even prior to the notes on *Mind,* and marked with the characteristics of youthfulness and immaturity, is this introductory essay:

OF BEING

That there should absolutely be nothing at all is utterly impossible, the Mind Can never Let it stretch its Conceptions ever so much bring it self to Concieve of a state of Perfect nothing, it put's the mind into mere Convulsion and Confusion to endeavour to think of such a state, and it Contradicts the very nature or the soul to think that it should be, and it is the Greatest Contradic-

---

[1] H. N. Gardiner, *Jonathan Edwards: A Retrospect,* New York, 1901, p. 116.

[2] E. C. Smyth, *Jonathan Edwards' Idealism, American Journal of Theology,* October, 1897, p. 950.

tion and the Aggregate of all Contradictions to say that there should not be, tis true we Cant so Distinctly show the Contradiction by words because we Cannot talk about it without Speaking horrid Nonsense and Contradicting our selve at every word, and because nothing is that whereby we Distinctly show other particular Contradictions, but here we are Run up to Our first principle and have no other to explain the Nothingness or not being of nothing by, indeed we Can mean nothing else by nothing but a state of Absolute Contradiction; and If any man thinks that he Can think well Enough how there should be nothing I'll Engage that what he means by nothing is as much something as any thing that ever He thought of in his Life, and I believe that if he knew what nothing was it would be intuitively Evident to him that it Could not be. So that we see it is necessary some being should Eternally be and tis a more palpable Contradiction still to say that there must be being somewhere and not otherwhere for the words absolute nothing, and where, Contradict each other; and besides it Gives a great a shock to the mind to think of pure nothing being in any one place, as it Does to think of it in all and it is self evident that there Can be nothing in one place as well as in another and so if there Can be in one there Can be in all. So that we see this necessary eternall being must be infinite and Omnipresent [1]

This Infinite And omnipresent being Cannot be solid. Let us see how Contradictory it is to say that an infinite being is solid, for Solidity surely is nothing but Resistance to other solidities. Space is this Necessary eternal infinite and Omnipresent being, we find that we can with ease Concieve how all other beings should not be, we Can remove them out of our Minds and Place some Other in the Room of them, but Space is the very thing that we Can never Remove, and Concieve of its not being, If a man would imagine space any where to be Divided So as there should be Nothing between the Divided parts, there Remains Space between notwithstanding and so the man Contra-

---

[1] Between this paragraph and the next are the words: 'Place this as a Lemma where it suits best and Let it be more fully [d]monstr' [demonstrated]. The last word is very obscurely written. It seems to begin with an s, as though another word were in mind than the one adopted, as suggested by the following letters, if these are rightly read. In the margin, running down from against the first line of the second paragraph are these words: 'Place this somewhere else.' A mark drawn above 'Place this as a Lemma,' etc., seems to indicate that this direction refers to the same paragraph. (Note by E. C. Smyth.)

dicts himself, and it is self evident I believe to every man that
space is necessary, eternal, infinite, & Omnipresent. but I had
as Good speak Plain, I have already said as much as that Space
is God, and it is indeed Clear to me, that all the Space there is
not proper to body, all the space there is without yᵉ Bounds of
the Creation, all the space there was before the Creation, is God
himself, and no body would in the Least stick at it if it were
not because of the Gross Conceptions that we have of space.

A state of Absolute nothing is a state of Absolute Contradiction
absolute nothing is the Aggregate of all the Absurd [?] contradictions in the World, a state wherein there is neither body nor
spirit, nor space neither empty space nor full space neither little
nor Great, narrow nor broad neither infinitely Great space, nor
finite space, nor a mathematical point neither Up nor Down
neither north nor south (I dont mean as it is with Respect to
the body of the earth or some other Great body but no Contrary Point, nor Positions or Directions [)] no such thing as
either here Or there this way or that way or only one way;
When we Go About to form an idea of Perfect nothing we must
shut Out all these things we must shut out of our minds both
space that has something in it and space that has nothing in it
we must not allow our selves to think of the least part of space
never so small, nor must we suffer our thoughts to take sanctuary
in a mathematical point, when we Go to Expell body out of
Our thoughts we must Cease not to leave empty space in the
Room of it and when we Go to Expell emptiness from Our
thoughts we must not think to Squeese it out by any thing Close
hard and solid but we must think of the same that the sleeping
Rocks Dream of and not till then shall we Get a Compleat idea
of nothing.

a state of nothing is a state wherein every Proposition in Euclid
is not true, nor any of those self evident maxims by which they
are Demonstrated & all other Eternal truths are neither true
nor false when we Go to Enquire whether or no there Can be
absolutely nothing we speak nonsense in Enquiring the stating
of the Question is Nonsense because we make a disjunction where
there is none either being or absolute nothing is no Disjunction
no more than where a tiangle is a tiangle or not a tiangle there
is no other way but Only for there to be existence there is no
such thing as absolute nothing. There is such a thing as nothing
with Respect to this Ink & paper there is such a thing as nothing
with Respect to you & me there is such a thing as nothing with
Respect to this Globe of Earth & with Respect to this Created
universe there is another way besides these things having exist-

ence but there is no such thing as nothing with Respect to Entity
or being absolutely Considered we don't know what we say if
we say we think it Possible in it self that there should not be
Entity

and how Doth it Grate upon the mind to think that something
should be from all Eternity, and nothing all the while be Conscious of it let us suppose to illustrate it that the world had a
being from all Eternity, and had many Great Changes and
Wonderfull Revolutions, and all the while nothing knew, there
was no knowledge in the Universe of any such thing, how is it
possible to bring the mind to imagine. yea it is Really impossible
it should be that Any thing should be and nothing know it then
you'll say if it be so it is because nothing has Any existence
any where else but in consciousness no certainly no where else
but either in Created or uncreated Consciousness Supposing there
were Another Universe only of bodies Created at a Great Distance from this Created in excellent Order and harmonious motions, and a beautifull variety, and there was no Created intelligence in it nothing but senseless bodies, nothing but God knew
anything of it I Demand in what Respect this world has a being
but only in the Divine Consciousness Certainly in no Respect
there would be figures and magnitudes, and motions and Proportions but where where Else but in the almightie's knowledge
how it is possible there should, then you'll say for the same
Reason in a Room Close Shut Up that no body sees nor hears
nothing in it there is nothing any otherway than in Gods knowledge I answer Created beings are Conscious of the Effects of
what is in the Room, for Perhaps there is not one leaf of a tree
nor Spire of Grass but what has effects All over the universe
and will have to the End of Eternity but any otherwise there is
nothing in a Rom shut up but only in Gods Consciousness how
Can Any thing be there Any other way this will appear to be
truly so to Any one that thinks of it with the whole united
strength of his mind. Let us suppose for illustration this impossibility that all the Spirits in the Universe to be for a time to
be Deprived of their Consciousness, and Gods Consciousness at
the same time to be intermitted. I say the Universe for that
time would cease to be of it self and not only as we speak
because the almighty Could not attend to Uphold the world
but because God knew nothing of it tis our foolish imagination
that will not suffer us to see we fancy there may be figures and
magnitudes Relations and properties without any ones knowing
of it, but it is our imagination hurts us we Dont know what
figures and Properties Are.

Our imagination makes us fancy we see Shapes an Colours and magnitudes tho no body is there to behold it but to help our imagination Let us thus State the Case, Let us suppose the world Deprived of Every Ray of light so that there should not be the least Glimmering of light in the Universe Now all will own that in such Case the Universe would be immediately Really Deprived of all its Colours. one part of the Universe is no More Red or blue, or Green or Yellow or black or white or light or dark or transparent or opake there would be no visible Distinction between the world and the Rest of the incomprehensible Void yea there would be no Difference in these Respect between the world and the infinite void, that is any Part of that void would really be as light and as Dark, as white and as black as Red and Green as blue and as brown as transparent and as opake as Any Part of the universe, or as there would be in such Case no Difference between the world and nothing in these Respects so there would be no Difference between one part of the world and another all in these Respects is alike confounded with and undistinguishable from infinite emptiness

At the same time also Let us suppose the Universe to be altogether Deprived of motion, and all parts of it to be at perfec Rest (the same supposition is indeed included in this but we Distinguish them for better Clearness) then the Universe would not Differ from the void in this Respect, there will be no more motion in one than the other then also solidity would cease, all that we mean or Can be meant by solidity is Resistance Resistance to touch, the Resistance of some parts of Space, this is all the knowledge we Get of solidity by our senses and I am sure all that we Can Get any other way, but solidity shall be shown to be nothing Else more fully hereafter. but there Can be no Resistance if there is no motion, one body Can [not] Resist another when there is perfect Rest Amongst them, but you'll say tho there is not actuall Resistance yet there is potential existence, that is such and such Parts of space would Resist upon occasion, but this Is all I would have that there is no solidity now not but that God would Cause there to be on occasion and if there is no solidity there is no extension for extension is the extenddness of the solidity, then all figure, and magnitude and proportion immediately Ceases. put both these suppositions together that is Deprive the world of light and motion and the Case would stand thus with the world, there would [be] neither white nor black neither blew nor brown, bright nor shaded pellucid nor opake, no noise or sound neither heat nor Cold, neither fluid nor Wet nor Drie hard nor soft nor solidity nor Extension, nor figure, nor magnitude nor Proportion nor body nor spirit, what then [is] to become of the Universe Certainly it exists no where but in the Divine mind this will be Abundantly Clearer to one after having Read what I have further to say of solidity &c

So that we see that a world without motion Can Exist no where Else but in the mind either infinite or finite

Corollary. it follows from hence that that those beings which have knowledge and Consciousness are the Only Proper and Real And substantial beings, inasmuch as the being of other things is Only by these. from hence we may see the Gross mistake of those who think material things the most substantial beings and spirits more like a shadow, whereas spirits Only Are Properly Substance.[1]

Here is an expression of idealism which has been declared akin to, if not identical with, that of Berkeley, though it is not generally understood precisely what that relation is.[2] Composed before Edwards read Locke's *Human Understanding,* this essay on *Being* was soon more fully elaborated in those notes on *Mind,* which are, in themselves, indications of the early and perhaps independent origin of Edwards' idealistic beliefs. In this second series there is evident reference back to the initial arguments concerning the inconceivability of the state of nothingness, the infinity and divinity of space, and the spirituality of substance. As given in the corrected literary form, for access is denied to the originals, the following early sections from the paper on *Mind* will indicate the consistent development of Edwards' idealism:

Space, as has been already observed, is a necessary being, if it may be called a being; and yet we have also shown, that all existence is mental, that the existence of all exterior things is ideal. Therefore it is a necessary being, only as it is a necessary idea, so far as it is simple idea, that is necessarily connected with other simple exterior ideas, and is, as it were, their common substance or subject. It is in the same manner a necessary being, as anything external is a being.

Coroll. It is hence easy to see in what sense that is true, that has been held by some, That, when there is nothing between any two bodies, they unavoidably must touch. . . . . .

---

[1] *Proceedings American Antiquarian Society,* October, 1895, pp. 241-245.
[2] Gardiner, *Retrospect,* p. 117.

The real and necessary existence of Space and its Infinity, even beyond the Universe, depend upon a like reasoning as the Extension of Spirits, and to the supposition of the reality of the existence of a Successive Duration, before the Universe: even the impossibility of removing the idea out of the mind. If it be asked, If there be Limits of the Creation, whether or no it be not possible that an Intelligent being shall be removed beyond the limits; and then whether or no there would not be distance between that Intelligent being and the limits of the Universe, in the same manner, and as properly, as there is between Intelligent beings and the parts of the Universe, within its limits; I answer, I cannot tell what the Law of Nature, or the Constitution of God, would be in this case.

Coroll. There is, therefore, no difficulty in answering such questions as these, What cause was there why the Universe was placed in such a part of Space? and, Why was the Universe created at such a Time? for, if there be no Space beyond the Universe, it was impossible that it should be created in another place; and if there was no Time before, it was impossible it should be created at another time.

The idea we have of Space, and what we call by that name, is only *Coloured Space,* and is entirely taken out of the mind, if Colour be taken away. And so all that we call Extension, Motion, and Figure, is gone, if Colour is gone. As to any idea of Space, Extension, Distance, or Motion, that a man born blind might form, it would be nothing like what we call by those names. All that he could have would be only certain sensations or feelings, that in themselves would be no more like what we intend by Space, Motion, &c., than the pain we have by the scratch of a pin, or than the ideas of taste and smell. And as to the idea of Motion, that such a one could have, it would be only a diversification of those successions in a certain way, by succession as to time. And then there would be an agreement of these successions of sensations, with some ideas we have by sight, as to number and proportions; but yet the ideas, after all, nothing akin to that idea we now give this name to.—And, as it is very plain, Colour is only in the mind, and nothing like it can be out of all mind. Hence it is manifest, there can be nothing like those things we call by the name of Bodies, out of the mind, unless it be in some other mind or minds.

And, indeed, the secret lies here: That, which truly is the Substance of all Bodies, is *the infinitely exact, and precise, and perfectly stable Idea, in God's mind, together with His stable Will, that the same shall gradually be communicated to us, and to other minds, according to certain fixed and exact established Methods and Laws;* or in somewhat different language, *the infinitely exact and precise Divine Idea, together with an answerable, perfectly exact, precise, and stable Will, with respect to correspondent communications to Created Minds, and effects on their minds.*[1]

This is the most striking passage in those initial notes on the *Mind,* in which Edwards sought to give a ' Natural History of the Mental World '; as emanating from a boy of sixteen or seventeen they have been declared truly marvellous, even if it be held that at this time Edwards was a veritable Berkeleian.[2] Whatever the sources of this juvenile idealism, as if repeating Berkeley's theory of the divine language of signs, Edwards at this point defines truth after the most strict metaphysical manner as the consistency and agreement of our ideas with the ideas of God. But should it be inquired, What is it for our ideas to agree with things as they are, seeing that corporal things exist no otherwise than mentally? . . . After all that has been said and done, the only adequate definition of Truth is: The agreement of our ideas with existence. To explain what this existence is is another thing. In abstract ideas it is nothing but the ideas themselves; so their truth is their consistency with themselves. In things that are supposed to be without us it is the determination and fixed mode of God's exciting ideas in us. So that Truth, in these things, is an agreement of our ideas with that series in God. It is existence; and that is all that we can say. It is impossible that we should explain a perfectly abstract and mere idea of existence; only we always find this, by running of it up, that God and Real Existence are the same.[3]

That the extracts given thus far are actually the productions of Edwards to the latter part of his sophomore or to his junior year has been argued from internal evidence, from characteristics more readily felt than described; for common to the pre-collegiate papers and those which stand first in the notes, there is

[1] *Mind,* §§ 9, 13.
[2] G. P. Fisher, *Discussion in History and Theology,* New York, 1880.
[3] *Mind,* §§ 10, 15.

an intensity which runs over into exaggeration of phraseology, a positiveness which in its own clearness and strength of conviction has not learned by experience how to introduce and adjust statements to the working and needs of other minds.[1]

Up to this point Edwards argues as if his idealistic system were quite of his own making; but he soon begins to take cognisance of the labours of others and refers to their speculations, at first in a general way, but soon more specifically. In the following passages it is noticeable that the first begins with a reference to a certain agreement among knowing philosophers; that the second seeks to adjust the new idealistic principle to the old way; that the third argues for the ideality of material existence by an appended description of Plato's subterranean cave, indicating that he considered sensible things as shadows and ectypes of the divinely conceived order; and that the fourth defends the mentality of motion against the objection that might be raised from what Newton says of the absolute and relative motion:

It is now agreed upon by every knowing philosopher, that Colours are not really in the things, no more than pain is in a needle; but strictly nowhere else but in the mind. But yet I think that Colour may have an existence out of the mind, with equal reason as anything in Body has any existence out of the mind, beside the very substance of the body itself, which is nothing but the Divine power, or rather the Constant Exertion of it. For what idea is that, which we call by the name of Body? I find Colour has the chief share in it. 'Tis nothing but Colour, and Figure, which is the termination of this Colour, together with some powers, such as the power of resisting, and motion, &c., that wholly makes up what we call Body. And if that, which we principally mean by the thing itself, cannot be said to be in the thing itself, I think nothing can be. If Colour exists not out of the mind, then nothing belonging to Body exists out of the mind but Resistance, which is Solidity, and the termination of this Resistance, with its relations, which is Figure, and the communication of this Resistance, from space to space, which is Motion; though the latter are nothing but modes of

[1] E. C. Smyth, *Some Early Writings of Jonathan Edwards, Proceedings of American Antiquarian Society,* October, 1895, p. 227.

the former. Therefore, there is nothing out of the mind but Resistance. And not that neither, when nothing is actually resisted. Then, there is nothing but the Power of Resistance. And as Resistance is nothing else but the actual exertion of God's power, so the Power can be nothing else, but the constant Law or Method of that actual exertion. And how is there any Resistance, except it be in some mind, in idea? What is it that is resisted? It is not Colour. And what else is it? It is ridiculous to say, that Resistance is resisted. That does not tell us at all what is to be resisted. There must be something resisted before there can be Resistance; but to say Resistance is resisted, is ridiculously to suppose Resistance, before there is anything to be resisted. Let us suppose two globes only existing, and no mind. There is nothing there, *ex confesso,* but Resistance. That is, there is such a Law, that the space within the limits of a globular figure shall resist. Therefore, there is nothing there but a power, or an establishment. And if there be any Resistance really out of the mind, one power and establishment must resist another establishment and law of Resistance, which is exceedingly ridiculous. But yet it cannot be otherwise, if any way out of the mind. But now it is easy to conceive of Resistance, as a mode of an idea. It is easy to conceive of such a power, or constant manner of stopping or resisting a colour. The idea may be resisted, it may move, and stop, and rebound; but how a mere power, which is nothing real, can move and stop, is inconceivable, and it is impossible to say a word about it without contradiction. The world is therefore an ideal one; and the Law of creating, and the succession, of these ideas is constant and regular. . . . When we say that the World, *i. e.* the material Universe, exists nowhere but in the mind, we have got to such a degree of strictness and abstraction that we must be exceedingly careful, that we do not confound, and lose ourselves by misapprehension. That is impossible, that it should be meant, that all the world is contained in the narrow compass of a few inches of space, in little ideas in the place of the brain; for that would be a contradiction; for we are to remember that the human body, and the brain itself, exists only mentally, in the same sense that other things do; and so that, which we call *place,* is an idea, too. Therefore things are truly in those places; for what we mean, when we say so, is only, that this mode of our idea of place appertains to such an idea. We would not therefore be understood to deny, that things are where they seem to be. For the principles we lay down, if they are narrowly looked into, do not infer that. Nor will it be found, that they at all make void Natural Philosophy, or the science of the Causes or Reasons of corporeal changes; for to find out the reasons of things, in Natural Philosophy, is only to find out the proportion of God's acting. And the case is the same, as to such proportions, whether we suppose the World only mental, in our sense, or no.

Though we suppose, that the existence of the whole material Universe is absolutely dependent on Idea, yet we may speak in the old way, and as properly and truly as ever. God, in the beginning, created such a certain number of Atoms, of such a determinate bulk and figure, which they yet maintain and always will, and gave them such a motion, of such a direction, and of such a degree of velocity; from whence arise all the Natural changes in the Universe, forever, in a continued series. Yet, perhaps all this does not exist anywhere perfectly, but in the Divine Mind. But then, if it be inquired, What exists in the Divine Mind; and how these things exist there? I answer, There is his determination, his care, and his design, that Ideas shall be united forever, just so, and in such a manner, as is agreeable to such a series. For instance, all the ideas that ever were, or ever shall be to all eternity, in any created mind, are answerable to the existence of such a peculiar Atom in the beginning of the Creation, of such a determinate figure and size, and have such a motion given it: That is, they are all such, as Infinite Wisdom sees would follow, according to the series of nature, from such an Atom, so moved. That is, all ideal changes of creatures are just so, as if just such a particular Atom had actually all along existed even in some finite mind, and never had been out of that mind, and had, in that mind, caused these effects, which are exactly according to nature, that is, according to the nature of other matter, that is actually perceived by the mind. God supposes its existence; that is, He causes all changes to arise, as if all these things had actually existed in such a series, in some created mind, and as if created minds had comprehended all things perfectly. And, although created minds do not; yet, the Divine Mind doth; and he orders all things according to his mind, and his ideas. And these hidden things do not only exist in the Divine idea, but in a sense in created idea; for that exists in created idea, which necessarily supposes it. If a ball of lead were supposed to be let fall from the clouds, and no eye saw it, till it got within ten rods of the ground, and then its motion and celerity was perfectly discerned in its exact proportion; if it were not for the imperfection and slowness of our minds, the perfect idea of the rest of the motion would immediately, and of itself, arise in the mind, as well as that which is there. So, were our thoughts comprehensive and perfect enough, our view of the present state of the world would excite in us a perfect idea of all past changes.

And we need not perplex our minds with a thousand questions and doubts that will seem to arise: as, To what purpose is this way of exciting ideas? and, What advantage is there in observing such a series? I answer, It is just all one, as to any benefit or advantage, any end that we can suppose was proposed by the Creator, as if the Material Universe were existent in the same manner as is vulgarly thought. For the corporeal world is to no advantage but to the spiritual; and it is exactly the same advantage this way as the other, for it is all one, as to anything excited in the mind. . . .

Since all material existence is only idea, this question may be asked, In what sense may those things be said to exist, which are supposed, and yet are in no actual idea of any Created minds? I answer, they existed only in Uncreated idea. But how do they exist, otherwise than they did from all Eternity, for they always were in Uncreated idea and Divine appointment? I answer, They did exist from all Eternity in Uncreated idea, as did everything else, and as they do at present, but not in Created idea. But it may be asked, How do those things exist, which have an actual existence, but of which no created mind is conscious?—For instance, the Furniture of this room, when we are absent, and the room is shut up, and no created mind perceives it; How do these things exist?—I answer, There has been in times past such a course and succession of existences, that these things must be supposed to make the series complete, according to Divine appointment, of the order of things. And there will be innumerable things consequential, which will be out of joint, out of their constituted series, without the supposition of these. For, upon the supposition of these things, are infinite numbers of things otherwise than they would be, if these were not by God thus supposed. Yea, the whole Universe would be otherwise; such an influence have these things, by their attraction and otherwise. Yea, there must be a universal attraction, in the whole system of things, from the beginning of the world to the end; and, to speak more strictly and metaphysically, we must say, in the whole system and series of ideas in all Created minds; so that these things must necessarily be put in, to make complete the system of the ideal world. That is, they must be supposed, if the train of ideas be, in the order and course, settled by the Supreme mind. So that we may answer in short, That the existence of these things is in God's supposing of them, in order to the rendering complete the series of things (to speak more strictly, *the series of ideas,*) according to his own settled order, and that harmony of things, which he has appointed.—The supposition of God, which we speak of, is nothing else but God's acting, in the course and series of his exciting ideas, as if they (the things supposed) were in actual idea. . . . If motion be only mental, it seems to follow that there is no difference between Real and Apparent motion, or that Motion is nothing else but the change of position between bodies; and then of two bodies that have their position changed, Motion may with equal reason be ascribed to either of them, and the Sun may as properly be said to move as the Earth. And then returns this difficulty. If it be so, how comes it to pass that the Laws of Centrifugal Force are observed to take place, with respect to the Earth, considered as moving round the Sun, but not with respect to the Sun, considered as moving round the Earth?—I answer, It would be impossible it should be so, and the Laws of gravitation be observed. The Earth cannot be kept at a distance from a body, so strongly attracting it as the Sun, any other way than by such a motion as is supposed. That body therefore must be reputed to move, that can be supposed so to do, according to the Laws of Nature universally observed in other things. It is upon them that God impresses that Centrifugal Force.[1]

While it may be allowed that this series of metaphysical definitions and discussions as emanating from an undergraduate are truly marvellous, yet it is now pretty well agreed that they were written before Edwards left college. Indeed, it has been argued from the forcing process of Edwards' youth, the stimulating atmosphere of theological speculation in which he was brought up, that there is no improbability that at seventeen he reached his idealistic conceptions, just as Berkeley himself began his *Commonplace Book,* containing the material for his *Theory of Vision* and his *Principles,* shortly after taking his first degree, at the age of nineteen.[2] But leaving aside all comparison in the somewhat futile problem of precocity, the contention that Edwards' idealism was as early as it has been traditionally claimed, receives further vindication by referring to the fourth series of notes which have been assigned to the last two years of college life

---

[1] *Mind,* §§ 27, 34, 40, 65.
[2] Gardiner, *Retrospect,* p. 144.

and the two following of graduate residence. It is the *Miscellanies* which possess that familiar air of retrospection, that way of pointing back to previous views, indicative of the fact that the youthful author's mind was already set in an idealistic direction. As taken from the originals, which are not in Edwards' collected works, two of these earlier observations may here be cited:

Spiritual happiness, as we have shown and demonstrated—contrary to the opinion of [most who believe] that nothing is substance but matter—that no matter is substance but only God, who is a Spirit, and that other spirits are more substantial than matter; so also it is true that no happiness is solid and substantial but spiritual happiness, although it may seem that sensual pleasures are more real, and spiritual only imaginary; just as it seems as if sensible matter were only real and spiritual substance only imaginary. . . . We know there was Being from eternity; and this being must be intelligent, for how doth the mind refuse to believe that there should be being from all eternity, without its being conscious to itself that it was; that there should be from all eternity, and yet nothing known, all that while, that anything is. This is really a contradiction; and we may see it to be so, though we know not how to express it. For in what respect has anything had a being, when there is nothing conscious of its being; for in what respect has anything a being that [of which] angels nor men, nor created intelligences know nothing, but only as God knows it to be? Not at all more than there are sounds where none hears it, or colour where none sees it. Thus, for instance, supposing a room in which none is; none sees the things in the room; no created intelligence. The things in the room have no being any otherways than only as God is conscious [of them]; for there is no colour there, neither is there any sound, nor any shape, &c.[1]

With these citations, which reaffirm the thought and even the argumentative illustration of the earliest essay on *Being*, the idealistic thinking of Edwards is brought through the year 1722, and thereby into the first probable point of historical connection

[1] E. C. Smyth, *Jonathan Edwards' Idealism, American Journal of Theology*, 1897, p. 953, quoting MS. copy of 'Miscellanies,' f. p. 1173, and pp. p. 1.

with the kindred immaterialism of Berkeley, for it was in the following year that Edwards' former tutor, Samuel Johnson, of Yale College, was reported to have first heard of Berkeleism when he went to England for episcopal ordination.[1] While the evidence that the American idealist drew on the Irish idealist prior to this date is highly problematical, one must needs review the arguments on both sides before proceeding to what may possibly furnish a new clue to the problem of Edwards' originality, namely, those mystic expressions which go far to explain the generation and growth of the later immaterialistic doctrines. As to the sources whence the young undergraduate derived his idealistic notions, it has been variously said [2] that in recent years there has grown up what may be regarded as a history of opinion on this difficult point. On the one hand, it is maintained that Edwards had no acquaintance with the writings of Berkeley, and that it is not necessary to suppose such an acquaintance in order to explain this reproduction, almost complete, of a philosophy which is identified with Berkeley's name. The former was the view of Dr. Sereno Edwards Dwight,[3] the latter the view of President Noah Porter of Yale College, who argued that, being surrounded as it were by similar logical and spiritual impulses, Jonathan Edwards drew the same conclusions as Berkeley had done from the same data in Locke's *Essays*.[4]

On the other hand, those who hold that Edwards may have read Berkeley's works can bring no direct evidence to substantiate their opinion. Professor A. Campbell Fraser, the biographer and editor of Berkeley, was the first to advance the opinion that Edwards, the most subtle reasoner that America has produced, adopted and professed Berkeley's great philosophical conception,[5]

---

[1] Noah Porter, *Discourse at Yale College on the 200th Birthday of Bishop Berkeley,* New York, 1885, p. 71.

[2] This summary is taken chiefly from the views of Allen, Curtis, Fisher, Gardiner and Smyth.

[3] Cf. his *Life of Edwards,* p. 40.

[4] *Discourse at Yale College on the 200th Birthday of Bishop Berkeley,* 885, p. 71.

[5] *Life of Berkeley,* p. 182; Berkeley's *Principles,* 1871, p. xviii.

but is now less disposed to this conjecture than formerly.[1] So, too, Professor Fisher was once of the opinion that it was from Berkeley that the youthful American philosopher imbibed his views, but further investigations have proved it to be in the highest degree probable that this inference is a mistaken one. It was owing to the powerful stimulus imparted to the young Yale student by the writings of Locke that he was prompted to move on in a path of his own, while the ' new philosophy,' to which Edwards afterwards refers with approval, appears to have been the publications of Sir Isaac Newton.[2] So, too, Professor George Lyon in treating of Edwards as a representative of the English idealism of the eighteenth century has declared that the dependence on Berkeley is unmistakable, and has even undertaken to point this out in some detail. He quotes, for example, the following: ' The ideas we have by the sense of feeling are as much mere ideas as those we have by the sense of seeing,' remarking that this is precisely the position whereby Berkeley in his *Principles* did away with what was equivocal in his *Theory of Vision*. He refers to Edwards' arguments for the merely mental existence of all the objects of vision, because, namely, ' all these things . . . do exist in a looking-glass,' as almost a phrase of Berkeley's, and, at any rate, one of his favourite proofs. He also considers the argument to be similar to Berkeley's in which Edwards maintains the unlikeness between our ideas of space and those which a man born blind would have.[3]

But in view of the later negative evidence, the dissimilarities between the principles of Berkeley and of Edwards, it has been asserted that these parallelisms of language and argument cited by Lyon appear trivial. How could any idealist fail to observe that ideas of touch are as much ideas as those of sight? And,

---

[1] Fraser's 1901 edition of Berkeley's *Works,* Vol. 3, p. 393. Compare also a letter to the writer, 9th July, 1906, in which Professor Fraser says: ' Edwards too (at least in his youth) embraced Berkeley, although I do not think he has named him.'

[2] G. P. Fisher, *An Unpublished Essay of Edwards on the Trinity,* New York, 1903, p. 18.

[3] Gardiner, *Retrospect,* p. 138.

what more natural illustration of the ideality of objects of vision than their reflection in a looking-glass? Or, what more likely an observation than the difference between a blind man's idea of space and ours? This last, moreover, he could have got, and probably did get, from Locke.[1]

Thus far all the evidence for this alleged influence of Berkeley is entirely internal. There is no external evidence that is worth considering. The suggestion that Edwards may have become acquainted with Berkeley's philosophy through Samuel Johnson, who was tutor at Yale between 1716 and 1719, fails when it is put to the test. Johnson was *persona non grata* to Edwards, for he remained at New Haven while Edwards withdrew, with other disaffected students, to Wethersfield. Nor is there any evidence that Johnson was at this time acquainted with Berkeley's writings. Johnson's own manuscript, entitled 'A Catalogue of Books read by me from year to year since I left Yale Colledge,' contains no mention of anything of Berkeley's before 1727-28. In that year and the year following the *Principles* are entered, and in 1729-30 the *Dialogues* and the *Theory of Vision*.[2] Finally certain recently discovered manuscripts confirm one's opinion of the lateness of the date in Johnson's mastery of Berkeley's works, for on September 10, 1729, he writes to the Dean 'a letter . . . upon reading his books of the *Principles of Human Knowledge* and *Dialogues*.' [3]

If it now seems highly improbable that Edwards could have become acquainted with the Irish metaphysician through his casual tutor Johnson, there nevertheless remains the possibility that he could have known Berkeley's works at first hand, for from four to seven years elapsed between the publication of Berkeley's early philosophy and the earliest date claimed for these writings of Edwards.[4] But here the suggestion of Johnson's biographer, Beardsley, that the 'new philosophy,' against which the students were warned, when Johnson graduated in 1714, was Berkeley's, has been demolished; [1] and the opinion of President Porter that there is no evidence that any of Berkeley's works were known at

[1] Gardiner, *Retrospect*, p. 147. [2] *Ib.*, p. 141.
[3] See preceding chapter. [4] Gardiner, *Retrospect*, p. 140.

Yale College when Edwards was a student is hardly tenable,[2] for the fact that a book is not catalogued is no proof that it was not in a library. So, too, with the argument from silence in Edwards' own works. He paid an ample tribute to Locke, but nowhere does he mention Berkeley, to whom lay the greater indebtedness. Although in his relations to other writers Edwards may have been candid in some respects, he was not in all. In corroboration of the opinion that he was not the man to conceal a real obligation has been cited his remark at the end of his notes in *Natural Science:* ' This has been thought of before.' But as a sort of psychological explanation as to the silence on the name of Berkeley, it has been said that, frank as these early writings of Edwards may seem, they contain intimations of a reserved and even secretive temperament. He has recourse now and then to shorthand, in which he buried in oblivion his most intimate thoughts or feelings. He charges himself not to allow it to appear as if he were familiar with books or conversant with the learned world. He seems to feel that he has a secret teaching which will create opposition when revealed and clash with the prejudices and fashions of the age.[3] In all this quandary one is not helped out by the articles and meagre references to Edwards' unpublished writings. What has been called the most interesting manuscript of the Yale collection, a memorandum book labelled simply ' Catalogue,' has as the opening leaf a record of ' legenda,' but what was the complete list of philosophical works mentioned in this reading list the editor has not divulged.[4]

Under these various difficulties and limitations as to the external evidence, one is forced to fall back upon the internal, the similarities or discrepancies between the immaterialistic doctrines

---

[1] E. C. Smyth, *Proceedings American Antiquarian Society*, Vol. 10, p. 251.

[2] Porter, *Discourse*, p. 71.

[3] Allen, *Edwards*, p. 19 note.

[4] F. B. Dexter, *The Manuscripts of Jonathan Edwards*, p. 15, reprint from the *Proceedings of the Massachusetts Historical Society*, March, 1901.

of Edwards and of Berkeley. Here, too, the evidence is mainly negative as to any direct dependence of the younger upon the older idealist. In a general way it has been argued that the student who had read Berkeley must surely have felt himself under a real obligation. But there is nothing whatever of this in Edwards. On the contrary, there is evident consciousness of independence. He is preparing to write a book in which these views of his will be given to the world. He is aware of their novelty. He is careful, therefore, to guard himself against misapprehension, especially in the matter of the seeming denial of the existence of bodies outside the mind. ' It is from hence I expect the greatest opposition,' he writes.[1] Interpreting this as an expression of a sense of personal ownership in his ideas, it is further argued that, if Edwards had derived his idealism from Berkeley, we should expect a much more direct reflection of Berkeley's thought and language. How, for instance, could he have written as he did on the subject of universals, if he had been acquainted with Berkeley's vigorous polemic against the doctrine of abstract ideas? No ideas are more characteristic and oft-repeated in the early works of Berkeley than the following: The impossibility of perceiving distance by sight, the arbitrariness of God in connecting ideas of sight and ideas of touch, the influence of suggestion in perception, the objects of sight a divine visual language. Is it conceivable or to be regarded as a mere accident that a young student, reproducing ideas derived from the reading of Berkeley, should have given no hint of being affected by such all-pervading and altogether fascinating conception?

. . . But we can go further. Not only is there no proof that Edwards derived his idealism from Berkeley, but it is clearly evident that his idealism has, to say the least, a different accent and character from that of the author of the *Principles of Human Knowledge* and the *Dialogues of Hylas and Philonous.* Berkeley's early doctrine is, as everyone knows, that the *esse* of material things consists in their *percipi.* Now it is no doubt true that in urging this doctrine his main object was to establish the reality of the divine being and action, and the sub-

[1] Gardiner, *Retrospect,* pp. 145-146.

stantiality and causality of spirit. That spirit is alone substantial and causal is indeed the real Berkeleian idealism. But the relation of things sensible to spirits, and especially to the mind of God, is hardly considered by Berkeley in his early writings; he contents himself with the thought that God imprints the ideas of material things on our senses in a fixed order. To the objection that material things when not actually perceived by us must be non-existent he can only reply that ' there may be some other spirit that perceives them, though we do not.' The *esse* of things is thus their *percipi*. Later in life Berkeley went beyond this, and taught that the *esse* of things is not their *percipi*, but their *concipi;* that the world in its deepest truth is a divine order eternally existing in the mind of God. But it is this doctrine which, along with the phenomenalism which he shares with Berkeley, is the characteristic doctrine of Jonathan Edwards. It is implied in his conception of the real, as distinguished from the nominal, essence, in his conception of truth as the agreement of our ideas with the ideas of God, and it is definitely expressed in various passages, best perhaps in the formulation of his idealism already quoted: ' That which truly is the substance of all bodies is the infinitely exact, and precise, and stable Idea, in God's mind, together with His stable Will, that the same shall gradually be communicated to us, and to other minds, according to certain fixed and established Methods and Laws.' The phenomenalism in Edwards is relatively subordinate. But similar ideas are not at all prominent in Berkeley before the *Siris,* which was not published till 1744.[1]

Further divergences between Edwards and Berkeley which have been pointed out do not especially concern the early idealism, for the doctrine that space is divine, which Berkeley denounces as absurd, is traceable to Newton, and the doctrine of necessitated volition, wherein Edwards differed from both Berkeley and Johnson, is to be referred to the later determinism of the *Inquiry Into the Freedom of the Will.* But if the hypothesis of Berkeleian influence be surrendered, although it is not certain that Berkeley had absolutely nothing to do with Edwards' early ideal-

[1] Gardiner, *Retrospect,* pp. 147-149.

ism,[1] that surrender weakens but does not necessarily preclude the hypothesis of a borrowing from other sources. Here four philosophers have been suggested. These are, in their historical order: Descartes, with his problematical idealism in the early part of the *Meditations;* [2] Malebranche, with his supposition that God is the only agent and does everything upon occasion of certain events in the mundane sphere; [3] Norris, whose *Theory of the Ideal or Intelligible World,* published in 1701, reproduced ideas of Malebranche; and Arthur Collier, whose *Clavis Universalis* of 1713 propounded a theory of absolute idealism.[4] Between these thinkers and Edwards there are affinities, yet as actual connections they have been declared highly problematic and quite gratuitous,[5] and for such reasons as these. Against Descartes the students of Yale had been warned as early as 1714 as one of those bringing in a corrupting new philosophy; [6] in behalf of Malebranche there is no proof positive, for Edwards makes no reference to him; [7] and the same is true of Norris, except for Edwards' chance use of the phrase, ' the ideal world '; [8] while as for Collier's pamphlet, which, like Edwards' early note on ' Existence,' compares the sensible world to a looking-glass,[9] at this time that rare work was unknown even in England and Scotland.[10]

Although these arguments from silence may be deemed inconclusive, since the tendency among writers to assume that the New England scholars cannot have been acquainted very largely with the literature of their times is unfounded,[11] nevertheless, in the absence of definite references, recourse must be had to those

---

[1] So H. N. Gardiner in a letter to the writer, 14th May, 1906.

[2] Gardiner, *Retrospect,* p. 151.

[3] Foster, *New England Theology,* p. 64.

[4] J. H. MacCracken, *Jonathan Edwards' Idealismus,* Halle, 1899, p. 32.

[5] M. M. Curtis, *Kantean Elements in Edwards,* Berlin, 1906, p. 40.

[6] Smyth, *Early Writings,* p. 234.

[7] Lyon, *Idéalisme,* p. 433.

[8] *Mind,* § 40.

[9] *Mind,* § 27.

[10] Curtis, *Kantean Elements,* p. 40.

[11] Foster, *New England Theology,* p. 48 note.

authors whom it is known that Edwards read as an undergraduate. These were Cudworth, with his diffused Platonism; Newton, with his doctrine of colours; Locke, with his doctrine of ideas. As to the last of the given authorities, it is well argued that, when one considers the nature of the mind of Edwards, there is no difficulty in believing that although isolated in a new world he advanced upon Locke in a way similar to that of Berkeley, and propounded elements of idealism that have entered into the most recent thought. That there is no difficulty in drawing idealism from the writings of Locke has been pointed out by Sir William Hamilton, and Reid thought it strange that Locke, who wrote so much about ideas, should not see those consequences that Berkeley thought so obvious.[1] However, this is arguing from mere probability. Therefore, in default of a careful re-editing of the unpublished manuscripts and since it is impossible to determine all that was in the air of the Connecticut Valley in Edwards' youth, it has been similarly declared that we need, in order to account for his idealism, to recognise only these forces: The early fascination for him of Newton's discoveries respecting light and colours; the philosophy of Locke, especially the stress laid upon sensation as explaining the origin of ideas; his own extraordinary deductive power, so early exhibited and henceforth at once his strength and his weakness, and his wonderful sense of the Divine Presence and agency.[2]

Assuming these three factors as making up the character of Edwards as idealist, one may say that his learning appears to have been less than his logical powers and his intuitive greater than either. Such an evaluation has at least the merit of correlating the various opinions of the man and his works. First, there is the native opinion that since he knew Plato but partially, Aristotle hardly at all, could not read French and was ignorant of the Schoolmen and the Catholic theologians since Augustine,[3] and since the search for his indebtedness to others has been vain, his early notes are all the greater warrant for

---

[1] Curtis, *Kantean Elements*, p. 40. Cf. below book V, Chapter VI.
[2] Smyth, *Early Writings*, pp. 235-236.
[3] F. B. Sanborn, *Journal of Speculative Philosophy*, October, 1883.

ranking him among the great, original minds.[1] Again, there is
the foreign opinion of Dugald Stewart that in logical acuteness
and subtlety Edwards does not yield to any disputant bred in the
universities of Europe;[2] this is borne out by Edwards' early
confession that one reason why, at first, before he knew other
logic, he used to be mightily pleased with the Old Logic, was
because it was very pleasant to see his thoughts, that before lay
in his mind jumbled without any distinction, ranged into order
and distributed into classes and subdivisions, so that he could tell
where they all belonged and run them up to their general heads.[3]
Finally there is the opinion of Sir James Mackintosh, that Edwards' power of subtle argument was joined, as in some of
the ancient mystics, with a character which raised his piety to
fervour. This sentiment is repeated in the most recent study of
Edwards, which contends that it was not in the realm of the
discursive but of the intuitive understanding that he has his pre-
eminence; for his mind in early years seems to have been dominated by the sense of the sublime and beautiful, proportion and
symmetry.[4]

Whether or not this element of the mystical and transcendental
thought was at variance with his own logic, that element has
received considerable recognition. Most pertinent is the opinion
that in the critical analysis of the mental outfit of Edwards it
would be a gross mistake to overlook the spiritual insight and
capacity of feeling, which is one part of the truth in the remark
of Mackintosh concerning him, that he was a rationalist and
mystic. . . . Let any discerning student take up the treatise
on the *Will* and observe the sharp, unrelenting logic in which the
author hunts down his opponents, and then let him take up the
same author's sermon on the *Nature and Reality of Spiritual
Light,* or passages in his book on the *Affections,* or some of the

[1] F. J. E. Woodbridge, *Philosophical Review,* Vol. 13, p. 407.

[2] Cf. W. H. Squires, *The Edwardean,* October, 1903, pp. 32-50, for
the panegyrics of Maurice, Blakey, Morrell, A. Campbell Fraser, Leslie
Stephen, Fichte, etc.

[3] *Mind,* § 17.

[4] Curtis, *Kantean Elements,* p. 35.

extracts from his *Diary*. It is like passing from the pages of Scotus or Aquinas to Thomas à Kempis or Saint Augustine or Saint Francis of Assisi.[1] This is a suggestion of the psychological side of Edwards' mysticism; what was its correlated philosophical significance has also been recognised. For example, in the early note on ' Excellence,' it is argued that God being Infinite Being, all other being must necessarily be considered as nothing, that ' in metaphysical strictness and propriety, He is and there is no other.' In the latest of the treatises the whole system of created beings is spoken of ' as the light dust of the balance (which is taken no notice of by him that weighs), and as less than vanity. . . . In harmony with these views, Edwards' type of piety is thoroughly the mystic type, the enjoyment of God in complete self-surrender to His Spirit and the communication of God himself to spirits directly by an immediate illumination. Now, this conception of God is what underlies Edwards' conception of the ideality of the material universe. It is not that the phenomenalism brings with it the idealism: it is the deeper idealism of the thought of God which brings in the phenomenalism.[2] Further recognition of the significance of Edwards' mysticism is given in the suggestion that Edwards may have drawn his conclusion that all existence is mental, the existence of all things ideal, by combining his idea of God as universal existence with the principle derived from Locke that all ideas begin from external sensation; and that with Edwards' premises the transition seems an easy one from the popular belief in the externality of the objects of our sense to a disbelief in the existence of matter.[3]

That Edwards' mysticism was behind his idealism has received abundant recognition, yet what were the more precise relations between the two elements needs fuller elaboration. In a general way, the belief in God as universal existence has been attributed to an high æsthetic interest as the most prominent characteristic. Thus, in the very first of the notes on the *Mind,* essaying to

[1] Fisher, *Edwards on the Trinity*, pp. 14, 21.
[2] Gardiner, *Retrospect*, pp. 158-159.
[3] Allen, *Edwards*, pp. 12-13.

define Excellency, or that which is beautiful and lovely as a thing he is concerned with more than anything else whatsoever, the youthful enthusiast concludes: ' As nothing else has a proper being but spirits, and as bodies are but shadows of being, therefore the consent of bodies one to another, and the harmony that is among them, is but the shadow of excellency. The Highest Excellency, therefore, must be consent of spirits one to another.' [1] In this initial definition there is, indeed, much of the æsthetic; at the same time there is more of the mystical, for the personal insight or direct intuition of the truth is based upon a feeling of union between the self and the absolute. Here Edwards' universal definition of excellency, as the consent of being to being, falls in with his definition of inspiration as an absolute sense of certainty, a knowledge in a sense intuitive, wherein such bright ideas are raised, and such a clear view of a perfect agreement with the excellencies of the Divine Nature, that it is known to be a communication from him; all the Deity appears in the thing, and in everything pertaining to it. [2]

How subtle, pervading and profound was this transcendental element in the development of Edwards' thought may be gathered only in a final review of his system; meanwhile, how fundamental it was, is to be seen in the very earliest of his idealistic fragments, that essay on *Being* which concluded that spirits only are properly substances. In a complete retrospection it is seen that all of Edwards' reflections are marked by æsthetic, intuitive, transcendental characteristics. Upon what were these characteristics based? Leaving aside the external sources as problematical, recourse may be had to the internal, those precocious mystic experiences which have been broadly likened to those of Thomas à Kempis and Francis of Assisi. In their highest manifestations these are ecstasies, transports of feelings, in which thought and will are merged; [3] in their origin and development they pass through a prescribed course or succession. Here the true mystic figures his path as a ladder reaching from earth to heaven; this

---

[1] *Mind*, § 1.   [2] *Ib.*, § 20.

[3] G. P. Fisher, *History of Christian Doctrine*, New York, 1896, p. 12.

scala perfectionis is usually divided into three stages: the first, the purgative, brought about by contrition and amendment, is valuable in teaching self-discipline and the meaning of order and limitation; the second stage, the illuminative, being the concentration of all the faculties upon God, assumes that to the individual there are vouchsafed intuitive visions of truth, and that feeling is a direct source of knowledge; the last stage, the contemplative, or intuitive, is one wherein man beholds God face to face and is joined to him. The means by which this vision is manifested to consciousness is in ecstasy, which begins where thought ceases to our consciousness; it differs from hallucination because there is no organic disturbance and because it claims to be, not a partial disintegration, but a temporary enhancement of the mental faculties.[1]

Whether or not the Saint of New England was familiar with this mystic progression as presented in the ancient manuals,[2] the record of his interior life, written for his own private benefit, some twenty years after the earliest of the events narrated, falls most naturally into the three given stages, purgative, illuminative and intuitive. As to the first, he tells how he had a variety of concerns and exercises about his soul from his childhood, and two remarkable seasons of awakening before he was brought to that new sense of things which he had since had. But after great and violent inward struggles and the gaining of a spirit to part with all things in the world, there came the first instance of that sort of inward sweet delight in God and divine things.[3] This was the illuminative stage, intimately conjoined and blended with the intuitive. Along with this new sense,—a kind of vision or fixed ideas and imaginations of being alone in the mountains or some solitary wilderness far from all mankind,—there came a thought of being wrapt up to God in heaven, being, as it

---

[1] W. R. Inge, *Christian Mysticism,* London, 1899, Chapter I.

[2] In his *Diary,* December 18th, 1722, Edwards says that he does not remember that he experienced regeneration exactly in those steps, in which divines say it is generally wrought, but in his *Affections* he refers to the ancient anchorites and hermits.

[3] Edwards, *Diary,* pp. LIV, LV.

were, swallowed up in Him forever.[1] This is the extremity of mysticism. What was its entire significance had best be given in Edwards' very words:

After this my sense of divine things gradually increased, and became more and more lively, and had more of that inward sweetness. The appearance of every thing was altered; there seemed to be, as it were, a calm, sweet cast, or appearance of divine glory, in almost every thing. God's excellency, his wisdom, his purity and love, seemed to appear in every thing; in the sun, moon, and stars; in the clouds, and the blue sky; in the grass, flowers, trees; in the water, and all nature; which used greatly to fix my mind. I often used to sit and view the moon for continuance; and in the day, spent much time in viewing the clouds and sky, to behold the sweet glory of God in these things: in the mean time, singing forth, with a low voice, my contemplations of the Creator and Redeemer. And scarce any thing, among all the works of nature, was so sweet to me as thunder and lightning; formerly, nothing had been so terrible to me. Before, I used to be uncommonly terrified with thunder and to be struck with terror when I saw a thunder-storm rising; but now, on the contrary, it rejoiced me. I felt God, so to speak, at the first appearance of a thunder-storm; and used to take the opportunity, at such times, to fix myself in order to view the clouds, and see the lightnings play, and hear the majestic and awful voice of God's thunder, which oftentimes was exceedingly entertaining, leading me to sweet contemplations of my great and glorious God. While thus engaged, it always seemed natural to me to sing, or chant forth my meditations; or, to speak my thoughts in soliloquies with a singing voice. Holiness, as I then wrote down some of my contemplations on it, appeared to me to be of a sweet, pleasant, charming, serene, calm nature; which brought an inexpressible purity, brightness, peacefulness, and ravishment to the soul. In other words, that it made the soul like a field or garden of God, with all manner of pleasant flowers; all pleasant, delightful, and undisturbed; enjoying a sweet calm, and the gently vivifying beams of the sun. The soul of a true Christian, as I then wrote my meditations, appeared like such a little white flower as we see in the spring of the year; low, and humble on the ground, opening its bosom, to receive the pleasant beams of the sun's glory; rejoicing, as it were, in a calm rapture; diffusing around a sweet fragrancy; standing peacefully and lovingly, in the midst of other flowers round about; all in

[1] *Diary*, LV.

like manner opening their bosoms, to drink in the light of the sun. There was no part of creature-holiness, that I had so great a sense of its loveliness, as humility, brokenness of heart, and poverty of spirit; and there was nothing that I so earnestly longed for. My heart panted after this,—to lie low before God, as in the dust; that I might be nothing, and that God might be ALL.[1]

In the concluding passage of this exquisite ecstasy, with its implication of union with the deity, of absorption into the inmost essence of the divine, there appear what have been called the unmistakable marks of the mystic in every age. But in Edwards' full narrative there are also to be found the marks of mysticism from the more modern point of view, and it is by combining the old and the new that there may be gathered some hints as to the idealistic bases of Edwards' philosophy. The psychological marks of mysticism have been recently given as four in number: Ineffability,—the subject of it immediately says that it defies expression, that no adequate report of its contents can be given in words. In this peculiarity mental states are more like states of feeling than like states of intellect. The noetic quality,—although so similar to states of feeling, mystical states seem to those who experience them to be states of knowledge; they are states of insight, illuminations, revelations, full of significance and importance, all inarticulate though they remain. Transiency,—mystical states cannot be sustained for long, their quality can be but imperfectly reproduced in memory, yet this is susceptible of continuous development in what is felt as inner richness and importance. Passivity,—the oncoming of mystical states can be facilitated by preliminary voluntary operations, yet when the characteristic sort of consciousness has once set in, the mystic feels as if his own will were in abeyance.[2]

To apply these criteria to the record of Edwards' inner life is to gain a further insight into those mental processes leading to his idealism. The mark of transiency may be neglected. The brief duration, the constant intermittance, is an accident not an

---

[1] *Diary*, p. LV.

[2] William James, *Varieties of Religious Experiences,* Boston, 1902, pp. 380-381.

essential of the mystic state. Edwards complained that his earlier affections were lively and easily moved, and that it was only after he had spent most of his time, year after year, in meditation and soliloquy that his sense of divine things seemed gradually to increase. Leaving aside, then, the mark of transiency, one comes to the more important mark of passivity. Here Edwards says in his early notes on the *Mind:* Our perceptions or ideas that we passively receive through our bodies are communicated to us immediately by God. There never can be any idea, thought or action of the mind unless the mind first received some ideas from sensation, or some other way equivalent, wherein the mind is wholly passive in receiving them.[1] Although these particular notes were probably written under the influence of the *Human Understanding,* yet the virtual contradiction of the Lockean sensationalism was not so easy a transition unless the young thinker had some other and deeper basis upon which to rest. This basis appears to have been the mystic experience indirectly referred to in the alternative offered in the foregoing passage; for besides the reception of ideas ' from sensation ' there was ' some other way equivalent, wherein the mind is wholly passive in receiving them.'

It is in this emphasis on the passive attitude in the reception of ideas that one fundamental source of Edwards' idealism is to be found. Being essentially subjective, the quietistic state readily lends itself to a sense of the unreality of the external world. In Edwards' language this takes the form of a belief that corporeal things could exist no otherwise than mentally, and that other bodies have no existence of their own; in modern psychological terms the recognition of the unreal sense of things may be laid to a temporary absence of conaesthesia, a transient loss of the sense of the compact reality of the bodily organism. Furthermore, this indirect phenomenalism, this extreme subjectivism, being carried to its logical extreme, might well lead to the conclusion embodied in Edwards' first fragment, the corollary of the essay on *Being,* which protested against the view that material things are the most substantial, and affirmed that spirits only are properly substances.

If these conjectures be true, if Edwards' mystic ecstasies fur-

[1] Allen, *Edwards,* pp. 12-13.

nished a personal ground for the earliest of his idealistic fragments, the question of originality receives a new light, for that
question is shifted from external to internal sources, from a later
period of general learning to an earlier period of individual
experience. The reading of other authors may have given a form
of expression, but a vivid, intense, personal impression furnished
in largest measure the substance of Edwards' idealism. Here
the convincement of the sovereignty of God had as its philosophical equivalent the belief in the universality of the divine
existence, and the ravishment of the spirit, the corresponding
assurance of the superiority of the ideal over the material world.
Now, if these inferences be true, the probability of the use of
external authorities assumes less importance. It may be granted,
indeed, that some of the notes on the *Mind* were written so much
later than is traditionally allowed, that Edwards was already
enabled to learn of Malebranche, with his vision of all things
in God, of Norris, with his kindred doctrine of the ideal world,
and even of Berkeley, with his divine language of signs. These
writers may have furnished Edwards with the outward form of
his philosophy, they do not entirely account for the inner substance.
In fine, whatever the dress in which his thoughts were clothed,
the body of philosophy was the author's own.

This supposition is strengthened by the air of personal assurance with which Edwards set forth his next work of speculative
interest, his maturer treatise on the *Religious Affections*. In a
general way this treatise was an *Apologia* for his inner life, an
attempt to express the manner and means of his conviction of that
'new sense' of things quite different from anything he ever
experienced before. This sense must now be defended on the
broadest grounds. To call it a kind of ravishment would satisfy
the mystic, but to call it an inexpressible ravishment would not
satisfy the rationalist, because to the latter the conjoining of the
negative and positive would be simply nugatory.

So being by nature rationalist as well as mystic, Edwards realises that to speak of inexpressible knowledge within the mind is
quite meaningless, unless others may look within. To this end
free access must be given to the inquirer. As if allowing access

to the very penetralia of his nature, Edwards now presents his
beliefs in a sermon entitled 'A Divine and Supernatural Light,
immediately imparted to the Soul by the Spirit of God, shown to
be both a Scriptural and a Rational Doctrine.'[1] Omitting the
exegetical portion of this discourse, a few extracts may be made
to exhibit Edwards in the character of a metaphysical preacher.
As a manifestation of the thoroughness of his scholastic divinity,
he is at pains, at the very outset, to present the negative side;
First in order is to show, in a few things, what the spiritual and
divine light is not. As the original has it:

This does not consist in any impression made upon the imagination. It is no impression made upon the mind, as though one
saw anything with the bodily eyes: 'tis no image or idea of an
outward light or glory, or any beauty of form or countenance,
or a visible lustre or brightness of any object, as when one's
imagination may be entertained by a romantic description of the
pleasantness of fairy-land; or be affected by what one reads in
a romance, or sees acted in a stage-play. . . But I proceed to
show positively what this spiritual and divine light is. In general
it is not merely a rational belief that God is glorious but a
sense of the gloriousness of God in one's heart. There is a twofold knowledge of good of which God has made the mind of
man capable. The first, that which is merely notional; as when
a person only speculatively judges that anything is, which, by
the agreement of mankind, is called good or excellent, viz., that
which is most to general advantage, and between which and a
reward there is a suitableness,—and the like. And the other is,
that which consists in the sense of the heart; as when the heart
is sensible of pleasure and delight in the presence of the idea
of it. In the former is exercised merely the speculative faculty,
or the understanding, in distinction from the will or disposition
of the soul. In the latter, the will, or inclination, or heart are
mainly concerned.

Thus there is a difference between having an *opinion,* that
God is holy and gracious, and having a *sense* of the loveliness
and beauty of that holiness and grace. There is a difference
between having a rational judgment that honey is sweet, and

[1] As recently emended from the original manuscript, this is here extracted from H. N. Gardiner's *Selected Sermons of Jonathan Edwards,*
New York, 1904.

having a sense of its sweetness. A man may have the former that knows not how honey tastes; but a man cannot have the latter unless he has an idea of the taste of honey in his mind. So there is a difference between believing that a person is beautiful, and having a sense of his beauty. The former may be obtained by hearsay, but the latter only by seeing the countenance. When the heart is sensible of the beauty and amiableness of a thing, it necessarily feels pleasure in the apprehension. It is implied in a person's being heartily sensible of the loveliness of a thing, that the idea of it is pleasant to his soul; which is a far different thing from having a rational opinion that it is excellent. . . .

It not only removes the hindrances of reason, but positively helps reason. It makes even the speculative notions more lively. It engages the attention of the mind, with more fixedness and intenseness to that kind of objects; which causes it to have a clearer view of them, and enables it more clearly to see their mutual relations, and occasions it to take more notice of them. The ideas themselves that otherwise are dim and obscure, are by this means impressed with the greater strength, and have a light cast upon them; so that the mind can better judge of them. As he that beholds objects on the face of the earth, when the light of the sun is cast upon them, is under greater advantage to discern them in their true forms and natural relations, than he that sees them in a dim twilight. . . . The mind being sensible of the excellency of divine objects, dwells upon them with delight; and the powers of the soul are more awakened and enlivened to employ themselves in the contemplation of them, and exert themselves more fully and much more to purpose. The beauty of the objects draws on the faculties, and draws forth their exercises; so that reason itself is under far greater advantages for its proper and free exercises, and to attain its proper end, free of darkness and delusion. . . . God, in letting in this light into the soul, deals with man according to his nature, and makes use of his rational faculties. But yet this light is not the less immediately from God for that; the faculties are made use of as the subject, and not as the cause. As the use we make of our eyes in beholding various objects, when the sun arises, is not the cause of the light that discovers those objects to us.

In the second part of the sermon on the *Realty of Spiritual Light,* the author appears less successful than in the first. To maintain the rationality of his thesis, he has recourse in order to a rhetorical question, to a doctrine of the cosmic gradation of being; to a veiled pantheism—a suggestion of a union between the individual and the absolute—and finally to such a definition or limitation of reason as well nigh to stultify his whole argument. Proceeding he says:

It is rational to suppose, that there is really such an excellency in divine things—so transcendent and exceedingly different from what is in other things—that, if it were seen, would most evidently distinguish them. We cannot rationally doubt but that things divine, which appertain to the Supreme Being, are vastly different from things that are human; that there is a high, glorious, and God-like excellency in them, that does most remarkably difference them from the things that are of men; insomuch that if the difference were but seen, it would have a convincing, satisfying influence upon any one, that they are divine. What reason can be offered against it? unless we would argue, that God is not remarkably distinguished in glory from men.

It is rational to suppose, that this knowledge should be given immediately by God, and not be obtained by natural means. Upon what account should it seem unreasonable, that there should be any immediate communication between God and the creature? It is strange that men should make any matter of difficulty of it. Why should not He that made all things, still have something immediately to do with the things that He has made? Where lies the great difficulty, if we own the being of a God, and that he created all things out of nothing, of allowing some immediate influence of God on the creation still? And if it be reasonable to suppose it with respect to any part of the creation, it is especially so with respect to reasonable intelligent creatures; who are next to God in the gradation of the different orders of beings, and whose business is most immediately with God; and reason teaches that man was made to serve and glorify his Creater. . . It is rational to suppose, that this blessing should be immediately from God, for there is no gift or benefit that is in itself so nearly related to the Divine nature. Nothing which the creature receives is so much a participation of the Deity: it is a kind of emanation of God's beauty, and is related to God as the light is to the sun. . . . It is rational to suppose, that it should be beyond man's power to obtain this light by the mere strength of natural reason; for it is not a thing that belongs to reason, to see the beauty and loveliness of spiritual things; it is not a speculative thing, but depends on the sense of the heart. Reason indeed is necessary in order to it, as it is by reason only that we are become the subjects of the means of it; but if we take *reason* strictly—not for the faculty of mental perception in general, but for ratiocination, or a power of inferring by arguments—the perceiving of spiritual beauty and excellency no more belongs to reason, than it belongs to the sense of feeling to perceive colours, or to the power of seeing to perceive the sweetness of food. It is out of reason's province to perceive the beauty or loveliness of anything: such a perception does not belong to that faculty. Reason's work is to perceive truth and not excellency. It is not ratiocination that gives men the perception of the beauty and amiableness of a countenance, though it may be many ways indirectly an advantage to it; yet it is no more reason that immediately perceives it, than it is reason that perceives the sweetness of honey: it depends on the sense of the heart.—Reason may determine that a countenance is beautiful to others, it may determine that honey is sweet to others; but it will never give me a perception of its sweetness.[1]

Of Edwards' sermon on the *Reality of Spiritual Light* it has been said that there was nothing essentially new in the principle itself; that God directly influences the soul, that the soul is capable of an immediate intuition of divine things, had been the common teaching of all, and especially of all the Christian mystics. Indeed, it may be doubted whether religion as a form of personal experience does not universally involve a consciousness of some such transcendent reality. But despite the lack of originality in the treatise in question, there lies in its transcendent relationship a retroactive proof of the originality of the earlier essays. For example, the doctrine of immediate divine communication of spiritual light has been referred back to the early paper on *Being,* whose idealism constituted a fitting philosophical counterpart to a main article in Edwards' belief.[2] Or to give these productions more fully and in their more proper order, it may be seen how peculiarly interrelated were the various idealistic phases in Edwards' life. At the age of eight came the first vivid spiritual insight; at the age of twenty, the first series of notes on the *Mind;* at another interval of twelve years, the

---

[1] *Spiritual Light,* pp. 14-15.
[2] Smyth, *American Journal of Theology,* Vol. 1, p. 951.

treatise on *Spiritual Light* was completed; in twelve more, the kindred treatise on the *Religious Affections*. The chronology in this series of events is accidental, the congruity is not. Of one piece, of like substance, was the unfolding mind of Edwards. The first episode shows a precocious convincement as to the un-substantiality of the world; the second, a tentative expression of a kindred immaterialism; the third, a rational advocacy of the mystical principle of intuitive apprehension; the fourth, a laboured vindication of the dialectic of the heart, whereby the soul is enabled to progress from the world of shadow to the world of substance.

It was in his *Treatise Concerning Religious Affections,* of 1746, that Edwards presented what has been described as an attempt to answer the question which confronted him in his youth as to the nature of true religion. He then determined, as is recorded in his *Resolutions,* ' that he would look most nicely and diligently into the opinions of our old divines concerning conversion.' Now, in what were in reality his *Confessions,* he answers that the bond of union between the human and the divine is beheld intuitively; the saint feels and sees plainly the union between his soul and God.[1] For all its subjectivity and profound introversion, this work on the *Affections* has a philo-sophical value. In it the recluse of Northampton presents the elaboration of his doctrine of spiritual light, or what may be called a theory of mystical knowledge. To himself, looking back on his earlier impressions, the objects of such knowledge were doubtless as substantial realities as the mountains of Berk-shire; to others, who lacked his emotional sensibility, these objects had to be made real by the aid of reasoning. Answering, there-fore, the prime inquiry as to the nature of such affections, Ed-wards broadly argued that a state of knowledge, which is at the same time a state of feeling, furnishes the means for the mystic insight. Described in terms of sensation, as well as in terms of intellection, ardent sensibility being added to cold ratio-cination, this peculiar noetic quality constitutes a veritable dia-lectic of the heart. The author has, indeed, much difficulty in conveying to the reader his doctrine of sensible knowledge. Un-

[1] Allen, *Edwards,* pp. 220-225.

consciously thwarted by the clumsy Lockean classification, which confuses affections, heart and will, he nevertheless contends for the proper recognition of the emotional element. In his previous remarks he says:

God has endued the soul with two principal faculties: The one, that by which it is capable of *perception* and speculation, or by which it discerns and judges of things; which is called the *understanding*. The other, that by which the soul is some way *inclined* with respect to the things it views or considers: or it is the faculty by which the soul beholds things—not as an indifferent unaffected spectator, but—either as liking or disliking, pleased or displeased, approving or rejecting. This faculty is called by various names: it is sometimes called the *inclination;* and, as it respects the actions determined and governed by it, the *will:* and the *mind,* with regard to the exercises of this faculty, is often called the *heart.*

The *exercises* of this last faculty are of two sorts; either, those by which the soul is carried out towards the things in view in *approving* them, being pleased with and inclined to them; or, those in which the soul opposes the things in view, in *disapproving* them; and in being displeased with, averse from, and rejecting them.—And as the exercises of the inclination are various in their *kinds,* so they are much more various in their *degrees.* There are some exercises of pleasedness or displeasedness, inclination or disinclination, wherein the soul is carried but a little beyond a state of perfect indifference. And there are other degrees, wherein the approbation or dislike, pleasedness or aversion, are stronger; wherein we may rise higher and higher, till the soul comes to act vigorously and sensibly, and its actings are with that strength, that (through the laws of union which the Creator has fixed between soul and body) the motion of the blood and animal spirits begins to be sensibly altered: whence oftentimes arises some bodily sensation, especially about the *heart* and vitals, which are the fountain of the fluids of the body. Whence it comes to pass, that the *mind,* with regard to the exercises of this faculty, perhaps in all nations and ages, is called *the heart.* And it is to be noted, that they are these more vigorous and sensible exercises of this faculty, which are called the *affections.*[1]

With all his emphasis on the physical, Edwards' doctrine is here not of the materialistic, but of the idealistic, type. The motions of the animal spirits and fluids of the body, he con-

[1] *Affections,* p. 237.

tinues, are not anything properly belonging to the nature of the affections; they are only the effects or concomitants of the affections. As it is the soul only that has ideas, so it is the soul only that is pleased or displeased with its ideas.[1] The nature of the affections then, resting upon the fervent exercises of the heart, it cannot yet be supposed, when this affection of love is spoken of, that the exercise of the understanding is excluded. There are two elements to be considered: As on the one hand, there must be light in the understanding, as well as an *affected* fervent heart; or, where there is heat without light there can be nothing divine or heavenly in the heart; so, on the other hand, where there is a kind of light without heat, a head stored with notions and speculations, with a cold and unaffected heart, there can be nothing divine in that light, that knowledge is no true spiritual knowledge of divine things.[2]

Having propounded his dual theory of mystical knowledge, Edwards now proceeds to its defence in the second part of his treatise. Here the theory is liable to misinterpretation, either from an over-emphasis of the ratiocinative, or from a misunderstanding of the affective element. On the one side, says the apologist, there are many in these days who condemn all affections which are excited in a way that seems not to be the natural consequence of the faculties and principles of human nature; to them there is no distinguishing by sense between the influences of the Spirit of God and the natural operations of our own minds. On the other side, are those of a weak and vapoury habit of body, and the brain easily susceptive of impressions, who may have strange apprehensions and imaginations, and strong affections attending them, unaccountably arising, which are not voluntarily produced by themselves. We see that such persons are liable to such impressions, about temporal things; and there is equal reason why they should about spiritual things. As a person asleep has dreams, of which he is not the voluntary author, so may such persons, in like manner, be the subjects of involuntary impressions, when they are awake.[3] But the true saint belongs to neither of these classes. In him the divine spirit may

[1] *Affections*, p. 237.   [2] *Ib.*, p. 243.   [3] *Ib.*, p. 249.

co-operate in a silent, secret, and undiscernible way, with the use of means, and his own endeavours, and yet even that is not all. Spiritual light may be let into the soul in one way, when it is not in another; in a dead carnal frame, it is as impossible that it should be kept alive in its clearness and strength as it is to keep the light in the room when the candle that gives it is put out, or to maintain the bright sunshine in the air when the sun is gone down.[1] What then are the distinguishing signs of truly gracious and holy affections? Affections that are truly spiritual and gracious arise from those influences and operations on the heart which are spiritual and divine, is the answer. They are spiritual, because they give to the soul a relish, to the mind an enlightening, different from any mere immediate suggestion of ideas. They are supernatural and divine because not only is the manner of the coming into the mind extraordinary, but the sensation is totally diverse from all that men have, or can have in a state of nature.[2] They are divine because they are not merely ideas of external objects, of the outward sensitive kind, such as are common to us with the beasts, but because through a vital communication and indwelling of the spirit, the saints have their light. Here one would be tempted to think that many of the heathen philosophers had great illuminations and inward fervours and elevations of mind, as though they were truly the subjects of divine illapses.[3]

In describing the above distinguishing characteristics of the affections, Edwards has presented both the subjective and objective sides of mystic knowledge. The latter he dismisses with the scant statement that the objective ground of gracious affections is the transcendently excellent and amiable nature of divine things as they are in themselves.[4] But the subjective characteristics cannot be formulated in so brief a fashion; a prime distinction must be made between a mere notional understanding, wherein the mind only beholds things in the exercise of a speculative faculty, and the sense of the heart, wherein the mind not only

[1] *Affections*, pp. 248-259.   [2] *Ib*., pp. 268-271.
[3] *Ib*., pp. 268-295.   [4] *Ib*., p. 274.

speculates and beholds, but relishes and feels.[1] Here is an inevitable recurrence to the peculiar noetic quality of the mystic state, a state of knowledge which is at the same time a state of feeling. This, then, continues the author, is the distinguishing characteristic of gracious affection, that there is given a new supernatural sense, a certain divine spiritual taste. This is, in its whole nature, diverse from any former kinds of sensation of the mind, as tasting is diverse from any other of the five senses, and something is perceived by a true saint in the exercise of this new sense of mind, in spiritual and divine things, as entirely different from anything that is perceived in them by natural men, as the sweet taste of honey is diverse from the ideas men get of honey by looking on it, or feeling of it.[2]

In further defining this spiritual insight as sensible knowledge, the writer is not using a mere figure of speech, but is evidently referring to an actual experience of his own. Like the previous conæsthesia, or loss of the compact sense of bodily reality, is this veritable synæsthesia, or blending of two mental processes into a sense of higher reality. As the former led to a doctrine of the insubstantiality of the material world, so the latter led to a conviction of the superior substantiality of the supersensible world. In both these convictions, the one of youth, the other of maturity, there is, moreover, a common ideality, since both are rooted in the same ground, a kindred temperamental origin. In a word, Edwards was an idealist because he was a mystic, and the early theory of being has vital connection with the later theory of knowledge because of that persistent fact. Corroboration of this is to be found towards the end of the treatise on the *Affections,* in an attempted synthesis of both the subjective and objective grounds of the new understanding. The former is when the soul has a kind of intuitive knowledge of the divinity of things, but it is without any long chain of arguments; the latter is the transcendentally excellent and amiable nature of divine things as they are in themselves.[3] But how, the rationalist may ask, is the noetic connection to be made between the human and the divine?

[1] *Affections,* p. 283.   [2] *Ib.,* p. 280.   [3] *Ib.,* pp. 274, 290.

At this point Edwards is in great straits and acknowledged difficulties. To use his initial confession, language is here somewhat imperfect, the meaning of words in a considerable measure loose and unfixed. Does the illuminated understanding of the sanctified arise through the mere operations of the sensible knowledge of the heart, combined with a speculative knowledge of the mind, or is there of necessity something further required? In a word, must the intuitive be added as a necessary concomitant of the illuminative stage? In his verbal distinctions Edwards appears to lean to the former view; in his figures of speech, to the latter. As he had affirmed that to the natural man God never, in any of his influences, communicates himself to them in his own proper nature, so now he says that the soul of a saint receives light from the sun of righteousness in such a manner that its nature is changed, and it becomes properly a luminous body. Not only does the sun shine in the saints, but they also become little suns, partaking of the nature of the fountain of their light.[1] In this approach to a doctrine of an hypostatic union between the individual and the absolute, the idealist has well-nigh reached the fatal dilemma—the pitfall of mysticism— a pantheistic doctrine of the universe. In the endeavour to grasp the ultimate reality of things, he presents an almost Platonic doctrine of the transcendence of the divine ideas, the superiority to the *bonum utile* of the *bonum formosum,* the beautiful good in itself. That doctrine is thus eloquently expressed:

He that hath the spiritual sense sees the fulness of all things without which all the world is empty, yea, worse than nothing. Unless this is seen, nothing is seen that is worth the seeing; for there is no other true excellency or beauty. Unless this be understood, nothing is understood worthy the exercise of the noble faculty of understanding. This is the beauty of the Godhead, the divinity of divinity (if I may so speak), the good of the infinite fountain of good. Without this, God himself (if that were possible) would be an infinite evil, we ourselves had better never have been; and there had better have been no being.[2]

That Edwards' thinking is thus far of one texture, that his mysticism and his idealism are most intimately interwoven, is

---

[1] *Affections,* pp. 265, 303. [2] *Ib.,* p. 281.

clear from this familiar recurrence, this repeated reminder of the problem of being. Yet, although in his doctrine of the transcendence of divine archetypes, the philosopher has drawn legitimate conclusions from his early idealism, this has not yet issued in a correlated pantheism. Up to this point his interests have lain rather in an illuminative theory of knowledge than in an intuitive theory of being. To explain the impartation of the spiritual sense he has used such significant terms as the communication of the divine, that fulness of all things, that infinite fountain of good, but he has not yet essayed to make an identification of his divinity with the totality of existence. In his posthumous *Dissertation Concerning the End for Which God Created the World,* it would appear that he would fain make that identification, but in the next treatise published in his lifetime there is apparent a certain conscious fear of an issue so fatal to his orthodoxy. In the most famous of his public writings, the *Inquiry on the Will,* there is evident that diversity of thought, that vacillation between two poles of speculation—Augustinianism and pantheism—which renders Edwards liable to the charge of metaphysical duality, a fatal diremption in an otherwise coherent system. This is the duality between Edwards the theologian and Edwards the philosopher. In the one case there is a tendency toward a consistent monism, a doctrine of the absolute based on the mystic longing for the ultimate unity of all existence; in the other, there is a tendency toward an uncritical dualism, a doctrine of immanence being sacrificed to the conventional Calvinistic transcendence. The former doctrine, based on his more personal and more ultimate experiences, may have been one which Edwards preferred for himself; but the latter, being called for by the exigencies of his theological position, he was obliged to teach to others. Nevertheless, beneath this well-worked mine there lay hidden a most precious vein of speculative metal. The chief value of this careful and strict inquiry was long considered to be in its demolition of the Arminian notion of contingency; its chief interest now consists in its disclosure of the personal idealism of its author. Here, it has been asserted that the two elements of this work, its determinism and its idealism, are discrepant and irreconcilable, because they are juxta-

posed, not united.[1]   But a more genetic view of Edwards' system,
as not to be fully understood, except in connection with his inward experiences, makes this position untenable.   Traces of Edwards' previous thought have been recognised in the very beginning of the essay, for the initial definition of cause is but the
expansion of the former definition in the notes on *Mind*.   The
latter had briefly said: Cause is that after or upon the existence of which, or the existence of it, after such a manner, the
existence of another thing follows.   And the former continues:

Therefore I sometimes use the word *Cause*, in this inquiry,
to signify any *antecedent*, either natural or moral, positive or
negative, on which an Event, either a thing, or the manner and
circumstance of a thing, so depends, that it is the ground and
reason, either in whole, or in part, why it is, rather than not; or
why it is as it is, rather than otherwise; or, in other words, any
antecedent with which a consequent Event is so connected, that
it truly belongs to the reason why the proposition which affirms
that Event is true; whether it has any positive influence, or not.
And agreeably to this, I sometimes use the word effect for the
consequence of another thing, which is perhaps rather an occasion
than a Cause, most properly speaking.[2]

What is the significance of these kindred definitions some
three decades apart?   The most recent investigation of the *Inquiry* has brought the pertinent conclusion that upon the idea
of cause as thus defined the whole treatise rests, for an event
in the realm of mind without a cause is as inconceivable to Edwards as such an one in the realm of matter.   This is a great
positive argument of the discussion, though rather an assumed
axiom than the subject of prolonged elaboration.   And thus it
comes to pass that into the very foundation of the whole argument there is inserted an ambiguity which, doubtless, deceived
Edwards himself, and has given rise to two distinct interpretations of the work.   Motives are ' causes ' determining the will.   Is
the motive an occasion upon which the efficient will acts, or
itself an efficient cause operating upon the will?   Edwards' defi-

[1] F. J. E. Woodbridge, *Jonathan Edwards, Philosophical Review*, Vol.
13, p. 399.
[2] *Will*, p. 15.

nition gives no answer to this question, for he has wrapped up in one term both efficient and occasional causes. It is doubtless true that his idealism had much to do with this. If God were the only agent; if, according to the occasionalism of Malebranche, God does everything upon occasion of certain events in the mundane sphere, then there is no essential difference between the occasional and what seems to us to be the efficient cause. But, however the ambiguity was introduced into his thinking, there it was, at the very foundation of the edifice he was about to rear, and destined to make its whole structure insecure to the highest pinnacle.[1]

That the necessarian's earlier metaphysics blended with the later theology is further illustrated by the congruity between his theory of causality and his theory of perception. Here it has been well argued that in Edwards' idealistic opinion as to all external things, perception by created beings is owing to the stable will of God, who not only produces ideas, but, as to things perceived, causes them to be the objects of perception. The question naturally arises whether motives, the antecedents of voluntary action, and their relative strength, are not likewise understood by him as the effect of the stable, constant exercise of the divine will? It must be borne in mind that his usual answer to the objection that if there were no power of alternative choice we should not be responsible for wrong moral choices, is that the wrong of a choice lies not in its cause, but in its nature.[2]

Although the idealistic elements in Edwards' best known treatise may be thus correlated, such a correlation does not explain the occasion, the animus or the extent of that work. Written hurriedly in some four months, while engaged in his missionary labours among the Indians at Stockbridge, the writer acknowledges his purpose to be the bringing of the late objections and outcries against Calvinistic divinity to the test of the strictest reasoning. Here, against the objection that such reasoning is metaphysical and abstruse, he proceeds:

[1] Foster, *New England Theology*, pp. 65-64.   [2] Fisher, *Trinity*, p. 39.

The question is not, whether what is said be metaphysics, physics, logic, or mathematics, *Latin, French, English,* or *Mohawk?* But whether the reasoning be good, and the arguments truly conclusive? The foregoing arguments are no more metaphysical, than those which we use against the papists, to disprove their doctrine of transubstantiation; alleging it is inconsistent with the notion of corporeal identity, that it should be in ten thousand places at the same time. It is by metaphysical arguments only we are able to prove, that the rational soul is not corporeal, that lead or sand cannot think; that thoughts are not square or round, or do not weigh a pound. The arguments by which we prove the being of God, if handled closely and distinctly, so as to show their clear and demonstrative evidence, must be metaphysically treated. It is by metaphysics only that we can demonstrate, that God is not limited to a place, or is not mutable; that he is not ignorant, or forgetful; that it is impossible for him to lie, or be unjust; and that there is one God only, and not hundreds or thousands. And, indeed, we have no strict demonstration of anything, excepting mathematical truths, but by metaphysics. We can have no proof, that is properly demonstrative, of any one proposition, relating to the being and nature of God, His creation of the world, the dependence of all things on Him, the nature of bodies or spirits, the nature of our own souls, or any of the great truths of morality and natural religion, but what is metaphysical. I am willing my arguments should be brought to the test of the strictest and justest reason, and that a clear, distinct, and determinate meaning of the terms I use should be insisted on; but let not the whole be rejected, as if all were confuted, by fixing on it the epithet, *metaphysical.*[1]

That in this relish for metaphysics the scholastic theologian was in his element is clear from this defence of his philosophic method; but that he had more than a dialectical interest in his subject is proven by the relentless rigidity with which he pursued the opponents of Calvinism. Owing to the prevailing deism the danger Edwards feared was that men would think that God had left the world to take care of itself.[2] Moreover, as the Arminian idea of freedom of the will seemed an assertion of

[1] *Will,* p. 85.

[2] For an exposition of Edwards' anti-deistic opuscle, 'The Insufficiency of Reason as a Substitute for Revelation,' cf. Curtis, *Kantean Elements,* p. 49 ff.

man at the expense of God, and a self-determining human will a limit placed by the finite upon the infinite, Edwards' object was to bring liberty within limitations, to establish ultimately the absoluteness of the deity. However, before this ultimate purpose can be affected, the ground must be cleared of the old issues. Here the specific question was the Arminian notion of liberty, which is the will's power of determining itself in its own acts, the being wholly active in it without passiveness and without being subject to necessity.[1] Expressed in more modern phrase, the question at issue might be framed as to whether the will be not itself a creative first cause, endowed with the power of initiating acts, of choosing between motives *de novo*.

To this question Edwards' answer was in general that philosophical necessity belongs to the very nature of the will, there having been no loss of liberty, no forfeiture of a prerogative once possessed. Now, as always, man's will is guided by the last dictate of his understanding, and those last dictates depend upon a Providential disposing and determining of men's moral actions.[2] Here the will is defined as that power or principle of the mind by which it is capable of choosing, and the last dictate, as that motive which, as it stands in the view of the mind, is the strongest; that is, the will always is as the greatest apparent good is, the good being that which is agreeable, pleasing and suits the mind. Furthermore, in every volition there is a preference or a prevailing inclination of the soul, whereby at that instant it is out of a state of perfect indifference. These inclinations depend upon moral necessity or causes such as habits and dispositions of the heart, whence moral inability consists in a want of inclination or the strength of a contrary inclination, being opposed to natural inability or some impeding defect or obstacle that is extrinsic to the will.[3]

Given these definitions, one may meet the Arminian notions concerning the will's self-determination, indifference, and contingence. As to the first possibility, it is to be argued that the will is not a self-determining power in and of itself, because we must consider how the person came to have such a volition,

[1] *Will*, p. 40.   [2] *Ib.*, pp. 17, 40, 68, 78.   [3] *Ib.*, pp. 5-11.

whether it was caused by some external motive or habitual bias. Then, too, if the dictate of the understanding be the same as the determination of the will, this is to make the determination of choice prior to the dictate of the understanding. But how can the mind first act and by its act determine what motives shall be the ground for its volition and choice?[1] Arguing against those who say that spirits, which are spirits of an active nature, have the spring of action within themselves, and can determine themselves, the strict necessarian is forced to identify a logical statement with the steps in a chronological process, and, at the same time, artificially to separate volition and determination, as if they were separately process and product. This was a weak argument against those advocates of the sovereignty of the will, who said that the determination of volition must be itself an act of the mind; for an act of the will being a mode of the mind's functioning, if it be free in this functioning, it is free in the act.

But secondly, continues Edwards, to suppose the will to act at all, in a state of perfect indifference, not inclining one way more than another, is to assert that the mind chooses without choosing, whereas the mind must be influenced in its choice by something that has a preponderating influence. Here there is no great difficulty in showing not only that it must needs be so, but also how it is so; for example, being asked to touch some square on a chessboard, my mind is not given up to vulgar accident, but makes the choice from foreign considerations, such as the previous determination to touch that which happens to be most in my eye.[1] In this criticism Edwards appears safe in asserting that the mind can ever be in a perfect state of equilibrium, for, as he says, even the involuntary changes in the succession of our ideas, though the cause may not be observed, have as much of a cause as the continual, infinitely various, successive changes of the unevennesses on the surface of the water. Thirdly, against the belief that an event is not dependent on a cause but, as it were, loose from its influence, it may be argued that the will is not contingent as opposed to all necessity, for the voli-

---

[1] *Will*, pp. 14, 26, 27.   [2] *Ib.*, pp. 12, 20, 21, 22, 41.

tion must come to pass from some adequate cause, or otherwise the mind would be given up to a wild contingence, as the smoke that is driven by the wind.[1]

With arguments like these does Edwards fill his polemical treatise against such writers as Whitby and Collins, who hold loosely defined notions of free will as including the choosing of choices, choice from a previous indifference or choice apart from all influence of motives. Now, in all this minute and painstaking argumentation, it is evident that recourse has been had to the author's earlier studies, for between Edwards and Locke, as has been pointed out, there is substantial similarity: in both the idea of liberty is the same; of determination by motive; of the different weight of different motives; of the causal relation between motive and action; the argument from causation is in Locke, though obscured by his sensational philosophy; the general conception of the inconceivability of the Arminian position is Locke's; and even the argument of the *reductio ad absurdum*.[2]

And yet for all these similarities and agreements, Edwards' most laboured work cannot be pronounced entirely unoriginal. The weapons of his dialectic may have been borrowed, but the ardour with which he wielded them sprang from a personal conviction. The sharp and relentless determinism of this treatise is one thing, its inward and impelling spirit another. Outwardly the author seems but a man in an iron mask; within there were impulses and feelings more congruous with the beaming eye and sensitive mouth of his portrait. Between Edwards the logician and Edwards the mystic there is here an apparent, but not a real, duality. The view of moral necessity as determining voluntary action appeared hard and mechanical, yet it had a vital connection with that profound belief of the immanence of the deity which was Edwards' earliest achievement. The steps in this conviction are somewhat involved; they may nevertheless be explicated. In giving a double definition of the will, as both that by which the mind chooses anything, and also that by which

[1] Will, p. 41.
[2] Foster, *New England Theology*, p. 76.

it desires or inclines to anything, Edwards superimposes the emotional upon the voluntary. This has been generally considered the ordinary eighteenth century confusion between the sensibility and the will, but for that confusion there was more than a conventional reason. It is indeed a fatal logical error to confound the feelings, the action of which is necessary, with the will, the action of which is free; but that error lay at the bottom of Edwards' peculiar personal experiences. As in his doctrine of mystical insight through sensible knowledge, he had blended the functions of sensibility and intellect, so in his use of the word inclination, as both a preferring and a choosing, he introduces an ambiguous middle term which partakes of the nature of both the involuntary and the voluntary. But to Edwards that ambiguity was no undesirable thing; the identification of inclination with the will, of the passive with the active, was a reminiscence of the receptive attitude of him who sought spiritual co-operation with the deity. That this twofold theory of the will, like a twofold theory of knowledge, seemed no incongruity, is borne out by two previous statements of the author. As he had already said that in sense-impressions the mind is abundantly active, so he had defined an inclination as nothing but God's influencing the soul according to a certain law of nature.[1] In fine, Edwards' ambiguities, the duplications both in his theory of causation and in his theory of knowledge, are to be explained from his idealistic mysticism, for both are founded in a conviction that with complete self-surrender there come not only pure impulses, but attendant reflection.

While in such a double occasionalism Edwards' indebtedness to his mystic experiences has been neglected, his resemblance to other idealists has nevertheless been pointed out. In subordinating his system to the divine will, he has been likened to Berkeley and Johnson; in combining the Platonism of the notes on *Mind* with the moral theory of the treatise on the *Will,* to Malebranche.[2] With these resemblances acknowledged, there still remains the further question of the ultimate issues of this treatise, since it has been suggested that the idealism of Ed-

[1] *Miscellanies,* No. 301 (MS.). [2] Lyon, *Idéalisme,* pp. 435-437.

wards, his view of the immanence of God, and his doctrine of moral necessity as connected with voluntary action would seem to involve pantheism.[1] Edwards, like Geulincx, might seem to teach that men's actions are but modes of the divine mind, but as for teaching a doctrine of blind necessity, the author is at pains to defend his treatise. As he answered the objection to being a Hobbite, by saying that it happens that he never read Hobbes, so he answers the charge of being one of the Stoics, by saying that if they held any such doctrine of Fate, as is inconsistent with the world being in all things subject to the disposal of an intelligent, wise agent, that presides—not as the *soul* of the world, but—as the Sovereign *Lord* of the Universe, governing all things by proper will, choice, and design, in the exercise of the most perfect liberty conceivable, without subjection to any constraint, or being properly under the power or influence of anything before, above, or without himself; I wholly renounce any such doctrine.[2]

In spite of the author's denial of the charge of Stoicism, the tendency of the treatise on the *Will* toward pantheism has been declared probable, because in both earlier and later writings he uses language which identifies God with the world. In his early Notes on the *Mind* he writes: ' God and real existence are the same; God is and there is none else. . . . It is impossible that God should be otherwise than excellent, for He is infinite, universal and all-comprehending excellence.' In his treatise on *Virtue* he writes, that God ' is, in effect, being in general, and comprehends universal existence.' In his late posthumous treatise on the *End of God in Creation* he says of God, that His ' being and beauty is, as it were, the sum and comprehension of all existence and excellence,' much more than the sun is ' the comprehension of all light and brightness of the sky.' [3] Similar views, which would identify God with the totality of the world, have been pointed out as follows: In his initial note on Excellency in *Mind,* as in his sermon on *Divine and Supernatural Light,* Edwards has been said to have manifested his deep æsthetic contemplation, whereby nature, man and God

---

[1] Fisher, *Trinity*, p. 40.   [2] *Will*, p. 69.   [3] Fisher, *Trinity*, p. 40.

are synthesised, or, more exactly, man and nature are one in God.[1] In like manner, concerning a very early *Observation* that ' the mere exertion of a new thought is a certain proof of a God, and that the substance which brings that thought forth is God,'[2] it has been asserted that such an occasionalistic view might easily pass on to an idealistic pantheism.

In view of these numerous citations, it can hardly be allowed that the grand heroic conception of God comprehending and fulfilling the existence of the infinite variety of the concrete was too sublime a conception for Edwards to have continued to hold.[3] It is true that in the treatise on the *Will* he momentarily forsakes the argument for the existence of God based on the category of substance for the more commonplace argument based on the category of causation; but it is not true that he loses the more poetic and more pantheistic notion of God's all-comprising substance. Indeed, Edwards' most boldly speculative work, *God's Last End in Creation,* has been more adequately described as one whose whole trend is toward a comprehensive idealism which makes God all in all.[4] Here, as Edwards' chief expositor affirms, there appeared, with something of the beauty which had fascinated the vision of his youth, that other element of his thought which, though subordinated, was never annihilated, that conception of God which Plato, Spinoza or Hegel might have held,—the idea of the good, the one substance, the absolute thought unfolding itself or embodying itself in a visible and glorious order. Furthermore, the very title of the work is declared to suggest the profound speculations of Gnostic theosophies, to recall the mystic thinkers of the Middle Ages, for throughout this treatise the Neo-Platonic word ' emanation ' is the one about which the thought revolves, and the old phrases, such as the overflow of the divine fulness,

---

[1] Curtis, *Kantean Elements,* p. 36.

[2] Smyth (*American Journal of Theology,* Vol. 1, p. 957), thinks that this *Observation* was composed not far from the year 1727.

[3] J. H. MacCracken, *The Sources of Jonathan Edwards' Idealism, Philosophical Review,* Vol. 11, p. 32.

[4] Gardiner, *Retrospect,* pp. 156-157.

diffusion of the divine essence, emanation from God compared with the light and heat which go forth from the sun,—these constitute the verbal signs of Edwards' thought. It is possible that he might have avoided them had he known their earlier association. But they represent truly the tendency of his mind; they stand for principles which had been lying for years beneath his practical theology.[1]

Further corroboration of the opinion that this same treatise represents an intellectual growth towards a pantheistic form of belief is to be found in the assertion that it was not an unpremeditated work, but largely a construction from his earlier writings, exhibiting a real simplification of his thought and suggestive indications of almost conscious attempts at unification. This intellectual growth, it is further explained, would remain altogether enigmatic were it not for the early notes on the *Mind*. Here the trend of Edwards' thinking is not so much disclosed in such Berkeleian expressions as that the ' material universe exists nowhere but in the mind,' as in such pantheistic expressions as these: ' Seeing God has so plainly revealed himself to us, and other minds are made in his image, and are emanations from him; we may judge what is the excellence of other minds by which is his, which we have shown is Love. His Infinite Beauty is his Infinite Mental Love of himself. Now God is the Prime and Original Being, the First and Last, and the Pattern of all, and has the sum of all perfections. We may, therefore, doubtless conclude, that all that is the perfection of spirits may be resolved into that which is God's perfection, which is Love.'[2]

How close is the connection between Edwards' earliest and latest thinking, is now to be seen in this passage from the *Chief End in Creation:*

As there is an infinite fulness of all possible good in God—a fulness of every perfection, of all excellency and beauty, and of infinite happiness—and as this fulness is capable of communication, or emanation *ad extra;* so it seems a thing amiable and

[1] Allen, *Edwards*, pp. 21, 327-331.
[2] Woodbridge, *Philosophical Review*, Vol. 13, pp. 399-407.

valuable in *itself* that this infinite fountain of good should send forth abundant streams. And as this is in itself excellent, so a *disposition* to this in the Divine Being, must be looked upon as an *excellent* disposition. Such an emanation of good is, in some sense, a *multiplication* of it. So far as the stream may be looked upon as anything besides the fountain, so far it may be looked on as an *increase* of good. And if the fulness of good that is in the fountain, is in itself excellent, then the emanation, which is as it were an increase, repetition, or multiplication of it, is excellent. Thus it is fit, since there is an infinite fountain of light and knowledge, that this light should shine forth in beams of communicated knowledge and understanding; and, as there is an infinite fountain of holiness, moral excellence, and beauty, that so it should flow out in communicated holiness. And that, as there is an infinite fulness of joy and happiness, so these should have an emanation, and become a fountain flowing out in abundant streams, as beams from the sun.

Thus it appears reasonable to suppose, that it was God's last end, that there might be a glorious and abundant emanation of his infinite fulness of good *ad extra,* or without himself; and that the disposition to communicate himself, or diffuse his own FULNESS, was what moved him to create the world. But here I observe, that there would be some impropriety in saying, that a disposition in God to communicate himself *to the creature,* moved him to create the world. For an inclination in God to communicate himself to an *object,* seems to presuppose the *existence* of the object, at least in idea. But the diffusive disposition that excited God to give creatures existence, was rather a communicative *disposition* in general, or a disposition in the fulness of the divinity to flow out and diffuse itself. Thus the disposition there is in the root and stock of a tree to diffuse sap and life, is doubtless the reason of their communication to its buds, leaves, and fruits, *after* these exist. But a disposition to communicate of its life and sap to its *fruits,* is not so properly the cause of its *producing* those fruits, as its disposition to diffuse its sap and life in general. Therefore, to speak strictly according to truth, we may suppose *that a disposition in God, as an original property of his nature, to an emanation of his own infinite fulness, was what excited him to create the world; and so, that the emanation itself was aimed at by him as a last end of the creation.*[1]

In this remarkable exposition it is declared that mystic pantheism could not be more explicit, and that Edwards himself appears not to have been wholly insensible to the possibility of

<hr />

[1] *Creation,* pp. 99-100.

such an interpretation.[1]   The dissertation, after an explanation
of terms, had begun with a consideration of 'what reason dictates in this affair,' although it is admitted that the affair is
'properly an affair of divine revelation.'   In this primary section Edwards had announced that no notion of God's last end
in the creation of the world is agreeable to reason, which would
truly imply any indigence, insufficiency and mutability in God;
or any dependence of the Creator on the creature for any part
of his perfection or happiness.[2]   But now, in an apologetic section, after the mystical passage which reads like some disciple
of Plotinus or a Christian Spinoza, the author proceeds to a
section wherein it is considered how, on the supposition that
God's making the forementioned things his last end, he manifests a supreme and ultimate regard to himself in all his works.[3]

It cannot be said that this line of argument is entirely successful as a defence, because to the original figures of speech
there are added qualifying clauses of the most subversive character.   For example, with respect to the fourth and last particular, namely, God's being disposed to an abundant communication and glorious emanation of that infinite fulness of good
which he possesses, it is argued as follows:

This propensity in God to diffuse himself, may be considered
as a propensity to himself diffused; or to his own glory existing
in its emanation.   A respect to himself, or an infinite propensity
to and delight in his own glory, is that which causes him to
incline to its being abundantly diffused, and to delight in the
emanation of it.   Thus, that nature in a tree, by which it puts
forth buds, shoots out branches, and brings forth leaves and
fruit, is a disposition that terminates in its own complete self.
And so the disposition in the sun to shine, or abundantly to diffuse its fulness, warmth, and brightness, is only a tendency to
its own most glorious and complete state.   So God looks on
the communication of himself, and the emanation of his infinite
glory, to belong to the fulness and completeness of himself; as
though he were not in his most glorious state without it. . . .
God acting for *himself,* or making himself his last end, and his

[1] Woodbridge, *Philosophical Review,* Vol. 13, p. 401.
[2] *Creation,* p. 97.
[3] *Creation,* Chapter 1, § 3.

acting for *their* sake, are not to be set in opposition; they are rather to be considered as coinciding one with the other, and implied one in the other. But yet God is to be considered as first and original in his regard; and the creature is the object of God's regard, consequently, and by implication, as being as it were comprehended in God, as it shall be more particularly observed presently.[1]

What were Edwards' subsequent observations, and how he answered the objections against the reasonableness of what has been said of God's making himself the last end, may be seen in two other passages, which recall not only the earlier illuminative and unitive states of the mystic, but even that primary idealistic essay on *Being*:

And it is farther to be considered, that what God aimed at in the creation of the world, as the end which he had ultimately in view, was that communication of himself which he intended through all eternity. And if we attend to the nature and circumstances of this eternal emanation of divine good, it will more clearly show HOW, in making this his end, God testifies a supreme respect to himself, and makes himself his end. There are many reasons to think that what God has in view, in an increasing communication of himself through eternity, is an *increasing* knowledge of God, love to him, and joy in him. And it is to be considered, that the more those divine communications *increase* in the creature, the more it becomes one with God: for so much the more is it united to God in love, the heart is drawn nearer and nearer to God, and the union with him becomes more firm and close: and, at the same time, the creature becomes more and more *conformed* to God. The image is more and more perfect, and so the good that is in the creature comes forever nearer and nearer to an identity with that which is in God. In the view therefore of God, who has a comprehensive prospect of the increasing union and conformity through eternity, it must be an infinitely strict and perfect nearness, conformity, and oneness. . . . God and the creature, in the emanation of the divine fulness, are not properly set in opposition; or made the opposite parts of a disjunction. Nor ought God's glory and the creature's good, to be viewed as if they were properly and entirely distinct, in the objection. This supposeth, that God having respect to his glory, and the communication of good to his creatures, are things altogether different; that God communicating his fulness for

[1] *Creation*, pp. 100, 101.

himself, and his doing it for *them,* are things standing in a proper disjunction and opposition. Whereas, if we were capable of more perfect views of God and divine things, which are so much above us, it probably would appear very clear, that the matter is quite otherwise: and that these things, instead of appearing entirely distinct, are *implied* one in the other. God in seeking his glory, seeks the good of his creatures; because the emanation of his glory (which he seeks and delights in, as he delights in himself and his own eternal glory) implies the communicated excellency and happiness of his creatures. And in communicating his fulness for them, he does it for himself; because their good, which he seeks, is so much in union and communion with himself. . . . In this view it appears, that God's respect to the *creature,* in the whole, *unites* with his respect to *himself.* Both regards are like two lines which at the beginning appear separate, but finally meet in one, both being directed to the same centre. And as to the *good* of the creature itself, in its whole duration and infinite progression, it must be viewed as *infinite;* and as coming nearer and nearer to the same thing in its infinite fulness. The nearer anything comes to infinite, the nearer it comes to an identity with God. And if any *good,* as viewed by God, is beheld as infinite, it cannot be viewed as a distinct thing from God's own infinite glory. . . .

But now, with respect to the Divine Being, there is no such thing as confined selfishness in him, or a love to himself *opposite* to general benevolence. It is impossible, because he comprehends all entity, and all excellence, in his own essence. The eternal and infinite Being, is in effect, *being in general;* and comprehends universal existence. God, in his benevolence to his creatures, cannot have his heart enlarged, in such a manner as to take in beings who are originally out of himself, distinct and independent. This cannot be in an infinite Being, who exists alone from eternity. But he, from his goodness, as it were enlarges himself in a more excellent and divine manner. This is by communicating and diffusing himself; and *so,* instead of *finding,* he *makes* objects of his benevolence—not by taking what he finds distinct from himself, and so partaking of their good, and being happy in them, but—by flowing forth, and expressing himself in them, and making them to partake. of him, and then rejoicing in himself expressed in them, and communicated to them.[1]

In these passages the New England saint has reached a system more mystical than rational, more in the nature of the ineffable knowledge than in harmony with what reason dictates

[1] *Creation,* pp. 101, 105.

in the affair. This he appears to realise in a subsequent question-begging defence, and in a final confession of the inadequacy of his previous answer: If any are not satisfied with the preceding answer, he continues, let them consider whether they can devise any other scheme of God's last end in creating the world but what will be equally obnoxious. . . . I confess there is a degree of indistinctness and obscurity in the close consideration of such subjects, and a great imperfection in the expressions we use concerning them, arising unavoidably from the infinite sublimity of the subject and the incomprehensibleness of those things that are divine.[1]

With its final note of ineffability, which marks the transition from the rationalistic to the theological portion of his dissertation, Edwards has reached the height of his philosophical speculation, inasmuch as the other posthumous treatises offer no real solution of the dualistic problem involved, but only a specious promise of an advance in speculation. It has been said that if the Calvinistic theology should be eliminated from the dissertation on the *Nature of True Virtue*, there would remain a conception almost identical with that of Spinoza,[2] but such an elimination was not made.

Disinterested love of God on the part of man, love to being in general on the part of God, are presented as the respective ideals; but it can scarcely be held, as the younger Edwards held, that this is a successful union of two heretofore supposedly mutually exclusive explanations of the universe, as created either for happiness of finite beings, or as a manifestation of the glory of God.[3] These two contrasted views, the one Arminian, the other Calvinistic, were not harmonised by Edwards, unless a certain passage expounding a sort of æsthetic mysticism be considered the key to the dissertation.[4] After having shown how that love, wherein

[1] *Creation*, pp. 102, 106.

[2] Woodbridge, *Philosophical Review*, Vol. 13, p. 402.

[3] Jonathan Edwards, Jr., in Williston Walker, *Ten New England Leaders*, New York, 1901, p. 254.

[4] A. T. Ormond (*Philosophical Review*, Vol. 13, p. 181) considers the key to Edwards' philosophy to be found in his treatise on *Decrees and Election*, § 58, in a passage similar to the above.

true virtue consists, respects both the Divine Being and created beings, it is added: That consent, agreement, or union of being to being, which has been spoken of, namely, the union or propensity of *minds* to mental or spiritual existence, may be called the highest and primary beauty; being the proper and peculiar beauty of spiritual and moral beings, which are the highest and first part of the universal system, for whose sake all the rest has existence. . . . The reason, or at least one reason, why God has made this kind of mutual agreement of things beautiful and grateful to those intelligent beings that perceive it, probably is, that there is in it some image of the true, spiritual, original beauty, which has been spoken of, or the union of spiritual beings in a mutual propensity and affection of the heart.[1]

These reasonings constitute an attempt to solve the dualistic problem of God's relation to the ideal and actual worlds, of the infinite to finite minds, yet they are no advance on previous thought. Indeed, they are little but a combination of the author's former conclusions, and may be referred, first, to the incipient Platonism of his essay on *Being,* whereby he puts in the divine mind infinite archetypes, on which the creation is fashioned; next, to the initial topic in his Notes on *Mind,* wherein excellency is defined as the loving consent of spirits one to another; and finally, to his mystical epistemology, a sensible knowledge, or knowledge of the heart, expounded in the *Religious Affections.* Dealing then, as he does, with the immanence of God in nature, Edwards should logically reach the issue of a speculative mysticism which makes the relation of the individual to the absolute less an ethical harmony of two mutually exclusive wills than a fusion of personalities, a union in which there is no longer a consciousness of a distinct life, but a real substitution of divine for human nature.[2] Nevertheless, to make such a transfusion or identification, even the mystic hesitated. His ecstatic desires tended towards the unitive state, his Calvinistic beliefs resulted in a dualism. How his theology thus overshadowed his philosophy has been pointed out in a certain contradiction in the treatise on *Virtue.* If Edwards had said plainly

---

[1] *Virtue,* pp. 125, 127, 128.
[2] Cf. Inge, *Christian Mysticism,* pp. 28, 29.

what his theology implies, that the creature has no existence outside of God, his attitude would have been clear and consistent. But he seems also to grant an infinitesimal portion of an independent existence to humanity. He halts between these two opinions, neither of which is quite acceptable to him.[1]

So, too, a certain vacillation on the allied question, whether the creation was an eternal necessity in the nature of the divine being, receives no corrective in the other treatises. A recently recovered manuscript on the *Trinity* deals with the problem of God and his relation to the mundane sphere, but here the author reasons more as a thelogian than a philosopher. In the opening section there is indeed an implication of a cosmic principle immanent in the world, but the unity of that principle is sacrificed to a conventional duality, for that immanence is rendered possible only by supposing that:

God Perpetually and Eternally has a most Perfect Idea of himself, as it were, an exact Image and Representation of himself ever before him and in actual view, & from hence arises a most pure and Perfect act or energy in the Godhead, which is the divine Love, Complacence and Joy. . . . However, if God beholds himself so as thence to have delight & Joy in himself he must become his own Object. There must be a duplicity. There is God and the Idea of God, if it be Proper to call a conception of that that is purely spiritual an Idea.[2]

By adopting a traditional doctrine of the logos as a mediating principle between Creator and creation, Edwards has sacrificed the philosophical unification of his system to theological teaching. Moreover, he finally confesses that he does not pretend to explain his subject so as to render it no longer a mystery, for he thinks it to be the highest and deepest of all divine mysteries still.[3] With this note of ineffability, denoting a certain metaphysical impotence, one may leave the writings of Jonathan Edwards. His unpublished manuscripts may afford some corrective to the grave deficiencies of his philosophical system, but, until they are given to the public, one is forced to the abrupt conclusion that, while the Saint of New England was a precocious idealist and a profound mystic, he was not a consistent philosopher.

[1] Allen, *Edwards*, 319 note.   [2] *Trinity*, pp. 77, 80.   [3] *Ib.*, p. 117.

BOOK III—DEISM

CHAPTER I

DEISM

DEISM was a product of eighteenth century rationalism, an attempt of the Enlightenment to reduce religion to ethics, revelation to a spiritual law in the natural world. Seeking for evidences of design and imbued with optimism, it found sermons in stones and good in everything. Discarding mystery and miracle, it had for its creed: 'Allegiance to the Creator and Governor of the Milky-Way, and the Nebulæ, and benevolence to all His creatures.' Deism was thus summed up by President John Adams. Its literature was represented, on the conservative side, by such names as Cotton Mather and Bishop Berkeley, and on the radical by Benjamin Franklin and Thomas Jefferson.

The movement affected the lives of eminent men; it was perhaps best defined by one of its minor prophets, a disciple of the notorious free-thinker, Thomas Paine. Said Elihu Palmer: Deism declares to intelligent man the existence of one Perfect God, Creator and Preserver of the Universe; that the laws by which he governs the world are like himself immutable; and that violations of these laws, or miraculous interference in the movements of nature must be necessarily excluded from the grand system of universal existence.[1] Whence this system was derived the popular writer of a century ago had nothing to say. It remained for a Boston encyclopedist of the time to give the sources of the belief and the classes of its adherents. In brief these were Lord Herbert of Cherbury's five points common to all religions, as given in the Stoic and Ciceronian 'common notions,' and Samuel Clarke's four varieties of deists,—from the Epicureans who fancy that God does not at all concern himself in the gov-

[1] Elihu Palmer, *Prospect, or View of the Moral World,* New York, 1804.

ernment of the world, to the mortal deists who deny a future
state.[1] The article concluded with the statement that deism began
in England and spread over all Europe. It had nothing to say
as to how it started and how it spread in America.

American deism began in a reaction against Puritan determinism. The belief in a deity separate from the world, an idle
spectator, an absentee landlord, was a logical rebound from the
belief in a deity constantly interfering with the world, a magical
intervener, a local busybody. Thomas Paine's *Age of Reason,*
with its notion of a creator whose ' arm wound up the vast
machine ' and then left it to run by itself, formed a kind of counterpoise to Cotton Mather's *Magnalia Christi Americana,* with its
faithful record of many illustrious, wonderful providences, both
of mercies and judgments, on divers persons in New England.
In a way, also, these two books marked the transition between
two different political points of view, one standing for class
favouritism, the other for the natural rights of man. The Calvinistic doctrines of sovereign grace and an elect people savoured
too much of the claims of British supremacy to be long acceptable. Hence the five points of Calvinism became so many points of
irritation. Total depravity might apply to effete monarchies, but
not to the new world; absolute predestination to the land of passive obedience, but not to the land where men sought to be free.
In a measure, then, the preaching of the New England divines
became unwelcome to the people. Even the master of those who
thought offended the national instincts. Jonathan Edwards' philosophy was overshadowed by his theology. In his private journal
he might seem to prefer the idea that man is free to will as he
pleases; in his *Inquiry into the Freedom of the Will* he belied
his title and concluded that the pleasure of his fallen nature is to
do evil. This determinism, this fatalistic scheme of necessity,
with its inference of man as absolutely dependent, was a paramount cause leading to the disintegration of Calvinism. Yet it
was not until the next century that Channing could replace the
idea of a bound and predestinated will by the freedom of the in-

[1] Hannah Adams. *A View of Religions,* Boston, 1801.

dividual life, and natural depravity by the assertion of the inherent
nobility of man.[1]

If Calvinism, as the doctrine of necessity, had transcendentalism
as its ultimate effect, with its corollaries it was a proximate cause
of deism. The notion of a partial and arbitrary deity prepared
for the religion of humanity, the system of inscrutable decrees for
a religion of reason. These humanitarian and rationalistic tendencies may be briefly traced in the development of New England theology, from the half-way Covenant of 1662 to the Unitarian manifesto of 1815. That Covenant was a compromise in
favour of those who, it was remarked, did not wish to go the whole
way on the road of strict discipline.[2] The high Calvinists had insisted that only the elect should be considered members of the theocracy. They were opposed by a strong party who desired that all
persons of regular and blameless life might be admitted to full
communion in the churches. This more lenient view of what might
be morally demanded was checked by the revivals of 1736 and such
disturbing sermons as that of Edwards at Enfield. But talk
about creatures infinitely sinful and abominable, wallowing like
swine in the mire of their sins, brought about a reaction, and the
next generation went from the extreme of puritanic pessimism to
the extreme of deistic optimism, the belief in the perfectibility of
the human race. The change in sentiment is recorded in the
attacks on the Berkshire divinity. The consistent Calvinists merely
filed smooth the rough edges of a cast-iron system, but the forerunners of the Unitarian movement boldly threw the dead weight
overboard. Jonathan Mayhew of Cambridge said that to speak
in reproachful language of the moral virtues, comparing them to
filthy rags, was absurd, and Charles Chauncy of Boston maintained that the Calvinistic doctrine of the tendency of man's
nature to sin as implying his utter and eternal ruin and the
torments of hell fire, was shocking to the human mind and contradicted all the natural notions both of justice and benevolence. So,
too, President Andrew Eliot quotes with approval the statement of

[1] *Moral Argument Against Calvinism,* Baltimore, 1819.
[2] F. H. Uhden, *The New England Theocracy,* Boston, 1858.

Howe that it is a black conception of God that He should be supposed irresistibly to determine the will of man. He adds that it is a conclusive argument against such a fatal necessity, that it is contrary to the perceptions of the human mind. We have a consciousness of liberty, we perceive no external influence.[1]

These protests against determinism were characteristic of early American deism; but behind these acute personal reactions there were larger and quieter forces at work, for the dogmas of an unnatural religion were giving way to the principles of natural religion. In a word, rationalism had at last a chance to assert itself. Here deism constituted the moving cause, and the colonial college the vehicle in the transaction.

[1] *Discourse on Natural Religion,* Boston, 1771.

CHAPTER II

HARVARD COLLEGE

DEISM, as a form of rationalism, had been hanging on the skirts of Puritanism during the last quarter of the seventeenth century, but it was not until the eighteenth that it took to an independent growth and hastened the intellectual emancipation of New England. The Boston platform of 1680 in its opening section had stated that the light of nature and the works of creation and providence do so far manifest the goodness, wisdom and power of God as to leave men unexcusable. Now this belief that natural reason is greatly impaired was based upon the assumption that after the first transgression man retained no more of the light of reason than would conduce to tormenting reflections on his own misery.[1] These doctrines of the Puritan fathers were a virtual recognition of the rationalistic principle, but more in the way of a forlorn negation than a hopeful affirmation. Hence from these timid limitations there arose the desire for a change from a gloomy theology to a cheering theodicy, from the doctrine of inscrutable decrees to the belief in rational purpose and benevolent design in the universe. This change is marked by two such representative works as Mather's *Reasonable Religion* and Chauncy's *Benevolence of the Deity*.

Cotton Mather (1663-1728) did not attain his rationalistic results without considerable mental perturbation; in fact, his attitude seemed, at the first, that of a sheer obscurantist, violently opposed to the pursuits of reason. In his *Student and Preacher,* addressed to the studious youths in academies, he speaks in an abusive manner, fashioned somewhat after the comic writer whom he impersonates: Hearken ye of Harvard and Yale College to old Eubulus, exhorting you with his counsel. In most academies of this world nothing is acquired but worldly wisdom; the phi-

[1] D. C. Williams's preface to Cotton Mather's *Reasonable Religion,* London, 1713.

losophy taught in them is nothing but *foolosophy*. Listen not to that smoke-selling chandler, that muddy-headed pagan, Aristotle, to whose yoke souls called rational have submitted their necks and written prodigious cart-loads of stuff to explain the Peripatetic philosophy. . . . The vulgar logic, instead of leading the mind into truth, merely enables one to carry on altercations and logo-machies, to exhibit in the pompous forms of art, with trifling application and illustration, what every one does by nature and custom. It might with equal solemnity be shown what points of regular management are exemplified by the boys playing at their marbles. What I say of logic, I say of metaphysics, which a learned man too justly calls, *disciplinarum omnium excrementum.* . . . Over ethics the academies spend too much time, plough too long; it is an *impietas in artis formam redacta;* it is all over a sham; it presents you with a mock happiness, a life of piety without a living principle, a good life with no other than dead works filling it. . . . Tired with academic futilities betake yourself to that best school of Mosaic philosophy; read the *Philosophia Vetus ac Vera* of the rare Dickinson rather than the hypotheses of the inquisitive sons of the wild asses' colt. Avoid philosophical romances and get as thorough an insight as you can into the principles of our perpetual dictator, Sir Isaac Newton. . . . I hope it will be no indecency for me to say, that if you desire to see the largest collection of the discoveries which the last age has made in philosophy, adapted unto the general capacity of the reader, you have this prepared in a book entitled the *Christian Philosopher.*[1]

Before passing to the book so modestly mentioned, there are to be noticed in this curious document two contradictory points of view: on the one hand the author's dislike of discursive reasoning and, on the other, an inconsistent appeal to reason itself. The former is based on a realistic theory of knowledge, which insists on universal instinctive principles. As Mather expressed it, the belief of a God implanted in the hearts of all the world is a sufficient reason for the belief of a God. As there is in the eye an innate faculty of seeing by which it will acknowledge the being of the light, so there is an innate faculty in the mind of man

---

[1] *Student and Preacher,* pp. 35-125, London, 1789.

which acknowledges the being of God. Indeed the notion of deity is engraved in the breast of man as with the point of a diamond. Moreover, the works of the deity command the belief of his being—the world's various parts, curious ends, incomparable order are the sensible stamps of an universal power and wisdom and goodness. The world had not a beginning from a casual concourse and jumble of atoms, more. than ten thousand wheels casually thrown together would form a well contrived watch. Nor did it build itself. Dull matter could never produce itself. The matter of the world being everywhere in motion, we must unavoidably come to a First Mover. This First Mover can be no other than deity. If the pagan Galen could not read his anatomy lectures without breaking forth into a hymn of praise unto his maker, it may suffice to say, ' O, man, look upon thyself.' . . . The works of Providence which are continued creation will further satisfy the reason. The preservation of the world, like an army preserved in exact order, though composed of different and quarrelsome nations, must be ascribed unto a God.[1]

In all this Mather exhibits the change that was impressing itself upon his mind. In his previous strictures against philosophy, he had shown himself intolerant of reason; now he strives to satisfy its demands and yet not without further inconsistencies. Declaring that it is an inconsiderate thing to pay so much of a compliment to atheism as to bestow solemn treatises full of learned arguments for the refutation of a delirious frenzy, he nevertheless does the same thing himself in his *Christian Philosopher,* or *A Collection of the Best Discoveries in Nature with Religious Improvements.* While this is a rejection of deism in name, it is an acceptance of it in principle and still not in its fullest measure. The book has not the cold tone of extreme rationalism, but may be regarded under that phase of deistic development which was stimulated by the growing interest in the external world. And yet because of the author's love of mysticism, his longing for the *aisthesis pneumatike,* that interest is less scientific than æsthetic. Mather takes the imperfect current notions of natural science, presents them in a somewhat fan-

[1] *Reasonable Religion,* p. 8.

tastic Elizabethan style, and withal leaves the impression of a thorough appreciation of the beautiful. Thus he quotes with approval the statement of an English writer that the divine reason runs like a golden thread through the whole leaden mine of brutal nature. Applying this principle to whatever he saw about him he exclaims: How charming the proportion and pulchritude of the leaves, the flowers, the fruits. How peculiar the care which the great God of nature has taken for the safety of the seed and fruit! When the vegetable race comes abroad, what strange methods of nature are there to guard them from inconveniences. How nice the provision of nature for their support in standing and growing, that they may keep their heads above ground and administer to our intentions; some stand by their own strength, others are of an elastic nature, that they may dodge the violence of the winds: a visible argument that the plastic capacities of matter are governed by an all-wise infinite agent. Oh! the glorious goodness of our deity in all these things![1]

The optimism of this passage is one of the distinguishing marks of deism; the purposiveness of nature is another; in this regard a final statement reads: Never does one endowed with reason do anything more reasonable than when he makes everything that occurs to him, in the vast fabric of the world, an incentive to such thoughts as these: Verily there is a glorious deity!

In its sense of the beautiful and its cheerful outlook upon the world, Mather's little work was strangely at variance with the Puritanic spirit as ordinarily conceived. Only once does the writer betray the effects of the morbidities of the day. In one place he speaks of men being utterly destitute of any principle to keep them honest in the dark, but in another he tells how the inspection of the things of nature compels us to confess the glorious maker of them all. Of Mather's excursions into the animal kingdom and into the realms of astronomy, ethnology and physics, little need be said, for, to use his own figure, he was trying to make short work of all the sciences and find out a north-west passage to them. In this attempt to make all knowledge his province, the author showed himself provincial to a degree. Nevertheless he sounded a note that did not die; the book with its scien-

[1] *Christian Philosopher*, pp. 126, 131, London, 1721.

tific arguments for design fell flat, but its æsthetic element lived on; it anticipated by a century the transcendentalists' love of nature for its own sake. In fine, Mather would have agreed with Emerson when he said, ' Come into the azure and love the day.'

Belonging to the same school of apologetic deists as Mather, but of far higher rank, was Charles Chauncy, (1705-1787). A great-grandson of that puritanical president of Harvard who opposed on pain of exile the measures of Archbishop Laud, he might have been expected to draw the long face of the Calvinistic pessimist; instead he wrote a book whose optimism was as pronounced as its style was elevated. In his *Benevolence of the Deity*,[1] in place of a being cruel, inscrutable, acting by particular providences, he puts a being benevolent, rational, acting in harmony with wise goodness and accurate justice. Hence the divine benevolence is not to be considered as a mere instinct mechanically and blindly urging to the communication of happiness, but rather a natural state of mind, necessarily inhering in the deity, disposing and prompting him to the communication of good, for the deity has within himself a boundless source of benevolence, a perfection inexhaustible, not capable of being exerted to a *ne plus,* but visible in the immense quantum of happiness seen in the support of innumerable animated creatures in our world and in the preservation of millions of creatures rendered comfortable and happy in other worlds.[2] This benevolence, furthermore, is not to be judged merely from the actual good we see produced, but according to the tendency of those general laws conformably to which it is produced. The deity does not communicate being or happiness to his creatures by an immediate act of power, but by concurring with an established course of nature. He makes them happy by the intervention of second causes, operating in a stated, regular, uniform manner. The operation of these causes is obstructed

[1] Although not published until 1784, this work probably antedated the Dudleian lectures. Writing to President Stiles of Yale, Chauncy said that he had ' a piece upon the Benevolence of God, its nature, illustration and consistency with evil, both natural and moral, written many years ago.' *Mass. Hist. Soc. Proc.,* Vol. 10, p. 163.

[2] *Benevolence of the Deity,* pp. 11-48, Boston, 1784.

by the intervention of ourselves, since the good that we are originally formed for, and which our implanted capacities tend to, is
put very much into our own power. This is one of the general
laws according to which the deity operates in the communication
of good. This is perhaps better adapted to produce the greatest
good, rather than the other method, by interpositions continually
repeated, for such interpositions would put a final bar to man's
activity, industry and foresight, and would totally destroy the
whole business of life which is carried on upon this supposition—
that such and such actions will be followed by such and such consequences in virtue of those established laws which uniformly
take place in the world. In short, the deity's not interposing, in
the manner pleaded for, is an instance of goodness and not an
argument in proof of the want of it.[1]

After utilizing the very language of Pope, that the deity acts
not by partial but by general laws, and anticipating the sacred
formula of Bentham as to the greatest good of the greatest number, Chauncy proceeds to fortify his scheme by the psychology of
Locke and the morality of Hutcheson. The gift of sensation, he
continues, is the capacity by means of which impressions from without become perceptions within, variously affecting the mind and
giving rise to sensible ideas. In vain had our bodies been so
curiously fitted with organs and external objects fitted by their
mediation to make the impressions on our minds, were it not for
this capacity. Barely a susceptibility of impressions from material
nature would not have been sufficient for the purposes of intelligence. . . . The other power furnishing us with the materials of knowledge is reflection, or the mind's ability to look
within and take notice of its own operations; these give rise to
another set of ideas, different from those we received from sensation; from these we rise above the material world and are
enabled to turn our view to moral objects, in the mental survey
of which we may entertain ourselves with the highest satisfaction.
Though these are the only inlets to the mind, though the simple
ideas originally let into the mind by sensation or reflection are
but few, yet they are capable of being put together with such
variety as to make new complex ones almost to infinity. So adding

[1] *Benovelence of the Deity*, pp. 60-61.

the other faculties—memory, will, discernment, imagination, or those which qualify us for the use of these materials of knowledge, there are given us those various excellent productions of art and genius which are so variously fitted both for the service of life and the entertainment of the mind. This intellectual pleasure is always at hand, and it will not, like animal delight, pall the desire and bring on satiety and disgust, for it is in itself a noble exercise and fitted to yield continually growing satisfaction to the mind. In fine, it is from hence that we are capable of rising in our thoughts to the existence of some uncreated, original being at the head of all, endowed with the highest possible perfection, in the contemplation of whom the mind may take the greatest complacency. The forming us with faculties, whereby we are qualified for such noble intellectual attainments, carries with it the marks of benevolence. Nothing, indeed, but supreme and perfect goodness could have so wonderfully adorned and endowed our nature. . . . The benevolence of the deity is further illustrated in the endowment of those powers fitting us for moral happiness. The first power in our nature, call it common sense, or moral sense, or moral discernment, or what you please, is that by which we are enabled at once, without the labour of a long train of reasoning, to distinguish between moral good and moral evil, virtue and vice, between which there is a difference, which cannot be inverted even by the power of the supreme ruler himself.[1]

These fervid arguments have a familiar sound; they might have belonged to a home-bred English deist of the apologetic school. And that such were Chauncy's affiliations he practically acknowledges in the casual mention of his authorities from Addison and Cumberland to Law and Maxwell. And yet pointing out these obligations of the New Englander to authors of the old country does not render him entirely unoriginal or unresponsive to native thought, for in the concluding portion of his work he makes a direct attack on the ineffectual attempt of Edwards to preserve the liberty of the creature. Another power in our nature, he continues, is that of self-determination, which gives rise to our volitions and consequent actions, and is in true propriety the cause

[1] *Benevolence of the Deity,* pp. 97-120.

of them. The benevolence of the deity is shown in the possession of our conscious perceptions, that we are the subjects of an inward governing power over our faculties, in virtue of which we are constituted free agents and not mere passive instruments, unavoidable effects of an established concatenation of exterior causes, over which we have no more dominion than over the palpitation of our hearts. Herein we are not mere machines, but causes and effects that are ascribed. Such agents are we men and we are as certain of this self-determination as that we possess existence. We do not ordinarily make ourselves so ridiculous as to endeavour by reasoning to prove that we exist. We know that we do without argumentation, because we feel that we do. So we feel that we are efficiently the causes of our own volitions and activities, and not that all effects take rise from a chain of causes with the deity at its head as the only efficient. We do not consider mankind as so many links in this adamantine chain, no one of which can possibly fail in the production of the effects assigned to it. Such a scheme would graft free agency upon the doctrine of fatality and the ill desert of men upon the operation of causes over which they have no power; it would fix vast multitudes in the place where they shall be tormented day and night without intermission, forever and ever. Such a scheme is debasing to the nature of man and dishonouring to the perfectly benevolent deity.[1]

Combining sound matter with a noble style, Chauncy's work marks a notable advance in the progress of rationalism. To teach that man is free and not determined; active and not passive; perfectible and not depraved, was to sum up the three great tenets of deism gained by way of painful reaction against the harsher doctrines of Calvinism. The process by which this reaction came about may be traced more intimately in the later writings of the Harvard worthies who had two great means for the public expression of their views. One was the Alvord professorship of 1789, whose purpose was declared as not merely to show the coincidence between the doctrines of revelation and the dictates of reason, but to state the absolute necessity and vast utility of a divine revelation. The other was the Dudleian lectureship of

[1] *Benevolence of the Deity*, pp. 128-130.

1755, for the proving, explaining and proper use and improvement of the principles of natural religion. Of these two foundations the earlier has the greater philosophical significance; for like the Boyle lectures in England, there is here presented not only the rise and progress of deism, but its destruction through a complex of powerful solvents. Thus while the eighteenth century lecturers, in this quadrennial cycle of discourses, argued for revealed religion as a necessary supplement to natural, those of the nineteenth century found it difficult to fulfil the purposes designated in the will of the colonial founder.

The first of the Dudleian discourses furnishes an appropriate introduction to the whole course by giving an historical summary of the problems of dualism as connected with cosmology. Here President Edward Holyoke was the initial speaker:

There were three opinions as to the existence of the world. One was that it was from Eternity, & Plato it seems, was the Father of it, and thought it flowed from God as Raies do from the Sun, where, by the way, we may note, That tho' they tho't the world to be eternal, yet that it proceeded from God; his Scholar also, Aristotle, propagated the same Notion & asserted that the world, was not generated so as to begin to be a world, which before was none. He supposes preexistent & eternal Matter as a Principle and thence argu'd the world to be eternal. . . . Another Opinion as to the Existence of the world, was that it came into this beautiful Form, by Chance, or a fortuitous concourse & jumble of Atoms, This is by all known to be the Philosophy of Epicurus, & his Notion was, that the Universe consisted of Atoms or Corpuscles of various Forms & Weights, which having been dispers'd at Random thro' the immense Space, fortuitously concur'd, into innumerable Systems or Worlds, which were thus formed, & afterward from time to time increased, changing & dissolving again without any certain, Cause or Design, without the Intervention of any Deity, or the intention of any Providence. And yet this Philosopher did not deny the Existence of a God, but on the Contrary asserted it, but tho't it beneath the Majesty of the Deity to concern himself with humane affairs. . . . But the most prevailing *Opinion* . . . was, *That the world had a beginning,* & was form'd by some great and excellent Being whom they called God. And this indeed is a Tho't that is perfectly agreeable to Reason.[1]

[1] *Natural Religion,* 1755, pp. 1, 10. (MS. in Harvard University Library.)

Holyoke's opinion that the cosmological argument is a rational belief was held by the next Dudleian lecturer of importance. The evidence of the being and perfection of God from his works, said Andrew Eliot, is not only conclusive, but clear and level to the meanest capacity. The rudest barbarian feels the absurdity of proposing that he himself and everything around him were produced by chance, that is, by nothing, a mere non-entity, that they were effects without a cause. There is One, and only One great and adequate cause of all, and this cause is God.[1]

In making the evidences of design palpable to the meanest mind, the lecturer runs the risk of making them cheap. To obviate this danger he adds a scholastic caution: to say that God has exerted his power or his wisdom, *ad ultimum posse,* so that he can proceed no farther, is to say a great deal too much. But he has discovered infinite wisdom and infinite power,—none but a Being possessed of these perfections in the highest possible degree could have created this stupendous universe.[2] As if recognising the inconsistency of arguing from a finite creation to an infinite creator, Eliot now strives to tone down the antinomies in this passage. He declares that the high a priori road is too intricate for men of common understanding, and that the argument a posteriori is the most generally useful. Every effect must have some cause; the structure and constitution of the world, the accurate adjustments of its various parts, and the uses and ends to which they are mutually adapted, prove this cause to be intelligent, wise and good. Some may dispute the goodness of God, when there is such a mixture of sorrow, distress and misery. But there is enough good to preponderate the evil in the universe. The most enjoy a great degree of comfort, very few being reduced to such a state of extreme misery as to be willing to exchange it for a state of non-existence. Possibly at the winding up of the drama, those things that are at present dark may have quite a contrary aspect.

In his modified optimism Eliot resembles the more moderate of the British deists such as Butler; in his stress upon the a pos-

[1] *Discourse on Natural Religion,* Boston, 1771.   [2] *Ib.*   [3] *Ib.*

terori argument, he resembles such empiricists as Locke. He is not so rash as to say, with a later lecturer, that the origin of innate ideas and principles is now almost universally given up,[1] yet he does hold that one would imagine by the exalted terms in which some men speak of the light of nature, that the whole system of moral truth arose spontaneously in the mind of man, without any help at all. The author of *Christianity as Old as the Creation* says that the most ignorant have a clear perception of the whole of religion and duty. On the contrary, concludes Eliot, the most acute philosopher, at his first entrance into life, has scarce any ideas of consciousness at all.[2]

Views similar to the last lecturer's were expressed by President Samuel Langdon in 1775. Defining the religion of nature as that investigatable by the natural powers of the human mind, without the assistance of any revelation from heaven, he gives, in a sort of imaginary conversation, the arguments for what he calls a coincidence of natural and revealed religion:

Reason would say: ' Surely this stupendous universe is the work of some invisible agent, beyond all comparison & conception superiour to man; for such a grand complete System so infinitely complicate, & yet so exactly adjusted in all its parts, the most minute as well as the grandest, that all kinds of symmetry and perfection concur to complete the whole, could never be the effect of chance or the product of endless essays & mutations of matter. This Agent must have an unlimited mind, to comprehend these vast innumerable works in one perfect Idea, before they were made. His *power*, also, must be equal to his unlimited understanding. And he is evidently as *good* as he is wise and powerful; otherwise malignity against his creatures would appear in universal discords through nature, perpetually generating all manners of evil.' . . . In some such manner as this Reason in its perfect state might be supposed capable of arriving at the knowledge of the *One True God*, & deducing from thence a compleat system of natural religion. Yet it can hardly be conceived, according to our experience of the labour of searching out truth, that the human mind, in its utmost strength, could by one glance of thought discover all the essential characteristics of the Deity, or the proper acts of worship & obedience which

[1] Gad Hitchcock, *Discourse*, p. 20, Boston, 1779.
[2] *Natural Religion.*

he requires. We might as well affirm, that unimpaired reason must naturally, at the first view of the heavenly bodies, have a clear knowledge of their magnitudes, distances and revolutions: or by looking round on the earth, immediately be acquainted with the innumerable gradations of animal life, & vegetable productions & fossils of all forms & kinds. . . . Therefore it may be justly questioned whether . . . it would not have cost the labour of Ages to demonstrate a true System of religion, as it has taken nearly six thousand years to search out the laws of the material system & bring natural philosophy to its present perfection.[1]

These opinions, somewhat antagonistic to the claims of unassisted reason, were expressed in the year before the Declaration of Independence; there now settled down upon the college at Cambridge an incubus of conservatism which was not lifted until a full generation. It was said, after the Revolution, that the deistic system is patched up of the dictates of reason and revelation blended together. . . . Natural sense and reason are not wanting to the natives of this northern part of America; in these poor Americans we have a just and lively image of nature, but they believe in the worship of devils.[2] About this time there was uttered a similar qualification, namely, that it is owing to the greater improvements which later ages have made in general science and literature than the former ages had done, that the modern deists know more than their predecessors.[3]

Passing over the sterile and unproductive period of Harvard philosophy during the last of the eighteenth century, it was not until after the second war with England that the Dudleian lectures show the weakening of the old conservative scheme under the assaults of the destructive deists. It remained for William Ellery Channing to attack the current scepticism, but with an effectiveness more oratorical than philosophical. In behalf of the great principle, that every effect must have an adequate cause, he contends that the fact that a savage in the woods could not compose the *Principia* of Newton, is about as plain as that he could not

[1] Samuel Langdon, *Discourse*, 1775, pp. 8-11.
[2] Samuel Wigglesworth, *Discourse*, p. 32 (MS.).
[3] Gad Hitchcock, *Discourse*, p. 30, Boston, 1779,

create the world. Furthermore, in opposition to the celebrated Humean argument against miracles, he declares that infidelity has seldom forged a weaker weapon: This argument affirms that the credibility of facts is to be decided by their accordance with the established order of nature; now if nature comprehended all existences and all powers, this position might be admitted.[1] Living on the verge of the transcendental movement, Channing's hypothetical approach out of deism into pantheism is of high significance, yet that approach is more obvious in the case of the lecturer of 1835. Familiar with authorities from Butler and Brougham to Cousin and Coleridge, John Brazer clearly recognises the drift of a priori arguments for natural religion as leading to the self-sufficiency of nature: abstract arguments, he reasons, are objectionable because they virtually assume the point to be proved. Thus, the axiom that every effect has a cause avails little with those who deny that the universe is an effect; the axiom that whatever begins to exist must have had a cause of its existence, will have no pertinency with those who, like the ancient and modern Epicureans, assert that the universe is eternal and the creative power, whatever it be, only plastic. Again, the statement that every contrivance must have a contriver is no argument to him who denies that there is any proof of contrivance further than the particular instances in question is concerned, as did Hume. Finally, the principle that nothing can be a cause of its own existence will conclude little against him who asserts that the world is an exception to this general rule,—it being self-existent, as Spinoza maintained.[2] Dissatisfied with Locke, Clarke, Paley and the Bridgewater treatises, Brazer now seeks consolation in the philosophy of Boethius and help in the idealism of Cudworth, and at last pulls himself up out of the *cul de sac* of design by transcendental intuitions of the perfect and absolute as essential states of human thought.

But this is anticipating Emerson and going beyond bounds.

[1] *A Discourse on the Evidences of Revealed Religion*, pp. 14, 19, Boston, 1821.
[2] *Review of the Arguments in Support of Natural Religion*, pp. 5-16, 1835.

So keeping within the proper limits of the early schools, one may summarise the tendencies of deism at Harvard by taking those three representatives who stood at intervals of precisely fifty years apart. First, in Mather is found universal purposiveness: all things prove an all-wise God, from man for whom ' to question the being of God would be exalted folly,' to the worm which ' adores the divine workmanship appearing in the constitution of his brethren.' Second, in Eliot is found a modified purposiveness: at the least ' the structure and constitution of the world and the accurate adjustments of its various parts prove an intelligent, wise and good Cause.' Third, in Channing no purposiveness is found, or rather, the order of nature is so lost in generalities as to constitute an hypothetical approach to pantheism. Unable to bridge the dualistic gap between creator and creation, this apologist gives but a half-hearted denial to that which the transcendentalists affirmed, namely that nature, comprehending all existence, may be its own cause.

CHAPTER III

YALE COLLEGE

THE rise of deism in the second oldest of the New England colleges was much like that in the first. At Harvard deism as a movement of enlightenment developed through opposition. Cotton Mather, with his eye upon the ethical free-thinkers, had pronounced the employing of so much time upon ethics in our colleges a vile piece of paganism; he put his finger on the trouble by declaring that the students of New Cambridge were eclectic in their tastes. That characteristic tendency was also noticed by another opponent of rationalism. George Whitfield, apostle of emotionalism, asserted that bad books were becoming fashionable in the college, the deistic Tillotson and Clarke being read instead of the pietistic Shepard and Stoddard. In reply Dr. Wigglesworth said that for almost nine years Tillotson's works had not been taken out of the library by any undergraduates, and Clarke's works not for two years; whereas writers reckoned evangelical were so often borrowed by undergraduates as scarcely ever to be in the library. Moreover upon the publication in Boston of the *Enquiry* of Emlyn, a minor English deist, the professor of divinity hopes it won't have much of a run among the students, but if so, he is ready to give the youth of the college the best preservative in his power against it.

Similar academic attempts to stem the tide of rationalism were made at Yale. In spite of them the freshening currents came stealing in. Rector Thomas Clap avowed that the great design of founding this school was to educate ministers in our own way; nevertheless he based his moral philosophy upon the deistic Wollaston's *Religion of Nature*. In his *Short Introduction to the Study of Ethics for the Use of Students* he taught that reason was insufficient as the basis of moral obligation, yet that God when he

209

makes a creature, communicates to him some degree of his own perfection. The sources of this cheerful outlook upon human nature are somewhat evasive. While a student at Harvard, Clap may have got it from reading the suspected Tillotson; or it may have come from the author's model, the *Ideal World* of Norris, who in turn acknowledged his indebtedness to Malebranche; or, finally, it may have been derived from a certain Cartesian optimist who managed to live in the reputed land of the blue laws. While Clap was president at Yale, a former tutor, Samuel Johnson, wrote as follows in his *Introduction to the Study of Philosophy*:

From the Natural World we evidently demonstrate the Being, Wisdom, Power and Goodness of God. From being perfectly Happy himself and Self-sufficient to his own Happiness, He could have no selfish Views, no other View in Creating and Governing the moral world than that it might be, in the whole, a happy system.

In the days of colonial conservatism Johnson was a marked example of the progressive. As an undergraduate at Yale, he was warned against reading Descartes, Locke, and Newton; becoming a tutor, he introduced these works into the college library. As a theological student he was cautioned against a certain new philosophy that was attracting attention in England, being told that it would corrupt the pure religion of the country and bring in another system of divinity.[1] The warning was ineffective, for Johnson as a clergyman took orders in the Church of England and embraced Berkeleism. The student who by the reading of Bacon had had opened to him a new world of thought was now on intimate terms with Berkeley, to whom Pope, the poet of deism, had attributed every virtue under heaven. Now the Irish idealist, while in Rhode Island, had composed what Principal

[1] Cf. *Proceedings of the American Antiquarian Society*, October, 1895. Professor E. C. Smyth claims that the warning was against Locke, but Locke was used as a text-book at Yale from 1717 to 1825. See President Noah Porter in the chapter on *Mental and Moral Science*, in *The History of Yale College*, New York, 1879.

Cairns has declared to be the only product of the deistic controversy born in the new world. *Alciphron* was the most thorough,
although not the only, work of the kind. In his advertisement the
author gave as his design the consideration of the free-thinker in
the various lights of atheist, libertine, enthusiast, scorner, critic,
metaphysician, fatalist, and sceptic. In its mere sub-title *Alciphron, or the Minute Philosopher* exposed the essential weakness
of deism, namely, the tendency to reduce every thing to littleness,
to microscopic evidences of design.

This work, which was reprinted as an apologetic seventy years
later in New Haven by the elder President Dwight, was called by
President Porter a criticism of the negative opinions of the times,
an attempt to arrest the tide of atheistic and anti-Christian opinion
then at its flood, a sketch of a Protean unbelief from the pothouse
ribaldry of Mandeville to the ambitious Platonism of Shaftesbury,
from the daring acuteness of Collins to the subtle insinuation of
Hume.[1] But it must be added that, at the same time that Berkeley
disposed of the crowd of English freethinkers, he did much to
stimulate colonial free-thought. It was he who indirectly nour-
ished the hopes of President Stiles that America might be a land
of British liberty in the most complete sense. How that influence
was exerted has not yet been precisely shown. It now appears
that the idealistic Johnson was the connecting link.

From being occasionally acquainted with Berkeley between 1729
and 1737, Johnson persuaded the Dean to believe that Yale College would soon become episcopal, and that it had received his
immaterial philosophy.[2] As a result of these representations,
Berkeley was induced to patronize this infant seminary by presenting it with some eight hundred and eighty volumes. This
formed the best collection of philosophic works then in the colonies. As a local rhymester expressed it, it was to Berkeley's liberal
hand that ' *Yalensia* owes the power of knowing more, than all
her *Sisters* on the western shore.' To his readers Johnson recom-

---

[1] Noah Porter, *Bishop George Berkeley*, p. 50, New York, 1885.
[2] *The Literary Diary of Ezra Stiles*, January 22, 1772, edited by F. B.
Dexter, New York, 1901.

mended many of these books, while Rector Clap issued a Catalogue of them.[1]

What use the latter made of the thirty-odd deistic books may not be known, as a large chest of the rector's manuscripts was among the plunder taken from New Haven in the Revolution. But another head of the college utilised these works. Ezra Stiles, in turn, student, tutor, and president, left an account telling how he was allured by the inviting circumstances of the college library, how he was led into the darkness of scepticism, and how he finally emerged from deism.[2] As an undergraduate he apprehended that his religious principles were settled, but about the year 1747, till which time he was full of the sentiments of Calvinism, he had great solicitude about being of the happy number elected to mercy. In his Birthday Memoir he continues:

In the year 1748 I had not indeed a disbelief, but I was in a state of scepticism, and ardently sought a clear belief of the being and attributes of God. Close attention to Dr. Clarke's demonstration, and above all, to the views of surrounding nature, at length pretty fully established me in this fundamental doctrine. . . . In 1750 a conversation with a young gentleman, of an amiable and virtuous character, first raised in me scruples and doubts respecting Revelation, which have cost me many a painful hour. But I most assiduously applied to the study of the evidences of revelation and by 1754 it appeared to be the best system, on the foot of natural religion.

To this view of his mind, Stiles added in 1768 a Review of those Authors, which he read during the rise, height and decline, of his scepticism. This may be given in detail as exhibiting both the persuasive influence of English thought and the mental independence of a young colonial. In 1747, the narrator continues:

I read with attention Doctor Clarke's Demonstration of the being and attributes of God; but did not find entire satisfaction. I proceeded through his evidences of Natural and Revealed Religion; but did not find his arguments conclusive for either. I

---

[1] Cf. Clap, *Catalogue of the Library of Yale College,* to which was appended Johnson's *Introduction to the Study of Philosophy, with a Catalogue of some of the most valuable Authors,* New London, 1743.

[2] Abel Holmes, *The Life of Ezra Stiles,* Boston, 1798.

did not perceive his reasonings so strong and conclusive as I had been accustomed to perceive those for the solar system, mathematics, and experimental philosophy. For many years I had been fed with demonstrations as to science. In 1748 I read Shaftesbury's Characteristics, and admired them as sublime views of Nature, and of the moral government of the Most High. I was particularly charmed with his rhapsody. At this time I had no thoughts of deism, and least of all that this was the deists' Bible, or their favourite author, though some passages, in the third volume, shocked me. At the same time I read and was so highly delighted with Pope's Essay on Man, that I committed to memory the first Epistle, and large paragraphs of the other Epistles; and repeated portions of it frequently by myself, in my chamber, and when I walked or rode abroad. I read also Castrell's and Whiston's Boyle's Lectures. Scott's preliminary discourses to the defence of Revelation seemed to give up too much of Revelation, and reduced it to Platonism, and a republication of natural religion. About 1751 I read Turnbull's Moral Philosophy. I was pleased with his scheme of treating moral, as Newton had treated natural, philosophy. I had previously to this read Butler's Analogy, which is a masterly production; but it served little more than to remove some rubbish, and to shew that there are no greater absurdities to be charged against revealed religion, than against some of the most acknowledged principles of natural religion; and so it still left me destitute of the positive evidence of Revelation. By all these authors I had advanced so far as to see, that Revelation was a most rational and sublime scheme, far exceeding natural religion. I only wanted to see that it was true, and positively of divine original. I had hitherto not seen Tindal, nor been conversant with any books, that directly attacked Revelation. In 1756, I read Tindal, Collins, and Bolingbroke.

As a result of ten years' reading, Stiles answered that he found himself able to obviate, to his own satisfaction, any and all objections, the most of which are very trifling. He gives evidence of this by scrutinising those sceptical lights which were just coming over the horizon of the western world. In a hitherto unpublished letter of 1759,[1] speaking of Lord Kames's Essays as curiosities in this country, he says:

[1] As given in a folio volume of the Stiles manuscripts, at Yale University, p. 436; this is the first draft of a letter to Mr. Bennett, of Edinburgh, September 14, 1759. Stiles adds: 'This letter not sent but an amended copy.'

I do not know what is his Lordship's opinion of Revelation—but am by no means certain but that a Man may entertain his Lordship's Speculations with respect to Liberty & Necessity and yet Confirm Believers of Revelation; I think I may add, that I am acquainted with such. I am in no doubt but there are more Christians & honest Revelationists of this opinion, than Deists. I am so far from thinking it a general principle of Deism, that I question if there are ten Deists in the World carry their idea of moral Necessity so high as his Lordship.

The Mr. Hume whom Dr. Leiland confutes directly opposes a supernatural Revelation—& strongly denies the Possibility of those Things which are the proper Evidences of Christianity: and I think treats the Subject with Caprice & Insolence: self-confident, nobly full of his own Discernment, he enjoys the supreme complacency of believing himself entrusted at last with the grand Secret imparted but to the happy few that the Basis or one main found^n of Christianity is an absolute Delusion. And truly it is a new Discovery that it is beyond the reach of Omnipotence to suspend, alter, or counteract the general Laws he himself has established in the Creation. . . . . Shall a King be able by a Seal and other infallible Signatures to evince his Proclamations to his Subjects so that they shall have no doubt of his Majesty's Will: and shall the Great Omnipotent King of the Universe be unable to evidence & ascertain his Will to such a Handful of Intelligences the small System of Man? . . . . So the Newtonian philosophy tho founded on Demonstration is yet disbelieved in many foreign Universities. A Man of less Science & less prepossession will rationally believe & receive, what sublimer Minds of great Learning in vain attempt to comprehend. There is a moral Jaundice, which some peculiar Refinements in Speculation always bring on that tinges all Objects. The Removing of this is the first Step to descerning the Truth. I think Dr. Leeland deserves highly of the Christian world. The Self sufficiency of the Deists will be a very great Obstacle to their seeing the Truth. Men of Sense ought to be treated with Candour & politeness—whatever be their Religion.

To this dissertation there were shortly added some remarks on two more of the deistic leaders, and, what is especially significant, a virtual confession of the influence of their optimism upon one brought up in the darkened chambers of Calvinism. Writing further to his Scotch correspondent, Stiles continues:

It is to be wished that Dr. Middleton, tho' a Sceptic if not an Unbeliever, had examined & discussed the Evidences of the Miracles of the first century in the same masterly manner he has done those of the second and third, methinks the Competition would burst forth irresistible Conviction. . . . . Lord Bolingbroke appears to be better acquainted with political, than theological Learning. He that perfectly understands the natures and connexions of the several Kingdoms and Polities in Europe, is very ignorant of the Administration of God. . . . . I doubt not the universe is very generally happy, an omnipotent & most benevolent Being had not else given it Birth. the Infelicity of this world would be in the universe' plan but as spots only scarcely perceptible spots in the Sun's bright orb.[1]

Having described the deistic movement in old England, Stiles as Anglus-Americanus turns to the movement in New England and gives a vivid account of the agitations of local thought during the French and Indian War:

As we are in the midst of the struggle of Infidelity I expect no great Reformation until that [Revelation] is demonstratively established. . . . . From the Conduct of the Officers of the Army you entertain an Expectation favorable to Virtue. Far from this I imagine the American Morals & Religion were never in so much danger as from our Concern with the Europeans in the present War. They put on indeed in their public Conduct the Mark of public Virtue—and the Officers endeavor to restrain the vices of the private Soldiery while on Duty. But I take it the Religion of the Army is Infidelity & Gratification of the appetites. . . . . They propagate in a genteel & insensible Manner the most corrupting and debauching Principles of Behavior. It is doubted by many Officers if in fact the Soul survives the Body—but if it does, they ridicule the notion of moral accountableness, Rewards & Punishments in another life. . . . . I look upon it that our Officers are in danger of being corrupted with vicious principles, & many of them I doubt not will in the End of the War come home minute philosophers initiated in the polite Mysteries & vitiated morals of Deism. And this will have an unhappy Effect on a sudden to spread Deism or at least Scepticism thro' these Colonies. And I make no doubt, instead of the Controversies of Orthodoxy & Heresy, we shall soon be called to the defence of the Gospel itself. At Home the general grand Dispute is on the Evidences

[1] Stiles MS., pp. 465-67.

of Revelation—some few of your small Folks indeed keep warming
up the old Pye, & crying Calvinism, Orthodoxy &c—these are
your Whitefields, Romaines, &c that make a pother: but the
greater Geniuses among the Ministers are ranging the Evidences
of Revelation to the public View, expunging the Augustine Interpretations of Scripture with the other corruptions of the Latin
Chh, yet retained among protestants—and endeavoring a just &
unexceptionable, rational Explication of the great Doctrines of
the Gospel.   The Bellamys &c of New England will stand no
Chance with the Corruptions of Deism which, I take it, are spreading apace in this Country.   I prophesy your *Two Witnesses* will
avail more towards curing the Contagion than thousands of Volumes filled with cant orthodox phrases & the unintelligible Metaphysics of Scholastic Divinity, which is a Corruption of Christianity
with *arabian* philosophy.[1]

The work here referred to is Jared Eliot's *Two Witnesses; or,
Religion Supported by Reason and Divine Revelation.*[2]   The Conclusion drawn by its author, that the overvaluing of reason tends
to promote atheism, was one not held by Stiles.   The story of the
latter's efforts to foster liberty of thought in Yale has been told
before, but not in its entirety.[3]   Mr. Henry Collins, a merchant
of Newport, R. I., had offered a dozen books,[4] to the college
library on the condition of their being deposited there for the free
use of the students.   He had, however, been informed that Rector
Clap would not suffer the volumes, because they contained heresy.
But when Stiles endeavoured to represent the college as an excellent and generous institution both for science and religion, the
books were forwarded, but only to be suppressed.   Hereupon,
Stiles wrote to the rigid rector what was not only a defence of a
promising college patron, but an appeal for unrestrained thought.[5]

---

[1] Stiles MS., pp. 469-71.   Letter from Newport, R. I., September 24,
1759.

[2] New London, 1736.

[3] L. Van Becelaere, *Philosophie en Amérique*, p. 55, quoting G. Stanley Hall.

[4] Mostly Baptist, viz., Sternwell's *Sermons*, 4 vols; *Answer to Rusen*,
Foster's *Sermons*, 4 vols.; *Answer to Tindal, Of Heresy*, etc., Cornthwaits'
Tracts.

[5] Stiles MS., p. 460; postscript of letter of August 6, 1759.

Mr. Collins remarkt strongly on the taking Dr. Clark's Sermons out of the Library: who told him of it I dont know. And I have heard those who are no friends to Clark say, they tho't it had not so generous an aspect in an Academy for Liberal Education. I have been hard put to it to defend it, for it is known to particular persons all over the Country. The Quakers & Baptists say they read any of our Books, but we prevent our Children reading theirs—and some have retorted and said it is the same principle as that on w^c the Romanists keep protestant Books from the ᵖple & from their Universities too. I believe the same reflexion would be made if Baxter's Works, or Calvin's Institutions, or Dr. Twiss, or Dr. Ridgely was to be taken & kept out of the Library. Different men indeed object from different motives, some from the Love of Orthodoxy & some from the Hatred of it, & some from the generous Sentiments of that generous & equal Liberty for which Protestants & Dissenters have made so noble a Stand. It is true with this Liberty Error may be introduced; but turn the Tables the propogation of Truth may be extinguished. Deism has got such Head in this Age of Licentious Liberty, that it would be in vain to try to stop it by hiding the Deistical Writings: and the only Way left to conquer & demolish it, is to come forth into the open Field & Dispute this matter on even Footing —the Evidences of Revelation in my opinion are nearly as demonstrative as Newton's Principia, & these are the Weapons to be used. Deism propogates itself in America very fast, & on this Found^n, strange as it may seem, is the Chh of Engld built up in polite Life. A man may be an excellent Chhman & yet a profound Deist. While public popular Delusion is kept up by Deistical Priests, sensible Laymen despise the whole, & yet, strange Contradiction! joyn it, and entice others to joyn it also.—and they say all priests are alike, we all try to deceive Mankind, there is no Trust to be put in us. *Truth* & this alone being *our* Aim in fact, open, frank & generous we shall avoid the very appearance of Evil.

The reason for the rejection of these New-Side books lay not so much in Clap's anti-deistic sentiments, and his scornful references to the light of nature[1] as in what was suggested in the last part of the foregoing passage. In the eyes of the Old Lights, Anglicanism meant tyranny. Having in mind the defection of Samuel Johnson, an alleged Arminian plot against the college was laid

[1] *History of Doctrines of New England*, New Haven, 1755.

bare. A supposititious Episcopalian had written a pseudonymous
' Letter from a Gentleman in the West,' which said that:

if once a Professor of Divinity, according to their Design is settled
in the College, good-bye to our Schemes. The Old Religion of
the Country, the Colonial Doctrines, as they are called, will be
establish'd in the House, there perpetually taught and rivetted in
the minds of the Pupils' and they will go out into the world
trammell'd with those trite doctrines of the Insufficiency of Human
Reason.[1]

Measures were now taken to stop the infiltration of that Arminianism so kindred to deism. By a vote of the president and
fellows, students were to be established in the principles of religion according to the Assembly's Catechism, Dr. Ames's *Medulla,* and *Cases of Conscience.* Yale was now outwardly a
stronghold of orthodoxy; how it came to be called a hotbed of
infidelity is a matter of later times. It was not until after the
Revolutionary War that the satirist could describe undergraduate
scepticism, could tell how the clockwork gentleman was made
'twixt the Tailor and the Player, and Hume, and Tristam and
' Voltaire.' All this might have been expected. Action and reaction were equal. As at Harvard opposition had brought electi-
cism, so at Yale the policy of suppression brought an explosion of
free-thinking upon the advent of the Franco-American deism of
Citizen Paine and President Jefferson.

Meanwhile it is in order to follow the fortunes of deism outside of New England, and to see how the other colonial colleges
of the first rank were laid open to the advances of rationalism.

[1] This letter was written by Noah Hobart of Fairfield.

CHAPTER IV

KING'S COLLEGE AND PRINCETON

WHEN Samuel Johnson became the head of King's College, New York, he found the new institution in a measure prepared for his advanced opinions. Another graduate of Yale had had a bit to do in the liberalising of the future Columbia University. William Livingstone, in his *Remarks upon Our Intended College*, wished to have the rules free to all, offensive to no sect. Fighting the efforts of the Episcopalians to obtain control of the institution, he was charged with deism and atheism.[1] He thereupon retorted upon his opponents with a travesty of the Thirty-Nine Articles, whose tenor may be judged from the following: ' I. I believe the Scriptures of the Old and New Testaments, without any foreign comments or human explications but my own: for which I should doubtless be honoured with Martyrdom, did I not live in a government which restrains that fiery zeal, which would reduce a man's body to ashes for the illumination of his soul. . . . XXXIX. I believe that this creed is more intelligible than that of St. Athanasius, and that there will be no necessity for any to write an exposition of the Thirty-Nine Articles of *my* faith.' [2] This rather inconsiderate example of rationalism was matched by Livingstone's article on *Primitive Christianity Short and Intelligible*, but elsewhere he shows himself a deist of a devouter kind, as when, in his *Philosophic Solitude*, he says:

> None but a Pow'r omnipotent and Wise
> Could frame this earth, or spread the boundless skies.
> He made the whole; at his omnific call
> From formless chaos rose this spacious ball,
> And one Almighty God is seen in all.[3]

[1] Tyler, *History of American Literature*, vol. 2, p. 221.
[2] *Independent Reflector*, No. 46.
[3] T. Sedgwick, *Memoir of William Livingstone*, p. 30, New York, 1833.

Livingstone's productions were of little weight, yet like straws they showed how the wind was blowing in the deistic direction. Of more significance was an article of Johnson's own, published in New York, some years before his presidency, as a defence of natural religion. Taking as his motto *Jovis omnia plena,* and as his purpose to excite our homage and adoration towards the Great Author of all things, the writer proceeds as follows:

Unaccountable, I say, it is, That Rational Creatures should have their Eyes open upon this vast & Stupendous Fabric of Heaven & Earth, & (I don't say, not be convinced of the Being, for that seems utterly impossible, but) not be struck with the strongest Impressions asserting, admiring, & adoring Apprehensions of the DEITY.

Say, (as it is sometimes said in this case) that the frequency & perpetual presence of these Objects to our Minds, is the Occasion of our being no more strongly affected by them; that hence it is, (to use this Authors Instance) that we do not so much admire the Sun, which we see every day, as a Comet, which is rarely seen once in a great many years; and that we do not so clearly discern, & are not affected with so strong a sense of the power & presence of GOD, in the constant and regular course of Nature, as we should in extraordinary & miraculous Interposition: However this shews our Great unattentiveness & want of reflexion; for if we do but a little consider & reflect, our Reason would soon convince us, That GOD does as really & as powerfully exert & Discover Himself in One as in the Other.

If indeed these Appearances were not so very many so noble August & magnificent, it were not so much to be wondered at, that we are so stupid, & so little affected by them; But when every thing that occurs to both our senses & Thoughts, every thing that we see, hear, tast, smell, or feel, either from without or within, exhibits the clearest & most obvious, the strongest & most affecting Indications of Wisdom unsearchable of Power ineffable, & of Goodness immense, how can it be that the Minds of men are not continually fixed with the deepest Admiration & Reverence, & inflamed with the highest Love & Devotion, towards that Mighty Being, who is perpetually presenting Himself to their view, in such great & noble productions on every hand of them, by whom they are environed on every Side, & in whom they Live move & have their Being.

Now therefore to affect one [our] Minds the more strongly with a Sense of these things, let us in the first place suppose a poor peasant, who had never seen anything greater or finer than a little mean Thatcht House or hut under Ground should at once be translated out of his despicable Cottage, into one of the Statliest Palaces in Europe, & there shewn, in such a magnificent Building, the exquisite Architecture, the fine Statuary, the Beautiful painting, the surprising clockwork, the curious waterworks, & delightful Gardening, & other the like noble productions of Art with what an Extacy of Ravishment would he be surprized amazed & astonished!

In like manner, in the Case before us. Let us imagine a Man shut up in the dark from his Youth, till he comes to Ripeness of Understanding; or let us suppose him in a State of perfect Manhood, first to enter into Being, (like Adam in Milton) & then on a Day when the Face of the World appears in the Height of its verdure & Beauty, to have all Nature in a moment open upon him, with all its Glory; What a mighty, beautiful scene, full of a boundless variety, in the midst of a most agreeable & pleasing Uniformity, at once entertains his ravisht Eye & astonish't Mind? . . . . Let us now make this our own Case, & awake out of our Insensibility, as tho' we had but this Moment first stept into Being, & imagine ourselves to begin the World anew, taking our first Prospect of this noble & beautiful Landskip of universal Nature with all her Grandure, & every one of us methinks must thus reason with himself. ' I am encompassed here, with a vast number & variety of Curious & Stately Objects, a Spacious Earth, an Ample Sea, & Immense Heavens, & all these garnished with a boundless plenty of gaudy Furniture; among all which I observe Unity of Design, Exactness of Order, beautiful Harmony, proportion & fitness of one thing to another, which certainly must be the Effect of mighty power & wonderful Art & Contrivance;— which necessarily infer the Universal Presence of a widely-Designing & All-powerful MIND.'

For in the next place, to be a little particular; if we essay to examine the Make & Fixture of any of the Bodies about us, tho' we are presently lost in impenetrable Mysteries, yet the further we extend our search, the more we discern of the presence & Agency of this Almighty Mind: If we take a Body & break, or file, or in anyway dissolve it, we find it consists of a Combination of numberless extremely fine & minute particles which strongly cleave together,: But how? Not by any force of their own. If we take up a Stone, & let it go, it immediately falls to the Ground again: But why downwards rather than upwards? It has no principle of Activity in it or Counsel to direct itself: Some Invisible Cause, there must therefore be, of this Strong Tendency of the parts of

Bodies one to another, and the Bodies themselves to the Earth visibly exerting itself in these Effects.

This Cause does not act mechanically, for all the Laws of mechanism suppose it: It does not act on nor according to the Surface of Bodies, but penetrates their Demensions, & every where equally pervades all things: These Effects, therefore, being unmechanical, the Cause of them must be Immaterial; & there evidently appearing in them all a plain Design & Tendency towards some Aim & End, the Cause of them must always act by Counsel. Whenever therefore we see these & the like Effects, even all the productions of Nature, we may be as evidently Certain of the Presence & Agency of a most Wise & powerful Spiritual Being, as we can of the presence of a Man, when we hear him Speak, & see him Walk.

If we survey the curious Structure & Contrivance of the Bodies of plants & Animals, & especially of this wonderful machine which we carry about us, how can we fail of being smitten with Astonishment at the power & Art by which they were so Fearfully & wonderfully made? For in all these productions, it is evident that the matter whereof they are made is meerly inert & passive, & has not the least Glympse of any power to move it self. There must therefore be present an Almighty Being who has the power of Beginning Motion & in every Instance not only First sets, but likewise Still keeps the wheels of Nature agoing.

It is no less evident that Matter is, in Fact, wrought into a various multitude of most wisely contrived systems; but if it could not move itself, much less, could it contrive & direct itself into such a variety of wonderful structures: There must therefore be everywhere present a Superintending designing MIND, an Alwise Contriver, as well as an Almighty Mover, who is the Author of all that Stupendous variety, that exquisite Harmony, that exact & beautiful proportion & Fitness of one thing to another, which so clearly shine forth among the vast numbers of all Sorts of Beings that are round about us.

If we now pass off from this our Globe of Earth, & take a survey of the boundless & unmeasurable Heavens, what an innumerable multitude of Stars are there, which doubtless are so many suns to their several systems! Our Sun a prodigious & amazing Globe of Fire, 900,000 times as big as this Globe of Earth, is attended with a noble Chorus of planets, each one of which, (like this our Earth, which is one of them) is unquestionably furnished with Rational Inhabitants, by the Great Author of All, to admire his Works, enjoy his Beneficence & adore his Majesty: Now what a Mighty Idea does this system of the Universe give us of the DEITY.

For, (as I argued before) These prodigious bulky Globes, (Some of which, are above an 100 times as big as our Earth) are utterly inert, & could never have moved themselves, they must therefore have been at first put into Motion by the Almighty Mover, exerting a prodigious Force, & the *vis centripeta,* or Tendency of these great Bodies to the Sun, by which (universally proportioned to the Quantity of their Matter, & the Squares of their distances from Him,) they are continually drawn from their Rectilinear projectile Motion, & retained in their Orbits, going their perpetual Bounds, can be ascribed to no Mechanical Cause, & therefore must be ascribed to the immediate Agency of an Almighty Mind, powerfully pervading the Universe, & continually exerting it self in the Government & Regulation of every System; And the wonderfully wise adjustment of these two motions, & the precise Situation of every Globe, so as to render it a proper Mansion for Inhabitants fitted to it, demonstrate that Almighty Cause to be Infinitely wise & Good.

And besides, since it is evident that the same Boundless Wisdom Power & Goodness are everywhere alike exerted & displayed in every System of the Stupendous Universe, throughout all these Immense Spaces; & Since nothing can act where it is not, we have hence an incontestible Evidence of the Universal Presence, & Surpassing inconceivable Greatness of that Glorious Being, who must of necessity be the Only One, Universal Cause of all these astonishing phenomena.

If now, lastly, we return home & look into our own Minds, these wonderful Thinking Beings which we feel within us, in which we are conscious of the noble powers of Perception, Apprehending, Judging, Reasoning, Knowing & Remembering, of Liberty, Willing, Chusing, refusing, Loving, Hating & Acting &c; we may from them discover, & even feel the Being, Perfections & Presence of the Divine Nature: For since we & all other Rational Beings, are conscious that the Exertion of these powers in us had a Beginning; Since nothing can begin to be & act without a cause; & since no Cause can give what it has not, or produce an Effect more noble than it Self; It is hence evident, both that these powers had a Cause, & likewise that the Author of our Beings & all our powers, must Himself be possessed of them in the Greatest Perfection & independent of any other, & consequently must be a Being of Infinite Perfection. (And since the Objects of these Powers of ours, the Ideas in our Minds, can be Resemblances of nothing but of Ideas existing in Some other Mind; & Since there is nothing but some Active Being that can produce these ideas in us; we are hence most certain to the Constant presence & Agency of an Almighty & All-Comprehending Mind, who possesses the

Originals of our Ideas in the highest perfection, & continually exhibits to our minds all those Ideas or Resemblances of them, which are the Objects on which our powers are perpetually exerted & employed.)[1]

And as to the Nature of these Souls of ours, we may determine, That seeing Matter consists of multitudes of particles divisible, nay, actually divided, each of which is a distinct & Separate Substance, & that it is capable of nothing but Figure & motion, & what results therefrom; & Seeing these Noble powers have no connexion with, & cannot be derived from matter, howsoever figured, moved or modified; It therefore follows that our Souls, are of intirely another Sort of Substance, *toto Coelo,* different from Matter: And seeing they are Immaterial, they must be indiscogitable [?] & consequently Immortal.

O Happy Day! when we shall be delivered from these Gross, sickly & unweildy Bodies, when we shall get a Liberty from these Prisons of Flesh & Blood, & be furnished with perpure, fine, & Æthereal Bodies, & with perfect, clear & exquisite senses & Understandings, & when without lett or hindrance, with the utmost freedom, vigor & agility, we shall in Company with other pure, philosophical & Devout Spirits, be under Advantage, at pleasure, to waft our Selves any where thro' the vast Fields of Æther, & more nearly survey the Mighty Systems of the Works of God: When we shall have nothing to interrupt our Contemplation of those Multitudes of most agreeable & Delightful Objects, from which His Immense Wisdom, Power & Goodness, will perpetually shine in, with the brightest Lustre, upon our ravish't Minds; strongly inducing & engaging us to the Reasonable Service, of Acknowledging, Loving, & adoring that Almighty, Alwise & Beneficent Author of all Things, in the Knowledge of, Union with, & conformity to whom, consists our highest perfection & Happiness.[2]

Johnson's New York letter appears more sentimental than systematic, more in the nature of a rhapsody than a philosophy; never-

---

[1] Note. That what is between those brackets is Dr. Berkeley's notion, but was not printed. [Addendum by Johnson, who wrote this passage February 25, 1728-9; Berkeley, it may here be noted, arrived in Newport January 23, 1728-9.]

[2] From Johnson's original MS. in Columbia University entitled 'The Copy of a Letter I sent to Mr. Bradford, printer, at New York, and which was published in the New York Gazette on Monday, March 17, 1728-9.'

theless, it has the merit of presenting colonial deism from three several points of view, together with their sources and their tendencies. Thus, in its astronomical references, it reproduces Newtonism, for the great Sir Isaac had presented his works to the college where Johnson had been a student; again, in its idealistic arguments, it is the earliest presentation of Berkeleism in America, for the Bishop of Cloyne had been in the country now less than five weeks; finally, in its critical remarks on materialism, it anticipates the author's controversy with Lieutenant-Governor Cadwallader Colden, for it was this speculative patron of King's College who, stimulated by both Newton and Berkeley, drifted from the current dualism into the inevitable monism of an attempted synthesis between the two.[1]

But without considering these later developments in New York, another Anglican, who exerted an influence upon the college, was William Smith (1727-1803). A graduate of the University of Aberdeen, coming to America in 1751, he wrote, one year before the installation of Johnson, a pamphlet entitled *A General Idea of the College of Mirania*. In this anonymous production there is given an imaginary scheme for the education of young men much after the fashion of More's *Utopia*. Its Raphael Hythlodaye is an impossible pedagogue, who dresses like a divine and talks like a deist. Here are some of his projects, given with an assumed air of retrospection. Speaking of the method of the Miranians of inculcating good morals or natural religion from the study of Homer, he says:

How strongly woul'd the good Man take occasion from the Sentiments even of this Heathen-Author, to inculcate the Belief of *One Supreme* GOD, *Father and Disposer of all Things*. . . In the next class what fresh Opportunities did he find of leading us from Wonder to Wonder and bringing the *Deity* before our Eyes in the Study of his Stupendous Works . . . in the Study of Astronomy how woul'd we stand astonish'd at our own Littleness, and the Grandeur of that GOD whose Hand fram'd all those clusters of Systems; kindled all their Suns; and feeds their immense Fires from Age to Age . . . from that single branch of Physics called Micrography we were forc'd to acknowledge the Almighty Author still greater, if possible, in the smallest

[1] Compare below, Book IV., Chapter II.

than the greatest. 'Tis impossible to express what a Fund of Piety and Natural Religion may be laid in, by a few Words dropt on these occasions. . . . In the Study of Agriculture he cou'd not explore the mineral Kingdom without shewing us the same Agreement and Fitness in the Disposition of Things. . . . There is only one thing wanting to improve and perfect the whole; and that is the Study of *reveal'd Religion,* by which a Society of fall'n *Adam's* Race may be restor'd and correspond for ever with the *general Harmony.*[1]

William Smith's *Sketch of the Method of Teaching Science and Natural Religion* reads like Fielding's imaginary conversation between Square and Thwackum on the eternal fitness of things. But the scheme of *Mirania* turned out to be no mere educational romance. The pamphlet being read by Benjamin Franklin,[2] its author was invited to become the first provost of what became eventually the University of Pennsylvania, for the New Yorker's ' plan of education calculated for an infant country ' was exactly what the flattering Philadelphian was seeking for in his ' perfect institution, suitable to the state of an infant country.'

Before passing from the college in New York to that in Philadelphia, a word must be said of the institution lying half way between. More properly the representative of the later Scottish realism,[3] the College of New Jersey was nevertheless drawn into the earlier deistic controversy. Started in opposition to its Anglican neighbours, Princeton was the headquarters of the Presbyterians. Now the latter, in their first trial for unsoundness of belief, charged one Samuel Hemphill, a certain ecclesiastical Irish agitator, with plagiarising from the sermons of Dr. James Foster. They did not appear to object so much to the fact of Hemphill's stealing, as to the facts which he stole, for they added that he was in the deistic drift, because of his declaration that Christianity was nothing else but a revival or new edition of the laws of nature. At this point, curiously enough, Franklin came in and lent

[1] Mirania, p. 46.
[2] *Works,* vol. 2, pp. 288, 290 (Bigelow ed.).
[3] See below, Book V., Chapter II., The Princeton School.

Hemphill his pen. In two or three pamphlets and in an article in the *Gazette* of April, 1735, he ironically defended the culprit by intimating that the borrowed views were probably better than the preacher's own.[1] However slight was the value of these controversial scribblings, it was to them that Jonathan Dickinson, the first president of Nassau Hall, made forcible rejoinder, and thereby implied that, in opposition to the new upstart doctrines and schemes, he personally was firmly attached to the good old principles. And yet, the College of New Jersey was not of necessity under these obligations; it declined the aid and oversight of the synod which framed them; it declared in the advertisement of its charter that those of every religious profession had equal privileges and advantages of education; it at last made its lay equal to its clerical incorporators. On paper, the institution was saved from excessive ecclesiasticism; in practice, it showed itself from the first a defender of one particular faith. Its pioneer presidents joined the Presbyterian church and disclosed themselves as enemies of innovation; their successors continued a similar policy. President Aaron Burr, a graduate of Yale in 1735, attacked the hidden Unitarianism of Emlyn's *Enquiry*.[2] President John Witherspoon, an imported descendant of John Knox, drove out an incipent idealism. He ridiculed Berkeleism, which had gained a foothold in the college, and lectured against the deistic trio, Clarke, Collins, and Wollaston. A representative of the Scotch school of common sense, he cautiously defined the light of nature as ' what we can do or discover by our own powers without revelation or tradition.'

Of the heads of the College of Nassau Hall the first is the most interesting in the deistic connection. Jonathan Dickinson, another graduate of Yale, borrowing his title from Locke, wrote a short and incisive criticism of natural religion. In his *Reasonableness of Christianity*,[3] he first presents what his Boston editor calls ' the grand peculiars of the Christian revelation '; he then proceeds

---

[1] *Writings,* (Smyth ed.), Vol. 1, p. 346.

[2] W. B. Sprague, *Annals of the American Pulpit,* Vol. 3, p. 71, New York, 1858.

[3] Pp. 19, 42, 61, Newark, N. J., 1732.

to a logical demonstration of the being and attributes of God, and finally throws the burden of proof on the doubters. These specimens will give his method:

It is manifest to every observation, that the *Maker, Guide* and *Gouvernour* of the Universe, must be always *present* in every part of this incomprehensible space; (He could not else have made, nor could He otherwise superintend, order, and direct all the parts, operations, and influences of this stately *fabrick*) which is impossible to conceive of any but an *infinite Being*. . . . . Here let the Deist try his skill: Let him without the assistance of revelation, draw up a perfect system of the laws of nature. The *Light of Nature* enjoins the belief of *one* God alone, but which of our modern *pagans,* our *Oracles of Wit* has ever pretended to propose a method of our obtaining *inward peace* and purity, *happiness* here, and *salvation* hereafter?

CHAPTER V

PHILADELPHIA AND FRANKLIN

TRANSFERRED to the College of Philadelphia, William Smith carried with him those views of moderate deism which he had promulgated in New York. In his preface to Samuel Johnson's *Elements of Philosophy*,[1] he interprets the author as teaching that revelation never says one thing and reason another; nor does the religion of nature ever contradict the religion of Christ. Far from this, he thinks that the deeper the sound philosopher pushes his inquiries, the greater reason he will still find to account the Holy Scriptures the only system of philosophy that rationally vindicates the ways of eternal Providence to man and renders the Deity amiable to his creatures. But who and what is this Deity? Many years later, at the very time he became the provost of the new University, the Miranian philosopher answered as follows:

. . . . Yet, there are many who conceive this being to be so absorbed in his own greatness, as to be inattentive to man, a creature endued with reason. They in fact tell us (my readers, I hope, will pardon the comparison) that, after having originally wound up the grand clock of nature, he has resigned it to accident. Having established general law, the deity, they suppose, is, and has been, at least with respect to human affairs, entirely inactive; as if he, who performs all by his will, were incapable of effecting even what may appear to be most trifling.

Those who deny the immediate, the unremitting interposition of providence, are usually denominated *deists*. They have given to the world some arguments, (at least they presume to call them arguments) on which, I shall not at present particularly animadvert. Although our corporeal eyes cannot view the deity, yet our reason discovers him throughout that part of the universe, which we are capable of observing. The revolutions of our globe; the revolutions of the other planets; the successions of the seasons;

---

[1] Pp. iii-xv, London, 1754.

and all animated nature, however diversified, announce a creator, and proclaim a God. Can it be supposed, that he, who is all-powerful, all-wise, and all-merciful, does not preserve, according to those rules which he has prescribed to himself, all that he has created, or endued with life? He certainly does. Thus to conceive an inactive deity, whose will must be action, is the greatest evil incident to the human mind, one alone excepted, which is *atheism*.[1]

That William Smith never became a deist of the extreme type is to be laid, in part, to the influence of his academic sponsor. Franklin has generally been conceived as of all colonials the least averse to free thought, for the university which his hand shaped was noteworthy for requiring no religious test of its instructors, and for being so unprejudiced as to bestow an honourary degree upon the notorious Thomas Paine. A self-made deist, a friend of free-thinkers, Franklin was yet, in one sense, opposed to free thought. As Johnson said of him, his educational scheme was that of a tradesman; [2] as his *Autobiography* discloses, he had a distaste to speculation which led nowhere. In a word, he was by nature not an Aristotelian, who valued thinking for its own sake, but a true Socratic in his desire for practical results. Of a like type, and in hearty accord with these utilitarian views was William Smith. This was manifest in his educational suggestions for the new academy.[3] Here not only did he emphasise the acquisition of solid wisdom, in the Socratic way, but actually conceived it very practicable by some plain definitions, to give the young *mechanic* right apprehensions concerning the nature of the Deity and the creature, and concerning the relation between *finite* and *infinite*.[4] For these reasons, then, and in three several respects, Johnson's treatise deserves the highest encomium, for his Metaphysics are not fine-spun notions, visionary and unimportant to

[1] *An Essay on Irreligion, Columbian Magazine*, July, 1791.
[2] Franklin, *Writings*, Vol. 3, p. 29, note (Smyth ed.).
[3] H. W. Smith, *Life and Correspondence of the Reverend William Smith*, Philadelphia, 1879, Vol. 1, p. 344. Compare Montgomery, *History of the University of Pennsylvania*, p. 240.
[4] *Elements*, p. 5.

mankind, but calculated to shew us what *we are* and *with what powers endued*; his Logic is not idle sophistry and unmeaning jargon, but teaches the right application and conduct of those powers in searching after truth, which is their proper object, that so the mind may be filled with substantial knowledge, and not puffed up with airy speculations; his Ethics are on the same useful plan with his Metaphysics and Logic. Those who have not time for tedious researches, 'tis hoped will find in them a short system of truths and duties arising necessarily from the relations in which we obviously stand. That they will be rationally instructed in what they owe to God, themselves, their country and mankind; and thence be convinced that the *injunctions of right reason* and the *precepts of Christianity* are invariably the same.[1]

Not to educate the recluse scholar, but the commonalty, who are the active part and support and strength of the commonwealth, was Provost Smith's ideal for the College of Philadelphia. With such an ideal he might approve the body of Johnson's book, yet at the same time, disapprove its final issues. Our author, he continues, from a sincere zeal to vindicate the rights of the Deity, and a just abhorrence of the absurd system of the materialists, has gone farther towards the opposite extreme than will be justified by some philosophers.[2] The extreme here referred to was, of course, Berkeleism, against which the Philadelphian argues in substance as follows: The Dean, while at Newport, might have been justified in putting into his *Minute Philosopher* rural descriptions exactly copied from those charming landskips that presented themselves to his eye in the delightful island at the time he was writing; that was all very well; but for the Dean's disciple to attempt to introduce into the schools and infant seminaries in America the unadulterated Irish idealism was another thing. Doctor Johnson, explains his critic, only pretends to teach Logic and Moral Philosophy, . . . his Logic and his Morality are very different from ours. There is no Matter by his Scheme; no Ground of Moral Obligation. Life is a Dream. All is from the immediate impressions of the Deity. Metaphysical Distinctions which no Men, & surely no Boys, can understand, I fear

[1] Preface to *Elements*.   [2] *Ib.*

much will come in the Place of fixing virtue on her true Bottom.[1]

For this personal attack the head of the Philadelphia Academy may be excused on the ground that the rival institution in New York was drawing off some of his pupils; but for his patronising attitude toward idealism in general, Smith had his own ingrained conservatism to blame. This is evident when he says that, lest students should spurn his teachings, he sought to avoid, on the one hand, a gloomy temper and starch behaviour, and, on the other, the small tincture of philosophy which makes free-thinkers. In accordance with this policy, in the year 1756, the provost recommended certain books to be read by candidates for the baccalaureate. In addition to Locke and Bacon, there were works whose long-winded titles suggest the very ideas and phrases found in the *Mirania*. As here given there was the *Spectacle de la Nature, or a Course of Natural and experimental Philosophy calculated for the Instruction of Youth, to create in their Minds an exalted Idea of the Wisdom of the Great Creator*. There was also *Religious Philosopher: or, The Right use of contemplating the Works of the Creator: (1) In the wonderful structure of Animal Bodies, and in particular Man. (2) In the no less wonderful structure and wise Formation of the Elements, and their various effects upon animal, and vegetable Bodies; and, (3) In the most amazing structure of the Heavens, with all its Furniture. Designed for the Conviction of Atheists and Infidels*. Besides these misconstrued and misconstructed volumes from the French and Dutch, there were offered the *Ecclesiastical Polity* of the Elizabethan Hooker, who treats of the law of nature as the stay of the whole world; the *Metaphysics* of the Scotch Hutcheson, who speaks of the capacity of the mind for the idea called Harmony; and lastly the *Ontology*, and *Essays* of the hymn writer Watts, the last being plainly in the nature of mental soporifics, agreeable to the Miranian principle that the professor of philosophy should take care to guard the youth against everything in which the authors might stand singular.[2]

[1] Letter to Rev. Richard Peters, July 18, 1754, from the original in the Pennsylvania Historical Society.

[2] *Discourses*, p. 225; *Mirania*, p. 46.

Concerning these suggestions one of the Pennsylvanians avowed that their first head drew up the most comprehensive scheme of education in any college in the American colonies.[1] That may have been true in a general way, it was not so in a philosophical. In his view of the philosophy schools, Smith gives a list of books which has the triple defect of being only intended for reading in private hours; of omitting idealistic authorities like Cudworth and Berkeley, such as were given in Johnson's Catalogue of 1743; and of defining philosophy and the encyclopædia of the subject, in a manner far less comprehensive than that of the president of King's College.   Here is Smith's dry and juiceless scheme:

This is what we call Philosophy in general; comprehending in it the knowledge of all things Human and Divine, so far as they can be made the objects of our present enquiries.   Now, the genuine branches of this Philosophy, or great system of practical Wisdom, together with the necessary instrumental parts thereof, may be included under the following general heads, it appearing to me that the nature of things admits of no more.   (1) Languages &c, which have been already mentioned rather as an Instrument or Means of Science, than a Branch thereof.   (2) Logic and Metaphysics, or the Science of the Human mind; unfolding its powers and directing its operations and reasonings.   (3) Natural Philosophy, Mathematics, and the rest of her beautiful train of subservient arts; investigating the Physical properties of Body, explaining the various phenomena of Nature; and teaching us to render her subservient to the ease and ornament of Life.   (4) Moral Philosophy, applying all the above to the business and bosoms of men, deducing the laws of our conduct from our situation in life and connexions with the Beings around us, settling the whole Economy of the Will and Affections, establishing the predominancy of Reason and Conscience, and guiding us to Happiness, through the practice of Virtue.[2]

Of the branches of learning enumerated by Provost Smith, the second and third were most assiduously cultivated at the hands of his successors, logic being exemplified in the compends of Samuel Magaw and John Andrews, natural philosophy in the

[1] J. C. Stillé, *Memoir*, Philadelphia, 1869, p. 56.   Compare Charles F. Thwing, *A History of Higher Education in America*, New York, 1906. p. 114.

[2] *Discourses*, Part II., pp. 157-158.

lectures of John Ewing. It was the latter who, on a visit to England before the Revolution, disarmed the great Samuel Johnson by the retort courteous: After liberally applying the terms 'rebels' and 'scoundrels' to the people of America, Johnson turned rudely to Dr. Ewing, demanding, 'What do you know in America? You never read; you have no books there.' 'Pardon me, Sir,' said Dr. Ewing, 'we have read the *Rambler*.'[1] If Ewing's remarks were relished by his contemporaries, his lectures were not. As they have been handed down, they present but an unappetising mixture of natural philosophy and natural religion: Here is an excerpt:

By the phenomena of nature, we mean all the situations, motions, and appearances of natural bodies, which are evident to the senses, and not immediately dependent upon the voluntary agency of an intelligent being; by which we do not exclude those appearances, which are found in animal bodies, so far as they do not depend upon the volition of the animal, but arise by the instrumentality of second causes. All these situations and motions are produced by certain fixed and determinate rules, which are denominated the laws of nature; as they are the invariable appointment of the First Cause of all things, whereby he determined that certain natural causes should always, in the same circumstances, invariably produce the same effects. And in the production of the effect, they constantly observe this fundamental rule: that the effect shall be always proportionate to the whole power and efficiency of the cause. Thus the same quantity of fire always burns, by a natural necessity, with the same degree of intensity; and gravitation always causes a heavy body to descend from a given height with the same invariable force. In this consists the difference between a natural and an intelligent cause: as the latter may produce its effects, very much disproportioned to the whole of its power.[2]

From the speculative point of view, Ewing's lectures presented little but dessicated deism; equally dry fodder was furnished by his successors in a series of compends on logic for the use of the University of Pennsylvania. According to a recently recovered manuscript, Samuel Magaw thus introduced his lectures of 1788:

[1] S. D. Alexander, *Princeton College*, p. 28.
[2] *Lectures on Natural Philosophy*, Philadelphia, 1809.

PHILOSOPHY is the study of truth and wisdom. It hath been defined, The " Science of all things possible, together with the manner and reason of their possibility." This definition respects, and supposes that kind of investigation, in the field of knowledge which natural reason itself is competent to; establishing the several steps of the mind's progress on principles undeniably certain. In order to be successful in Philosophical enquiries, the first step we are to take is, to consider the nature of the Human Understanding—its powers and the manner of its procedure in the search after and communication of truth. The branch which teaches this, is Logick, which Mr. Watts has defined ' The art of using reason well in our inquiries after truth, and the communication of it to others.' LOGICK is partly theoretical, and partly practical. The former contains a view of the intellectual powers, from their earliest exercise and simplest perceptions, through all their combinations and deductions, together with the rules by which the process is conducted. The latter directs to a proper application of those rules. LOGICK may be distinguished into the natural and artificial. We need insist upon this no farther, than just to remark, that one differs not essentially from the other; the latter being only a more distinct and full explanation of what common sense and nature originally suggest. All our knowledge consists in representing objects to the mind, and in judging concerning them. We judge in two ways: First in comparing objects together we discern at once their agreement or disagreement, we appropriate immediately to anything whatever we clearly discern to be contained in it; we separate as immediately whatever we perceive to disagree—in the next place infer one judgment from another. The first is called intuitive judgment, the latter discursive. As the understanding then advances from one step to another, it puts forth various acts, or expresses itself by different operations: perceiving, judging, reasoning: and lastly arranging the discoveries and materials of knowledge which it is in possession of. So that Logick hath usually been laid out in four parts, corresponding to these operations respectively, and explaining them viz. Simple Perception, Judgment (or rather Intuition,)´ Reasoning and Method. We shall sketch these parts pursuing their natural order.

Simple Perception is barely the attention of the Understanding to the objects impressing it. Hereby it is furnished with distinct notices of things and all those first characters, or, as it were, elements of knowledge, which it is enabled to make such a wonderful use of. Just in the instant that any object is acting upon the mind, through one or another of the organs of sense, 'tis observable, that the perception is more forcible and lively. When the object is removed, the perception may be recalled or reflected on; but it is much weaker than before differing both in kind and degree; thus the perception when we are beholding a man, a tree, a river, while we are hearing musick; feeling the heat of fire, smelling a rose, tasting an apple—is very different from the perception, or impression barely recollected. This recollected Perception therefore or renewed representation in the mind, is called an Idea. Before we proceed to view ideas with regard to their nature, and division, which Ideas are all the result of perception; it may be well enough by the way to mention the general objects of Perception. The object of Perception in its simplest operations is Being and in some respects Not Being. Being is whatever actually exists, the word substance seems to include all the kinds of Being, that come within the reach of our comprehension at present, and these are divided into *material* and *Spiritual* (or to vary the expression) into *Solid* and thinking Substances.[1]

Of the same empirical stripe with Magaw was Provost John Andrews. Assuming that the mind can avail itself of no other materials than those which are furnished by sensation and consciousness, and that the utmost bounds of human knowledge cannot exceed the limits of our simple ideas and their various combinations, he nevertheless holds that the mind, by its power of combining these materials, finds itself in possession of an inexhaustible treasure, sufficient to employ it to the full extent of its powers.[2] What the undergraduate thought of this kind of teaching may be a side issue, but it is one so unexpectedly lighted up by a bright flash of wit as momentarily to compel the attention. Francis Hopkinson, the first pupil to enter the Academy, thus gave vent to his feelings in some orations which purported to be written for, and at the request of, young gentlemen of the University, and delivered by them at public commencements in the College Hall:

As to *metaphysics,* it is a visionary system, wherein uncertain

[1] Magaw's *Compend of Logick,* from notes taken by Caesar A. Rodney, February 1-July, 1788; property of Watson Beatty Lenderman, Wilmington, Del.

[2] *Compend of Logic, for the Use of the University of Pennsylvania,* pp. 15, 18, Philadelphia, 1801.

conclusions are drawn from uncertain premises, and in which the very terms used have no determinate meaning. The whole is an ingenious fabric built in air; having no real, known foundation, whereon to rest: not unlike the Pagan creed, that the world stands upon the horns of a bull, the bull on the back of an elephant, the elephant on a great tortoise; and the great tortoise upon nothing.

It must be owned, however, that we are indebted to metaphysics for some very curious and entertaining riddles: such as—that *infinite* carried beyond *infinity* becomes *finite*—that one *infinity* may be twice as long as another *infinity*—that *soul* is not *matter,* and that *matter* is not *soul;* and in short, that it is no matter whether there be any soul or not—Oh! the heights and the depths of learning.

But of all the systems of complicated nonsense, that ever puzzled the busy brains of mortal man, *logic* is surely the most insignificant. An art which no ingenuity can apply to any one useful purpose of life. Imagine to yourselves, gentle hearers, a society of *logicians,* whose conversation in the common occurrences of life should be conducted in *syllogistic* mode and form. The learned housekeeper goes to market, and endeavours to persuade the butcher to lower the price of his mutton in *celarent;* the butcher enforces his demand in *barbara.* The logical lover also attacks his dulcinea in form. He assures her, in *particular affirmatives,* that he is enamoured of her charms; and from these premises, draws an artful conclusion, that she ought to encourage his passion, and return his love. The lady replies, in *universal negatives.* The gallant then plays off his whole battery in a compacted *sorites.* The lady answers only in the *simple form*—a weakness is discovered in her *middle* term—she is reduced to a *dilemma,* and surrenders at discretion.[1]

This diatribe of the Pennsylvania satirist might be called Attic salt in a Bœotian province, were it not for the fact that the learning against which it was directed was actually a stimulus to further philosophical developments. For example, Magaw's remarks on simple perception prepared the way for Beasley's notable defence of Locke on the question of representative perception;[2] and Andrew's remarks on man's power to multiply his conceptions was of like service in regard to Rush, on the pleasures of the mind. It was in this last named lecture, delivered in the

[1] Hopkinson, *Miscellaneous Essays,* pp. 8-10, Philadelphia, 1792.
[2] See below, Book V., Chapter VI.

medical school of the university, that Rush essayed to revive the older deism from the naturalistic side: Is it probable, he asks, that a wise and good Being, whose means and ends are so exactly suited to each other in such parts of his works as we are able to comprehend, will finally waste or throw away the costly and beautiful apparatus he has given us for the enjoyment of corporeal and mental pleasures?[1] These arguments of Rush, like his other arguments for the goodness of the deity manifested in Animal Life,[2] constituted more or less unsuccessful academic attempts to harmonise religion and science. Meanwhile, outside of university circles, deistical arguments were finding expression in a popular way. In the last decade of the century, Charles Christopher Reiche published his *Discourses on the Marvellous Works in Nature*. Rush praised this work as calculated to beget a grateful admiration of the power, wisdom and goodness of the Supreme Being, as manifested in the vegetable and animal creation; Rush's successor, Benjamin Barton, claimed that the *Discourses* possessed advantages over the similar works of Derham and the Abbé Pluché, being less voluminous than the last and nearly a century more modern than the first of these performances.[3] These praises were evidently for local consumption; but, to show to what a sorry pass the later deism had come, one has but to read the first of Reiche's *Discourses,* entitled ' On the Universe ':

Since by the laws of nature, as far as you observe them, material things must either be held up from above, or supported from below, or else fall to the ground; you might conclude that this globe, our earth, must therefore either fall into the abyss, or be held up by a kind of chain, or have whereupon to rest its stupendous weight. But where is that chain to which the earth hangs, or the basis which sustains this ponderous mass?

But supposing, what some have imagined, that the materials for all these globes existed from eternity, either dispersed, or gathered into one enormous heap; you may still question: who gathered and distributed these materials to every marvellous frame in this multitude of innumerable, yet different spheres; who cemented or con-

[1] Rush, *Pleasures of the Mind,* p. 455, Philadelphia, 1811.
[2] *Ibid,* p. 82.
[3] Reiche, *Discourses,* Preface, Philadelphia, 1799.

nected those in every sphere, so as never to destroy or jar against each other or even to separate; who also fashioned their shapes, rounded them all, and filled them for their circular courses; who gave to the weight and extent of each a just proportion to that space, which they were intended to occupy, and that orbit which each of them should describe?

Reiche's *Discourses* furnished a sort of deistic game of twenty questions for infant intellects. Of equal puerility were Thomas Dobson's *Letters on the Existence and Character of the Deity,* ' written at the request of a young friend.' [1] Without referring to the authors from whom his arguments were gleaned, the Philadelphia bookseller gives these ' hints for thinking ':

It has often been urged that the consideration of ourselves and all around us, must lead us to think that there must be a powerful and intelligent being who made and directs all things. For instance, when we see a piece of mechanism we must infer that it was the work of a mechanic; but do we know of any person making a rock, a hill, a river or a tree? Have we been accustomed to see worlds made, that when we see them we necessarily infer their maker? Here the case is widely different, we have neither experience nor observation to direct our conclusion. These things have been as they are, as far back as we can recollect. The most natural conclusion, therefore, would be that these things never had a beginning, but had always been as we now perceive them, allowing for such occasional variations as we may observe in our own day and that as the change and succession of seasons and the general order of the universe are pretty uniform, they have always been so. These things may be matters of curiosity and astonishment, but we are possessed of no data to furnish any hints for solving the phenomena, and consequently nothing to give rise even to a conjecture of a first cause producing and directing the course of the universe. In fine, these things contain little evidence of the existence and government of a Supreme Being without that revelation which is the source of all the most valuable knowledge we possess.[2]

Published in the last year of the eighteenth century, Dobson's *Letters* may serve as an index to the fate of deism in the nine-

---

[1] Philadelphia, 1799. Reviewed in *American Review,* September, 1800.
[2] Dobson, *Letters,* pp. 9-23.

teenth. When the deist started with Paley, but grew weak as he approached the goal of pantheism, it shewed that he was at his last gasp; or, in more general terms, when natural religion had to lean on supernatural, it presaged the logical collapse of a dualistic system in the face of a monistic. Although it is running ahead of deism proper, it should here be pointed out that a transcendental monism, such as was developed in the North, was impossible in these parts. There were, indeed, certain groups of men headed in this direction, but their progress was unsteady, and their influence on formal philosophy slight. Taking as representative the Quakers of English, and the Pietists of German stock, the following brief sketch may be given as to their speculative trend. In respect to the first, while the Hicksite party, originating in Philadelphia in 1827, stood for much the same tendencies in the Society of Friends, as the Unitarian movement among the orthodox churches of New England,[1] yet that party possessed little of its intellectual ability and less of its power to think things through. This was particularly true of its leader. Elias Hicks was a man with great natural force and energy,[2] but without academic culture or learning; hence the expression of his peculiar doctrines was inadequate, being rather emotional than rational, a thing of the heart rather than of the head. Taking the traditional Quaker aspiration for a union of the self with a larger whole, he attempted to turn that feeling regarding ' the universal divine principle,'[3] into a proposition concerning a ' fullness of God in us and in every blade of grass.' Suspecting that this was but a false logical conversion, the orthodox Friends refused to be converted to it, while harsher critics pronounced it either a fanatical deism,[4] or a wandering off into the dreary wastes of pantheism.[5] Both these statements were true in part, for Hicks' doctrine contained both divisive and unitive tendencies;

[1] H. B. Adams, *Life of Jared Sparks*, Vol. 1, p. 15, note.

[2] Henry Augustus Riley, *Reminiscences and Events*, p. 130 (MS.).

[3] Elias Hicks, *Journal*, p. 122, New York, 1832.

[4] Baird, *Religion in America*, 1856, p. 528.

[5] Robert Barclay, *The Inner Life of the Religious Societies of the Commonwealth*, p. 557, London, 1876.

the one being represented by the mystical, the other by the rationalistic leaders in the movement. On the one side, for example, were Anthony Benezet with his 'innocent simplicity,' and John Woolman with his 'inward fellowship, received immediately from the divine fountain'; [1] on the other side, were Robert Barclay, who had much to say of natural reason, and William Penn, who was repeatedly charged with being in the deistic way. [2] Yet even with these advanced scholars the old influences seemed to be stronger than the new, for Barclay preserved his attachment for the Cambridge Platonists, and the founder of Pennsylvania went back for inspiration to the mediæval quietists. [3] Hence it came about that American Quakerism, with all its admixture of deism, had an effect more ethical than philosophical. In fine, when the later rationalism was dissolved in the earlier mysticism, there was left not a crystallized system of thought, but rather a residue of spirituality, a state of tender sensibility, an appreciation of the higher morality. [4]

Similar negative results from the systematic side, followed in respect to a kindred branch of sectaries. Like the Quakers, the so-called Pennsylvania Pietists attempted an explanation of the universe as an expression of spiritual principles, seeking by magical intuitions of transcendental truth to get at the world behind this world. Such, at least, was the actual aim of Conrad Beissel, head of the monastic community at Ephrata, near Philadelphia. Unfortunately these singularly interesting speculations of the cloistered followers of Tauler, were hidden behind a veil of theosophic lore,—the esoteric doctrine of the *Sophia*. As a writer of the day expressed it: Cabbalists and Quietists all affect a mystic language, a dark kind of canting; they talk much of a light within

---

[1] *Journal,* Philadelphia, 1845, p. 354. Compare John Greenleaf Whittier, *The Inner Life,* Boston, 1899, p. 351.

[2] William Tallack, *George Fox, the Friends, and the Early Baptists,* London, 1868, p. 62. Compare Joseph Beese, *A Confutation of the Charge of Deism, wherein the Christian and Orthodox Sentiments of William Penn are fully Demonstrated,* London, 1734.

[3] Compare, *No Cross, No Crown,* p. 34, Philadelphia, 1845.

[4] Compare below, *Notes.*

them, instead of common sense,—whoever shall reconcile all these must be an Oedipus indeed.[1] With this essentially Anglo-Saxon way of regarding mysticism and nonsense as convertible terms,[2] it is no wonder that the neighbouring pietists remained a remote and unfriended brotherhood without palpable influence on the leaders of thought in the city of brotherly love. It is true that Richard Peters of the University was reputed to have adopted the fantastical notions of Jacob Boehme,[3] yet Franklin, who printed some of the 'Dutch' books, had only contempt for those quietists who had removed hither from Germany.[4] Franklin's prejudices were here unfortunately strengthened and propagated by peculiar local conditions. Not only were the Germans in Pennsylvania isolated by language and religion, but the type of civilisation with which they were confronted was too conservative to admit much play of sentiment and imagination.[5]

But without further gropings in this unexplored field,[6] there emerges at this point a final reason that made a philosophical monism impossible in these parts. Philadelphia itself was the abode of conservatism; not in a practical way, for here medical materialism had its stronghold, yet withal in a philosophical way, for here thought for thought's sake was anything but welcome. The place, as John Adams sarcastically observed, considered itself the pineal gland of the United States; but that it was the Athens of America, as a local rhapsodist proudly observed, was a most inappropriate comparison. The treatment accorded to the books

[1] *Remarks on the Spread of the Present Enthusiasm,* United States Magazine, Philadelphia, 1779; signed Phila-Aletheias, Lewes (Matthew Wilson, of Lewes, Delaware?)

[2] Leslie Stephen in *Dictionary of National Biography,* art., William Law.

[3] Appleton's *Cyclopaedia of American Biography,* Vol. 4, p. 743.

[4] *Works,* Vol. 2, p. 261. (Bigelow adds: 'This is the only evidence in our literature, so far as I know, that any of this sect, for whose principles Fénelon suffered and Molinos died, ever found a refuge in the United States'). Does this exclude the issues of the Ephrata press, dating from before the Revolution? Compare the notable Cassel Collection in the Pennsylvania Historical Society.

[5] Compare F. H. Wilkens, *Early Influence of German Literature in America,* (Americana Germanica, Vol. 3, No. 2, 1899).

[6] Compare below, *Notes.*

in Franklin's Library Company is a curious commentary on this aversion to hearing and learning new things. Founded in 1731, this library possessed the largest collection of rationalistic literature in the country; but according to the Catalogue of 1764, such literature was not left alone without corrective or counter-irritant. As against Tillotson and Wollaston there were offered Mather's *Christian Philosopher,* and an American reprint of *The Second Spira; being a fearful example of an atheist who had apostatized from the Christian Religion, and died in despair at Westminster.* Among the other volumes the fate of the foreign works was especially curious. The most noteworthy were disregarded or distorted. Fénelon's *Demonstration of the Existence of God from Proofs purely Intellectual,* had no appreciable influence on native thought; Hume's *Enquiry Concerning the Principles of Morals,* awoke no Philadelphian from his dogmatic slumber, while the sceptical trend of Spinoza's *Tractatus Theologico-Politicus* was disguised under the title, *A treatise partly Theological and partly Political, to prove that the liberty of Philosophizing (that is, making use of Natural Reason) may be allowed without any Prejudice to Piety.* So much for the real philosophers; as might be expected, the citation of the secondary writers indicated the wider influence of the philosophic middlemen. As at Harvard and Yale, Clarke and Cudworth were to be found, while Conyers Middleton's *Free Enquiry into the Miraculous Powers* became a rich mine of information for Thomas Paine, and the Boyle Lectures started the thinking of the most precocious of American sceptics, Benjamin Franklin (1706-1790).

' I was scarce fifteen,' narrates Franklin, ' when, after doubting by turns of several points, as I found them disputed in the different books I read, I began to doubt of Revelation itself. Some books against Deism fell into my hands; they were said to be the substance of sermons preached at Boyle's Lectures. It happened that they wrought an effect on me quite contrary to what was intended by them; for the arguments of the Deists, which were quoted to be refuted, appeared to me much stronger than the refutation; in short, I soon became a thorough Deist.'[1] In further explanation of his belief, Franklin now adds, with characteristic

[1] *Writings,* Vol. 1, 295, (ed. Smyth).

inclusiveness, the complex factors of heredity and environment: he was a free-thinker because of a free-thinking ancestor, and a deist because of a youthful overdose of Calvinism. Thus he relates how his maternal grandfather had written some home-spun verse in favour of liberty of conscience, and that his father's little collection of books consisted mostly of polemical works of divinity. But although he considered that some of the dogmas of the Presbyterian persuasion, such as the eternal decrees of God, election, reprobation, appeared very unintelligible and others doubtful, yet he never doubted, for instance, the existence of the Deity; that he made the world and governed it by his Providence; that the most acceptable service of God was the doing good to man; that our souls are immortal; and that all crimes will be punished, and virtue rewarded, either here or hereafter.[1]

In making himself out a moderate deist, for this creed was nothing but Herbert of Chebury's five points common to all religions, Franklin was inclined to slur over those earlier metaphysical flights, which began with a deistic fatalism and ended with a Platonic polytheism. Resuming his narrative, he tells how he was made a doubter from reading Shaftesbury and Collins; then how he left Boston when his indiscreet disputations about religion began to make him pointed at with horror by good people as an infidel and atheist;[2] and finally, how being employed in London, at the age of nineteen, in composing for Wollaston's *Religion of Nature Delineated,* and some of the author's reasonings not appearing well founded, he wrote a little metaphysical piece entitled, *A Dissertation on Liberty and Necessity, Pleasure and Pain.* The purport of this was to prove the doctrine of fate from the supposed attributes of God; in some such manner as this: That in erecting and governing the world, as he was infinitely wise, he knew what would be best; infinitely good, he must be disposed, and infinitely powerful, he must be able to execute it: consequently all is right.[3] Of this deistical pamphlet of 1725, Franklin had one hundred copies printed, of which he gave a few

---

[1] Vol. 1, p. 325. [2] *Ib.,* p. 249.

[3] Vol. 7, pp. 411-412. Letter to Benjamin Vaughan, 9th Nov., 1779. For the reprint of James Parton (*Life and Times of Benjamin Franklin,* Boston, 1884, Vol. I., Appendix II.), see below *Notes.*

to his friends; but afterwards, disliking the piece, as conceiving it might have an ill tendency, he burned the rest.[1] Franklin's latest editor has seen fit not to print this exceedingly rare pamphlet, declaring that it has no merit, and that the author would have been distressed at its republication.[2] Both these opinions may be valid, and yet such an omission is unwarranted; the printing of the pamphlet may have been an ' erratum ' in the book of Franklin's life, yet without it the knowledge of that book is incomplete. It shows not only the author's escape from one extreme of Calvinistic pessimism into the other extreme of deistic optimism, but his inconsequential conclusion that philosophy is but a blind guide to the understanding. So the narrator continues: My London pamphlet, printed in 1725, which had for its motto these lines of Dryden:

> ' Whatever is, is right. But purblind man
> Sees but a part o' the chain, the nearest links;
> His eyes not carrying to that equal beam,
> That poises all above,'

and which from the attributes of God, his infinite wisdom, goodness, and power, concluded that nothing could possibly be wrong in the world, and that vice and virtue were empty distinctions, no such things existing, appeared now not so clever a performance as I once thought it; and I doubted whether some error had not insinuated itself unperceived into my argument so as to infect all that followed, as is common in metaphysical reasonings.[3]

Dedicated to his fellow printer, James Ralph, Franklin's ' wicked tract ' had little influence except on himself. It indeed led Priestley, in his zeal to bolster up determinism, to ask for a copy;[4] it also led to an introduction to Dr. Mandeville, author of the *Fable of the Bees*, but it is doubtful if this versified bit of philosophy had anything to do with Franklin's own beliefs.[5] Mandeville was a pessimist, who rejected the cosmic harmony of Shaftesbury, but Franklin was an optimist and was already familiar with

---

[1] Vol. 1, p. 277.   [2] *Ib.*, p. 296, note.
[3] *Ib.*, p. 296.   [4] Vol. 7, p. 411, note.
[5] As suggested by Curtis, *Philosophy in America*, p. 5.

this latter exponent of the Leibnizian world-scheme.   In other words, affecting to despise his first metaphysical piece as so much 'youthful nonsense,' this piece still served to register his earlier opinions and to presage his later thinking.   In its introductory attempt to give some thoughts on 'the general State of Things in the Universe,' it was an unconscious repetition of Franklin's satire on the Harvard student of his day,—the ambitious Plagius who was diligently transcribing some eloquent paragraphs out of Tillotson's works to embellish his own[1].   Likewise in its general syllogistic form, the pamphlet points back to a study of the *Art of Thinking,* by Messrs. du Port Royal, and its doctrines of sensationalism and representative perception to the contemporary reading of Locke *On Human Understanding.*[2]   It was this residual portion of his work which contained the germs of Franklin's subsequent speculations; its eudaemonism reappearing in the Dialogues on *Virtue and Pleasure,* its equating of pleasure and pain in what he was wont to call his moral algebra.   Meanwhile, in the year 1728, Franklin had compiled his *Articles of Belief, and Acts of Religion.*   Drawn up among the regulations of the Philadelphia Junto, or club for mental improvement, this document formed a kind of shop-keeper's litany, or home service for young mechanics.   Among its parts were the First Principles, Adoration and Petition, of which the last begged that the petitioner might be preserved from atheism and infidelity; the second urged the reading of deistic authors like Ray, Blackmore and the Archbishop of Cambray; while the first, as if in conscious opposition to the Anglican creed, taught the doctrine, not of one God without parts and passions, but of many gods endowed with human passions.   Here, then, follow Franklin's peculiar,

First Principles.

I believe there is one supreme, most perfect Being, Author and Father of the Gods themselves.   For I believe that Man is not the most perfect Being but one, rather that as there are many Degrees of Beings his Inferiors, so there are many Degrees of Beings superior to him.

[1] Vol. 2, p. 13.   [2] Vol. 1, p. 243.

Also, when I stretch my imagination thro' and beyond our System of Planets, beyond the visible fix'd Stars themselves, into that space that is every Way infinite, and conceive it fill'd with Suns like ours, each with a Chorus of Worlds forever moving round him, then this little Ball on which we move, seems, even in my narrow Imagination, to be almost Nothing, and myself less than nothing, and of no sort of Consequence.

When I think thus, I imagine it great Vanity in me to suppose, that the *Supremely Perfect* does in the least regard such an inconsiderable Nothing as Man. More especially, since it is impossible for me to have any positive clear idea of that which is infinite and incomprehensible, I cannot conceive otherwise than that he the *Infinite Father* expects or requires no Worship or Praise from us, but that he is even infinitely above it.

But, since there is in all Men something like a natural principle, which inclines them to DEVOTION, or the Worship of some unseen Power;

And since Men are endued with Reason superior to all other Animals, that we are in our World acquainted with;

Therefore I think it seems required of me, and my Duty as a Man, to pay Divine Regards to SOMETHING.

I conceive then, that the INFINITE has created many beings or Gods, vastly superior to Man, who can better conceive his Perfections than we, and return him a more rational and glorious Praise.

As, among Men, the Praise of the Ignorant or of Children is not regarded by the ingenious Painter or Architect, who is rather honour'd and pleas'd with the approbation of Wise Men & Artists.

It may be that these created Gods are immortal; or it may be that after many Ages, they are changed, and others Supply their Places.

Howbeit, I conceive that each of these is exceeding wise and good, and very powerful; and that Each has made for himself one glorious Sun, attended with a beautiful and admirable System of Planets.

It is that particular Wise and good God, who is the author and owner of our system, that I propose for the object of my praise and adoration.

For I conceive that he has in himself some of those Passions he has planted in us, and that, since he has given us Reason whereby we are capable of observing his Wisdom in the Creation, he is not above caring for us, being pleas'd with our Praise, and offended when we slight Him, or neglect his Glory.

I conceive for many Reasons, that he is a *good Being;* and as I should be happy to have so wise, good, and powerful a Being my Friend, let me consider in what manner I shall make myself most acceptable to him.

Next to the Praise resulting from and due to his Wisdom, I believe he is pleas'd and delights in the Happiness of those he has created; and since without Virtue Man can have no Happiness in this World, I firmly believe he delights to see me Virtuous, because he is pleas'd when he sees Me Happy.

And since he has created many Things, which seem purely design'd for the Delight of Man, I believe he is not offended, when he sees his Children solace themselves in any manner of pleasant exercises and Innocent Delights; and I think no Pleasure innocent that is to Man hurtful.

I *love* him therefore for his Goodness, and I *adore* him for his Wisdom.

Let me then not fail to praise my God continually, for it is his Due; and it is all I can return for his many Favours and great Goodness to me; and let me resolve to be virtuous, that I may be happy, that I may please Him, who is delighted to see me happy. Amen![1]

Franklin's *First Principles* form an astonishing document; they teach a veritable polytheism in a land monotonously monotheistic. As to the sources for this pluralism of divinities several conjectures may be made: in a general way, there was the Leibnizian law of continuity,[2] from which was derived the prevalent belief in a graded scale of reasoning life, as when Pope sought to discover ' what varied being peoples ev'ry star.'[3] More particularly, there was the familiar cosmology of Wollaston, who spoke of ' the fixed stars as so many other suns with their several sets of planets about them ';[4] them was, finally, inserted in the midst of Franklin's document, the *Hymn to the Creator,* wherein Milton sang of ' Sons of light, angels, fixed stars.' But these conjectures are inadequate: neither

[1] Vol. 2, pp. 92-4. With this compare the so-called *Franklin's Prayer Book,* a curious abridgment of the Book of Common Prayer which Franklin undertook in 1772, at the request of Sir Francis Dashwood, Lord Le Despencer, a notorious roué and deist. (Ford, *Bibliography, p.* 37.)

[2] Compare Bowen, *Modern Philosophy,* p. 104.

[3] *Essay on Man,* Epistle I., line 27.

[4] *Religion of Nature,* London, 1750, p. 143.

the general notions, nor the specific authorities of the day will furnish the exact doctrines here promulgated by Franklin. His pluralism was an anachronism, a fragment of the ancient gnosticism with its hierarchy of demiurge and archons, strangely out of place in the eighteenth century philosophy. For these reasons other ground has been explored to find the root of the Philadelphian's *Articles of Belief*. It is known that the original manuscript was his daily companion to the end of his life,[1] but it seems to have escaped notice, for a full century after his birth, how far he was indebted to Plato.[2] Nevertheless it has been shown how Franklin's writings give evidence that in his youth he fell under the spell of the ancient charmer. Only once in his published works does he quote from Plato and then his reference is dubious;[3] only once does he quote the kindred *Memorabilia* of Socrates, but in his *Autobiography* he mentions that in his sixteenth or seventeenth year he procured that memoir and soon adopted the Socratic method of dispute, dropping abrupt contradiction and positive argumentation and putting on the humble inquirer and doubter.[4] As the results of this early study, Franklin tells how he published in his newspaper little pieces of his own, which had first been composed for reading in the Junto. Of these are a Socratic dialogue, tending to prove that, whatever might be his parts and abilities, a vicious man could not probably be called a man of sense; and a discourse on self-denial, showing that virtue was not secure till its practice became a habitude, and was free from the opposition of contrary inclinations.[5]

Despite the scantiness of his references, Franklin's speculative

---

[1] Vol. 2, p. 92 (Note by Smyth).

[2] C. M. Walsh, *Franklin and Plato*, Open Court, March, 1906.

[3] "One of the philosophers, I think it was Plato, used to say that he had rather be the veriest stupid block in nature than the possessor of all knowledge without some intelligent being to communicate it to." (Vol. 2, p. 70.) A secondary reference is to be found in Franklin's Journal (11th July, 1781), where he quotes from Hamlet's Soliloquy.

[4] Vol. 1, p. 244. From Franklin's use of the title "The Memorable Things of Socrates," it is presumable that he read the translation of Edward Bysshe of 1702, which is here used.

[5] Vol. 1, p. 343.

writings betray a free use of the Platonic literature. For instance, the description in the *First Principles* of the Father of the gods themselves embodies the doctrines of the *Timaeus* concerning the Father who begat the world and made the eternal gods, who formed the universe and assigned each soul to a star, who was good, and being free from jealousy, desired that all things should be as like himself as possible.[1] Similarly, Franklin's dialogues between Philocles and Horatio concerning *Virtue and Pleasure,* resemble Xenophon's use of a dialogue of Prodicus, where Virtue and Pleasure make their court to Hercules under the appearance of two beautiful women. In borrowing from the ancient moralist, Franklin evinces his wonted skill as an adapter of the ideas of others. In place of the mythological hero, who had arrived at that part of his youth when young men commonly choose for themselves,[2] he puts a contemporary Anglo-American of about two-and-twenty, with a healthful, vigorous body, and a fair plentiful estate of about five hundred pounds a year. This is the young Horatio who, supposing Philosophy in general so favourite a mistress that he will take her as men do their wives, for better, for worse, without regard to consequences, asks: 'Why should I not do it? Pray, what have you to say, Philocles?'

Phil. This my dear *Horatio,* I have to say.; that what you find Fault with and clamour against, as the most terrible Evil in the World, Self-denial; is really the greatest Good, and the highest Self-gratification: if indeed, you use the Word in the Sense of some weak sour Moralists, and much weaker Divines, you'll have just Reason to laugh at it; but if you take it, as understood by Philosophers and Men of Sense, you will presently see her Charms, and fly to her Embraces, notwithstanding her demure Looks, as absolutely necessary to produce even your own darling sole Good, Pleasure: For, Self-denial is never a Duty, or a reasonable Action, but as 'tis a natural Means of procuring more Pleasure than you can taste without it so that this grave, Saintlike Guide to Happiness, as rough and dreadful as she has been made to appear, is in truth the kindest and most beautiful Mistress in the World.

Hor. Prithee, *Philocles!* do not wrap yourself in Allegory and

[1] *Timaeus,* §§ 29, 37, 41, translation of Jowett, 1871.
[2] *Memorabilia,* Book II., Chapter I.

Metaphor. Why do you teaze me thus? I long to be satisfied, what this Philosophical Self-denial is; the Necessity and Reason of it; I'm impatient, and all on Fire; explain, therefore, in your beautiful, natural easy Way of Reasoning, what I'm to understand by this grave Lady of yours, with so forbidding, downcast Looks, and yet so absolutely necessary to my Pleasures. I stand ready to embrace her; for you know, Pleasure I court under all Shapes and Forms.

Phil. Attend then, and you'll see the Reason of this Philosophical Self-denial. There can be no absolute Perfection in any Creature; because every Creature is derived and dependent: No created Being can be All-wise, All-good, and All-powerful, because his Powers and Capacities are finite and limited; consequently whatever is created must, in its own Nature, be subject to Error, Irregularity, Excess and Disorder. All intelligent, rational Agents find in themselves a Power of judging what kind of Beings they are; what Actions are proper to preserve 'em, and what Consequences will generally attend them, and what Pleasures they are form'd for, and to what Degree their Natures are capable of receiving them. All we have to do then, *Horatio,* is to consider, when we are surpriz'd with a new Object, and passionately desire to enjoy it, whether the gratifying that Passion be consistent with the gratifying other Passions and Appetites, equal if not more necessary to us. And whether it consists with our Happiness To-morrow, next Week, or next Year; for, as we all wish to live, we are obliged by Reason to take as much Care for our future, as our present Happiness, and not build upon the Ruins of t'other. But, if thro' the Strength and Power of a present Passion and thro' want of attending to Consequences, we have err'd and exceeded the Bounds which Nature or Reason have set us; we are then, for our own Sakes, to refrain, or deny ourselves a present momentary Pleasure for a future, constant and durable one; So that this Philosophical Self-denial is only refusing to do an Action which you strongly desire; because 'tis inconsistent with your Health, Fortunes, or Circumstances in the World; or, in other Words, because 'twould cost you more than 'twas worth. You would lose by it, as a Man of Pleasure. Thus you see, *Horatio!* that Self-denial is not only the most reasonable, but the most pleasant Thing in the World.

Hor. We are just coming into Town, so that we can't pursue this Argument any farther at present; you have said a great deal for Nature, Providence, and Reason: Happy are they who can follow such divine Guides.

Phil. Horatio! good Night; I wish you wise in your Pleasures.

Hor. I wish, *Philocles!* I could be as wise in my Pleasures as you are pleasantly Wise; your Wisdom is agreeable, your Virtue is amiable, and your Philosophy the highest Luxury. Adieu! thou enchanting Reasoner! . . . .

Hor. . . . in our last Conversation, when walking upon the Brow of this Hill, and looking down on that broad, rapid River, and yon widely-extended beautifully-varied Plain, you taught me another Doctrine: You shewed me, that Self-denial, which above all Things I abhorred, was really the greatest Good, and the highest Self-gratification, and absolutely necessary to produce even my own darling sole Good, Pleasure. . . . . . .

Hor. But now, my Friend! you are to perform another Promise; and shew me the Path which leads up to that constant, durable, and invariable Good, which I have heard you so beautifully describe, and which you seem so fully to possess: Is not this Good of yours a mere Chimera? Can any Thing be Constant in a World which is eternally changing! and which appears to exist by an everlasting Revolution of one Thing into another, and where every Thing without us, and every Thing within us, is in perpetual Motion? What is this constant, durable Good, then, of yours? Prithee, satisfy my Soul, for I'm all on Fire, and impatient to enjoy her. Produce this eternal blooming Goddess with never-fading Charms, and see, whether I won't embrace her with as much Eagerness and Rapture as you.

Phil. You seem enthusiastically warm, *Horatio;* I will wait till you are cool enough to attend to the sober, dispassionate Voice of Reason.

Hor. You mistake me my dear *Philocles!* my Warmth is not so great as to run away with my Reason: it is only just raised enough to open my Faculties, and fit them to receive those eternal Truths, and that durable Good, which you so triumphantly boasted of. Begin, then; I'm prepared.

Phil. I will. I believe, *Horatio!* with all your Skepticism about you, you will allow that Good to be constant which is never absent from you, and that to be durable, which never Ends but with your Being.

Hor. Yes, go on.

Phil. That can never be the Good of a Creature, which when present, the Creature may be miserable, and when absent, is certainly so.

Hor. I think not; but pray explain what you mean; for I am not much used to this abstract Way of Reasoning.

Phil. I mean all the Pleasures of Sense. The Good of Man

cannot consist in the mere Pleasures of Sense; because, when any one of those Objects which you love is absent, or can't be come at, you are certainly miserable: and if the Faculty be impair'd, though the Object be present, you can't enjoy it. So that this sensual Good depends upon a thousand Things without and within you, and all out of your Power. Can this then be the Good of Man? Say, *Horatio!* what think you, Is not this a checquer'd, fleeting, fantastical Good? Can that, in any propriety of Speech, be called the Good of Man which even, while he is tasting, he may be miserable; and which when he cannot taste, he is necessarily so? Can that be our Good, which costs us a great deal of Pains to obtain; which cloys in possessing; for which we must wait the Return of Appetite before we can enjoy again? Or, is that our Good, which we can come at without Difficulty; which is heightened by Possession, and which never ends in Weariness and Disappointment; and which, the more we enjoy, the better qualified we are to enjoy on? . . . .

Phil. I think, *Horatio!* that I have clearly shewn you the Difference between merely natural or sensual Good, and rational or moral Good. Natural or sensual Pleasure continues no longer than the Action itself; but this divine or moral Pleasure continues when the Action is over, and swells and grows upon your Hand by Reflection: The one is inconstant, unsatisfying, of short duration, and attended with numberless Ills; the other is constant, yields full satisfaction, is durable, and no Evils preceding, accompanying, or following it. But, if you enquire farther into the Cause of this difference, and would know why the moral Pleasures are greater than the sensual; perhaps the Reason is the same as in all other Creatures, That their Happiness or chief Good consists in acting up to their chief Faculty, or that Faculty which distinguishes them from all Creatures of a different Species. The chief Faculty in a Man is his Reason; and consequently his chief Good; or that which may be justly called his Good, consists not merely in Action, but in reasonable Action; . . . . for, as the Happiness or real Good of Men consists in right Action, and right Action cannot be produced without right Opinion, it behoves, above all Things in this World, to take Care that our Opinions of Things be according to the Nature of Things. The Foundation of all Virtue and Happiness is Thinking rightly. He who sees an Action is right, that is, naturally tending to Good, and does it because of that Tendency, he only is a moral Man; and he alone is capable of that constant, durable, and invariable Good, which has been the Subject of this Conversation.

Hor. How, my dear philosophical Guide, shall I be able to know, and determine certainly, what is Right and what is Wrong in Life?

Phil. As easily as you can distinguish a Circle from a Square, or Light from Darkness. Look, *Horatio,* into the sacred Book of Nature; read you own Nature, and view the Relation which other Men stand in to you, and you to them; and you'll immediately see what constitutes human Happiness, and consequently what is Right.[1]

As to the sources of these delightful colloquies little need be said; except for some current deistic phrases, they are conceived in the pure spirit of Plato, for Franklin, like his master Shaftesbury, has recourse to the antique harmony of self-limitation, the antique confidence in nature.[2] And so his teachings are in close accord with the Platonic teachings that the rational is higher than the animal soul;[3] that temperance is the same with self-knowledge;[4] that pleasures are evil because they end in pain; and that all things are knowledge including virtue itself.[5] These opinions doubtless furnished the ground and inspiration for Franklin's Dialogues in the classic style, yet however slight their originality they were remarkable performances for a self-educated youth not much older than his second interlocutor; indeed, it is fair to say that they were the work of an enchanting reasoner; nothing to equal them for charm and fancy had heretofore appeared in the colonies, for Berkeley had not as yet published those Platonic conversations whose scene was laid in Rhode Island.[6] With these ideal affiliations there was yet little of the idealist hereafter in the life of the young Pennsylvanian; he had first referred to Plato in describing his homeward trip from London to Philadelphia; but after his return to that utilitarian city, there were no more speculative voyages. As he admitted at this very period, the great un-

1 Vol. 2, pp. 161-169.
2 Höffding, *Modern Philosophy,* Vol. 1, p. 392.
3 *Republic,* Book 4, § 441.
4 *Charicles,* § 164.
5 *Protagoras,* §§ 353, 361.
6 Berkeley's *Minute Philosopher,* first edition, London, 1732.

certainty he found in metaphysics disgusted him, and he quitted that kind of reading and study for others more satisfactory.[1]

Henceforward, then, one may perceive in Franklin not a further logical advance upon the Socrates of Plato, but a retrogression to the more practical and unimaginative Socrates of Xenophon, the Socrates who harps on the mischiefs of intemperance and the advantages of sobriety, and, seeing no difference between an irrational animal and a voluptuous man, urges his disciples to avoid the bad and embrace the good.[2] In a word, recalling the various errata he had committed in the past, Franklin now sought to mend his life, much as his latest editor has tried to expurgate his writings. He tells how, after his first foreign trip, he conceived the bold and arduous project of arriving at moral perfection, and, wishing to live without committing any fault at any time, tried to conquer all that either natural inclination, custom, or company might lead him into.[3] In this scheme for moral improvement Franklin has been called an ascetic philosopher, with the regimen of a Pythagorean,[4] but that scheme need not be repeated, except as it marks the change that had come over his speculative spirit. When he wrote the *First Principles* he had given as one of the rules for his fellow members in the Junto, that they love the truth for the truth's sake;[5] now he takes for his general principle

---

[1] Vol. 7, p. 412. The rest of the passage reads: 'In 1730, I wrote a piece on the other side of the question, which began with laying for its foundation the fact: That almost all men in all ages and countries have made use of prayer. Hence I reasoned, that if all things are ordained, prayer must among the rest be ordained. But as prayer can procure no change in things that are ordained, prayer must then be useless and an absurdity. God would therefore not ordain praying if everything else was ordained. But praying exists, therefore all other things are not ordained, etc. This pamphlet was never printed and the manuscript has long been lost.'

[2] *Memorabilia*, Book IV., Chapter V.

[3] Vol. 1, p. 326.

[4] Philarète Chasles, *Le Dix-Huitième Siècle en Angleterre*, Paris, 1846, p. 309.

[5] Vol. 2, p. 90.

the line of Cicero concerning philosophy as the guide of life, and for particular application the advice of Pythagoras in his *Golden Verses,* that daily examination would be necessary for moral perfection.[1]   In thus applying to himself the revival of the Dorian ideal of abstinence and hardihood, Franklin has again had recourse to the ancients, but in a most uninspiring way; it is no longer theoretical, but applied morals in which he is interested. At this juncture, as if he were a sort of ethical bookkeeper, he opens up an account with each of his thirteen virtues, beginning with Temperance and ending with Humility or the imitation of Socrates.[2]

With the compilation of his list of practical virtues, the retrogression in Franklin as a speculative philosopher is complete. Instead of advancing to the Aristotelian view that thinking is in itself a good, he returns to the Socratic standpoint which values only the present good, in so far as it leads to the redemption of the individual and the regeneration of society from the disturbances of life. Here the Philadelphian showed the same homely sense and practical knowledge as did the Athenian sage. For example, in his small scheme for private moral improvement, Franklin compared himself to a man who, having a garden to weed, does not attempt to eradicate all the bad herbs at once, which would exceed his reach and strength, but works on one of the beds at a time. Moreover, in his more extensive project for public improvement Franklin, in a letter to the Scotch moralist Lord Kames, refers to his desire of writing a book on the ' Art of Virtue,' [3] but not without some proper vehicle to convey his lessons. Such a vehicle he conceived to exist in his Society of the Free and Easy, a sect that should be begun and spread at first among young and single men, each one of whom should exercise himself with the thirteen weeks' examination of the thirteen virtues, and only then should the existence of the Society be made a matter of public knowledge. Franklin was always of the opinion that this was a practicable scheme, for as he wrote in his *Observations on Reading History in the Library,* he inferred from the fact that the great affairs of the world, the wars and revolutions are carried on and effected by parties, there seemed to him to be great

[1] Vol. 1, p. 329.   [2] *Ib.,* pp. 327, 328.   [3] Vol. 4, p. 12.

occasion for raising a united party for virtue. But the printer's then narrow circumstances, and the necessity of sticking close to business and his later multifarious occupations, public and private, induced him to continue postponing his scheme until he had no longer strength or activity sufficient for such an enterprise.[1]

With the year 1731, Franklin's metaphysical activities ended; hereafter he showed himself a man of parts, but with one part missing; he was educator, scientist, politician, essayist, diplomat, but no philosopher in the strict sense of the word. A kind of Socrates in small clothes, he preserved to the last the ancient irony, the mastery of dialogue, the habit of ingenious exposition; but all traces of the Platonic idealism, of the love of wisdom for its own sake, had disappeared, when he was capable of asking such a question as this: ' What signifies philosophy that does not apply to some use? ' [2] In the face of this crass utilitarianism, of this disparaging attitude towards pure speculation, it has nevertheless been argued that Franklin underwent a recrudescence of his youthful metaphysics during his old age. On his mission to France in 1776, the American minister showed a remarkable liveliness of spirits for a man of seventy, but the little essays of the Passy period were anything but serious productions. Written to give relaxation to an over-worked official, they might be called mere *feux de joie,* mere literary fireworks to amuse ' la societé choisie de Franklin.' [3] Hence to reason that the paper entitled ' The Ephemera: An Emblem of Human Life,' was a presentation of phenomenalism, or that the alleged letter from the Elysian fields to Madame Helvétius was an attempted revival of paganism, would be to miss the light Gallic spirit in which they were conceived. But though these bagatelles had as little substance as the magic squares with which Franklin amused himself, they served to put their author on terms of desirable intimacy with his sceptical hosts. What the old diplomat was thought to believe at this time is told in a conversation which John Adams recounts

[1] Vol. 1, pp. 339-342.

[2] Vol. 4, p. 15.

[3] Compare *Franklin à Passy,* in C. A. Sainte-Beuve, *Causeries de Lundi,* 3d ed., Paris, Vol. 7, pp. 167-185.

having had with De Marbois, later secretary of the French legation in the United States: ' " All religions are tolerated in America," said M. Marbois, " and the ambassadors have in all courts a
right to a chapel in their own way; but Mr. Franklin never had
any." " No," said I, laughing, " because Mr. Franklin had no "—
I was going to say what I did not say, and will not say here. I
stopped short and laughed. " No," said M. Marbois, " Mr.
Franklin adores only great Nature, which has interested a great
many people of both sexes in his favour." ' " Yes," said I, laughing, " all the atheists, deists, and libertines, as well as the philosophers and ladies, are in his train,—another Voltaire, and thence—"
" Yes," said M. Marbois, " he is celebrated as the great philosopher and the great legislator of America." ' [1]

It was Franklin as a philosopher, in the eighteenth century use
of the word as a natural philosopher, who chiefly stimulated the
interchange of ideas between France and the western world. Thus,
had it not been for the Philadelphian's electrical experiments,[2]
there would have been fewer points of contact between the two
republics. The modern Prometheus drew lightning from the
clouds, as Turgot's famous lines expressed it; he also drew ideas
from men, and despite that non-conducting medium, the Anglo-
American mind, succeeded in introducing into the colonies many
of the stimulating notions of his French acquaintances. Among
those of a philosophic turn who had a transatlantic influence were
Buffon, whose *View of Nature* fortified the American deists; [3]
Cabanis, whose materialism influenced Jefferson; [4] Chastellux, who
anticipated the philosophic travels of De Tocqueville; [5] Condorcet,
whose *Progress of the Human Mind* received an early printing in
Maryland; [6] Crèvecœur, whose letters on America fascinated and

---

[1] John Adams, *Works*, Vol. 3, p. 220.

[2] Compare *American Museum*, March, 1788; Miller, *Retrospect*, 1803,
Vol. 1, pp. 441-4; *Franklin Bicentennial Celebration*, Philadelphia, 1906,
articles by E. L. Nichols, and Ernest Rutherford.

[3] Compare *Philadelphia Monthly Magazine*, 1796, p. 38.

[4] Compare next chapter, *Virginia and Jefferson*.

[5] *Travels* 1780-82.

[6] Baltimore, 1802.

misled Europeans;[1] du Pont de Nemours, who projected a settlement of philosophers on the Mississippi;[2] Lavoisier, whose pneumatic theory was used to explode the phlogistic views of Priestley in Pennsylvania;[3] Quesnay, a follower of Lafayette, whose grandson sought to found a kind of French Academy in Virginia;[4] Rochefoucauld duc d'Enville, who translated the Constitutions of the thirteen original States;[5] Volney, whose *Ruins, or Revolutions of Empires* stirred up even Philadelphia.[6]

As the friend of their *gens de lettres,* Franklin naturally received the enthusiastic admiration of the French from first to last. Upon his arrival, being publicly introduced to Voltaire, he was hailed as the Solon embracing the Sophocles of the age; when the news of his death reached the French Academy, Condorcet made the remarkable eulogy which contains the parallel between these two men as representatives of philosophy rescuing the race of man from the tyrant fanaticism.[7] Whether these estimates were not exaggerated, and whether Franklin was as much of a promoter of rationalism as the French thought, are difficult questions to answer. At the least, in his relations to the British and Anglo-American philosophers, something might be said on one side, as well as the other. Leaving out of account an intimacy with David Hume, which was more political than metaphysical,[8] Franklin went beyond that easy sceptic in the firm stand he took against intellectual and religious coercion. This was shown in the aid he extended to the radical Samuel Priestley, author of the *Corruptions of Chris-*

---

[1] Tyler, *Literary History of the American Revolution,* Vol. 2, p. 357.

[2] John Adams, *Works,* Vol. 8, p. 596.

[3] *Columbian Magazine,* September, 1788.

[4] Quesnay de Beaurepaire, *Mémoire, Statuts et Prospectus concernant l'Académie des Sciences et Beaux-Arts des États-Unis de l'Amérique,* Paris, 1788.

[5] *La Grande Encyclopédie,* Vol. 28, p. 782.

[6] C. F. Volney, Philadelphia, 1799. For other French writers of influence in America at this time, compare *Notes.*

[7] E. E. Hale, *Franklin in France,* Boston, 1888, Vol. 2, p. 140.

[8] Hume referred to Franklin as the first philosopher of America, but this was apparently in reference to his physical experiments. Vol. 3, p. 189 (F).

tianity; [1] in his request to Cadwallader Colden to stop the prosecution of the editor of the *New York Gazette,* for publishing a defence of deism; [2] and finally in his letter to Ezra Stiles of Connecticut, wherein he reiterates the deistic creed of his youth, confesses that he believes that primitive Christianity has received corrupting changes, and concludes with the observation that he does not perceive that the Supreme takes it amiss by distinguishing the unbelievers in his government of the world with any peculiar marks of displeasure. [3] In this same letter Franklin encloses another, supposed to be written to Thomas Paine, who several years after this published the first part of his notorious *Age of Reason.* [4]

To whomsoever this epistle is addressed, it discloses another side of the writer, his cautious attitude towards religion as a public institution. He tells his anonymous friend that he has read his manuscript with some attention, but that the arguments it contains against the doctrines of a particular providence, strike at the foundation of all religion. He therefore gives as his opinion, that though the author's reasonings are subtle, and may prevail with some readers, yet he will not succeed so as to change the general sentiments of mankind on the subject, and the consequence of the printing of the piece will be a great deal of odium drawn upon himself, and no benefit to others. He that spits against the wind, spits in his own face. [5] Of the same nature as this homely piece of advice was Franklin's ' Information to those who would remove to America,' in which he said that in the new world, religion under its various denominations is not only tolerated, but respected and practised. Atheism is unknown there; infidelity rare and secret; so that persons may live to a great age in that country without

[1] Vol. 7, p. 10 (F).   [2] Vol. 3, p. 87.   [3] Vol. 10, p. 194.

[4] Letter to ————, July 3, 1786 (?) Note that the first draft of the *Age of Reason* was not written earlier than 1793 (Conway, *Life of Paine,* Vol. 2, p. 100). Sainte-Beuve suggests that the MS. in question was that of Volney's *Ruins* (*Causeries,* Vol. 7, p. 179). In a letter to Rochefoucauld in 1787, Franklin refers to Paine as an ingenious, honest man (Vol. 9, p. 565).

[5] Vol. 9, p. 521.

having their piety shocked by meeting with either an atheist or an infidel.[1] This is a jesuitical generalisation, its truth being invalidated by the single fact, that, when Franklin made a motion for the holding of prayers in the Constitutional Convention, as a means of correcting the melancholy imperfections of the human understanding, he added, in a satirical note, that the convention, except three or four persons, thought prayers unnecessary.[2]

These are contradictory statements, but there was a reason why Franklin's writings and private beliefs did not hang together. That reason was his utilitarian point of view: he might consider freethinking as a thing good in itself, but like his electric fluid, it was to be guided and conducted into safe channels. This explanation fits a further discrepancy between individual opinion and outward utterance, in one of the most curious episodes in Franklin's life, namely his relations to that popular craze, Mesmerism. In reviewing the services of his countryman, Jefferson said that the animal magnetism of the maniac Mesmer had just received its death wound from Franklin's hand in conjunction with his brethren of the learned committee appointed to unveil that compound of fraud and folly.[3] Whatever the element of truth in this alliterative exaggeration, to Mesmer himself, who claimed that magnetic and healing effluvia emanated from his person, Franklin was at first not particularly hostile. In fact, he seemed to think there might be something in those claims, for he allowed that the delusion might, in some cases, be of use while it lasts. There are in every great, rich city, he explains, a number of persons who are never in health, because they are fond of medicines and always taking them, whereby they derange the natural functions, and hurt their constitutions. If those people can be persuaded to forbear their drugs, in expectation of being cured by only the physician's finger, or an iron-rod pointing at them, they may possibly find good effects, though they mistake the cause.[4] In this, his private opinion, the American minister seemed almost to favour Mesmer's anticipated form of mental healing; but after he had made a series of experi-

[1] Vol. 8, p. 614.   [2] Vol. 9, p. 601.
[3] *Works*, Vol. 5, p. 291 (F).   [4] Vol. 9, p. 182.

ments at Passy, he signed the adverse report of the royal commission.[1] This report, which for almost a century was accepted as a final exposé of Mesmerism, declares that all the phenomena observed might be explained by three chief causes,—imitation, imagination, and contact; it concludes that imagination, apart from magnetism, produces nothing.[2]

In lending the weight of his authority, by heading the signatures to this report, the American minister showed too much of that common sense and too little of that imagination against which he inveighed. Herein he inadvertently did a disservice to his country, for back of the 'medicine of the imagination' lay the unsuspected field of psycho-therapeutics which has since suffered almost entire neglect in the United States. Had Franklin taken an opposite course, obtained some insight into the meaning of the magnetic-sympathetic medicine of the eighteenth century, far different results might have followed in the nineteenth. But in this matter the Philadelphian blew both cold and hot. In so far as Franklinism, or the theory which considers electricity as a single, subtle and universally diffused fluid, bolstered up the popular notion of a transferable curative principle, its author was right in denying objective existence thereto. But, on the other hand, he was not right in denying the possibilities of a correlative subjective factor, namely, that through suggestion, the subject may regain his nervous stability, relieve himself of mental overtension, and thus hasten the recuperative processes. Of this truth Franklin's fellow townsman, Dr. Benjamin Rush, gained an inkling from his private practice.[3] and also had the mesmeric therapeutic principle explained to him during a visit from Brissot de Warville.[4] But to the kindred

---

[1] Ford, *Bibliography*, p. 169.

[2] Binet and Féré, *Animal Magnetism*, New York, 1898, pp. 16, 17. Hale (op. cit., Vol. 2, p. 302) suggests that the translation of *attouchment*, as contact, fails to give the subjective side of the original, the French word carrying with it the complementary sense of feeling by him who is touched, and of the feeling which results from touching.

[3] Compare my article, *Benjamin Rush as Materialist and Realist*, Johns Hopkins Hospital Bulletin, March, 1907.

[4] Compare Brissot's *New Travels in the United States*, London, 1794.

system of Thouret of Paris, Franklin turned a deaf ear,[1] and thereafter the true principle of therapeutic suggestion at the bottom of animal magnetism was lost sight of. In all this there was a striking contrast between France and America: in the one country, the academic successors of Mesmer ultimately developed out of the magical beliefs of the day the real phenomena of hypnotism, hysteria and suggestion;[2] in the other, the incredible mixture of religion with medicine led to the almost entire neglect of mental healing in the medical profession.[3] The result of this was that the little which had been established was soon forgotten, and that the promising era of scientific enlightenment was eclipsed by the dark age of occultism. For example, Rush's notable work on *Diseases of the Mind;* his colleague Beasley's recognition of the interrelation of psychical and physical; Buchanan's hints as to mental causes of disordered physiological functions; Cooper's translation of the work of Broussais,—all these serious investigations were almost completely ignored. So in place of the academic materialists of Philadelphia and the South, came the popular occultists of the North,[4]—Poyen, disciple of the eccentric Deleuze, Grimes, the inventor of electro-biology, Quimby, the forerunner in the present most widely known movement for drugless healing.[5] As this bizarre group of sectaries, this strange line of backdoor philosophers grew, in one way or another, out of animal magnetism, it is not without reason to connect their perversions and distortions of that principle to Franklin's original opposition to Mesmer and his school. This was really most unfortunate, for that opposition was of such weight that it prevented what might otherwise have

---

[1] Among the MSS. in the American Philosophical Society's Collection is a note and a publication on Animal Magnetism from J. A. Thouret, 748-1810), director of the École de Médecine. (Hale, op. cit., Vol. 2, p. 310.)

[2] Compare Pierre Janet, *L'Automatisme psychologique*, Paris, 1903, Chapter III., § 1, *Résumé historique de la théorie des suggestions.*

[3] From a conversation with Professor Pierre Janet, 20th November, 1906.

[4] Compare Joseph Jastrow, *Fact and Fable in Psychology*, New York, 1900; Frank Podmore, *Modern Spiritualism*, Book II., London, 1902.

[5] Compare my article, *The Personal Sources of Christian Science*, *Psychological Review*, November, 1903.

been a fruitful grafting of the psychical branch upon the physical tree of knowledge.[1] In this unsympathetic attitude toward the more fugitive and elusive mental phenomena Franklin was but an example of that dominant American type which seeks merely the palpable and immediately practical. But although this hard-headed way of looking at things had as its deficiencies, blindness in matters of the spirit, absence of imagination and passionate emotion,[2] it had as its excellences that desire for physical improvement and material welfare without which even philosophical culture languishes.

With these deficiencies and excellences in mind, one may attempt a final estimate of Franklin's services to American philosophy. Despite the crude and fragmentary nature of his own speculative system, he was nevertheless an indirect promoter of speculation. Starting in what has been described as a small and unpretending intellectual sphere in a remote part of the English colonies,[3] the Philadelphian conceived the scheme of organising a learned society whose attention was to be devoted to all philosophic experiences that let light into the nature of things, tend to increase the power of man over matter and multiply the conveniences or pleasures of life.[4] In this Original Proposal for Promoting Useful Knowledge among the British Plantations in America, it has been implied that Franklin, after the manner of Bacon, by identifying philosophy with the natural sciences, was the chief representative of that conception of philosophy which has until recently been current in America as well as in England.[5] The comparison is suggestive, but not complete; it needs to be supplemented by a contrast. To utilise, in a reverse form, the description of another, Franklin was unlike the typical

---

[1] As an example of Franklin's casual interest in psychological problems is his observation that ' green glasses removed give a book a blush of red. This I know not how to account for.' (Vol. 2, p. 469).

[2] Compare Sainte-Beuve, *Causeries,* Vol. 7, p. 136.

[3] *Greetings from the Royal Society of London to the American Philosophical Society,* 1906 (MS).

[4] Vol. 4, p. 228.

[5] M. M. Curtis, *Philosophy in America,* p. 5.

British man of science.[1] There may have been something casual and accidental about his first discoveries, but he did not communicate novel ideas in unintelligible language, retain an isolated position, attach little or no importance to the labours of others; it must rather be said that, in the clearness of his expression, and the sureness of his touch, his scientific writings were akin to those of the French; while in his attempts to correlate and diffuse scientific knowledge and become acquainted with the views of others, by means of a central society with local ramifications and literary organs, his scheme resembled the German university system.

[1] Described by J. T. Merz, *European Thought in the Nineteenth Century*, London, 1904, Vol. i, p. 277.

CHAPTER VI

VIRGINIA AND JEFFERSON

A S Philadelphia was intellectually dominated by Benjamin Franklin, so was Virginia by Thomas Jefferson (1743-1826). But while the former represented utilitarian ambition for palpable results, the latter stood for liberty of thinking for its own sake. This was manifest in the President's express desire to have inscribed on his tomb: 'Author of the Declaration of American Independence, of the Statute of Virginia for Religious Freedom, and the Father of the University of Virginia.' As the advocate of free-thought in the Old Dominion, Jefferson was but the embodiment of his class. In contrast to the heresy-hunting Calvinists of the North, he typified the fox-hunting Arminians of the South; his earliest intellectual impressions were gained from that local species of Anglican clergy who, from reading the fashionable, sceptical literature of the mother country, came to be considered as lax in thought, as they were reputed to be loose in living. But without entering into the respective moral merits of Roundhead and Cavalier,[1] it was the latter who furnished the initial stimulus for Jefferson's most fundamental form of belief, since his deism had its rise in his education in the College of William and Mary. This, the second oldest of the chartered institutions in the colonies, had an ecclesiastical origin; at the same time, rationalism received adequate expression. The founders of the College, according to the charter of 1758, earnestly desired that the orthodox Christian faith might be propagated, but they

[1] Compare John Fiske, *Old Virginia and Her Neighbours*, New York, 1898, Chapter X., *The Coming of the Cavaliers*. Compare also Miller, *Retrospect*, Vol. 2, p. 334, for the 'low state of literature and religion in Virginia,' from the Princeton point of view. Somewhat apocryphal tales are quoted from McConnell's *American Episcopal Church*, by Émile Boutmy, *Eléments d'une Psychologie politique du Peuple américain*, Paris, 1902, p. 278.

added, in respect to the philosophy school: For as much as we see now daily a further progress in Philosophy, than could be made by Aristotle's Logick and Physicks, which reigned so long alone in the Schools, and shut out all others, we leave it to the President and Masters, to teach what systems of Logick, Physicks, Ethicks and Mathematicks they may think fit.[1]

In addition to this liberty of philosophising, the scientific spirit prevailed in the place. William Small, friend of Watts, the inventor of the steam engine, and of Erasmus Darwin, the grandfather of the evolutionist, came to the Virginia institution in 1758, and Jefferson, who attended his lectures in natural philosophy, declared that he fixed the destinies of his life.[2] Adding to these liberalising forces the elective system of studies, and the naturally volatile temper of a Southerner, it was inevitable that Jefferson should develop that receptive spirit which made him the typical progressive of his times. As he wrote in regard to the proposed University of Virginia, the Gothic idea that we are to look backwards instead of forwards for the improvement of the human mind, is not an idea which this country will endure.[3] These were glittering educational generalities, but Jefferson backed them up by specific details. In his *Notes on Virginia,* replying to the assertion of the Abbé Raynal [4] that America had not produced one man of genius, he retorted that he expected such progress to be made here, under our democratic stimulants, on a grand scale, until every man is potentially an athlete in body and an Aristotle in mind. For the education of the young Stagirite there was now offered a scheme of Jeffersonian simplicity: it was to start the inquiring student with books of a harmless sort, but finally and insidiously to wean him away from orthodoxy. The list recommended was headed by Hutcheson's *Introduction to Moral Philosophy,* Locke's treatise on the *Conduct of the Mind in Search*

[1] *The Charter, etc.,* Williamsburg, 1758, pp. 9, 133.

[2] Lyon G. Tylor, *Early Courses and Professors at William and Mary College,* 1904, pp. 5, 6.

[3] Vol. 7, p. 415 (F).

[4] In his *Philosophical and Political History of the Establishments and Commerce of the Europeans in the Two Indies,* 1770.

for Truth, and Dugald Stewart's *Philosophy of the Human Mind.*
These were followed by Lord Kames' *Natural Religion* and Buck-
ner's adaptation of Enfield's *History of Philosophy.* The latter
volume presented certain insinuations against revealed religion; it
spoke of the low state of moral philosophy among the Jews and
declared that the early teachings had been perverted from the
principles of a pure deism. Jefferson now sought to instil into
the youthful mind, what his countrymen came to look upon with
suspicion,—the principles of French rationalism. These were to
be found in an anonymous *Traité de Morale et Bonheur,* in *La
Sagesse de Chavron,* the production of the sceptical follower of
Montaigne, and in Condorcet's *Progrés de l'Esprit Humain,* a
revolutionary brief for the rule of reason. Finally came the *Corruptions of Christianity,* by Dr. Samuel Priestley, the Anglo-American free-thinker.

Although he compiled this reading list for another, the sage of
Monticello was but indicating, in miniature, the elements and
phases of his own philosophy. In brief, the Scotch realists represented the common-sense scheme of his old age, the French the
materialism of his halcyon days, and the work of Priestley the
fundamental deism of his whole life. By his own confession
the *Corruptions of Christianity* established the groundwork of the
President's creed,[1] and also opened to him a view of the subject,
which, to his mind, ought to displease neither rationalists, Christians nor deists.[2]   But in this fruitful line of inquiry the apologetic
deist of the White House was anticipated by another work of his
prolific friend. It was Priestley's *Comparative View of Socrates
and Jesus,* which excited in Jefferson the desire to see the author
take up the subject on a more extended scale.[3]   As an explanation
of this desire Jefferson adds: In consequence of some conversation
with Dr. Rush, in the year 1798-99, I had promised some day to
write him a letter giving him my view of the Christian system. I
have reflected often on it since, and even sketched the outlines in

[1] Compare H. S. Randall, *Life of Thomas Jefferson,* Vol. III., Chapter
14, *Jefferson's Religious Views.*
[2] Vol. 7, p. 460 (F).
[3] Vol. 8, p. 244 (F).

my own mind. I should first take a general view of the moral doctrines of the most remarkable of the antient philosophers, of whose ethics we have sufficient information to make an estimate, say of Pythagoras, Epicurus, Epictetus, Socrates, Cicero, Seneca, Antoninus. I should do justice to the branches of morality they have treated well; but point out the importance of those in which they are deficient. I should then take a view of the deism and ethics of the Jews, and show in what a degraded state they were, and the necessity they presented of a reformation. I should proceed to a view of the life, character, and doctrines of Jesus, who sensible of incorrectness of their ideas of the Deity and of morality, endeavoured to bring them to the principles of a pure deism, and juster notions of the attributes of God, to reform their moral doctrines to the standard of reason, justice and philanthropy, and to inculcate the belief of a future state.[1]

Jefferson's views of the Christian religion were more fully disclosed by him in a subsequent letter, which was both a vindication of the public charges of atheism brought against him, and a private explication of his really moderate deism. Writing to Benjamin Rush, he says: My views are the result of a life of inquiry and reflection, and very different from that anti-Christian system imputed to me by those who know nothing of my opinions. To the corruptions of Christianity I am, indeed, opposed; but not to the genuine precepts of Jesus himself. I am a Christian, in the only sense in which he wished any one to be: sincerely attached to his doctrines, in preference to all others; ascribing to himself every *human* excellence; and believing he never claimed any other. At the short interval since these conversations, when I could justifiably abstract my mind from public affairs, the subject has been under my contemplation. But the more I considered it, the more it expanded beyond the measure of either my time or information. In the moment of my late departure from Monticello, I received from Dr. Priestley, his little treatise of *Socrates and Jesus Compared*. This being a section of the general view I had taken of the field, it became a subject of reflection while on the road, and unoccupied otherwise. The result was, to arrange in my mind a syllabus, or out-

[1] Vol. 8, p. 224 (F).

line of such an estimate of the comparative merits of Christianity, as I wished to see executed by someone of more leisure and information for the task than myself. This I now send you, as the only discharge of my promise I can probably ever execute: *Syllabus of an Estimate of the Merit of the Doctrines of Jesus, compared with those of others.*

In a comparative view of the ethics of the enlightened nations of antiquity, of the Jews and of Jesus, no notice should be taken of the corruptions of reason among the ancients, to wit, the idolatry and superstition of the vulgar, nor of the corruptions of Christianity by the learned among its professors.

Let a just view be taken of the moral principles inculcated by the most esteemed of the sects of ancient philosophy, or of their individuals; particularly Pythagoras, Socrates, Epicurus, Cicero, Epictetus, Seneca, Antoninus.

I. Philosophers. 1. Their precepts related chiefly to ourselves, and the government of those passions which, unrestrained, would disturb our tranquillity of mind. In this branch of philosophy they were really great.

2. In developing our duties to others, they were short and defective. They embraced, indeed, the circles of kindred and friends, and inculcated patriotism, or the love of our country in the aggregate, as a primary obligation: toward our neighbours and countrymen they taught justice, but scarcely viewed them as within the circle of benevolence. Still less have they inculcated peace, charity, and love to our fellow men, or embraced with benevolence the whole family of mankind.

II. Jews. 1. Their system was Deism; that is, the belief in one only God. But their ideas of him and of his attributes were degrading and injurious.

2. Their ethics were not only imperfect, but often irreconcilable with the sound dictates of reason and morality, as they respect intercourse with those around us; and repulsive and anti-social, as respecting other nations. They needed reformation, therefore, in an eminent degree.

III. Jesus. In this state of things among the Jews, Jesus appeared. His parentage was obscure; his condition poor; his education null; his natural endowments great; his life correct and innocent; he was meek, benevolent, patient. firm, disinterested, and of the sublimest eloquence.

The disadvantages under which his doctrines appear are remarkable.

1. Like Socrates and Epictetus, he wrote nothing himself.

2. But he had not, like them, a Xenophon or an Arrian to write for him. I name not Plato, who only used the name of Socrates to cover the whimsies of his own brain. On the contrary, all the learned of his country, intrenched in its power and riches, were opposed to him, lest his labours should undermine their advantages; and the committing to writing his life and doctrines fell on unlettered and ignorant men, who wrote, too, from memory, and not till long after the transactions had passed.

3. According to the ordinary fate of those who attempt to enlighten and reform mankind, he fell an early victim to the jealousy and combination of the altar and the throne, at about thirty-three years of age, his reason having not yet attained the *maximum* of its energy, nor the course of his preaching, which was but of three years at most, presented occasions for developing a complete system of morals.

4. Hence the doctrines which he really delivered were defective as a whole, and fragments only of what he did deliver have come to us mutilated, misstated, and often unintelligible.

5. They have been still more disfigured by the corruptions of schismatising followers, who have found an interest in sophisticating and perverting the simple doctrine he taught, by engrafting on them the mysticisms of a Grecian sophist, frittering them into subtleties, and obscuring them with jargon, until they have caused good men to reject the whole in disgust, and to view Jesus himself as an impostor.

Notwithstanding these disadvantages, a system of morals is presented to us which, if filled up in the style and spirit of the rich fragments he left us, would be the most perfect and sublime that has ever been taught by man.

The question of his being a member of the Godhead, or in direct communication with it, claimed for him by some of his followers, and denied by others, is foreign to the present view, which is merely an estimate of the intrinsic merits of his doctrines.

1. He corrected the Deism of the Jews, confirming them in their belief of one only God, and giving them juster notions of his attributes and government.

2. His moral doctrines, relating to kindred and friends, were more pure and perfect than those of the most correct of the philosophers, and greatly more so than those of the Jews; and they went far beyond both in inculcating universal philanthropy, not

only to kindred and friends, to neighbours and countrymen, but to all mankind, gathering all into one family, under the bonds of love, charity, peace, common wants, and common aids. A development of this head will evince the peculiar superiority of the system of Jesus over all others.

3. The precepts of philosophy, and of the Hebrew code, laid hold of actions only. He pushed his scrutinies into the heart of man; erected his tribunal in the region of his thoughts, and purified the waters at the fountain-head.

4. He taught, emphatically, the doctrines of a future state, which was either doubted, or disbelieved by the Jews; and wielded it with efficacy, as an important incentive, supplementary to the other motives to moral conduct.[1]

This *Syllabus* was a hasty performance, a matter of a dozen days in the strenuous year of the Louisana purchase. Moreover its subject was not seriously resumed for as many years, and then in a greatly altered and diminished form. So, too, in the political agitations of the times, Jefferson appears to have conveniently forgotten his earlier project, for he declares that of publishing a book on religion he never had an idea; he should as soon think of writing for the reformation of Bedlam as the world of religious sects.[2] In a word, then, the former ambitious project for a study of comparative religions had dwindled to a home-made harmony of the gospels. Yet these two productions were essentially connected. In regard to the former, considering Christianity the most sublime and benevolent, but at the same time the most perverted system that ever shone upon man, the Virginian had set to work to mend it. His plan was first to take a general view of the moral doctrines of the most remarkable of the ancient philosophers, then of the deism and ethics of the Jews, finally to proceed to a view of the life, character, and doctrines of Jesus, who, sensible of the incorrectness of their ideas of the Deity, and of morality, endeavoured to bring them to the principles of a pure deism. As to the harmony, Jefferson's object was merely to take the four Evangelists, cut out from them every text they had recorded of the moral precepts of Jesus, and there will be found remaining, he avers, the most sublime and benevolent code of morals which has ever been offered to man. . . . I have

[1] Vol. 8, pp. 223-8 (F).   [2] Vol. 14, p. 232.

performed this operation for my own use, he continues, by cutting verse by verse out of the printed book, and arranging the matter which is evidently his, and which is as easily distinguishable as diamonds in a dunghill. The result is an octavo of forty-six pages of pure and unsophisticated doctrine.[1]

This production issued by Congress in its four-fold polyglot form, a full century after its inception, is the so-called Jefferson Bible.[2] Bearing the title *The Life and Morals of Jesus of Nazareth,* the compiler acknowledges that it was attempted too hastily, being the work of two or three nights only at Washington, after getting through the evening task of reading the letters and papers of the day.[3] Having, therefore, collated the *Syllabus of the Doctrines of Jesus,* ' a precious morsel of ethics, somewhat in the lapidary style,' Jefferson never went back to his larger undertaking, for as he said of his friend Van der Kemp's projected *Encyclopedia of the Christian Philosophy* it would require a Newton in physics and a Locke in metaphysics.[4] Here also Jefferson may have taken a lesson from Priestley, who had neglected his discovery of oxygen for his *Doctrines of Heathen Philosophy, Compared with those of Revelation,* while all the time, as an opponent remarked, he was a better doctor of chemistry than of divinity. So, perhaps, it was that Jefferson seemed at last to have realised, that the rôle of a philosophical higher critic was an impossible one, that to distinguish between primitive Christianity and later accretions was a task beyond the scholar of that age.

Jefferson's imperfect comparative studies remain as the most formal, but not as the sole expression of his beliefs, for in addition the ' Syllabus ' and the ' Bible ' there is a voluminous corre-

---

[1] *Works,* Vol. 13, p. 390.

[2] Washington, 1904, with an introduction by Cyrus Adler.

[3] Vol. 15, p. 2 (L).

[4] Judge Fr. Adr. Van der Kemp, a political refugee from the Revolution in the Netherlands, also published a *Sketch of a Desired Work.—Moral and Physical Causes of the Revolutionary Spirit in the latter part of the Eighteenth Century, in their Probable Issues in both continents,* (General Repository, 1813, Cambridge, Vol. 4, p. 390).

spondence, from which the Virginian's somewhat motley philosophy may be reconstructed. In general, that philosophy was an eclecticism of a pronounced deistic type, since it was the very peculiarity of the deist to wear a patchwork philosopher's cloak, yet to wear it in the fashion of the day. Thus, when, on different occasions, Jefferson exclaimed: 'I am an Epicurean,'[1] 'I am a Materialist,'[2] 'I am a sect by myself,'[3]—there was discoverable beneath these various disguises the strut and swagger of the age of reason. With all its modern setting, Jefferson's first phase of belief had an ancient origin. Writing to William Short he declared: I too am an Epicurean. I consider the genuine (not the imputed) doctrines of Epicurus as containing everything rational in moral philosophy which Greece and Rome have left us. Epictetus, indeed, has given us what was good of the Stoics; all beyond, of their dogmas, being hypocrisy and grimace. I have sometimes thought of translating Epictetus by adding the genuine doctrines of Epicurus from the Syntagma of Gassendi.[4] To his correspondent, Jefferson confesses that with one foot in the grave, these are now idle projects; but he fortunately included in his letter another of his documents in the lapidary style:

The Syllabus of the Doctrines of Epicurus.

Physical.—The Universe eternal. Its parts, great and small, interchangeable.

Matter and void alone.

Motion inherent in matter which is weighty and declining.

Eternal circulation of the elements of bodies.

Gods, an order of beings next superior to man, enjoying in their sphere, their own felicities; but not meddling with the concerns of the scale of beings below them.

Moral.—Happiness the aim of life.

Virtue the foundation of happiness.

[1] Vol. 15, p. 244 (L).
[2] Vol. 10, p. 143 (F).
[3] Vol. 7, p. 172 (W)
[4] Vol. 10, pp. 143-145 (F). Query: Did Jefferson have anything to do with the publication of the Encheiridion of Epictetus in the Greek, at Philadelphia, about this time?

Utility the test of virtue. Pleasure active and In-dolent.
In-do-lence is the absence of pain, the true felicity.

Active, consists in agreeable motion; it is not happiness, but the means to produce it.

Thus the absence of hunger is an article of felicity; eating the means to obtain it.

The *summum bonum* is to be not pained in body, nor troubled in mind, *i. e.* In-do-lence of body, tranquillity of mind.

To procure tranquillity of mind we must avoid desire and fear, the two principal diseases of the mind.

Man is a free agent. Virtue consists in 1. Prudence. 2. Temperance. 3. Fortitude. 4. Justice. To which are opposed, 1. Folly. 2. Desire. 3. Fear. 4. Deceit.[1]

The two parts of this syllabus had an unequal influence on the mind of its compiler. In the moral sphere, he remained a utilitarian, and in his old age, when every avenue of pleasing sensation was closed, and athumy, debility and malaise left in their places,[2] he sought to attain the Epicurean *summum bonum,*— ease of body and tranquillity of mind. But in the physical sphere, the Virginian did not hold strictly to the Epicurean doctrine of the eternity and self-sufficiency of the material universe. He now questioned whether the movements of nature are in a never ending circle. A particular species of unorganised matter, he reasons, might disappear for a while and be restored by the fortuitous concourse and the combination of the elements which compose it, but organised being cannot be restored by accidental aggregation of its elements.[3] These doubts of the ancient atomism seem inconsistent in the face of previous declarations. They nevertheless have an explanation in what was the most interesting of Jefferson's philosophical experiences. It was his five years' residence in France, before the outbreak of the Revolution, that gave the free-thinking Southerner an insight into the possibilties of materialism when carried to a logical outcome. As American minister, Jefferson had the fortune of enjoying the society of the

[1] Vol. 10, p. 146 (F).
[2] Vol. 10, p. 216 (F).
[3] To Van der Kemp, February 19, 1818, Buffalo Historical Society Proceedings, Vol. 7, p. 23.

same lively set of spirits as did his predecessor, Franklin. Thus he could recall to Cabanis the pleasant hours he passed with him at the house of Madame Helvétius; confess that the French literati are half a dozen years ahead of the American,[1] and yet make no effort to catch up with them.

Here Jefferson's fundamental deism held him back; for, like the more moderate exponents of the Enlightenment, while disbelieving in a revealed, he was at the same time convinced of the advantages of a natural theology. So it was that 'the savage from the mountains of America,' living in the midst of the intellectual seductions of Paris could still remain a believer in the Être Suprême. The system of Diderot, D'Alembert and D'Holbach was designated by his friend Baron Grimm, an exposition of atheism for chambermaids and barbers. Jefferson, not so witty but more wise, criticized this extreme presentation more broadly and more soberly. Remarking that the atheistic was a more numerous school in the Catholic countries, while the infidelity of the Protestant took generally the form of deism, he puts the arguments of both sides thus: When the atheist descanted on the unceasing motion and circulation of matter through the animal, vegetable and mineral kingdoms, never resting, never annihilated, always changing form, and under all forms gifted with the power of reproduction; the theist pointing " to the heavens above, and to the earth beneath, and to the waters under the earth," asked, if these things did not proclaim a first cause, possessing intelligence and power.[2] But Jefferson's belief does not rest solely on a calmly reasoned assurance of an abstract cause. He returns with ardour to an attack on the extremists and offers a brilliant personal defence of deism. He desires to give a complete *gain de cause* to the disciples of Ocellus, Timaeus, Spinosa, Diderot and D'Holbach. The argument which they rest on as triumphant and unanswerable is, that in every hypothesis of cosmogony, you must admit an eternal pre-existence of something; and according to the rule of sound philosophy, you are never to employ two principles to solve a difficulty when one will suffice. They say, then, that it is more simple to believe at once in the

[1] Vol. 4, p. 496 (W).   [2] Vol. 15, pp. 426-427.

eternal pre-existence of the world, as it is now going on, and may forever go on by the principle of reproduction which we see and witness, than to believe in the eternal pre-existence of an ulterior cause, or Creator of the world, a Being whom we see not and know not, of whose form, substance and mode, or place of existence, or of action, no sense informs us, no power of the mind enables us to delineate or comprehend. On the contrary, I hold (without appeal to revelation) that when we take a view of the universe in its parts general or particular, it is impossible for the human mind not to perceive and feel a conviction of design, consummate skill, and indefinite power in every atom of its composition. The movement of the heavenly bodies, so exactly held in their course by the balance of centrifugal and centripetal forces; the structure of our earth itself, with its distribution of lands, waters and atmosphere; animal and vegetable bodies, examined in all their minutest particles; insects, mere atoms of life, yet as perfectly organised as man or mammoth; the mineral substances, their generation and uses; it is impossible, I say, for the human mind not to believe that there is in all this, design, cause and effect up to an ultimate cause; a Fabricator, of all things from matter and motion; their Preserver and Regulator.[1]

That Jefferson's cosmology was that of a moderate deist was next shown by a characteristic compromise between the Epicurean eternalism and the puritanic doctrine of interference with the ordered course of nature. Calling himself a sceptical reader, he nevertheless reasons on the supposition that the earth has had a beginning, yet he does not agree with those biblical theorists who suppose that the Creator made two jobs of his creation, that he first made a chaotic lump and set it in motion and then, waiting the ages necessary to form itself, stepped in a second time to create the animals and plants which were to inhabit it.[2] In this

---

[1] Vol. 7, p. 281 (W).

[2] Did not Jefferson elsewhere oppose Leibniz, this might be considered a renewal of that cosmology which holds that there are not successive acts of creation, but that the universe is completed by the original act of the divine will, and thereafter moves on by its own inherent forces.

modified materialistic cosmology Jefferson bases his humdrum
notions chiefly on the old fashioned deist Waterland. In his
ontology, his sources are more varied and more modern. In fact,
he appeals to a kind of international tribunal of his own appointment, asserting that he was supported in his creed of materialism
by the Lockes, the Tracys, and the Stewarts.[1] This was a strange
association of authorities, yet that Jefferson could, in the first
place, lump together the English empiricist and the French ideol-
ogist was not altogether without reason: like Voltaire, who assumed from Locke that matter can think, he evidently adopted
the one-sided Gallic emphasis upon the sensational at the expense
of the reflective element. So he goes on to say: Mr. Locke and
other materialists have charged with blasphemy the spiritualists
who have denied the Creator the power of endowing certain
forms of matter with the faculty of thought. These, however,
are speculations and subtleties in which, for my own part, I have
little indulged myself. When I meet with a proposition beyond
finite comprehension, I abandon it as I do a weight which human
strength cannot lift, and I think ignorance in these cases is truly
the softest pillow on which I can lay my head. Were it necessary, however, to form an opinion, I confess I should, with Mr.
Locke, prefer swallowing one incomprehensibility rather than two.
It requires one effort only to admit the single incomprehensibility
of matter endowed with thought, and two to believe, first, that of
an existence called spirit, of which we have neither evidence nor
idea; and then, secondly, how that spirit, which has neither extension nor solidity, can put material organs into motion. These
are things which you and I may perhaps know ere long. We
have so lived as to fear neither horn of the dilemma.[2] So much
for Locke; of the second and third members of Jefferson's strange
triumvirate he considers Dugald Stewart and Destutt de Tracy
the ablest metaphysicians living, since the former has given the
natural history of the thinking faculty from facts and observations, the latter its modes of action and deduction, which he calls
logic and ideology. Along with these men are to be put Cabanis,
who in his *Physique et Morale de l'Homme*, has investigated

[1] Vol. 15, p. 274.   [2] Vol. 7, p. 153 (W).

anatomically and most ingeniously the particular organs in the human structure which may, most probably, exercise the thinking faculty. And they ask, continues Jefferson: Why may not the mode of action called thought have been given to a material organ of a peculiar structure, as that of magnetism is to the needle, or of elasticity to the spring by a particular manipulation of the steel? They observe that on ignition of the needle or spring, their magnetism and elasticity cease. So on dissolution of the material organ by death, its action of thought may cease also, and that nobody supposes that the magnetism or elasticity retires to hold a substantive and distinct existence.[1]

Jefferson's relations to the philosophers last named was of the utmost importance, since he knew them all personally and was profoundly influenced by their views. While the Virginian was in Paris, Cabanis had delivered before the Academy the series of lectures on the relations between mind and body which contained the famous apothegms: ' the brain secretes thought,' ' the nerves make the man.' A few years later Jefferson wrote to the lecturer on reading his completed volumes: That thought may be a faculty of our material organisation has been believed in the gross, and though the *modus operandi* of nature, in this, as in most other cases, can never be developed and demonstrated to beings limited as we are, yet I feel confident you will have conducted us as far on the road as we can go.[2] However, it was the less known side of Cabanis that had a greater influence on Jefferson's mental development. As has been pointed out, this *idéologue* does not lay stress exclusively on the external senses, for in addition to the passive reception of the organism, there is, to his mind, an inner activity, the vital feeling, an obscure instinct independent of the outer sense impressions.[3] Because of this emphasis on the inner rather than the outer, on the instinctive rather than the sensational, Jefferson was led to disagree with Cabanis' adherent, Tracy. The latter's supplement to his *Elements of Ideology,* the President caused to be translated and pub-

---

[1] Vol. 15, p. 240.   [2] Vol. 4, p. 496 (W).
[3] Höffding, *Modern Philosophy,* Vol. 2, p. 299.

lished in America;[1] he also kept in his possession the manuscript of Tracy's *Logique,* which he described as a compendious demonstration of the reality and limits of human knowledge, occupying exactly the grounds of Locke's work on the understanding.[2]   For the former of these works Jefferson expressed particularly high regard, since it makes our perceptions of whatever we actually feel, perfectly, completely and necessarily sure.   But with Tracy's *Ethics,* which adopts the principles of Hobbes that the sense of justice is not derived from our natural organisation, but is founded on convention only, the American realist does not agree, but is forced to confess that, for his own part, he believes that the moral sense is instinctive and innate.[3]

Here is an apparent contradiction, not only of Jefferson's second, but of his prime authority for nativism, an explicit denial of the Lockean denial of innate ideas.   But even this reversal of judgment as to the *tabula rasa,* is not so much an inconsistency as a sign of progression, a mental change with a valid cause.   The change may be attributed to the last, but not the least of the given authorities.   Jefferson had read Locke, listened to Cabanis, and corresponded with Tracy, but with Dugald Stewart he was on singularly intimate terms.   When the exponent of Scottish realism was called to France to combat the rampant materialism and sensationalism, he met the American plenipotentiary, and the two visited one another daily for some months.   Considering him 'a great man and among the most honest living,' the receptive Scottish-American readily absorbed the pre-digested philosophy of common sense.   This was a peculiar performance, yet not without its justification.   For one who early prided himself on being naturally incredulous and sceptical, realism would have been weak intellectual diet, but for one who had reached the age of quietism, it furnished sufficient nourishment.   When he was young, Jefferson recalls that he was fond of speculations which seemed to promise some insight into the hidden country; after

[1] Prefixed to Tracy's *Treatise on Political Economy,* Georgetown, D. C., 1817; from a copy in the possession of Dr. R. B. Warfield, Baltimore.
[2] Vol. 10, p. 174 (F).
[3] Vol. 10, p. 32 (F).

his retirement from active life, he rests content in the belief that there is a reality which we directly recognise in beings, and that we are guided unconsciously by the unerring hand of instinct.[1]

While these sentiments were attributed to Stewart, it is evident that they were but echoes from the founder of the Scottish philosophy, repetitions of those so-called original, fundamental principles of the human mind, comprising the belief in a material world and in a moral sense. In his *Inquiry into the Human Mind on the Principles of Common Sense,* Reid had used these convenient principles against Berkeley's doubts concerning the reality of the external world, and against Hume's scepticisms concerning the reality of the Ego; it was only afterwards that Stewart had combined them in his dictum that there is first a sensation, then a belief in self. Armed, then, with these handy principles, Jefferson found them most useful in warding off the dubeities with which John Adams assailed him; so he replies to the latter: The crowd of scepticisms in your puzzling letter on matter, spirit, motion, &c., kept me from sleep. I read it and laid it down; read it and laid it down, again and again; and to give rest to my mind I was obliged to recur ultimately to my habitual anodyne, I feel, therefore, I exist. I feel bodies which are not myself: there are other existences then. I call them matter.[2]

A thorough realist in his metaphysics, it was in the field of ethics that Jefferson found the greatest service for these instinctive pre-suppositions. Reid had declared that as by the external senses we have the original conception of the various qualities of bodies, so by our moral quality we have the original conceptions or right and wrong in conduct.[3] Jefferson repeats: man was endowed with a sense of right and wrong, which is as much a part of his nature as the sense of hearing, seeing, feeling.[4] These striking resemblances between the father of the common-sense school and his transatlantic follower were to be expected, not only because the pupil of one was the teacher of the other, but because Stewart injected Reid's views into Jefferson's mind before his own views had been put into print. The first part of Stewart's

---

[1] Vol. 10, p. 107 (F).   [2] Vol. 15, p. 274.
[3] Höffding, Vol. 1, p. 451.   [4] Vol. 4, p. 428 (F).

Elements of the Philosophy of the Human Mind was not published until 1792, some four or five years after he made the acquaintance of Jefferson. It is for this reason that the American represents the earlier and more undeveloped stage of Scottish realism. In the second volume of his *Elements* Stewart had used the phrase ' the fundamental laws of belief.' This, as one of his critics has said, was a great improvement on ' common sense,' which labours under the disadvantage of being ambiguous, inasmuch as it usually denotes that untaught sagacity which is found only in certain men and which others can never acquire, whereas it can be admitted into philosophical discussion only when it denotes principles which are regulating the minds of all.[1]

With this distinction between the primitive and developed realism, it is not hard to understand the crudity of Jefferson's remarks on the moral sense, his preference for a morality based on sentiment and not science, on the heart and not on the head. A few facts, he argues, will suffice to prove that nature has not organised reason for our moral direction. . . . If our country, when pressed with wrongs at the point of the bayonet, had been governed by its heads instead of its hearts, where should we have been now? Hanging on a gallows as high as Haman's. The heads began to calculate and compare numbers; the hearts threw up a few pulsations of their warmest blood; they supplied enthusiasm against wealth and numbers; they put their existence to the hazard when the hazard seemed against us, and they saved the country.[2] . . . I think it is lost time to attend lectures on moral philosophy. He who made us would have been a pitiful bungler, if He had made the rules of our moral conduct a matter of science. For one man of science, there are thousands who are not. What would have become of them? Man was destined for society. His morality, therefore, was to be formed to this object. He was endowed with a sense of right and wrong, merely relative to this. This sense is as much a part of his nature, as is the sense of hearing, seeing, feeling; it is the true foundation of morality, and not the *to Kalon,* truth, etc., as fanciful writers have imagined. The moral sense, or conscience, is as much a

[1] McCosh, *Scottish Philosophy,* p. 290.   [2] Vol. 6, p. 320 (F).

part of a man as his leg or arm. It is given to all human beings in a stronger or weaker degree, as force of members is given them in a greater or less degree. It may be strengthened by exercise, as may any particular limb of the body. This sense is submitted, indeed, in some degree, to the guidance of reason; but it is a small stock which is required for this; even a less one than what we call common sense. State a moral case to a ploughman and a professor. The former will decide it as well and often better than the latter, because he has not been led astray by artificial rules.[1]

Written during his stay in Paris, these philistine sentiments were nevertheless repeated by Jefferson after his return to the United States. Writing to the Abbé Correa in 1815 he says that he fears from the experiences of the last twenty-five years that morals do not necessarily advance hand in hand with the sciences. This pessimistic admission was clearly due to the fact that during the previous year the sage of Monticello had tried to systematise his ethical principles, but had reached only paltry conclusions. Corresponding with one of the lesser American realists and seeking to define the foundations of morality, Jefferson tells what they are not, but as to what they are, he can scarcely get beyond a shallow utilitarian realism. To him morality is not founded on abstract truth, nor love of God, nor the love of self, but nature has constituted utility to man as the standard and test of truth. This is the summary of a letter written to Thomas Law of Washington, in acknowledgment of the latter's *Second Thoughts on Instinctive Impulses*.[2] The letter should be given at length as a final example of Jefferson's philosophising, and as containing what he called his own creed:

On the Foundation of Morality in Man.

. . . . It is really curious that on a question so fundamental such a variety of opinions should have prevailed among men, and those, too, of the most exemplary virtue, and first order of understanding. It shows how necessary was the care of the Creator in making the moral principle so much a part of our constitution

[1] Vol. 4, p. 428 (F).
[2] Compare below Book V., Chapter VII.

as that no errors of reasoning or of speculation might lead us astray from its observance in practice. Of all the theories on this question, the most whimsical seems to have been that of Wollaston, who considers *truth* as the foundation of morality. The thief who steals your guinea does wrong only inasmuch as he acts a lie in using your guinea as if it were his own. Truth is certainly a branch of morality, and a very important one to society. But presented as its foundation, it is as if a tree taken up by the roots, had its stem reversed in the air, and one of its branches planted in the ground. Some have made the *love of God* the foundation of morality. This, too, is but a branch of our moral duties, which are generally divided into duties to God and duties to man. If we did a good act merely from the love of God and a belief that it is pleasing to Him, whence arises the morality of the Atheist? It is idle to say, as some do, that no such being exists. We have the same evidence of the fact as of most of those we act on, to wit: their own affirmations, and their reasonings in support of them. I have observed, indeed, generally, that while in Protestant countries the defections from the Platonic Christianity of the priests is to Deism, in Catholic countries they are to Atheism. Diderot, D'Alembert, D'Holbach, Condorcet, are known to have been among the most virtuous of men. Their virtue, then, must have had some other foundation than the love of God.

The *to Kalon* of others is founded in a different faculty, that of taste, which is not even a branch of morality. We have indeed an innate sense of what we call beautiful, but that is exercised chiefly on subjects addressed to the fancy, whether through the eye in visible forms, as landscape, animal figure, dress, drapery, architecture, the composition of colours, etc., or to the imagination directly, as imagery, style, or measure in prose or poetry, or whatever else constitutes the domain of criticism or taste, a faculty entirely distinct from the moral one. Self-interest, or rather self-love, or *egoism,* has been more plausibly substituted as the basis of morality. But I consider our relations with others as constituting the boundaries of morality. With ourselves we stand on the ground of identity, not of relation, which last, requiring two subjects, excludes self-love confined to a single one. To ourselves, in strict language, we can owe no duties, obligation requiring also two parties. Self-love, therefore, is no part of morality. Indeed it is exactly its counterpart. It is the sole antagonist of virtue, leading us constantly by our propensities to self-gratification in violation of our moral duties to others. Acordingly, it is against this enemy that are erected the batteries of moralists and religionists, as the only obstacle to the practice of morality. Take from man his selfish propensities, and he can have nothing to seduce him from the practice of virtue. Or subdue those propensities by education, instruction or restraint, and virtue remains without a competitor. Egoism, in a broader sense, has been thus presented as the source of moral action. It has been said that we feed the hungry, clothe the naked, bind up the wounds of the man beaten by thieves, pour oil and wine into them, set him on our own beast and bring him to the inn, because we receive ourselves pleasure from these acts. So Helvétius, one of the best men on earth, and the most ingenious advocate of this principle, after defining ' interest ' to mean not merely that which is pecuniary, but whatever may procure us pleasure or withdraw us from pain, [*de l'esprit* 2, 1,] says [*ib.* 2, 2,] ' The humane man is he to whom the sight of misfortune is insupportable, and who to rescue himself from this spectacle, is forced to succour the unfortunate object.' This indeed is true. But it is one step short of the ultimate question. These good acts give us pleasure, but how happens it that they give us pleasure? Because nature hath implanted in our breasts a love of others, a sense of duty to them, a moral instinct, in short, which prompts us irresistibly to feel and to succour their distresses and protests against the language of Helvétius, [*ib.* 2, 5,] ' What other motive than self-interest could determine a man to generous actions? It is as impossible for him to love what is good for the sake of good, as to love evil for the sake of evil.' The Creator would indeed have been a bungling artist, had he intended man for a social animal, without planting in him social dispositions. It is true they are not planted in every man, because there is no rule without exceptions; but it is false reasoning which converts exceptions into the general rule. Some men are born without the organs of sight, or of hearing, or without hands. Yet it would be wrong to say that man is born without these faculties, and sight, hearing, and hands may with truth enter into the general definition of man.

The want or imperfection of the moral sense in some men, like the want or imperfection of the senses of sight and hearing in others, is no proof that it is a general characteristic of the species. When it is wanting, we endeavour to supply the defect by education, by appeals to reason and calculation, by presenting to the being so unhappily conformed, other motives to do good and to eschew evil, such as the love, or the hatred, or rejection of those among whom he lives, and whose society is necessary to his happiness and even existence; demonstrations by sound calculation that honesty promotes interest in the long run; the rewards and penalties established by the laws; and ultimately the prospects of a future state of retribution for the evil as well as the good done while here. These are the correctives which are supplied by education, and which exercise the functions of the moralist, the preacher, and legislator; and they lead into a course of correct action all those whose disparity is not too profound to be eradicated. Some have argued against the existence of a moral sense, by saying that if nature had given us such a sense, impelling us to virtuous actions, and warning us against those which are vicious, then nature would also have designated, by some particular ear-marks, the two sets of actions which are, in themselves, the one virtuous and the other vicious. Whereas, we find, in fact, that the same actions are deemed virtuous in one country and vicious in another. The answer is, that nature has constituted *utility* to man, the standard and test of virtue. Men living in different countries, under different circumstances, different habits and regimens, may have different utilities; the same act, therefore, may be useful, and consequently virtuous in one country which is injurious and vicious in another differently circumstanced. I sincerely, then, believe with you in the general existence of a moral instinct. I think it the brightest gem with which the human character is studded, and the want of it as more degrading than the most hideous of the bodily deformities.[1]

Taking this, the last of his formal dissertations as an index of his philosophic character, Jefferson shows himself to be more legal than logical, more of a special pleader than an exact philosopher: so it might be said of him what he said of Cicero, that he was, ' diffuse, vapid, rhetorical, but enchanting.' In brief, he who professed to be an utter sceptic turns out to be considerable of a dogmatist. But to bring his philosophy into bolder relief he may be compared with John Adams, the cautious speculator and taster of systems, who, even in the days of their political rivalry, Jefferson considered, ' as disinterested as the being who made him.' Now it was after their reconciliation through Benjamin Rush that the correspondence between the Whig and the Federal ex-presidents discloses two gentlemen of the old school, both omnivorous readers, both averse to Calvinism and clerical obscurantism, both interested in the rising study of comparative religion, both tinged with the current deistic thought. Of the two the Southerner was more prone to generalisations, more im-

[1] *Works,* Vol. 14, pp. 139-144.

patient of other men's beliefs; the Northerner more tolerant, not inclined to go beyond ' New England guesses.' ' The Philosophical Chief of Monticello is such a heterodox and hungry fellow,' so runs a doggerel couplet of the day; Adams appears equally versatile but far less ardent. Confessedly afflicted with a kind of Pyrrhonism, he numbers himself among those Protestants *qui ne croyent rien*. So he considers Rousseau and Helvétius as absurd as Athanasius; condemns Rousseau and Rochefoucauld and Franklin for their gross ideology; disavows belief ·in Diderot and Condorcet; disagrees with the reasoning machine Priestley; is grievously disappointed in Plato,—in short ' philosophers, ancient and modern, appear to me as mad as Hindoos, Mohametans, and Christians. No doubt they would all think me mad and for anything I know, this globe may be a Bedlam, le Bicêtre of the universe.' [1] These are universal negatives with a vengeance, but Adams has a reason for them. For more than sixty years, he remarks, he had been attentive to controversies between Calvinists and Arminians, Trinitarians and Unitarians, Deists and Christians, and can now say he had read away bigotry, if not enthusiasm. He adds that he had been a student in books whose titles Jefferson had never read, from the *Light of Nature Pursued* and Ezra Styles Ely, to Leland's view of the Deistical writers and Van der Kemp's vast map of the causes of the revolutionary spirit;—and yet, these things are to me, at present, the marbles and nine-pins of old-age; I will not say the beads and prayer books.[2]

Adams' ironical deprecation of his own knowledge, which even left him ' not wholly uninformed of the controversies in Germany,' doubtless acted as a check on Jefferson. It seems to have been one reason for the abandonment of his projected view of the Christian system, supplementary to Priestley's works. Adams grants that Priestley has not given a satisfactory account of Pythagoras, Zoroaster, Confucius and all the founders of religions before Christianity. He ought also to have told us of the profound philosophy of the introduction to the Shasta, which teaches

[1] *Works* (ed. C. F. Adams), Boston, 1856; Vol. 10, pp. 45, 53, 102, 105, 409.
[2] *Works*, Vol. 10, pp. 56-58.

that God governs all the Creation by a general providence, resulting from his eternal designs. Priestley has his defects, yet
he is ' really a phenomenon, a comet in the system like Voltaire,
Bolingbroke and Hume.'¹ Such praise was the gentle hint that
Jefferson was scarcely prepared to carry out his elaborate scheme
of comparing Christianity with the ethnic religions. Moreover
in regard to the syllabus of ethical teachings extracted from the
text of the Evangelists, Adams agrees that the Christian philosophy is the most sublime and benevolent, but whether it is more
perverted than that of Numa, of Mahomet, of the Druids and
the Hindoos, he cannot as yet determine, because he is not sufficiently acquainted with these systems.² Adams' caution is unusual
in view of the contemporary habit of making odious comparisons.
Moderating his deism, it aided him to steer clear of the more
obvious difficulties of materialism. This was the stream of thought
where Jefferson had struck snags, but where the Northerner was
helped out by his constitutional agnosticism. He remembers that
when he was a junior sophister at Harvard he was a mighty metaphysician, or thought himself such, until he ran against the materialistic inference that the universe was both infinite and eternal.
And now, reading Leibniz and Berkeley and Hume, he finds that
matter is as much of an abstraction, a chimera, a conjecture, as
spirit; and reading Baron Grimm he discovers that the philosophy
of the Encyclopedists is nothing but pure, unadulterated atheism.
He is sensible of their services to Liberty and Fraternity, yet he
cannot but think they were all destitute of common sense. ' They
all seemed to think that all Christendom was convinced as they
were, that all religion was ' visions Judaicques,' and that their
effulgent lights had illuminated all the world. They had not
considered the force of early education on the millions of minds
who had never heard of their philosophy. And what was their
philosophy? The universe was matter only, and eternal; spirit
was a word without a meaning. All beings and attributes were
of eternal necessity; conscience, morality, were all nothing but

¹ *Works,* Vol. 10, p. 57.
² Jefferson's *Works,* Vol. 14, p. 316.

fate. Who, and what is this fate? He must be a sensible fellow. He must be a master of science. He must calculate eclipses in his head by intuition, and what is more comfortable than all the rest, he must be good natured, for this is upon the whole a good world.'[1] In these jocular criticisms there was a sly dig at Jefferson's deism. The French fate bore a striking resemblance to his benevolent deity, trust in whom would bring the philosophic millenium. And so Adams writes again: Let me now ask you very seriously, my friend, where are now, in 1813, the perfection and the perfectibility of human nature? Where is now the progress of the human mind? Where is the amelioration of society? . . . I leave those profound philosphers to enjoy their transporting hopes, provided always that they will not engage us in French Revolutions.[2] And so throughout the correspondence,—the impartial Novanglian meets the strenuous Virginian with whimsical advice. When as Epicurean he becomes too stoical, he urges him to eat his canvasback duck; when as deist he becomes too dogmatical, he remarks: 'It has been long, very long, a settled opinion in my mind, that there is now, never will be, and never was but one being who can understand the universe. And that it is not only vain, but wicked, for insects to pretend to comprehend it.'[3]

It was easy for Adams to write in this way; an agnostic's apology was tolerated in the case of one who would leave ' metaphysics in the clouds.' But with Jefferson things were different; politics complicated the situation and faction spoiled philosophy. The Federalists linked together Jeffersonianism, atheism and the excesses of the French revolution. They called the President a Jacobin, an infidel and a republican villain. They spoke of a dangerous, deistical and Utopian school of which a great personage from Virginia was a favoured pupil. They said his principles relished so strongly of Paris, and were seasoned in such a profusion of

[1] Jefferson's *Works*, Vol. 13, p. 371; Vol. 14, pp. 438-440; Vol. 15, p. 121.
[2] Jefferson's *Works*, Vol. 14, p. 426.
[3] *Works*, Vol. 10, p. 69.

French garlic that he offended the whole nation.[1] In these attacks the Federal clergy of New England were implicated. When Jefferson had brought over from France the arch-infidel Thomas Paine in a government ship, they spoke of him as an Ephraim who had become entangled with the heathen. Jefferson's defenders did not mend matters. The author of the *Hamiltoniad, or an Extinguisher of the Royal Faction of New England* dismisses the worn out tale of the President's irreligion by retorting that he has thrown into the lap of Morality the purest apothegms of the Apostles and Fathers; he confounds the politicians by calling them Tory bloodhounds, yelping upon the dangers that may arise from the Virginian or southern influence. These mixed metaphors betray a political confusion in which Jefferson found it hard to preserve a philosophic calm. He asserted that the priests, to soothe their resentments against the act of Virginia for establishing religious freedom, wished him to be thought atheist, deist or devil, who could advocate freedom from their religious dictations. Having opposed the scheme of a state supported church—'Christianity for pence and power'—he pronounced Massachusetts and Connecticut the last retreat of monkish darkness and bigotry. But the 'pious young monks of Harvard and Yale' were too much for him. In his old age, when urged to declare his views, he gave up the fight and confessed that he did not dare to thrust his head again into a hornet's nest, the *genus irritabile vatum*.[2]

Had it not been for this politico-clerical opposition, Jefferson might have been a more powerful agent in the intellectual development of the times. Hence to make an estimate of his academic influence, it remains to be shown what were his real purposes, and what the opposing forces. In the plan for university education which he proposed to the Legislature, he intended to place the entire responsibility for religious training upon an ethical basis,

[1] Joseph Dennie in the *Portfolio*, Number 1, 1805, quoted in Stedman and Hutchinson's *A Library of American Literature*, 1890, Vol. 4, p. 250.

[2] Vol. 15, pp. 60, 108; Conway, *Life of Thomas Paine*, Vol. 2, p. 310.

where all sects could agree. As he explained the matter: The proofs of the being of a God, the creator, preserver and supreme ruler of the universe, the author of all the relations of morality, and of the laws and obligations these infer, will be within the province of the professor of Ethics; to which adding the development of these moral obligations, of those in which all sects agree . . . a basis will be found common to all sects.[1] In the face of this declaration and because of his plan of having no professorship of divinity, but allowing independent schools of theology to be established in the neighbourhood of the University, Jefferson complained that a handle had been made to disseminate an idea that this is an institution, not only of no religion but against all religion.[2] This reputation of the University for being a ' seminary for atheists ' was an ingenious misrepresentation of two facts in the life of its founder, namely, his earlier friendship with French literati, and his later with English free-thinkers. With his conspicuous versatility, liberality and sanguine disposition, the Virginian was the proper representative both of America in France, and of France in America, the very embodiment of the belief that of all nations, the French and the Anglo-Americans were the most free and most exempt from prejudices.[3] This, at the least, was the sentiment of Condorcet, whose *Political Progress* Jefferson deemed a work of high value, since the eye of the author was a natural achromatic which divests every object of the glare of colour.[4] And so, in palpable imitation, Jefferson imagines a philosophical observer commencing a journey from the savages of the Rocky Mountains, eastwardly to our seacoast. These he would observe in a state of nature; he would next find those on our frontiers in a pastoral state; then would succeed our semi-barbarous citizens, the pioneers of the advance

---

[1] H. B. Adams, *Thomas Jefferson and the University of Virginia,* Washington, 1888, pp. 90-91.

[2] *Ib.,* p. 91, note.

[3] So Condorcet in his *Outlines of an Historical View of the Human Mind,* Baltimore, 1802. p. 210.

[4] Vol. 2, p. 799 (F)

of civilisation, and so in his progress he would meet the gradual shades of improving man until he would reach his, as yet, most improved state in our seaport towns. This in fact, is equivalent to a survey, in time, of the progress of man from the infancy of creation to the present day. I am eighty-one years of age, born where I now live, in the first range of mountains in the interior of our country. And I have observed this march of civilisation advancing from the sea coast, passing over us like a cloud of light, increasing our knowledge and improving our condition, inasmuch as that we are at this time more advanced in civilisation here than the seaports were when I was a boy.[1]

In tracing the steady steps of amelioration in his locality, Jefferson employed French historical methods; he utilised similar educational suggestions in the construction of his University. Two representative men, from whom he derived useful hints, have been well described as follows: the Chevalier Quesnay de Beaurepaire, one of those enthusiastic Frenchmen, who, like Lafayette, had come over to this country to aid in the war of the Revolution, had a scheme for planting in Richmond a kind of French academy of arts and sciences to be affiliated with the royal societies of London, Paris and Brussels and with other learned bodies of Europe. The scheme fell through, but living in Paris at this very time, and mentioned by Quesnay among the supporters of the proposed Academy, Jefferson must have been familiar with this early project for introducing the higher education of France into his native state. His original idea of a University for Virginia was to develop the curriculum of his *alma mater,* William and Mary College, but we hear nothing more of the idea after Jefferson's return from Paris; instead, his ideas of university education began to take such cosmopolitan form as actually to lead to a correspondence with General Washington about the feasibility of removing bodily to Virginia, the entire faculty of the Swiss College of Geneva, which was thoroughly French in its form of culture.[2]

Another of his Gallic correspondents, from whom Jefferson derived liberalising notions, was the French economist du Pont

[1] Vol. 7, p. 377 (W).
[2] H. B. Adams, *op. cit.,* pp. 21-27.

de Nemours. An associate of the physiocrats Turgot, Mirabeau and Quesnay the elder, du Pont was one of the delegates from the National Institute to go to the United States with a view to improve, and extend the sciences.[1] At the request of Jefferson, du Pont not only prepared a scheme of national education for the young republic, but also proposed a plan for the state University,[2] composed of distinct schools for the most advanced instruction.[3] Along with these educational suggestions were several highly characteristic philosophical views. In his published *Philosophie de l'univers,* du Pont had said, ' Dieu et la matière sont nécessaires et co-relatifs; '[4] in a private letter he referred to the Deity as ' le sublime Président de l'univers,[5] and urged the instituting of a national festival in which pæans shall be sung, one of which shall be consecrated to the country, our common mother, and to God, the father of the Universe.[6] It was well perhaps for the peace of mind of the hermit of Monticello, that these sentiments did not get abroad, for the first was too much like his youthful materialism borrowed from Gassendi, the second despite its subtle flattery too much of a democratising of the Deity, and the third too closely akin to the discredited scheme of Thomas Paine to found a society of theo-philanthropists.[7] And it was, Jefferson's Franco-American alliance brought him only trouble and irritation, for whenever he tried to introduce French literature he was invariably criticised. Thus, when he welcomed Flouren's experiments on the functions of the nervous system as a ' terrible tub to the Athanasians,' it was objected that incision knives will never discover the distinction between matter and spirit; [8] when he based his schematisation of the sciences on d'Alembert's system, by

[1] John Adams, *Works,* Vol. 8, p. 594, note.
[2] Franklin, *Works,* Vol. 4, p. 194, note (F).
[3] H. B. Adams, *op. cit.,* p. 51.
[4] Paris (ed. 1798), p. 46.
[5] Dated Philadelphia, April 12th, 1800, in Jefferson Papers, I., Vol. 7, No. 336, p. 12 (MS. Johns Hopkins University).
[6] Letters to Jefferson, Paris, 17 Dec., 1800, 5 Sept., 1808 (pp. 41, 217, MS).
[7] Compare Conway, *Life of Thomas Paine,* Vol. 2, Chapter XIII.
[8] John Adams, *Works,* Vol. 10, p. 414.

dividing moral philosophy into ethics and jurisprudence, it was argued that by so doing religion comes to be no more than a part of jurisprudence; [1] when he thought Becourt's *Sur la Création du Monde* to be merely an innocent attack on the Newtonian philosophy, he was mortified to find that certain persons contemplated its censorship by the government as an offence against religion. [2]

In these affairs, Jefferson's countrymen showed themselves in a bad light; once they had been willing enough to receive French gold, now they seemed to fear the Gauls even when they were bearing gifts. What this narrow attitude led to, and how the Gallic invasion was checked another has pointed out: if French ideas had really penetrated Virginian society they would have become as dominant in the South as German ideas became later in the North. It was one of the difficult tasks in Southern educational history to dislodge French philosophy from its academic strongholds in North and South Carolina; it was done by a strong current of Scotch Presbyterianism proceeding from Princeton College southwards. [3] And so it was that after all his endeavours to introduce the philosophical culture of France, the President's plans seem to have met with defeat. Leading to an attack from the same quarter, and to equally negative results, was his championship of English free-thought. Here but one representative thinker need be taken. Accompanying the apostle of radicalism, Samuel Priestley, was his son-in-law, Thomas Cooper, who proved a veritable stumbling block to Jefferson. The first appointment to the University faculty, this former Chartist was known to have been obnoxious to the prevailing religious sentiment of England, and partly for that reason to have sought refuge in America. Prejudice and suspicion were naturally aroused against him in orthodox and conservative Virginia, for he had supplied an arsenal of attack upon his philosophical and religious opinions

[1] A. E. B. Woodward, *A System of Universal Science*, Philadelphia, 1816.

[2] Vol. 6, p. 340 (W).

[3] H. B. Adams, *op. cit.*, p. 28. Compare below Book V., Chapter II., The Princeton School.

by editing and annotating the writings of his father-in-law, Dr. Priestley. Considered as a propagandist of new and strange doctrines, Cooper was so persistently attacked by the Virginia clergy that he felt constrained to offer his resignation.[1] At this performance Jefferson [2] was naturally highly indignant, called Cooper's assailants ' satellites of religious inquisition, who charged him with unitarianism as boldly as if they knew the facts, and as presumptuously as if it were a crime, and one for which, like Servetus, he should be burned. In all this hue and cry the Presbyterian clergy are loudest, most intolerant, and most tyrannical; when they condemn Doctor Cooper for being a monotheist in opposition to their tritheism, they want to re-establish by law the holy inquisition which they can now only infuse into public opinion, that lord of the universe. But in despite of their fulminations against endeavours to enlighten the general mind, to improve the reason of the people, the liberality of this state,' concludes the Virginian humanist, ' will support this institution and give fair play to the cultivation of reason.'

[1] H. B. Adams, *op cit.*, p. 109. For the influence of Priestley and Cooper, compare below Book IV., Chapters IV. and V.

[2] Vol. 15, pp. 246, 247, 254.

CHAPTER VII

POPULAR DEISM

IN examining the books of the early colleges and the thoughts of their representative men, there have been found numberless signs of colonial free-thinking, of mental independency before political independence. In addition to these academic studies there must now be made a search for the more elusive traces of the spreading of infidelity, before the actual outburst of revolutionary thought. As has been already intimated, this movement, beginning as a popular reaction, was more felt than avowed, more a matter of subtle distrust than of precise knowledge; it was the faint smoke in the air, presaging the coming forest fire; it was a time when the clergy might warn against ' the insidious encroachments of innovation,' but when the laity preferred the Indian summer of indifference. Toleration was pervasive. It has been described as gradually diffused over the land by such fostering circumstances as colonial impatience with prescription and custom, and that original adventurous spirit which, combined with dissatisfaction with home conditions and voluntary exile insensibly fitted the mind for the propositions of liberty.[1] Of these propositions, the liberty to think as one liked was the most conducive to the coming of free-thought. Paine's *Age of Reason* would never have been so acceptable had it not been for the liberty of conscience granted or implied in the revolutionary documents. To what extent this liberty was a native production, and to what a foreign acquisition, has been elsewhere considered.[2] Yet the deistic movement played some part in the matter. There are many phrases and expressions such as might have come from Locke's *Essay on Toleration,* or Spinoza's *Politico-Theological Tractate,* or from those countless minor works of

[1] S. H. Cobb, *Pioneers of Religious Liberty in America*, Boston, 1903, p. 14.

[2] Compare before, Chapter on *Philosophy and Politics.*

296

the *sæculum rationalisticum* which put forward as a cardinal article of faith the supremacy of reason. The lesser documents of liberty show this.[1] Patrick Henry in his Bill of Rights of 1774 said that religion can be directed only by reason, and Madison added that all men are equally entitled to the full and free exercise of religion according to the dictates of conscience. This was followed in 1785 by Jefferson's Declaratory Act establishing religious freedom in Virginia, and by the Pennsylvania constitution, advocated by Franklin, which contained the clause as to the natural and inalienable right to worship according to the dictates of the understanding. In brief, twelve out of the thirteen original States allowed an increased measure of mental freedom. It was only in Massachusetts that a dread of liberty was expressed. There the question was debated whether public offices might not be held ' even among those who have no other guide in the way to virtue and heaven, than the dictates of natural religion.'

The political expressions of rationalism in the revolutionary period are many, the philosophical few. Between the Stamp Act and the adoption of the Constitution, there was but one native work worth mentioning in the deistic connection. But Ethan Allen's *Reason the Only Oracle of Man* did not arrest the popular attention. So it remained for a naturalised American to turn the tide of thought. It was the *Age of Reason* of Thomas Paine (1737-1809) which marked high water in the deistic movement, being carried up on the wave of enthusiasm caused by the author's revolutionary pamphlets *Common Sense* and the *Rights of Man*. Now by the year 1794, the radical writer affirms that, as his motive in his political works had been to rescue man from tyranny and false systems and false principles of government, so in his religious publications it was to bring man to the right reason God has given him, unshackled by fable and the fiction of books.[2] The animus of this bellicose work, written in the expectation that a revelation in the system of government would be followed by a revolution in the system of religion, has been

[1] Compare *Pioneers of Religious Liberty in America*, Boston, 1903.
[2] *The Writings of Thomas Paine*, (ed. Moncure D. Conway), New York, 1894-6, Vol. 2, p. 374.

strangely laid to a non-belligerent sect.　Paine being of Quaker parentage, it is surmised that his inspiration was due to the quietists.　His partisan editor says that he was the spiritual successor of George Fox, a keener critic that he was a Quaker minus the orthodox creed, his mysticism being replaced by eighteenth century deism.[1]　The former statement appears dubious, the latter paradoxical.　It is true that, like Fox, Paine had a contempt for the vanities of the world, enthusiasm for the brotherhood of man, and a reverence for the rights of conscience, but as a pietist he is an anomaly.　He had some of the light, but none of the sweetness of that persuasion.　He talks as if his inner spark were a beacon, and from his ineffable conceit got the nickname of Citizen Egotism.　In a suppressed passage of his private thoughts concerning reason, he thanks Heaven that he has been given "a large share of that divine gift.'[2]　In a loud aside, Paine now recounts the story of his life.　He acknowledges that his father being of the Quaker profession, it was his good fortune to have an exceedingly good moral education, but he explains that his natural bent of mind was to science.　He allows that the religion of the Quakers approaches the nearest of all others to true deism, in the moral and benign part thereof, but that they have contracted themselves too much by leaving the works of God out of their system. Although he reverences their philanthropy, he cannot help smiling at the conceit that, if the taste of a Quaker could have been consulted at the creation, ' what a silent and drab-coloured creation it would have been!'[3]　By his own account Paine was not a born mystic but a born sceptic.　He boasts that from the time he was capable of conceiving an idea or acting upon it by reflection, he doubted the truth of the Christian system.　Nor did he have a high opinion of his school education at Thetford, in Norfolk; it merely served to put him in the way of beginning learning for himself afterwards.　The use of the globes and the orrery gave him an idea of the infinity of space and of the eternal divisibility of matter,

---

[1] Leslie Stephen, *English Thought in the Eighteenth Century,* New York, 1881, Vol. 1, p. 253.

[2] *Works,* Vol. 2, p. 370.

[3] *Ib.,* pp. 65, 66.

but it was something else that gave him almost all the knowledge that he had. Any person, he runs on, who has made observations on the state and progress of the human mind, by observing his own, cannot but have observed that there are two distinct classes of what are called thoughts; those that we produce in ourselves by reflection and the act of thinking, and those that bolt into the mind of their own accord.[1]

This is the only bit of introspection, the only example of the interior attitude in the book. Despite such crude psychologising, Paine's editor considers his ' reason ' only an expansion of the Quaker's inner light; it might better be called a mere reflection of current deism. The *Age of Reason* has the same method of so-called mathematical proof, the same mechanical view of nature, the same disregard of the problem of evil, the same aversion to mystery, the same iridescent dream as to mankind's perfectibility, the same delusion as to monotheism being a primitive belief,— ' Adam was created a deist ' says this prehistoric higher critic. In a word, the book is anything but original. With the exception of a phrase or two like the ' religion of humanity,' there is not an idea in it which cannot be matched in the writings of the English free-thinkers of the Georgian era. Like the belated deism of Gibbon's chapters on Christianity, Paine simply repeats, in the language of the street, the arguments of Collins against prophecy, of Woolston against miracles, of Tindal against revelation, of Morgan against the Old Testament, of Chubb against Christian morality. Unaware of his plagiarisms Paine's admiring editor calls him a Prometheus who stole his fire from heaven, whereas, in fact, his sources were considerably lower. John Adams alleged that Paine's billingsgate was taken from Blount's *Oracles of Reason,* from Bolingbroke, Voltaire and Bérenger.[2] This is well found, but too specific to be true. Citizen Paine, although resident in France, was no French scholar.[3] As for the English

---

[1] *Works,* Vol. 2, p. 64.

[2] *Works,* (ed. C. F. Adams), Vol. 10, p. 58; Vol. 9, p. 567, Boston, 1851.

[3] Hence the futility of the attempt to trace his later doctrine of the plurality of worlds to such a work as that of Fontenelle's. Compare *Carey's American Museum,* Vol. 12, p. 241.

authorities, he got his information at second hand, with but a single exception. That exception was Conyers Middleton, who made out that Christian theology was nought but heathen mythology.[1] Since most of the arguments of the Anglican divine's *Letters from Rome* were probably taken from a little known work on the conformity of modern with ancient ceremonies, it was with a twice-told tale that Paine would rout his enemies. Thus he proceeds: The Mythologists had gods for everything; the Christian Mythologists had saints for everything. The church became as crowded with the one, as the pantheon had been with the other; and Rome was the place of both. The Christian theory is little else than the idolatry of the ancient mythologists, accommodated to the purpose of power and revenue; and it yet remains to reason and philosophy to abolish the amphibious fraud.[2]

In the place of these 'bases of Christianity' the iconoclast would therefore put what he designates as the true theology. He cannot see how men can hold to a system where Satan is deified and given power equal to that of the Almighty; where man is an outcast, a beggar, a mumper, calling himself a worm and the fertile earth a dung-hill, and all the blessings of life but the thankless name of vanities.[3] But there is a substitute for all these corruptions 'from Moloch to modern predestinarianism,'—it is eighteenth century optimism, thus grandiloquently set forth: If objects for gratitude and admiration are our desire, do they not present themselves every hour to our eyes? Do we not see a fair creation prepared to receive us the instant we are born—a world furnished to our hands, that cost us nothing? Is it we that light up the sun; that pour down the rain; and fill the earth with abundance? Whether we sleep or wake, the vast machinery of the universe still goes on.[4] Turning again to the Bible, the author treats it in the ordinary unhistoric deistic fashion, by attempting to turn it into a code of ethics. For example, he asserts that the Proverbs are an instructive system of ethics, but inferior in keenness to the proverbs of the Spaniards, and not more wise and œconomical than those of the American Franklin. The chapters

[1] L. Stephen, *op. cit.*, Vol. 1, p. 253.
[2] *Age of Reason*, p. 25. [3] *Ib.*, p. 61. [4] *Ib.*, p. 31.

on the Old and New Testaments, as also their enlargement in part
two of this work, have thus been summarised by the author in his
dotage: Thomas Paine has written to show that the Bible is not the
Word of God, that the books it contains were not written by the
persons to whom they are ascribed, that it is an anonymous book,
and that we have no authority for calling it the Word of God, or
for saying it was written by inspired penmen, since we do not know
who the writers were. This is the opinion not only of Thomas
Paine, but of tens and tens of thousands of the most respectable
characters in the United States and Europe.[1] At this point there
is offered another substitute. Instead of the book called the
scripture, which any human hand might make, there is the book
of Creation, the only true and real work of God. In answer to
those who ask if we are to have no word of God, the self-ap-
pointed apologist gives the twice repeated passage: Do we want to
contemplate his power? We see it in the immensity of the creation. Do we want to contemplate his wisdom? We see it in
the unchangeable order by which the incomprehensible Whole is
governed. Do we want to contemplate his munificence? We see
it in the abundance with which he fills the earth. Do we want to
contemplate his mercy? We see it in his not withholding that
abundance even from the unthankful.[2]

By utterances like these Paine shows that his Quaker antecedents have been left far behind, that the voice in the soul has
been succeeded by the tom-tom of reiteration. So he closes the
first half of his book in a temper of coarse hostility, concluding
that the Christian system of faith is a species of atheism, a sort
of religious denial of God, for it includes the whimsical account
of the creation—the strange story of Eve, the snake, and the
apple—the amphibious idea of a man-god—the corporeal idea of
the death of a god—the mythological idea of a family of gods,
and the Christian system of arithmetic, that three are one, and
one is three.[3] But to hasten on, Paine now offers his final substitution; in place of Christianism he would put the pure and
simple profession of deism. The true deist, he explains, has

---

[1] *Works*, Vol. 4, p. 342.
[2] *Age of Reason*, p. 46. [3] *Ib.*, pp. 50, 58.

but one Deity, and his religion consists in contemplating the power, wisdom and benignity of the Deity in his works, and in endeavouring to imitate him in every thing moral, scientifical, and mechanical. . . . Deism then teaches us, without the possibility of being deceived, all that is necessary or proper to be known. The creation is the Bible of the deist. He there reads, in the hand-writing of the Creator himself, the certainty of his existence, and the immutability of his power, and all other Bibles and Testaments are to him forgeries. The probability that we may be called to account hereafter, will, to reflecting minds, have the influence of belief; for it is not our belief or disbelief that can make or unmake the fact. As this is the state we are in, and which it is proper we should be in, as free agents, it is the fool only, and not the philosopher, nor even the prudent man, that will live as if there were no God.[1] As to the meaning of the problems involved in all this owlish wisdom, the author seems half blind. He appears to be content with mere intimations of immortality and slight implications of freedom of the will. He expresses a hope for happiness beyond this life, but does not trouble himself about the manner of future existence. It is enough of an argument for him to perceive the progressive changes in the winged insects, their little life resembles an earth and a heaven, a present and future state, and comprises an immortality in miniature.[2] As for a belief in the future life Paine offers the trite arguments of analogy and probability. For a belief in moral freedom he offers his own word. Moreover in respect to morality he assumes that the knowledge of it exists in every man's conscience: Here we are; the existence of an Almighty power is sufficiently demonstrated to us. We must know also, that the power that called us into being, can if he please, and when he pleases, call us to account for the manner in which we have lived here.[3]

In thus disposing of the inextricable problems of freedom and necessity, Paine acts as if his mind had water-tight compartments, but in preparing for his longest speculative voyage, the search for

[1] *Age of Reason*, pp. 65, 188, 189.
[2] *Ib.*, p. 179.   [3] *Ib.*, p. 188.

the proofs of the existence of a Deity, he positively overloads his
decks with metaphysics. In his *Discourse to the Theophilan-
thropists* he points out that the universe is composed of matter,
and, as a system is sustained by motion, God is the power of first
cause, nature is the law, and matter is the subject acted upon.[1]
He further enlarges on the topic by announcing that the only
idea man can affix to the name of God, is that of a *first cause,*
the cause of all things. And, incomprehensibly difficult as it is
for a man to conceive what a first cause is, he arrives at the belief
of it, from the tenfold greater difficulty of disbelieving it. .
. . The Almighty lecturer, by displaying the principles of
science in the structure of the universe, has invited man to study
and to imitation. . . . It is only by contemplating what he
calls the starry heavens, as the book and school of science, that
he discovers any use in their being visible to him, or any advantage resulting from his immensity of vision. But when he contemplates the subject in this light, he sees an additional motive for
saying, that *nothing was made in vain;* for in vain would be this
power of vision if it taught man nothing.[2]

Disentangling these passages, they are seen to offer, in a popular way, the familiar theistic arguments. The ontological is given
in a negative form; the cosmological in a mechanical form; the
teleological in a utilitarian form. An attempt is now made to re-
inforce these arguments. To the first is added the corollary of
the regressive series: Everything we behold carries in itself the
internal evidence that it did not make itself, and carries us on,
by necessity, to the belief of a first cause eternally existing.[3] To
the second argument is added a reference to that invisible agency
by which all the component parts of the immense machine of
the universe have influence upon each other.[4] To the third argument Paine adds some fanciful embellishments. He had represented that when young, he had repressed rather than encouraged
his imagination. He now offers a chapter on the advantages of
the existence of many worlds in each solar system. As therefore
the Creator made nothing in vain, so also must it be believed that

---

[1] *Works*, Vol. 4, p. 240.
[2] *Age of Reason*, pp. 47, 55.　　[3] *Ib.*, p. 47.　　[4] *Ib.*, p. 53.

he organised the structure of the universe in the most advantageous manner for the benefit of man; and as we see, and from experience feel, the benefits we derive from the structure of the universe, formed as it is, which benefits we should not have had the opportunity of enjoying if the structure, so far as relates to our system, had been a solitary globe, we can discover at least one reason why a *plurality* of worlds has been made, and that reason calls forth the devotional gratitude of man, as well as his admiration.[1] The followers of Leibniz, chasing after the rainbow of final ends, are outdone by this cockney speculator of common sense, who concludes his philosophising by these dogmatic statements: The belief of a God, so far from having anything of mystery in it, is of all beliefs the most easy, because it arises to us out of necessity. . . . It has been by wandering from the immutable laws of science, and the light of reason, and setting up an invented thing called ' revealed religion,' that so many wild and blasphemous conceits have been formed of the Almighty.

[1] *Age of Reason*, p. 72.

CHAPTER VII

THE DECLINE OF DEISM

THE effect of the *Age of Reason* on the community may be easily imagined. The clergy attacked it, the colleges criticised it, the populace grew sick of it. Nevertheless, this did not happen before the book had enjoyed a decided run of popularity. Dedicated to the author's fellow citizens of the United States of America, it was sold for a few pence the copy or given away gratis. The first edition, printed in France, was spread broadcast through the free-thinking societies affiliated with the Jacobin Club of Philadelphia.[1] Within two decades the pamphlet was to be found on the banks of the Genesee and Ohio;[2] within two more it was circulated among the readers of Volney and Voltaire in those places in Tennessee and Kentucky whose names still attest the French sympathies of the first settlers. It is astonishing how far the light of nature threw its beams. The president of Transylvania University was suspected of teaching an unrestrained naturalism, and a friend of Abraham Lincoln reported that in Indiana, the *Age of Reason* passed from hand to hand, furnishing food for the evening's discussion in tavern and village store. The spread of rationalistic opinion was one thing, the channel of transmission another; this channel was said to be Illuminism, a supposed combination of masonry and infidelity. As a branch of the French Grand Orient, the order of Illuminati, starting in 1786 in Portsmouth, Virginia, was reported in the year 1802 to have numbered seventeen hundred agents.[3] This is a palpable exaggeration, yet it is safe to say that the influence of the *Age of*

[1] E. H. Gillett, *History of the Presbyterian Church,* 1864, Vol. 1, p. 420.
[2] David Nelson, *The Cause and Cure of Infidelity,* New York, 1841, p. 396.
[3] Seth Payson, *Proofs of the Existence and Dangerous Tendency of Modern Illuminism,* New Haven, 1802, p. 205.

Reason was increased by the Franco-mania, prosaic rationalism being augmented by an insidious naturalism, and both by the common Lockean sensationalism of the day. However, the ' System of Nature,' as Albert Sorel has explained, pushed to its logical results, meant a subtle poison of sensuality impregnating the air.[1] In America this naturalism found effective advocates among the Frenchmen in the revolutionary struggle. These were described by the elder President Dwight of Yale as men of polished manners, improved minds and superior address, who knew how to insinuate the grossest sentiments in a delicate and inoffensive manner, and were at the same time friends and aids of the American cause—*nos très chers et très grands Amis, et Alliés*.[2]

In spite of this encomium the influence of French ideas on American thought should not be drawn out of perspective. That might, perhaps, bear too close a resemblance to the symbolism indicated in those pictures at Versailles, in which Layafette and his officers overtop Washington and his staff. There existed a racial difference between the Anglo-Saxon deist and the French doctrinaire. The writer last quoted considers that the English infidel has some reverence for the Creator, and admits that man is an accountable being, and that there may be an existence hereafter; but the French infidel only despises the Creator, knows a priori that there is nothing beyond the grave, and holds that God exercises no moral government over man.[3] The contrast here presented might have been used in favour of the author of the *Age of Reason*. Poor ' Tom ' Paine had himself argued in behalf of God, of freedom and of immortality. Once being denounced as a Jacobin and revolutionary, he asserted that he had caused his dissertation to be translated into French in order to stop the people of France in their headlong career into atheism.

If Paine is to be put in any school it is that of the *emigré* Volney, who, disgusted with the French revolution, came to America in search of the ideal republic. Volney was a populariser, among other things, of the study of comparative religion; his *Ruins, or*

[1] *L'Europe et la Révolution Française,* Paris, 1885, Vol. 1, p. 235.
[2] Dwight, *Travels,* Vol. 4, p. 368.
[3] *Ib.,* p. 366.

Meditations on the Revolutions of Empires was published in 1793 as the 'French Citizens' Catechism.' Translated by Joel Barlow, and printed both in New York and Philadelphia, it explored nearly the same ground as the *Age of Reason,* but went somewhat deeper. Discussing the problems of religious contradictions, it sought the origin of various worships, such as that of the elements of Sabeism, of the Demi-Ourgos or grand artificer of the world machine, and of Christianity or ' the allegorical worship of the sun.' Volney's method was sound, but his resources were scanty, and his results dubious. Possessing but an imperfect acquaintance with oriental thought, he came to the trite conclusion that the object of all religions was identical, namely to gain power and wealth by priestcraft. Associated with his popular book of travels, the *Ruins* helped the *Age of Reason* and the twin volumes, hand in hand, went wandering through the woods. By this coincidence Paine gained countless rustic admirers,[1] yet his chief advocate was an academic, Elihu Palmer, a graduate of Dartmouth, who became head of the Society of Columbian Illuminati and, while in New York, wrote that early definition of American deism, which is found in his *Principles of Nature, or a Development of the Moral Causes of Happiness and Misery Among the Human Species.*[2] This work being launched at the opening of the nineteenth century, marks the drifting away from the old speculative issues. The chief philosophical inquiry is said to be this: Are the evils incident to human life the result of the operation of the laws of nature, or are they special judgments from God? Effects have been attributed to the chimerical combinations found in the distorted brain of an enthusiastic religious zealot. The simplicity, uniformity and grandeur of the physical universe have been abandoned for the doctrine of special judgments; the application of the law of power in surrounding objects and the law of sensation for special interventions of divine power.[3] Palmer was wrong in his pathetic remonstrances; had he exactly

[1] Compare W. H. Venable, *Beginnings of Literary Culture in the Ohio Valley,* 1891, pp. 232, 238.
[2] London, 1802.
[3] *Principles of Nature,* pp. 191-2.

reversed his judgment he would have been nearer the truth. The
system which taught special providences had about it, by this
time, a general flavour of mild decay. The doctrines which were
growing strong were those of applied sensationalism and of human
self-sufficiency. Palmer confesses as much when he uses as his
chief authorities the *Système de la Nature,* and William Godwin's *Political Justice.* Of these two volumes the former, repeating the error of the London edition, is attributed to Mirabaud instead of D'Holbach; but the latter has more than a negative interest. It was Godwin who inspired Shelley in his ideal
Pantisocracy which the poet sought to found on the banks of
the Susquehanna. Godwin also was the means of propagating
French naturalism[1] in the most strait-laced circles through that
popular romance concerning the marvellous boys Sanford and
Merton. Intrinsically these references are valueless; historically
they indicate some of the remote and indirect results of Locke's
sensational philosophy, as it was carried to France by Voltaire,
returned to England in the guise of the principles of 1789, and
was finally transferred to America by the obscure disciples of free-
thought. Of the other publications fostering the so-called Paine
panic only brief mention is needed. Palmer supplemented his
Principles of Nature by his *Prospect,* or *View of the Moral
World for the Year 1804.* According to the allegorical thunder
and lightning frontispiece, the Book of Saints and Ten Commandments are being dashed to the ground from the Altar of
Truth and Justice to be supplanted by the *Age of Reason* and the
Rights of Man. Of an equally destructive aspect was George
Houston's New York *Correspondent* of 1829, containing lectures delivered before the Free Press Association on the inconsistencies, absurdities and contradictions of the Bible. This journal also presented the advanced views of Fanny Wright, a sort
of Wilhelm Meister in petticoats, who wandered over the country
from Woodstock, Vermont, to Cincinnati, Ohio.

These things are incidental and trivial, yet they mark
ginning of the end of popular deism. Free-thought now

[1] Compare Edward Dowden, *The French Revolution and English Literature,* New York, 1897, p. 61.

itself open to a double assault by becoming involved with the incipient socialism of Robert Dale Owen. The latter's pronouncement coming from the Fourier Colony at New Harmony, that ' focus of the lights of scepticism ' was entitled by Lyman Beecher the infidel trumpet call to all the envious and vicious poor. Likewise the free-thinking societies spread through New England and the Middle States were designated the banded Goths and Vandals of political atheism. Attacks similar to these were what Paine received from the start, for his minor clerical opponents were most bitter. As in England they had been the trained fighters in the deistic trouble, so in America, they furnished the bulk of the ammunition of which much was of but small calibre. There were reprints like Wakefield's *Examination of the Age of Reason*, or Williams' *Age of Infidelity;* there were also anonymous pamphlets like the *Folly of Reason* and the *Sceptic's Manual.* The latter published in Philadelphia in 1811, contained in part one Leslie's *Short and Easy Method with the Deists,* in part two Fletcher's *Letters on Spiritual Manifestation,* in part three *Exemplifications of the Contrasted Lives of Saints and Sinners.* To read the petty and malicious gossip concerning the last days of Hobbes and Hume, Voltaire and Paine, one would be led to think that the compilers had gone mad to meet their private ends.

Of a not much higher type were the works of the clerical chemist Joseph Priestley, who had discovered oxygen but could find very little good in deism. As an expatriated Unitarian he might be expected to have had some sympathy with free thought, outside of Great Britain, but his faith was of the hard-shell variety, and his views remained petrified. His *Answer to the Age of Reason* was but a continuation of his *Letters to the Philosophers of France, and to a Philosophic Unbeliever,* while his *Increase of Infidelity* was a mere series of negations. He contended that there was no solid argument to be found in any of the works of Gibbon or D'Holbach, Paine, Volney, or Voltaire. As for Mr. Hume, he has not advanced a single step in metaphysics. Nevertheless, concludes Priestley, it must be acknowledged that the evidences of natural religion are more difficult to understand, and require more of what is called metaphysical reasoning, than

those of revealed religion.[1]   Of these polemical works the one
which seems to have caused especial irritation was an *Antidote
to Deism,* published by Uzal Ogden, an Episcopal minister of
Newark.   Possibly in recollection of some of his disagreeable
experiences in East Jersey, Paine retorts upon its title, by saying
that an antidote to deism must be atheism,—for what can be an
antidote to the belief of a God but the disbelief of a God?'[2]
Ogden's book has for its sub-title the 'Deist Unmasked, or an
ample Refutation of all the Objections of Thomas Paine'; it
contains an appendix of the concessions and recantations of several deists from Toland to Voltaire; it winds up with the frequently reprinted work of Leslie.   This complete arsenal against
infidelity has over its portals a quotation from Berkeley's *Minute
Philosopher,* to the effect that, if the age is singularly productive
of infidels, it is not because it is more knowing, but only more
presuming than former ages.   The author now follows the ideal
bishop's line of argument, namely that the deist's conceit is not
the effect of the exercise of the powers of reason.   He intimates
that, notwithstanding their pretensions to philosophy, the deists
have been extremely sterile in the invention of new objections to
Christianity, even Lord Bolingbroke quoting deistical objections
to the truth from the twentieth hand.[3]   No such charge can
be brought against Ogden.   If he quotes, he quotes with authority, offering sixty-three topics in favour of Christianity, with
references to the authors under each topic.   In a passage much
like that of Samuel Clarke upon the four varieties of deists, the
author has drawn up a table of the contradictory sentiments of
those who appeal to the eternal reason and nature of things and
yet cannot explain what is the uncorrupted religion of reason and
nature.   Some, it is pointed out, believe that the world was
created; others that it is eternal; some that our souls are parts
of God, others that they are created spirits; some found moral
obligation upon the perfections of God, others on the eternal
differences and relations of things independent of God; some

---

[1] *Increase of Infidelity,* Philadelphia, 1797, p. 131.
[2] *Works,* Vol. 4, p. 311.
[3] *Antidote to Deism,* 1795, p. x.

believe in the immortality of the soul and future rewards and punishments, others believe the soul is mortal and perishes with the body.[1] The *Antidote to Deism* betrays not a spark of originality, descends to wretched personalities, and concludes with an appeal to political animosities. Ethan Allen is called an ignorant and profane deist, Paine a drunkard, to reason with whom would be like the casting of pearls before swine. Then it is asked with a rhetorical flourish: What American patriot, of the Senate or the Field, suffered himself to be so infatuated with revolutional ideas, as to cause him to imagine, because it was necessary he should wage war against tyranny, he must therefore wage war against God?[2] Ogden, writing in 1795, said he was the first American to answer Paine. The following year the second part of the *Age of Reason* was roughly handled by James Tytler in a pamphlet which attempts to identify deism with atheism. Atheism, so runs the tale, consists in a belief that the present system of nature is eternal and self existent, and that it will continue to eternity. As there is no being distinct from nature, we must take nature for the guide of our actions. The principles of strict deism differ in nothing but a pure speculative point from those of the atheists. A true deist believes that there is a being, distinct from this world, whom he calls God. Mr. Paine calls the system of nature the work of God. Others have said that matter as well as God is eternal; that matter has laws to which it is immutably subject, and which God himself cannot reverse. All deists agree in asserting that the character of the Deity can only be known from the works of nature. As to any future state, it seems to be a matter of doubt; so that the morality of the deist and atheist ought to be precisely the same.[3]

The most prolific of the writers against deism, and the materialism which happened to be associated with it, was president Timothy Dwight of Yale. As one of the Hartford wits, he had composed a sort of American Dunciad, the *Triumph of In-*

[1] *Antidote*, p. 97.
[2] *Ib.*, p. 3.
[3] *Paine's Second Part of the Age of Reason Answered*, Salem, 1796, pp. 93, 95, 96.

fidelity, which was ironically dedicated to Voltaire. How that poem confined the deist in the pillory of his own terms, and flung into his teeth his own arguments, is to be seen from these lines:

'His soul not cloath'd in attributes divine;
But a nice watch-spring to the grand machine.

.   .   .   .   .

Enough, the Bible is by wits arraigned,
Genteel men doubt it, smart men say it's feigned.' [1]

In contrast to this effusion, were the earlier poems of Dwight's salad days which showed a decided leaning to the philosophy of the Encyclopedists. In the *Columbia* and the *Conquest of Canaan,* French phrases are curiously wrought into a sort of biblical epic on the new world. The sons of this 'blissful Eden bright' are urged to 'teach laws to reign and save the Rights of Man.' The author subsequently explained that these were the mock heroics of a time, when the strong sympathy toward the leaders of the French revolution prepared to make us the miserable dupes of their principles and declarations.[2] But the doctrines of the 14th of July were not to be confused with those of the 4th of July. As the head of Yale College, Dr. Dwight became the leader of the clerical forces against deism. His *Century Discourses* gives a trenchant account of the progress of infidelity,—its descent from the lofty philosophical discourse to the newspaper paragraph, its spread among the masses, and the ultimate return to more sober thought. Infidelity, the discourse proceeds, was first theism, or natural religion, then mere unbelief, then animalism, then scepticism, then partial, and finally, total atheism. The infidel writers have used terms so abstract, and a phraseology so mysterious, as to attract readers fond of novelty, but the common people, never honoured by Voltaire with any higher title than the rabble or the mob, have been caught by these writers, who volunteered to vindicate their wrongs and assert their rights. Happily, it was soon discovered that the liberty of infidels was not the liberty

[1] *Triumph of Infidelity,* 1778, p. 31.
[2] *Century Discourse,* New Haven, 1801, p. 32.

of New England; that France instead of being free, merely changed through a series of tyrannies; and that man, unrestrained by law and religion, is a mere beast of prey. Even sober infidels began to be alarmed for their own peace, safety and enjoyments.[1]

The air of gravity and severity about this passage is explained by what men remembered of the events following the peace of 1783, the intrigues of Genet, the terrorism incited by Freneau, when Market street in Philadelphia was filled with a mob, the distrust of Napoleon implied in President Adams' proclamation. Despite these events at home and the excesses of the revolutionists across the sea, the Federalist clergyman takes care to distinguish between French citizens and French doctrinaires. The Frenchmen whom he had found deserving of esteem and respect have been Catholics and loyalists; but the philosophy of the French school, with which it was intended to overwhelm these states, is a system of abstract declarations, delivered in an abstract style, equally violating all good taste and sober criticism. The language in which it is uttered is like the signs of unknown quantities in algebra; the arguments by which it is professedly supported are usually of the a priori kind, attended with no evidence, and conducting the mind to no conclusion. At their side Behmen and Swedenborg would lose their distinction, and return far toward the character of common sense.[2]

This attack against what has been called a mathematics dealing with society[3] was contained in Dr. Dwight's *Travels in New England*, published in 1822. The author had already set to work to overthrow the system in question, for matters were in a bad way in his locality. As a contemporary remarked, wild and vague expectations were everywhere entertained, especially among the young, of a new order of things about to commence, in which Christianity would be laid aside as obsolete.[4] So, too, one of the

---

[1] *Century Discourse*, p. 33.

[2] *Ib.*, pp. 4, 5.

[3] Edward Dowden, *The French Revolution and English Literature*, New York, 1897, p. 4.

[4] Daniel Dorchester, *Christianity in the United States*, New York, 1888, p. 323.

historians of Yale College asserted that in the exultation of political emancipation, infidel philosophers found ready listeners when they represented the restraints of religion as fetters of the conscience, and moral obligations as shackles imposed by bigotry and priestcraft.[1] The anecdote recounted by Lyman Beecher that his classmates nicknamed themselves Voltaire and Rousseau,[2] is substantiated by the fact that English and French deism brought orthodox believers down to eight or ten. At this point President Dwight met both undergraduate whim and serious doubt. On the one hand, sarcastic observations were made regarding striplings scarcely fledged, who suddenly found that the light of wisdom had just begun to dawn on the human race;[3] on the other, chapel sermons endeavoured an appeal to reason as well as to faith, and there was offered a thorough discussion of English free-thought from the ' pompous insinuations of Shaftesbury to the wire-drawn metaphysics of Hume.' In his *Nature and Danger of Infidel Philosophy*,[4] two discourses addressed to the candidates for the baccalaureate, Dr. Dwight presents a brief criticism of those schools which professed such an intimate acquaintance with Universal Order, and the great First Cause. The great machine of Providence, he contends, is infinitely more complex, the proportion of the parts unknown to those which are known is infinitely greater than in the machine supposed. Again we know not thoroughly the nature of those beings and events with which we are best acquainted; philosophy cannot answer what are the uses and purposes they are destined to accomplish. In such a state of things analysis must plainly be of little use. They are the attempts of a clown undertaking to interpret the designs of a statesman, in the management of a great empire. Finally, the character of God cannot be perfectly known from creation and providence; his designs can never be learned from his works. From a priori results He may be admitted of infinite perfection, but the real state of creation and providence shows the existence of moral and

---

[1] *Annals of Yale College*, New Haven, 1838, p. 145.
[2] *Autobiography*, p. 40.
[3] *Travels*, Vol. 4, p. 376.
[4] New Haven, 1798.

natural evil,—the death of one-half mankind under the age of five years; the frozen, burnt and barren state of the land.

There is here presented a refreshing attitude of criticism toward the shallow books of ' evidences,' the far-fetched ' analogies ' then prevalent in the country,[1] but elsewhere the author's criticism of the rationalists of England, France and Germany shows a certain lack of penetration. Yet for these deficiencies there were somewhat special and personal reasons. An ardent Whig would naturally denounce Godwin's *Political Justice* with its impossible revolutionary reforms; an advocate of a state supported church would distrust D'Holbach's *Système de la Nature* with its prediction of the new world of the enlightenment as free from tyrants and priests. This suspicion of the Illuminati may be explained for it rested on a strange confusion between illuminism and infidelity, but how any president of Yale College, where the idealism fostered by Berkeley was again to flourish, could assert that Kant's publications were formed to diffuse loose principles, is almost incomprehensible.[2]

Turning to Harvard College, the academic attitude toward the declining deism was peculiarly complicated. Federal in politics and Unitarian in religion, it was doubly averse to the enthusiasms and raptures of Franco-American rationalism; it deplored the foul spirit of innovation, and sought some check to the infuriated steeds of infidelity.[3] So ran Buckminster's Phi Beta

---

[1] Compare J. J. Gurney, *The Portable Evidences of Christianity*, Hartford, 1833. T. H. Gallaudet, *Class Book of Natural Theology for Common Schools and Academies*, Hartford, 1837. Edward Hitchcock, *Religious Lectures on peculiar Phenomena in the four Seasons*, Amherst, 1850.

[2] Compare *Century Discourse*, 1801, p. 50: ' The present state of literature and morals in Germany conspires to show that the principles of the Illumines (*sic*) respecting morality and religion have an extensive prevalence in that country. From the philosophy of Kant to the plays of Kotzebue, their publications appear to be formed to diffuse loose principles.' This sentiment is perhaps based on the popular confusion between illuminism and infidelity, as in the case of Samuel Miller's attack on the Könisberg philosopher. (See below, Book V., Chapter V.) At any rate this passage appears to contain the first reference to Kant in American literature.

[3] Henry Adams, *History of the United States during the First Administration of Thomas Jefferson*, New York, 1890, p. 204.

Kappa oration of 1809; however, not long after this Channing was introducing certain innovations and Emerson some enthusiasms and raptures. To the movements here suggested deism stood in a peculiarly unfortunate relation; Unitarianism seemed in part due to the 'Old English' rationalism presented in the Alvord lectures, yet it was now hostile to the developed rationalism brought over from France; transcendentalism seemed contrary to the Harvard teachings on natural religion, which were more in the temper of the rationalising Tillotson than of the platonising Cudworth, yet it, too, was hostile to Franco-American infidelity. So between the Boston liberals and the Concord mystics, the philosophy of Paine was bound to suffer. The Unitarians under the lead of Priestley held to the sensationalism of the school of Hartley, but despised the sensualism of the plebeian follower of Rousseau and Diderot; the transcendentalists in attacking Priestley attacked Paine's kindred materialism and the whole weak line of utilitarian arguments. Thus, Margaret Fuller,[1] of Brook Farm, asserted that New Englanders disgusted with the materialistic workings of 'rational religion' are becoming mystics; they quarrel with all that is, because it is not spiritual enough. Their hope for man is grounded on his destiny as an immortal soul, and not as a mere comfort-loving inhabitant of earth, or as a subscriber to the social contract.

If at Cambridge the age of reason was succeeded by the age of intuition, at Princeton it was opposed by the philosophy of common sense. Where Berkeleian idealism had been driven out, the Bridgewater Treatises came in. According to its catalogue, the library abounded in volumes like Dick's *Celestial Scenery Illustrating the Perfections of the Deity,* and Prout's *Chemistry, Meterology and the Functions of Digestion considered with reference to Natural Theology;* the favourite text book, as in the majority of conservative colleges, was Dugald Stewart, and Stewart's aim was declared to be to stem the inundation of the sceptical, or rather atheistical publications which were imported from Eu-

[1] O. B. Frothingham, *Transcendentalism in New England,* New York, 1876, p. 291.

rope.[1]   But a conservative literature does not alone explain the
stringent policy of Princeton; behind the books were such facts
as that, after the revolutionary war when they had been ' freed
from all sanctuary and Sabbath restraint,' there were only a handful of students who professed themselves Christians, and that, in
1802, the trustees in their ' Address to the Inhabitants of the
United States,' declared that their purpose was to make this institution an asylum for pious youth, in this day of general and
lamentable depravity.

Judging from the experiences of the leading colonial seats of
learning, it is safe to repeat a former generalisation, namely, that
the outcome of formal deism in America was to have the clergy
reject it, and the colleges thrust it out.   It remains to be seen how
the public first accepted, then grew tired of it.   Chancellor Kent
said that, in his younger days, there were very few professional
men who were not infidels; Ezra Ripley that a large portion of
the learning not possessed by the clergy leaned to deism.[2]   A few
specific events will illustrate how this rapid growth of the army
of free thinkers was followed by an equally rapid defection from
the ranks.   In 1801, James Dana of Connecticut said that infidelity appeared to be gaining ground;[3] by 1810, it was reported
that infidelity abounded to an alarming degree and in various
shapes in the district west of the Military Tract in New York.[4]
In 1822, an anonymous ' letter to a Deist in Baltimore ' stated
that deism is taking root rapidly and soon will grow up surprisingly and become the only fashionable religion.   In Virginia about
the same time Bishop Meade asserted that in every young man he
met he expected to find a sceptic, if not an avowed unbeliever.[5]
This was the advance of the movement.   Attempts to check it
among the people were already coming from the church, the state,
and the professions.   In 1798, the Presbyterian General Assembly
uttered a warning against the abounding infidelity which tends to
atheism itself; in 1800, the President referred to the dissemination

[1] McCosh, *Scottish Philosophy*, p. 391.   [2] Dorchester, *op. cit.*, p. 323.
[3] *Century Sermon*, New Haven, 1801.
[4] Gillett, *op. cit.*, Vol. 2, p. 110.   [5] Dorchester, p. 316.

of principles subversive of the foundation of all religious, moral and social obligations, that have produced incalculable mischiefs in other countries; in 1824, Dr. Charles Caldwell thought fit to write a *Defence of the Medical Profession against the charge of Infidelity and Irreligion.* These expressions of the leaders had their effect on the rank and file; the resulting unpopularity of deism is exhibited in the light literature of the day. Fenimore Cooper describes one of his heroines as being properly impressed with the horrors of a deist's doctrines, and another as shrinking from his company.[1] Harriet Martineau wrote back to England how she was told of one and another with an air of mystery, like that with which one is informed of any person being insane, or intemperate or insolvent, that so and so was thought to be an unbeliever.[2] This social ostracism is incidentally presented in such titles as Hinton's *Lectures to Despisers of Religion,* especially the last chapter on the nature and criminality of unbelief. Similar evidence is found in a current magazine, in an anonymous letter from one who professed himself a sceptic and said that when he was formerly apt to mention his scepticism to clergymen and laymen, the former expected that a few weak reasons should eradicate at once strong and deep-rooted prejudices, and the latter looked upon him as if he had the plague, for owning he did not believe the religion they pretended to believe; the writer now confesses that he has dropped into the horrible pit of deism; he attempts to extricate himself, but in vain; he examines the fitness of things which deism boasts of, discerns the beauty and wisdom in the inanimate parts of creation, but considers the animate as a great rolling globe covered over with slaughter houses; man surveyed in a state of nature is a kind of executioner-general.[3]

This passage is worth noting because so unlike the spirit of the times,—the flamboyant optimism of the era of good feeling; at that period most of the writer's countrymen were attracted to the imported naturalism because it was so rose-coloured; they accepted the deistic dictum 'whatever is, is good,' because it

[1] T. R. Lounsbury, *Life of Fenimore Cooper,* New York, 1883, p. 26.
[2] *Society in America,* 1837, p. 335.
[3] *American Moral and Sentimental Magazine,* 1797.

seemed so eminently fitted to their own land; just as they were flattered by foreign writers who represented the new world as a scene of pastoral simplicity. But while deism appealed to the majority of the people as a matter of sentiment, it was soon found to be not sentimental enough; Franklin's philosophy, which was little but collateral security for virtue, might appeal to the business but not the bosoms of men; a cold and formal system, which externalised the deity and lacked a continuing enthusiasm, failed to satisfy the cravings of emotional excitement. Consequently, among the mass of the American people, as among the English, rationalism, to put the matter in a word, was swept away by revivalism.[1] This apparent defeat of the cause of reason was, of course, more the result of abnormal neurotic conditions than of legitimate criticism; from the standpoint of orthodoxy it was magnificent, but from the standpoint of philosophy it was not war. A saying of the day that the battle in behalf of infidelity had been the desultory attack of a barbarian, not of a civilised soldier, might with more truth be applied to the onset against the free-thinker, for that onset was carried on by all sorts of irregular recruits, by the Methodist and his saddle bags education, by the Campbellite and his new light, by the Spiritualist and his celestial rapping, and even by the Mormon and his gold bible.[2]

The results of deism in America may now be briefly summarised. Among the people the majority were drawn off by an emotional substitute for thought; among the colleges, those who were not affected by revivalism were held in check by circumscribed courses presenting the similarities between natural and revealed religion; finally, among the clergy, the great part stood for orthodoxy. As expressed by one of the numerous century sermonisers,[3] there was no neutral ground to be taken between evangelical doctrines and infidelity. These results of a hundred years' war might be counted philosophically negative, except for one thing, —deism was for a time a popular movement, yet it was not the com-

---

[1] Compare H. Howe, *Historical Collections of the Great West*, Cincinnati, 1857, p. 216.
[2] Compare the writer's *Founder of Mormonism*, London, 1903, p. 153.
[3] Charles Backus, Hartford, 1801.

mon people, but the uncommon people that profited by it. The programme of the New England transcendentalists was on its negative side almost precisely what the deists had been denying; on its positive an assertion of what they had been lacking. Transcendentalism denied the need of miracle, revelation, dependence upon an objective standard of faith; it affirmed the need of intuition, mystic ecstasy, subjective dependence upon an immanent life. In conclusion, then, it may be pointed out how deism in America had an outcome peculiarly like that of rationalism in Germany. As without the illuminism of Wolff there had been no Kant, so without the deism of Paine there had been no Emerson. In fine, what the philosopher of Königsberg said concerning religion within the limits of mere reason, might have been said by the philosopher of Concord as to the communications of the Over-Soul: ' Here is now a perfect religion, which can be set in an intelligible and convincing manner before all men by their reason.'

BOOK IV—MATERIALISM

CHAPTER I

MATERIALISM

MATERIALISM in America was at first chiefly described by those who were hostile to the movement. The earliest of these adverse expositors was Benjamin Waterhouse, a medical graduate of the University of Edinburgh and a founder of the Harvard medical school. Discoursing *On the Principle of Vitality* he said of the ancient materialists that, having postulated a universal change or mutation of all things into all, they not only reasoned that there must be one primary matter, common to all things, out of which they were made, but went further and enquired into the moving principle, the efficient cause which associates the elements of natural substance. This moving principle they called the *anima mundi*. Thales maintained that water was the subtile principle that moved all things, Heracleitus that fire was the vivifying principle, Anaximenes that air was the first mover, the Stoics that there was one infinite, eternal, almighty mind, which being diffused through the whole universe of well ordered and regularly disposed matter, actuates every part, and is, as it were, the soul of this vast body. Modern philosophers say matter is inert, yet that there are certain powers which the particles of matter have of acting on one another, as gravitation, cohesion, the attraction of crystallisation, of magnetism, of electricity, of chemical attraction. But none of these merit the name of vitality, nor in them is the origin of intelligent ideas to be looked for. Sensible objects may be the destined medium to awaken the dormant energies of man's understanding, yet these energies are no more contained in sense than the explosion of the cannon in the spark which gives it fire.[1]

[1] *On the Principle of Vitality,* Discourse before the Humane Society of the Commonwealth of Massachusetts, Boston, 1790. (Waterhouse gives as his sources, Bacon, Harris, C. Manilius and Whytt.)

Another hostile critic was Noah Webster, who opposed the imported English materialism in *Some Doubts concerning Darwin on the Laws of Organic Life*. The author of the *Zoonomia,* says the lexicographer, by merely observing the phenomena of animal motions might trace them to fibrous contractions, and fibrous contractions to irritation of external objects, to pleasure, pain, volition or association; but, at last, he is compelled to inquire *why* and *how* th'e fibres become obedient to the impulses of stimulus, and, mounting a step higher in the catenation of causes, to create or imagine a certain something to reside in the medullary substance of the brain to which he gives the denomination of the *spirit of animation*. What this principle is he makes no attempt to explain; and the very existence of it is rather assumed than proved. . . . He should have determined whether this primary source of the animal functions is an active agent or a passive capacity or faculty of the brain, producing effects only, in consequence of the impressions or influence of causes external to itself. If the spirit of animation is the former, an active substance, or ethereal substance in the brain, separate and independent of the medullary substance of that organ, how does this theory differ from the old hypothesis of a nervous fluid in the brain and nerves, by which motion is communicated to all parts of the body? Upon the other hypothesis, that the sensorial power is a passive quality, dependent on the structure of the brain and acting in obedience to stimulus, the author at length arrives at a phenomenon or effect for which he can find no cause or none which he has the power to comprehend.[1]

These opinions of Webster and Waterhouse represent the jealous attitude of the North toward a materialism prevalent in the South. A fairer attitude and one significant of an actual mediating position was taken by Samuel Miller of Princeton. He reviews the opinions of the principal materialists of the eighteenth century and shows how they differ in some of the details of their opinions from those philosophers of preceding times who held the same general doctrine. Epicurus supposed the soul of man to be a material substance, but a very refined and attenuated kind of

[1] Letter to Dr. Edward Miller, January, 30, 1804, in *New York Medical Repository*, Vol. 8, pp. 25-27.

matter. He taught that this substance, notwithstanding the extreme subtlety of its texture, is composed of four distinct parts: fire, which causes animal heat; an ethereal principle which is moist vapour; air; and a fourth principle which is the cause of sensation. This sentient principle he supposed to differ essentially from the three former, but to be like the rest, corporeal, because it is capable both of acting and being acted upon by bodies. From the union of the soul, thus constituted, with the body, he believed life and sensation to result. Something like this seems to have been the opinion of almost all the ancient materialists. Spinoza and Hobbes held a system of materialism quite as gross as any of their predecessors; for they seem to have thought that every material atom is, in a greater or less degree, animated or endowed with sensation. Dr. Hartley (if he be ranked in this class, and it is not easy to give him any other place) sometimes appears to recognise a sentient principle, which if not wholly immaterial, differs from any ideas which he seems to have formed of ordinary matter. The two grand principles on which his whole system rests are those of Vibration and Association. Newton had taught that the rays of light falling upon the bottom of the eye excite vibrations in the retina, and that these vibrations, being propagated along the optic nerves into the brain, produce the sensation of seeing. Dr. Hartley adopted this hypothesis, and applied it with ingenious additions and modifications of his own to the other senses. Mr. Locke had thrown new light upon the doctrine of association, and shown its great influence and importance in the operations of the human mind. Dr. Hartley also adopted the leading ideas of this great metaphysician on this subject, and by uniting them with the Newtonian opinions, formed a system on which the praise of great ingenuity and plausibility has been bestowed. According to this theory, the nerves are divided into two classes, sensory and motor; the former being the immediate instruments of sensation, the latter of motion. Both originate in the medullary substance of the brain, and their vibrations influence and modify each other. In short, every sensation, idea, muscular motion, affection, and internal feeling whatever, is supposed by Dr. Hartley to correspond with some vibratory state of the medullary substance, so that the one may be regarded as the exponent of the other.

Dr. Priestley's opinions on this subject, considered as a connected system, are new. He denies that there is any ground for making a distinction between the soul of man and the body; supposing the whole human constitution to be made up of one homogeneous substance. He denies that we have any evidence that the Deity himself is immaterial, in the commonly received sense of this word; and, finally, by the adoption of Father Boscovich's theory, he so refines and spiritualises matter, as to make it an extremely different thing from that gross and impenetrable substance which it is generally represented to be. He differs from preceding materialists, then, in his views of the nature of matter, and, in rejecting the idea entertained by most of them, that the sentient principle is a species of matter peculiarly refined and attenuated.[1]

So much for English materialism as viewed by American eyes; of its extreme development among the French philosophers native writers had far less to say. Jefferson indeed wrote to Cabanis, that it is not improbable that thought is a faculty of our material organisation; and Buchanan of Kentucky, accepting the physiology of the Gallic school, reduced ideas of whatever kind to motions excited in the brain and there felt or perceived. But these adherents of materialism were too immediately engrossed in its principles to recognise its final outcome. So it remained for a Southern writer of a later day to give a brilliant yet somewhat bitter review of the Anglo-French sensationalism which so extensively permeated his part of the country. By Robert Dabney of Virginia Hobbes is considered as the first modern expounder of what is called the sensualistic philosophy. According to this intellectual giant of Malmesbury, philosophy has for its object all bodies which are formed and possess qualities. The only definition of a soul, then, which philosophy can admit, is ' a natural body of such subtility that it does not act upon the senses, which fills a place, as

[1] Samuel Miller, *Retrospect of the Eighteenth Century*, New York, 1803, Vol. 2, pp. 18-19, 456-457.

would the image of a visible body and has figure (without colour) and dimension.' Our souls have two faculties, conception and movement. Sensation is nothing else than a movement of certain parts, which exist in the interior of the sentient being, and these parts are those of the organs by which we feel. Sensations are the principle of knowledge, and all knowledge is derived from them. Thus, memory consists in our having a sensation that we have had a sensation. Imagination is a sensation which continues with a feebler force, after its cause has ceased to act, like the wavelets which roughen the surface of a pool for a number of moments after the stone has fallen upon it. All the acts of generalising, naming our ideas, comparing and reasoning, are but associations of these sense-perceptions.[1] . . . The real agent for naturalising the ideas of Hobbes and Locke in revolutionary France was Condillac. Bolder than Locke, he announces it as his purpose to show that every process of the soul is reducible to a single principle, and that is sensation. The simplification which seems to be promised by this result is seductive to the superficial thinker, but such a design cannot but make havoc of the modest and humble rules of true, inductive science. With Condillac, all the faculties, including what Locke distinguished as faculties of reflection, are generated by experience, from the one faculty of sensation, the only real power of the human soul. Thus Condillac precludes himself from those wholesome, though inconsistent, returns to rational views of the a priori powers of the soul, which Locke gains through the vagueness of his definition of the reflective act. With Condillac, the favourite phrase is to call every operation of mind 'a transformed sensation.' Reflection itself is a transformed sensation—attention, memory, comparison, judgments, desires, volitions —all are transformed sensations.[2] . . . According to Helvétius, as according to his predecessors, the problem of philosophy is to investigate, not the properties, but the origin of our ideas. Man has but two mental powers, sensation and memory, which are both passive powers. Sensation is purely a physical suscepti-

[1] Robert L. Dabney, *The Sensualistic Philosophy of the Nineteenth Century,* New York, 1875, p. 8.

[2] *Ib.,* p. 25.

bility; and memory is but sensation prolonged and enfeebled. Judgment is also but sensation modified; to say ' I judge ' is the same thing as saying ' I feel.' Our ideas of space, duration, spirit, infinitude, are but illusions of thought. We really know nothing of space but extension, of infinitude but the indefinite. Errors of judgment arise wholly from passion and ignorance. Our mental processes are essentially the same with those of the brutes; and the only reason that man is in a higher state than they is that his corporeal organisation gives him a superiority, and especially the capabilities of his hands, as compared with their hoofs and claws. Liberty is an illusion, save as it is the liberation of our bodily members from material bonds; freedom of will is an idea of which philosophy can know nothing, and which can only be held, if held at all, on the authority of theology. As all ideas are merely relative to our own susceptibility of impression, certainty is impossible, and absolute or necessary truths there are none. All ideas are but probable appearances; and a calculation of probabilities is the only reasoning possible.[1]

[1] *The Sensualistic Philosophy of the Nineteenth Century*, p. 40.

CHAPTER II

CADWALLADER COLDEN

CADWALLADER COLDEN (1688-1776), the first and foremost of the early American materialists, had a career as varied as his accomplishments. Born in Ireland, the son of the Reverend Alexander Colden, intended for the ministry of the Church of Scotland, obtaining a medical degree from the University of Edinburgh and continuing his studies in England, he was allured by the flattering accounts of William Penn's colony and came to Philadelphia in 1710. Confessing that on his arrival he had some knowledge of books, but was absolutely a stranger to the world, and finding that the encouragement to a mere scholar was very small in any part of North America, he shortly returned to London, where his paper on *Animal Secretion* was read by Dr. Halley before the Royal Society. Again journeying to Philadelphia, he removed in 1718 to New York, where he gave up the practice of medicine, entered politics, and became in succession, Surveyor-General of the Province, Master in Chancery, Member of the Council, and Lieutenant-Governor.[1] Settling at Coldengham near Albany, at a time when the country from his own account was the habitation of wolves and bears and other wild animals, he entered upon an active career which began with the publication of his *Five Indian Nations,* consequent upon his adoption into the Mohawk tribe, and which ended with his attempts to start in the province of New York, with King's College as a mother, and under the patronage of His Majesty, an American University, whose object should be the prevention of the too prevalent growth of republican principles.[2] Yet in all this Colden was no mere Tory politician, but, as a French critic has

[1] Samuel Miller, *Retrospect of the Eighteenth Century,* New York, 1803, Vol. 2, p. 366, note. New York Historical Society, *Colden Papers,* 1876-1877.

[2] *History of Columbia University,* New York, 1904, p. 208.

329

acknowledged, a very learned man. As he himself put it, he enjoyed an acquaintance with bookish men in several parts of North America, and in addition had a foreign correspondence which included Linnæus of Upsala, Gronovius of Leyden, Portersfield of Edinburgh, and Peter Collinson of London. The results of this scientific comity ranged from a suggestion to Franklin for the organisation of the American Philosophical Society,[1] to the introduction into the colonies of the Linnæan system of botany.[2]

This was the man whose very existence has been declared almost a myth and whose philosophical system he himself feared would die in obscurity along with him. Constantly employed in business, he regretted that he could not pursue these studies otherways than by way of amusement, by fits and starts. This apology is somewhat pathetic, but now, after the lapse of a century and a half, with the recovery of his printed works and with access to the original autographs,[3] the Coldenian system may be reconstructed in its entirety. In general this system was a kind of dynamic panpsychism, somewhat in the manner of Toland's *Pantheisticon,* for Colden's works, taken in their order, are to be characterised in their own language as follows: *The First Principles of Morality* (1746?) presents a materialistic hedonism, body being a machine whose actions are determined by man, and pleasure being the final cause of the virtues. *The Principles of Action in Matter* (1751) presents a dualistic dynamism, matter being extended, active and unintelligent, and mind extended, active and intelligent. The *Introduction to the Study of Physics* (1756?) presents a phenomenalistic occasionalism, substance being power and force, known, not in itself but only by its effects, and the operations of

[1] As reported in the *American Medical and Philosophical Register*, New York, 1811, Vol. 1, p. 30.

[2] The *Plantae Coldinghannenses*, in the *Acta Upsalensia*, 1743-4, has been declared by Asa Gray 'a truly remarkable performance.' Compare *Selections from the Scientific Correspondence of Cadwallader Colden; American Journal of Arts and Sciences*, New Haven, 1843.

[3] In the possession of the New York Historical Society, and of H. F. De Puy, Esquire, of New York. According to the *Medical Repository*, Vol. 13, p. 78, the great mass of Colden's papers were preserved through his grandson, Cadwallader D. Colden.

mind being not caused, but only occasioned by the actions of material powers. The *Enquiry into the Principles of Vital Motion* (1766) presents a physiological atomism, both vitality and mentality being attributed to a fermentation or intestine motion of the atoms which compose the elastic fluid of the nerves. The *Reflections* (1770?) presents a psychological hylozoism, intelligence being a universally diffused substance in nature, and in it all other beings contained.

How far these works, of which only the second was printed, formed a consistent whole, how far they failed in their approach to a genuine materialistic monism, is a subject for later consideration. Meanwhile the first of them may be dismissed in a few words because of its lack of originality. Doubtless the earliest of Colden's philosophical ventures, Dr. Samuel Johnson of Yale College called it a beautiful little draught of the first principles of morality,[1] possibly because it so largely agreed with his own views. Like his *Ethica*,[2] it presents the same definition of morality as the art of living so as to be happy, and the same division of moral knowledge into three classes: 1, of the relation between God, the infinite, intelligent being or mind of the universe, and his creatures as he is the supreme governor of them; 2, of ourselves or of mankind in general, for procuring happiness as men are social creatures; 3, of things as necessary for life or to make it more comfortable.[3] The materialist also holds the same view of ethical liberty as his idealistic friend, asserting that we have the power of determining or altering our own actions of ourselves, without the force of compulsion of anything external to us. Without this power, he adds, the precepts of morality would be as ridiculous as in the maker of a clock to preach to it in order to correct its motions.[4] With this general agreement, there is, however, one point of dif-

---

[1] In a letter dated April 15, 1747, in reply to Colden's letter of January 27, 1746-7. In the latter Colden refers to the ethical teachings of his own *Principles of Natural Philosophy;* this presumably means the deistical arguments finally incorporated in the *Principles of Action in Matter.*

[2] Cf. *Elementa Philosophica*, Philadelphia, 1752, Part II, Introduction.

[3] *Principles of Morality*, De Puy MS., pp. 131, 133.

[4] *Ib.*, p. 126.

ference. Johnson thinks the sense of right and wrong intuitive, and derives it from the perpetual presence and irradiation of the Deity in our minds,[1] Colden cannot go to such heights, but confesses that in what manner does the spirit act, or in what manner its actions are determined by final causes, he cannot explain, any more than how matter acts when it moves.[2] This touch of agnosticism is to be explained by the author's deistic aversion to the doctrine of interferences. He allows that Providence may act for the unity of the universe and for the preservation of the actions of the universal system, but he cannot conceive how the Deity can act in opposition to the actions of material beings, for this would suppose that they wanted perpetual correction and amendment.[3] From such a passage as this it is evident that the materialist's system of morality is built on a lower level than the idealist's. This is more especially shown in the *Reflections* of Colden's old age, when worldly wisdom had rubbed the lustre from his earlier beliefs. Here he grants that the relations of things may be discovered intuitively, yet, at the same time, he perceives that the morals of all men in their childhood and of the common herd of men at all times differ little from the conduct of brute animals. They are entirely directed by their appetites or by habits which they have acquired. Men in general are good by authority or custom and habit, and very little by reason; for example, the military gentleman will defend the least charge on his veracity by his life and yet defraud a soldier of his poor pittance; and the lawyer, under the mask of a gown and band, will for a fee disguise truth and oppress the widow and orphan. Such evils could not happen in a society where men from infancy are enured in the use of reason.[4]

In addition to his ethical writings, and exclusive of his systematic works, the lieutenant-governor leaves 'to his dear children,' as the fruits of fifty years of life, the greatest part of which was spent in speculation, a quantity of treatises, of which all but the last was unpublished. These included *An Introduction to the Doctrine of Fluxions* (1743) ; *Of the Primary Material Agents,*

[1] *Ethica,* Introduction, § 15.　　　　[2] *Morality,* p. 128.
[5] *Ib.,* p. 147.　　　　[4] *Reflections,* §§ 28, 30.

or corrections and additions to the second edition of the *Principles of Action in Matter; Some Reflections on Dr. Berkeley's Treatise on Tar Water adapted to Diseases frequent in America; A Summary Account of the Principal Functions in the Animal Œconomy;* and *An Explication of the First Causes of Action in Matter and of the Cause of Gravitation.* Among these strangely miscellaneous articles only the last is of philosophic interest. The *First Causes* is at the same time an attempted criticism and enlargement of the Newtonian system and a starting point for Colden's own speculations. Newton, says he, in the last editions of his writings, holds that the agent which makes all bodies gravitate toward each other acts by pulsion, but his manner of explaining this is not satisfactory. . . . The apparent attraction or gravitation is more properly the effect of the joint actions of the moving, resisting, and elastic powers.[1]   There was a certain air of presumption about the Scottish-American's first brochure, and of this he was apparently conscious, for as he claimed, his was that liberty of philosophising assumed by Descartes, that bold assertion that we must receive nothing in philosophy on mere authority. Moreover, as he explained later, Newton nowhere in his writings attributes an attractive power to bodies or to matter, but tells us that this attraction is only apparent, only a perpetual effect of a cause of which he is ignorant.[2] Then, too, since Newton did not promulgate his theory of a possible cause of gravitation until his famous letters to Bentley, and since these letters were not made public until some time after the *Principles of Action in Matter,* Colden feels that his own works are justified in their publication.[3]

While these works were comparatively well received abroad, they apparently fell flat at home. Franklin assures Colden that they met with a good reception in England,[4] and there are indications

---

[1] *First Causes,* pp. 17, 27.

[2] *Natural Philosophy,* pp. 7, 17.   [3] See Notes.

[4] Franklin's Works (Bigelow Edition), Vol. 2, pp. 103, 330; compare (Smyth Edition) Vol. 3, p. 163, where Franklin tells Colden of extracts from the *First Principles* being printed in the *Monthly Review* and other journals.

of their translation into German and French, but in the colonies they were unknown and unhonoured. To this undeserved neglect there was one exception and that of the highest significance. Both the *First Causes* and the *Principles* aroused the keen interest of Dr. Samuel Johnson of Connecticut, the friend and follower of Bishop Berkeley during the latter's stay in Rhode Island. Consequently when in 1744 Johnson sent the principal Berkeleian treatises to Colden, there ensued an interchange of ideas between the materialist and idealist which read like veritable dialogues between Hylas and Philonous. Due attention has been given to this discussion,[1] but not to the writings around which it centred. In fact, Colden's printed works have been declared of no philosophic concern,[2] his doctrines dubious,[3] and his manuscripts as either lost or unknown.[4] And yet these productions, taken together, present a scheme of thought not without interest in the history of philosophy. In brief, the materialist of New York stands as a variant type in relation to the great system builders of his age. A reactionary against Descartes, Colden was neither a local Leibniz nor a colonial Spinoza; opposing the doctrines of the passivity of matter, he neither granted it the perceptions of the monad nor treated it as a necessary mode of the one only substance. A follower of Hobbes, he was a materialist and yet not a total determinist; in his physics he limited the activities of matter in accordance with their created essence, and in his metaphysics granted freedom of will to intelligent agents. Finally, a disciple of Newton, he was a dualist and yet not without a tendency to

---

[1] E. E. Beardsley, *Life and Correspondence of Rev. Samuel Johnson, D.D.*, First President of King's College, New York, 1874, pp. 129-142, 181-188.

[2] A. L. Jones, *Early American Philosophers*, New York, 1898, pp. 17-18.

[3] Georges Lyon, *L'Idéalisme en Angleterre*, Paris, 1888, pp. 377-383. Lyon describes Colden as an incurable realist and an inconsequent causalist. This characterisation is perhaps justified by the correspondence with Johnson but not by Colden's other writings, for these show that the materialist followed the Hobbite doctrine of causation, and the Newtonean, if not the Humean phenomenalism, in carrying to its logical conclusion the scholastic doctrine of representative perception.

[4] See Notes.

monism; he granted the existence of intelligent agent and unintelligent matter, and still comprehended both in a loose framework of cosmic activity.

From this summary one may estimate Colden's position in the development of American thinking. His system in general was in advance of the ordinary eighteenth century deism, anticipated to a degree the New England transcendentalism, and issued in a movement essentially modern,—the resolution of matter into the mechanics of energy. Colden is thus akin to Franklin, to Emerson and to Count Rumford. His benevolent being, who governs the great and small in a way most conducive for the well being of the universal system of nature, suggests Poor Richard's benevolent deity, who is said to be all-wise, all-good, all-powerful.[1] His doctrine of the specific forces of nature, as ever guided by fixed principles of design, suggests Emerson's doctrine of nature as the present expositor of the divine mind, whose serene order is inviolable to us.[2] Finally, his simplification of the concept of matter into force and quantity suggests, if it does not anticipate, that native theory of the correlation and conservation of energy which has been attributed to Benjamin Thompson of New Hampshire.[3]

Here is a paradox: a deist drifting toward a pantheistic absolute, a materialist with an irresistible tendency to eliminate matter. In a word, there is a motley look about this colonial thinker, but that has its legitimate explanation: Colden attempted to serve two different masters, and at the same time to harmonise the one with the other. Accepting both the Hobbite principle that the cause of all events can be reduced to motion, and the Newtonian speculations regarding the ether,[4] he tried to overcome the conse-

[1] Benjamin Franklin, *A Dissertation on Liberty and Necessity.*

[2] Essay on *Spirit*, p. 68.

[3] Rumford, *Works*, Vol. 2, p. 188, *Historical Review of Heat*, compare J. T. Merz, *A History of European Thought in the Nineteenth Century*, London, 1903, Vol. 1, p. 103.

[4] Compare *American Medical and Philosophical Register*, Vol. 1, p. 400; among Colden's early papers was found a copy of an original letter from Newton, dated Cambridge, February 28, 1678-9: 'First I suppose

quent dualism of the mental and physical worlds by the composition of his *Principles of Action in Matter*. The outcome of this philosophico-mathematical treatise was this: matter as a sublimated force, mind as spiritualised matter are not opposed substances, but possess a common denominator in a universal elastic medium, a vaguely diffused ether.

Advocate of energy and force, Colden at the outset attacks the problem of human understanding in a manner opposed to Locke. The prevalent belief that knowledge is a cognisance of inert and inactive objects, passively received by the senses, is contradicted by the introductory statement of the *Principles*. Here it is asserted that all the primary or simple ideas we have of things external to us arise from the impressions or actions of these things on our senses, that the knowledge we have of things is no other than the perception of these actions, and that thinking is a kind of action of a peculiar kind differing from all other kinds of action.[1] Postulating the need of a joint activity of bodies and minds in sense perception—for everything that we know is an agent or has a power of acting—Colden adds to this dynamism a touch of phenomenalism. As we know nothing of anything but its action and the effects of that action, the moment anything ceases to act it must be annihilated as to us. But herein the author is no mere subjectivist. Still insisting that all our knowledge of anything consists in the perception of the power, or force, or property, or manner of action of that substance, being, or thing,[2] he enters the ontological jungle of objective existence. Returning from his struggle with the thing-in-itself, he declares that it is wrong to speak of matter as passive, since each species of matter hath a force peculiar to itself. These species are three in number: the resisting, moving, and expansive, and are represented in the *vis inertiae,* moving bodies, especially light, and the elastic ether.[3]

What is the origin of these three forces? Matter being reducible to motion, whence came that motion? Before he gave

that there is diffused through all places an ætherial substance, capable of contraction and dilatation, strongly elastic, and, in a word, much like air in all respects, but far more subtile.'

[1] *Principles*, pp. V., 7.   [2] *Ib.*, p. 2.   [3] *Ib.*, p. V.

his final answer to these questions, Colden had considered them in his earlier *Principles of Morality*. Discussing certain statements in the latter, Johnson had said that his chief objection was against Colden's using the term action as expressing anything in matter, which is merely a passive thing, whereas he himself held that all the actions in all nature that affect our senses are really the action of the great supreme Being or Spirit.[1] Here was an immediate occasionalism, facile solution of the problem of cosmic activity, but Colden did not avail himself thereof. He could not derive motion immediately from the deity, for he had in his mind a lurking notion of the self-sufficiency of the universe. He could not assume a perpetual primary cause, for thereby secondary causes would be obviated. To inject such an arbitrary principle as personality into matter would make investigation impossible, since matter acts uniformly. To admit the capriciousness of voluntary action among material agents would be to destroy the possibility of exact investigation. Such appears to be the burden of the following passages: It is commonly supposed that a certain degree of motion or velocity was communicated to each of the planets at the creation. But it is a very unphilosophical method of reasoning to suppose that motion comes immediately from the Divine Being, or that he is the immediate cause of all motion, as he must be if no other thing have the power of moving in itself; and therefore that every new motion, at least, is generated by the immediate power of the Creator. This indeed would make any inquiry into the causes of the phenomena arising by the motion of the planets very short, by saying that their motions are directed by the Spirit which governs them. The laws of action of such an agent can never be discovered by any mathematical inquiry, because quantity is its sole object.[2] Thus far Colden's ontology is a combination or rather a permutation of the views of Descartes and Leibniz. To the former matter is extended and passive, spirit unextended and active, to Colden matter is extended and active. To the latter each species of matter has an inherent principle of activity, uniform, necessary and invariable, to Colden this principle is the same, yet, unlike the monads which possess certain perceptions, it is not intelligent. Purpose and ultimate design

[1] Beardsley, pp. 137-138.   [2] *Principles*, pp. 72, 73.

in things material are supplied from without, room being thus left for immediate control through second causes, but not for an immediate concourse of the deity. But the materialist's position is not yet fully determined. In treating of the elementary parts of matter as acting uniformly and necessarily, he appears to favour an atomism which makes ' the smallest parts of which matter is supposedly compounded ' to be substances existing in and of themselves. He had previously denied that the motions, for example, of the planets were due directly to the Divine Being, and thereby implied that bodies have a power of movement independent and self-originated. From this contention there might seem to follow a double implication: that matter is somehow intelligent, and, being self-moved, needs no prime mover. Colden briefly dismissed the first point as incomprehensible. He asserted that there is no intelligence or perception in matter, but that these are the properties of some kind of being distinct from matter. Johnson had held that consciousness and intelligence were essential to all agents that act from a power in themselves. Colden replied that intelligence to him was not a concomitant to all action, else he could not conceive of the action of a mill without supposing it endowed with mentality. But herein he was not possessed of such a dull apprehension as he so complaisantly informed his correspondent. Foreseeing at least two consequences of his first implication, he was forearmed against the later charges of pantheism. These consequences may be interpreted as follows: to grant activity to matter, and, at the same time, to deny it any rational faculty is to suppose a doctrine of the unconscious; but this is obviated by postulating a sort of deistic control. Thus, in a thousand objects of our senses does Colden discern power and force, nevertheless the action of matter is determined by efficient causes always external to itself.[1] Again to speak of a soul of the world is to suppose a doctrine of hylozoism. Regarding this Colden explains that passive matter being synonymous with nothing, some of the ancient philosophers asserted that all nature is alive; but he hastens to add that he did not think of the old opinion of the soul of the world when he wrote that paragraph, and therefore requests Johnson to put in its place ' infinitely Intelligent Being.'[2]

[1] Beardsley, p. 138.   [2] Ib., p. 140.

Against the second inference, that matter being self-moved needs no prime mover, the materialist utters an explicit negative. He contends that the first formation of all things was made by some intelligent being and that God at the creation gave to different kinds of matter different and distinct kinds of action.[1] By this statement is met the objection of one of the fellows of Yale College, reported by Johnson, that there was a tendency in the New Yorker's system toward atheism. Johnson himself had escaped such a charge by supposing matter to be a mere passive thing, whereas it was spirit that pervaded and agitated all. To him the ancient notion, the principle of Vergil's philosophy—*mens agitat molem*—meant that there was one self-exerting, active principle Who pervades all things.[2] The idealist had reached this monistic point of view by denying activity, or, what was the same thing to Colden, essential reality to matter. He therefore urged his friend to join him in this, his comfortable conclusion: You say very truly we have no idea of matter, by which it is plain that by matter you mean something that is not the object either of our sense or minds. Of what use then is it in philosophy? Why may we not wholly drop it, and do as well without it, perhaps much better? And suppose what you call the action of it to be the action of that Almighty Spirit in whom we live, move, and have our being, and consider all nature as being the glorious system of his incessant exertions and operations, with which by his own action governed by fixed rules of his most wise establishment called the laws of nature, He perpetually and with endless variety of objects affects our senses and minds. This will sufficiently account for everything, whereas matter, whereof we can have no idea, can account for nothing.[3] To the voice of the tempter, to the idealistic blarney caught from the good bishop of Cloyne, Colden gave but half an ear. He had indeed allowed that we have no immediate knowledge of matter,[4] but in this attempt to twist his phe-

[1] Beardsley, p. 136, and *Principles*, p. 161.

[2] *Ib.*, p. 134.

[3] *Ib.*, p. 139, compare also a partial copy of this letter of April 15, 1747, in Colden's hand, among the manuscripts of the New York Historical Society.

[4] *Principles of Morality*, § 9.

nomenalism into immaterialism he protested that Johnson had not given sufficient attention to his fundamental argument, nor to the distinction which he makes between the substance and the action of the substance. Consequently he reiterates his former contention that we have no ideas of substances, but only of their actions, or the ideas are the effects of their actions on the mind. . . . So although this power or force should be only apparent and the consequence or effect of some other primary cause, yet I am cer tainly to be excused in my thinking it real till it appears otherwise to me, as I believe every man is to be excused who does not understand astronomy, and thinks that the sun moves.[1]

So far Colden's ontology is of a piece with his epistemology. It is a science of the real based upon a theory of knowledge which emphasises active processes. Or to compare it with another reactionary against the Cartesian view, this theory resembles that of Cudworth when he said all perception is a vital energy and not a mere dead passion.[2] Hence with the Cambridge Platonist Colden is led on into the larger questions of how this perception arises and what is the interaction between spirit and matter. Here he distinguishes between material and spiritual agents, as did Leibniz between material and spiritual monads. Like him he refuses the help of the Cartesian occasionalism, the continuous assistance or perpetual concourse of the deity, such as Johnson taught to be essential to the rise of ideas in the human mind. But unlike Leibniz, at this juncture Colden makes no use of the doctrine of preestablished harmony to solve the problem of concomitance. Difficulties consequently arise from his assumptions: granted that matter acts to the extent of its created properties—but all without self-determining purpose—and that spirit determines and directs its own actions, how far does the latter determine and direct the former? In this perplexing situation a compromise is offered: spirit and matter are opposite in their essential nature, yet not antagonistic in their actions; the intelligent agent never acts in opposition or contradiction to the material agent, but so disposes of the parts of the system that their complicated actions shall

---

[1] Beardsley, p. 132.   [2] Cf. *Intellectual System of the Universe.*

serve the purposes which the intelligent being has in the forming
of the system. When the action of the material agent is not determined by anything external to it and its action is indifferent to
any direction, then the intelligent being gives the action such
direction as best suits its own purpose. Thus in the voluntary
actions of animals the ether in the nerves has its elasticity equal
through the whole length and therefore the mind can direct or
stop the reaction at pleasure.[1] This is the extent of Colden's
psychological principles as given in his chief published work; he
apologises for their meagreness because they are among the dark
things hereafter to be discovered, and are as yet seen only with
a very glimmering light. The author's ultimate beliefs as to the
origin of ideas are to be found in the hitherto unpublished treatise on the *Principles of Vital Action*. Being products of his old
age and supplementary to his *Principles of Action in Matter*,
they may be left for later consideration.

In his earlier psychology Colden ran into a sheer absolutism of
mind over body. It was otherwise in the sphere of cosmology.
Here he asserted that perfect intelligence will not act in contradiction to the action of matter, because the latter has its active
principle in itself.[2] To this statement Johnson strenuously objected, and tried to make the offensive passage read as follows:
Perfect Intelligence will not, in the settled course of things, act
in contradiction to the laws He hath established, according to
which He wills matter to act, because the action of matter, as
well as matter itself, is entirely dependent on the constant free
exertion of the divine will and power.[3] In this attempted toning
down of a doctrine advocating the independency and consequent
eternity of matter, Johnson misread Colden's other passages. As
an astronomer the latter was willing to allow that there may have
been a time when the present solar system did not exist; but as a
metaphysician, considering systems in the universal, why object to
the infinite duration of matter? Matter, it is ingeniously argued,
may exist as well at one time as another, therefore we might as
well consider it as existing at all times.[4]

[1] *Principles of Matter,* p. 163.   [2] *Ib.,* p. 164.
[3] Beardsley, p. 186.   [4] *Principles,* p. 165.

Before considering the sources of these notions, the query may be raised whether the materialist was at all conscious of his drift toward pantheism. He criticised Johnson for such a tendency, entitled his immaterialism a kind of Spinozism, and claimed that, if all action be attributed immediately to the Almighty Spirit in whom we live, move, and have our being, all nature being a system of his incessant exertions, it is impossible to see how any thing or action can be morally evil in a proper sense.[1] In thus pointing out another's trend towards an idealistic monism, it may be answered that Colden was evidently aware of the implications of his own thought. And that was further evidenced from the manner in which he hedged on his materialistic monism. In order to show that he was no pantheist in the Spinozistic sense, he attached certain alternatives to his favourite tenets of the self-sufficiency and eternity of matter. To nature, whether considered as *naturata* or *naturans,* he added a creator, ruler, and governor, and further postulated a limitation in time for this present world. Nature, he explains, or more properly speaking the infinite, intelligent Archæus, has ordered so that, since the several individual systems must in time fail from their natural constitution, this defect is supplied by the generation of new and similar systems under the direction of the intelligent agent. The duration of all solar systems probably is infinite in respect to the duration of any small system on this earth whose period we knew; and yet the duration of the solar system may be infinitely small in respect to the duration of the universe. The Egyptian priests, and Pythagoras from these, seem to have had speculations of this sort, which they delivered out in mystic terms to the people, and explained clearly to the initiated only.[2]

What were the sources of this cosmology, as given in this the concluding passage of philosophic significance in the *First Principles of Action in Matter?* An attempt to answer that question was made by a contemporary. Johnson compares Colden's recrudescence or rejuvenation of the world, by a perpetual return of the ethereal fluid to the sun or by the operations of the elastic fluid manifest in gravitation, to Hutchinson's doctrine of the ethereal fluid or fire of the sun as it returns to its fountain. Ac-

[1] Beardsley, p. 141.   [2] *Principles*, p. 167.

cording to the idealist, Hutchinson, Bishop Berkeley and the Abbé Pluché agree that this ethereal fire is the light and life of the whole sensible world, the grand agent in all nature, the immediate engine from whence all the phenomena mechanically derive, and that this was the original philosophy of Moses and in all the Hebrew scriptures, and taught man from the beginning. 'Your demonstrations,' he concludes, ' and Mr. Franklin's experiments illustrate and confirm it to be the only true and original philosophy.' [1] These references of Johnson are interesting but only half correct. Franklin, indeed, conveyed to Colden an opinion in support of his theory regarding a subtle elastic fluid filling universal space, but as for identifying such a theory with the *Philosophica Sacra* of Samuel Pike, the follower of Hutchinson, that manner of philosophising, he protested, was much out of his way.[2] Then too, it was Samuel Pike, who in the appendix to his work of 1753, tried to harmonise the Coldenian system with his own, but with only nominal success. He claims that the treatise of the ingenious and laborious American is a vindication of his own philosophy of nature, which was in its turn drawn from the scripture plan. As the scriptural expansion is Colden's expansive or elastic force of ether, so the universal commotion is his moving power, and the universal compression his resisting power. But although the first three principles of Mr. Colden are thus exactly accounted for from revelation, his deductions therefrom do not necessarily exhibit a rational account for the universal law of gravitation, and for these reasons: 1, no particle of matter can be of itself elastic, because it is in itself absolutely dead and inactive; 2, no particle of matter can be self-moving, because to suppose this is to make out matter a living and not a dead thing; 3, no particle of matter can have in itself a power of resistance, because it being dead is merely passive and therefore can only receive a motion impressed. . . . But how came dead matter to have such active properties belonging to it? As the penetrating author of the *First Principles* has made it appear that the three forementioned principles will account for gravitation and other phe-

[1] Beardsley, pp. 186, 187.
[2] *Works* (Bigelow Edition), Vol. 2, pp. 254, 341.

nomena, and the scripture plan will fairly account for his three principles, there will be no necessity of recurring to three distinct hidden, unexplained qualities as he does.[1]

To this incoherent and reactionary bit of criticism, from the half-educated and fanciful disciple of Hutchinson, Colden seemingly made the following reply: I never looked into the bible for the principles of philosophy, thinking it was only to instruct us as moral agents, and not understanding Hebrew. . . . My aim is to discover what are the simple, uncompounded powers which produce action on all the mechanical natural compositions. For an analytical examination of the phenomena of the effects of these powers, they may be reduced to three principles or powers of action. Now there is nothing not perfectly consonant with scripture in the belief, 1, that God created three distinct substances with these powers, for as Sir Isaac Newton observes, *virtus sine substantia subsistere non potest;* and 2, that God formed and ranged these three different substances into innumerable systems, in the proper shapes, figures and proportions, so as to produce the effects, according to his purposes, in their formation necessarily arising from the mechanical disposition and complication of these several powers. . . . But the universal opinion of dead, inert matter is an universal error. How do we first receive the idea of this dead matter otherwise than by action on our sense?[2]

To return to Johnson's original conjecture: in comparing the Coldenian to the Hutchinsonian method of reasoning, the idealist was committing the very fault with which he charged the latter school, the fault of carrying the humour of allegorising too far. Johnson's accomplishments as an Hebraist doubtless led to this endeavour of his to connect the non-connectable, to identify a contemporary system with an imaginary prehistoric philosophy, but how vain was that endeavour. As a deist, a materialist and a Newtonian, Colden was the very antithesis of his alleged original, for Hutchinson considered deism an engine of the devil,

---

[1] *Philosophica Sacra: or The Principles of Natural Philosophy*, London, 1753, pp. 135-150.

[2] Colden's copy of an undated and unaddressed letter, presumably to Samuel Pike. (New York Historical Society.)

denied that inert matter was capable of active qualities, and wrote a book entitled *Moses' Principia,* in which an ill-defined universal fluid was substituted for the principle of gravitation.[1] To these discrepancies, however, Johnson was not wholly blind; he asks Colden's pardon for his incoherent and rambling way of writing and yet, in conclusion, esteeming the philosophical part of Hutchinson entirely right, again attempts to identify Coldenianism with it. He points out that these views were set forth by his friend's countryman, Lord President Forbes, and thus seeks to trace them to a native source. But to cut these futile conjectures short; the sources of Colden's system are not so much Scotch as English. In brief, he was an inconscient follower of Hobbes and an avowed disciple of Newton. His psychology, epistemology and theory of causation were drawn from the philosopher of Malmesbury, his ontology and cosmology were written as a defence of the great Sir Isaac.

It is now in order to make an exact comparison of the Coldenian system with its manifest originals. While in but a single incidental reference does the author mention the father of English materialism, yet his indebtedness to him is palpable. The very title of Colden's *Principles* suggests the postulate of Hobbes's *De Corpore,* that the universal cause of all things is motion.[2] Again Colden's tripartite division of material beings resembles the Hobbite division of matter in general into object, medium, and the sentient itself.[3] Besides these minor correspondences there are closer resemblances in the subdivision of each scheme. The primitive psychology of the colonial is that of his predecessor's work of precisely a century before. Colden's statements that thinking is a kind of action, and that our ideas are only excited by the actions of things on our senses, find their equivalent in Hobbes's preliminary definition of sense as some natural motion in the sentient, generated by some internal motion of the parts of the object.[4] The fuller explication of sense as a phantasm due to the perpetual propagation of pressures made by motions outward and

[1] Chandler, *Life of Samuel Johnson,* p. 74.
[2] Chapter 6, § 5 (Calkins' Edition), Chicago, 1905.
[3] *Ib.,* § 9.   [4] *Ib.,* Chapter 25 § 2.

inward was not followed by the American materialist. Yet it was not until later that he expressed his dissatisfaction with that explanation of the origin of ideas which attributes them, as it were, to an attenuated series of material forces. Meanwhile in the inception of a crude physiological psychology, Colden had employed the peculiarly Hobbite phrases as to an ethereal spirit involving both the brain and nerves. In his *Medical Piece* of 1745 which he had sent to Franklin, he presents a theory of fermentation in the capillaries as explaining vital motion analagous to Hobbes's theory of the fermentation of the fluid parts of the body to explain vital heat. Here Colden was making no particular advance, since his predecessor had already maintained that the vital spirits were stirred by diseases, purified by the heart, and carried off by the arteries.[1] In a word, neither master nor follower rose above the vulgar, figurative conception of the animal spirits as so many volatile gases in a retort,—subtle and invisible fluids similar to the products of the alchemist's distillation.

Colden's early psychology was rudimentary and derivative; it was not so with his epistemology. That the knowledge we have of the qualities of things arises from the power or force of these things on our senses, that we have no ideas of substances or of things themselves,[2]—such a theory of knowledge begins indeed like Hobbes but ends in a manner like Kant. Standing nearly half way between the two subjectivists, Colden was innocent of the absolute distinction between phenomenal and noumenal, yet he went beyond the first of them in insisting upon the non-identity of the external and internal worlds. Hobbes had asserted that there is nothing without us (really) which we call an image, and that this said image is but an apparition unto us of the motion, agitation, or alteration, which the object worketh in the brain.[3] Colden went further in his contention that our ideas may not be true or perfect images of the things they are supposed to represent; for he held that we have no ideas or conceptions of substances or of things themselves, nor have we any conception in what manner substances or things exert their action; our ideas

---

[1] *De Corpore*, Chapter 34.   [2] *Principles*, pp. 1, 24.
[3] *Human Nature*, Chapter 2, § 4.

are only excited by the actions of things on our senses.[1] This passage is not to be interpreted as teaching the unreality of consciousness, but merely the non-identity of idea and object. In other words, Colden's epistemology leans to a knowledge which is relational rather than factual. As the phenomenalism of a mathematician it approaches the belief of Hume that the only objects of real knowledge and demonstration are number and quantity. It was the conviction of Colden that whatever differences exist in the actions of things arise from their different quantities, for otherwise this action could not be the object of mathematical enquiry.[2] Against the Coldenian theory of knowledge may be raised the same objection as against the Humean:[3] Whence arises the certainty assumed in mathematics, if there is nothing in the intellect which was not previously in the senses? This difficulty does not seem as yet to have occurred to Colden; therefore not deeming it necessary to validate the principles of the understanding, he reverts to experience as the sole source of knowledge, and employs the very language of Hume in asserting that no simple ideas can be explained, no definition or explication can give a blind man any ideas of colours, or a deaf man of sounds.[4]

In his epistemology Colden carried out the subjective relativity of knowledge taught by Hobbes; in his ontology he was less radical. While the English materialist declared that we cannot form any idea of an immaterial substance, and that to speak of incorporeal substances is to speak of four cornered circles, the American held a theory of being which included along with the material, the spiritual. Yet the latter has a starved look, for the hope expressed in the introduction to his *Principles* of giving as clear and distinct an idea of spirit as of matter is not fulfilled. The definition of the essence of things as their manner of acting, when applied to the mind, brings forth the incomplete and unsatisfactory deduction that thinking is a kind of action of a peculiar sort. This inadequate ontology is due in part to the author's

---

[1] *Principles*, p. 25.   [2] *Ib.*, p. 157.
[3] Cf. Weber, *History of Philosophy*, p. 432.
[4] *Principles*, p. 9. Compare Hume's *Inquiry*, § 2, p. 15. (Open Court Edition).

sticking too closely to his predecessor's theory of causality. In making the reality of being dependent upon the effects as judged by the sentient, he adopts the Hobbite principle that the knowledge of the essence of anything is the cause of the knowledge of the thing itself.[1] Moreover he follows the Baconian principle, also used by Hobbes, that physics deals with *causae efficientes*, metaphysics with *causae finales*.[2] This distinction, together with further causal definitions, is thus carried out in the *Principles*: As our ideas frequently arise from the complicated actions of intelligent and material agents, a mixture of mathematical and metaphysical principles becomes necessary in our enquiries. . . . Of these two agents the former deserve the name of efficient causes, because they alone are able externally to alter the action or direction of those material agents which have no power in themselves to increase their force of action or to determine it to one direction more than to another. They have no will, purpose, view or design in their action. But the intelligent being directs its own actions, by the purpose, design or views which it has, and therefore its actions are said to be determined or directed by final causes.[3] Adding to these passages the previous statement as to the self-activity of matter and there appears an obvious parallelism between the two materialists in respect to the problem of causality. Colden's power or force peculiar to each species of matter was Hobbes's power of the patient or material cause; while the latter's contention that the efficient and material causes are both but partial causes was carried out in the former's postulate regarding the complicated actions of intelligent and material agents. Finally Colden re-echoes his predecessor's assertion that a final cause has no place but in such things as have sense and will, but this without making the final cause equivalent to the efficient cause or even the final cause.[4]

In both the initial classification and terminology of causation there is manifest agreement between the author of the *Principles* and the author of the *De Corpore;* it is not so in their conclu-

---

[1] *De Corpore,* Chapter 10, § 7.   [2] *De Augmentis,* III., 4.
[3] *Principles,* pp. 162, 163.
[4] Compare *Principles,* pp. 27, 163, with *Inquiry,* Chapter 9, § 4.

sions. While Colden starts with the postulate that the essence of reality consists in the principle of action, essence Hobbes would designate to be formal cause and identify it with efficient cause, agreeably to the argument that all mutation consists in motion only.[1] And so the question arises how with this likeness at the start there was unlikeness at the finish. The reason undoubtedly lay in a certain constitutional difference between the determinist and the deist; there being in the one a desire for unity and system, in the other a shrinking from too thorough an application of any single principle. Colden was in evident trepidation of following the chain of causation to its end; for one thing that would bring mechanism into morals by destroying free will and the liberty of choice; for, as he says, in all actions of intelligent beings, which are likewise called moral actions, the intention, purpose or will is principally to be considered.[2]

In his equating of the various partial causes to the end of gaining in a single grasp plenary power or entire cause, Hobbes, so to speak, pushed the joints of the telescope together. Colden, on the other hand, left them apart. In other words, while the monist gained consistency by this arbitrary method of synthesis, the pluralist exposed the breaks in his system. Here was matter: extended—active—unintelligent, and mind: unextended—active—intelligent, and yet the term common to each does not make them co-ordinate. But even if matter be active within the limits of its essential nature, why does it not, in some degree, deserve the name of efficient cause? If it act uniformly, invariably and according to fixed laws, why should it be called entirely unintelligent and lacking the characteristics of final cause? These were the flaws picked out by the sharp eye of Johnson, consistent monist from the idealistic point of view. The scrutiny led Colden to return to his prototype. It is in his section on Sense and Animal Motion that Hobbes cites philosophers, and those learned men, who have maintained that all bodies are endued with sense; and at the same time objects, that, unless those bodies have organs, as living creatures have, fit for the retaining of such motion as is made in them, their sense would be such, as that they should never remember

[1] *Principles*, § 6.   [2] *Ib.*, p. 162.

the same.[1] The argument and the rebuttal are now repeated.
Colden agrees with Johnson that an unactive cause and no cause
are synonymous, but he is not convinced that intelligence is an
essential concomitant to all action. ' Now, Sir,' he concludes,
' these are fundamental differences. One of us must be under a
very great mistake.'[2] The misunderstanding between the two
men is to be attributed to their having, the one monistic, the other
dualistic, leanings. Johnson would submerge matter in spirit,
Colden would keep them separate. In this discussion it is seen
that whereas Johnson has outgrown his earlier deism, Colden falls
back upon his other principal authority. To his correspondent
he continues in this strain: You seem likewise to think that the
words *inert* and *unactive* are synonymous. Sir Isaac Newton
was certainly of a different opinion, as appears by the third definition in the beginning of his *Principles,* viz.: *materiae vis inerta est
Potentia resistendi.* We certainly can have no conception of Force
or Power devoid of all kinds of action.[3] Causality is now carried
over into cosmogony and the discussion is in substance as follows:
You may start a machine, but if it consists of dead parts, how,
pray, is it to be kept running? Johnson answered to the effect
that the shifting cosmic phenomena are to be regarded as manifestations of a divine will, activities of a supreme intelligence.
Colden replied that there was no necessity of going so far, that
material agents need not be endowed with sense, will or intelligence, but that essential activity is all that is called for. Johnson
still insisted that his opponent had made a considerable approach
towards his own master's way of thinking, in allowing that all
our ideas of sensible things are the effects of the actions of something external to our minds, and that even resistance is an action.
. . . All that Berkeley contends for is that there are no
other than two sorts of beings, the one active, the other passive,
—that spirit, the Deity, and created intelligence alone are the
active beings, and the objects of sense alone are merely passive;
and that there is no active medium intervening between the actions
of the Deity and our minds whom He has made to be perceptive

[1] *Physics,* Part IV., Chapter 25, § 5.
[2] Beardsley, p. 182.   [3] *Ib.*

and self-active Beings.[1] In the last letter of this amicable controversy Johnson tries to reconcile his friend to himself. He argues that a blind principle or power of action without Intelligence seems repugnant and useless. However, it seems a question of little real consequence, he concludes, after what you allow in the chapter of the Intelligent Being; the action of what you call matter being according to you derived originally from and directed by the Intelligent Being. And so matter is no more than merely His instrument, so that what you call the action of a mill or watch is really only a successive series of passions till' you come to the principle of Intelligence, which will ultimately prove also to be the principle of the action.[2]

In all his correspondence with Colden, Johnson was unconsciously trying to win him over to an older idealism, to the school of Henry More, who differed from the Cartesian concept of substance in including in the mind original activity, in matter imparted activity.[3] In this dynamic conception of the philosophy of nature there was a general agreement between the idealist and materialist, but Johnson does not seem to have recognised a palpable disagreement in method. The difference between the follower of the Cambridge Platonist and the follower of Newton was the difference between the magical and the mathematical explanation of cosmic phenomena. Both men postulated an initial impulse, but one made this imparted activity continuous only through the perpetual miracle of the concourse of the deity, the other only through the self-perpetuating character of motion. In a word, Colden energised matter at creation and left it to itself, Johnson called for the divine assistance whenever occasion arose. In carrying out the doctrine of the self-sustaining power of matter Colden laid himself open to that very charge of Spinozism which he brought against Johnson. As has been previously noted, with all his deistic creationism he hovers dangerously on the brink of hylozoism. The word matter, he protests, when it represents a mere being without power, force, or action, or property, is syn-

[1] Beardsley, p. 143.   [2] Ib., pp. 185, 186.
[3] Harald Höffding, A History of Modern Philosophy, New York, 1900, Vol. 1, p. 290.

onymous with nothing. For this reason some of the ancient philosophers asserted that all nature is alive, that is, all nature is active.[1] This statement, together with a brief reference to the mystic speculations of Pythagoras, may be due to Colden's lively interest in the ancient mathematics, or they may be more specifically traced to the opening section in Newton's *System of the World*. Whatever the source of these notions, they exhibit in Colden, materialist and deist, much the same mental oscillation as in Newton, mathematician and theologian. As the latter held that matter may be endowed with innate gravity and yet in addition be controlled by a supernatural guiding power,[2] so the former asserted that the systems of the universe are regenerated by nature or more properly speaking, by the infinite, intelligent Archæus.[3] By such timid alternatives, the lieutenant-governor tried to square his beliefs as churchman with his beliefs as scientist. But the effect was not attended with entire success. The earlier machiavellian argument that, if the deity so desired, matter might be coeval with himself was based on the assumption that the activities of matter are uniform and persistent. This implying that the world of gravity lives in itself was one step toward pantheism, another was to be found in etherialising the cosmic substance, and turning it into a vague, unitary substance: the parts of every system, it is urged, have some general reference or connection, with one, single point, by which they become a kind of unity or one system; this reference is commonly, if not always, done by means of the ether.[4] In thus attempting an explanation of the principle of gravitation Colden rushed in where others feared to tread. While Hobbes utilised the ether only as a possible cause, and Newton took care to distinguish between the *vis gravitatis* and the *causa gravitatis,* he himself presumes to think that he has discovered an error which has slipped from the sagacious Sir Isaac by his not knowing the cause of the apparent attraction of bodies.[5] Either Colden had lost his own sense of gravity or he was as yet unfamiliar with all of Newton's writings. He knew

[1] *Principles,* p. 27.
[2] Letter to Bentley, February 25, 1692-3, in Sir David Brewster, *Memoirs of Newton,* London, 1855, Vol. 2, p. 128.
[3] *Principles,* p. 167.   [4] *Ib.,* p. 164.   [5] *Ib.,* Preface, p. II.

the *Principia,* for in his postulate concerning the inherent activity of matter he acknowledges his indebtedness to the third definition in the beginning of that work. He likewise knew the *Optics,* for he lent a copy of it to Franklin, but evidently not the second edition, where the author returns to his earlier guesses regarding a proposed etherial medium,—much of the same constitution with air, but far rarer, subtiler and more strongly elastic.[1] But this conjecture was repeated in Newton's addendum of 1708 in which he surmised that perhaps the whole frame of nature may be nothing but various contextures of certain ethereal spirits, wrought into various forms, at first by the immediate hand of the creator and ever after by the power of nature.[2] It was on this later passage, then, that Colden obviously based his supposition regarding an ethereal stuff pervading all things, and also that summary statement regarding the generation of new and similar systems under the direction of the intelligent agent.

At this point it is possible to venture an estimate of Colden's highly involved cosmology. In the last letter of their correspondence, Johnson charged his friend with being a natural philosopher and not a metaphysician, because he did not refer his principles of action in matter to a single great principle.[3] That charge was in a measure just; Colden did not think things through; he had certain impulses towards monism, but these were checked by dualistic compromises. There were in his system hypotheses which pointed to a theory of the absolute, but over against these lay conflicting negations: for example, causality might be reduced to the principle of motion, but not in the sphere of free will; the principles of action in matter might be independent, but not previous to creation; all nature might be alive, but not so as to include a rational faculty in matter; matter might be eternal, but not so as to divest the individual systems of the world of the need of regeneration and superintendence. There are glaring inconsistencies in this scheme, and yet they only repeat the Newtonian philosophy of nature as it included the ultimate dependence of self-active matter upon a creator, the non-identity of the soul of the universe with the deity, and even that arbitrary interference

[1] Merz, Vol. 1, p. 340.   [2] Compare *Open Court,* No. 231, p. 1.
[3] Beardsley, p. 184.

in the world-machine, which Leibniz derided as the Almighty's wanting to wind up his watch from time to time.[1]

These inconsistencies Colden himself came to recognise. His unpublished correspondence shows that he was alive to foreign criticism, and his later unpublished treatises that he was able to present a more consistent notion of the absolute than was given in his *First Principles*. Learning of one critic who turned up his nose because a man in the woods of America pretended to teach the sublime parts of philosophy, he retorts that his situation deprives him of a monitor and corrector, and he therefore expects great indulgence, especially from those in the universities.[2] But Colden was no mere apologist; conscious that he did not understand astronomy as well as he ought, he made a year's observations in Lord Macclesfield's observatory; living in a remote part of the country and realising the lessening commerce between his province and Scotland, he renews correspondence with his countrymen and sends for such books as Maclaurin's *Newtonian Philosophy*. Refreshed by this dip into the stream of European thought, he now returns to a defence of his views. He still thinks matter to be active despite the objections of Professor Kastner of Leipsic and Professor Euler of Berlin. It was the latter who said that the treatise of the American philosopher contains many ingenious reflections in its endeavours to explain the physical cause of universal gravitation, but that the explication founded on the elasticity of the ether is so imagined that it is absolutely contrary to the first principles of hydrostatics. To these strictures Colden replies that the Berlin professor looks with contempt on any attempt in America to improve our notions in philosophy, but that there is nothing in Newton's *Principles* which is contradicted in the *Principles of Action*.[3]

Of all his foreign readers Colden received the fairest treatment

[1] Brewster, Vol. 2, p. 284.

[2] MSS., New York Historical Society, letter to Dr. Gordon, Charleston, S. C., 1755.

[3] Euler's letter of November 21, 1752, and Colden's reply of June 27, 1753; from MSS. in the possession of Mr. H. F. De Puy of New York City.

at the hands of a certain anonymous correspondent, whose criticism ran as follows: The greatest mathematicians have hitherto found no other notions of inertia than that it only acts at the time when an alteration happens in the body. They have compared it to a sentinel who does not discover himself until an enemy appear. This comparison may be made more excellent by comparing it to a corps of observation. Mr. Colden perhaps is the first who makes his corps of observation to consist of hussars continually in action. This power no one can explain unless infected by Leibnizian metaphysics with its talk of a passive power and of monads. The phenomena of the power of inertia has its cause in the essential properties of body, which are yet unknown to us— 'werl sich unser Aug am Kleid der Dinge stockt!' . . . Mr. Colden derives new consequences from the incomprehensible operations of inertia, like believers in the *primum mobile* which carries the other crystalline spheres along with it. . . . Leibniz himself confesses that the original power of body is not sufficient to explain all the phenomena. So Baron van Wolfe says that the phenomena of motion in the corporeal world are not to be explained from Leibniz's representative power in the monads. . . . If I believe that the phenomena which I call inertia and motion arise from an idea which my soul has of a multitude of monads, yet I dare not venture to explain how a multitude of monads can produce that idea in us. The leap from monads to motion is greater than from the coloured rays to sunlight. . . . In explaining gravitation from electricity—a description which appears not to have been done in New York but Pennsylvania—Mr. Colden has done nothing particular. We have philosophers enough in the old world who have endeavoured to explain gravitation from matter, and whose efforts are more easily to be understood than Mr. Colden's ether.[1]

It was in answer to such criticisms as these that in the year 1759 Colden wrote to a friend in South Carolina: In Leibniz's *Specimen Dynamicum* I find an extract which had entirely escaped my memory. Although my principles of action are not to be identified with his monads with their representative powers, it confirms my opinion that an active principle constitutes the essence of

[1] De Puy MSS.

matter. I suspect this agreement with Mr. Leibniz will not recommend my performance to the gentlemen in London. . . . The men of learning among the English have sometimes been charged with want of politeness to strangers.[1] This complaint of academic incivility was called forth by the neglect of Colden's London agent in publishing the manuscripts correcting the second edition of his *Principles*. So the author is forced to make clear how unfounded are the objections to his work, which, he contends, is not contradictory to Newton's *Principia,* for Sir Isaac does not show the cause of gravity. His own attempt, he explains, gave offence to those who thought the mutual attraction of bodies to be an innate quality or power in matter; but since the publication of the *Principles of Action in Matter,* Newton wrote to Dr. Bentley that gravity is innate, inherent and essential to matter, so that one body may act on another at a distance through a vacuum. This is an absurdity; gravity must be caused by an agent acting constantly, although it is uncertain whether that agent be material or immaterial.[2]

Becoming more conversant with the literature of the day, the Scottish-American advances to a further criticism of the Newtonian system and to an exposition of the popular misconceptions thereof. Writing to Professor Whytt of Edinburgh, he claims that in that system the first projectile motion of the planets can only be accounted for by the will of God, as the first motions of machines by the will of the mechanic. To Dr. Portersfield he declares that to attribute the motion of the celestial bodies to the immediate action of the deity is the common refuge of ignorance. It seems strange to him that any philosopher should attribute gravitation of bodies to the immediate operation of the deity. It only serves the same purposes which the occult qualities of the ancients did. If all action in matter proceed from an Intelligent Being, Dr. Berkeley's arguments against the existence of matter are unanswerable, and nothing can go wrong.[3] Colden like Newton dismissed as occult, views opposed to a mechanical explanation of natural phenomena. Such was the Cartesian occasionalism of which he is ultimately forced to make partial use, and such the

---

[1] Letter to Dr. Gordon. [2] MSS. n. p.; n. d. [3] *Ib.*

Leibnizian pre-established harmony to which he now adverts. Discussing with the correspondent last mentioned the difficulties in the problem of the interaction of body and mind, he says that the common answer is that these mutual effects are produced by the law of the creator at the uniting of the soul and body. This you say is a mere evasion, a law of itself can do nothing, there must be some agent which has power to put it in motion; but this law is no better than an occult quality, a covering of our ignorance. You say this agent which puts the laws of union between soul and body in execution, can be no other than either that eternal, omnipotent cause on whom everything else depends, or some subordinate active intelligence acting under him and by his appointment. But I am afraid that, although the deity be allowed to be everywhere substantially present and to be always acting, this supposition of his acting and concurring in all our ideas, lusts and passions, which are evidently excited in the mind by material objects, will meet with violent objections, and the supposition of a subordinate intelligence does not remove the difficulty. We can as little conceive how a body can act on any one kind of intelligence as any other, or how any one kind of intelligence can give motion to any body rather than any other kind. My solution is that action is caused by some intelligent being universally present; it has generally obtained the name of *nature,* sometimes that of universal mind or *anima,* sometimes instinct. By it are guided the actions of the vital intestine motion; it also gives direction to the action of the material powers.[1]

The closing words of this passage suggest the two treatises on which Colden's activities were henceforth largely engaged. By 1766 he had completed his *Enquiry into the Principles of Vital Motion,* and some ten years before he had begun his *Introduction to the Study of Physics or Natural Philosophy.* Drawn up for the use of the lieutenant-governor's grandson, Peter DeLancey the younger, this latter semi-philosophical pamphlet has an air of intimacy and pleasing directness. It explains to the undergraduate at King's College the curious sources of his grandfather's knowledge, the useless doctrines which are to be avoided, and the current philosophies of Europe and America,—in a word, the pet

[1] Letter to Dr. Porterfield, 1761.

speculations of a retired materialist. In the opening section it is declared that Pythagoras was the best instructed of any of the Greeks in the Egyptian learning, knew what of late times has been called the Copernican system, and also that general apparent attraction between bodies which has been rediscovered in the last century by Newton. After regretting that we know very little of the true principles of that ancient philosophy, it is inquired why two or three years of the best time of life should be thrown away in acquiring such learning as is given in the scholastic definitions of substance, quality, mode and accident. For example, to find out the substance of the candle, or to discover what the candle really is, we must remove all those qualities, modes and accidents, which are only outside coverings and mere appearances. . . . But after you have removed the shape, the colour, the greasiness and stiffness, and its being capable of burning, what idea of the candle have you remaining? Have you any kind of conception of the substance? [1]

Having presented the meagreness of the ancient philosophy and the futility of the school logic, from the useless stuff of Cardinal Bellarmine to the enthusiasm of Robert Barclay, the materialist proceeds to a brief exposition of modern thought as related to his own system. My present purpose, he tells his young reader, does not allow me to give you a particular account of Descartes, his system. I shall only mention his general distinction of matter and spirit. The essence of matter, he says, consists in extension, that it cannot be conceived but as of some length, breadth and thickness. And the essence of spirit consists in thinking. But can anything be conceived to exist, to be anywhere, or to occupy any part of space, and to be of no length, breadth or thickness? That would be to say it exists somewhere, but in no part of space; for no part of space can be conceived without breadth, length and thickness. I cannot conceive anything to exist, but either by an universal extension or expansion through all space, or by a limited extension in some part of space; otherwise it exists nowhere, which to me is to say, it does not exist. Extension therefore can make no distinction between

[1] *Natural Philosophy,* pp. 1, 6. New York Historical Society, MS.

matter and spirit, unless it be said that spirit is universally extended and matter confined within limits. Again, all the properties of anything depend on its essence and may be evidently deduced from it; but I think nobody has attempted to deduce all the properties and phenomena of matter from mere extension, and it is impossible to do it, for mere extension gives no idea of any power or force from which any effect may be produced. To avoid these difficulties and just exceptions the present teachers in the schools tell us that the essential difference between matter and spirit is in inactivity and activity. Matter, they tell us, is an absolutely passive substance which can do nothing of itself; it receives all action from the active substance or from spirit. . . . For these reasons Dr. Berkeley denied the existence of matter and affirms that everything which we call matter exists nowhere but in our mind. That neither our thoughts, passions, nor ideas formed by imagination exist without the mind, he says, is evident; nor is it less evident that the various ideas or sensations imprinted on the senses, however blended and combined together (that is, whatever objects they compose), cannot exist otherwise, than as in a mind perceiving them. What are hills and trees but things perceived of sense? And what do we perceive but our own ideas and sensations? And can any one of these or any combination of them exist unperceived? Thus your body, head, hands, &c., is only the idea of body, head, hands, &c., which exists only in my mind, and my body is only an idea which exists in your mind, or in the mind of others which perceive it. You will hardly believe, I suppose, that he was in earnest when he wrote these things. Yes, he was; he wrote a large and learned treatise in proof of this doctrine, and he obtained disciples who formed a sect in philosophy called *Idealists* which has extended even to America, where you will find men of sense advocates of it [and, if I mistake not, the President of your College was once strongly of Dr. Berkeley's opinion.[1]] . . . In consequence of the maxim, that activity is peculiar to spiritual substances, and that the material are entirely passive, it is said that God, in the beginning, created a certain quantity of motion and distributed

[1] This reference to President Samuel Johnson is erased in the original,

it, in certain proportions, through the universe. . . . It is said God created motion, because it is not to be imagined that he communicated motion by impulse or by projection, for thereby we would reduce our conception of God to that of some finite being. . . . When God created motion, they tell us, he did not create any being or thing; for then there must be some active thing besides spirit. He created only a quantity or an action which he distributed through the universe. Can anything be more ridiculous in all the exploded school learning than this is?[1] Thus abruptly dismissing the scholasticism of his day as teaching false maxims, Colden repeats his familiar materialism compounded by dynamism and phenomenalism: matter in some degree or other resists our touch; from this resisting power we form a clear conception of its impenetrability; this power is called substance, but we have no conception of this substance, either by immediate perception or by reason, other than its power of producing certain effects. . . . The table now before me is hard to my touch, reflects rays of light to my eyes, &c., but what that thing is, other than its producing such effects or sensations in my mind, I in no manner know.; I have no kind of idea of the thing itself which causes these effects.[2]

The last quarter of the tractate on *Natural Philosophy* exhibits the author as not wholly satisfied with his earlier explanation of the origin of ideas. Like Hobbes he rejects the notion that ideas are copies of things, since to imagine that something similar to the ideas which we have exists in the objects or bodies which occasion them, is the source of most of the errors in physics. Like Hobbes, also, he reduces consciousness to changes in the nervous system and brain, defining it as the perception of the communication of action by the nerves from every part of the animal system to one place in it, called the common sensory.[3] Nevertheless, as previously intimated, the American materialist does not remain content with the Hobbite reduction of sensation to motion. A reaction of motions outward and inward, a perpetual propagation of pressures, a series of motions however attenuated,

[1] *Natural Philosophy*, pp. 8-14.
[2] *Ib.*, pp. 10, 13, 23.   [3] *Ib.*, p. 28.

this is the fallacy of substituting differences of degree for differences of kind. Or, as Colden himself expressed it, in a somewhat lengthy way: the ideas which the mind excites, in consequence of any material action communicated to the common sensory, have nothing in common with or similar to the actions of the material substances, and it is impossible that they should, as the material and intellectual beings are essentially different. . . . The great difficulty is to conceive how matter can act on the intelligent being, or how the intelligent being can give motion to matter, for there is nothing in common between them by which the one can act on the other. Since the power of the several kinds of matter consists in resisting any change of its present state, or in motion, or in reaction, it cannot be conceived that any of these can produce any kind of sensation or idea, because in mere thoughts or ideas there is nothing either of resistance, or of motion, or of reaction included. For example, we can conceive no reason why a ray of light, which is less bent in passing between air and water, should produce the idea of red, and a ray which is more bent, should produce the idea of blue, because there is nothing in common or of similitude between the greater or less bending of a ray of light and the ideas of blue and red. The same difficulty arises when it is supposed that the difference in the rays proceeds from their different velocity. . . . These difficulties are removed by considering that these ideas or sensations are not properly the effects of any of the material powers, but are only the effects of the operations of the mind in consequence of the actions of the material powers. The actions of the material powers are the occasions of the operations of the mind, but not the efficient causes. Unless changes happen in the actions of matter, these changes cannot be perceived, but the perception of them is truly the operation of the mind itself.[1]

Here is an occasionalism of a limited, if not a peculiar kind. It does not go so far as Johnson when, in the section in his *Noetica* on the origin of our ideas, he makes the human mind passive and the perceptions of sense due to the incessant activity of the great parent mind. Nor is it so radical as the Berkeleian notion of no efficient or active cause other than spirit. It rather resembles

[1] *Natural Philosophy*, pp. 27, 28.

that doctrine against which the Irish metaphysician was arguing, the contention of Hylas in the *Dialogues* that, subordinate to the Supreme Agent, there is a being, a limited and inferior nature, which concurs in the production of our ideas; and yet it differs from the further definition of matter as an inactive, unthinking being, at the presence whereof God excites ideas in our minds.[1] In short, Colden's is a partial occasionalism, limited to a mere concomitance of active matter and active mind, and opposed to the postulate of a constant divine agency. Hence with his deistic creed, being averse to interferences with the cause of nature, he remains content with the simple statement that certain and distinct ideas always accompany certain and distinct material actions. By such an unimaginative conclusion two extremes are avoided; in the problem of perception turning the trivialities of mental life into miracles; in the problem of volition turning ordinary men into a set of paralytics supernaturally galvanised into activity. In both these problems, then, Colden rejects the occasionalism developed by the Cartesian school, but in regard to volition he reverts to the original views of Descartes concerning the reciprocal action of mind and body. It is true that he designates Descartes's *Physics* an amusing philosophical romance rather than a true natural history. Nevertheless his own *Physics*, like the *Traité des passions,* declares mind and matter to be heterogeneous, their action incomprehensible, and yet avails itself of the doctrine of animal spirits, or the intestine motion of the animal fluids, as the medium of communication between the two substances. Colden declares that this is a difficulty of which no satisfactory account has been given; still his own solution resolves itself into the *influxus physicus* of the later Cartesian anthropology. As given in the last section of the *Natural Philosophy,* a recapitulation is followed by a conclusion: the first difficulty is to conceive how matter can act on the intelligent being; the other difficulty is to conceive how the mind, or any intellectual being, can give motion to any body or stop motion in any body by its will or purpose, or other intellectual action or operation. There is nothing of motion or of resisting motion included in any conception we have of intelligence, and if the intellectual power

[1] Second *Dialogue*, p. 71. (Open Court Edition.)

be supposed to have the power of moving and resisting, all distinction between the material and intellectual beings must cease. We observe, however, every moment that we move our hands and other parts of our bodies and give motion to and stop motion in other bodies, as often as we will, or by the action of our mind. How can anything give that which it has not, or do that which it has no power to do? . . . In the first place, it is to be observed that no instance can be given where the mind gives motion to any body wherein motion is not discovered to have existed previously to the action of the will, by which any animal, voluntary motion is supposed to be produced. Thus we may constantly observe that an intestine motion in the fluids of animals is previous to all their animal actions, and that when this intestine motion ceases by cold all animal actions likewise cease. . . . In the next place, supposing two moving powers acting in opposite directions, or that their force is equal, these opposite actions can produce no effect without the assistance of the intellectual power in giving a direction in which both these opposite actions can produce their proper effect. Thus the first direction of the planets cannot be given on the principles of any system of physics otherwise than by the will of the deity.[1]

These unfinished speculations, written for the eye of an undergraduate and evidently high over his head, furnish a transition to another of Colden's fragmentary documents: *An Enquiry into the Principles of Vital Motion.* This was perhaps the 'medical piece' submitted to Franklin, and described by its author as proving that the mind of man acts by material organs. Written in 1766 it had for its central principle the Cartesian notion of the animal-machine, or, as the materialist expressed it, that the Animal Œconomy may be explained mechanically, or according to the laws of matter in motion. This proposition had been enun·ciated by Colden in a manuscript,[2] presumably offered as a thesis for the degree of medicine in the University of Edinburgh. As the youthful treatise abounded in learned quotations ranging from Hippocrates in the original to Wislow's *Exposition Anatomique,* so the mature work presented an equally formidable list of authori-

---

[1] *Natural Philosophy,* pp. 29, 30.
[2] New York Historical Society.

ties.   The writer complains that he is almost too far advanced
in age to take up the subject of the phenomena of the animal
system, yet here, in his seventy-eighth year, he quotes the observations of Harvey, Rede, Leuwenhoeck, Malpighi, Ballini, Jussieu,
Monro and Linnaeus[1].   Like the previous treatise written for
the instruction of his grandson, Colden's *Enquiry* begins with
a word in favour of the wisdom of the ancients; they are declared not so ignorant of the general principles or laws of nature,
but as having as their principal object of hope, like the philosophers of all ages, to discover the primary powers which produce all
the phenomena in nature.[2]   That hope, Colden now declares
with unaccustomed temerity, is not vain, for those primary powers
have already been given in the *First Principles of Action in Matter*, as the resisting power or matter, the moving power or light,
and the reacting power of the universal medium—that subtle elastic ether, which, being equally distributed between the compound-
ing parts of any body, or quantity of matter, becomes fluid and
forms a sort of electric atmosphere which fills up the meshes and
empty interstices.[3]   This explanation may do for the phenomena
of matter in general, but to explain the phenomena of life a finer
distinction is necessary.   The vital action in the veins is not strictly
mechanical, but is due to a fermentation of a peculiar kind; in the
mechanical account of the circulation, the impulse of the blood
gives motion to the animal spirits or fluid of the nerves.   This fermentation is the principle of animal and vegetable life, yet it is
not a primary or simple power of anything.   As Newton assumed
gravitation in explaining the phenomena of the solar system, though
allowing it to be only a perpetual effect of an unknown cause, so
we assume fermentation as a principle, without being able to explain in what manner the primary powers produced it.   Nevertheless, the same powers, which retain the fixed stars in their places,
may retain the minutest particles of bodies in their places.   Therefore, while we can as little form a picture of the sun in its real
magnitude, as we can of the minute elementary particles of bodies,
yet, supposing these to be like little suns, consisting of matter of
the greatest degree resisting, and surrounded by still more minute

[1] *Vital Motion*, § 1.   [2] *Ib.*, § 32.   [3] *Ib.*, §§ 32, 53.

and elastic atmospheres, it is not difficult to conceive that these minute little suns may be the leaven which gives the intestine motion to animal and vegetable fluids, and that they compose the elastic fluids of the nerves by which the vital fermentations are produced. . . . Now, if we further suppose that the air is the principal agent in all fermentation, and that it consists of exquisitely small bodies surrounded by an atmosphere of ether or electric fluid continually emitting light, the light emitted by their respective atmospheres must continually repel these little bodies from each other. The emission of light, as before observed, and consequently all motion, is by repeated vibrations at exceedingly small intervals; therefore the intestine motion of fermenting fluids must likewise be by repeated vibrations. Thus it is easy to conceive that by the vibration of the air being alternate with the vibrations of the fermenting fluids, the vibrations of the latter may be greatly increased and its action continually renewed.[1]

Breaking off abruptly at this point, Colden's theory of vital motion presents a curious medley of hints from many quarters. In it are to be found intimations of Euler's doctrine of the ether as a universal elastic medium, of Hobbes' definition of fermentation as the change of parts of the fluid medium called air, of Leuwenhoeck's discovery of the spermatozoa, of Newton's assumption that vibrations are connected with the material rays emitted from shining bodies, and, lastly, of Berkeley's controversies regarding the infinitely little and the infinitely great which called forth Colden's own *Introduction to the Doctrine of Fluxions* and his *Ideas on the Conception of the Finite and Infinite.*[2] In

[1] *Vital Motion,* §§ 58, 59. Cf. Colden's addition to his *Principles,* Chapter x. On the Cohesion of the Parts of Bodies: There may be parts of matter infinitely, infinitely small, or parts of the second order. These infinities of the first order may have infinities around them consisting of infinities of the second order. These things I propose only as possible, and as hints for more sagacious inquirers. There may be the same variety of contrivances in the infinitely little systems as in the great solar system. (Such may be Aristotle's conception of substantial forms). So the sun and stars may only be the constituent or fundamental particles, or elemental parts of some infinitely, infinitely greater system or animal. This is a subject of extent enough or the most fertile imagination. De Puy MS. p. 285.

[2] Written in 1743, so De Puy MSS., p. 37.

brief, the treatise on *Vital Motion* is a mere fragment for whose undigested state the author apologises from lack of time, lack of books, and especially such recent authorities as he hears are to be found lodged in the library of his old university. So, leaving these as possible hints for some other person of greater abilities, knowledge, and application, and craving indulgence for them as being made by way of amusement, to fill up a vacant hour in a solitary part of the country, the aged philosopher passes on to the last of *Treatise on the Eye*. This hitherto unmentioned document opens his speculations, the *Reflections,* from reading Dr. Porterfield's with a query whether the ideas which we receive from our senses do truly and really represent things as they are. We affirm, for example, that heat and cold exist as little in the bodies which excite these sensations, as pain does in the pin which pricks the finger. Yet are the ideas given merely to deceive us? No, but to serve the common uses of life. If we perceived all things only really as they are, we might be fine philosophers, but we could not be men.[1] To this touch of realism Colden suddenly opposes philosophic scepticism, averring that Descartes doubts too much, and yet as suddenly does he defend the general Cartesian method of investigation. Since he believes that the study of primary causes, by an accurate observation of effects, has improved our knowledge of physics, he inquires if the same method is not likely to succeed in the investigation of the intellectual powers of intelligent beings in the several animal systems. The question answers itself, provided one accepts the Coldenian definition of mind as consisting of the operations of intelligence in that particular system suited to its peculiar purposes, these purposes being adapted to the vital fermentation of the fluids in the animal systems.[2] With this rough definition in hand, the retired materialist starts to rake over his stores of knowledge, medical experiences, every day observations, popular superstitions, historical events—all of which tend to substantiate the thesis, so like that of the *Enquiry*. For example, that the operations of intelligence vary as the vital intestine motions of the fluids vary, is evident in the same man when the fermentation is low and when it is brisk, when it is weak and languid from too much fasting, and when invigoured and strengthened by a glass of

[1] *Reflections*, § 1.   [2] *Ib.*, § 12.

generous wine. So, too, in the hydrophobia from the bite of a mad dog, the intestine vital motion becomes similar to that of the mad dog, and in consequence of it their ideas and imagination become similar.[1]

Even if this is the Hobbite principle of animal motion carried to absurd extremes, Colden is elsewhere more successful in his endeavours to give a natural history of the emotions. To the physical conditions of abnormal phenomena he adds the more purely psychic processes of what we still call mental contagion, and even comes to suggest the fruitful principle of suggestion. For instance, that kind of madness called enthusiasm he ascribes to a chain of ideas continued long and without intermission: weak judgments, he says, being unconscious of the ideas which produce these passions, or of the actions of the body which accompany them, attribute their terror or joy to supernatural influences. When this enthusiasm happens in hysterical constitutions, it may be accompanied by the most surprising convulsions of the body. Furthermore, by a social, sympathetic instinct, enthusiasm is propagated like a contagion through a large assembly. Thus Cromwell's enthusiastic preachers and their terrible denunciations of damnation, accompanied with surprising action and vociferation, repeated every day of the week, and confirmed by long prayers morning and evening in the same train of ideas, and by long graces at meals, produced the most mischievous enormities, with the total loss of the social pleasures.[2] Citing as further instances of enthusiasm the Popish plot in the days of Charles II., and the revolutionary agitation in the American colonies, the lieutenant-governor turns from cases of national hysteria to those of individual hyperæsthesia. Next, for an explanation of these strange psycho-physical occurrences, he reverts to his earlier principles, supposing that the common sensory is not confined to a single point, but is a vesicle from which all the nerves take their origin, and that it is filled with the same elastic fluid, by which the impulse on the extremity of the nerves is conveyed. He further supposes the impulse to be conveyed by some elastic fluid, the same or similar to the electric fluid, then the impulse on the common sensorium will be more or less vivid and strong, as the nervous fluid is more or less elastic. In old age the elasticity is les-

[1] *Reflections*, § 21. [2] *Ib.*, § 66.

sened, in hysteric cases greatly increased; for this reason women of the quickest sensibility are the most subject to hysteric disorders, as in the case where the hysteric person could distinguish the lowest sound, which none else, nor she herself, could have distinguished in her natural state.[1]

In his search for the ultimate principles back of these abnormalities of mind, the materialist has practically adopted the Cartesian hypothesis of the pineal gland. For all that he sees the embarrassments arising from a strict application of such an hypothesis, and acknowledges that there are insurmountable difficulties to the prevalent interpretation of a common sensory in the brain. If this, he reasons, be the seat of the intelligent being, if the soul be confined to any one place, it must be of the same shape, or figure, or quantity; but this would destroy all distinction between matter and spirit. So, too, if the soul be said to be a single point, this will not remove the difficulty with those who understand the doctries of infinities. . . . Where did this distinct being, confined within certain limits and yet of no quantity, shape, or figure, exist before its union with the body? Where does it exist after the death of the individual? Can we have any conception of its operations in its state of separation? . . . We know nothing of the operations of intelligence otherwise than as its operations are connected with some material system; we cannot conceive of it as divisible into parts; its whole power acts in every place, or according to the School phrase, it is *tota in toto et tota in qualibet parte.* . . . These difficulties are removed only by a conception of intelligence similar to that of space. Space of itself is indivisible, cannot be conceived as existing of parts separable from each other, contains all other beings, exists everywhere, and is not any quantity, shape, or figure. This conception of intelligence is very ancient, and is allowed to be very just and true—in Him we live, move, and have our being. Suppose space is really the intelligent Being, in which all other beings are contained, and that there can be no distinct parts, and that no part can have different powers from any other part, then all the different operations of intelligence must arise from the different material systems in it. As the mutual attraction of bodies in the planetary system is the effect of

[1] *Reflections,* § 13.

the action of some universal medium, and the unity of that system is preserved by the gravitation of all toward the sun, so the unity of the animal system is preserved by the intestine motion of the fluid in the nerves which meet in the common sensory of the brain.[1]

These speculations of the aged materialist are somewhat peculiar, yet they are not unconnected with his earliest writings. As he began in his first *Principles* with an astronomical view of nature in general, seeking the cause of the motion of the planets in the larger atomism of the world-soul, so here in his last *Reflections* he ends with a sort of Copernicising of human nature, seeking a central principle in a common sensory. In fine, this is one of those numerous abortive efforts to correlate the macrocosm with the microcosm. With Colden an explanation of the former is sought in the Newtonian doctrine of space as the divine sensorium, and an explanation of the latter in the Hobbite notion of some vesicle as a receptacle for animal spirits. But this attempt to unite spiritualistic ideas with atomistic and mechanical doctrines is manifestly doomed to failure. Space, by a bold metaphor, may be considered the organ which God makes use of to perceive things by, yet the common sensory in the individual cannot be subsumed under any concept of an intelligent essence. Colden himself is evidently aware of this quandary; he confesses that he knows that it will shock the understanding of most people that there is an intelligent being universally diffused, and yet he cannot help going back to the ancient doctrine of a plastic principle, that intelligent Being by a perpetual effect of whose power new things are being formed every day, from the species of animals, to the ideas, the appetites, and even the social affections of men.[2]

This is the end of the Coldenian system, which finally approaches a doctrine of panpsychism. Upon it a brief judgment may be passed. As a unitary scheme it failed to reduce mind and matter to phenomenal modifications of the same common substance, but such finality was obviously impossible under the circumstances. The aged materialist, indeed, asserts that the philosopher should perform the duties of worship without in the least suffering his philosophical opinions to be affected thereby. Yet both his earlier beliefs, and his official relations to the Church of England would

[1] *Reflections,* §§ 12, 32, 33, 35.　　[2] *Ib.,* § 39.

not allow of a thorough-going pantheistic conception of the *unica substantia*. Fettered by the dualism of deism, he failed to attain a pure monism. This lamentable conflict between philosophy and religion was accentuated by another struggle. The Revolution came on, the lieutenant-governor's house was burned down, and his philosophical treatises, although fortunately rescued, remained utterly ignored. As the speculations of an outspoken Tory official, they could not have been popular, nor were they in accord with the serious spirit of the times; they were made, as Colden put it, by way of amusement to fill up a vacant hour, as some gentlemen play at chess. And yet, even if for reasons religious, political and social, Colden's speculations lay forgotten in unconsidered books and undeciphered manuscripts, they served a useful purpose. To continue his own figure of speech, he made certain openings, set certain problems to be finished by those who came after him. Bred in an ancient university, familiar with historic systems of thought, the Scottish-American inadvertently suggested lines of investigation which were to be taken up by the later materialists in America. Such were Joseph Priestley of Pennsylvania, with his doctrine of the homogeneity of matter and spirit; Thomas Cooper of South Carolina, with his theory of mental development founded on the history of the body; Joseph Buchanan of Kentucky, with his dictum that mind is no more than an organic state of matter; Benjamin Rush of Philadelphia, with his insistence on the study of the diseases of the brain; and Samuel Clark of Connecticut, with his reversion to a plastic principle in nature.

Colden boasted of his acquaintance with bookish men in several parts of North America, but of his unconscious successors he knew not one; they came too late for him. But despite that fact, the colonial materialist possessed some significance in the country of his adoption. It might appear hazardous to make him a profound thinker, yet he was at least an acute observer. His various theories were, so to speak, so many trial balloons, indicating the drift and direction of coming speculations. In conclusion, then, it may be shown what the New Yorker did as a prognosticator of currents of thought in both the lower and higher levels. In general his semi-pantheistic absolute, like that of Ethan Allen, put him half way on the road toward the transcendentalism of New England; but in particular he was even more advanced. As a *materialist* he reduced psychology to a physiology of the nerves, and was precursory to the French sensationalism which came in after the Revolution and lasted until the arrival of the Comtean positivism. Here was the promise of a valid experimental psychology, yet connected with this tendency was one somewhat reactionary. By turning the supposed animal spirits in the nerves into a sort of fine matter, and mediating its movements by an electric ether, Colden presaged the popular relish for that local variety of animal magnetism called electro-biology. This was the penalty for dabbling in those occult speculations concerning the essential properties of matter against which Newton had sounded a warning. Again, as a *phenomenalist* Colden's epistemology taught the relativity of knowledge, and thus to a degree anticipated the strictures of the New England idealists against the uncritical Scotch realism with its simple empirical intuitions. Here the beliefs of the subjective astronomer are somewhat akin to the utterances of Emerson concerning that appearance we call the world, our impotence to test the authenticity of the report of the senses, our doubt whether Orion is painted up there in the heaven, or some god paints the image in the firmament of the soul.[1] Lastly, as *physicist* Colden's ontology and cosmology, being subsumed under a conception of dynamism, presaged the advancing belief in a universe of force. His principle that matter and mind possess the common quality of activity was again prophetic of Emerson in his doctrine that the world proceeds from the same spirit as the body of man.[2] But while the Concord philosopher held that once we inhale the upper air, we are admitted to behold the absolute nature of things, the New Yorker recognised that such high abstractions were liable to fade away. Authors, he said, are apt to be vain of their own conceits, and to put forth romantic theories, which make a glaring show like a meteor, but in a short time leave no track behind.

Here in a figure of speech Colden foretold the obscuration of his system. As a strict system it may have deserved this, for with the

[1] *Nature,* Chapter VI., *Idealism,* p. 52.
[2] *Ib.,* Chapter VII., *Spirit,* p. 68.

exception of a few of his son's corroborative experiments, it lacked scientific precision and empirical verification. Yet as an hypothesis the Coldenian system was far in advance of colonial thinking. Benjamin Thompson of New Hampshire is alleged to have first taken the discussion of the nature of energy out of the domain of metaphysics, where it had been speculated upon since the days of Aristotle.[1] It is true that Rumford, as early as 1778, demonstrated the falsity of the prevailing view of the materiality of energy, but he did not go so far as did Colden, who laid it down as a fundamental principle that the properties or qualities of things are nothing else but their various actions or modes of activity. In fine, the author of the *Principles of Action in Matter,* by resolving matter into the mechanics of force, has left himself on record as one of the pioneers in the development of the latest phase of scientific materialism.

[1] George E. Ellis, *Memoirs of Sir Benjamin Thompson,* Boston, 1871, p. 469.

CHAPTER III

JOSEPH BUCHANAN

JOSEPH BUCHANAN (1785-1812) of Kentucky is the next writer to exhibit the development of materialistic thought in America. An obscure physician, whose one published work was practically unknown, except to omnivorous readers like Jefferson and John Adams, Buchanan was yet not without significance. Like Priestley, his associationist psychology betrays an original dependence on the Hobbite catenations of motion. Like Colden, his theory of nerve vibrations is to be carried back to Newton's queries in the *Optics*. But while the materialist of New York remained content with a simple co-ordination of the two substances, the Kentuckian emphasised matter at the expense of mind, attempted to construct a materialistic monism, and thereby reached the other extreme from the opposed idealistic monism of Samuel Johnson of Connecticut.

Of Buchanan's life, the details are as scanty as were his means. Reputed a man of great and varied powers, want of concentration is said to have prevented him from becoming eminent in medicine as in other pursuits which divided his attention. Educated in the embryonic Transylvania university and in Philadelphia under Dr. Samuel Brown, he was obliged to leave his medical course unfinished. Returning on foot to Lexington and commencing the practice of physic, he attempted the establishment of a medical school in his home institution. On reviewing the lectures he had prepared, after the contemplated school had miscarried, it appeared, as he ingenuously confesses, that they contained original matter. Though he was unable to mature them into a system more perfect and complete, being forced to relinquish the unprofitable pursuits of literature and science, they were nevertheless published in Richmond, Kentucky, in 1812, under the title of the *Philosophy of Human Nature*.

The authors from whom Buchanan specifies having drawn the

most are Locke, Hartley, Hume, and Erasmus Darwin. As a 'metaphysical investigation of human nature,' the book bears few traces of the father of English sensationalism, inasmuch as it was he who disavowed meddling with the physical consideration of mind and its essence. But the writer's remaining authorities, with the addition of Pestalozzi, furnish in order the four salient points of the work. Briefly, its view of sensation is materialistic; of cognition, sceptical; of volition, necessitarian; of mental development, genetic. Of the given authorities, again, Hume and Darwin play the chief parts in the *Philosophy of Human Nature*. Its value, therefore, lies in its being the earliest native exposition and application of the great criticist's method; its novelty in the juncture of sceptical doubts concerning the operations of the understanding with the doctrine of palpable vibrations—the notion, in short, that ideas are but the equivalent of sensual motions. It would be forced to interpret Buchanan as holding the modern conceit that ideas are nothing but cortical events subjectively viewed, yet he was well abreast of his time. With his emphasis on the laws of association, his ingenious experiments to prove the early formation of habit, and his final conjectures on the physiology of the brain, he fulfilled the prophecy of the editor of the first American edition of the *Zoonomia,* who was disposed to search for the future Darwin of America in some secondary town or even village of the country.[1]

In his introductory disquisition Buchanan presents an ontology more monistic than that of the colonial exponents of materialism. Starting with the alternative opinions that the human mind is an independent existence, mysteriously connected with the body, or, on the other hand, merely an organic state of matter, he concludes that there is no immaterial principle in man which forms the basis of his mind, but that mind and matter are substantially the same, each possessing one common nature. This conclusion is reached by what is called the inductive method; it might better be called the argumentative. To overthrow the doctrine of immaterialism, the materialist reasons in a way reminiscent of the debating societies of his youth. Obtaining opinions from all quarters, he attempts to define whatever he finds in his own interests. First,

[1] Charles Caldwell, Part 2, Philadelphia, 1797.

adopting the Humean theory of cognition, he declares that our notions of matter and mind are both relative and imperfect, obtained merely by inference, and not by direct perception. By our senses we perceive certain qualities—extension, solidity, figure, coexisting in nature, and we refer them to an unknown substratum called matter, a connective substance in which we suppose them to inhere. By consciousness, again, we apprehend certain operations—feeling, thought, volition—transpiring in ourselves, and we refer them to an unknown substratum or connective medium called mind. Unable to acquire a direct and complete knowledge of either mind or matter, we can neither positively decide that they are radically the same, nor that they are radically different.[1]

This is an ingenious use of the sceptical argument, but it is likewise dangerous. The author has succeeded in bringing mind down to an equality with matter, but it is the equality of nescience, the common plane of negation. Lest the argument prove doubleedged and cut the ground from under his feet, he proceeds to transfer to the lower substance the qualities commonly attributed to the higher. He therefore passes abruptly from the older doubts to the more recent determinations of the positive characteristics of matter. Mr. Davy's chemical discoveries, he says, made by means of electricity, suffice to convince us that every material particle in nature is essentially active. Instead of concluding from his experiments that matter is intrinsically passive, we should rather believe that the inert mass perceived by our senses is composed of elements which might properly be called *spiritual energies,* elements possessing active powers adequate to any celerity and subtleness of action in the human mind.[2] In thus opposing the popular argument that matter is too sluggish and inactive ever to display more than mechanical effects, being wholly unequal to the activity and subtleness of mental operations, Buchanan is but expanding what Hartley had said of the arguments which are usually brought for the immateriality of the soul from the subtlety of the internal senses.[3]

In pursuing his demonstration that the elements of matter are capable of combining together in an infinite variety of forms, the

[1] *Human Nature,* p. 4.   [2] *Ib.,* p. 6.   [3] *Observations,* p. 345.

author turns from contemporary researches back to the Platonic doctrine of the hierarchy of nature, the theory of a scale of beings which, to use his own figure, are changed into each other like the colours of the solar spectrum, by unnoticeable variations. The spiritualists grant matter at one extreme of the series, but find at the other a substance totally different, a spiritual intellect combined with it. Between the block of marble and the man of genius they put a chasm in the series; but the materialists—considering how minerals rise by insensible degrees into vegetables, and these again into animals—find no calculable difference; no being which does not interlock with another. Now, the greater part of this ascending series of beings is material, hence the whole series is material.[1] This too generous interpretation of the law of continuity is, however, partially modified by the statement that when the materialist affirms that mind is material, he does not mean that the terms matter and mind are synonymous, but that the ultimate principles of the objects they indicate are the same—mind being merely an organic state of matter, a peculiar combination of material elements capable of displaying the attributes of intellect.[2] And yet from this approximation between the two substances, they are not to be considered co-ordinate, for the mind's connection with certain organic states of matter amounts to an actual subordination and dependence, the mental act being secondary and consequential to the physical.[3] The primacy of mind is further invalidated by its dependence on a material organ. If the intellect were purely spiritual, it is improbable that changes in the mere instrument of its operations could make an important difference in its powers; but if mentality be only an attribute of the living brain, then every disease which affects the nervous system, affects proportionately the functions of the mind.[4]

This line of argumentation is doubtless taken from Darwin; but whereas his *Laws of Organic Life* had postulated two essences or substances in nature, of which spirit possesses the power to commence or produce motion,[5] here it is held that mind is a mere creature of the brain, entirely unable to think and feel within itself, or

[1] *Human Nature*, pp. 6, 7.   [2] *Ib.*, p. 8.
[3] *Ib.*, p. 9.   [4] *Ib.*, p. 11.   [5] American Edition, p. 3.

to commence thought, sentiment, or motion.[1] If, then, it be proven that the intellectual transactions, made known to us by consciousness, correspond as their shadows to the physical transactions of the brain discovered by our senses, may we not conclude that they are identically the same things perceived by us in different ways and thence thought different?[2]

Realising the weakness of this conjectural monism—a sort of crude double-aspect theory, in which the mental and bodily facts are considered as parallel aspects of a single underlying unity— recourse is had to the difficulties of dualism, and especially the problem of the interaction of unlike substances. If all these arguments were sophistical and the doctrine of spirituality did accord as well with facts as the organic theory, yet that doctrine is darkened by a mystery. How a spirit can be connected with a mass of matter, so that they shall mutually act upon each other, is not only an inexplicable fact, but philosophically absurd. To suppose that two substances, mind and matter, which are so essentially and totally dissimilar that they have no common properties, can be so connected as to operate on each other, is inconsistent with all the analogies of nature. Nor is this the whole amount of the absurdity. According to the spiritual theory, mind and matter operate on each other without possessing common properties, yet two minds whose natures are congenial and all their qualities similar in every respect, are wholly incapable of a direct reciprocal influence. Peculiarly adapted for direct intercourse, they choose to communicate circuitously through a medium on which they seem unqualified to act.[3] So it is unauthorised to concede to the spiritualists that the act of consciousness, which apprehends our intellectual attributes, is a peculiar and distinct exertion of the mind; rather is it a mere attention to past experiences; a repetition of perceptions, which, according to the organic theory, are only acts of the living brain, excited by the external object to be perceived.[4] And yet what is it that makes the act of thinking in the brain, perceived as a physical event by our senses, seem to be a thing entirely different from the same act apprehended by our consciousness? It is due to our 'mental imperfection,' our prejudice against believing mind and

[1] *Human Nature*, p. 3.   [2] *Ib.,* p. 13.   [3] *Ib.,* p. 14.   [4] *Ib.,* p. 15.

matter to be substantially the same; our inadequate knowledge of the efficient elements and energies of nature. Thus we can arrive at no rational view on the subject of causation. Experience here is our only guide. We never could affirm that any one event might not be caused by any other, unless through the customary connections. It is merely the association of ideas produced by the constant conjunction of particular events which induces us to view them as connected by causation. Applying this to the prejudice in question, our mental deficiency is such that we cannot readily observe, or have direct experience of that connection which does exist between the action of the brain and the act of thinking. The acts of consciousness by which we recognise our thoughts give no intimation of their physical concomitants; and the perceptions of sense by which we learn the properties of matter and the actions of the brain give no intimation of thought as known to us by consciousness. The act of thinking and its physical cause, being thus discovered by us in different ways, do therefore not become associated in our minds, and thence must naturally be believed by us to be distinct and independent and entirely unconnected by causation. On the contrary, if we had always by the same percipient action apprehended both our thoughts and the physical events on which they are dependent, we could no more doubt the act of thinking to be a physical effect than the motion of the second billiard ball to be effected by the impulse of the first.[1]

To uphold his thesis that there is no immaterial principle in man which forms the basis of his mind, Buchanan is manifestly obliged to return to Hume's sceptical doubts concerning the operations of the understanding. But while the latter contended that objects constantly conjoined with each other are simply inferred by experience to be causally connected, the former assumed that, were that causal connection known, we should be justified in believing in the identity even of two such apparently different substances as mind and matter. With this double supposition, and as if realising the embarrassments of holding to a single unitary principle, the introductory disquisition closes, much in the cautious style of Hartley's general remarks on the mechanism of the

[1] *Human Nature*, pp. 19, 20.

human mind.[1] As the latter deems it sufficient for physicians and philosophers to allow that there is a certain connection, of one kind or another, between soul and brain, so Buchanan admits that whatever his preferences, the materialist can investigate the physical principles and laws of human nature without reference to his own opinion.[2] At this point one may understand an apparent reversal of judgment, by summarising the writer's arguments against the spiritualists, and noting therein certain underlying defects. He had said that mind is an unkonwn substratum; that matter possesses subtle spiritual energies; that the organic theory of gradation is alone in accord with the order and connection of nature; that the particular mode of the composition of material elements is sufficient for the intellectual operations; that the mind is a mere creature of the brain as shown by diseases and accidents; that it possesses no real primacy, consciousness being a secondary process, an unreal shadow of a real substance; that interaction is impossible between two dissimilar substances; and finally that, comparing the properties of matter as known through the agency of sense, with the attributes of mind as known through the medium of consciousness, we find them substantially the same, each consisting in perceptions, sentiments, and ideas which possess one common nature.[3]

This is perhaps the most systematic presentation of the case in behalf of materialism that the country had yet afforded. For all that, it leaves unanswered certain important questions; the author has fished in many waters, yet the spoils have escaped him, and he himself points out, as it were, the hole in his drag net of argumentation. What is the one common principle? What is the particular mode of composition that can explain mentality? What is an organic state? These questions Buchanan tries to answer in his second chapter entitled an Outline of Physiology. Matter, he contends, is universally imbued with active qualities which, though evanescent, are essentially indestructible. Again, the human system is a machine entirely material, composed of a great variety of elementary particles possessing various energies incessantly exerted. Finally, organisation is a vitalised state of matter,

---

[1] *Observations*, pp. 245-6.   [2] *Human Nature*, p. 20.
[3] *Ib.*, 11, 13, 17.

or the radical source of animal life, but what are the ultimate conditions of animality may not yet be discovered.[1] Here is the rift in the Buchanian system: if the ultimate conditions of animality may not be known, what of the ultimate conditions of mentality, so confidently assumed? The problems so intimately connected remain unsolved, and yet the materialist still pursues his inquiries and goes on to state that the final causes in the construction of every animal system are pleasurable existence, and the perpetuity of its vital state.[2] This second section of his work the physiologist treats much in the style of his predecessors. He repeats Darwin in attributing the spirit of animation, or sensorial power, to organisation, or that adjustment of parts to each other such as form a regular system—the peculiar composition of elements which is the radical source of animal life; in defining excitability as that property of organised matter, or that principle inherent in a living animal, which is the source of all spontaneous or proper motions; and in imagining that the renovation of excitability is brought about by the oxygen in the blood.[3] And yet Buchanan considers Darwin fanciful in supposing that it is the new arrangement, or combination of elements in the organism, produced by stimulation, which constitutes the alteration itself; while as to excitability he would prefer to call it a condition of the organic structure of the fibre—not a distinct principle, an immaterial something, an occult and self-existent quality.[4] Next, considering the different kinds of excitement—muscular, sensual and sensorial—Buchanan adopts Darwin of Shrewsbury's experiments as to eye movements and after-images,[5] and considers with Hume that the sensorial excitement, being originally derived from the sensual, has much less vivacity, precision, and force, and concludes that these differences between our perceptions and ideas is the source of the common delusion respecting the difference between the properties of matter and the attributes of mind.[6] We are conscious that our ideas are creations of our own; our per-

---

[1] *Human Nature,* pp. 31, 36, 37.   [2] *Ib.,* p. 21.
[3] *Ib.,* pp. 31, 60.   [4] *Ib.,* p. 31.
[5] The American Edition of the *Zoonomia* contains hand-coloured plates illustrating these experiments.
[6] *Human Nature,* p. 109.

ceptions, on the contrary, appear to be nearly independent of us. Being the archetypes of our ideas we regard them as things external, or mistake them for the regular, fixed, external causes by which they are produced, and of whose existence we are certified alone by an influence founded on causation.[1]

With the exception of this temporary return to his old metaphysical interests the chapters immediately succeeding the outline of physiology contain little of interest. The actions of the organs of sense are divided into two classes; that is, from sensual motions come sensation and perception, while derived from them are the sensorial motions comprising sentiment and idea. This is but a dry repetition of the *Zoonomia,* yet in the attempt to bind together these various processes considerable ingenuity is shown. The chief factor is the unity of excitement, or the reciprocal influence and dependence of our actions upon each other. This unity is illustrated by a train of gunpowder, ramified into various branches representing the nervous system. As fire in the one is quickly communicated to all the combustible materials, so a stimulus in the other rouses the whole sensorium. The second unifying factor is association, or that principle which artificially connects the scattered portions of excitement. Here a channel is traced by repeated stimulation in which the current of excitement may glide through the common sensory, from one organ of sense or motion to another. Thus the actions of the muscles moving the eyeball have become associated with certain motions of the retina.[2] While Darwin had defined association as a society or convention of things in some respects similar to each other, Buchanan considered it an assemblage or convention of things naturally distinct. And he further diverges from his chief authority on the point of associate motions, not dividing them into the indefinite sensorial faculties, but more simply into the two classes of collateral and consecutive, the former being exemplified in the perception of the written character of a word, the idea of its sound, the sentiment it represents, whereby the action of the vocal organs is all collaterally embraced in a common bond of union; the latter in an act of respiration, in which, when finished, the deficiency of oxygen excites a disagreeable sensation, this, in turn, producing the as

---

[1] *Human Nature,* p. 108.   [2] *Ib.,* p. 117.

sociated act of inspiration.[1] In passing from sensation to cognition Buchanan now follows the lead of Darwin, but here again he but agrees in order to disagree. The former had bluntly rejected the various meanings of idea in the writers of metaphysics and crudely resolved it into a sensual motion, a contraction or configuration of the fibres which constitute the immediate organs of sense. So Buchanan rejects the notions of the metaphysicians who believed the idea to be a distinct existence, and regards it as being nothing more than a repetition of the sensorial action. At the same time he holds that the intrinsic motion of an organic fibre which constitutes excitement can never resemble the powers of external bodies which produce it, or the essential and active properties of those very elements in which it occurs.[2]

Passing to his epistemology, in his opposition to the scholastic realism, Buchanan acknowledges his indebtedness to Locke, whom he interprets as considering an idea as an intellectual something, generated in the mind by its sensitive intercourse with external nature, and not anything distinct from the mind, or deposited in the memory by an act of sensation.[3] The materialist has now reached his theory of knowledge. Introduced to Berkeley through Darwin,[4] he agrees with the idealist regarding the lack of resemblance between our ideas and their correspondent objects, and also regarding the origin of the conception of space as suggested by its association with the voluntary movements of the eye. Still he does not go so far as Berkeley in affirming that ideas may serve as a language of signs, a means of interpretation between the internal and the external. Our ideas, he protests, considered as the representatives of external things, and the materials of human knowledge, are fundamentally defective. They have in general no resemblance to the objects by which they are excited. No objects in nature can be more dissimilar than a process of change, say in an organic fibre, and the elementary powers on which it is dependent. Our ideas, therefore, cannot individually afford a perfect knowledge of their external objects.[5] If they could, however, possess the same relative properties with respect to one an-

[1] *Human Nature*, p. 146.   [2] *Ib.*, p. 153.   [3] *Ib.*, p. 152.
[4] *Zoonomia*, p. 76, § 14, 1.   [5] *Human Nature*, p. 154.

other that exist between their exciting causes, our knowledge would still be practically perfect; the ideal system would still be an adequate representation of the real state of external things. But this kind of perfection is apparently as impossible as the former.[1] The inference that we actually can gain no knowledge of external objects either real or relational would be pure agnosticism, if the author were consistent; but he is not. He accepts at least one section of knowledge as trustworthy and finally adopts the Humean validation of experience through the principle of association. Having demonstrated the general lack of correspondence between ideas and objects, he adds that there is one kind of knowledge to which these imperfections cannot be attributed. All our mathematical ideas have properties which perfectly resemble the properties of nature to which they correspond. Our abstract, unalloyed conceptions of this kind, and the objects they represent, are in reality the same kind of existences and possess the same properties. The ideas of number, extension, figure and motion are really numerical, extended, figured and motory in the mind; or the sensorial actions, of which these abstract ideas are integral parts, are performed by portions of the brain of which these mathematical properties may be affirmed. The idea, for example, of three is performed by three distinct parts in that organ; the idea of a triangle consists of a triangular train of action; in the conception of geometrical solidity a solid portion of the brain is excited; and in the idea of motion the idea does actually traverse the region which conceives it. To this perfect coincidence of these ideas and their objects we are to refer the superior perfection of the mathematical and physico-mathematical sciences.[2]

This deliverance reminds one of the passage in the *Zoonomia* regarding the certainty of the mathematical sciences as they explain these properties of bodies, which are exactly resembled by our ideas of them.[3] But the ‘fanciful’ Darwin is outdone in this curious reversal of his doctrine. It is not that certain ideas resemble external objects, but that the internal motions of the brain resemble certain ideas. Nevertheless, in the face of this

[1] *Human Nature*, p. 154.   [2] *Ib.*, p. 155.   [3] § 14, 2.

literal application of materialism, Buchanan next avails himself of a more idealistic theory of cognition. His belief in the superiority of mathematical ideas is really based upon a conviction of their subjective worth as modes of the mind's functioning. Our elementary conceptions, he explains, are so accurate and complete, that we are able to develop all their properties and relations without recurring to their objects for experimental assistance. Another circumstance tributary to this perfection is the frequent recurrence of mathematical ideas in all the operations of the mind. Thus number, magnitude and time are component parts in every sensational perception we can experience; geometrical solidity with all the attributes it involves, must recur in every perception by sight and touch; and motion, though not essential in any case, is yet incessantly perceived. Our mathematical ideas in fact, like the skeleton in the human system, compose an intellectual framework which pervades and upholds the whole fabric of human knowledge.[1] Here is a hint of subjective principles spoiled by a figure of speech; a clue to the regulative principles of pure reason lost in a thicket of physiological terms. So in his bewilderment the materialist falls back on sheer empiricism. We have no ideas, he continues, but those of mathematical qualities, which afford complete scientific information by adequately representing their objects. All the rest of our knowledge is radically composed of those conceptions which are termed ideas of sensible qualities, and which are merely effects produced in the sensory by certain powers of external objects, to which they bear not the slightest resemblance. We must therefore acknowledge that we are substantially ignorant of all those powers and energies in the material world which produce the incessant changes of nature in the order of causation. Hence experience, as Hume has demonstrated, is our only guide in all those affairs, in which causation or the energies of nature are concerned. And the principle of association in the human mind is the basis on which the acquisitions of experience are built. It is the only representative in the ideal system of all the efficient principles of nature. When the effects are evolved by their causes, the efficient agency eludes our discernment; but the principle of association connects their ideas in the mind ac-

[1] *Human Nature*, p. 156.

cording to the manner in which they stand connected in nature; and thus performs in the intellectual sense a function corresponding to the energies of external things. Wherefore, concludes the American, the theatre of nature in which we live does not display a stationary scene, but is incessantly revolving by its own energies, in conformity to the established laws of causation. Hence the adult finds all his ideas naturally associated in tribes and trains, corresponding to the natural combination and succession of their objects.[1]

To sum up Buchanan's epistemology: in the treatment of the origin and validity of ideas he argues against scholastic realism, and yet in behalf of a sort of cerebral realism; against relative knowledge, and yet in behalf of associative knowledge. These contradictions may be attributed to the meeting of two divergent tendencies. As a materialist, he assumed an identity between mind and matter; as an associationist, a harmony between association and reality. For all that, we may finally ask, what makes the shifting scenes of the mind correspond to the outward theatre of nature? That was a question which the obscure disciple answered no more than the master. Hume concluded that the power or force which actuates the whole machine is unknown to us, save as it arises from reflecting on the operations of our own mind,[2] Buchanan that in the transition of thought from the conception of a cause to the ideas of its effect we obtain a very inadequate conception of power, at the most a mere kind of forcible progression of the mind.[3]

Before resuming the unsolved noetic problem of the nature of causality and the conformity between idea and reality, the author turns to such topics as the nature of attention, the classification of ideas, and the meaning of sentiment and temperament. The chief peculiarity of attention is said to be its relative situation in the sensorial department; for example, the seat of attention in the eye is the centre of the retina. Another peculiarity is the association of such ideas and sentiments in one department with those which are simultaneously regarded in all the others.[4] In the classification of ideas Locke is judged to be greatly mistaken

[1] *Human Nature*, p. 158. [2] *Enquiry*, pp. 65-6, § 7, Part I.
[3] *Human Nature*, p. 163. [4] *Ib.*, p. 167.

in the opinion that our simple ideas are primary and our complex artificial. On the contrary we never experience even a single sensation which is perfectly simple. The first perception of an object has doubtless a uniform and homogeneous appearance in the mind, but the repetition of perceptions, in which the same constituent parts are variously combined, interrupts this uniformity and enables us to recognise the complexity of the conception.[1] Next in his chapter concerning sentiment, the materialist gives the current definitions and repeats the previous crass notions of cerebral localisation. The excitement of the organ is said to constitute a sensation whose attributes are pleasure and pain. Propagated to the sensory, and reiterated in the appropriate sensorial department, it becomes sentiment. Hence the common confusion of sentiments with emotions or passions is erroneous, for the latter are combinations of simple sentiments sprung from sensation by the law of association. Thus Darwin has explained how in the adult every distinct and energetic sentiment is associated with particular modifications of countenance and gestures of body which constitute the language of nature. Further, each organ of sense having a portion of the brain consecrated to the repetition of excitement, the sentiment has some particular portion of the sensory destined to perform the predominating action. Thus, the perceptions of sight are utilised by the union of the optic nerves in their passage to their departments, the sentimental actions of the hemispheres by their communication through the anterior commissure and the corpus callosum, the auditory sensations by the termination of the auditory nerves in the central parts of the basis of the brain.[2]

These physiological observations applied to the subject of conception now furnish the author a sort of rudimentary psychology of religion. As the temper of mind often assumes a character directly the reverse of that which immediately prevailed—just as after the perception of red we perceive the colour of green with peculiar facility—so in the abuse of religion the enthusiast, feeling the tumults of hell, and exhausted by dismal sensations, suddenly experiences an ecstatic libration of sentiment and mistakes the natural fluctuations of sentimental excitement for the inspiration of heaven.[3] In these examples the Kentucky philosopher

[1] *Human Nature,* p. 175.   [2] *Ib.,* pp. 246, 190, 324.   [3] *Ib.,* p. 219.

had half an eye on the revivalistic excesses of his locality.[1] The
interest in his next topic, on the contrary, is more speculative than
practical. He devotes three chapters to belief, its nature, limits,
and consistency with facts. His excuse for giving so much space
to the ' standard of truth ' is that it is disclaimed by the most
popular treatise on the subject. This remark, as is subsequently
clear, is directed against the realism of Dugald Stewart. What
follows, therefore, is interesting not so much for what it repeats
from Hume, but as a defence of the living against the dead, a
duel of vindication between a Scotch opponent and a Scottish-
American follower, over the body of the critical Patroclus. Assuming the weapons of Hume, Buchanan makes a vigorous onslaught upon the common sense position. He holds that belief
does not depend on any intrinsic, constituent property in our ideas,
or in the manner of their combination together, or on the per-
spicuity of their conception; the energy of their conception is the
essential foundation. In a word, the only sensible property or
immediate effect of belief consists in a higher grade of feeling, sentiment or, passion than the imaginative conception could excite.[2]
Moreover, Buchanan follows Hume not only in language but in
illustrative figures. The latter had said that the causal inference
was not intuitive, or demonstrative, but founded on custom or
habit, as when a man finding in a desert the remains of pompous
buildings would conclude that it had been cultivated in ancient
times by civilised inhabitants.[3] Buchanan in turn says we have
no direct knowledge of the intrinsic powers by which causes and
effects are connected together, nor can we assign any reason why
the one should be conjoined with the other. Our inference is

[1] For a description of the Kentucky revivals see the writer's *Founder of
Mormonism,* London, 1903, p. 46. Compare also *Account of a Singular
Convulsive Affection in Tennessee,* by Felix Robertson, M. D., (Philadelphia Medical and Physical Journal, 1805, Vol. 2, Part I., p. 86) ; (*Ib.,* 1808,
Vol. 3, Part I., p. 110), *Thoughts on the Exercises at Camp Meeting* by
William Young, who says these ' jerks ' are due not to *chorea sancti viti,*
or a special visitation from the Deity, or Rush's influence of a convulsive
operation of the moral faculty upon the bodily system, but a propensity
to imitation arising from the sympathy of association.

[2] *Human Nature,* p. 243.

[3] *Enquiry,* § 5, Part I., p. 43.

entirely founded on habit.[1] Thus if one should undertake to prove that Kentucky was formerly inhabited by people more civilised than the present American savages, he would do it by describing visible memorials more considerable than the present Indians possess.[2] Again, following closely the Humean analysis that belief in matter of fact is a more forcible sentiment or feeling than what the imagination can attain, and is derived from a memory of sense object and a customary conjunction between that and some other object,[3] Buchanan holds that energy of conception is the essential foundation of belief; that the only sensible quality consists in a higher grade of feeling, sentiment or passion than the imaginative conception could excite; and that the two general causes by which the credential excitement can be produced are the action of a stimulus and the agency of association.[4] Accordingly, belief in matters of fact is produced by the evidence of the senses, and the individual must abandon an instinctive, internal, or immediate standard of truth for the sake of an external criterion—the conformity of his ideas to nature. Thus the conception that Lexington, Kentucky, is composed of houses formed of wood and brick, and not of marble palaces, is true because conformable to reality. Again belief depends on the agency of association: we no sooner perceive the objects of nature than we perceive them succeeding in a regular order, and this succession is reiterated in our thoughts as often as we advert to the objects of sense or revive their ideas by memory or imagination. Hence the veriest infant is led by the sway of habit or the association of ideas to infer causes and effects from each other. This association is connate and incorporated with the elements of thought, grows with their growth and strengthens with their strength.[5]

There are accordingly two varieties of belief, representative and inferential; the former, as conformable to the realities of nature, is the infallible standard of general truths,—as that matter is geometrically solid; the latter, as consisting of ideas involving causation, is but probable assurance,—as that animal life is the effect of organisation, or that mind is merely an organic state of

---

[1] *Human Nature*, p. 266. [2] *Ib.*, p. 265. [3] *Enquiry*, pp. 37, 46, 48.
[4] *Human Nature*, pp. 243, 251. [5] *Ib.*, pp. 252, 253, 266.

matter.[1] Notwithstanding this distinction between the two kinds of belief, the author does not hold to their essential difference. Belief in the validity of the causal relation becomes positive assurance not through an outward perception, but an inward principle. The system of our ideas, he asserts, is copied entirely from the system of nature which it is destined to represent. The efficient powers which are supposed to bind the elements of things together and to direct them in the routine of causation, are undiscoverable by the senses; but the principle of association performs a corresponding function in the ideal system. It combines our elementary ideas in collateral and consecutive tribes and trains, comformably to the natural concourse and succession of the sensible properties from which they are copied. And this intrinsic harmony of our ideas, in unison with the regularity of nature, is the source and essence of consistency.[2]

But what is this conformity? How do we know what is natural? What validity is there in our belief in the orderly succession of the external world? The American criticist has sought, like Hume, to trace up these phenomena to principles still more general and has come to the latter's conclusion, namely, that Nature has implanted in us an instinct which carries forward the thought in a correspondent course to that which she has established among external objects; though we are ignorant of those powers and forces on which this regular course and succession of objects totally depends.[3] To his theory of belief Buchanan now adds some apparently contradictory principles, which carried him over into the controversy with the Scotch realists. Similar to the influence of consistency is the power which illustration possesses: by a well chosen figure, says Blair, even conviction is assisted. Thus, if an abstract proposition be compared with some sensible object that resembles it, the mind mistakes the clearness and coherency of this likeness for the real attributes of the idea itself— as when Dr. Rush enforces his doctrines of animal life by an ingenious comparison of the vital system to a violin.[4] Again ideas

---

[1] *Human Nature,* pp. 253, 268. [2] *Ib.,* p. 272. [3] *Enquiry,* pp. 51, 56.
[4] *Human Nature,* p. 274. Buchanan's later unpublished essays are said to have met the approval of Rush.

in sleep are accompanied by the most implicit conviction. Though
our dreams are incoherent and unsupported by any kind of evidence, they arouse belief; their falsehood is only discovered by their
inconsistency with the facts of causation previously perceived and
remembered. So is it with reveries, day-dreams and the wandering
imaginations of a brain affected by a fever, when it becomes so
irregular that its internal, irregular excitement exceeds the force
of ordinary perception.[1] But the most plausible objection against
the theory of the credential energy of conception is the contrary
theory of attention. Stewart contends that we constantly believe
in the ideas to which we attend, since the subject is limited which
can be at once clearly and fully apprehended. To this objection
Buchanan concludes that he cannot fully agree; it confuses per-
spicuity with force; and yet he is ready to concede that attention
tends to invigorate our ideal conceptions, and thus to harmonise
the two views.[2]

Given Buchanan's previous theories of sensation and cognition,
it may be easily imagined what was his theory of volition. Supposing that man is a machine whose final cause is pleasure, and
that the causal inference is not rational, but due to habit or association, there followed a necessitarian view of the will. As before,
the interest here lies not in the repetition, but in the defence of
the Humean doctrine. Again is the opposition brought out between
the critical and the common-sense methods. Hume, says his disciple, considered the sentiment of a nisus which we feel in volition,
to compose the vulgar notion of power; whilst he viewed the sentiment, of which we are conscious in the transition of our ideas
in the order of causation, as its true philosophical conception.[3]
Furthermore, volition is commonly considered as an exertion of an
innate power, or constituent faculty of the mind; concerning
whose intrinsic nature it is fruitless and unnecessary to enquire.
The propensity of the grave and infallible metaphysician to affirm
that every mental transaction requires a simple and fundamental
faculty of the mind was exposed and ridiculed by Locke. Yet
the practice has continued. According to the popular school every
active verb in the English language, to which mind can be a nom-

[1] *Human Nature*, p. 277.   [2] *Ib.*, pp. 281, 284.   [3] *Ib.*, p. 316.

inative, should indicate a particular faculty which performs the action affirmed. They seem entirely to have forgotten that philosophy consists not in multiplying but in simplifying general principles.[1] To show how we might naturally acquire all our knowledge was deemed by Locke a sufficient argument against innate ideas; to show how associations must have been formed, sufficient to produce all our voluntary actions, must likewise disprove the existence of any innate, simple faculty.[2] In short, there is no property in the mind of man which can be denominated a faculty in the common meaning of the term, except perhaps the powers of perception and association, and it is probable that future discoveries will diminish rather than increase their number. So volition does not consist in the operation of any simple, constituent principle, but is an acquirement made at the expense of much labour. In the infant there is no trait of voluntary power until months elapse. It has no command of a single muscle in the body, except through the need of what has been denominated instinct, and when it does commence, its first attempts are crude and abortive.[3]

Coming to the more positive aspects of volition, Buchanan follows the lead of Hartley in the latter's contentions that the doctrine of association explains the rise and progress of the voluntary and semi-voluntary powers; that muscular motion is performed in the same general manner as sensation and the perception of ideas; and that in voluntary motions the power of obtaining pleasure and removing pain is generated early in children.[4] These general principles are now applied not only with clearness but with some approximation to a sound genetic psychology. Without reading too much of the future into the past, it may be said that Buchanan has anticipated to a considerable degree the modern notions of volition. It is, he suggests, an acquirement, and consists in the association of a muscular action with an energetic conception of that action and a predominating desire to perform it; its essential parts are three: an idea of some action to be performed, a desire of performing it, and ultimately the action itself. The antecedent idea and desire have not generally been considered as integral

---

[1] *Human Nature*, p. 298.   [2] *Ib.*, p. 307.   [3] *Ib.*, pp. 299, 300.
[4] *Observations*, pp. 26, 29, 40; prop. 14, cor. 5; prop. 15.

parts of volition, our attention being naturally attracted to the muscular motion which seems to be produced by a specific effort of the will. So it is necessary to demonstrate that the idea of the motion is first conceived with that degree of energy which constitutes belief, that this idea becomes connected with a predominating desire to perform it, and that the concurrence of the two produces the motion; that is, that the process of volition embraces all the principal kinds of excitement,—sentimental, ideal and muscular. Hence no special faculty is required, the whole consisting in a combination of the ordinary modes of excitement.[1] These things, continues the writer, are obvious to the adult, yet it is difficult to demonstrate the formation of these earliest rudiments of volition, unless we go back of the records of memory and consider the human system in its infancy. This period is characterised by an extraordinary degree of mobility from which great irritability is to be inferred. But as muscular motions commonly procure relief from the pain which produced them, the natural desire of this relief will presently be transferred by association to those objects by which it is procured. Again, infancy being the peculiar season of association, those actions which the child learns to associate in the order of causation with some agreeable event must soon become desirable for themselves. Thus all the trivial actions of boyish play are performed in consequence of this association. The excitability of the child in the morning suggests to its vacant mind the idea of some voluntary movement, immediately revives the associated pleasurable desire of performing it, and the action is instantly performed. But the original involuntary motions, by which the first rudiments of volition were established, commenced in pleasure and terminated in pain; when they become voluntary their sentimental tendency is reversed; they now commence in pleasure and generally terminate in the pain of fatigue.[2]

Having brought the argument to an hedonistic issue, in accordance with the prevailing tendency of the associationist school, the *Philosophy of Human Nature* is concluded with an application of this theory of the will to imitation; with a case of illusory volition; with a few experiments on the formation of habit; and finally with some conjectures on the physiology of the brain. Using a

[1] *Human Nature*, p. 302.   [2] *Ib.*, pp. 308, 309, 312.

genetic method which is suggestive of the Pestalozzian system as applied by Joseph Neef of Philadelphia,[1] Buchanan says that the idea, the desire, and the association of the muscular contractions form the three steps in the process invariably pursued in the formation of voluntary actions. This is illustrated in a boy's learning a mechanic art. The lad first carefully observes the movements of his teacher. Having thus gained a clear idea of the manual motion and an energetic desire of performing it, he proceeds to attempt its execution. But his first efforts are crude and abortive, for his muscles are not yet associated to the complex idea which is now to direct their operations. But repetition renders it familiar and associates with precision to its idea in his mind.[2] The acquirement of habits through imitation and repetition disposes of a large part of the so-called voluntary actions; another section is cut out by considering the phenomena of illusory volition. Instead of this being excited by the concomitant determination of a supposed faculty called the will, another explanation is simpler: a strong irritation passes to the sensory, is reflected into the irritable muscles, and produces a convulsion. In this case we are conscious of exactly the same sentiment that we feel in a common volition, though we try to refrain from the exertion by which it is caused. We must therefore be conscious of an effort of the will to perform a certain action, and from another to refrain from it at the same time—an absurd complication.[3]

In his *Additional Remarks on Volition* the materialist offers some simple experiments, in part adapted from Hartley, in order to meet those metaphysicians who have written against Hume. They have contended that experience, habit, or the association of ideas cannot be the cause of the inference founded on causation, for the infant infers effects and causes from each other from so early an age that such habits could not be previously established. But we attempted to prove that such associations were among the earliest acquisitions of infancy. In addition the following experiments shew with what quickness and ease associations may be established. For example, in turning on the heel from left to right till gid-

---

[1] Cf. Neef's *Sketch of a Plan and Method of Education*, Philadelphia, 1808.

[2] *Ib.*, p. 313.   [3] *Ib.*, p. 315.

diness occurs, a habit of muscular action speedily arises, for when we stop, the muscles of the eyeball, unconsciously to us, continue to turn the eye slowly to the left and quickly again to the right. So, too, fixing one's eyes immovably on a swift brook will generate a habit of perceiving other objects moving in a contrary direction. In brief, no period can be assigned too early for the previous institution of irresistible habits, for these experiments prove that habits, both in muscular and sensual excitement, are established almost instantaneously. These are indeed not permanent, but by constant repetition they might become not less firm than those early and powerful habits which have improperly been denominated instincts.[1]

Here ends Buchanan's *Philosophy of Human Nature.* In thanking Jefferson for a copy of the work, John Adams said he could not foresee much utility in reviewing in this country the controversy between spiritualists and materialists. Why should time be wasted in disputing about two substances, when both parties agree that neither knows anything about either.[2] This is but captious questioning on the part of the Northern critic. To it the answer may be given that Buchanan had a real value, his significance lying in his attempt to carry out the materialistic monism latent in the systems of Darwin and Hartley. The cautious English writers were ostensibly dualists, but their drift was toward a physical interpretation of psychic events. The former with his tribes and trains of motion, the latter with his location of the rational soul in the brain, were actually reasoning in favour of the existence of but a single basic substance. Hence their disciple was more or less justified in arguing against the existence of any such mind as the spiritualists maintained—an immaterial, intrinsically active, independent being. By thus rejecting the immaterial element, Buchanan has left on his hands not the inert and lifeless thing which superficial inspection imagines, but that which by a deeper scrutiny develops energies and operations able to perform the quick and subtle acts of intellect itself.[3] What was the nature of this remarkable entity it can scarce be said that Buchanan ade-

---

[1] *Sketch of a Plan and Method of Education,* pp. 321-3.
[2] Jefferson's *Works,* Vol. 15, p. 121, May 26, 1817.
[3] *Ib.,* p. 15.

quately set forth. When, for example, he confessed that it was not yet discovered what were the ultimate conditions of animality, he upset his larger calculations as to the ultimate conditions of mentality. Searching for a single underlying principle, he was forced back to the point whence he started—the unknown substratum of the Humean speculation. Notwithstanding his failure to construct a monistic system out of the implications of his foreign authorities, the Southern materialist stands in a suggestive position as regards the native disputants in the body-mind controversy. While Samuel Johnson of Connecticut favoured occasionalism and pre-established harmony, and Cadwallader Colden of New York a causal theory of the *influxus physicus,* the Kentuckian was an epiphenomenalist. Mind to his thinking was but the creation of the brain, consciousness only the shadow of a real substance. Furthermore, while his definition of matter as ' spiritual energies ' might have pleased both the idealist Johnson and the dynamist Colden, the application of the definition would have pleased neither. Buchanan's ultimate object was not to spiritualise matter, but to materialise mind, and all to the end of showing that the two are substantially the same, each part possessing ' one common nature.' Although it may be concluded that the Kentucky philosopher was unable to prove his thesis, and exposed in many ways the defects of a pure materialism, he performed a peculiar service in his insistence on the indissoluble connection between the psychical and physical processes. For this he may be called the earliest native physiological psychologist. However imperfectly expressed, there were in his work certain adumbrations of modern doctrines—in sensation, a presentation of the nerve-tract theory; in cognition, an emphasis on the genetic; in volition, an approximation to the law of kinaesthetic equivalents— ' reflection disclosing that no voluntary action can be performed without its preconception in the mind.'

CHAPTER IV

JOSEPH PRIESTLEY

JOSEPH Priestley, metaphysician and materialist, came to America in 1794. Fleeing, as Jefferson said, from the fires and mobs of Birmingham, a welcome was assured the distinguished chartist and chemist for such widely varying reasons as his championship of free thought,[1] his discovery of oxygen, and his eminent praise of Franklin in his *History of Electricity*. The purpose of the ' honest heretic,' as the Philadelphia philosopher called him, was to found a large settlement for the friends of liberty near the head waters of the Susquehanna river,[2] a project which succeeded as little as did Shelley's Pantisocracy on the banks of the same stream. Moreover, the proposed college of Northumberland had to be abandoned,[3] and the proffered chair of chemistry in the University of Pennsylvania declined. Nevertheless in spite of ill health and political complications Priestley accomplished much in this last decade of his life. Confining the inquiry to what was written by him in America and about him by Americans, an estimate may be made as to what he accomplished for the cause of materialism in the new world. In these ten years he made large additions to the astonishing bulk of his writings. On the voyage over he wrote *Observations on the Cause of the Present Prevalence of Infidelity,* which served as a preface to the new edition of his *Philosophers and Politicians of France,* the third part of which contained an *Answer to Mr. Paine's Age of Reason.* Within the next two years appeared two works in defence of Unitarianism as against both Calvinism and Arianism.[4] In 1797

[1] Compare Rutt's *Life of Priestley,* Vol. 2, p. 235, for the fulsome address of welcome by the Democratic Club of New York.

[2] H. B. Adams, *Thomas Jefferson and the University of Virginia,* Washington, 1883, pp. 46-49.

[3] Franklin, *Works,* Vol. 7, p. 10 (Ford Edition).

[4] Extracts from Dr. Priestley's *Catechism,* Salem, 1795, *Unitarianism Explained,* Philadelphia, 1796.

came the *Outline of all the Evidences in Favour of Revelation* and the *Controversy with Mr. Volney,* the last being composed in a single day, as he deemed Volney's shallow deism unworthy of a grave argument.[1] In the same year Priestley began the *Comparison of the Institutes of Moses with those of the Hindoos,* besides contributing various papers on phlogiston and electricity to the *Medical Repository* [2] of New York and to the *Transactions* [3] of the American Philosophical Society. In 1803, the year before his death, he completed his *Notes to All the Books of Scripture,* thus carrying his grand total to over one hundred publications. From the remains of this intellectual mastodon on the banks of the Susquehanna one can almost reconstruct his mental habits, can almost hear his ponderous tread as he pushes through the opposing jungle of ancient and modern thought. Thus it was that in three months he read through all the works quoted in his *Doctrines of Heathen Philosophy Compared with Those of Revelation,* for, as he said: ' My labour was the shorter as I had nothing to do with the logic, the metaphysics, or the physics of the writers, all equally trifling and absurd.' [4] But Priestley's astonishing output, even in his declining years, can be laid to his old and easy method of adapting the works of others to his own purposes. As he had edited Hartley's *Observations on Man* by dropping the essential but obnoxious hypothesis of vibration, so he compiled his *Socrates and Jesus Compared,* by confining himself to Xenophon's *Memorabilia.*

As the products of a philosophical middleman, Priestley's works met with a varying reception in America.[5] By John Adams they were subjected to a merciless criticism, by Thomas Jefferson they were received with the utmost enthusiasm. To the hermit of Mon-

[1] W. B. Sprague, *Annals of the American Pulpit,* New York, 1865, Vol. 8, p. 308.

[2] Cf. *Ib.* Vol. 8, pp. 300, 430; Vol. 13, p. 260.

[3] Cf. Volume of 1804, for Priestley's attack on Darwin's *Equivocal or Spontaneous Generation.*

[4] Preface, p. VI.

[5] See H. B. Adams, *Life and Writings of Jared Sparks,* New York, 1893, Vol. 1, p. 119 note; C. C. Everett, *The Old Unitarianism and the New,* Philadelphia, 1889. O. B. Frothingham, *Boston Unitarianism,* p. 249.

ticello, wandering in the dismal swamp of clerical obscurantism, Priestley had come as a breeze to drive away 'the foggy mists of Platonism.' Some correspondence had already passed between the two educators relative to the proposed University of Virginia.[1] So Jefferson welcomes the foreign Unitarian to 'our country— the asylum for whatever is good and great,' but regrets that he had not visited in some valley of the Blue Ridge and 'met the homage of universal reverence.' He concludes: 'Those who live by mystery and *charlatanerie*, fearing you would render them useless by simplifying the Christian philosophy, endeavoured to crush your well-earnt and well-deserved fame. But it was the Lilliputians upon Gulliver. . . . But I can cover you under the protection of those laws which were made for the wise and good like you, and disdain the legitimacy of that libel on legisla- tion which, under the form of law, was for some time placed among them.'[2] The reference here is to an unfortunate episode during Priestley's stay at Northumberland. Owing to certain po- litical essays of his son-in-law, Thomas Cooper, who had injudi- ciously attacked the administration, the two Englishmen came under the provisions of the notorious alien and sedition laws. This aroused the ire of the Federal President, and at the very time of his coolness with Jefferson. Upon Priestley, then, succeeding the warm praises of the Southern statesman, there blew a chilling blast from the North. Adams averred that the chartist was a discon- tented and turbulent spirit, 'weak as water, as unstable as Reu- ben, or the wind, and his influence not an atom in the world.' This estimate can hardly stand; it was biassed by political animos- ity and contradicted by other statements of the writer. After the renewal of the friendship with Jefferson, Adams recalls how he had liked Priestley the first time he met him in London, and how he considered him a great and extraordinary man—really a phenom- enon, a comet in the system like Voltaire, Bolingbroke, and Hume. For all this, there were certain things about the dogmatic divine that irritated the retired scoffer. He did not like being charged by

[1] Jefferson, *Works* (Ford Edition), Vol. 10, p. 220; Vol. 7, p. 408, 415, 407.
[2] *Ib.* Vol. 8, pp. 21-22 (March 21, 1801).

him with being a mere church-going animal, and protested that if Priestley dedicates his discourses to him, it will give him the character of an heretic. It was, perhaps, Priestley's attitude of inconsistent infidelity, of free-thinking orthodoxy, that most offended the logical Northerner. Writing to Jefferson he asked: What does Priestley mean by an unbeliever, when he applies it to you? How much did he unbelieve himself? Gibbon had him right when he denominated his creed scanty.[1] Then, too, Priestley was carried away by the French revolution, and actually told Adams that Bonaparte was the instrument of providence prophesied in the Apocalypse; yet when it came to Dupuis and his *Origine de tous les cultes,* on which the *Corruptions of Christianity* was largely based, Priestley pronounces him an atheist and his work the *ne plus ultra* of infidelity.[2] Inconsistencies such as these led Adams to a more particular criticism of the Englishman's American publications. The *Doctrines of Heathen Philosophy Compared with Those of Revelation,* which Jefferson had praised so highly, Adams considered extremely imperfect. In it he found no notice of Cleanthes and his hymn of divine sovereignty, no satisfactory account of the Pythagorean philosophy, nor of Ocellus, Timaeus, Archytas, Zaleucus, Zoroaster, Sanchoniathan and Confucius.[3]

Except to air his own knowledge, Adams found little use for Priestley's works. It was far different with Jefferson. Upon Priestley, together with Middleton and Waterland, he rested the basis of his faith. But although the work last mentioned was executed perhaps a little hastily, yet that may be excused, Jefferson urges, on the ground that the author felt himself pressed by the hand of death.[4] For this charitable view, as in the case of Adams' strictures, certain personal reasons may be imputed. The *Comparative View of Socrates and Jesus* had been a direct incentive to what turned out to be the Jefferson ' Bible '; and the American continuation of the *General History of the Christian Church* had been dedicated to Jefferson as the ' advocate of religious liberty.'

[1] John Adams, *Works,* Boston, 1856, Vol. 9, pp. 6, 14; Vol. 3, p. 396: Vol. 10, p. 57; Vol. 9, p. 636; Vol. 1, p. 488; Vol. 10, p. 57.
[2] *Ib.,* Vol. 10, pp. 229, 71.   [3] *Ib.,* pp. 83-5.
[4] *Works* (Ford Edition), Vol. 9, pp. 416-418; Vol. 8, p. 293.

It was doubtless for these more intimate reasons that Jefferson, upon learning that a life of Dr. Priestley had been published, expressed his conviction that in politics, religion, and physics no man had rendered more service.[1] But this estimate was higher than Priestley put upon himself. He wrote to his friend, Benjamin Vaughan, who likewise tended to overrate his importance, that he had kept out of the way of politics, and yet had met with more coarse abuse in America than in England, and in a newspaper most patronised by the governing people—the courted and popular Tories. So, too, in religion; the proposal for his *Church History* gets him only seven subscribers in Philadelphia, and among them was not Mr. Adams. All that he can do here, as the day draws near a close, is to complete his exposition of the books of Revelation and of Daniel.[2] But these plans came to little. The cause may be found in the contradictions which existed not only between his favourite subjects, but within them. In physics he discovered the gas carbon monoxide,[3] but he still persisted in upholding the obsolescent doctrine of phlogiston. In religion his *Corruptions of Christianity,* as a New Hampshire editor expressed it, was beneficial in cutting off the gangrened excrescences of tradition; but what must Benjamin Rush have thought when the clerical chemist wrote to him: ' I wish I could give you as much satisfaction with respect to the *prophecies* as you do to me with respect to *medicine* and *physiology.* The present time shows us where we are in the great chain of events. I expect the downfall of all the states represented by the *ten toes* in the image of Nebuchadnezzar, and the *ten horns* of the fourth beast of Daniel, before the present war be over '? [4]

Jefferson's high estimate of Priestley's influence in politics, religion and physics may be discounted in every particular,[5] nevertheless there was one field of thought in which his activities in

[1] *Works*, Vol. 9, p. 102.

[2] Letter of April 19, 1798, in H. C. Bolton, *Scientific Correspondence of Dr. Priestley,* New York, 1892, pp. 153-4.

[3] *Ib.,* p. 153, notes.

[4] *Ib.,* p. 156. Letter to Rush, August 8, 1799.

[5] Compare Mitchell's *Medical Repository,* New York, 1804, p. 430, in which Priestley is called ' the favourite of science, the advocate of civil and religious liberty, and the first metaphysician of the age.'

America were of positive importance. Although complaining that he lived quite insulated from learned society,[1] as a metaphysician he had a stimulating relation to the Philadelphia school of thinkers, and through his influence upon his troublesome but brilliant colleague, Thomas Cooper, spread the cause of materialism in the South. It was the latter who wrote, while at Northumberland, a valuable account of the Priestleyan metaphysics and traced the growth of his ideas relating to matter and spirit.[2] Priestley, it is asserted, had at first only occasional doubts on the intimate union of two substances so entirely heterogenous as soul and body, but objections did not impressively occur to him till the publication of his treatise against the Scotch doctors. But in editing Hartley's *Observations,* the doctrine of the homogeneity of man had followed from that author's thesis, that all the phenomena of mind may be accounted for from the known properties and laws of an organisation. Hence in the *Disquisitions* of 1778 Priestley defined matter as a substance, not only with the property of extension, and the active powers of attraction and repulsion, but, like Boscovich, admitted the penetrability of matter.[3]

Cooper has given some, but not all, of the steps in his master's progress toward the doctrine of an ' attenuated kind of matter.' The account needs to be supplemented, for it is not improbable that the initial impulse to this doctrine came from America. Priestley did not acknowledge this, yet it must be considered that in the mental habits of the professional plagiariser the unconscious memory plays its rôle. The facts are these: In his *History of Light,* Priestley confesses that he adopted personally from Boscovich the notion that matter is not impenetrable, but that it consists only of points of force.[4] This was in 1772, yet five years before in his *History of Electricity* he had described Franklin's theory of electricity as that of a subtile and elastic fluid dispensed through the pores of all bodies.[5] Here, then, was an inkling of the penetra-

---

[1] *Medical Repository,* p. 148.

[2] *Memoirs of Dr. Joseph Priestley to the Year 1745,* Northumberland, 1806.

[3] *Ib.,* pp. 310-312.

[4] Quoted in *Disquisitions,* p. 24.

[5] London, 1767, p. 456.

bility of matter based on experiments which Franklin had made as early as 1749, wherein he described the electrical matter as consisting of particles extremely subtile, since it can permeate common matter.[1] It cannot be determined precisely when Priestley obtained this notion of the extreme tenuity of the electrical matter, whether from these first experiments, or from the one described in the treatise of Beccaria which Franklin procured for him.[2] What use he made of the notion is, however, interesting to record. He protested that he had no sort of objection if Clarke and Price choose to call this matter by the name of spirit, his ultimate object being to shew that there is no real conflict between mind and matter, and that the doctrine of the soul is not affected by the death of the body, since one substance may admit all the properties of man, if that substance be characterised by active powers and impenetrability.[3]

It was this peculiar combination of Franklinism with materialism that led a contemporary critic to pronounce this system a new one. In refining and spiritualising matter, said Samuel Miller of Princeton, Priestley makes it an extremely different thing from that gross and impenetrable substance which it is generally represented to be, and so far differs from preceding materialists.[4] But while the novelty of this doctrine attracted the critic, its application he considered hazardous. By supposing the whole human constitution to be made up of one homogeneous substance, Priestley denies that there is a distinction between the soul of man and the body; that the idea of the natural immortality of the soul is wholly fallacious; and that the properties of sensation and thought must be extinguished by the dissolution of the organised mass in which they exist, and, therefore, that the only reason which men have to expect a state of consciousness or enjoyment hereafter is derived from the scripture doctrine of the resurrection.[5] This was a

[1] *Works* (Smyth Edition), Vol. 2, p. 427.

[2] *Elettricismo Artificiale,* Turin, 1771, Capo I, Art. III. Compare Smyth, Vol. 4, p. 163 for letter of Franklin to Beccaria, dated London, July 13, 1762.

[3] *Doctrines of Materialism,* 1778, pp. xii-xiii, 23.

[4] *Retrospect of the Eighteenth Century,* New York, 1803, Vol. 2, p. 456.

[5] *Ib.,* p. 32.

strange fate that befel the doctrine of the homogeneity of man. It was rejected by the conservatives because it put what was scriptural above what was natural; it was accepted by the radicals because it conjoined the two. As presented in Cooper's later tractate, the *Scripture Doctrine of Materialism,* it met the hearty approval of Jefferson. To him it seemed a new idea, yet unquestionably proved, and effective in putting a quietus upon the orthodox immaterialists.[1]

While the doctrine of anthropological materialism was disallowed originality by Cooper, since Priestley, as he held, was but following the path set by Blount in his *Anima Mundi,*[2] yet that doctrine appeared so novel to most Americans that it was little appreciated and less understood. Thus James Purves, a student but not a graduate of Princeton, attacked this doctrine with the following lengthy arguments:

The doctrine of materialism, as held by this author, is perhaps tolerably innocent, considered by itself; since he allows that matter may be so modified as to be capable of perception and thought. For, if matter be capable of intelligence now, and shall become intelligent after the resurrection, notwithstanding its being deprived of that property while lying in the grave, it might have been intelligent in a pre-existent state, for anything we know, though it had remained a long time in a state of insensibility, and may, in its intelligent state, possess all the volatility that has generally been ascribed to the spirit. . . . To prove that matter is not solid, it must be seen, or demonstrated, that two or more of the ultimate particles thereof can occupy the same place; and this will surely be very difficult to do, if, as he says, every one of these particles has internal forces of repulsion, preventing their contact, which cannot be overcome by any known power. If it be so difficult to bring them into contact, it will surely be impossible to bring them to occupy the same space; we may therefore conclude that it is impossible for Dr. Priestley to prove that matter is not solid, upon his own principles. . . . .
. . . Modern philosophers seem to despise the ancients, as ignorant of the laws of nature, and unintelligible in their explanations of what they pretended to know; but, is there anything in

---

[1] To Cooper, December 11, 1823, *Works* (Ford Edition), Vol. 10, p. 285.
[2] *Observations on Doctor Priestley's Doctrines of Philosophical Necessity and Materialism,* Philadelphia, 1797, p. 3; *Memoirs,* Vol. 2, p. 303.

antiquity more unintelligible or absurd than the doctrine of attraction and repulsion as taught by many moderns? Attraction, repulsion, and extension are the only properties that Dr. Priestley allows to matter; and yet it has never been proved that either attraction or repulsion are properties of matter, nor has it been explained how they operate, supposing them to be such properties. Mathematical calculations have been made to ascertain the centripetal and centrifugal forces of bodies; but they have not been in every respect satisfactory to those who wished to support the Newtonian system, and others have denied that any such forces exist. But supposing matter to possess the powers of attraction and repulsion, ' by which the ultimate particles of bodies are prevented from coming into contact,' as is said in the *Disquisition on Matter and Spirit,* what are these powers of attraction and repulsion? And by what are these opposite powers excited? According to Dr. Priestley's own definition, they must be distinct from matter; for they not only repel bodies of matter, but the very ultimate particles of these bodies, so as to prevent their coming into contact. He says, ' It has been asserted, and the assertion has never been disproved, that, for anything we know to the contrary, all the solid matter in the solar system might be contained within a nutshell, there is so great a proportion of *void space* within the substance of the most solid bodies. . . .' This is bringing solid matter into a very small compass; but the *ultimate particles* of matter, solid or unsolid, seem to be contained in an inconceivably less *space,* in his opinion; for, instead of filling a nutshell, he says, ' It consists of *physical points* only, endued with power of attraction and repulsion.' This seems to be a refining as much upon matter as ever any did upon spirit; for, as mathematical or physical points are supposed to occupy no space, this definition denies extension to matter, as much as ever any denied extension to spirit. And if the *ultimate particles* of matter consist in *physical points,* and these points occupy no space, then these particles will be found in no space, or nowhere.[1]

If Priestley's anthropological materialism was scarcely comprehended by Americans, a like bewilderment was aroused by the twin doctrine of philosophical necessity. William Allen of Massachusetts could see why Priestley should make all volitions the necessary results of previous circumstances, but why he should be opposed to the Calvinistic doctrine of predestination he could not comprehend. It seemed to him an inconsistency that the author

[1]James Purves. *Observations on Doctor Priestley's Doctrines of Philosophical Necessity and Materialism,* Philadephia, 1797, pp. 13-18.

should embrace optimism—the belief that all evil results in the good of the whole—in order to escape ascribing the existence of sin to the will of God.[1] It cannot be said that Priestley's advocate meets this objection with much success. He cites Edwards as one who wrote in tedious defence of the same side of the question as his master; but he thinks that the New England divine did not understand the problem when he connected the doctrine of necessity with all the bigotry of Calvinism.[2] This is special pleading, and no answer to the difficulty involved. Indeed, Cooper is so ignorant of the Edwardean system that he defends Priestley in the very terms of the *Freedom of the Will*, which the latter admits having read in his younger days. Priestley, he concludes, shows that from the nature of cause and effect every volition must be the necessary result of previous circumstances; that the *scientia contingentium*, the great and insuperable difficulty of God's pretended foreknowledge of uncertain events, can on no other hypothesis be avoided; and that the doctrine of necessity is perfectly consistent with the great plan of divine benevolence, and avoids considering God Almighty as the author of sin. Like Leibniz in his *Theodicée*, granting the goodness of God, it follows that He has adopted that system which is most conducive to general and individual happiness upon the whole; and that moral evil and consequent physical evil are necessary to produce the greatest sum of good to the system at large. . . . The question must now be considered as settled, for those who can resist Collins' philosophical enquiry, the section of Hartley on the mechanism of the mind, and Priestley's review of the subject, are not to be reasoned with. *Interest republicae ut denique sit finis litium* is a maxim of law applicable to letters, hence the time has arrived when the separate existence of the human soul, and the freedom of the will, like the doctrines of the trinity and transubstantiation, may be regarded as no longer entitled to public discussion.[3]

That Priestleyism in America meant the overthrow of immaterialism and of the metaphysical doctrine of voluntarism, was

---

[1] *American Biographical and Historical Dictionary*, Cambridge, 1829, p. 486.

[2] Cooper, *Memoirs*, Vol. 2, p. 322.   [3] *Ib.*, pp. 324-335.

disproved by the intense interest excited by the pursuit of these perennial doctrines among the transcendentalists. Of this, Cooper knew nothing, but he exposed the extravagance of his conclusion by eating his own words. Having, like Priestley, abandoned an heterogeneity between the physical and bodily processes, and having attempted to replace psychology by nerve physiology, he yet proceeds to discuss immaterialism and voluntarism in a series of publications extending from 1806 to 1831. As these carried him over from the British to the French materialism, and were in turn directed against the Scotch realism, they call for separate treatment.

CHAPTER V

THOMAS COOPER

THE career of Thomas Cooper (1759-1840), disciple and companion of Joseph Priestley, may well be described in the words of John Adams as that of a ' learned, ingenious, scientific, and talented madcap.'[1] Writing violently against the Federal party when in Pennsylvania, losing his judgeship on representations of overbearing temper; attacked by the clergy when proposed by Jefferson as first professor of natural science and law in the University of Virginia,[2] and finally engaging in the nullification agitation in South Carolina, he was a living exemplification of his materialistic doctrine of irritability. Mentally, Cooper was a combination of dogmatist and agnostic. His portrait shews this, so do his letters; the one exhibiting the keen and eager face of the fighter against the ' Adams dynasty,' the other a series of doubts and denials, infinitely shocking to the 'orthodox ontologists.' Writing from Columbia in 1832 to a political friend, he says: ' I take great interest in S. Girard's will and his college, which I greatly fear the Black-coats will contrive by some rascally scheme or other to defeat. You have heard, I suppose, that the battle rages furiously between the ch[urch mili]tant and your humble servant, even to extermination. Bellum [internec]inum. I am not yet conquered, and expect yet to bivouac on the field of battle. I have no objection to a moral governor of the universe, but how came he in that character to create the Priesthood? Moral! You might as well apply squareness to virtue. I wish I knew how to account for moral and physical evil, and then I should be able to account for malaria, dyspepsia, yellow fever, the plague, cholera, rattlesnakes, mosqui-

[1] *Dictionary of National Biography,* Vol. 12, p. 152.
[2] H. B. Adams, *Thomas Jefferson and the University of Virginia,* Washington, 1888, p. 59.

toes, and faquirs of all classes and orders, Asiatic and European, Papist and Protestant.'[1]

With so caustic a pen it might be expected that Cooper's academic career in America was as disturbed as his political. Such was the case. Occupying in succession the chair of chemistry in Dickinson College, the University of Pennsylvania, and the South Carolina College, in the North he left behind him the reputation of a 'sturdy sceptic'[2] and in the South was formally tried for heresy.[3] And yet in the midst of these varied and perturbed activities the former Chartist still found time to edit a magazine entitled *The Emporium of Arts and Sciences,* to compile an *English Version of the Institutes of Justinian,* to deliver some of the earliest lectures in the country on the *Elements of Political Economy,* and to write a pamphlet *On the Connection of Geology and the Pentateuch,* the point of which was that there was no connection. In addition to these juridical and miscellaneous writings, and in spite of his economic arguments against overproduction, Cooper nevertheless published during these twenty-five years five works of considerable philosophical significance. For this tendency to excessive output Cooper has been called the Priestley of the South.[4] But he was not like his master in all his mental habits. Priestley's historic method was as diffuse and porous as that homogeneous matter for which he contended. There were gaps in it, due to his leaving out what he did not like. It was otherwise with the disciple. Although he complained that American libraries seldom contained the means of tracing the history of questions,[5] he was able to supplement the deficiencies of proper historical references. For example, in his *Review of the Metaphysical System of Dr. Priestley,* he scrupulously notes the omission of such foreign publications as *Le système de la nature,* attributed to Mirabaud, and of *Le vrai sens du système de l'univers,* attributed to Helvétius.[6] Although he may not have been 'the greatest man in America in the powers

---

[1] *American Historical Review,* Vol. 6, pp. 734-5.

[2] G. P. Fisher, Life of Benjamin Silliman, Philadelphia, 1866, p. 287.

[3] Compare *The Trial of Dr. Thomas Cooper for Infidelity,* Columbia, S. C., 1831.

[4] H. B. Adams, *Jared Sparks,* New York, 1893, p. 119.

[5] *Some Information Concerning America,* London, 1795, p. 164.

[6] *Memoirs,* Vol. 2, 310.

of his mind and in acquired information,' as Jefferson enthusiastically exclaimed, Cooper was yet conversant with the literature of
materialism from Blount to Broussais. But with him too much
knowledge was a dangerous thing. Owing to his fatal familiarity
with the progress of Gallic thought from the Encyclopædists to the
Idéalogues, he inadvertently undid much of the work that his master had accomplished for the defence of the deistic faith. His
Scriptural Doctrine of Materialism, according to which ' with the
death of the body, the whole soul dies,' was a logical inference
from Priestley's materialistic anthropomorphism; but the accompanying strictures against natural religion would have been too
much for the optimism of the old teleologist. Thus Cooper flatly
denied the existence of the Law of Nature, claiming that it was a
system fabricated by the theoretical writers from Grotius and
Puffendorf to Rutherford and Burlamaqui, none of whom knew
by whom it was enacted, or by what power it was sanctioned. No,
the universal, primary law of nature is the law of force, according
to which, if there were two shipwrecked men on a plank, the
stronger may push off the weaker.[1] Here was rank utilitarianism
supplanting one of the cherished ideals of the times. And there
was another ideal of the same sort to which the belligerent chartist
was equally opposed. As an antidote to the sickly sentimentality
attached to the belief that all men are born free, Cooper asks: Is a
puling infant born free? Leave him free from despotic control for
a few hours and he dies. Are all infants born equal? Equal in
what? In size, health, strength, mental capacity? Independent?
Of what and whom? Do the various circumstances to which two
persons are liable to be exposed make no difference between them?
A child, for example, educated among the priests of Juggernaut
and another among the Sçavans of Paris? Our Creator has not
thought fit to make every man six feet high, or to distribute brain
or intellect in precise or equal proportions. In the distribution of
these in all possible portions and varieties it is not society, but nature, that is in fault.[2]

From this private declaration of independence, so essentially re-

[1] *Lectures on the Elements of Political Economy,* 2nd edition, London,
1831, p. 64.
[2] *Ib.,* pp. 359-60.

lated to Cooper's subsequent defence of States' rights, it might be supposed that such an extreme individualist was unable to see both sides of a question. But his work of chief philosophical interest disproves that supposition. In his *View of the Metaphysical and Physiological Arguments in Favour of Materialism* his legal training stands him in such good stead that he does not argue the case in behalf of materialism before he has offered a brief for the other side. The chief arguments for immaterialism, he explains, are these: From matter and motion nothing but matter and motion can result. As no configuration or disposition of the particles of which our bodies are composed can amount to anything more than varieties of position, we have no reason to ascribe perception, memory, thought or will to any form of matter or motion, however varied, for the phenomena of intellect are too dissimilar to these. So the source of intellect must be something that cannot be the body, something immaterial, having no relation to matter; otherwise some arrangement of carbon, azote, hydrogen or oxygen might produce a syllogism. And modern immaterialists go further. They say the tendency to organisation itself must have been originally imparted and communicated to inert matter, which could not have assumed this tendency by any effort of its own. So life and the properties connected with it must have been originally impressed by that being to whom all creation is to be ascribed. Hence the intellectual phenomena are owing to a separate and distinct communication from the author of our common existence. They are not ascribable to any form of organisation, but to some separate being of a different and superior nature. This separate being is the soul. Finally, we are not here to argue from the possibility of any thing to its actual existence—*a posse ad esse non valet consequentia*. But when the phenomena cannot be explained by any known properties of organised or unorganised matter, something besides matter is needed to explain appearances which are not matter.[1]

Having reviewed the case of his opponents, with touches of scholastic reasoning suggestive of his reputed Oxford training, Cooper proceeds to exhibit the arguments in favour of materialism. These are of two classes—metaphysical and physiological. Under

[1] *Arguments in Favour of Materialism*, p. 335.

the former it is urged, first, that one thing is the property of another because of the universality with which they accompany each other. Such is the necessary connection between the nervous system of animals and the property of sensation and of perception. When the sentient extremities of a nerve are excited, perception is the certain and instantaneous result. These properties are inseparable, yet how this perception results from the stimulations of the nervous system, no one can any more explain than how an immaterial soul can act on a material body, without having one property in common with it. We feel in ourselves that perception is a function of the visible organ, the body, but of the existence of a separate soul we know nothing but by conjecture. Certainly the universality of concomitance is the sole ground for asserting the necessary connection between the phenomena.[1] Again, we may consider the impossibility of the existence of an immaterial and indiscerptible, immortal soul. Here either the soul is material, partly material, or in no respects material. The last case is the only one of the alternatives that the hypothesis of immaterialism can consistently maintain. But let the soul have no property in common with matter, then neither can act upon the other but by means of some common property, else one might conceive of erecting the Coliseum of Rome by playing Haydn's Rondeau. There is further proof from the impossibility of conceiving how the opposite proposition can be true. The disappearance of intellectual phenomena is explained by materialism as due to their dependence on the nervous system in its usual state of excitement. During derangements caused by sleep, swooning, drugs, and the like, the soul is dead, for all its properties—perception, memory, judgment, volition— are extinguished. But if intellectual phenomena furnish the evidences and properties of a separate immaterial being, where is the subject itself, when all its evidences and properties are annihilated, though but for a day or an hour? Therefore, if sensations, ideas, and volitions are produced, modified, or extinguished by involuntary organs, disease, and medicine, these effects, produced by means of the body, are bodily effects. But these are the essential, incommunicable properties of the soul, according to the immaterialists, and yet we have here these very properties under the control of

[1] *Arguments in Favor of Materialism*, p. 336.

accident, subject to the articles of the materia medica, and slaves of the pharmacopœia.[1]

Leaving the difficulties of the abnormal and unconscious to be settled by the other side, the Southern materialist now turns to the second class of arguments, the physiological. We need not resort, he says, to psychological doctrines of some distinct and superadded being, such as the *anima intellectualis, sensitiva,* and *vitalis* of the ancients, for that would give an immortal soul to an opossum or an oyster. Nor need we resort to the separate faculties of the Scotch school, for that would mean a species of entities most accommodating, ready for all work and always in waiting. Nor, finally, need we resort to some being of analogous existence to the immaterial soul of the orthodox, for, if the seat of the soul be in the medullary substance, then has it all the properties of matter. On the contrary, all the mental phenomena are explicable as the phenomena of the body, or attributable to the nature of the society in which we are thrown. For example, a man born and educated in Constantinople will have one set of impressions and associations, one habit of sensation and volition, and a man with a similar arrangement of nervous apparatus, born among the Quakers of Philadelphia, will have another. All this is the result of generating causes extraneous to the system.[2] In this separation of causes into external and internal, Cooper was but applying what he had learned of Hartley's division of motives into those *ab extra* and *ab intra*—the action depending on the compound force of the motions from without and the physiological state of the animal organs at the moment.[3] Of these determining impulses Cooper emphasises the external or environmental. The intellectual faculties, he repeats, vary with education and from habitual difference in the stimuli applied. Suppose the original intellect of two infants exactly the same, the one among the thieves of Broad St. Giles in London, and the other among the best class of Philadelphia Quakers; would their intellect be the same at one and at twenty? Is the soul thus mouldable and changeable? Is the soul infantile as well as the body? [4]

In setting up and knocking down such a man of straw as the

[1] *Arguments in Favour of Materialism,* pp. 339, 352-3.   [2] *Ib.,* p. 351.
[3] *Memoirs,* p. 322.   [4] *Arguments in Favour of Materialism,* p. 352.

ever adult soul, the materialist runs counter to the teachings of his own authorities regarding the activities of the growing mind. But besides losing sight of the possibility of a genetic development, as suggested in Hartley's *Observations* and Darwin's *Zoonomia,* Cooper gives an equally one-sided interpretation to his argument from environment: Man, he holds, is the creature of circumstances in which he is placed, because according to the acknowledged axioms of the schools, the character of the recipient determines the mode of reception of the thing received—*quicquid recipitur, recipitur ad modum recipientis.* Thus a Mussulman and a Calvinist differ in their intellectual powers because of the different impressions and associations to which their nervous system is exposed.[1] Cooper here places the temperamental upon a par with the environmental, and approaches consequently what might be considered a subjective interpretation of his scholastic maxim. At the same time, there is an evident disinclination to consider the subject in any dualistic fashion, and a consequent return to a crudely objective monism—the doctrine of the materiality of the soul, or the singleness of human nature as consisting of the organised body only. All the faculties of an immaterial soul, it is insisted, may be resolved into one simple law of animal organisation, for all the intellectual powers and processes, whether *in potentia* or *in actu,* are dependent on the state of the brain, and, therefore, on the circumstances which have produced this involuntary state of the organ, whatever these circumstances may have been.[2]

But these circumstances—what are they? A suspicion seems to occur to the dogmatic materialist that things may not be altogether what they seem; that the outward and visible reality is, after all, not so easy to grasp. Yet he opines that it is not in favour of Berkeley's hypothesis to say that the external world is an hypothesis to account for our sensations, for it is an hypothesis to which we are driven by the laws of an animal economy. There is, indeed, as much difficulty involved in the fact of sensation or perception as in any powers of reasoning. Both processes are dependent on the properties of the bodily organ employed in them—properties no more explicable than the cause of life, electricity, or gravi-

[1] *Arguments in Favour of Materialism,* p. 371, note.
[2] *Ib.,* p. 371.

tation. If the latter require a soul to explain them, so do the former. If gravitation be an essential property of any given mass of matter, so is perception and thought an essential property of the nervous apparatus of a human being.[1] Cooper clearly fails to realise the force of the Berkeleian contention that ideals may build themselves into the brain, as new forms grow in a crystal. So, with but a momentary glimpse of the part played in the fashioning of the external reality by the constitutive principles of the understanding, he returns to his original attack upon the subjectivists, and concludes by arguing against taking one of the minor Cartesian conjectures with an absurd seriousness: Let us take for granted a soul. Then if the brain can modify the soul, and the soul the brain, are not both the one and the other material—subject to the laws of organic matter? In fine, no light is thrown on the functions of the brain by the supposition of its connection with a being totally and essentially dissimilar in its nature, and having no common property with the matter of which the brain is composed. But if the seat of the soul be in the medullary substance, then has the soul all the properties of matter, and is material. Occupying space, it has solidity, extension, and figure. As the soul is placed there to act on the brain, she has the common properties of all matter, attraction and repulsion, into which all matter can be resolved.[2]

It cannot be said that Cooper's first tract on materialism is a good specimen of his mental furniture. For one thing, it was warped with age. Originally published in England in 1789, it was republished with alterations in Philadelphia some two score years later. Nor can it be held that these alterations were an improvement, when they took the form of local references ranging from the education of young Quakers to the souls of opossums. The treatise, however, is significant as representing a stage in the author's progress toward a pure materialism. Written against the immaterialists Malebranche, Leibniz, the Cambridge Platonists and Descartes,[3] it rid the author's mind of such rubbish as a

---

[1] *Arguments in Favour of Materialism*, p. 372, note.

[2] *Ib.*, pp. 371, note; p. 374, note.

[3] *Tracts, Ethical, Theological and Political*, Warrington Edition, p. 207.

belief in the soul as separate, immaterial, and immortal—*a parte ante* or *a parte post*. Meanwhile, influenced by Hartley's 'great work,' he inveighs against a gratuitous theory of the soul in addition to the visible, corporeal frame,[1] and finally reaches an explicitness of negation not previously known in America. That explicitness is due to a mass of fresh material pouring in from a new source. Sojourning in France, and coming again under French influences in South Carolina, Cooper published in 1831 a translation of Broussais' *On Irritation and Insanity*. That volume, he claimed, was the most recent exposition of the physiological doctrines of medicine of the modern French school, and a refutation of the metaphysical doctrines of psychology. The author therein examines the ontological and psychological notions which clerical metaphysics have introduced into physiology, and shows that we have no right to assume the existence of any hypothetical entity to account for the intellectual phenomena.[2] Fortified in publishing such a work by the earlier approval of the sage of Monticello, the translator is emboldened to remark that only those who have studied Hartley, Priestley, Cabanis, Destutt de Tracy and Broussais, will know how to estimate the vague and wordy discussions of the Scotch school. To the translation of Broussais Cooper appends his last and liveliest brochure, an essay *On the Association of Ideas*. This, he tells us, originated from reading Blair and Lord Kames during his course of lectures in the University of South Carolina, and noting their deficiencies. Appealing to his favourite triumvirate—Hartley, Darwin, and Priestley—and in addition to Archbishop King in his *Origin of Evil*, and to Locke in his chapter on the association of ideas, Cooper seeks to oust from the seat of authority the orthodox psychologists who offend no popular prejudices, run counter to no clerical doctrines. To this end, he revises his former animadversions against 'Reid and Company,' who, employing common sense as a *clavis universalis*, have appealed to innate and instinctive principles, and have criticised Hartley without understanding him. Reid, Oswald, Beattie, Dugald Stewart, and Thomas Brown have had their day; their system, having enjoyed the decided suffrage of modern authority in the universities

---

[1] *Memoirs*, p. 316. [2] Preface, p. vi.

of Europe and our country, is fast losing ground. But the anatomists and physicians of England and France, together with the followers of Dr. Priestley, are of the opinion that mental phenomena can be explained from the properties of the organised body, without the intervention of any distinct, immaterial principle—such as the soul is described to be—provided the property of perception or feeling be allowed to belong to or arise from our organisation. Here there is a constant concomitance on which to build the case of necessary connection, for mental phenomena have never been observed unless in conjunction with a corporeal organised system, depending on the healthy state of the nervous system, disordered by its derangement, growing old with the body, and ceasing to be when the body dies.[1]

Having kicked the props from under his opponents, the controversialist proceeds to undermine the fundamental principles of his very authorities. When Locke, treating of trains of motions in the animal spirits, implies that the physiological explanation of mentality was inadequate,[2] Cooper still holds to his persuasion that no theory of the mind can be satisfactory which is not founded on the history of the body.[3] So far as he can yet see, every intellectual fact is no other than the usual normal function or mode of action of the brain, some modification of the cerebral viscus. And yet it may be asked: When these motions along the course of the nerves reach the brain, is there in that organ any common sensorium, any seat of perception located in some particular part? Newton, Hartley and Broussais adopt the opinion that there is such a spot. Darwin's opinion makes it pervade the whole nervous system, his sensorial power being coextensive with nervous ramifications. And yet, for all that, there is no proof either from anatomy or physiology, that will establish such a locality.[4] Cooper next doubts the theories of his predecessors not only as to the location of intellectual motions, but as to their modes of representation. That the impression or stimulation is propagated by some kind of motion along the course of the brain is true, but the hypotheses

[1] *Association of Ideas*, pp. 380-383.
[2] *Human Understanding* (Fraser Edition), Vol. 1, p. 530.
[3] *Memoirs*, p. 333.   [4] *Association of Ideas*, pp. 384, 385.

as to the kind of motion are dubious. There is no proof that it is a vibratory motion, an oscillation of the body or of the cord of the nerve, because the nerves are nothing like the stretched cords of a harpsichord. Nor is there any proof that the particles of which the nerves are composed are put into a vibratory motion by the ether. And while it is also true that the nerves secrete some kind of subtle fluid, which is the subject of these successive impulses or vibrations, yet what this fluid is has never been shown. It is probable that the galvanic fluid is the agent on this occasion, but this is only an opinion as yet. So although no theory can be framed on this subject, yet the motion of something or other must take place. When it does so, and is in some way or other communicated from the sentient extremity to the medullary substance of the brain, it is there felt, or, as the now adopted phrase is, perceived. Every sensation is therefore essentially a motion of the brain perceived.[1] After all these negations something positive might be expected from so dogmatic a thinker as Cooper, but he candidly says he advances no theory of his own or of others, but simply gives facts familiar to every physiologist who has ever turned his attention to the catenation of stimulations and motions in the nervous fibre. Such facts are the Hobbite conception of idea, the Hartleian of sensation, and the Humean of the association of ideas.

The rest of Cooper's treatise is somewhat of a réchauffé, at the same time it exhibits his knack of making stale materials appetising. Thus he tells how, when an idea is very complex, the combination may overpower the particular parts, just as in a well made punch we do not recognise the acid, the sugar, the spirit or the lemon flavour particularly, but find them all merged in the combination. This sounds trivial, but with all his illustrations and analogies the South Carolinian was by no means a mere populariser of prevalent notions. As he had expressed doubts of his predecessors, so he questions the results of contemporary researches. For example, he contends that the doctrine of equivocal generation, or of life being the result of any form of organised matter to which it did not previously belong, is not established by the few dubious

[1] *Association of Ideas*, pp. 381-382.

instances of Darwin, Baillie, and Lamarck. In fact, it is not known whether perception be a property of organisation in those animals that have a nervous system, or whether it belong essentially to life; whether life owed its existence to the organisation with which it is connected, or to the original gift of the creator, in which case organisation will be a property or result of life previously imparted, and not life a property or result of organisation.[1] While this seems like materialistic heresy yet these dubieties in the application of materialism do not invalidate the doctrine itself. In a final passage Cooper throws the burden of proof on the other side and leaves the question open: How, by what organic mechanism, this association and catenation of sensations, ideas, volitions, and cerebral motions with each other takes place—what is the immediate rationale of the process—who can tell? I do not pretend to offer any explanation of this, but the facts will be facts. The combinations of matter and motion that we can put together will no more explain the life of a plant, than the volition of a man; but in neither case do we see anything else. To say that it is impossible that matter and motion should produce the timid shrinking of a sensitive plant, or the retreat of a child from a disagreeable object, is, to say the least, a very presumptuous limitation of the powers of nature, within the limits prescribed by our own ignorance.[2]

Here end the philosophical musings of a remarkable man, the former chartist and perennial agitator whom President Adams had wished to have removed from the country. And now denounced and tried as an infidel, forced by the legislature to resign his presidency of the South Carolina College, Cooper's last days were troubled and his influence not what it should have been. As he put it, he led the life of a toad under a harrow. In philosophy, particularly, he was as much of a nullifier as he was in politics. A final review of his speculative writings will disclose the wide range of his negations. Starting with a denial both of pure spirit and of matter as an inert, lifeless thing, he doubted both the immaterialist's conception of a soul as separate and distinct from the body,[3] and the Hartleian conception of the same entity as a very fine etherial substance, added to the body and surviving it.[4] In the

[1] *Association of Ideas*, p. 397.   [2] *Ib.*, p. 408.   [3] Broussais, p. 37.
[4] *Association of Ideas*, p. 383.

next place, questioning the existence of any consciousness different from feeling or perception of motions excited in the brain, he asserted that we do not know positively whether the instrument of motion or that substance in which the movement takes place be the particles of the nerve, or an unknown secreted nervous fluid, or a secreted galvanic fluid.[1] But in spite of the difficulty of conceiving how any mere modification of unthinking matter can become thinking matter; and in spite of the uncertainty as to Newton's ether, or its modern substitute, the electric fluid, being any essential part of the nervous mechanism, some kind of motion there certainly is; its existence in the brain is unquestionable; and this, with the law of association, will explain all the activities of the human system of organised matter, with its visible parts and sensible properties.[2]

Cooper is indeed both agnostic and dogmatist. After a complex series of negations, he has ended in a simple assertion. This tendency toward simplification is further exhibited in his favouring the mechanical theory of the will as against the libertarian; in his hostility to the realistic multiplication of the faculties; and lastly, in resolving his system of human nature into a sort of positivistic religion of humanity. These basic principles are illustrated by such passages as the following: For the confutation of what is ignorantly called freedom of the will, one may read Hartley and Collins, Priestley and Hobbes, and Jonathan Edwards of New England. But to the physiologist all this reading will be superfluous. . . . The faculties of the soul have no existence; they are words only, the counters employed in reasoning, convenient signs of arrangement like the plus and minus. . . . The time is approaching when metaphysics will rank among the sciences that lay claim, if not to absolute demonstration, yet to an approximation to certainty sufficient for all the purposes of ethical reasoning and all the practical duties of human life.[3]

This anticipation of positivism twenty years before Comte began his lectures, fifty years before his system was introduced into the country by Harriet Martineau, is certainly remarkable. At

---

[1] *Association of Ideas*, p. 397.
[2] *The Scripture Doctrine of Materialism*, p. 310.
[3] *Arguments in Favour of Materialism*, p. 408; *Memoir*, p. 336.

the same time its appearance was unseasonable. An important endeavour to work out the principles of the Anglo-French sensationalism, it had no tangible results. Conceived in a decidedly Gallic
section of the South, it exerted not a fraction of the influence of the
later Comteanism of the North.[1] There was a double reason for
this. Cooper raised up enemies in front and rear by opposing all
a priori speculations and by attempting to sift everything down to a
few general principles. In particular, by casting reflections on the
existence both of the faculties and of the soul itself, he stirred up
both the Scotch-American realist and the New England transcendentalist. Consequently, what was left of his remains by the
one, was torn to shreds by the other. The associational side was
mangled by the Princeton school in their strictures upon the Hartleian and Priestleian tenets; the sensational by the Concord school
in their onslaught upon a philosophy which located the sentient
principle in man in the material substance of the brain. Instead
of immortality and liberty being the *species intelligibiles* of the old
schoolmen—as Cooper expressed it—they counted them realities
provable by the most valid arguments. So it was that the materialist's extremity was the transcendentalist's opportunity. In
place of a reliance upon organised matter, the motions of nervous
fluids, the changes of the cerebral viscus, they put their trust in a
substantial soul, subjective intuitions, the ideas of pure reason.
The physiologist might relish the former, they preferred the latter.

But this is anticipating the movements of a later day. In spite
of this constitutional incompatibility of thinking between the North
and the South, there was a place where materialism and its opposites could meet. This middle ground was, curiously enough, to be
found in one of the Middle States. It was the philanthropic physician, Benjamin Rush, of Pennsylvania, who, trained as a realist,
confirmed in his belief in spiritual realities, nevertheless found materialism a most useful working hypothesis. To this mediating
scholar of the Philadelphia school we shall next turn our attention.

[1] Compare also John Fiske, *Cosmic Philosophy*, 1874.

CHAPTER VI

BENJAMIN RUSH

DR. BENJAMIN RUSH, (1745-1813) of Philadelphia, was the most conspicuous of the American medical materialists of the eighteenth century. Born of English stock in Pennsylvania, at school under the Reverend Samuel Finley, the later head of Nassau Hall, then at Princton itself under President Samuel Davies, he learned the rudiments of medicine from Dr. John Redman. Obtaining his medical degree in Edinburgh University, walking the London hospitals, and helped by Franklin to study in Paris, he returned to America in 1769 and became in turn professor in chemistry in the Medical College of Philadelphia, physician-general of the continental army of the middle department, and professor of the institutes of medicine in the new University of Pennsylvania.[1]

Subjected to the varying influences of Anglo-American deism, Scottish realism, and British and French materialism, Rush's philosophical remains range from an undergraduate transcription of the metaphysical system of Dr. Davies, and a translation at the age of seventeen of the *Aphorisms of Hippocrates,* to his *Thoughts on Common Sense,* and a final volume on the *Diseases of the Mind.* It was in regard to this last work that he made the interesting statement that the diseases of the brain should be watched, since they often produce discoveries of the secret powers of the mind; like convulsions of the earth, which throw up metals and precious stones, they would otherwise have been unknown forever.[2]

As in his speculations Rush was a living compromise between various divergent schools of thought, so in his numerous public activities he was a personal paradox: in politics a signer of the Declaration, yet a maligner of the military genius of Washington;

[1] Reprinted from the *Johns Hopkins Hospital Bulletin,* March, 1907.
[2] Purnell MS., p. 50.

in education an agent in bringing President Witherspoon to Princeton and President Nisbet to Dickinson, yet a philistine as regards
the study of the classics; in philanthropy an opponent of capital
punishment and of slavery, yet a believer in the most drastic measures to stamp out the yellow fever; in medicine a pioneer in psychiatry, yet the originator of a species of phrenology. The dual
nature of the man is outwardly shown in his portrait, which represents him in a pensive and yet self-conscious attitude, his head in
his hand, but one eye cocked on the observer. So, from his works
and his looks Rush may be judged to be rather profuse than profound,—a hard-headed philosopher, dealing in what he was pleased
to call the practical metaphysics of the mind. Mere theories did
not disturb him. When at Edinburgh he was thrown with David
Hume, but no traces of that subtle sceptic are to be found in his
thought. At home he received from Jefferson a confidential copy
of the *Syllabus of the Doctrines of Jesus,*[1] but that did not shake
his orthodox beliefs.

In a word, Rush was an eclectic. He took what he wanted and
left what he did not like. Consistency was not his, for he was
influenced in turn by deism, realism, and materialism. The influence of the first appears in the teleological trimmings of his system,
the moral bearings he gave to his physiology and psychology. Like
Hartley, he was not content with examining man's frame, but extended his observations to his duty and his expectations. Likewise
in his realism the good doctor was wont to pick and choose. For
common sense he found use at first rather in a political than in a
philosophical way. He had suggested the term as a title for
Thomas Paine's revolutionary pamphlet of 1775, but by 1791 he
writes that he had long suspected the term to be applied improperly to designate a faculty of the mind.[2] Here he will not repeat
the accounts which have been given of it, from Cicero and Berkeley to Hobbes and Hume, but will confine himself to differing
with Reid's account of the matter. Instead, then, of considering it
a faculty or part of a faculty, possessing a quick and universal perception of right and wrong, truth and error in human affairs—he

---

[1] Jefferson's *Works,* Ford. ed., Vol. 8, p. 223. Letter to Rush, April 21,
1803.

[2] *Thoughts on Common Sense,* p. 249.

will define it simply as opinions and feelings in unison with the opinions and feelings of the bulk of mankind. From this definition it is evident that common sense must vary with the progress of taste, science, and religion. Thus it is contrary to common sense to speak in favour of republicanism in Europe or of monarchy in America; it is contrary to common sense to use opium, bark, mercury, or the lancet, but agreeable to it to revenge public and private injuries by wars and duels; common sense in Great Britain and the United States is in favour of boys spending four or five years in learning Latin and Greek, whereas it is contrary to right reason to teach them words before they are taught ideas. In fine, to say that a man has common sense, is to say that he thinks with his age and country, in their false, as well as their true opinions. After all that has been said in its favour, one cannot help thinking that it is the characteristic only of common minds. Had this common sense depended upon the information of the five external senses, one would have no difficulty in admitting Dr. Reid's account of it. But to suppose it the first act of the reason, and afterwards to suppose it to be universal is to contradict everything that history and observation teach us of human nature. And yet in the progress of knowledge, when the exact connection between the senses and reason is perfectly understood, it is probable that the two will be in unison with each other, but this unison as in the case of vision—where the reason connects the distance of objects with the evidence of the eye—must be the result only of experience and habit.[1]

To judge from this diatribe against the doubtful faculties of taste and intuition,[2] Rush must have suffered from that overdose of realism which he got in his undergraduate days and while a student at the Scottish capital. The reaction sent him over into the English materialism. The transition between the two is exactly marked by the title of his best known essay, the *Influence of Physical Causes upon the Moral Faculty*. Delivered before the American Philosophical Society in 1786, this exhibits a vocabulary borrowed from speculative Edinburgh, but an application suitable to utilitarian Philadelphia. The moral faculty, to borrow the term

[1] *Thoughts on Common Sense*, pp. 251-4.
[2] Purnell MS., p. 81.

of Beattie, may be called the moral sense of Hutcheson, the sympathy of Adam Smith, the moral instinct of Rousseau, the regula regulans of the schoolmen; it may be a native principle, a capacity in the human mind of distinguishing good and evil, a faculty quick in its operations, and like the sensitive plant acting without reflection—it may be all these things, and yet, at the same time, be subject to physical influences. Do we observe a connection between the intellectual faculties and the degrees of consistency and firmness of the brain in infancy and childhood? The same connection has been observed between the strength as well as the progress of the moral faculty in children. Do we observe instances of a total want of memory, imagination, and judgment, either from an original defect in the stamina of the brain, or from the influence of physical causes? The same unnatural defect has been observed, and probably from the same causes, of a moral faculty. A nervous fever may cause the loss not only of the memory but of the habit of veracity. The former is called amnesia, the latter unnamed malady will compel a woman, be she even in easy circumstances, to fill her pocket secretly with bread at the table of a friend.[1]

For instances and reasonings like these, drawn from his own experience and practice, Rush has been designated the father of psychiatry in America.[2] In venturing upon this untrodden ground the doctor confesses that he feels like Æneas when he was about to enter the gates of Avernus, but without a Sibyl to instruct him in the mysteries before him. He therefore begins with an attempt to supply the defects of nosological writers by naming the partial or weakened action of the moral faculty *micronomia,* its total absence *anomia.* But to name these derangements is not to explain them; they may be caused not only by madness, hysteria, and hypochondriasis, but also by all those states of the body which are accompanied by preternatural irritability, sensibility, torpor, stupor, or mobility of the nervous system. It is vain to attack these accompanying vices, whether of the body or of the mind, with lec-

---

[1] *Moral Faculty,* pp. 6, 7.

[2] W. Pepper. *Journal of the American Medical Association,* April 26, 1890, p. 6, note 2.

tures upon morality. They are only to be cured by medicine and proper treatment. Thus the young woman, previously mentioned, that lost her habit of veracity by a nervous fever, recovered this virtue as soon as her system recovered its natural tone.[1] Furthermore, it makes no difference whether the physical causes that are to be enumerated act upon the moral faculty through the medium of the senses, the passions and memory, or the imagination. Their action is equally certain whether they act as remote, predisposing, or occasional cases. For instance, the state of the weather has an unfriendly effect upon the moral sensibility, as seen in the gloomy November fogs of England; so does extreme hunger, as in the case of the Indians of this country, who thus whet their appetite for that savage species of warfare peculiar to them. Again, the influence of association upon morals is strong. Suicide is often propagated by the newspapers and monstrous crimes by the publication of court proceedings. And as physical causes influence moral, so do they influence religious principles. Religious melancholy and madness will yield more readily to medicine than simply to polemical discourses or casuistical advice.[2]

In this presentation of the influence of physical causes upon the moral faculty, its advocate anticipates the objection raised to it, from its being supposed to favour the materiality of the soul. And yet he does not see that this doctrine obliges us to decide upon the question of the nature of the soul, any more than the facts which prove the influence of physical causes upon the memory, the imagination, or the judgment. The writers in favour of the immortality of the soul have done that truth great injury, by connecting it necessarily with its immateriality. The immortality of the soul depends upon the will of the Creator, and not upon the supposed properties of spirit. Matter is, in its own nature, as immortal as spirit. It is resolvable by heat and mixture into a variety of forms; but it requires the same almighty hand to annihilate it, that it did to create it. It would be as reasonable to assert that the basin of the ocean is immortal from the greatness of its capacity to hold water, or that we are to live forever in this world, because we are afraid of dying—as to maintain the immortality of the soul from

[1] *Moral Faculty*, p. 26.   [2] *Ib.*, pp. 42, 47.

the greatness of its capacity for knowledge and happiness, or from its dread of annihilation.[1] On another occasion and in a less figurative way, Rush strove to disentangle the popular confusion between these two concepts. The writers to whom he now specifically refers are Plato and Cicero, Locke and Priestley. Regarding the nature of the mind, he says, the two first suppose it to be immaterial and independent of the body. Locke supposes it to consist of a matter, exquisitely fine, and connected with the body; that it is incapable of existence without the body, but that it does not perish with the body. Priestley supposes that there is no such thing as a mind either material or immaterial. With this meagre reference to the Northumberland advocate of the homogeneity of man, the student who took these notes passes with unconcealed delight to a doctrine apparently different from all the variant forms, ancient and modern. Dr. Rush, he explains, believes that the mind is immaterial, that it can exist independently of the body, and that there is no necessary connection between the immateriality and immortality of the mind, the one being a divine attribute, the other a divine gift.[2]

Returning from this digression, the immaterialistic materialist comes to a defence of his main proposition—the universal and essential existence of a moral faculty in the human mind. He apologises for presuming to differ from such a justly celebrated oracle as Locke, yet holds that the latter has confounded this moral principle with reason, just as Lord Shaftesbury has confounded it with taste, since all three of these faculties agree in the objects of their approbation, notwithstanding they exist in the mind independently of each other.[3] One may admit with Locke that some savage nations are totally devoid of the moral faculty, yet it will by no means follow that this was the original constitution of their minds. As well might we assert, because savages destroy their beauty by painting, that the principles of taste do not exist naturally in the human mind. It is with virtue as with fire. It exists in the mind as fire does in certain bodies, in a latent or quiescent state. As collision renders the one sensible, so education renders the other visible. It would be as absurd to maintain, because olives

[1] *Moral Faculty*, p. 19. [2] Purnell MS., p. 81.
[3] *Moral Faculty*, p. 17.

become agreeable to many people from habit, that we have no natural appetite for food, as to assert that any part of the human species exists without a moral principle, because in some of them it has wanted causes to excite it into action, or has been perverted by example. There are appetites that are wholly artificial. There are tastes so entirely vitiated as to perceive beauty in deformity. There are torpid and unnatural passions. Why, under certain unfavourable conditions, may there not exist also a moral faculty, in a state of sleep, or subject to mistakes? [1] Ending with one of the author's habitual rhetorical flourishes this passage leaves an impression of weakness. But while it makes the moral principle a poor thing, incapable of effecting positive results, leading to nowhere in particular, the suggestion as to artificial and vitiated tastes opened a fruitful line of inquiry, leading indirectly to the last and most important work on the diseases of the mind.

Having considered the influence of physical causes upon the moral faculty, Rush next takes up ' the influence of physical causes in promoting an increase of strength and activity of the intellectual faculties of man.' Delivered as an introductory lecture to his students in 1799, it exhibits a growing tendency towards materialism, together with a more cautious avoidance of metaphysical speculations. The writer confines himself only to those agents which increase the quantity of mind, leaving the causes which lessen it to a later pathology. He then passes by the knotty questions of the theoretical nature of the mind, deeming it sufficient for his present inquiry to believe that all its operations are the effects of bodily impressions, a belief according with the axiom of the schools— *nihil est in intellectu quod non prius fuit in sensu.*[2]

In employing the trite maxim of sensationalism and treating the mind as if it were a pint measure, the speaker is but adapting his remarks to the capacities of his hearers. Desiring to present facts intelligible to the youngest student of medicine, he brings in anecdotes which savour more of natural history than of mental philosophy. Such are the bits of information that Jonathan Edwards rode a trotting horse to stimulate his thoughts; that Joseph Priestley, in order to strengthen his faculties, used to write upon every subject which he wished to understand perfectly; that in republics

---

[1] *Moral Faculty,* pp. 15, 16.   [2] *Intellectual Faculties,* p. 88.

mental vigour is increased by the frequency of general elections. In citing these miscellaneous cases with all their triviality Rush, nevertheless, has a serious purpose. It is to calculate the degrees of vigour, and the number and exility of motions which the mind is capable of receiving. It is by the exercise of the body and the collision of our intellects, by means of business and conversation, that we impart to them agreeable and durable vigour. The effects of this action and reaction, in making addition to the intellects and knowledge, lead us to admit the assertion of Condorcet that the time will come, when all the knowledge we now possess will appear to the generations that are to succeed us, as the knowledge now possessed by children appears to us. . . . From what has been delivered, gentlemen, it appears that the enlargement and activity of our intellects are as much within our power as the health and movements of our bodies.[1] This is the characteristic conclusions of an introductory lecture to the study of medicine. To judge from certain manuscript notes of one of the doctor's pupils the others resemble it in being full of wise saws and modern instances: for example, the brain is like the lower limbs, if exercised it lasts; as the body is stimulated by air, so the mind is stimulated by motives; the faculties may be compared to a well-organised government: the memory and imagination to the House of Representatives, the understanding to the Senate, in which the transactions of the House of Representatives are examined, the moral faculties to the Courts of Justice, the conscience to the Court of Appeals.[2]

The works of the Philadelphian thus far are popular and superficial. With their abundant illustrations, from classical allusions to local anecdotes, they bear out John Adams' estimate of Rush as an elegant and ingenious body, but too much of a talker to be a deep thinker.[3] But this stricture can only in a measure be passed upon the next production of Rush's middle period, the *Three Lectures upon Animal Life*. The author is here more modest in his claims, in proportion as he is more thorough in his results. He disclaims being the source of the great and original conception upon which they are founded, confessing that he has done little more than carry the hod to assist in completing a part of the fabric

[1] *Intellectual Faculties*, pp. 114, 117.   [2] Purnell MS., p. 96.
[3] *Works*, Vol. 2, p. 427.

of which the foundations were already laid.[1] It was while a student in the University of Edinburgh in 1766 that he heard Dr. Cullen deliver the opinion that the human body is not an automaton, or self-moving machine, but is kept alive and in motion by the constant action of stimuli upon it. This opinion, which Rush repeated in one of his own lectures as early as 1771, he now enlarges into three general propositions concerning the human body, namely: that every part of it is endowed with sensibility; that it is a unit, a simple and indivisible quality of substance; and finally, that life is the effect of certain stimuli acting upon the sensibility and excitability, which are extended in different degrees over every external and internal part of the body. These stimuli are as necessary to its existence as air is to flame. Included, moreover, in animal life are motion, sensation, and thought. These three, when united, compose perfect life. The term motion is here preferable to those of oscillation or vibration, as employed by Dr. Hartley in explaining the laws of animal life, because it is more simple and better adapted to common apprehension.[2]

To this modified materialism the American now proceeds to attach a peculiar form of realism. In opposition to the Hartleian leaning toward monism he sets a form of pluralism: man is not a machine whose parts, however complex, are homogeneous, but he is rather a number of entities acted upon by a variety of forces. Or as Rush puts it, in addition to the external stimuli like heat and light, and the internal like the action of the brain, and the pulsation of the arteries, there are the intellectual stimuli arising from the exercises of the faculties of the mind itself. Thus the imagination acts with great force upon the body, and the passions pour a constant stream upon the wheels of life.[3]

Like a good realist the author has hypostatised the faculties. Yet he does not leave them hovering in mid air as mere empty quiddities. To the mind of the materialist, thought itself is the effect of stimuli acting upon the organs of sense and motion. Furthermore, the exercises of the faculties of the mind have a wonderful influence in increasing the quantity of human life. They all act by reflection only, after having been previously excited into action by impressions made upon the body. This view of the reaction of

[1] *Animal Life,* preface, p. v.   [2] *Ib.,* pp. 5-7.   [3] *Ib.,* p. 6.

the mind upon the body accords with the simplicity of other operations in the animal economy. Finally, common language justi-
fies the opinion of the stimulus of the understanding upon the
brain, hence it is common to say of dull men, that they have
scarcely ideas enough to keep themselves awake. And so, contrary to the picture of the Indian character drawn by Rousseau,
their vacant countenances are to be attributed to the effects of the
want of action in their brains from a deficiency of ideas. Again,
atheism does violence to the mental faculties by robbing man of
his most sublime beliefs, abstracting his thoughts from the most
perfect of all possible objects. This is demonstrated by the theophi-
lanthropists, who, after rejecting the true God, have instituted
the worship of nature, of fortune, and of the human race.[1]

In these curious illustrations of a quantitative conception of
mentality Rush's psychology threatens to degenerate into a sort of
arithmetic of the mind, for along with the minus side in his table of
values there is the plus. Thus the whole animal machine may be
set in motion by the love of money, as was shown in the Philadelphia panic of 1791, when speculation over the scrip of the United
States Bank excited febrile diseases in three of the doctor's patients.
Similar mental stimuli are furnished by political conditions; many
facts prove animal life to exist in a larger quantity in the enlightened and happy State of Connecticut, in which republican liberty
has existed above one hundred and fifty years, than in any other
country upon the surface of the globe.[2] These strange generalisations, concerning the larger aspects of animal life, do not prevent
the author from taking up the smaller phenomena, the minuter influences in the psychic life. Speaking of slight sounds which it is
not necessary should excite sensation or perception, in order to
their exerting a degree of stimulus, he adds: there are a hundred
impressions made daily upon the body, which from habit are not
followed by sensation; the stimulus of the blood upon the heart
and arteries probably ceases to be felt only from the influence of
habit. It is unfortunate that we forget what passed in our minds
the first two or three years of our lives. Could we recollect the
manner in which we acquired our first ideas, and the progress of
our knowledge with the evolution of our senses and faculties, it

[1] *Animal Life*, pp. 19, 20, 67.   [2] *Ib.*, pp. 64, 62.

wouid relieve us from many difficulties and controversies upon
this subject. Perhaps this forgetfulness by children of the origin
and progress of their knowledge might be remedied by our attending more closely to the first effects of impressions, sensation, and
perception upon them as discovered by their little actions, all of
which probably have a meaning as determined as any of the actions
of men or women.[1]

By piecing together the broken hints of his authorities, from
Leibniz on minute perceptions to Reid on how the infant faculties
begin to grow, Rush in a measure advances the genetic point of
view. But that suggestive method is again unfortunately spoiled
by a quantitative misconception. In his attempt to be precise, the
materialist verges toward an accurate arithmetic rather than a
trustworthy psychology. In other words, the American realist,
following the lead of the Scotch, has attempted to obtain a distinct
and full history of the mind of the child; but the result is scarcely
'a treasure of natural history.' Nor is the succeeding disquisition,
which seeks to establish the principle that animal life in every species depends on the same causes as in the human body. But what
is of interest here is the cautious conclusion reached by the former
dogmatist: From a review of what has been said of animal life in
all its numerous forms and modifications, we see that it is as much
an effect of impressions upon a peculiar species of matter, as sound
is of the stroke of a hammer upon a bell, or music of the motion
of a bow upon the strings of a violin. I exclude, therefore, the
intelligent principle of Whytt, the medical mind of Stahl, the
healing powers of Cullen, and the vital principle of John Hunter
as much from the body, as I do an intelligent principle from air,
fire, and water. . . . It is not necessary to be acquainted with
the precise nature of that form of matter which is capable of producing life from impressions made upon it. It is sufficient for our
purpose to know the fact. It is immaterial moreover whether this
matter derive its power of being acted upon wholly from the brain,
or whether it be in part inherent in animal fibres. The inferences
are the same in favour of animal life being the effect of stimuli,
and of its being as truly mechanical as the movements of a clock
from the pressure of its weights. . . . Should it be asked

[1] *Animal Life,* p. 11.

what is the peculiar organisation of matter, which enables it to emit life, when acted upon by stimuli, I answer, I do not know.[1]

Notwithstanding his agnostic conclusion regarding man as a machine, Rush has something to say on the practical application of his doctrine to metaphysics and morality. It enables us to reject the doctrine of innate ideas, and to ascribe all our knowledge of sensible objects to impressions acting upon an innate capacity to receive ideas. Were it possible for a child to grow up to manhood without the use of any of its senses, it would not possess a single idea of a material object; and as all human knowledge is composed of simple ideas, this person would be as destitute of knowledge of every kind, as the grossest portion of vegetable or fossil matter.[2] Again, the account which has been given of animal life furnishes a striking illustration of the origin of human actions by the impressions of motives upon the will. As well might we admit an inherent principle of life in animal matter, as a self-determining power in this faculty of the mind. Motives are necessary not only to constitute its freedom, but its essence; for without them there could be no more will than there could be vision without light, or hearing without sound. It is true they are often so obscure as not to be perceived, and they sometimes become insensible from habit, but the same things have been remarked in the operation of stimuli; and yet we do not on this account deny their agency in producing animal life. In thus deciding in favour of the necessity of motives to produce actions, I cannot help bearing testimony against the gloomy misapplication of this doctrine by some modern writers. When properly understood it is calculated to produce the most comfortable views of the divine government and the most beneficial effects upon morals and human happiness.[3]

Thus far the system of Rush exhibits the three familiar marks of materialism, namely, a phenomenalistic view of substance, a sensationalistic of perception, a deterministic of volition. Now there are added certain incongruous elements. Seeking to apply his doctrine to the sphere of theology, the Philadelphian embellishes it with remnants both of an earlier deism and even of that Edwardean occasionalism, which had not been obliterated when

[1] *Animal Life*, pp. 73, 74, 75.   [2] *Ib.*, p. 78.   [3] *Ib.*, pp. 79, 80.

Rush was an undergraduate at Princeton. The best criterion of the truth of a philosophical opinion, he continues, is its tendency to produce exalted ideas of the Divine Being and humble views of ourselves. The doctrine of animal life which has been delivered is calculated to produce these effects in an eminent degree. It does homage to the Supreme Being as the governor of the universe, and establishes the certainty of his universal and particular providence. Admit a principle of life in the human body and we open a door for the restoration of the old Epicurean or atheistical philosophy, which supposed the world to be governed by a principle called nature, and which was believed to be inherent in every kind of matter. The doctrine I have taught cuts the sinews of this error, for by rendering the continuance of animal life, no less than its commencement, the effect of the constant operation of divine power and goodness, it leads us to believe that the whole creation is supported in the same manner.[1]

To this last observation of the last lecture on *Animal Life* Rush at some later period added a disquisition on *Liberty and Necessity.* As extracted from his unpublished *Letters and Thoughts,* and containing an erased passage of no small originality, it will bear generous quotation:

Is it not absurd to talk of *past* or *future* when we speak of the knowledge of the Deity? Can anything be *past* or *future* to a being who exists from eternity to eternity? Are not past, present, and future to *Him,* one eternal *now?* Is not time a finite idea only, and past and future knowable only to finite beings? May not the moral actions of men then have appeared as complete to the Deity at the creation as the *material* world? I see the objects of a plain before me as distinctly as if I were near it. My view of it has no influence on its form or distance; the same probably occurs to the Deity with respect to pre-existing actions. Imperfect man by *memory sees* past events—a wonderful power in a finite mind! May not a perfect being see future events in the same manner? They all have an existence in the eternal mind. *There is nothing truly new* in actions, any more than in truths *under the sun.* There can be no contingency with the Deity—all is fixed and immutable with Him; cause and effect, *motive* and *action,* creation and preservation, all one simple object and act. . . . The perfections of the Deity require this solution of this doctrine. *Prescience* is

[1] *Animal Life,* p. 81.

only a human term, but, like many others applied to the Deity in
accommodation to our weak capacities. Prophecies are to Him
things present; to us things to come—hence their great accuracy.
It is improper and dishonourable to His glorious Oneness in existence as well as nature. It is impossible matters should be otherwise. Succession belongs only to man. God can do and know
nothing in succession. So far for necessity. But all this is compat-
ible with the most perfect liberty. The knowledge of God of actions flows from a perfect knowledge of the union between cause
and effect in creation. All is still free. An artist can tell from
the construction of a machine exactly its strokes, etc., without
touching it after its wheels are set in motion, although he still upholds it in his hand. We still live, move and have our being in
God. . . . Nor does this idea destroy man's responsibility.
He is still free. His liberty is essential to the necessity—otherwise
his action would have no moral nature and could not be the object
of pardon, and for this purpose alone evil existed. It must be free
to be a crime, and crimes existed, not for a display of vindictive
justice in endless punishment, but for the display of love in justice
in endless and universal happiness. This removes all the fears and
difficulties about moral necessity. It was necessary that man should
fall—it was likewise necessary that he should be *free,* or he could
not have fallen. Liberty and necessity are, therefore, both true,
and both necessary to advance in due consistency all the glorious
attributes of God. This union of liberty and necessity may be
illustrated by a simple example: [1. I walk on the deck of a
ship. Here is one free motion—the helmsman steers the ship in
the direction in which I walk, and yet I am not influenced by his
helm, nor he by my walking; we both direct our course the same
way—he, by pointing the bow of the ship, makes me keep the
same course with him, but without my knowledge or his influence
over my will. 2. I resolve to take a walk to an adjoining village.
This is the first act of my will. On my way I forget the original
act of my will and occupy it upon twenty other objects, none of
which have any connection with the first. Here then is a will
within a will.] I require a perfect knowledge of a man's taste
in building, and then convey secretly into his hands a plan of a
house. Every act of this man in building this house is foreknown
by me, and yet no influence is exercised over his will. Here is
necessity and liberty united.[1]

This is a reactionary document, betraying the conflict between
the spirit of orthodoxy and the spirit of free inquiry. As a projected addition to the essays on *Animal Life* it explains the oppo-

[1] Ridgway MS., *Letters and Thoughts,* pp. 28-30.

sition to the revival of the ancient ' atheism ' and also the closing confession that the author feels as if he had waded across a rapid and dangerous stream. The figure is a good one; it exhibits Rush as conscious of the drift of his speculations. And yet in opposing his dualistic occasionalism to a monistic hylozoism, he was but vainly struggling against the tendency of materialism toward a single unitary principle—the reduction of both mind and matter to modifications of the same common substance. That tendency as regards anthropology, if not cosmology, is manifested in the opening passage of the next lecture *On the Utility of a Knowledge of the Faculties and Operations of the Mind to a Physician.* Here man is said to be a compound of soul and body. However this language may be in religion, it is not so in medicine. He is, in the eye of a physician, a single and indivisible being, for so intimately united are his soul and body that one cannot be moved without the other.[1] This is the doctrine of the homogeneity of man. In substituting it for his earlier dualism, Rush was undoubtedly influenced by his friend Priestley, who had read the Philadelphian's earlier lectures and called them sublimely speculative.[2] But while this supplementary lecture begins with a decided monistic turn, its force is speedily dissipated by the intrusion of pluralistic arguments—the dividing up of an indissoluble being into separate faculties. Among these are included not only memory, imagination, and understanding, but in addition, the principle of faith, the passions, the moral faculty, conscience, and a sense of deity.[3] Disregarding Locke's warning against supposing the faculties to stand for some real beings in the soul,[4] Rush has weakened his initial plan by the assumption that there are minds within a mind, extra agents within a single agent. Nevertheless, this complexity has its practical side. Like the modern assumption of selves split off from the self, multiple personalities within one body, it calls attention to the intimate relations subsisting between the psychical and

[1] Lecture XI., 1805, p. 256.
[2] Compare Bolton, *Scientific Correspondence of Dr. Priestley,* letters of August 8, 1799, and January 27, 1802.
[3] *Utility*, p. 257.
[4] *Human Understanding*, Bk. 3, Chapter 21, § 6.

the physical, and leads to a fruitful study of the abnormal and pathological. Or, as Rush himself puts it, a knowledge of the faculties and operations of mind furnishes many useful analogies by which we are enabled to explain or illustrate the actions of the human body. Like the will and its motives, these actions do not occur without the influence of external and internal impressions, association and habit; indeed, as pathology shows, the different faculties of the mind, when unduly exercised, act specifically upon certain systems and parts of the body.[1] Moreover, this science of mind can be applied to abnormal as well as normal. Since the operations of the understanding act upon the brain, and vary with sex, rank, profession, climate, season, time of day, they will explain morbid phenomena of the body and mind, particularly the causes of dreams, phantasms, and supposed voices; all of which have been superstitiously ascribed to supernatural influence.[2] For example, unfavourable changes discovered in diseases in the morning are often the effect occasioned by the disturbing dreams of the night before; while the pain of a surgical operation is often lessened by telling the patient that the worst part of it has been performed.[3] Having touched on suggestive anæsthesia some forty years before the application of material anæsthetics in America, and having mentioned the influence of the passions in curing the diseases of the body, the lecturer now maintains that their efficacy is much greater in curing the diseases of the mind. To compose and regulate the passions, there are to be found means ranging from the physical influence of music to the removal of painful associations of ideas, as when a fever, caught while out gunning, was cured by removing the gun from the ill man's room.[4]

It is at this point that Rush's underlying quantitative conception of mentality again crops out. In his *Animal Life* he had spoken of the tempers and dispositions of the mind as if they were so many psychical quarts and pints. Here the faculties and their operations are presented as if they formed a parallelogram of forces, a framework of calculable energies. Thus, by opposing a new and fresh to an exhausted passion, by combining two passions against one, by giving a passion, that has operated in a retrograde

[1] *Utility*, p. 258.   [2] *Ib.*, p. 259.   [3] *Ib.*, p. 263.   [4] *Ib.*, p. 267.

course, its natural direction, madness, from the influence of the passions upon the understanding and will, has often been cured, without the aid of any other remedy.[1] Granted that this way of looking at things may appear strange, it still has its advantages. It renders the science of mind an exact science, not a chimerical and uncertain thing. While it bore the name of metaphysics, and consisted only of words without ideas, of definitions of nonentities, and of controversies about the ubiquity of spirit and space, the materiality and immateriality of mind—it deserved no quarter from the rational part of mankind. But the science I am now speaking of is as real as any of the sciences that treat upon matter, and more certain and perfect than most of them. Note the changes and improvements that have taken place in the theories of every branch of what is called physical science within the last two thousand years. Very different is the state of phrenology, if I may be allowed to coin a word to designate a science of the mind. Most of the leading opinions and observations of Locke, Condillac, Hartley, and Reid may be found in the writings of Aristotle and Plato, and discoveries in this science are now as rare as they are in anatomy. The reason of this certainty and near approach to perfection is obvious. The mind is the same now as it was in the time of those illustrious Greek philosophers, and of course exhibits the same phenomena in all its operations to the moderns, that it did to them. It is moreover always present with us, and always subject to our observations. It requires no excursions from home, no apparatus of instruments or agents, to develop its operations; hence there is nearly the same coincidence of opinion concerning them that there is of the qualities of bodies that act upon the senses.[2]

This is the concluding passage of the lecture of 1805. It is interesting and eloquent, but at the same time disappointing. Rush's analogies sound like original discoveries and promising anticipations; but they are neither. His hints regarding suggestive therapeutics were to be traced back to the Zoönomic philosophy, his suggestions regarding the localisation of cerebral functions became involved in phrenology. The Philadelphian appears to have utilised the word a decade before Hunter applied it to the system

[1] *Utility*, pp. 264-5.   [2] *Ib.*, pp. 271-2.

of Gall and Spurzheim.[1] Unfortunately his use of this 'history of the faculties of the human mind,' as he elsewhere defined it,[2] betook of the nature of a pseudo-science. In a lecture of this period on *Dreams,* he said: whatever part of the brain is affected, the dream that takes place is of that nature—different parts of the brain being allotted to the different faculties and operations of the mind. Thus, if the moral part is affected, we dream of committing crimes, at the very thought of which we shudder when awake.[3] So, too, the closing part of the lecture, defending a knowledge of the faculties, is neither original nor sound. Rush confesses that he is not singular in considering such lectures as a branch of physiology, these faculties having been considered by Dr. Haller in his large work, under the title of *sensus interni.*[4] While the American, then, did service in differentiating his science of mind from speculative metaphysics, yet he did not succeed in carrying it over into the safer field of psycho-physics. His method was vitiated by the obstinate misconception that reflection is the chief avenue to knowledge. Here he might be contrasted with Franklin, follower of no subjective school, but believer in any objective experiment. One can imagine what the latter would have made of Judge Hopkinson's suggestion regarding the composition of a scale of pleasurable sensations by the fingers, analogous to the musical scale, by means of objects of different degrees of softness and smoothness.[5] Rush considered his friend's thought an ingenious one, but did not carry it into execution. For this his earlier training was to blame. For instruments of precision he preferred simple introspection. On the verge of possible discoveries realism bandaged his eyes.

Notwithstanding this preference for inward over outward observation, hints for a primitive experimental psychology are given in the ensuing lectures *Upon the Pleasures of the Senses and of the Mind.* Having described the offices of the senses, the author now intends to enumerate their pleasures, and to inquire into their

---

[1] Compare *Baldwin's Dictionary of Philosophy and Psychology, sub verbo.*
[2] Lecture XII, on Hippocrates, p. 295.
[3] For an adverse opinion of Gall's Craniology, compare *Medical Repository,* Vol. 2, p. 438, N. Y., 1808.
[4] *Utility,* p. 272.   [5] *Pleasures of the Senses,* p. 409.

causes, that is, into the changes which are produced in the nerves by the sensation of pleasure.[1] Of these two inquiries the former, as might be expected, leads to a perfect medley of facts and fancies. Among the senses of touch are given the sensation of perfect health which the Germans call self-feeling;[2] the joy of fear which the Indians experience after surviving a bloody victory; the sensation of tickling which partakes of both pain and pleasure. An illustration of the pleasures of sight is Hogarth's line of beauty which delights the eye because it consists of an unbroken curve; an instance of the pleasures of sound that of the winds, rains, and streams of water—all doing homage to the ears of man. More important than this enumeration of the pleasures of the senses, is the inquiry into the accompanying changes produced in the nerves. The fundamental proposition here is that the pleasure we enjoy from music is derived from a certain order and relationship of vibration, which are excited in the ear, to each other; while the pain we feel from discord is produced by the want of order, or relationship, in the vibrations which strike the ear.[3] Rush had once decried the Hartleian theory of vibrations, here he makes a particularly unhappy application of it. Assuming that the pleasure we derive from our ears is ascribable to impressions and vibrations of a peculiar kind, and pain to an excess or dissonance of similar impressions, he states that it is from this organ that he borrows his analogies to explain the causes of pleasure and pain in all the other organs.[4] For example, the pleasure derived from contemplating a beautiful face is produced by certain harmonious motions in the retina of the eye; the pleasures of the table by a harmony in the relations of the aliments, provided, of course, that there is no mixture with indelicate toasts and bacchanalian songs; the pleasures of smell by a difference in harmony imparted to the nerves of the nose by the scale of odours. Here magnolia may be said to resemble bass, the rose tenor, the wall-flower the treble tones! In fine, all the pleasures of the senses being produced from

---

[1] *Pleasures of the Senses,* p. 399.

[2] Compare Rush's essay on the *Manners of the German Inhabitants of Pennsylvania.*

[3] *Pleasures of the Senses,* p. 428.   [4] *Ib.,* p. 432.

greater or less degrees of harmony analogous to the vibration of musical sound, our bodies may be compared to a violin; the senses are its strings; everything beautiful and sublime in nature and art is its bow; the Creator is the hand that moves it; and pleasure, nearly constant pleasure, their necessary effect! [1]

To these ridiculous analogies the other materialists made more or less direct answer. Buchanan, of Kentucky, protested against turning the human system into a violin; Cooper, of South Carolina, ironically mixed a sort of vibratory punch in which the spirits and the lemon were blended in harmonious proportions. But aside from Rush's figures of speech, attributable to the pedagogue's propensity to make matters clear to the meanest intelligence, the lecture on the *Pleasures of the Senses* contained a number of valuable observations, summed up in the form of laws of sensation. Such were the statements that some pleasures are increased, others lessened by repetition; that motion in the organ increases the sensitivity of touch; that the loss of the use of one sense often increases the pleasures of another, the blind enjoying music more than those who possess their eyesight; finally, that we are able to receive only a single sensation in our minds at once, the impressions of yellow and blue, for example, exciting the green color.[2] These laws, for one thing, lead Rush to disagree with the theory of Edmund Burke, presented in his treatise on the *Sublime and Beautiful,* that relaxation is so extensive a source of pleasurable sensations. Rather should one conclude that motions of a moderate degree of force, and in regular order, constitute pleasure; and that motions in excess, and out of order, constitute pain.[3] Or, to use an obvious simile, pleasure may be compared to a clear stream of water, flowing with rapidity through a straight and narrow channel; pain to the same stream rendered turbid by flowing with accumulated velocity and in every possible direction.[4]

Rush's laws of sensation appear the more safe as they are the less specific. When freed from such latent metaphors as the senses being so untuned by diseases as to emit no tones of pleasure, they stand as suggestive contributions to current knowledge. Such

[1] *Pleasures of the Senses,* pp. 424-5. [2] *Ib.*, pp. 425-6.
[3] *Ib.*, p. 432. [4] *Ib.*, p. 428.

are the closing remarks that the pleasures of the senses are of short duration; that they are of limited nature as to their degree —no ingenuity being ever able to raise them so high as to perfectly satisfy the mind; finally, that they are so nearly related to pain that they often teminate in it. In the last of these summary negations the materialist has well nigh formulated a law of diminishing return, applicable to the psychical field. But herein his first aim is apparently not so much to uphold exact science, as practical piety. He means to show that numerous and delightful as are the pleasures of the senses, they have their alloy, and yet that, in these evils, heaven is still kind—since we are taught by them to aspire to more sublime and durable pleasures of the mind, the subject of the next lecture.[1]

In this supplementary treatise the author pursues the same order as before. He enumerates the pleasures of each of the faculties; inquires into their proximate cause; and concludes with some general remarks. As another introductory address the subject must be made interesting at all hazards. So, under the first of these topics there appears the customary mixture of rhetoric and anecdote. By the memory we command, as it were, the suns that have gone down to rise again; by the understanding we gain the most delicate and sublime pleasures. The nature of this may be conceived from the fact that Mr. Rittenhouse fainted upon perceiving the transit of Venus on the third of July, 1760. Again, the pleasures of the association of ideas are of so peculiar a nature that an old African slave, who saw a lion conducted as a show through New Jersey, was transported with joy, being carried back to the days of his boyhood in his native country.

Having pointed his moral with provincial tales, and brought the subject down to his hearers, Rush returns to his original quest, the higher hedonism of intellectual pursuits. Here he emphasises the pleasures of the will as consisting in contemplating the mysterious union of free agency and necessity in all its operations. We are barely pleased with what we understand; but the exercise of admiration is necessary to our intellectual happiness, and this can be employed only upon subjects which are removed beyond our comprehension. While we thus contemplate, with a

[1] *Pleasures of the Senses,* p. 436.

delightful wonder, the union of free agency and necessity, we derive pleasure from a sense of each of their respective operations. The pleasure we enjoy in free agency is felt in the sacrifices that we make for the attainment of liberty, and in reflecting that we are masters of ourselves. The pleasure we enjoy in a belief in the will acting from necessity, is in disposing us to view the hearts of all the men that move our world by their powers or their talents, as under the direction of a wise and good being; and it assures us that all the events that relate to our individual happiness, whether from moral or physical causes, are in his hands, and that his hand is in every event. I am aware that I dissent from two popular and rigid sects of philosophers and divines, in thus admitting the truth of the opinions held by each of them. But an exclusive belief in either of them, so far from being attended with pleasure, is calculated to excite misery and despair. I repeat, therefore, what I said formerly in speaking of the operations of the will, that both opinions appear to me to be alike true; and that we act most freely when we act most necessarily, and most necessarily when we act most freely.[1]

Here are the paralogisms of the pure reason considered, not as mutually exclusive, but as actually complementary. And nothing could better exemplify Rush's habit of looking on both sides of the shield at once. The only ground and justification for reaching such a cross-eyed conclusion lay in his private paper on *Liberty and Necessity*. But this, as previous inspection showed, left the matter decidedly undecided, the best argument being a suppressed simile. Equally unsatisfactory is the author's treatment of the problem of personality, incidentally subsumed under the pleasures of consciousness. Identity, it is asserted, may be conceived of from a single fact. There never was a man who was willing to change his own mind for that of any other person, however willing he might be to exchange his condition, limbs, and face with him.[2] In thus generalising from a single instance Rush seems to ignore the perversions of consciousness. It was apparently not until later that he met with the anomaly of double personality, in the reputed two minds of the somnambulist. This one-sided-

---

[1] *Pleasures of the Mind*, pp. 441-3.   [2] *Ib.*, p. 449.

ness is exceptional, for in treating of his favourite faculty, the moral sense, Rush takes a broader outlook and includes both the extreme and abnormal manifestations of this activity. He holds that the intensity of the pleasures derived from this source is so great, that it may destroy bodily pain—as in the case of the primitive martyrs to Christianity, who had joys even in the flames of fire. And the perversions of the same faculty are so remarkable that it may become a veritable idiosyncrasy—as in the case of the Parisian in the reign of Robespierre, who declared that the most delightful music he ever heard was the sound of the guillotine.[1]

Having enumerated the pleasures of the mind and some of their perversions, the author comes to his second inquiry—their proximate cause. This may be summed up in a few words. They are the effects of impressions of a certain definite or moderate degree of force, accompanied with motions of a regular or harmonious nature in the brain and heart and communicated by them to the mind. This is to be inferred from dissections, which discover marks of undue or irregular excitement in the brain and of rupture or disorganisation in the heart, where death has been the consequence of an excess of intellectual or moral pleasure.[2] In his extreme zeal for palpable results the materialist has here assumed a cause too great for its effects. His contention, however, may serve as a fitting transition to his last and most extended work of philosophic interest, the *Medical Inquiries and Observations upon the Diseases of the Mind*. Published in 1812, at the solicitation of the author's pupils, this volume is said to be a supplement to materials already collected, a set of new principles founded upon old facts.[3] Unfortunately for his claims to originality, Rush neglects to refer to the books from which he drew these facts. Then, too, he repeats many of his former borrowings. Again are the faculties lengthily enumerated, and a special plea made for the sense of deity according to Lord Kames; again are they defined, in the manner of Haller, as internal senses, depending wholly upon bodily impressions to produce them. Indeed, it

---

[1] *Pleasures of the Mind*, p. 445.
[2] *Ib.*, p. 452.   [3] *Observations*, Preface, p. v.

is said after the fashion of Locke, as well might we attempt to excite thought in a piece of marble by striking it with the hand, as expect to produce a single operation of the mind in a person deprived of the external senses.[1] With these resemblances to former doctrines there yet goes a difference; there is a similar combination of realism and sensationalism, but the materialism is slightly modified. The Hartleian figures of speech are dropped and a safer generalisation adopted. No longer is the body compared to a musical instrument, or the senses spoken of as untuned by diseases so as to emit no tones of pleasure. Refusing then, like Priestley and like his own colleague Frederick Beasley, of the University of Pennsylvania, to commit himself to any specific theory of vibrations, Rush carries out his previous implications in the following postulate: all the operations in the mind are the effects of motions previously excited in the brain, and every idea and thought appears to depend upon a motion peculiar to itself. In a sound state of the mind these motions are regular, and succeed impressions upon the brain with the same certainty and uniformity that perceptions succeed impressions upon the sense in their sound state.[2] Except for an unwarranted assumption of the priority of the physical over the psychical, Rush's thesis might almost be counted a rough formulation of the theory of psycho-physical parallelism. At the least it is a practical working hypothesis, or, as he puts it, a system of principles that shall lead to general success in the treatment of the diseases of the mind.[3]

Having considered the faculties and operations of the mind, it is in order to inquire into the proximate cause of intellectual derangement. Here the American alienist reviews the erroneous opinions on this subject, from the ancient notion that the liver is the seat of the trouble, to the modern belief in favour of madness being an ideal disease. The former theory Rush had met in his lecture on the *Opinions and Modes of Practice of Hippocrates;* the latter, as to madness being purely psychical, he objects to for three reasons: first, because the mind is incapable of any operations independently of impressions communicated to it through the medium of the body; second, because there are but two instances upon record of the brain being found free from morbid

[1] *Observations,* p. 445.   [2] *Ib.,* p. 11.   [3] *Ib.,* preface, p. vi.

appearances in persons who have died of madness; third, because there are no instances of primary affections of the mind, such as grief, love, anger, or despair, producing madness until they had induced some obvious changes in the body.[1]

In this same thorough manner the doctor next examines the remote and exciting causes of intellectual derangement. Briefly put, these are of two classes: first, those that act directly upon the body, as malconformations and lesions of the brain; second, those that act indirectly upon the body through the medium of the mind, as intense study over the means of discovering perpetual motion, or even researches into the meaning of certain biblical prophecies.[2] In the ten score pages following this preliminary section, Rush presents what he calls a new nomenclature of mental diseases, from tristimania to manalgia—a cobweb of technicalities as involved as the Zoönomic classification. Occasionally the author presents clear and illuminating psychological observations, as in his definition of demence as consisting, not of false perceptions, but of an association of unrelated perceptions, wherein the mind may be considered as floating in a balloon, and at the mercy of every object and thought that acts upon it.[3] But in general, Rush in this part of his work has been pronounced often discursive and sometimes inconsequential, with a tendency to expand and multiply rather than to condense and critically classify.[4] The last reference is especially applicable to the earlier articles on the *Different Species of Phobia and Mania.* Among the former are instanced the cat-phobia and solo-phobia, the phobia being excellently defined as a fear of an imaginary evil, or an undue fear of a real one. Among the latter are described the land-mania which is especially prevalent in the United States; and the liberty-mania which shows itself in visionary ideas of liberty and government—when men expect liberty without law, government without power, sovereignty without a head, and wars without expense.[5]

In these statements the American exhibits all the fanciful in-

---

[1] *Observations*, p. 16.   [2] *Ib.*, pp. 30-37.   [3] *Ib.*, p. 257.

[4] C. K. Mills, *Benjamin Rush and American Psychiatry, Medico-Legal Journal*, Dec., 1886, p. 34.

[5] *Columbian Magazine*, 1786-7, pp. 110-113, 177-180, 182-187, 305.

genuity of the modern French alienists with their movable arrangements of fixed ideas. But he has more solid parts, and, in his chapter on the derangement of the will, is declared to have led his generation and forecasted the later work of Ribot.[1] This estimate seems exaggerated. Rush enumerates but two ways in which the will is affected by diseases, one of which is treated too superficially, and the other too metaphysically. There is first a negative affection, aboulia, or what he would call a debility and torpor, or loss of all sensibility to the stimulus of motives. In this he says he has never been consulted, yet he has been informed by his friend Brissot that animal magnetism will cure light cases. He suggests, however, that persons afflicted with this disorder of the mind should be placed in situations in which they will be compelled to use their wills in order to escape some great and pressing evil. A palsy of the limbs has been cured by the cry of fire and a dread of being burned. Why should not a palsy of the will be cured in a similar manner?[2] But to proceed: there is, second, a privative affection of the will, when it acts without a motive, by a kind of involuntary power. Rush is here at pains to set forth the two opinions that have divided philosophers upon the subject of the operations of the will and to grant that freedom is as true as necessity. But in spite of his effort to reach a perfect metaphysical impartiality he finds himself on the necessitarian side of the fence. That derangement of the will in which it acts without a motive, by a kind of involuntary power, is exactly the same thing that occurs when the arm or foot is moved convulsively without an act of the will, or even in spite of it.[3]

Such notions of the diseases of the will as affecting the moral faculty had at the least a practical value in Rush's ideas of medical jurisprudence; his corresponding notions of the disease affecting the believing faculty has not even a theoretical worth. Assuming a realistic principle of faith he uses it, first, as a peg upon which to hang more anecdotes, then, as a club to throw at the idealists. Defining his favourite faculty as that principle in the mind by which we believe in the evidence of the senses, of reason,

[1] Mills, *op. cit.*, p. 10.
[2] *Diseases of the Mind*, pp. 268-270.   [3] *Ib.*, p. 263.

and of human testimony, he gives as an instance of its excess an old Revolutionary quidnunc, who, like Horace's character of Apella, believed everything he heard; and as an instance of its deficiency Burke's description of those who 'believe nothing that they do not see, or hear, or measure with a twelve-inch rule.' This incredulity, adds Rush, is not confined to human testimony. It extends to the evidence of reason and of the senses. The followers of Berkeley either felt or affected the last grade of this disorder in the principle of faith. That it is often affected, I infer from persons who deny their belief in the utility of medicine, as practised by regular-bred physicians, but believe implicitly in quacks.[1] Since it affects both his preaching as a realist and his practice as a materialist, the Scotch-trained doctor now offers a sort of logical prescription for this insanity of doubt. The cure for a weak mental digestion is to go back to a plain intellectual diet,—or as he puts it: the remedy for this palsy of the believing faculty, should consist in proposing propositions of the most simple nature to the mind, and after gaining assent to them, to rise to propositions of a more difficult nature.[2]

In the succeeding chapter on derangement in the memory there is presented a dry catalogue of the various forms of this disease. Lacking a technical nomenclature, it nevertheless contains implicit recognition of the various forms of amnesia. Among those given is an oblivion of names and vocables, of the sounds of words but not of the letters which compose them, of the qualities or numbers of the most familar objects, of events, time, and place. Instances of these lapses in the memory are forthwith presented—from Rush's own friends to his patients in the Philadelphia hospital —from the absent-minded Dr. Magaw of the university, to an Italian victim of the yellow fever, who in the beginning of his malady spoke only English, in the middle only French, and on the day of his death only the language of his native country.[3] Rush here obtained an insight into retrogressive amnesia, yet in treating of the results of the weakness and loss of memory he is

---

[1] *Diseases of the Mind*, pp. 276-7. [2] *Ib.*, p. 274.
[3] *Ib.*, p. 276. Compare W. B. Carpenter, *Principles of Mental Physiology*, London, 1879, p. 437.

even more superficial than before. He resorts to the once-rejected scholastic realism, speaking of the objects of knowledge as either sleeping or perishing in the mind. Finally, he gives a most inadequate account of the causes of these things. Among mental causes he mentions the oppressing the memory in early life with words and studies disproportioned to its strength, as prematurely crowding Latin and Greek into boys' minds; and also the undue exercise of memory upon any one subject, as in the case of the negro calculator, Thomas Fuller, of Virginia, who was famous in numbers, but could not recollect faces.[1]

The chapter on dreams and somnambulism is an equally hasty performance, yet may be happily supplemented from other sources. Dreaming is here said to be always induced by irregular or morbid action in the blood-vessels of the brain, hence it is accompanied with the same erroneous train, or the same incoherence of thought which takes place in delirium. This is so much the case that a dream may be considered as a transient paroxysm of delirium, and delirium as a permanent dream.[2] Again, somnambulism is nothing but a higher grade of the same disease; it is a transient paroxysm of madness. Like madness it is accompanied with muscular action, with incoherent or coherent conduct, and with that complete oblivion of both which takes place in the worst grade of madness. Coherence of conduct discovers itself in persons, who are afflicted with it, undertaking or resuming certain habitual exercises or employments. Thus, we read of the scholar resuming his studies, the poet his pen, and the artisan his labours, while under its influence, with their usual industry, taste, and correctness.[3] As a foil to these dogmatic definitions and unqualified assertions, Rush on other occasions made a number of additions and conjectures. Suggesting that dreams are useful to prognosticate incipient diseases and to prevent delirium from too great excitability, he goes on to say that we never dream of things the raw material of which did not exist in the mind previously. So dormant or lost ideas are often revived in dreams and recollected afterwards. The fact that I remembered the name of a forgotten classmate of the Jersey college after a dream proves, not that such

[1] *Diseases of the Mind*, pp. 281-2.   [2] *Ib.*, pp. 300-1.   [3] *Ib.*, p. 304.

a recollection was a preternatural occurrence, but simply that nothing exists in the brain but that which had previously entered through the medium of the senses.[1]

As Rush's sensationalism rescued him from a magical conception of the phenomena of dreaming, so did his materialism from a similar view of the phenomena of somnambulism. Here is given, in a remarkable anticipation of later French discoveries, a case of continuous memory in trances, of patching up recollections into an unbroken secondary series. Somnambulists, he reasons, recollect in each fit what they did in the preceding one, as in the case reported by Dr. Lentwork, [?] of Springfield, to the Reverend Dr. Stiles, of Yale. They appear to have two distinct minds, but may this not be owing to impressions made on the other parts of the brain by diseases and re-excited by the same stimulus?[2] It must be granted that Rush has here ingeniously approached the problem of dual personality, previously ignored, by a sort of anticipated nerve-tract theory. In his next topic he is not so modern. He defines an illusion as a sort of waking dream, a disease in which false perceptions take place in the eyes and ears from a morbid affection of the brain. The deception consists most commonly in hearing our own names, for the reason that we are accustomed to hear them pronounced more frequently than any other words. Hence, that part of the ear which vibrates with the sound of our names moves more promptly, from habit, than any other part of it.[3] This naturalistic explanation is put forward against the beliefs of superstitious people, who say that these false perceptions are premonitions of death. Yet the author is careful to add that it may not be applied to invalidate the accounts of the supernatural voices and objects that were seen or heard by individuals in the Old or New Testaments.[4]

Allowing no conflict between his science and his religion, Rush offers in his final chapter on the *Diseases of the Mind* a plea for what he calls a system of Christian jurisprudence. Though based on a cramped and narrow psychology, it was given a broad and fruitful application. The disease of the will, it is assumed,

[1] Purnell MS., p. 128. [2] *Ib.*, p. 133.
[3] *Diseases of the Mind*, p. 307. [4] *Ib.*, p. 308.

discovers itself only in the moral faculty and exists with a sound
state of the conscience and sense of the deity.   Hence, as the lecturer had previously declared, it would be as absurd to inflict the
punishment of death upon a fellow creature for taking away a life
under a deranged state of the will, as for a surgeon to cut off
an arm or a leg because in its convulsive motions it injured a
toilet or overset a tea table.[1]   Now, while these morbid operations of the will may include in their consequences even theft and
murder, yet they are to be considered, not as vices, but as symptoms of a disease.   Therefore, for persons thus afflicted legislators
should abolish the punishment of death, cropping, branding, and
public whipping, and substitute for them confinement, labour,
simple diet, cleanliness, and affectionate treatment.   As is shown
by the moral effects thus produced in the jail of Philadelphia, the
reformation of criminals and the prevention of crimes can be
better effected by living than by dead examples![2]

   This semi-political peroration concludes the last of Rush's phi-
losophisings.   Contrasted with the first, the undergraduate transcription of scholasticism, it illustrates his saying that it was time to
take science out of the hands of philosophers and put it into the
hands of the people.[3]   Here is a principle much in the spirit of
Franklin.   Applied as a criterion to Rush's own works, it shows
him to be a populariser rather than a speculator, an advocate of
concrete results rather than of abstract consistency.   So, however
much Rush accomplished as a practical reformer, the natural and
inevitable outcome of such a principle was to make his metaphysics
a thing of inconsistencies.   As a transitional thinker he strives to
be so impartial that he takes both sides at once.   His ' cold common
sense ' is offset by a phenomenalism in which ' ideas are mere
qualities, having no more reality than the sound of a hammer or a
bell.'[4]   So, too, the principle of animal life, excitability, is allowed
in one place to be either a quality or a substance;[5] in another it
is looked upon as a sort of vital phlogiston, which was to be drawn

---

[1] *Medical Jurisprudence*, p. 388.

[2] *Diseases of the Mind*, pp. 365-6.

[3] A. E. B. Woodward, *A System of Universal Science*, p. 239, Philadelphia, 1816.

[4] Purnell MS., p. 90.   [5] *Animal* Life, p. 6.

off from animal matter as freely as Rush himself drew blood from his patients.[1] Again, while diseases of the mind are counted as veritable derangements of a constituted order, real evils in this present world, still it is likewise held that ' all evil has wisdom in it, and every folly and vice, like every particle of matter, is necessary.' [2]

In fine, if these scattered inconsistencies be fitted into the divisions of epistemology, ontology, and cosmology, Rush's system is found to issue in a mutual cancellation of terms. That this was due to the varying influences of conflicting schools of thought—realism, materialism, and an obsolescent deism—becomes evident in a criticism of his main field of endeavour. Rush's psychology was vitiated by a kind of realistic phrenology, in which imaginary faculties are immured in so many water-tight compartments. Now such a confinement within arbitrary limits has a two-fold defect: it prevented the attainment of a correct view of precise cerebral localisation, and of the general activity of the brain in the higher thought processes. Rush is again but half right in his genetic methods. He recognises the growth of the child mind, and attempts to map out the steps in its mental development; but he fails to see that the decline of the intellectual powers occurs in an order the reverse of that of their acquirement. The doctrine of retrogression, which he touched upon in his mature essay on *Old Age,* is twisted by an earlier deistic bias. Giving the order in which the mind declines as, first, the memory, then the imagination and understanding, he adds, that the sense of the Deity is never forgotten.[3] A lost memory which never forgets something is a cause for astonishment, and yet in the face of this and other defects Rush was no more inconsistent than those upon whom he drew. Like the Zoönomic philosopher, he put in the same basket fragile innate faculties and lively vital movements. Like Hartley, he added teleological trimmings to a doctrine of philosophical necessity: nothing was made in vain; every power, principle and feeling of the body and mind must answer to the end of their creation.[4] For these things, Rush, as a transitional writer,

[1] Compare *Utility of a Knowledge,* etc., p. 258.
[2] Purnell MS., p. 90.   [3] *Ib.,* p. 96.
[4] *Thoughts,* MS., p. 47.

was hardly to blame. Struggling in the stream of conflicting currents, he was indeed in a poor position to estimate their relative forces. In other words, the times were against him. Historically, he was not so placed as to obtain the right perspective. No more than his masters could he be aware of the fact that his realism was a drawing away from his materialism, just as his materialism was from his deism.

Rush's system was a syncretism, a mode in which varied movements were fused. It was, therefore, capable of a variety of interpretations. These it received at the hands of both contemporaries and followers. An anonymous London deist wrote that, when it was said that medical men were enemies to the religious view, Dr. Rush was an example to the contrary.[1] So, too, a Philadelphia admirer attributed to Rush the statement that it remains yet to be discovered, whether all the moral, as well as natural attributes of the Deity may not be discovered in the form and economy of the material world.[2] And the same author, in his *Eulogium,* recalling Rush's methods of teaching, said that he urged his students to the study of the anatomy of the human mind, commonly called metaphysics, since the reciprocal influence of the body and mind upon each other can only be ascertained by an accurate knowledge of the faculties of the mind and their various modes of combination and action. To this end they should study Butler, Locke, Reid, Beattie, and Hartley.[3]

Interpreted, then, both as a realist and a deist, Rush was yet in the main a materialist. His followers and imitators at home and abroad show this. His own pupils outdid him in the application of the physical principle. One wrote on the effects of the passions of the body;[4] another on the morbid effects of grief and fear;[5] a third made voluntary motion the effect of irritability;[6] a fourth defined volition as a sensorial power secreted in the substance of the voluntary muscles.[7] These opinions were expressed

[1] *An Interpretation of the Sacred Scriptures,* p. 11, London, 1797.
[2] David Ramsay, *Eulogium* . . . *of David Rittenhouse,* p. 27, Philadelphia, 1796.   [3] *Eulogium,* p. 124.
[4] Henry Rose (Va.), 1794.   [5] William Hall (S. C.), 1806.
[6] John Hart (N. C.), 1812.   [7] Robert Mayo (Va.), 1808.

in the inaugural theses of the doctor's students at Philadelphia. A similar use of his name and opinions is to be found in the theses of the early American students in Edinburgh.[1] The contents of these treatises may be as dull as their Latinity is indifferent, nevertheless, they are of interest in that, while some of them refer to Hartley and Darwin, Franklin and Priestley, all of them refer to Rush and thus go to prove that as head of the Philadelphia school of materialists he was of no small influence. That influence, it should be noted, in conclusion, was chiefly exerted in the Southern States. From them came the great majority of Rush's pupils, and if to them be added open-minded thinkers, who, like Jefferson, Cooper, and Buchanan, knew either Rush or his works, the South may be looked upon as the most promising field for the spread of materialism. Why that movement failed to flourish there, and how it was rooted out, is another story, connected with the interplay of conflicting forces. But before taking up the important topic of the decline of the English and French materialistic influences, through the rise of natural realism, or the philosophy of common sense, consideration must be given, for the sake of thoroughness, to the case of the minor materialists.

[1] Such as C. Berkeley (Va.), 1793, *De Corpore Humano;* R. B. Screben, (S. C.), 1799, *De Vitae Humane Gradibus,* in the William Osler Collection, in the Medical and Chirurgical Faculty Library, Baltimore.

CHAPTER VII

THE MINOR MATERIALISTS

THE early American materialists, taken together, formed a sort of planetary system. There were the greater lights, grouped about Philadelphia as a centre; there were the lesser, whose beams diminished with their distance from that source of illumination; there were finally the mere speculative meteors—small minds subject to varying mental perturbations, but at the last drawn under the one controlling influence. Such were the deists who were attracted by materialistic monism, and the idealists who succumbed to the kindred sensationalism. Although the minor materialists had common interests they had not common acquaintanceship. Like the atoms with which they dealt, they did not act with immediateness upon one another. And although they had a common period with the major materialists, their chronological order was not their logical order. In point of time, from Richard Peters to Sheldon Clark was almost the same as from Cadwallader Colden to Benjamin Rush; but in similarity of thought, the first in each series resembled not the first but the last in the other.

It was the Reverend Richard Peters, a graduate of Oxford and a clergyman of Philadelphia, who spoke as follows at the opening of the Philadelphia Academy in 1750: ' In a State of Ignorance the rational Faculties of the Soul, for want of Use, may be so extremely weakened, as not to exert themselves whilst in union with the Body. As Exercise gives Strength to the Nerves, and preserves the Health, so Thinking strengthens the Powers of the Mind, and promotes the Health of the Soul; but if Knowledge, its natural Food, be with-held, it falls into a paralytick State, and becomes unable to make any vigorous Efforts. All that magnetical Force in the Affections and Passions, by which the Soul is with Violence carried towards Information, Merit, Excellence, Virtue, Goodness, Elegance, Decorum, find no Place

454

in an ignorant Mind; but in their Room one has the Mortifica-
tion to behold a perfect *Vis Inertia,* or inert Power.[1]

This passage in its beginning sounds like Rush, in its end like
Colden. In the former respect it anticipates the combination of
a realistic psychology with analogies drawn from physiology; in
the latter it goes back to the older problems of the substantial
powers. But while these hints of Peters were thrown out in the
very year in which Colden published his *Principles of Action in
Matter,* it was not until five and twenty years had passed that they
were taken up and more fully elaborated. In 1776 Matthew Wilson, of Lewes, Delaware, published *A Proposal for Reducing
Natural Philosophy to a System; with Remarks on the Cartesian
and Newtonian Theories.* Despite its pretentious title, this was
really a modest proposal in philosophising, for in it the author
hopes that some genius—perhaps an American—may arise to purge
both systems of their rust and mistakes, and either compound a good
one from both, or strike out a new one, which may unravel many
things which yet lie in perplexing obscurity.[2] As this remark indi-
cates, the Delawarean, like the majority of his countrymen, was
unaware of the work the lieutenant-governor of New York had
been doing in his attempts to reconcile these very cosmologies.
He therefore attempts to harmonise the two systems by a criticism of their principles. He reviews Descartes' definition of the
two substances, his mechanical explanation of the origin of the
world, the atheistical tendency of his doctrine of the eternity of
matter as counteracted by his belief in a creator who endued matter
with all its principles. Now, contends Wilson, philosophers have
advanced many things against Descartes' elements—his subtle
matter, hooked atoms, vortices, and other machines, and have compared them to the occult qualities. But what is better in the present system? Perhaps subtle matter and vortices will be found to
account for gravity better than gravity will account for many
actual demonstrations of several kinds of subtle matter lately discovered, and probably many more that may be found hereafter.
Definition and defence of Cartesianism is followed by a counter

[1] *A Sermon on Education,* Philadelphia, 1751, p. 7.
[2] *Proposal* in the *Pennsylvania Magazine,* March, 1776.

attack on Newtonianism. Any schoolboy, who has read half of Whiston's Euclid, may rail at the absurdity of Descartes' plenum, but is there any less absurdity in Newton's plenum which allows universal space to be the ubiquity of the divine nature? And as establishing a vacuum seems to be a fundamental principle of the Newtonian system, continues the critic, permit me to raise some doubts about it. We need not go back to the disputes of the ancient Pythagoreans, Epicureans, and Corpuscularians, who asserted a *vacuum coacervatum;*—for example, should God annihilate all the air and other bodies in this chamber, there would then be a vacuum between the walls. This is denied by others, as supposing such a vacuum would make it infinite, eternal, and uncreated. The Cartesians, however, deny any *vacuum coacervatum* at all, and assert, in the supposed case above, that the walls would become contiguous, and include no space; those things being contiguous which have nothing intermediate. If, therefore, there is no body between, there is no extension; and if no extension, the walls are contiguous, and where is the vacuum? But the kind of vacuum chiefly disputed among modern philosophers is called *vacuum disseminatum,* or *interspersum,* supposed to be dispersed among different bodies, and in the pores of the same bodies. I need not mention the Peripatetic great argument against it, from nature's abhorring a vacuum. The *fuga vacui* is justly superseded by the discoveries of the weight and elasticity of the air, the pressure of the atmosphere, and the like, which are justly calculated by the Newtonians, whether they assign a just cause or not. The Cartesians not only deny the existence of such a vacuum, but even the possibility of it; on this principle, that ' Extension being the essence of matter or body, wherever extension is, there is body; but mere space is supposed extended, therefore it is material.' Here ends the Delawarean's attempt to reduce natural philosophy to a system. As such it was about as insignificant as the state in which the author lived, or as Dr. Witherspoon expressed the thing, in a sarcastic attack upon this essay, a complete definition of it might be put into a lady's pocketbook.[1] The essay, however, is of peculiar interest as exhibiting a combination of scholasticism and materialism much like that of Colden. There are reasons for this.

[1] See below, Book V., Chapter III.

Wilson was a theologian as well as a physician, and the two sorts of training are patent in his thinking. As the former he engaged in what Dr. Rush considered unprofitable discussions over the ubiquity of space and time; as the latter he was attracted by a materialistic explanation of the cosmos. So he enters upon his discussions with a cautious disavowal of matter as either infinite or eternal; yet he leaves the impression that the ancient atomism, with all its pantheistic implications, is not wholly untrue.

The next of the minor materialists to attempt a similar explanation of the universe was an unnamed Philadelphian, as untrained as he was unknown. In 1784 there appeared an anonymous *Essay on Matter* whose postulates were as naïve as its conclusions were sweeping. In his prefatory apology the humble writer explains that when he had written his first two chapters he had never read any author who had considered matter in this way, nor did he even know that thoughts similar to these had ever been conceived; in his last chapter he grows bold enough to conjecture that creation, so far as we can trace it, would appear to be one infinite mass of matter.[1] Compiled as a sort of *vade mecum* for the common mind, the essay starts with a definition of matter as cautious as it is obvious. Simply considered, it includes everything that we can possibly see, hear, feel, taste or smell. Our minds can have no information or conception of that which is not material. Yet matter is not perishable; to suppose that it could waste, must carry with it the supposition that it must be constantly creating *de novo;* but this is taking from the Deity the attribute of omnipotence. Having started with this deistic premise, further inferences are consistently dualistic. In the second chapter it is held that matter as connected with the vital principle does not exclude that influence from the elements or compound parts of bodies, for to say that the elements alone give motion is to say that the elements give life; but this is denying an Universal Agent, or making him to act more by intermediate agents, than philosophy will allow. Matter and the living principle, therefore, are coexistent: the one as durable as the other, and both from everlasting to everlasting.[2]

With these initial principles, so fashioned as not to disturb the

[1] *An Essay on Matter*, Philadelphia, 1784, pp. 1, 23.
[2] *Ib.*, pp. 3, 7.

ordinary thinker, the unknown philosophiser enters upon bolder speculations. In his third chapter he considers that the generation and change of matter is due to the motions in the parts which are too small beyond our comprehension. These motions we cannot see any more than could a being, whose organ of seeing is gross, perceive, for example, that a solid square of men is composed of companies, files, and separate soldiers. So the form of matter can be changed to our gross sense, but matter cannot cease to be matter, so long as it emerges from one form or kind of existence into another.[1] Having somehow got hold of the Hobbite ontology and made it as plain as a pikestaff, the materialist goes on in the same easy way to popularise a kindred psychology. Under the finer composition and action of matter is included the soul and its operations. Thus reasoning is no more than the finest operation of matter and the comparing of material impressions or ideas. Just as matter and life are one and the same thing, so the soul is no more than the operation of matter, acquiring that power of operation from its particular kind of composition. Though we cannot know exactly how the action of thinking is performed, yet it comes under the universal principle which actuates all matter. It is like the action of a spring of iron or wood: the moment the force which holds the rod in its tortured position is removed, it recovers the place which the various forms of matter in its composition require and induce.[2] At the first glance these principles have the appearance of a safe simplicity, nevertheless their author is not of so simple a mind as to be ignorant of their consequences. Perceiving that they will disturb the idols of the market place, he endeavours to tread lightly on the forbidden ground. If the operations of matter, he continues, be thus made to have the same effect as the operations of that which has been called soul, why should it be so hateful to our pride to deny a soul which we have proved is denying nothing? Here we may modestly disagree with Mr. Locke that an immaterial something, the soul, can have acquaintance with material things. We cannot, for example, conceive of an idea of distance unconnected with matter. I have an idea of the distance from Philadelphia to Boston by the number of miles into which the road has been divided; but does it follow from this that I have an

[1] *An Essay on Matter*, pp. 10, 11.   [2] *Ib.*, pp. 16, 17.

idea of immaterial distance? Granting this would be giving parts to the infinite, carrying material impressions into infinity.[1] These metaphors may be good, but the deductions therefrom are badly mixed. The connection between the soul, Boston, and infinity is, in this particular case, hardly to be reckoned as clear. But this very inconsequence leads to interesting results. Living in the centre of materialism, subject to more varied influences than he could express in the compass of a short essay, the conclusions of the anonymous author are drawn with all the temerity of an unsigned article. From all that has been said, he concludes, it follows that what we call soul or life have the same origin with our bodies—the one as much as the other being a part of this world, this earth and its atmosphere. But as creation swells into infinity, we may conclude that this harmony and dependence, which we observe in things that we can see, accompany it into infinity. Creation, then, as far as we can see, would appear to be one infinite mass of matter.[2]

Here ends the second of the materialistic tracts for the times. If the previous essay was reducible to the size of a lady's pocket-book, this might be called a manual for the man in the street. That stricture could not be passed upon the next number in the series. In 1819 there appeared *An Original Essay on the Laws of Pleasure and Pain* by Thomas Ewell, a physician of Virginia and a surgeon in the United States Navy. Although the author was the editor of the first American edition of Hume's *Essays,* into which his own production was surreptitiously inserted, he did not dare to push his own principle so far as the sceptical method might allow. In his earlier work entitled *Plain Discourses on the Laws and Properties of Matter,* he had denominated heat, light, electricity, and galvanism as unconfinable elementary bodies, and implied their self-activity and self-sufficiency.[3] Now he says that both philosophers and common people agree that nature, in all her works, observes a remarkable uniformity operating by established rules in everything visible.[4] These initial statements, taken by themselves, give Ewell the look of an absolute materialist with pantheistic

---

[1] *An Essay on Matter,* p. 23.   [2] *Ib.,* p. 23.
[3] New York, 1806, p. 50.   [4] *Pleasure and Pain,* p. 525.

leanings. But nothing is further from his thoughts. Instead of
making his principles of matter self-active and self-sufficient, and
uniformity an independent principle immanent in nature, the natural system, order, and regulation is referred to a transcendent
source. These things are not the blind events of chance, but the
operations of a being of intelligence, benevolence, and impartiality.[1]
Changing thus quickly from an initial materialism to a convential
deism, Ewell, like the great eclectic of Virginia, makes an equally
rapid transition from his cosmology to his anthropology. Observing the unequal distribution of pleasure and pain among men, and
inferring that in these most important points there are no laws to
govern, no fixed rules of limitation, he strives to counteract the
universally acquiescent belief in the inequalities of suffering and
of happiness, and claims in a fine anticlimax that he has discovered
the great law upon this subject. He assures us that by preserving
the equilibrium of the mind, that is, keeping it fixed in its great
operations in pursuit of knowledge, never allowing it to be ruffled
with the trifling excitements of pleasure, we shall perfectly insure
the total exemption from every pang.[2] This law, furthermore,
teaches us that, having indulged in pleasure, pain will inevitably
ensue, and, therefore, that when under its operation, we should
endure whatever may happen with perfect resignation.

This simple theory, continues the author, is nothing but an
induction from facts. I had scarcely arrived to manhood before I
was impressed with its truth. In every situation where pleasure
was enjoyed, in defiance of every effort, pains equal in degree,
sooner or later would ensue. I could only preserve my mind from
suffering by preserving it from the operation of pleasure; when
preserved from pleasure, no occurrences could excite one painful
feeling.[3] Ewell's law is, of course, nothing but the Stoic doctrine
of tranquillity and undisturbedness taught by Jefferson. He acknowledges as much in asserting that the law was in conformity to
the oldest philosophers. While he thus vitiates any claim to originality, he is at pains to show that the ancient principle may be rein-
forced by the results of modern investigation.

For the ready comprehension of the law regulating the pleasures
and pains of the mind we may refer to the laws of the actions of

[1] *Pleasure and Pain*, p. 528.   [2] *Ib.*, pp. 526, 531.   [3] *Ib.*, p. 529.

our bodies. The great Dr. Brown has incontrovertibly established that the life, the actions of our body, called excitement, are produced by stimulants acting upon the excitability of the system. That for animal life to be in perfect state, excitement and excitability should be equal; that when excitement is too high, the excitability is exhausted, and that the healthy state can only be produced by the abatement of the excitement, so that the excitability shall return to its proper standard. In like manner, when excitement is too low the excitability is accumulated and requires exhaustion for the restoration of health. The doctrine is illustrated by supposing a scale of an hundred degrees of excitement and another of excitability, healthy action being when excitement and excitability are both fifty. Now this law of the body, extended to the mind, explains somewhat its pleasurable and painful excitements. Every mind has a capacity for pleasurable feeling, and the feeling, when indulged, exhausts this capacity or excitability, in proportion to the degree of indulgence. The restoration of this excitability is a retrograde motion which is called pain. Accordingly, when our intellect has the excitement of any pleasure to any fixed degree, we have afterwards a counter-action of pain corresponding precisely; when we have indulged in the excesses of joy we have to pass through the excesses of pain until the mind is restored to its natural equilibrium.[1] This has a familiar sound; it is Benjamin Rush's arithmetic of the mind which was itself in turn drawn from the Brunonian scheme of vital measurements. Lest it should appear too excessive in its materialism, too much in the nature of a physiologising of things spiritual, Ewell hastens to give it a teleological finish. Referring to his deistic introduction, he summarily concludes that this law of pleasure and pain presented itself as the only means of explaining the innumerable variety and sources of misery in others; it unfolded the whole secret of suffering; established the uniformity of the ways of providence, and ascribed to system and order what had been marked by confusion and folly.[2]

Ewell's *Essay on the Laws of Pleasure and Pain* marks the course of one of the lesser speculative bodies in a strange orbit, ranging from a conservative deism to an extreme materialism. A

[1] *Pleasure and Pain*, pp. 528, 529.　　　[2] *Ib.*, p. 530.

more pronounced example of the same kind is the last of the minor materialists, Sheldon Clark of Connecticut. A typical small farmer, he was at the same time a typical small philosopher. From his stony farm he saved a fund sufficient for the establishment of a chair of mental and moral science in Yale College, by which his name is still perpetuated. From an equally meagre stock of ideas he raised a surprisingly large stock of speculative questions, such as these: Whence comes matter and whither does it tend? Whether matter before creation was promiscuously diffused in a vacuum? What is there in the human mind different from the vegetative to make it immortal? These were strange questions to ask at the time when the college in New Haven was in a peculiarly petrified condition. So, although the authorities, with true academic freedom, took Clark's money, at the same time they scorned his ideas. His speculations indicated ingenuity, but he was often bewildered in the mazes of his own metaphysics,—this was the judgment passed upon him by the geologist Silliman.[1] Such a judgment may have been correct, but it was not wholly just. Clark indeed wandered in the by-paths of heterodoxy, but like another free-thinking Yankee, Ethan Allen, he did service by tracing out in the popular systems of the day such inconsistencies as the antitheses of two absolutes—an infinite God and infinite space, an eternal deity and eternal matter. Clark arrived at his conclusions with difficulty. He had tough obstacles to work against and generations of speculation to work through. When young he was allowed to read only on Sundays, stormy days, and in the long winter nights. Becoming his own master, he was yet unable to attend lectures in the neighbouring college except irregularly. Even with these limitations he learned to know Hume and Edwards, Reid and Franklin, Stewart and Jefferson. It was the last of these worthies who, in reviewing a sheaf of Clark's earlier essays, asserted that he found in them news both profound and instructive.[2] We may admit the one adjective without retaining the other. Clark's essays were instructive but scarcely profound. As in the case of Buchanan's writings, they were useful in showing how

[1] *American Journal of Science and Arts,* Vol. 41, No. 2, p. 15.
[2] Jefferson on Clark, December 5, 1825.

pervasive were the influences both of materialism and of philosophic scepticism, how Hobbes and even Hume had penetrated not only to the freshwater college, but also to the farm. But to discover the extent of the metaphysical maze through which Clark had to grope his way, we must begin with the earliest of his pamphlets, wherein he appears as the defender of Puritanism against Arminianism. Based on the greatest of the New England divines, this initial treatise was as pronounced in favour of determinism as the final materialistic tract was pronounced against it. So, while the *Cure for Arminianism* [1] did not call out the dangerous praise of the hermit of Monticello, it evidently gained the approval of the conventional Federalists of the college. In it the author discloses himself to be an orthodox traditionalist. He offers as the chief argument in behalf of predestination the fact that it was one almost universally believed by our forefathers. Moreover, this doctrine is founded upon the principle that God is the first cause, and that everything in the universe is entirely under his control, the planets and this earth, the mechanism of all animals, including man. God existed before he began to create either matter or spirits, over which he has sovereign indisputable right. Before he created these he determined how he would govern them, and how many suns, comets, and planets he would make. Being infinite in wisdom, power, and goodness, and perfect in happiness, nothing could happen but what was right in his sight. So we cannot choose differently from what we do, for we are necessarily actuated by motives to choose as we do. This does not destroy the whole moral law and reduce us to the condition of passive machines. This objection of the necessarians is invalid against those who hold that we are free moral agents, when we do what we have a mind to. The question of foreordination to salvation or damnation, like raising a crop of wheat, is a question of using the ordinary means. [2]

Here is Puritanism in bucolic trimmings, Edwards bound in half-calf. But Clark goes further in bringing high a priori speculations down to the common level. While he introduces his *Essays* of 1822 in a spirit full of the reverence and decorum of Puritanism, he nevertheless passes with unseemly haste into an attitude of

[1] New Haven, 1815.   [2] *Kingsley's Theological Miscellany*, Vol. 18.

bold, deistic rationalism. No moments, he begins in his opening section on meditating on the character of God, are more happily enjoyed than when we are thinking on the adorable character of that eternal, self-existent Being, who created matter and every active, immaterial being that has ever existed. But whence do we gain our knowledge of this Being? Our ideas of the attributes of God are, generally speaking, only an enlargement of the similar qualities in ourselves; when we think of his wisdom, we think of what constitutes wisdom in ourselves. For example, man's chief object is his own happiness and that of his fellow beings; he, therefore, that employs the best means to accomplish this is the wisest. So when we see that the best possible means have been used to accomplish the designs of God, and that everything is perfect in its kind, we affirm that the creator is infinite in his wisdom.[1] Besides making the New England system of divinity anthropomorphic, Clark abstracts from it that element of Platonic idealism with which it was tinctured. The construction of the universe may require archetypes, but these are not necessarily entities. An artist may have a clear, distinct, and perfect idea of all the parts of the most complicated new invention, before he proceeds to make it. So God from all eternity has had perfect ideas or patterns in his mind of all the beings he has ever created,—matter and its essence, immaterial beings and their powers and natures. But these ideas or patterns of beings in God's mind are not themselves real beings, but only his ideas of them.[2] Further modifications of the Edwardean scheme are to be seen in the distinctions between free and moral agency. It may be that there is a foreordination of men's actions, but unless volition enter in, the moral quality cannot be attributed to those actions. All that constitutes free agency is power to do as we choose or as we will, even in those cases where the mind, being in suspense, is decided by that mode which is called touching and taking, or luck and chance. Therefore, if from eternity it was foreknown and foreordained that we, in every instance, should do as we do; if from the operation of natural causes it were impossible for us to do differently, yet if, after we have chosen and determined to do anything, we have had power to do, then have we been free agents. Now the merit of actions is founded on their

[1] *Essay*, 1822, pp. 10, 13.   [2] *Ib.*, p. 14.

utility, but no actions deserve to be rewarded or punished unless they be voluntary, and such actions are essentially different from the necessary motions of a machine, such as a clock striking wrong.[1] Intimately conjoined with the question of moral determination is the problem of cosmic design. In this Clark again differs from the Puritan idealist of Connecticut. He believes in a direct creation, but not in direct interference; in a teleology, but not in an occasionalism. He contends, for instance, that the power of attraction which retains the planets in their orbits may have been infused into them by the creator for the purpose of executing his designs; but they keep their distinct distances not by the immediate agency of the Deity, but by the agency of their secondary powers.[2]

In rejecting a predestination which has no moral quality, and a teleology in which there is no room for arbitrary interference, Clark has unmistakably passed out of the puritanic into the deistic stage. Now he takes a more advanced position, by limiting the powers of the Deity through postulating the coexistence of a co-ordinate entity. Although God, he argues, has had power to create and govern the universe, it were impossible for him to create either himself or infinite space. Nor can we believe that God could cause all space to be filled with a solid, impenetrable substance, so that there is no possibility of it, or any part of it, being moved, even by God himself, for want of room. To believe this is too much for our weak capacities. One infinite being cannot create another, but more than one infinite being may exist, perfectly distinct from and independent from each other, for such are infinite God and infinite space.[3] Following the line of reasoning offered by the deistic dualism, Clark, like that other rural philosopher, Ethan Allen, has reached the absurdity of two absolutes. And so, too, being hampered by the deistic transcendence, he does not go on in the straight logical way, and, by making the two absolutes identical, reach a doctrine of transcendence. Instead, he is led off into the by-paths of pluralism, and chases the phantom of a plastic principle in nature. He tells how, from his experiences in attempting to move billet or stone and finding in them a resisting force, he came to believe that matter never existed in accordance with the common definition, as a solid, extended, inert substance, but that

[1] *Essays*, p. 16.   [2] *Ib.*, p. 23.   [3] *Ib.*, p. 15.

the active powers of attraction and many other powers were perhaps coeval with its very existence.[1]   From this supposition it follows that no hard and fast line can be drawn between the material and the spiritual worlds.   Matter, being active and not passive, is akin to those substances generally considered immaterial.   Thus, if we find it difficult to conceive of the souls of men existing in a disembodied state, it is equally difficult to deny that some arrangement of mind can produce thought.   Furthermore, the vegetative soul is no more distinct from matter than matter is from mind. Indeed, the vegetative and human souls resemble each other in both being produced by traduction, and in both possessing the power of self-healing.   But along with these resemblances there are differences.   While the vegetable has no power of perception, is fixed to one place, and cannot move itself by volition, the animal has powers of mind, active propensities, immutable and unchangeable in each species.   Surely all this depends on something entirely different from passive, inert matter.[2]   The speculative countryman, ruminating on what he saw in those long, solitary walks, described by his biographer, has well-nigh reached the ancient doctrine of the *anima mundi.*   But he is not enough of a pantheist fully to carry out the doctrine of the soul of the world, the possibility of his developing a natural monism being thwarted by his eighteenth century dualism.

Clark's next production, the *New Pamphlet,* published some years after the *Essays,* is likewise of a deistic cast, in returning to the argument for design and repeating the dreary round of Pope and Paley.   Under the caption that nature is an effect whose cause is God, it is argued that we ought not to confound the two and consider them as one and the same, for, by so doing, we cannot discriminate between efficient and physical causes.   If we do make no distinction between God and nature, we admit that, if there be an efficient cause to produce an effect, it ought to be considered only as another physical cause in a train of sequences, and not observed as an antecedence.   But God existed before nature, hence we can look from nature up to nature's God, for nature is as distinct from God as a watch is from him who made it.[3]   While Clark's cosmology is deism gone to seed, there is still something

[1] *Essays,* p. 23.   [2] *Ib.,* p. 27.   [3] *New Pamphlet,* p. 11.

vital in his ontology.   Instead of considering matter as a solid, inert substance, he conceives of it as the support of all the secondary and all the sensible qualities, a substance which no power in nature can destroy.   Moreover, if all bodies should perish by the war of the elements by which they are surrounded, yet the matter of which they were composed would still exist as a real being, even if there were no mind in existence.[1]   What is the meaning of this passage? While it does not exclude the existence of the divine mind as a necessary substratum of matter, an idealistic interpretation thereof is expressly set aside.   Matter includes sensible qualities, and all sensible qualities have need of a support.   And yet that which supports bodies is a really existent matter and not, as Berkeley defines it, merely that which is immediately seen and felt, merely a combination of sensible qualities.[2]   Again, there may be ideas in the mind separated from all real existences, ideas of the state, modes, and sensible qualities of bodies, viewed by the mind as entirely separated from body, yet such ideas are those of abstraction and have no archetypes in nature.[3]

In his theory of knowledge Clark is no Berkeleian, little trace of that form of thought being left in Connecticut since the departure of the ideal bishop from the neighbouring province and the discomfiture of his disciple, Samuel Johnson, at Yale College.   So Clark is more of a realist than of an idealist.   He believes, it is true, that there is a power in mind, as a cause, under given circumstances, to produce particular effects, as there is power in a coiled watch spring to expand.[4]   But from this power arise merely ideas of reflection; the most of our ideas originating from sensation, according to which, wherever an impression is made on the organs of sense-perception, we are as certain that a body exists out of our minds, as that we have an impression.[5]   In spite of its commonsense point of view, this essay of Clark's met with little favour. Jefferson in his latter days, after his conversion to realism through the person of Dugald Stewart, wrote to Clark that he revolted against the metaphysical reading to which the *New Pamphlet* belonged.   Locke, Kames, Hartley, Reid, Stewart, Brown, and

[1] *New Pamphlet,* pp. 9, 10, 12.   [2] *Ib.,* p. 4.
[3] *Ib.,* p. 12.   [4] *Ib.,* p. 7.   [5] *Ib.,* p. 7.

Tracy, he continued—these dreams of a day vanish in vapour, leaving not a wreck behind. The business of life is with matter; that gives us tangible results; handling that we arrive at the knowledge of the axe, the plough, the steamboat, and everything useful in life; but from metaphysical speculation I have never seen one useful result.[1]

These philistine remarks of the Southern sage may have been meant to dissuade the Northern farmer from the vain pursuit of philosophy. But Clark did not take the hint. Within two years there appeared a disputatious pamphlet *On the Immortality of the Soul*. Following the conclusion of the *Essays* of 1822, which denied to the soul any innate ideas, and arguing against both pre-existence and after-existence, by questioning the good of a soul without a body,[2] the author cynically asserts that to manage the multitude it makes no difference whether the soul be immortal or not, since they can easily be made to believe it is, and that will answer every purpose.[3] But to make the multitude believe was not Clark's purpose. He is less interested in the immortality of the soul than in its nature, and that he makes to consist in an active, immaterial being, which exists in the embryo of man immediately after he is conceived, is the cause of life, has a power to make the blood and keep it in circulation, to form the nerves, bones, and muscles of the body and all the various organs which are the means of sensations, appetites, imagination and thought.[4] This complicated definition is referred to Goldsmith's *History of Animals* and to Balfour's explication of the Stoic doctrine of the constituent parts of man. From the latter Clark is led off into his subsequent speculations regarding a plastic principle in nature and regarding a doctrine of the homogeneity of mind and matter approaching that of Priestley. Now he simply rests content in a dilemma, denying that matter itself can either perceive or think, yet affirming that without bodily changes there are no intellectual changes.[5]

Interesting and Important Truths [6] is the title of Clark's fifth

[1] Jefferson to Clark, Dec. 5, 1825.
[2] *Essays*, pp. 29, 31.
[3] *On the Immortality of the Soul*, 1827, p. 12.
[4] *Ib.*, p. 1.
[5] *Ib.*, pp. 6, 7.
[6] *Interesting and Important Truths;* 1834.

and last pamphlet. That title is belied unless the work be considered a sort of popular epitome of the speculative movements of the eighteenth century as they came to agitate the common mind. In it there is to be found a rejection of Puritanic determinism, yet an acceptance of transcendent design; a belief in materialism, yet an aversion to pushing its principles to the extreme. So first, despite the Edwardean conclusion of the *New Pamphlet,* that every volition of mankind, from the beginning, has necessarily been as it has, Clark here rejects the dogma of foreordination of whatsoever comes to pass, as inconsistent with moral accountability. Accountable to God for doing his will? Fine logic, indeed! he exclaims. Had no member of a commonwealth power to counteract the will of its legislature, there never would be a rebellion or any violation of its laws.[1] And further there is no proof that God exercises a particular providence toward man, any more than toward the rest of the animal kingdom, inasmuch as from eternity he could not foreknow and determine every impression that should be made through the medium of the senses on the countless millions of animals. On the contrary, all that we receive, enjoy and suffer from nature is produced by natural causes; no animal act, no act of man is the immediate act of God. The falling down of persons at camp meetings is no more the immediate act of God than the falling of water from the top of Niagara Falls; both are produced by natural causes; the first by the power of the passions and the imagination over the nervous system, through faith, the other by the attraction of gravitation. But although we receive nothing directly from God, yet nature is only a means, an instrument, or an agent by which God accomplishes his designs or purposes; it is not an independent being which purposes or wills anything of itself, but merely a passive agent which faithfully executes the will of God and is itself from God. In fine, the Book of Nature is the Word of God.[2]

While Clark utilises a special phrase from the *Age of Reason* he is evidently not satisfied with the shallow deism of Paine. Admit that there cannot be design and contrivance without a designer and contriver, admit that mere nothing could not have produced matter, yet this does not prove but that matter has

[1] *Interesting and Important Truths,* p. 11.   [2] *Ib.,* pp. 1, 2, 3.

eternally existed and was not created. Grant that matter has been eternally existent; that no arrangement of mere matter can produce either feeling, perception, thinking or volition; that mind could not possibly have been produced by matter; that the present beautiful and harmonious system of nature could not have arisen from a fortuitous concourse of atoms; yet this does not prove but that the universe, with all its suns and stars, may have existed from eternity. It implies no contradiction to suppose the universe self-existent and eternal, for how can it be proved but that there has been eternal sequence of antecedents and consequences, of causes and effects, similar to what is now occurring.[1] That Clark, in this question of his, knew whither he was tending is evidenced by his coming to an indirect defence of pantheism. The pantheist, he explains, who denies the personality of God, no more believes that the universe came into existence by chance, than the theist, who affirms the divine personality, believes that God came into existence by chance. The one believes that the universe is eternally self-existent, the other that God is eternally self-existent. Neither attributes the existence of anything to chance.[2]

Without definitely accepting a monistic cosmology, Clark proceeds to speculate upon the subject of a plastic principle in nature. This he tentatively defines as an active, immaterial substance producing effects not attributable to inert matter. An instance of this principle is to be found in the workings of the vegetative soul, as when a growing tree, slightly wounded, heals itself. A similar instance is to be found in the physical power of the human soul, by the which it arranges matter, forms the various parts of the body and heals it of sickness.[3] While technically ignorant of the *anima vegetativa* and the *vis mediatrix naturae,* the minor materialist has been beguiled into postulating those occult qualities which his materialistic predecessors, Colden and Cooper, were wont to decry as remnants of mediæval scholasticism. However, Clark goes on to argue that bodies cannot exist without their appropriate immaterial substances, or active powers, and their essential qualities; for example, ice from water cannot exist without cohesive attraction, and the qualities of hardness and coldness, nor can

---

[1] *Interesting and Important Truths*, p. 5. [2] *Ib.,* p. 5. [3] *Ib.,* pp. 15, 19.

these qualities exist in a disembodied state separately from ice. So too, if it be possible for ultimate atoms to exist without the power of attraction in them, then that power is not essential to the existence of matter. Such atoms may exist in farthest space, at as great a distance from the most distant stars as these are from the earth, in a chaos as vast and extensive as that over which Milton represents Satan to have journeyed, when he went from paradise to pandemonium.[1] With this flight of fancy the author returns to a more logical arrangement of his materials. He accepts in a preliminary way a current definition of matter as the substratum of sensible qualities, the concealed subject or support of visible and tangible qualities.[2] He then adds that substance is a being or subject which of itself is supposed to have essential qualities, and that bodies consist of matter, of an immaterial substance, and of qualities not essential to the existence of matter.[3] Leaving these definitions Clark comes to his last section wherein he makes the agnostic confession that it is impossible to explain the creation of matter. But although he realises that his metaphysical labyrinth ends in a blind alley, he amuses himself by peering through the hedge. Atoms and occult qualities have been misleading clues, but there remains the unexplored region of the ethereal world. In it there may be ultimate substances which are neither minds or bodies, as attractions, repulsions, and gravitation itself. Take one of the first category—magnetic attraction. If it be produced by an intervening, subtile fluid, what causes the motion of this fluid? Is it an active power, an immaterial substance within the fluid and yet not essential to the existence of matter? Matter itself cannot produce motion, therefore that which can produce motion is something different from matter, an active instead of an inert substance. Motion is not a real substance any more than time; neither is it a quality of matter, but only a particular state of it. There are consequently two kinds of substances, material and immaterial. Bodies may be produced and destroyed by the operations of nature, but matter cannot; candles and paper

[1] *Interesting and Important Truths*, p. 23.
[2] Quoted from the *English Encyclopaedia* (*Encyclopaedia Britannica?*).
[3] *Interesting and Important Truths*, p. 22.

can be destroyed by fire, but not the particles of matter of which
they are composed; they are bandied about by every active power
in nature, to be again arranged into other bodies and again dis-
arranged in succession, as long as the universe shall last. Now
the attractions and repulsions of bodies are conveyed and exerted
through the medium of an intervening, active fluid, but this does
not remove the necessity of admitting an active immaterial substance to cause the motion of the fluid.   But what causes its
motion?[1]

In his final abrupt query the last of the early American materialists ends where the first began.   But while Colden made a critical use of historical speculations, Clark's method was essentially
popular.   Puritanism and idealism, deism and materialism in succession attracted his attention, but he was able neither to get to
the bottom of the systems he rejected, nor to leave behind him a
strong and consistent structure of his own.   In fine, he was one of
those metaphysical castle-builders,[2] described by the father of
common-sense as adding colour and befitting ornament by the
imagination, but disdaining the mean offices of digging for a
foundation and carrying materials. So while the fabric pleases
the eye, it wants solidity and lasts only until it is blown into rubbish by some succeeding architect of the fancy.

[1] *Interesting and Important Truths,* p. 24.
[2] Thomas Reid, *Inquiry into the Human Mind,* New York, 1824, p. 8.

BOOK V—REALISM

CHAPTER I

REALISM

NATURAL Realism, according to an early American exponent, consists in the doctrine that the mind perceives not merely the ideas or images of external objects but the external objects themselves; that when these are presented to our senses, they produce certain impressions; that these impressions are followed by correspondent sensations; and these sensations by a perception of the existence and qualities of the objects about which the mind is employed, and that they possess the qualities which we witness, not by a train of reasoning, by formal reflection or by association of ideas, but by a direct and necessary connection between the presence of such objects and our consequent perceptions. In short the distinguishing peculiarity of such metaphysics is an appeal from the delusive principles of the idealism of Berkeley and the scepticism of Hume to the common sense of mankind as a tribunal paramount to all the subtleties of philosophy.[1] This is the definition of Samuel Miller, the Princeton historian of the eighteenth century in his exposition of the system of Reid; it may be supplemented by a defence of President McCosh, the pupil of Hamilton, two generations later. Realism, says the latter, is that system which holds that there are real things and that man can know them; that we have no need to resort to such theories as those of internal ideas or occasional causes coming between the perceiving mind and the perceived objects; but that the mind knows directly and intuitively three kinds of reality, first, matter, whether existing in the body or out of the body as external, extended and resisting; second, the perceiving self as thinking or willing, a reality as certain and definite as matter, but perceived by self-consciousness and not the external senses; third, the objects perceived by our conscience or moral perception, the higher knowledge of voluntary acts as being

[1] Miller, *Retrospect,* 1803, Vol. 2, p. 11.

morally good or evil. The mind perceives matter at once, but it also perceives benevolence, and perceives it to be good as clearly as the eye perceives objects to be extended. In brief, in all our cognitions, our intuitive convictions carry with them their own evidence and authority; adopt any other theory, say idealism, and make the mind add to things as it perceives them, or phenomenalism, which makes us know mere appearances, and we shall find ourselves ever knocking against intuitive convictions, as against obstinate facts facing us as rocks. By the help of these fundamental laws of belief, with their criteria of self-evidence, necessity and universality, we can stand up for the trustworthiness of the senses and do not require to call in to our help, ' ideas ' with Locke, or ' impressions ' with Hume, or ' phenomena ' with Kant, but may follow our natural convictions implicitly and regard the mind as perceiving things immediately and running no risk of deceptions or contradictions.[1]

Such, without further dilation, is that natural realism which has had the distinction of being considered by many as pre-eminently the American philosophy. This is true, if one considers its rapid growth, its wide spread and its tenacious hold upon the popular mind. Brought in as a transatlantic off-shoot of the Scotch school, it overran the country, had at one time an exclusive and preponderant influence, and has lasted until the present hour.[2] For this astonishing success many reasons have been given: not only was the common sense philosophy of Reid, Stewart, Brown and Hamilton in harmony with the practical note of the country, but it was also an aid to faith, a safeguard to morality as against the scepticism of Hume and the atheism of the Voltairians.[3] Granting the validity of such arguments, they may be more properly classified from two points of view: internally as intrinsic excellences; externally as adventitious aids. As to the former, natural realism is claimed to possess a unity, not only in the circumstances that its expounders have been Scotchmen, but also and

---

[1] James McCosh, *Realistic Philosophy,* New York, 1887, Vol. 1, pp. 5-10; Compare *The Scottish Philosophy,* New York, 1874.

[2] Becelaere, *op. cit.,* p. 54.

[3] *Ib.,* quoting John Fiske and G. Stanley Hall.

more especially in its method, its doctrines and its spirit: first, it proceeds on the method of observation and induction and not of analysis and deduction,—not explaining phenomena by assumed principles or bringing facts to support theories, or resolving the complexities of the universe by refined mental distinctions; second, it employs self-consciousness as the instrument of observation, professes to draw all the laws of mental philosophy from observations of consciousness and not from the observations of the brain or nerves, or generally from animal physiology.; here its instrument is our internal sense, our inward experience and not such subordinate and subsidiary knowledge as the estimation of the vital forces; third, by its observations, consciousness reaches principles which are prior to and independent of existence, principles of common sense which Reid characterises as natural, original and necessary, Stewart as fundamental laws. of human thought and belief. In fine, it is the great merit of this school that it puts a large body of truth on a foundation which can never be moved, throwing light on perception through the senses, the intellectual powers and classifications of the mental faculties and the peculiarities of man's moral and emotional nature, of his conscience, and of his taste for the beautiful.[1]

Thus far, merits ranging from the method of observation to a criterion of aesthetics were claimed to be the special possession of realism, as if materialism did not possess the one and idealism the other. But in addition to these intrinsic excellences, there were adventitious aids which contributed to the success of the movement. First, it happened to fit the needs of educational and ecclesiastical orthodoxy. It was not, as in Scotland, favoured by the union of church and state, but by the peculiar American combination of church and college, here not only was the philosophy of reality convenient, compact and teachable, appealing to a common sense of which every youngster had some spark, but it was also an eminently safe philosophy which kept undergraduates locked in so many intellectual dormitories, safe from the dark speculations of materialism or the beguiling allurements of idealism. Or, as the matter has been expressed by another, Hobbes because of his. atomism, was considered a guide to atheism, Hume

[1] McCosh, *Scottish Philosophy*, p. 9.

because of his scepticism, the arch-enemy of orthodoxy, while
Berkeley was always suspected to be a leader in the same direction.
Therefore, to prevent the undermining of the faith, college professors took philosophy seriously and not speculatively and a religious bias helped to determine the hold of realism in education.[1] A
second cause for the success of realism lay in the organisations
upon which it chanced to fasten. In its propaganda it used most
of the denominational colleges on the Atlantic seaboard, and was
also backed by the denominations themselves. Here the churches,
like well-constructed machines, turned out uniform sets of opinions
all fitting the same mould of common sense; for to obtain many
men of one mind, the Protestant clergy of these times were practically all formed from the Scotch pattern, the text-books of Reid
and Stewart, Beattie and Hamilton coming from the native press
in an almost unbroken series of editions. A third cause of the
success of realism was the character of the immigration into the
country. Between the New Englanders with their modified Calvinism, and the Southerners with their diluted Arminianism, there
came a wave of new settlers, which on touching the American
shore spread itself more widely than any other.[2] Whatever the
extent of the immigration, at any rate, the Scotch-Irish, entering
chiefly by way of the ports of the Middle States, carried along
with their Presbyterian connections their philosophy of common
sense. To trace this movement into the Alleghany Mountains and
down the valleys of Virginia and of the Cumberland, is to trace
a kind of intellectual glacier, an overwhelming mass of cold facts
which moved slowly southwards and ground out all opposition.
This glacial age in American thought was of the greatest significance. Because of it deism disappeared, save in the tide-water
counties where planters of English blood still remained, and materialism was wiped out, save in the Gallicised portions of the
country, such as the Carolinas, and the Bourbon sections of Kentucky.

That the union of church and college was a fortuitous aid to

[1] President Patton of Princeton Seminary in a conversation with the
writer.

[2] John DeWitt, *The Planting of Princeton College*, 1897, p. 179.

the spread of realism is clear from the fate of its rivals; deism lacked new blood because English pioneers of the cultured class had ceased coming to the country; idealism languished because its especial means of communication, the Anglican church, was practically a channel cut off; few scholars of Oxford and Cambridge, no ecclesiastic of the type of Berkeley came into the country after the second war with England. But it was materialism that suffered most for want of those auxiliaries under which realism flourished. As compared with realism the contrast is striking: immigration did not help it, and sparks struck out by men like Priestley and Cooper were a mere flash in the pan; nor were the colleges of much avail; the University of Pennsylvania by bad management, Transylvania University by its poverty and remoteness, and the University of Virginia by political complications were together rendered inoperative as aids to materialism. Even if Jefferson's late conversion from materialism to realism had been known, his political affiliations would have damaged him in the sight of the orthodox, for thus, by way of contrast, the elder President Dwight of Yale had more weight in the scales of orthodox philosophy than the President of the United States himself; the one standing for respectable federalism, the other for infidel democracy.[1] But the lack of efficient organisation was the great drawback for the materialistic cause. Had Jefferson succeeded in founding his central society after the model of the French Academy, had there been anything approaching the Royal Society of England in the whole land, scientific investigations like those of Colden and of Rush might have received the stamp of institutional approval.

If these are mere conjectures as to what might have happened, what did really happen was that materialism, left to itself as a mere speculative movement, practically disappeared from the field of thought, and that a rival movement which was backed up by a strong organisation, a rigid faith, and well trained agents, with all its faults, inconsistencies, contradictions and superficialities, remained as the dominant force in the field. Such a force was Scotch realism whose headquarters were at Princeton.

[1] Compare Jefferson's letter to Thomas Cooper, Nov. 2, 1822. *Works*, Vol. 10, p. 242, (Ford ed.).

CHAPTER II

THE PRINCETON SCHOOL

TRADITIONALLY Princeton is committed to a realistic metaphysics as opposed to agnosticism, materialism or idealism.[1] This is the opinion of one of its exponents at the one hundred and fiftieth anniversary of the founding of the institution. Amplified and put in slightly different terms this opinion sums up the early history of the College as it passed through successive reactions to the current phases of speculation. First, it was opposed to the agnosticism of extreme deism, considering the age of reason as little else but the age of infidelity;[2] next, it was opposed to materialism, whether that meant a no-soul psychology as with Buchanan, or a reduction of psychology to a physiology of the nerves as with Cooper, or an identification of body and mind as with Priestley. Lastly, it was opposed to idealism in all its forms, putting against the phenomenalism of the followers of Berkeley, Hume and Kant, the Scotch intuitionism which finds, in place of mediate perception, immediate cognition, and in place of the relativity of knowledge, a direct knowledge of real qualities in things and the unchangeable relations between them. In brief, the Princeton system was a complete dualism: in its cosmology between the world and deity; in its psychology between soul and body; in its epistemology between subject and object. Or, as one of them has expressed it, Princeton philosophers prefer to admit the existence of an *impasse* to a complete intellectual unification of the universe, than to purchase metaphysical unity at the cost of surrendering the judgments of common sense.[3]

[1] W. M. Daniels, *Princeton Traditions and Tendencies* (*The Critic*, Oct. 24, 1896).
[2] Compare Elias Boudinot, *The Age of Revelation, or the Age of Reason shown to be an Age of Infidelity*, Philadelphia, 1801.
[3] Daniels, *op. cit.*

480

It was this avoidance of the difficulties and embarrassments of a strict metaphysics, this accommodation of its teachings to the general intelligence, that led realists like McCosh to claim that such a natural realism as was taught at Princeton was what an American philosophy should be.[1] The claim may be disputed, yet it has in its favour the fact that the College of New Jersey, from its very foundation, had impressed upon it a national character, inasmuch as it was not the college of an established church, nor of a single colony, nor of a people sprung from a single nationality, but had for its charter an undenominational document, for its heads graduates of Harvard and Yale, Glasgow and Edinburgh, and for its students, the sons of English Friends, New England Puritans and Presbyterians from Scotland and Ireland.[2] But although in this connection it be granted that Princeton was the freest college in the country in its beginnings, it was hardly so in its development; a fatal polemic spirit seized hold of it, and, as the institution passed through three external stages, corresponding to the three speculative movements of the age, it grew more and more constricted and unreceptive. During the Revolutionary war Nassau Hall was a refuge for the military, but not for the intellectuals; it received Washington and his forces, but shut out the stray followers of Locke, Berkeley, Hume, Hartley and Darwin. In a word, the college which had been a defence of the faith against the attacks of the deists, became what one of the defenders of natural realism has called a bulwark of impregnable truth before which all forms of error and irreligion must give way.[3] To explain this state of affairs a parallel may be drawn: as Princeton, situated on the highway between New York and Philadelphia, was a critical battle-ground between the British and the Americans, so it became a position of strategic importance between the idealists of the North and the materialists of the South. But in the latter case, the victory over the opposing forces was gained only at considerable expense, the loss of a certain spirit of

[1] *Realistic Philosophy,* Chapter I.

[2] John DeWitt, *Planting of Princeton College.*

[3] W. H. Hodge, *Intuitive Perception, a New Philosophy of Natural Realism,* Lancaster, Pa., 1903, p. 380.

liberality due to the replacement of speculation by dogma, of philosophy by theology. Starting as a non-ecclesiastical body, formed by the broader men of the synod of New York, a Presbyterian form of belief came in with Witherspoon, increased with Stanhope Smith, until, with the appearance of Ashbel Green in 1812, the theological seminary so dominated the college, that the two were persistently identified and that up to the very sesquicentennial of the University.[1]

While these events may run past the period of the early schools, they are necessary for the understanding of the Princetonian claim that it was the Scottish-American realism, and not New England transcendentalism, that was to be considered, in largest measure, the peculiar philosophy of the country.   However, for the settling of these alternatives, one might ask which of the two systems best fulfilled the criteria of native origin, of progressiveness, of liberality of spirit and of toleration of other forms of thought. But these are questions to be answered only after one has gained the proper historical data, and these data are in turn furnished only by a consideration of the personal representatives of natural realism.

[1] So Professor John DeWitt in a conversation with the writer.

CHAPTER III

JOHN WITHERSPOON

AFTER the administration of its early heads, from the apologetic Jonathan Dickinson to the scholastic Samuel Davies, Nassau Hall entered upon a short period of speculative quiescence. But with the advent of President Witherspoon in 1768, the philosophical situation became as agitated as was the political, for now English deism vanished, an American form of idealism was driven forth, and Scotch realism became the official system of the place. From this time, arguments a priori, evidences of final cause and the whole machinery of teleology disappeared, along with Martin's *Newtonian Philosophy* and Watts' *Knowledge of the Heavens and Earth Made Easy*. In their stead came arguments a posteriori, obvious first principles, simple perceptions of necessary truth, and the works of Reid and Beattie, Thomas Brown and Hamilton. In brief, the era of deduction and design was succeeded by the era of induction and common sense, or as the new college head phrased the matter—it is safer in our reasonings to trace facts upwards than to reason downwards.

Like President McCosh, his successor, of precisely one hundred years later, John Witherspoon (1723-1794) was in point of ancestry a Covenanter, by birth a Lowland Scotchman, in his youth a student at the University of Edinburgh, in his manhood a minister of the Church of Scotland. As to his personality accounts differ: a recent biographer describes him as a man of extraordinary force, versatility and charm; eminent as a teacher, preacher, politician, law-maker and philosopher, and with the exception of Washington, as having more of the quality called presence than, perhaps, any other man of his time in America; on the other hand, Thomas Carlyle said that he was of a disagreeable temper; Jonathan Odell satirised him as ' fierce as the fiercest, foremost of the first '; John Adams declared him clear but a little heavy in his

speech; and President Stiles of Yale shrewdly remarked that while
the Doctor was of a reasoning make, his philosophical learning
was not great.[1]   In truth, Witherspoon was a man of action
rather than of reflection.   With his manifold duties in the New
Jersey College, the Provincial Convention and the Continental
Congress, he had little time for meditation and less for the production of philosophic works; it might indeed be said that from
his estate called Tusculum few Tusculan disputations came forth.
As a further hindrance to the free output of speculative productions Witherspoon had entered the country with his mind somewhat rigidly made up, and at the age of five and forty possessed
ideas more conservative than those of his predecessors.   The former
heads of the College, graduates of Harvard and Yale, had been
open to the influences of the earlier optimistic deism, they had
argued in favour of this being the best possible world, they had
looked on the workings of nature with such admiring eyes as to
be well nigh ready to grant it self-sufficiency.   But to the lineal
descendant of John Knox the external world bore a different aspect; in itself it was far from being perfect or self-sufficient; rather
was it a created thing, a limited thing, a thing full of defects.
If the apologetic deist chose to defend natural evil, see sermons in
stones and good in everything, he was no such complaisant reasoner.   That such was his attitude is evident in those vigorous
assaults he had already made in the old country on these feeble
compromisers.   In his *Ecclesiastical Characteristics* he described
the moderate man as one who ought to be filled with a contempt
for all kinds of learning except for the *Theodicée* of Leibniz, the
chief parts of which are so beautifully painted and so harmoniously
sung by Lord Shaftesbury.[2]   Moreover, for those who have great
charity for atheists and deists, Witherspoon draws up, in obvious
parody of the Anglicans, what he denominates his Athenian Creed:

---

[1] James McCosh, *The Scotch Philosophy*, New York, 1874, p. 184 ff.
John DeWitt, *Princeton College Administrations in the Nineteenth Century*,
in *Presbyterian and Reformed Review*, Oct., 1897, p. 665.   M. C. Tyler,
Literary History of the American Revolution, New York, 1900, Vol. 2, p.
320.   John Adams, *Works*, Vol. 1, p. 227.   Stiles, *Literary Diary*, Vol. 2,
p. 338.
[2] *Works*, Edinburgh, 1804-5, Vol. 6, p. 180.

I believe in the beauty and comely proportions of Dame Nature, and in almighty Fate, her only parent and guardian. . . . I believe that the universe is a huge machine, wound up from everlasting by necessity, and consisting of an infinite number of links and chains, each in a progressive motion towards the zenith of perfection and meridian of glory; that I myself am a little glorious piece of clockwork, a wheel within a wheel, or rather a pendulum in this grand machine, swinging hither and thither by the different impulses of fate and destiny; that my soul (if I have any) is an imperceptible bundle of exceeding minute corpuscles, much smaller than the smallest Holland sand. . . . I believe that there is no ill in the universe, nor any such thing as virtue, absolutely considered; that these things, vulgarly called sins, are only errors in the judgment, and foils to set off the beauty of nature, or patches to adorn her face.[1]

Harrassed by the host of enemies raised up by this anonymous satire of his, and finding from certain legal troubles that Scotland was too hot for him, Witherspoon took up with the repeated offer of the presidency of the New Jersey College, which was pressed upon him by Benjamin Rush, then a student of medicine at Edinburgh, and journeyed to America, where he was received as if he were the very prince after whom the college was named. But his duties at Princeton were not easy; in teaching alone, in addition to a course in moral philosophy, he included lectures to the juniors and seniors upon chronology and history, composition and criticism, Hebrew and French. Then, too, speculative troubles stared him in the face; on his arrival he found that the Irish idealism had obtained a footing in the locality. According to the later account of President Ashbel Green, the Berkeleian system of metaphysics was in repute in the college when Witherspoon entered. The tutors were zealous believers in it, and waited on the president with some expectation of either confounding him or making him a proselyte. They had mistaken their man. He first reasoned against the system, and then ridiculed it till he drove it out of the college. The writer has heard him state that before Reid or any other author of their views had published any theory on the ideal system, he wrote against it, and suggested the same trains

[1] *Works*, Vol. 6, p. 185.

of thought which they adopted, and that he published his essay in a Scotch magazine.[1]

The story of Witherspoon's fight against idealism is substantiated by the accounts of those who were implicated in it, President Stanhope Smith and his biographer Frederick Beasley being among that number; but the boast of being the precursor of natural realism has a very shaky foundation. Witherspoon's essay in the Scotch magazine has never been found, nor do the facts warrant the statements that he was the man who actually introduced Scottish thought into the new world,[2] or that he was the first man who taught in America the substance of those doctrines of the philosophy of the human mind which Dr. Reid afterwards developed.[3] The Scotch philosophers were read in the college some time before Witherspoon set foot in the country. Thus, in 1764 Kames' *Principles of Natural Religion* was read by Jefferson,[4] in 1760 Hutcheson *On Beauty and Virtue* was in the Princeton library;[5] in 1756 one of the same author's works was being used as a text-book in the philosophy school of the Philadelphia Academy;[6] and in 1748 Ezra Stiles in New Haven had read Shaftesbury's *Characteristics,* and Shaftesbury's constant appeal was to the *sensus communis.* Moreover, in 1751 Stiles expressed his pleasure with Turnbull's scheme of treating moral, as Newton had treated natural, philosophy.[7] If anticipations are looked for, here was an anticipation of the hope that Witherspoon expressed exactly two decades later, that perhaps a time may come when men, treating moral philosophy, as Newton and his successors have done natural, may arrive at greater precision.

Witherspoon did not actually introduce the Scottish philosophy

[1] McCosh, pp. 187-8.   [2] *Ib.,* p. 184.

[3] Samuel Miller, *Retrospect,* Vol. 2, p. 377. A more accurate statement is given in Appleton's Encyclopaedia, Vol. 6, p. 585: 'Witherspoon was the first teacher in America of the system of metaphysics that was contemporaneously expounded in Scotland by Thomas Reid.'

[4] *Works,* Vol. 14, p. 144.

[5] *Catalogue of Books in the Library of the College of New Jersey,* Jan. 29, 1776, Woodbridge (N. J.).

[6] William Smith, *Discourses,* London, 1759, p. 225.

[7] Compare above Book III, Chapter III; also the Yale Library contained a copy of Hutcheson's *Metaphysical Synopsis* as early as 1745.

into America; neither did he antedate the doctrines of Reid or his immediate followers. In the *Lectures on Moral Philosophy,* of which, like the *Nicomachean Ethics,* there remains only a dry syllabus, the author expresses but a hesitating acceptance of the doctrine of natural realism. He says that in opposition to such infidel writers as David Hume, who sought to shake the certainty of our belief upon cause and effect, upon personal identity, and the idea of power, some writers have advanced, with great apparent reason, that there are certain first principles or dictates of common sense, which are either first principles, or principles seen with intuitive evidence. These are the foundation of all reasoning, and without them, to reason is a word without a meaning. They can no more be proved than you can prove an axiom in mathematical science. These authors of Scotland have lately produced and supported this opinion, to resolve at once all the refinements and metaphysical objections of some infidel writers.[1] According to his later recapitulation the Scots to whom Witherspoon here refers are Beattie and Reid. From the former's *Essay on Truth* of 1773 Witherspoon draws his definition of impressions of common sense as axioms and first principles of all our reasonings on moral subjects, but from Reid's *Inquiry* of 1763 he fails to assimilate the distinction between simple apprehension and judgment or belief, consequent upon sensation. Instead, therefore, of forestalling the chief representative of Scotch realism, the Princetonian actually fails to hold to the characteristic differentiation between sensation and reflection; on the contrary, he leans to that view of the faculty of morality which makes it both a sense and a perception of moral excellence.[2] Then, too, he was unsuccessful in grasping the central principles of that system against which Reid had already written—the doctrine of representative perception through mediate images. In his criticism of Berkeley and Hume he exhibits an entire misconception of the doctrine of sensible reality. He asserts that the immaterialists say, that we are conscious of nothing but the impression or feeling of our own mind; but they do not observe that the impression itself implies and supposes something external that communicates it, and can-

[1] *Moral Philosophy*, p. 42.　　[2] *Ib.*, p. 21.

not be separated from that supposition. Sometimes such reasoners tell us, that we cannot shew the substance separate from its sensible qualities; no more can any man shew me a sensible quality separate from a particular subject. If any man will shew me whiteness without shewing me anything that is white, or roundness, without anything that is round, I will shew him the substance without either colour or shape. Immaterialism takes away the distinction between truth and falsehood. I have an idea of a house or tree in a certain place, and I call this true, that is, I am of the opinion, there is really a house or tree in that place. Again, I form an idea of a house or tree, as what may be in that place; I ask what is the difference, if after all, you tell me, there is neither tree, house nor place anywhere existing.[1]

With all his ignorances of the fine points of the earlier realism, Witherspoon was a true realist in the larger sense. His reference to that universal dictate of our nature, which we must take as true immediately, without further examination, smacks strongly of the principles of the Scottish school, from Shaftesbury's natural knowledge and fundamental reason, to Hamilton's scheme of the essential characters of the principles of common sense as incomprehensibility, simplicity, necessity and universality, comparative evidence and certainty.[2] Witherspoon's definitions contained, in an implicit way, the principles of the later representatives of the realistic type; at the same time, in their embryonic stage, they bore the traces of the earlier stages of development. Such was the notion that the universality of the dictates of our nature was due to the fact that they must have been communicated at first, and handed down by information and instruction from age to age.[3] Implying, as does Reid, that the practical principles of common sense are so many divine instincts, the Princetonian now seeks to apply them to morality to the exclusion of all other principles. To prove that the Scotch school is right, he would prove that the other schools are wrong; this he does by a process of counterpoise, or mutual cancellation. First he ingeniously gets rid of Ameri-

[1] *Moral Philosophy*, p. 18.
[2] Hamilton's Edition of Reid's *Works*, Vol. 2, p. 754, Appendix A.
[3] Witherspoon, *Moral Philosophy*, p. 43.

can rivals by opposing to them the opinions of foreign authorities: against Cotton Mather, who protested that moral philosophy is just reducing infidelity to a system, he puts most of the English writers of the last age who made reason the standard of virtue. Against Doctor Wilson of Delaware, who held that the first principles of knowledge are taken from information, he puts Doctor Clark, the champion of the law of nature. Finally, against Jonathan Edwards, who held that virtue consists in the love of being as such, he put his own opinion that there is in the nature of things, a difference between virtue and vice, and however much virtue and happiness are connected by the divine law, and in the event of things, we are made so as to feel towards them, and conceive of them, as distinct, we have the simple perceptions of duty and interest.[1]

In intimating that his idealistic predecessor in office was wrong, while he was right, Witherspoon stultifies his own introductory principle that from the different and opposite systems of philosophers, there is nothing certain in their schemes. And yet he goes on with his method of mutual destruction, for he has at least a negative purpose in view: let men think what they will of moral philosophy, they ought to acquaint themselves with it; they must know what it is, if they mean to shew that it is false.[2] And the same confusion obtains when we come to the proper division of the subject into ethics, politics and jurisprudence, for we are to consider how man in species is distinct from other creatures, and, as an individual, what are the parts which constitute his nature. As to the first, philosophers have generally contradicted one another in endeavouring to bring the distinction between man and the other animals to one incommunicable characteristic, for man is not necessarily divided from the brutes by reason, or foresight, or speech, or instinct, though he may be by the sense of religion and the sense of ridicule. As to man considered as an individual, we discover that he is a compound of body and spirit; yet, with regard to the influence of the body, there does not seem to be any such connection with morals as to require a particular description. Nevertheless it does seem plain that such are the

[1] *Moral Philosophy*, p. 27; Vol. 6, p. 29.   [2] *Ib.*, p. 8.

laws of union between the body and spirit, that many faculties are weakened and some rendered altogether incapable of exercise, merely by an alteration of the state of the body, as when memory is lost by old age and disease, and the judgment wholly disordered by a confusion of the brain in a fall.[1]

In first suggesting and then disregarding the reciprocal influence of the body and spirit, the realist is but pursuing his method of reduction for the sake of simplification. Man's entire nature may be dual, yet the body is properly but the minister of the soul, —the means of conveying perceptions to it, but nothing without it. So likewise man's mental nature may be triple, for the faculties of the mind are commonly divided into three kinds—the understanding, the will, and the affections—yet properly these are not three qualities wholly distinct, as if they were three different beings, but different ways of exerting the same simple principle. It is the soul or mind that understands, wills, or is affected with pleasure and pain.[2] In thus emphasising the mental at the expense of the physical, and the rational at the expense of the conative and affective, the moralist is inexorably leading up to a single organ as the basis of our knowledge of matters of fact. Thus against Shaftesbury, who makes affection the principle of virtue, he holds that it is the understanding that seems to have truth for its object, the discovering things as they really are in themselves and in their relations one to another.[3] But the process of elimination may be carried even further: not only as regards the capacity of human nature for knowledge, but as regards the way in which we become acquainted with reality. Here then are but two ways with which we come to the knowledge of things,—sensation and reflection; the first of these must be divided into two parts, external and internal; the external arising from the immediate impression of objects from without, in which are observable the impression itself, or the sensation we feel, and the supposition inseparable from it, that it is produced from an external object. That our senses are to be trusted in the information they give us, seems to me a first principle, because they are the foundation of all our after reasonings. The few exceptions of accidental irregularity in the senses can found no just objection to this, as

---

[1] *Moral Philosophy*, pp. 6, 8, 9, 13.   [2] *Ib.*, p. 13.   [3] *Ib.*, p. 14.

there are so many plain and obvious ways of discovering and correcting it.[1]

In reviewing Witherspoon's survey of human nature, it is safe to say that his method of common sense simplification led to a sterile system of ethics, and one which was no advance on either his immediate successors or predecessors in the Princeton circle. Ignoring the connection between body and mind in morals, he loses the clue which led Rush to the discovery of moral irregularities arising from a disordered state of the brain. Disregarding overmuch the Lockean element of reflection, he is unable to perceive the validating subjective principles of morality such as were insisted upon by Edwards. And so, failing to draw Reid's sharp distinction between sensation and perception, he goes back to Hutcheson's sensitive perceptions, and turns the moral sense into a reflex sense, an automatic law of nature, previous to all reasoning, and both intimating and enforcing duty.[2] Witherspoon has thus brought his morality into accord with his epistemology and made the moral sense, like common sense, a faculty or organ whereby even the artless clown may gain an immediate grasp of certainty. Yet even if the dictates of the moral sense are certain, we must search a little further for the principles of moral action. Now here arise many controversies regarding the nature, the foundation, and the obligation of virtue. As to the first, Clark makes virtue to consist in the nature and reason of things, Hutcheson in the good of the whole, Wollaston in the truth or falsehood of the proposition, Campbell in self-love, Adam Smith in sympathy, David Hume in utility, and finally we have an opinion published in this country that virtue consists in the love of being as such. Next as to the foundation of virtue there are four opinions, founded respectively upon the will of God, the reason and nature of things, public happiness, and private happiness; upon these opinions it is to be observed that there is something true in every one of them, but they may be easily pushed to excess.[3]

As to the obligation of virtue, we need not follow the author in his dessicated enumeration, for it is here that he proceeds on the dullest of all principles, or what he was fond of referring to as the genuine dictates of common sense. But in this dreary desert there

[1] *Moral Philosophy*, pp. 17, 18. [2] *Ib.*, p. 21. [3] *Ib.*, pp. 26, 28, 31.

is one oasis, a disquisition on the nature of space, wherein the Scottish-American shows both an unwonted diffidence and a rare catholicity of judgment. Discussing, under the head of our duty to God, the natural perfections of the deity, he says that immensity in the Divine Being is that by which he is everywhere and equally present. Metaphysicians, however, differ greatly upon this subject. The Cartesians will not admit that place is at all applicable to spirits. They say it is an idea wholly arising from extension, which is one of the peculiar and essential qualities of matter. The Newtonians, however, who make so much use of the idea of infinite space, consider place as essential to all substance, spirit as well as matter. The difficulties are great on both sides. It is hard to conceive of spirit at all, separating from it the qualities of matter, and after we have attempted to do so, it seems to be bringing them back to talk of place. And yet it seems not only hard, but impossible, to conceive of any real being without supposing it in some place, and particularly upon the immensity of the Deity, it seems to be putting created spirits too much on a level with the infinite spirit to deny his immensity. It is, I think, certain they are either confined to a place, or so limited in their operations, as is no way so well expressed as by saying we are here and nowhere else.[1]

This passage may serve as a point of transition to Witherspoon's only other paper of philosophic importance written on this side of the water, his answer to his Delaware friend Matthew Wilson's *Proposal for Reducing Natural Philosophy to a System*.[2] This article, explained the Jerseyman, was an attempt of an obscure writer to unsettle our belief of the Newtonian theory, which for nearly a century has been received by all Englishmen. Shall we then hear anything against the Newtonian principles in America? Yes, replies Witherspoon, as Descartes overthrew the occult qualities and substantial forms of Aristotle, and Newton destroyed or brought into disrepute the vortices and subtle matter of Descartes, so Sir Isaac sometimes assumed certain principles, forgetting his own plan to take nature just as it was by an induction of experiences.[3]

[1] *Moral Philosophy*, p. 45.
[2] See above, Chapter on the Minor Materialists.
[3] *Pennsylvania Magazine*, May, 1776, p. 226.

This is a laboured explanation, but Witherspoon does not make clear what the trouble was. The subject with both disputants was the Newtonian conjecture as to space, in its infinite extension, being the sensorium of the deity, and the concomitant inference that both space and the divine being were material. For the sake of the contrast between the two men there may be given the conclusion of Wilson's article, and, following it, Witherspoon's continuation of the discussion. Said the former: Whether there be pure space at the utmost boundary of the created universe, is a thought which plunges and confounds our reason in this state. The vacuum or void space seems to have actual extension as well as body; it seems, therefore, an absolute being, and not a mere negation, as Sir Isaac himself confesses. This has made some philosophers allege that if space was eternal and infinite, it was either God himself, or his attribute, his immensity. But this has been thought impious, because it admits of parts, which cannot be said of God; and to admit that space is infinite and eternal, and yet not God, is admitting two Gods, which is absurd and impious. Pure space, therefore, seems contrary to or above our reason. What if we should suppose there is no end to creation, but that it extends to infinity? Or shall we suppose that, beyond creation, universal space is indeed the divine immensity, not divisible into parts, considered as universally and eternally extended; though like eternity (which is also infinite and indivisible respecting God), it exists only in our imagination, as it respects our little world and small affairs, considered piecemeal in our finite minds, which are unable to grasp an object more disproportioned to our minds than the ocean to a nutshell? [1]

Treating rival theories with moderation, Wilson concludes his disquisition in a spirit of modest conjecture. On the contrary, Witherspoon approaches the matter aggressively, and reduces the arguments of his opponents to absurdities. He proposes to the Newtonians *A Few Thoughts on Space, Dimension and the Divisibility of Matter in Infinitum,* and continues in this wise:

I class these three together, because the two latter will serve to illustrate what is to be considered of the former. It is not with-

[1] Wilson, *Proposal,* etc.

out reason that, in the present philosophy, space is always considered in the first place; because without admitting space void of matter, the whole system falls to the ground of course. . . .
. . . . This same infinite space is the most wonderful thing within the whole range of being; to enumerate its contrary definitions is impossible. It is neither God nor his creature; and yet it is inseparable from the being either of God or of anything he can create. All matter is space whatever more it is; for space is an essential property of matter; it is in space, and space is in it. Wherever matter is, there is space; and there space would be, though matter were not there. The same holds just as true with relation to it and spirit, or it and God. It is infinite both in its extension and duration; it is immovable and indivisible! If a complete definition of it were put into a lady's pocketbook, I am persuaded there is not a woman that wears one but would positively guess it to be an enigma for Nothing; and she would be astonished to be told that, in the judgment of the learned, it is the quintessence of a most learned, most metaphysical, and most subtle argument maintained upon the subject of space, by one of the most celebrated divines and philosophers that the last or any age has produced. . . . The only positive idea applied to space is extension; but we can apply no idea to any subject which the subject itself does not impress. Matter forces upon our senses the idea or image of its dimensions or extension. It is philosophical felony to steal an image which nature gives us, and invest a subject with it that never excited any idea in us, and consequently has no existence to us. We create nothing into a being, by applying ideas to it which we derive from something. Space is only one of the ideas excited by matter, and by the power of the mind abstracted from its subject, just as we can imagine a colour to ourselves, without connecting in our apprehension a subject with it wherein it exists. A little more of the same metaphysics which can prove that nothing is extended, will prove that space is purple. But why should I say purple? Space is of all colours, if light is reflected by vacuum and not by matter. It is a very ingenious contrivance in philosophers to render Nothing a subject of enquiry and conception, by dressing it in a suit of cloaths borrowed from something.[1]

Witherspoon's facile use of satire in his *Few Thoughts on Space,* together with his ruthless employment of logical elimination in the *Lectures on Moral Philosophy,* shed much light on the most interesting philosophical event of his administration at Princeton. That

[1] *Thoughts on Space.*

event was his successful attack on idealism, which, as Ashbel Green said, he first reasoned against and then ridiculed till he drove it out of the college. A single tutor, Joseph Periam,[1] had been the unhappy vehicle for the Berkeleian metaphysics, and Stanhope Smith, the president's own son-in-law and successor in office, had become infected with the taint of what was described as that impious scepticism which wholly denies the existence of matter. According to one version, Periam, soon after his graduation in 1762, embraced the bishop's theory denying the existence of the material universe, and Smith, who was intimate with him, was thereby in great danger of making shipwreck of his religious principles.[2] Of the precise manner in which immaterialism was introduced into Nassau Hall we have no record. It is very unlikely that Samuel Johnson's Berkeleian *Elements of Philosophy* was used there, as it was in the Philadelphia Academy, for Johnson, as head of the Episcopalian King's College in New York, had called the rival Presbyterian College of New Jersey a fountain of nonsense. Nor did Edwards leave behind him any trace of his peculiar idealistic theory of perception. Had he completed his projected Calvinistic *History of Redemption,* he might have been said to have left the print of his iron heel, but all that was actually published by him during his lamentably short incumbency was but a paltry list of theological questions for the senior class.[3]

[1] Not Meriam, as wrongly given by McCosh, *Scottish Philosophy,* p. 184.

[2] J. Sanderson, *Biography of the Signers of the Declaration of Independence,* Philadelphia, 1824, Vol. 5, p. 113. Compare S. D. Alexander, *Princeton College during the Eighteenth Century,* New York, 1872, p. 79.

[3] Theological Questions by Rev. Jonathan Edwards, President of the College of New Jersey. He died 22d March, 1758, aged 54.

1. How does it appear that something has existed from Eternity?

2. How does it appear that this earth and the visible system are not from eternity?

3. How does it appear that the existence of man is derived and dependent?

4. How do you prove the natural perfections of God, viz., his intelligence, infinite power, foreknowledge, and immutability?

5. How do you prove his moral perfections, that he is a friend of virtue, or absolutely holy, true, just and good?

If President Edwards did not affect the college directly, it is yet possible that an infiltration of idealism may have found its way in by a roundabout way. There is record of one Ebenezer Bradford, a Connecticut student and a subsequent advocate of the Northern immaterialism, who wrote to Dr. Bellamy, one of the later Edwardeans, the following ingenuous tale: Dr. Witherspoon was a great enemy to what they call the Eastward or New Divinity, which was so much exploded by all in college that when I came here I was advised by a particular friend not to let my sentiments be known by any means, alleging it would be of great disservice to me. I found two or three, however, who dared to think for themselves, and we agreed to promote what we judged to be truth in as private and hidden a manner as possible. We ventured to read some of your books with the title pages cut out, which were much admired by those who professed themselves enemies to the New Divinity.[1] By whatever devious path idealism worked its way into Princeton, it is tolerably clear, from this naïve account, that Witherspoon was a high conservative, preferring above all things what the narrator terms ' notions which appear greatly confined.' The result of this bias was practically seen in the career of Periam, who, from being ' a very ingenious young man,' became ' a very serious man.' But before this change of mind had occurred, Princeton's earliest idealist had influenced a person of much greater importance than himself.

[1] *Proceedings of the New Jersey Historical Society,* Vol. 5, pp. 170-6.

CHAPTER IV

SAMUEL STANHOPE SMITH

SAMUEL STANHOPE SMITH (1750-1814), the son of an Irish Presbyterian divine, and in turn student, tutor, professor of moral philosophy, and president, coming to college at the age of sixteen, before President-Elect Witherspoon had arrived from Scotland, was consigned more especially to the care of tutor Periam. Now Periam, continues Smith's biographer,[1] had not confined himself to the study of mathematics, but had extended his inquiries to metaphysics also, and become infected with the fanciful doctrine of Bishop Berkeley, which consists, as is generally known, in denying the existence of a material universe, and converting every object of the senses into a train of fugitive perceptions. How this professor, who had been habituated to the hardy pursuits of mathematical science and the inductive philosophy, could ever have brought himself to embrace such a visionary theory, a theory so repugnant to common sense, and rather an object of ridicule than of serious consideration, it is difficult to explain, unless it be upon the principle that, having been accustomed to require the most conclusive proof of everything before he assented to its truth, he so far misconceived the subject as to imagine that he must have arguments drawn from reason, to convince him of the existence of an exterior world, before he would admit the reality of it; and this surely is an evidence which Nature would deny him, as she rests the proof of it solely and entirely upon the simple testimony of the senses. However this may have been, Periam had address and ingenuity enough to infuse the principles of the Bishop of Cloyne into the mind of Smith, and he began seriously to doubt whether there were in the world such real existences as the sun, moon and stars, rivers, mountains and human beings. While it was a proof of perspicacity that Smith, at his early age and un-

[1] Memoirs of Samuel Stanhope Smith, by Frederick Beasley, in Smith's *Sermons*, Philadelphia, 1821, Vol. 1, pp. 6-10.

skilled as he must have been in the grounds of human knowledge, perceived a real difficulty in proving by arguments derived from reason the existence of a material universe, or, in other words, inferring by necessary consequences the real existence of the objects of our perception, from our having perceptions of them; yet it must be admitted, at the same time, that the knowledge of that man must be extremely limited in the science of the human mind, who does not readily perceive the method by which he can extricate himself from that difficulty, and arrive at undoubted certainty from the testimony of the senses of the real existence *in rerum natura,* of external objects.   Accordingly Smith, although captivated at first by the specious fallacies of the Bishop of Cloyne, had too much sober sense and penetration to be long held in bondage by the silken chains of such a fantastic theory.   Dr. Witherspoon arrived from Scotland, and bringing with him the recently broached principles of Reid, Oswald, and Beattie, furnished him with a clue by which he was conducted out of the dark labyrinths into which he had been betrayed by Bishop Berkeley and his disciple, Periam.   From the cloudy speculations of immaterialism he was now brought back to the clear light of common sense.   Nature was again reinstated in her rights, and the external world, which had been banished for a while, returned and resumed its place in creation.

This account of the supersession of idealism by realism, which incidentally disproves Witherspoon's claims for being the anticipator of Reid, may be trusted for the reason that it was written by one who was declared to have no relish for the Scotch philosophers.   But Stanhope Smith's formal renunciation of idealism, and his assumption of a more practical and common sense view of things, had an institutional as well as an individual significance. Being the first alumnus of the college to become its head, by a sort of intellectual inbreeding the strain of realism tended to become fixed.   In the case of the new president's ethical works, at least, one can see how this fixity of type led to an actual philosophic sterility, for he goes so far in his reasoning as to decry the employment of reason itself.   Thus he defines the moral faculty as an internal sense, distinct from all others, imparting primary and ultimate ideas on the peculiar subject it was destined to enlighten, which cannot be acquired by any process of reasoning, nor by any other sense or power of our nature.[1]

It was evidently with a faculty as thus defined, and not with an unbiassed judgment, that Smith went on to attack the current forms of idealism and scepticism. Calling Berkeley's and Hume's denial of the existence of the material object a philosophic delirium of hypothesis, he explained that according to the scheme of Hume the vivacity of the idea is the only criterion of truth; the reality of the material world, therefore, perishes by the fairest inference, since according to the confession even of Locke and the peripatetic school, it is not the object of our perception. . . . Whatever medium, in the opinion of these philosophers, nature may employ to connect the object with the organ of sense, whether image or idea, or any other sensible phantasm, it is beyond a doubt the object itself, not its idea, which is discovered by the sense; any image or phantasm, in the case, being either unknown or unperceived, and at the time wholly unthought of. An idea is merely a conception of the fancy, or the reminiscence of the object.[2] Again, Hume's principle of the regular and constant course of nature is but a modification of the Aristotelian philosophy and leads to atheism. For, if our own experience is the sole and exclusive ground of judging of whatever is credible in the physical history of the world, it is unreasonable to believe that this globe ever had a beginning, or that it will ever perish. It must always have existed, and must always continue to exist in the same state in which we now behold it.

There can be no future condition of existence for human nature, no future judgment, no future retribution to the righteous and the wicked. For each of these states implies a condition of things such as has never come under our observation, or been the subject of our experience. There is, on this supposition, no foundation for religion. The order of the world must be eternal, immutable, necessary, and can have no dependence on a creating and intelligent cause. We must embrace the philosophical absurdity of

[1] *Lectures on Moral and Political Philosophy*, Philadelphia, 1812, p. 226.
[2] *Ib.*, pp. 19, 24.

an eternal succession of mutable and perishing beings; and are driven to the impious alternative of believing that there is no God; or, that the universe itself is God.[1]

These terrific consequences, drawn from the simple postulates of empiricism, savour more of extravagance than of common sense, and are consequently not a fair example of Smith's logical methods. In an earlier book, before his official position demanded the conventional onslaught upon scepticism in all its forms, he did a piece of work which made some stir at the moment and was, at the same time, connected with the realistic movement from both the negative and positive sides. The *Essay on the Causes of the Variety of Complexion and Figure in the Human Species* was directed against Lord Kames' *Discourse on the Original Diversity of Mankind;* its chief argument was that the unity of the race lay in the common principles of human nature, primitive man having been created with divinely endowed intuitions. For the probability of this supposition, the author reasons thus: Hardly is it possible that man, placed on the surface of the new world, in the midst of its forests and marshes, capable of reason, indeed, but without having formed principles to direct its exercise, should have been able to preserve his existence, unless he had received from his creator, along with his being, some instructions concerning the use and employment of his faculties, for procuring his subsistence, and inventing the most necessary arts of life. The American savage, for example, has been taught from his infancy the necessary arts for supplying his wants. But the primitive man, if we suppose him to have received no communication of knowledge from his creator, and to have been abandoned merely to his own powers, without the least aid from experience, or instruction, would have been nothing but a large infant. Reason, the supreme prerogative of our nature, and its chief distinction from that of the inferior animals, could have availed him little in that emergency. It would have required, in order to its exercise, a knowledge of principles, and of the nature of the objects around him, which could have been the result only of time, and a certain degree of experience. In the

[1] *Lectures on the Evidences of the Christian Religion*, Philadelphia, 1809, pp. 42, 43.

meantime, that recent mass of organised matter, called a man, would probably have perished.[1]

Here enters upon the scene the realistic primitive man; an American was its intellectual father, it had two Scotchmen for godfathers: one Beattie, who gave this large infant common sense as distinguished from reason; the other Reid, who endowed it with an almost adult brain. As Smith further described it, this lay figure stood for human nature in the beginning, which, as originally formed by a wise and beneficent Creator, was instructed by him in the duties and the most necessary arts of life. Hence, contends the writer, against the absurd opinion of an equivocal generation resulting from the united action of moisture and heat on the primitive mass of the world—an opinion which leads to the ancient theory of an infinite chaos of atomical actions, which have no other cause for their existence or their motions but the necessary nature of matter—against this gloomy opinion there is the highest reason to believe that the primitive man received such a knowledge of the qualities, powers, and uses of the various objects around him, together with such moral and religious principles, as would lay in his family and among his immediate descendants the true foundations of civilised society.[2]

But how is this contention to be sustained? Smith, borrowing the method of elimination from his master Witherspoon, now attempts to strengthen his own position by pointing out the mutual opposition existing between his rivals. Thus Leibniz's division of the different races of man is contrasted by that of Kant; Lamarck's theory of equivocal generation by those who ascribe an eternal succession to the human race upon this globe; Buffon's criterion of the fixity of the species by Monboddo's whimsical supposition that mankind originally had tails; Cardan's opinion that the effects of violence upon the body, or of any customs which affect it only externally, can never be transmitted by birth, by the contrary doctrines of Haller.[3] In brief, the conclusion to be drawn from all this variety of opinion is that it is hard to draw any conclusion. Nevertheless, with Smith, as with Witherspoon, the

[1] *Human Species*, pp. 17-20.   [2] *Ib.*, pp. 29-32.
[3] *Ib.*, pp. 13, 115, 131, 206, 240.

eclectic spirit turns out to be stronger than the destructive; so, going back over his list of previous incipient evolutionists, he picks out the following opinions: first, with Haller, he accepts the transmissibility of acquired characteristics, or, as he expresses it, any form of the body or of any of its parts, produced not only by climate or the means or modes of living, but by any habit, the result either of climatical influence like the contracted eyes and forehead of the negro, or of national custom like the flat heads of some of our Indian tribes, is communicable to offspring by natural inheritance.[1] Again, with Lamarck, the American holds that even though the variations transmitted in a single generation be very small, yet there is a cumulative effect from the factors of use and disuse, food, climate or the effort of the individual, or, as the author put it, of the causes which affect the most minute gradations in the intermediate grades of the several sections of mankind the chief are climate, the state of society, the manner of living.[2] Finally, notwithstanding his primary assumption of man being created with an almost supernatural intellectual endowment, the orthodox realist comes to employ the arguments of an advanced materialism. The varieties of human nature, he insists, are to be explained by the known operations of natural causes and the necessary laws of the material world.[3]

Of Stanhope Smith's *Essay on the Human Species,* his biographer says that, even if the author had not the honour of conceiving the original plan upon which the varieties in the race might be explained, which it is conceded had been sketched out by the philosophers of Europe, he is yet entitled to the merit of having reduced what they only conjectured, or feebly supported, to a finished and conclusive argument. His object in this treatment is to show that all the great variety exhibited among our race in their stature, complexion, and figure, from Tartar and European to Indian and negro, may be explained from the united action of climate, the state of society, and the manner of living. Besides, the doctrine would

[1] *Human Species,* p. 131.
[2] *Ib.,* pp. 33, 34. Compare H. W. Conn, *The Method of Evolution,* New York, 1900, pp. 108, 151.
[3] *Ib.,* pp. 9, 11.

seem to be evidently deducible from the scriptural account of the original of our race. If from a single pair, or from the family of Noah, the whole globe be speedily peopled, it would be against all the principles of a great philosophy to resort to the supposition of a diversity of origin in order to account for the varieties which exist.[1] This opinion is exaggerated and its animus obvious; Smith is inconsistent and his attitude unscientific. Like Witherspoon and his inaugural address on the *Union of Piety and Science,* his disciple's treatise is vitiated by an attempt to reconcile incompatibles, to harmonise the written word with the facts of nature, by a process of arbitrary rejection. This is shown by his contention that the hypothesis that the human kind was originally divided into various species, in a state of primitive and absolute savagism, is equally contrary to true philosophy and to the sacred literature.

Although in its methods the Princetonian's *Essay on the Human Species* has but slight scientific value, it is somewhat of a curiosity in the glimpses it affords of the use of the principles of evolution fully two generations before his college was ready to consider them.[2] Passing then from what is termed the more speculative to the more anatomical section of his book, the author applies to man the general principles of physical action. Given the causes for their variety, it is held that, long in growing to maturity, natural features, like natural manners, become fixed only after a succession of several generations. At last, however, they become fixed. And if we can ascertain any effect produced by a given state of climate, of society, or of the habits of living, it requires only to be repeated during a sufficient length of time, to give it a permanent character, and so to incorporate it into the constitution as to render it an hereditary property of the race.[3] Along with this fixity is a certain flexibility, for the human constitution is formed with such pliancy in its organisation that it is capable of accommodating itself to every situation on the globe. Thus the overseers of slaves in the Carolinas and Georgia, as compared with their

[1] Frederick Beasley, *Memoir,* p. 44.
[2] Compare H. W. Rankin, *The Philosophy of Charles Woodruff Shields,* 1905.
[3] *Human Species,* p. 45.

British ancestors, are but a few shades lighter than the aboriginal Iroquois or Cherokees. And conversely, two young Virginia gentlemen, members of the College of New Jersey in 1785, the fourth in descent from the princess Pocahuntis, had a countenance and form of face, except for the dark and vivid eye, perfectly Anglo-American.[1] Now this instance, continues Smith, militates against the pertinacious position of Lord Kames that mankind must have been originally created of different species, and fitted for the different climates in which they were placed.[2]

Holding to the unity of the race, Smith accounts for the diversities by further natural causes, and proceeds to illustrate the influence of the state of society and of the habits of living, in creating other varieties, or in aggravating or correcting those which are occasioned by climate. By these factors not only are all the features of the human countenance modified, but its whole expression formed. Here the physiognomonical science, although not very accurate, may furnish general principles in judging of the qualities of the understanding and the heart. Every passion, every emotion, every thought which passes through the mind has its peculiar expression; each single touch may be so fine as to be imperceptible, but frequent repetition will at length trace on the countenance very distinct lineaments.[3]

The same may be said of the conjectures of the physiologists, who have imagined that the figure of the skull, with its various protuberances and indentations, affords a criterion of the intellectual powers and moral disposition of men. Perhaps these pretensions have been carried too far, but as the passions which agitate the mind affect the muscles which give expression to the countenance, so, on the other hand, the original figure of the receptacle of the brain by giving it scope for a more ample expansion, or by compressing and thereby restricting the regularity and freedom of its motions, may affect the operations of the mind.[4]

By his favourable references to the physiognomy of Lavater and

[1] Compare p. 353 ff, the Appendix on the *Natural Bravery and Fortitude of the American Indians,* extracted from a larger dissertation entitled the *History and Philosophy of the Manners of the American Savage,* which Smith had in contemplation as an addition to his lectures on moral philosophy.

[2] *Ib.,* p. 333.   [3] *Ib.,* pp. 150, 159.   [4] *Ib.,* pp. 123, 124, 159.

to the empirical form of brain psychology of Gall, Smith has at length ranged himself on the side of the realistic materialists of the land. Like Rush, who conceived himself to have coined the word phrenology, he believes that there is a cerebral localisation of separate faculties; like Jefferson, that the state of society in which men live has a powerful influence in varying the countenance and habit of a whole people.[1] So against the aspersions of Buffon and of that rapid philosopher, the Abbé Raynal, who imputed great mental and physical debility to the people of the United States, he agrees with the author of the *Notes on Virginia* that men ranging the forest for game or occupied in perpetual labours in clearing and cultivating the soil of the new world have not produced, cannot be expected to produce, such poets as Homer or Pope, such philosophers as Aristotle and Locke. The true philosopher, instead of inferring that the American, like what was fabled of the Boeotian, air has hebetated the genius of this last and largest quarter of the globe, will be disposed rather to respect the energy and enterprise which has accomplished almost a new creation within a single century, over the face of a new continent.[2] These Jeffersonian arguments are valid as applied to Anglo- or Gallo-Americans; they are not as applied to the Afro-American. These may not be so much inferior to the whites in their faculty of memory, nor in their imagination so dull, tasteless and anomalous, as witness the letters of Ignatius Sancho, and the poems of Phillis Whately.[3] Negroes of clear and undoubted African descent, especially the domestic servants employed within the families of their master, insensibly receive the same ideas of elegance and beauty, and discover a great facility in adopting their manners.[4]

Smith's psychology of the negro, his attempt to minimise fundamental racial characteristics between blacks and whites, was violently attacked by critics at home and abroad.[5] But notwithstand-

---

[1] *Human Species,* p. 161.   [2] *Ib.,* p. 273.
[3] For the latter see Albert Smyth, *The Philadelphia Magazines,* p. 51.
[4] *Ib.,* p. 170.
[5] Compare Prof. J. A. Smith, professor of anatomy and surgery in the University of New York, in the *New York Medical and Philosophical Journal,* February, 1809; and Charles White, *Remarks* on the first edition of this *Essay,* before the Literary and Philosophical Society of Manchester.

ing the long list of essential varieties subsisting between the different tribes of mankind, to be drawn from the works of Cuvier, Hunter, Camper and Blumenbach,[1] the Princetonian returns to his original thesis of the substantial unity of the race, and repeats, in concluding his work, an observation made at the beginning. This is that the denial of the unity of the human species tends to impair, if not entirely to destroy, the foundations of duty and morals, and, in a word, of the whole science of human nature.[2]

Thus far the weakness of the *Essay on the Human Species* lay in the extremes into which the author was forced by his original apologetic principles that a just philosophy will always be found coincident with a true theology.[3] Its strength lay in the employment of naturalistic and well-nigh evolutionary principles that the divergences between men arise from the effects of climate, with its different proportions of light, heat and the electric fluid; of the manner of living, with its various kinds of food and shelter; and of the state of society. In this use of environmental influences Smith's book has some value as an early contribution to American anthropology. Taking a hint from the assurance of Dr. Witherspoon, that there are striking differences between the well-fed people in the eastern counties of Scotland and those in the western, who draw a coarse and scanty subsistence from a thin and ungrateful soil,[4] the pupil applies this hint to his native land. For example, there are the industrious and economical New Englanders who, with their composed countenance and serious gravity, are obviously distinguished from the natives of the Southern States; then there are those descendants of fairest Europeans, who, taken prisoner in infancy by Indians, grow up with the same apathy of countenance as their captors; finally, there is the case of a copper-coloured young Indian, a student in the College of New Jersey, who appears to be losing that vacancy of eye and that lugubrious wildness of features peculiar to the savage state.[5]

With its local illustrations of the powers of physical causes in the natural development of man, Smith's *Essay* might seem to put its author in the camp of the early American materialists. But

---

[1] *Human Species*, p. 294.   [2] *Ib.*, p. 243.
[3] *Ib.*, 1st ed., p. 242.   [4] *Ib.*, p. 164.   [5] *Ib.*, pp. 164, 172, 173.

such was hardly the case; instead of ranging himself on that side, he opposed. Priestley and his Hartleian doctrines by Reid and his principles of common sense. His former strictures on the inadequacy of the ancient atomism, to explain the system of the universe, are now followed by a diatribe against the inadequacy of the theory of vibrations to explain the workings of the human mind. This diatribe, in favour of whose authenticity there is every evidence,[1] appeared in the *Retrospect* of his friend, Samuel Miller. Amplifying the latter's valuable review of the materialistic movement, Smith proceeds as follows: If we are to account for all the varieties of thought upon mechanical principles, it will be necessary to consider the subject in the light of known mechanical laws. Whether we adopt the hypothesis that the nerves are like fiddle-strings, or that they are full of a medullary substance capable of vibrations, the fundamental principle of materialism is one. ' The vibrations of matter produce thought.' On this theory it may be observed: 1. It has never been proved that there *are* such vibrations. It is a mere hypothesis. It may serve for speculation; but to build a system on such a basis is credulity, not philosophy.   2. Granting, for argument's sake, the existence of vibrations, there is no necessary connection between vibration and thought. If there is not, there must be another hypothesis introduced, viz.: ' There *may* be a connection between vibrations and thought.' Upon this hypothesis I should be glad to see Dr. Priestley or Dr. Darwin give us a poem or dissertation upon the thoughts of the harpsichord while the strings are vibrating at the touch of a lady's finger; or upon the grave speculations of a mill-pond while the boys at play are throwing stones into it.   3. Suppose I again grant, for further argument's sake, this hypothesis to the materialists. It will be necessary to show that, in vibrations, considered abstractly, there is such a variety in kind and degree as corresponds exactly with all the varieties of thought. There are at least ten distinct intellectual powers. Not one of these can be accounted for by one or more of the others. The active powers, moreover, are numerous; and the mind, so constituted, is capable of a vast variety of thoughts, differing in kind and degree. Do vibrations afford an equal variety?   No: it is not possible that there should be any

[1] See Notes.

more than two kinds of vibrations in a uniform elastic medium; that is, they may be either quick or slow, or they may be strong or weak. These kinds admit of various degrees; and this is all the variety of which the laws of matter (however finely organised the machine) will admit. Now, he must certainly be ignorant of his own mental operations, or of the laws of motion in matter, who can be persuaded of an exact correspondence of the one to the other. Certainly credulity never appeared more conspicuous in the devotees of Popish superstition than it does in the advocates and believers of the material system. Shall vibrations in an elastic medium be supposed to account for all the original powers, intellectual and active? Put all these out of the question except one class, viz.: the powers we have of our external senses, and even then there is a manifest disparity. But how shall we find in vibrations a variety corresponding to the immense variety of sensations which we have from sight, hearing, taste, smell and touch? And how shall they account for all the ideas which we have from all the other sources and powers of thought, upon mechanical principles? Common sense, reason, and philosophy are in a lamentable condition when such theories gain ground among men. He who would be a materialist in the nineteenth century, would have been a believer in the doctrine of transubstantiation in the twelfth.

While this diatribe begins with an air of learned fooling and ends with an appeal to bigotry, it was on the safe side in denying a one to one correspondence between medullary vibrations and mental operations. The same caution was manifested by the author of the work in which this article appeared—Samuel Miller.

CHAPTER V

SAMUEL MILLER

S
AMUEL MILLER (1769-1850), was peculiarly well fitted to criticise materialism from the point of view of realism, for he was thrown into personal contact with the local leaders of both movements. He entered the university in Philadelphia at the time when the town was fairly vibrating with the Hartleian doctrines, and there met Joseph Priestley, who expressed great admiration for the character of his mind. Yet despite these subtle influences, Miller was insensibly drawn toward the Scottish way of thinking; here three Princetonians influenced him; Witherspoon by his preaching, Ashbel Green by his advice, John Ewing by his teaching. The latter, as provost of the university, expressed his preference for the common sense view of things when in his lectures on natural philosophy he said: by the phenomena of nature, we mean all the situations, motions and appearances of natural bodies, which are evident to the senses, and not immediately dependent upon the voluntary agency of an intelligent being.[1] This is but a hint of the formative influences in the intellectual life of Miller; of more importance were the lectures of his theological preceptor, Charles Nisbet, first principal of Dickinson College, and at one time a candidate for the presidency of the College of New Jersey. This remarkable man was called by Benjamin Rush a walking library; he left behind him a monument of learning in the shape of a metaphysical system, which for thoroughness of method and clearness of style was only surpassed, among the early schools, by Samuel Johnson's *Elements of Philosophy.* Miller fell under Nisbet's spell, but whether or no he got from this tremendous preceptor his alleged distaste for abstract study, he certainly derived from him his liking for concrete inclusiveness. This came out in his most ambitious work, which, although enti-

[1] John Ewing, *Natural Experimental Philosophy,* Philadelphia, 1809, Chapter I.

tled *A Brief Retrospect of the Eighteenth Century,* contained in its single published part a sketch of the revolutions and improvements in science, arts, and literature; and in its projected parts a review of the theology, moral theories, and politics during that period. Owing to the author's disposition to introduce American writers and publications, and to his unconsciously ironical humility in putting America among those 'nations lately become literary,' this volume is not only a mine of information regarding the general culture of the day, but a valuable index to the somewhat narrow philosophic temper of the newly emancipated colonies. Mentioning the early native writers, from the Mathers and Edwards to Johnson and Franklin, it also presents an orderly review of the current speculative movements and their antecedents, and leads up to natural realism as the best solution of the problem of perception.

Miller's friends called his *Retrospect* the funeral discourse of the eighteenth century. That title was more applicable to the germinal discourse of 1801, which hastily consigned to the philosophic potter's field the opinions of nations as well as of individuals. Such were the misnamed discoveries of Hartley that the soul of man was material; of the French that nature and reason are the only gods; of Godwin that gratitude is a vice and not a virtue; of the Germans that rationalism is superior to revelation. In brief, concludes this lugubrious discourse, the accomplishments of the age are to be deplored, inasmuch as its spirit of free inquiry has resulted in the horrors of the French revolution and the guillotine, its unrestrained liberty of thought in the opinion of the hollow-hearted infidel Jefferson, that twenty gods are as good as one god.[1] Miller's century sermon was indeed funereal, but the *Retrospect* of two years later discovers a more cheerful frame of mind. Those authors, previously buried with the unseemly haste of the victims of the yellow fever plague through which the author had passed, are now disinterred, if not resurrected. It is actually found that even abettors of heresy or infidelity may write profoundly and instructively on some branches of science highly instructive to mankind. Hartley's system of vibration and association may lead to Spinozism, but his theories have a consid-

[1] Miller, *Memoir of Nisbet,* p. 268.

erable claim to originality; Godwin's doctrine of perfectibility, borrowed from Helvétius and Condorcet, may lead to doubts concerning the immateriality and immortality of the soul, but for all that it conduces to the improvement of man in this world.[1]

If with increased acquaintance the Princetonian's former intellectual foes are discovered to be not so bad, how much better are his own intellectual kin. It is with a cheerful complacency that he informs his readers that the writers of the common sense school have contributed the most important accessions which the philosophy of mind has received since the time of Locke. Their first service was to cease the senseless prattling about occult terms, —phantasms, sensible species, substantial forms; next, in observing the sceptical conclusions which Berkeley and Hume had drawn from the old theory of perception, as it had been taught, in substance, by all writers, from Pythagoras down to their time, they were led to call this theory in question. Standing at the head of these North-British philosophers, Reid totally rejected the ideal system and maintained that the mind perceives not merely the ideas or images of external objects, but the external objects themselves.[2]

In his strictures against the Scottish historian and the Irish ecclesiastic—daring metaphysical revolutionists who deny the existence of a spiritual as well as of a material world, in opposition to the common sense and all the spontaneous and deepest impressions of mankind—the American confesses that he is but adopting the opinion of Stewart that, with respect to the process of nature in perception, philosophers are no less ignorant than the vulgar.[3] That Miller's opinion was ill-considered and at second-hand is obvious from his misinterpretations, not only of Berkeley but of Reid. In saying that the former contended that all the varied beauties of creation which we behold, are nothing more than fancies or images impressed on the mind, without reference to those prototypes of our ideas, usually called material objects,[4] the realist implies that such impressment is arbitrary and not in accordance with the lawful language of signs. Again,

[1] *Retrospect*, pp. xii, 17-19.   [2] *Ib.*, pp. 2, 3, 4, 10, 11.
[3] *Ib.*, Vol. 2, p. 10.   [4] *Ib.*, Vol. 2, p. 8.

in claiming that Reid maintains that the mind perceives not *merely* the ideas or images of external objects, but the external objects themselves, he disregards the realist's denial of representative perception through the mediation of sensible species. Nevertheless, for these misinterpretations the writer has already given an excuse, it is not to be supposed that he had read all the works concerning which he delivers opinions; hence he confesses that symptoms of superficial reading, or of striking unacquaintance with many works of which he speaks will often be discovered.[1] This is especially apparent in Miller's account of the Kantian system; based on a London review of an English edition of Adelung's *Elements of the Critical Philosophy*,[2] it is as full of mistakes as it is remote from the original text. And yet this account at third hand has its interest; with the exception of the sneering reference of President Dwight of Yale College to Kantianism as subversive of morality,[3] it is the first contemporary notice of the Königsberg philosopher by a native American. Moreover, it illustrates the philistine attitude of one born and bred in the British schools toward a continental system, and thus serves to explain the difficulties which the critical philosophy had to contend with in the United States until it found its first sympathetic interpreters among certain Pennsylvanians of German origin.[4]

Immanuel Kant, says Miller, about the year 1781, first published a system of metaphysics and moral philosophy, which has been ever since gaining ground among the literati of Germany, and is now much in vogue in that country. Professor Kant, we are told, was led to the train of thinking, which ripened in his mind into the system which bears his name, by the perusal of Hume's

[1] *Retrospect,* preface, p. xii.
[2] Translated by A. F. M. Willich, London, 1798.
[3] See above, Book III, Chapter VIII.
[4] Compare *Psychology, or a View of the Human Soul,* New York, 1840, by F. A. Rauch, president of Marshall College; *Psychology, or Elements of a New System of Mental Philosophy on the Basis of Consciousness and Common Sense,* New York, 1842, by S. S. Schmucker, professor in the Theological Seminary, Gettysburg. For a review of Rauch, compare James Murdock, *Sketches of Modern Philosophy, especially among the Germans,* Hartford, Ct., 1842, pp. 189, *seq.*

essay on the idea of necessary connection, and of Priestley's reply to Reid, Beattie and Oswald. But from whatever source his ideas are derived, he has formed them into a fabric which is extolled by his adherents as one of the most sublime efforts of human genius, and as ranking among the most important improvements ever made in science. If we may believe the extravagant panegyrics of these enthusiastic disciples, he has more successfully explored the darkest recesses of the human mind than any individual amongst all his illustrious predecessors, and his writings contain a development of precisely those truths after which mankind have been seeking for centuries in vain.[1] Still, however, says the London reviewer whom Miller now quotes, when inquiry is made among the followers of this singular man, respecting the general drift of his system, they answer chiefly in negations. It is *not* atheism; for he affirms that practical reason is entitled to infer the existence of a Supreme Intelligence. It is *not* theism; for he denies that theoretical reason can demonstrate the existence of an infinite intelligent Being. It is *not* materialism; for he maintains that time and space are only forms of our perception, and not the attributes of extrinsic existences. It is *not* idealism; for he maintains that noumena are independent of phenomena; that things perceptible are prior to perception. It is *not* libertinism; for he allows the will to be determined by regular laws. It is *not* fatalism; for he defines this to be a system in which the connection of purposes in the world is considered as accidental. It is *not* dogmatism; for he favours every possible doubt. It is *not* scepticism; for he affects to demonstrate what he teaches. Such are the indefinite evasions of this school.[2]

The complaint that all this is obscure and scarcely intelligible, continues the American, will probably be made by every reader. An English philosopher tells us that it would require more than ordinary industry and ingenuity to make a just translation, or a satisfactory abstract of the system in question, in our language; that for this purpose a new nomenclature, more difficult than the

---

[1] *Retrospect*, pp. 2, 22.

[2] *Ib.*, Vol. 2, p. 23, quoting *Monthly Review*, Vol. XXVIII., IV. S., p. 62, 1799.

Linnaean botany, must be invented. This circumstance itself affords strong presumption against the rationality and truth of the Kantian philosophy. Locke and Newton found little difficulty in making themselves understood. Every man of plain good sense, who is used to inquiries of that nature, readily comprehends their systems, in as little time as it requires to peruse their volumes. Even Berkeley and Hume, with all their delusive subtleties, found means to render themselves easily intelligible. Is there not reason, then, to suspect either that the system of Professor Kant is made up of heterogeneous, inconsistent and incomprehensible materials; or that, in order to disguise the old and well known philosophy of certain English and French writers, and to impose it on the world as a new system, he has done little more than present it under a new technical vocabulary of his own? Or, which is, perhaps, not the most improbable supposition, that, being sensible of the tendency of his philosophy to undermine all religion and morals, as hitherto taught and prized in the world, he has studied to envelope in an enigmatic language, a system which he wishes to be understood by the initiated alone; a system which has been pronounced ' an attempt to teach the sceptical philosophy of Hume in the disgusting dialect of scholasticism'? At any rate, notwithstanding all the unwearied pains which some of the disciples of this famous Prussian have taken, to rescue him from the imputation of being one of the sceptical philosophers of the age, the most impartial judges will probably assign him a place among those metaphysical empirics of modern times, whose theoretical jargon, instead of being calculated to advance science, or to forward human improvement, has rather a tendency to delude, to bewilder, and to shed a baneful influence on the true interests of man.[1]

When he based his opinions on the authority of others, Miller's conclusions were extreme, realism was the most rational, idealism the most absurd of schemes. But coming at last to a system in which he enjoyed a first-hand knowledge, he is more moderate and thereby more efficient in his criticism. The Zoonomic theory of materialism, he concludes in his *Additional Notes,* makes an important part of a medical work which is highly popular and has

[1] *Retrospect,* Vol. 2, pp. 26-27.

an extensive circulation in the United States. Now as there is reason to suppose that many superficial thinkers have been seduced into the adoption of its principles by the plausible aspect which it wears, the following remarks are submitted, not as a full refutation of the Darwinian doctrines, but as suggesting some hints worthy of the consideration of those who are disposed to embrace them: Dr. Darwin sets out with a singular inconsistency; he declares that by the spirit of animation, or sensorial power, he means only that animal life which mankind possesses in common with brutes, yet afterwards he shows how the sensorial power produces ideas of memory, imagination and abstraction which have always been considered as belonging to the rational and immortal mind of man. Again, his theory embraces a gratuituous assumption; its object is to reduce all the energies of intellectual and animal life to the operation of an invisible fluid secreted by the brain, and existing in every part of the body. But does this fluid exist? If so, it explains nothing; the whole business of causation is as much in the dark as ever, even after all the parade of development through contractions, fibrous motions and appetencies. Indeed, the sensorial power, as applied to explain the phenomena of mind, too much resembles the occult qualities, the phantasms and the essential forms of the schoolmen; for when using the word idea sometimes to signify the fibrous motion and sometimes the sensorial, it signifies both the cause and the effect. Again, the spirit of animation is said to have the power of producing certain motions in the animal fibre. But if the power of producing fibrous contractions be inherent in this spirit, then that portion of which it is in immediate contact with the fibre must induce contraction before the application of stimuli, unless the power be counteracted. But in this case, nothing is supposed to counteract its action, and as the effect is not produced, where is the inherent power of this subtle fluid? Another inconsistency appears in the account of the qualities belonging to sensorial power. To say that a substance can assume the property of solidity, and lay it aside; that it can occupy space, and cease to occupy it at pleasure, is to say that it can, at pleasure, exist and cease to exist. Next, upon the principles of this theory, association is impossible: association is a particular quality or state of sensorial power; but this power, or, which is the same thing, the spirit of animation, is in a perpetual state of flux. It is constantly secreted and expanded, being too subtle to remain any length of time in the system. The particles of this spirit, then, cannot form any habitual connections or associations with each other, because in the very act of association, they are expended and destroyed. According to any laws of matter with which we are acquainted, they can only be connected by means of repeated simultaneous action; but in their first action, according to this theorist, they expire and their places are supplied by new particles, which like them can only act once and fly off. The fibres, indeed, remain amidst this continual flux of the vital fluid, but without it they possess no other qualities than those of inanimate matter. So, too, this theory is insufficient to account for the phenomena which it is intended to explain. Can all our different and opposite states of mind—rapture and agony, horror and joy—be accounted for by any supposable changes in one homogeneous fluid? From what organs of sense do we derive our abstract ideas? What fibrous motions are excited when we call to mind the ideas of wisdom, benevolence, justice and truth? According to Dr. Darwin, these general ideas are repetitions of former particular perceptions, obtained through the organs of sense. But can general ideas be mere repetitions of particular ones? The simple statement of the doctrine is sufficient for its refutation. While, in general, it solves the phenomena of one class of ideas—those which we receive immediately from our external senses—all the rest, not only of memory and abstraction, but of imagination, taste, and moral perception, are left completely in the dark. In fine, the author falls into the grand mistake adopted by all the materialists, namely a belief that we are acquainted with the nature of causation. In the physical world we see events connected with each other, with respect to time and place; but we know not the relation which they sustain. At most a series of facts is all that we can determine. The links which bind them together, and the nature of the respective processes by which they succeed each other, in a word, the nature of causation, we can never understand.[1]

[1] *Retrospect,* Vol. 2, pp. 458-465.

In his last thrust at his opponents the Princetonian has flung against them an undeserved charge, for most of the materialists in the land were phenomenalists and did not pretend to explain the nature of causation but only to describe things caused; all they claimed was that nervous contractions and fibrous motions were not the efficients but merely the occasions of the accompanying mental phenomena. And so insisting upon the constant concomitance of the physical and psychical they anticipated in large measure the modern doctrine of parallelism and opened the way for a valid experimental psychology. But no such progress was possible for Miller and his school; instead of connecting the facts of association with a nerve tract theory, he denied all connection between the two; instead of throwing light upon psychic events by means of physical, he merely reasserted the opinion of Thomas Brown that the affections of the sentient principle are not rendered in the least degree more intelligible by resolving them into motions of solids or fluids, but the material changes can be known to us only by the changes of mind, and must, of consequence, be liable to all their uncertainty.[1]

In concluding with this opinion of a foreign reactionary, the American exposes the ground for his own adverse opinion at the beginning of his work, namely, that if the physical sciences have received great improvement during the century under consideration, it is feared the same cannot with truth be said respecting the science of the human mind; in this wide field, new experiences and discoveries, in the proper sense of the word, can have no place.[2] By such a denial the Princeton historian went far to impair the claim that realism was to be the coming philosophy of America, for such a denial ran counter to the inventive genius of his countrymen, cast reflections on such psychological experiments as were framed by Rush, and perhaps thereby prevented the rise of a school of experimentalists among such Princetonians as the electrician Joseph Henry. But fancies aside, the facts are that the spirit of common sense left little to the imagination, desired no novel inventions, but preferred to keep its adherents revolving in the

[1] *Reflections on Zoonomia,* Edinburgh, 1798.
[2] Miller, *Retrospect,* Vol. 2, p. 1.

treadmill of traditional thought. In fine, the policy of the New Jersey College was to turn out safe minds who were contented to mark time in the old way. But there was one character who kicked against this policy, the last of the early Princetonians, who began with a violent aversion to Reid, came to see much good in Hartley, and yet, in his inculcated mistrust of Berkeley, was forced to expunge all traces of idealism in the works of his favourite author Locke.

CHAPTER VI

FREDERICK BEASLEY

FREDERICK BEASLEY (1777-1845) was described by
one of his pupils as a very pleasant, affable man with a
sensitive, nervous system and as favourably known for his
metaphysical work in behalf of the philosophy of Locke.[1]
Born in North Carolina, entering Nassau Hall in 1793, and for
three years after graduation a tutor in the college and a student
of theology with President Stanhope Smith, Beasley subsequently
became an Episcopal priest in Baltimore, a member of the Philosophical Society of Philadelphia and provost of the University
of Pennsylvania. From his Southern affiliations and his long residence in the centre of materialism, Beasley came to accept the modified Hartleyism of his colleague Rush. But this approach to materialism, like his turning against realism, was only an apparent
and temporary lapse from the strict conservatism of Princeton.
The statement of the official college biographer that Beasley had
no relish for the Scotch philosophers, but admired John Locke
above all others, has its explanation in the fact that he considered
the latter sounder than the former, for, to his mind, Reid and
his followers, in their attacks on the real father of British idealism, had become themselves impregnated with the very poison
they sought to avoid. How the empiricist got this peculiar
notion into his head, is told in the preface to his chief work,—
a work which in its ultimate doctrine of crass common sense
outdoes the most extreme realists.

Beasley's *Search of Truth* [2] was dedicated to the companion of
his early studies, Bishop John Henry Hobart. To him the author
recalls their delightful days together under the direction of their

[1] Henry Augustus Riley, *Some Reminiscences and Events of a Life of
Three Score Years and Ten*, Vol. 1, p. 184. (MS. in the possession of the
writer.)

[2] Philadelphia, 1822.

519

venerable president. He continues: You are aware that in the College of Princeton, to which we were attached, after the fanciful theory of Bishop Berkeley, as a kind of philosophical daydream, had maintained its prevalence for a season, the principles of Reid, and the Scottish metaphysicians superseded it, and during the period of our residence in the seminary, acquired and maintained undisputed sway. At that time, I, together with all those graduates who took any interest in the subject, embraced without doubt or hesitation the doctrines of the Scottish school. Since, however, I came in possession of the station, which I at present occupy in the College of Philadelphia, my duty as well as inclination, led me to renew my inquiries into this branch of science. The farther I proceeded, the more interesting the subject became, and I determined, if possible to compass the whole ground, by consulting every author who had written upon it, both in ancient and modern times. I had advanced but a short distance upon this extended plan, before I thought I perceived that the Scottish metaphysicians had either inadvertently or wilfully, done their predecessors very great injustice in their animadversions upon their writings, ascribed to them opinions which they never held, and assumed to themselves the merit of broaching and promulgating the very doctrines which they taught.[1]

With the cry of back to Locke, Beasley now proceeds to raise against his adversaries what he calls the literary tomahawk. He does this with such cruel effect as to lay bare the skulls of his enemies and to discover to the world a brain capacity not so large as had been presumed. The propensity of the Scots, he exclaims, being to cavil at the doctrines of preceding philosophers, into what diminutive forms do Locke, Descartes and Malebranche sink in the writings of Reid, Stewart and Beattie! And yet the latter have fallen into the grossest errors in the new system of pneumatology, which they claim the credit of introducing. Foremost of these errors is Reid's assertion that Hume built his system of scepticism upon the principles of Locke, and that we must either call in question their principles, or admit his conclusion. But this is a capital mistake; the arch-sceptic may have held to a

[1] *Search of Truth,* Dedication, p. ii.

doctrine of idealism, that we do not perceive external objects directly, but the sage Locke, as Warburton says, did not dishonour himself by any whimsies. He indeed used the figure of a dark closet to explain his system of perception, but that did not necessarily imply that the immediate objects of perception are only certain shadows or films of external objects. It is an unfounded charge that he maintained that in perception, besides the object perceived, the mind that perceives, and the perception of mind, there is a fourth thing, called an idea, image or representative, the which alone is perceived by the mind.[1]

In his strictures on what might be termed a perceptual *quartum quid,* Beasley strives to relieve his master of being implicated in the opinion falsely ascribed to Aristotle by his misinterpreters, the schoolmen, that sensible species or films passed off from the object, and, impinging upon the senses, make their way into the mind and enable us to perceive. It is not denied that Locke often makes use of the term, impressions upon the mind, but he uses it only in the proper or figurative sense, as implying some effect produced upon it by the agency of the body; his doctrine is, that bodies through the instrumentality of their several media act upon the senses, and occasion certain motions in the nerves and brain, that become the cause of ideas in the mind; but he does not say that they make any impression upon the mind, such as that which they make upon the organs of sense.[2] Having relieved the English empiricist's system from any connection with the ancient heresy of representative perception though mediate images —the absurd opinion that the image of the object perceived enters by the organ of sense and strikes upon the mind—the American passes to the more difficult and more dubious portion of his defence, the contention that there is no taint whatsoever of idealism about the Lockean metaphysics, and therefore no connection between it and the principles of Hume and Berkeley. In regard to this matter, Reid had said that there was a single passage in Locke's *Essay,*[3] which may lead one to conjecture that he had a glimpse of that system which Berkeley afterwards advanced, but Beasley denies that there was any such meaning in that pas-

[1] *Search of Truth,* pp. vi, 139, 233.   [2] *Ib.,* p. 133.   [3] Bk. 4, Ch. 10.

sage. The Bishop, by making all the objects of an external world to consist only of those perceptions conveyed into the mind through the organs of sense, turns the world into a phantom. Again, if as he maintains also, all the objects of our knowledge in reference to the external world consist of those ideas which are perceived, by attending to the passions and operations of the mind, of consequence, the internal world or mind, as far as substance or any distinct subsistence is concerned, perishes also by just inference, and trains of unsubstantial images or ideas are all that survive this wreck of nature. But Locke commits no such glaring fallacy as to assert that the *esse* of things is their *percipi;* with him, the object that exists is one thing, and our perceptions of its properties another,—since there is the distinction to be made between the secondary and primary qualities of bodies; the former are admitted to be merely sensations in the mind; the latter exist in the bodies themselves, whether perceived by us or not. Indeed it was a difficult task remaining to the Bishop to show that the primary as well as the secondary qualities of body exist only in the mind that perceives them, for when strictly applied such reasoning leads to absurdity. Berkeley, for example, says that ' great and small, swift and slow, are allowed to exist nowhere without the mind, being entirely relative, and changing as the frame or positions of the organs of sense varies. The extension, therefore, which exists without the mind is neither great nor small, the motion neither swift nor slow, that is, they are nothing at all.' That is to say, continues Beasley, the College of Philadelphia, at which I now look, changes its apparent magnitude according to the distance and position of my eye, is not great when compared to the earth or sun, nor small, when compared to the houses around it; therefore, it is nothing, having no extension.[1]

Against such reasonings, which have been represented as legitimate deductions from the sound and just philosophy of the inimitable Locke, his disciple makes the short and easy answer that the testimony of our senses is the true and sole evidence in the case, and adds that we can give no reason why we place confidence in the certainty of intuitive truths, but that such are the laws of our constitution. As if this were not a clear case of reversion to type,

[1] *Search of Truth*, pp. 215, 217, 220.

a return to the obligatory realism of his undergraduate days, the Princetonian now turns the tables on Reid and charges him with being still attached to that form of idealism which he once so heartily embraced. After remarking that it is a dictate of common sense that the causes which we assign of appearances should be both true and sufficient to explain them, Reid tells us that what we call natural causes might with more propriety be called natural signs, and what we call effects, the things signified. But what advantage accrues to philosophy from this phraseology? Is it any better than the ordinary methods of speech to say that, when lightning rends the oak, the electric fluid is the sign and the rending of the oak the thing signified? The author is using the very language of Hume when he says that natural causes have no proper causality or efficiency in them as far as we know, and that all we can certainly affirm is, that nature hath established a constant conjunction between them and the things called their effects. But perhaps Reid meant this doctrine to apply solely to the events of the natural world, and not to what are properly denominated efficient causes, in which the energies of mind are always presupposed to be exerted. Yet such is not the case. As to the origin of our idea of power, active power, cause and effect, which are inseparably connected together, he is evidently of the opinion of Hume in believing that it cannot be explained upon the principles of Locke, not being derivable either from sensation or reflection. He maintains that the maxim—for every effect there must be an efficient cause—is not founded either upon reason or experience, but is to be traced to an original or instinctive principle in the constitution of our nature. How inconsistent is Reid here. As he formerly tried to introduce into the Lockean scheme of perception those aerial delegates, the shadows and substances of things, so now he would bring into his own scheme of causality a spurious bantling, that small instinct which so infallibly guides us. And yet not one proof has been exhibited for the existence of such an instinct. Will it be said that the fact of our having arrived at the conclusion, that for every change in nature there must be an adequate cause, is a proof of its existence *in rerum natura?* Instead of supposing that nature, or rather nature's God, found it necessary to confer upon us a separate instinct, in order that we might attain this single maxim, we should rather return to the first and unbiassed impressions of all mankind, that the causes which operate in the natural world are real efficients.[1]

In the critical portion of the *Search of Truth* it is hard to grasp the difference between Reid's original instincts and Beasley's first impressions, nor does the constructive portion clear up that difficulty. Assuming that the doctrine of innate ideas has been refuted by Locke, the writer would undertake to show that all our simple ideas are obtained through the inlets of sensation and reflection. To this end he makes a supposition: instead of the animated statue of Condillac, we will suppose a philosopher endowed with all the bodily and mental powers, bestowed upon our race by the Creator, and with a thirst for improvement, and a turn to scientific investigation, but entirely destitute of ideas, even of the original perceptions of sense—to set himself forth in the world in quest of information. Before he has proceeded far in his examination of nature, he discovers that he is possessed of powers that enable him to arrive at a new species of truth, not always depending upon experience, though posterior to it in the order of his attainments: namely, those truths which he discovers from tracing the connection of his ideas, or the immutable relations of things. These are called immutable and eternal truths, and properly constitute demonstration—such as those of mathematics, and some of those that come under the denomination of metaphysics, moral science and natural religion. These all have their foundation in what are denominated intuitive judgments, first principles or axiomatic truths, and lead us on frequently through the finest speculations of the human mind, to the most important and sublime conclusions.[2]

Immutable and eternal truths! Intuitive judgments and first principles! The opponent of idealism and realism has returned to the very language of Norris and Reid. But he goes even further and well-nigh reaches Beattie's extreme definition of common sense, as that power of the mind which perceives truth, not by progressive argumentation, but by an instantaneous, instinctive,

[1] *Search of Truth,* pp. 50-52, 58, 86, 87.   [2] *Ib.,* pp. 289, 290.

and irresistible impulse.[1] Or as Beasley himself expresses it: the
primitive man, passing from the shadowy regions of conjecture
and probability, comes to the clear and full light of demonstrative
certainty which rests ultimately upon intuition; here by intuition
is meant that act of the mind by which it perceives the truth of
any proposition, as soon as it is propounded, without exertion or
examination; and by intuitive truths—those axioms which are
at once perceived by the mind, by a single glance of attention, and
flash with a light upon it that is irresistible.[2]

Thus far it is evident that Beasley's primitive man was not only
of Scotch extraction, but at the same time, like his literary creator,
possessed a strain of English blood in his imaginary veins. Supposing our first philosopher to be in the state in which Adam was,
when he rose in the full perfection of his powers, but totally unin-
structed, and further supposing him to have been placed in this un-
tutored state in Eden; as soon as he opened his eyes on the scene
around him, every odour wafted to his nostrils and every object
presented to his vision would seem to be within himself. He would
be a whole world to himself and feel in a state of trance, enchant-
ment or reverie. But the spell would soon be broken by the impulses of nature. Possessed of muscular power, he would soon be
prompted to exert it, and stretching forth his hand, would be surprised to discover that nothing opposed its motion, and that there
was apparently an empty space before him. His legs would next
be moved with a similar result. Emboldened by these attempts,
our young adventurer would soon advance forward to any object,
say the tree that was before him, and beginning to examine it by
the touch, would soon make himself acquainted with its figure,
colour, and extension. Advancing from object to object, and subjecting them to the scrutiny of his sight and touch, he would soon
arrive at a knowledge of their qualities, and the sight, at first
under pupillage to the feeling, would soon learn to outstrip its
instructor in the information it gave its possessor, and enable him
to judge of things concerning which it could derive no light from
the touch. Thus commencing in a few simple notices would the
senses soon convey to him their numerous acquired perceptions.
He quickly becomes an adept in judging of sounds, tastes, odours,

[1] *Essay on Truth,* 1773. [2] *Search of Truth,* p. 331.

colours, extensions, figures. Next, impelled by hunger, and under the sure guidance of instinct, he plucks the fruit, enjoys it, and finds himself sated, and thence concludes that this, and things like it, to which he feels a similar propension, are his appointed sustenance. By a similar process of experiment and observation, he discovers that water will quench his thirst, fire will warm him at one distance and burn him at another, some fruits are wholesome and others noxious, some animals are innocent and others fierce and destructive. . . . In all this he reasons correctly and becomes, in the language of Lord Bacon, *naturae minister et interpres*.[1]

The American writer's primitive man has now become an international character. Built on a French model and endowed with Scotch common sense, feeling like an Irish idealist and acting like an English empiricist, he resembles in his instinctive and varied accomplishments a member of the Swiss Family Robinson. As yet, however, this hypothetical being, this metaphysical automaton, is, according to Beasley, by no means a philosopher in the true meaning of the word, but the simple pupil of nature. Hence the unsoundness of that philosophy which supposes an inductive principle to be one of the constituent powers of the human mind, because an original instructive principle of induction, which implies in its very terms the exercise of reason, is as palpable an absurdity as can be imagined. Upon Reid's principles, Adam, when he saw the sun rise and set on the first day of his life, would have a prescience that it would rise and set in future. If this were true, Adam must have possessed a sagacity and penetration, much surpassing those of the most enlightened philosopher at the present day; for it is impossible for us to decide upon any ground of certainty and demonstration that the sun will rise and set to-morrow. All the evidence which we have that these events will happen, is only probable evidence. How do we arrive at this probability, which at length becomes so strong and satisfactory, that we repose, and justly too, entire and unlimited confidence in it? Surely by frequent and invariable experience of the established constitution and course of nature.[2]

This is the last of Beasley's attacks on his Scotch foes, and it is

[1] *Search of Truth*, pp. 291-301.   [2] *Ib.*, pp. 301-306.

well it were so. He has destroyed the enemies' possessions, now it is time to repair the ravages of destructive criticism. So coming to his final section on the progress of the mind in the acquisition of ideas, he seeks to avoid the presumptive method of the common sense school. In place of attributing to humanity the possession of innate principles which instantaneously discover fundamental verities, he makes the attainment of truth a slow and operose process, ever subject to the method of trial and error. Let us return back, he says, for a few moments, upon our footsteps and retrace the progress of our primitive man or philosopher in attaining the first elements of human knowledge. We have seen that the number of his original perceptions would be extremely limited, and that he would be utterly unable to determine from what kind of objects they were derived. By sight he would perceive, at first, only a variously coloured superficies, but of figures, distances, and magnitudes would know nothing. All this time, however, he would be acquainted only with himself and his own sensations. His acquaintance with the objects around him would soon commence, and curiosity as well as enjoyment would prompt him to extend it. Subjecting the things which presented themselves to his sight to the examination of his touch, he would discover that, instead of exhibiting to him any longer only a plain surface variously coloured, they were formed in different figures, and situated at different distances. Marking the appearances which objects displayed to the sight, when thus examined by the sense of touch, and taking these appearances as the signs by which to designate and distinguish them in future, after repeated attempts, he would be able to perceive their figures and magnitudes by sight alone. This process by which the mind arrives at a perception of figures, magnitudes, and distances, is what the young man couched by Cheselden very significantly denominated learning to see. It is like the case of a woman in Pennsylvania who, having cataracts removed from both her eyes, declared that her sensations were indescribably delightful, but, at the same time, her newly recovered power of vision was for some time of very little use to her; she was perpetually stretching out her hands from fear of running against objects, being unable to distinguish their distances or magnitudes.[1]

[1] *Search of Truth*, pp. 391-2.

With a preliminary instance of this concrete sort, and after a short digression on the education of children, in which it is urged that they should be let alone in acquiring a knowledge of the external world, and not be subject to a hot-bed process of forcing, Beasley takes up some special problems in vision. To the question whether we do not originally perceive objects in an inverted position, as the image upon the retina is known to be inverted, and whether, of consequence, our seeing them erect is not an acquired perception, the answer is given that it is the established law of our constitution that rays passing from the upper parts of bodies, and falling upon the lower parts of the retina, present to our perception those upper parts, while those which come from the lower impinge upon the upper regions of the retina, and cause us to see the lower; and if from any cause, as pressing the eyeball, the effect can be produced upon the upper or lower parts of the retina, the corresponding portion of the object will appear to be exhibited, although it should not exist in reality.[1] A similar reply is given to the next questions on this subject. Do we see objects single or double originally with both eyes? Is our seeing an object single with both eyes an original or acquired perception? Every experiment which has been hitherto made in this matter leads to the conclusion that nature has endowed us with the power of seeing objects single with both eyes, immediately and without effort; since we are originally so constituted by our Creator as to see objects single with both eyes; that in order to this purpose, the muscles and membrane of the eyes are so adjusted as to enable us to move them in concert with each other; that images of objects are formed upon corresponding parts of the retina, and that a similar action upon the optic nerves leading to the brain must be produced, and that those actions must be made to mingle and coalesce in their progress to the sensorium. In fine, from the cases reported by Cheselden, and despite certain instances apparently to the contrary, Beasley comes to the conclusion that our seeing objects single with both eyes is not an acquired but an original perception, since the power of moving both our eyes in correspondence with each other seems to be instinctive.[2]

To the problem of visual inversion and duplication Beasley has

[1] *Search of Truth*, pp. 395, 404.   [2] *Ib.*, pp. 404-416.

given a solution somewhat after the manner of the question-begging realists, yet his is not that naïve realism which leaves no room for illusive perceptual references. He allows that in the mysterious union of mind and matter there may be deceptions of the senses, yet even here, that our senses sometimes deceive us, furnishes no argument against the truth of those informations which they give in their sound and natural state, and respecting those things concerning which their testimony ought to be trusted. Besides, admitting the veracity of their testimony as the reporters of matters of fact, the errors into which they lead may be all accounted for upon the strictest principles of philosophy. We have before illustrated the justness of the observation, that in all our acquired perceptions we proceed according to the interpretation of signs, and whenever the sign of any thing is presented, the mind naturally concludes that the thing signified is present. A gentleman passing along the streets of Philadelphia, imagines that he perceives a steamboat in the Delaware at a distance, but upon approaching it, finds that he was deceived, for that the object he saw was a sign-post before an inn, upon which the representation of a steamboat was rudely painted.[1]

After other pertinent illustrations of visual mistakes and delusions, which may be explained on the objective principles of perspective and refraction,—such as Jefferson's account of the looming of the mountains around Monticello, and the canoe in the bay of Yorktown which was taken for a war-ship—Beasley reverts to the subjective principles underlying the errors to which the perspective processes are liable. Disregarding his previous strictures on Berkeley's idealism, he attributes these phenomena to the wrong interpretation of signs, for none of them are original, but all acquired perceptions. Hence it is both with sight and hearing that they become liable to such an indefinite number of mistakes and delusions. For whenever, either by art and contrivance, or from mere contingency, the sign by which certain objects are exhibited to the mind can be presented, the objects themselves will appear to be present. Thus, for example, after our primitive man had learned to distinguish a globe by his sight from its peculiar appearance, if the painter had placed in his view a globe drawn in a pic-

[1] *Search of Truth*, pp. 417-418.

ture, he would have imagined it to be a real globe, and expected that it would seem such to his sense of touch.[1]

Beasley now passes from the simple misinterpretation of sensible signs in the waking life to the more ambiguous and doubtful interpretation of the symbols and hieroglyphics of dreams and deliriums. Here he draws on his former instructor, Stanhope Smith, for curious instances of spectral visions: one was that of a young woman whose disturbed imagination converted a white robe hanging on a chair into the image of a deceased friend; another was that of an inebriate who would hear strange voices, would ask and answer questions, as if engaged in conversation with visionary personages, so that Baron Von Swedenborg, in his most visionary moments, was never surrounded by more extraordinary assemblages of strange sights.[2] In thus treating of the progress of the mind in the acquisition of ideas, the realist has advanced from the normal interpretation of signs in ordinary perception to their abnormal misinterpretation in those extraordinary cases wherein an agitated mind, out of rude outlines presented by nature, may form complete and terrible pictures. He next inquires on what principles these things are to be explained. If crudities and indigestion, or whatever increases the irritability of the nervous system, produce frightful dreams, a similar solution may be given of other mental phenomena, such as alienations of mind, deliriums, the excitement which leads to somnambulism, ecstasies and trances, idiocy and madness. A conspicuous instance of mental alienation is to be found in the following singular case: A gentleman from the State of New York who had been for some time indisposed, had some business to perform at Norristown, in the State of Pennsylvania. Setting off from home, he went to Norristown, transacted the business which was assigned him, received a sum of money from the bank in behalf of a company with which he had some connection, and was just ready to return to his family, when, on a sudden, his mind became disordered. Without any apparent motive he commenced a journey on horseback to Baltimore of more than a hundred miles, and after remaining a short time in that city, equally without motive, he went from Baltimore to a small town upon Lake Erie, at a distance of more than two hundred miles,

[1] *Search of Truth*, p. 393.   [2] *Ib.*, p. 479.

travelling, too, at an inclement season of the year. Upon his arrival at the town upon Lake Erie, being probably greatly fatigued and exhausted, he obtained a refreshing sleep, and upon waking in the morning, appears to have come to his recollection, and was much surprised to find himself so remote from his family, and in pursuit of no object. He now hastened home, and his health was improved as well as his mind restored to its usual tone. Such an alienation of mind as this could have been occasioned by nothing but disease, which affecting those organs by which the mind performs its operations of reasoning, judging, remembering, leaves it, without their control, to become the sport of every vain imagination which for the time could take possession. As soon as that irregular action in the system was corrected, the mind returned to the performance of its functions.[1]

Beasley's explanation of this case of double personality seems very much like Rush's definition of a delirium as a permanent dream, and his reference of mental alienation to veritable derangements of a constituted order. The resemblance is a true one, for the head of the Philadelphia college refers with approval to his colleague's work on *Diseases of the Mind;* moreover, to the doctor's instances of mental aberration he adds several of his own choosing. Such were the visions of Nicolai, a member of the Royal Society of Berlin, a description of which he extracts from a German publication; but more pertinent was that of an apparently sensible and well-informed youth, who communicated to the provost what he considered a very important secret, namely, that he was the son of General Washington, but who, when he came to describe the particulars of the striking resemblance between himself and the president, and the honours, which on some occasions had been paid him by the military, discovered plainly his derangement.[2]

In his chapter on alienations of the mind the realist has almost hit upon a purely psychological explanation of obsessions and fixed ideas. At the same time, being insensibly influenced by the Philadelphia school, he inclines toward a physiological explanation of disordered mental functions. Yet even there he does not fall in with the extreme doctrines prevalent in his youth. Without enter-

---

[1] *Search of Truth,* pp. 465-6.   [2] *Ib.,* p. 472.

ing at all into the scheme of materialism, or Hartley's doctrines of vibrations, he inquires whether we may not consider ourselves as having good ground to conclude that in every case in which there is performed an operation of the mind, there takes place, at the same time, a correspondent, correlative or consentient change in the body.[1] In this clear and precise formulation of the principle of psycho-physical parallelism, Beasley has preserved a judicious balance between the extreme positions taken by the men of his time. Given the parallels of mind and matter, the realists like Witherspoon exaggerated the importance of the upper line, the materialists like Buchanan the lower, while the compromisers like Priestley made the two coalesce. But Beasley was a strict dualist, and took a peculiar position in respect to these alternatives: as to the third possibility, the homogeneity of man, he expressed a doubt whether there may be an intermediate substance between matter and mind, partaking of the properties of either the one or the other. To the second possibility, assumed chiefly by the anatomists, he says there is all imaginable difference between conceiving of mind, as performing all its operations through the instrumentality of the organs of sense, and conceiving all those operations as being nothing more than mere modes of motion in the corporeal organs. To the first possibility, that the science of mind is a pure pneumatology, he makes this answer: Taking the above stated theory to be true, of the soul's always acting, in its present state, through the instrumentality of the corporeal organs, but without the necessity of materialising the mind, we may account for the phenomena before mentioned, as the state of the soul in sleep, in dreaming, a swoon, a deliquium, of suspended animation by drowning, of alienation of mind, of ecstasies, trances, and all those idle superstitions of the vulgar which relate to spectres and apparitions.[2]

In utilising the researches of medicine to explain abnormal psychological problems, Beasley has passed into the domain of scientific research and out of the domain of dogmatic common sense. It is that transition which may explain the neglect of his work on the science of the human mind by the Princetonians, for, like the majority of realists, they sought to turn psychology into a pure pneumatology, made scornful references to mere physiologists, and

[1] *Search of Truth*, p. 452.   [2] *Ib.*, p. 454.

seemed actually afraid of investigating what Hamilton called present phantasms containing an illusive reference to an unreal world. So it was that, among Princetonians, Beasley's philosophical works appear to have had as little influence as his political *Dialogues of the Dead;* while he himself used Stanhope Smith's *Moral and Political Philosophy* in his own classes, in the New Jersey College, the *Search of Truth* was ignored. The latter, however, received a measure of recognition in the University of Pennsylvania. One of Beasley's own students, reviewing it a generation later, brought out its significance in relation to the transcendental movement at home and abroad. The *Search of Truth,* said George Sharswood,[1] was written to vindicate Locke from the charge of teaching the ideal theory—that every object of thought is but an impression or idea, a faint copy of some preceding expression. Hume went further, built a system of universal scepticism, denying all evidence of the existence of the mind itself, making it nothing but a succession of impressions and ideas. These conclusions aroused Reid and Kant. They took very different modes of combating the hypothesis in question; the one by appealing to certain fundamental principles of human belief, resting on the common sense of mankind: the other by an effort to prove that there exists knowledge a priori, not deduced from sensation or reflection, but by the criticism of Pure Reason. Kant's reasoning, however, tended to a subjective instead of an objective idealism. According to him, the mind imposes its own laws on the material universe. Space, time, cause and effect, are not in the universe itself, but merely in the mind, and are therefore but the forms or categories of knowledge. It was long, however, before the writings of the transcendental school attracted the attention of philosophers in England or this country. Dr. Beasley contented himself with showing, in opposition to Dr. Reid, that while Mr. Locke certainly traced the origin of all our knowledge to sensation and reflection, he nowhere taught that the perceptions of the mind are merely ideas, images or representations of outward things; but that, on the contrary, while admitting that the mode of perception is an unfathomable mystery, he held that external objects produce ideas or notions of them through the instrumentality of the senses,

[1] *Alumni Address,* Philadelphia, 1857, pp. 18, 19.

and expressly repudiated the doctrine that we have no sufficient evidence of the existence of a material universe.

In his *Search of Truth,* Beasley reached high tide in his investigations; in his minor works the scientific spirit is on the ebb. In his *Review of the Philosophy of the Human Mind by Thomas Brown,* he first uses the method of the heresy hunter of proving that a man is wrong, by assuming that those whom he resembles are not right: thus if Brown is like Hume in his theory of causation, Brown is no theist but an atheist. Again, Beasley takes up what might be called the trite argument of infection by proximity: thus, as Reid caught the taint of idealism from Berkeley, so does Brown in his theory of the external senses, for he frequently adverts to the Berkeleian theory and regards it as untenable; yet what is the sum of his own doctrine upon the external senses? In the case of vision, he maintains that we see only light and not objects themselves. . . . How then do we arrive at the idea of an external world and a belief that it exists? Not by the testimony of any of the five senses, but by a sixth sense—the muscular organ—forsooth a sort of metaphysical Atlas, of strength sufficient to support upon his shoulders an external universe.[1]

The last of Beasley's reactionary writings was one which reverts to deism, and yet, at the same time, in its classification of the various forms of pantheism points forward to the coming transcendentalism. In his *Vindication of the Argument a Priori,* assuming that the proposition that the eternal and necessary being must be a cogitative and intelligent mind would seem to be an undeniable truth, the writer yet allows that upon this point sceptics and atheists enter into controversy with him. One sect of philosophers ascribes all the order, and beauty, and nice contrivances which we find in the world, to an accidental concourse of atoms, and the subsequent workings of dead and senseless matter. This was the doctrine of Leucippus, Democritus, and their followers. Another sect alleges that there has been an eternal succession of such objects as are now exhibited to us. This is the doctrine of Hume, as far as his doctrine has any foundation in reason and common sense. A third supposes that the universe, as it now is, has existed necessarily from all eternity, and that the Deity himself is nothing more or

[1] *Review of Brown,* p. 5.

less than the illimitable frame of material things, which, from its
organisation, is capable of thought and intelligence. So held the
celebrated Spinoza. This is usually called pantheism. A fourth
opinion is, that an intelligent mind produced all that exists in the
universe. The second atheistical theory is the one which seems to
have accorded best with the views and to have most strongly laid
hold of the affections of the masters of the modern school of scepticism and deism. The world has always been, say they, as it is
now; events of a similar nature have followed each other, without
any beginning, and shall continue so to do without end. Nature,
or the material universe, produces all things by regular and established laws, and has continued steadily and invariably to evolve
similar forms, and give rise to diversified phenomena, from all
eternity. This is the substance of their doctrine, without any particular reference to the language employed by them. Hume's
opinions about cause and effect, when he maintains that all we know
concerning them is merely that they bear the relation of antecedent and sequence, and that we have no reason to believe that there
is any power in the one to produce the other, lead, inevitably, to
the system of an eternal succession. Hobbes, Helvétius and others
may be classed among the maintainers of this theory. . . . The
third view which may be taken of this atheistical scheme is, that
the world, or whole universe and everything contained therein, is
one uniform substance, eternal, uncreated and necessary. The only
difference between this and Spinoza's theory is that the one supposes mind and intelligence to belong to the material mass, while
the other excludes them. The same, or similar absurdities, are
involved in this system as in the foregoing. If the whole universe,
and all things contained therein, are necessary, it must be necessary that there should be the number of suns and planets which
are now found, the number of rivers, mountains, trees, men, flowers, plants. It must be impossible that any one of these should
not subsist. It is necessary that some objects should exist to-day,
and others to-morrow; that this year there should be in Philadelphia 120,000 inhabitants, and the next 5000 more—such is the
absurdity of this view of the subject. . . . Finally, the last
scheme is that of Spinoza. The only difference between this

and the one before mentioned is, that it introduces upon the stage an intelligent mind, as the origin and source of all while the last leaves it out. Spinoza makes the whole material universe to be eternal and necessary, but supposes this material system to be so organised as to think, and perceive, and be God. While it allows a God, however, it divests him of all his attributes, subverts his power and providence, and subjects him, as well as all things else, to the control of fate. A God, says Newton, without dominion and final causes, is mere fate or nature. All the operations of nature, then, the movements of the planets, the flux and reflux of the tides, all the laws of nature, are to God what the functions of our bodies, as, for instance, the circulation of our blood, our respiration through the lungs, the performance of our secretions, are to us. The Great Supreme has no more dominion in nature than we have—every event is brought about by an uncontrollable necessity. This scheme, then, although it ushers God upon the stage of being, binds him in chains, strips him of all his attributes, and is justly regarded, like that of Epicurus, as complete atheism. All final causes are excluded from it. This system is liable to all the objections, therefore, which were adduced against the other, and is traceable to the same absurdities. For, although intelligence is allowed, yet it is matter still which produces all results, and the whole material universe, which exists from necessity.[1] Here ends the last of the early Princeton realists; it remains to consider three of the lesser realists, Nisbet, Law and Ogilvie.

[1] *Vindication*, pp. 10-14.

CHAPTER VII

THE LESSER REALISTS

CHARLES NISBET (1736-1804), a graduate of the University of Edinburgh and a pupil of Beattie of Aberdeen, was another of the imported representatives of the Scotch school in America. Brought over by Benjamin Rush as a rival in scholarship to John Witherspoon, and appointed first principal of Dickinson College, Carlisle, Pennsylvania, Nisbet was described by his sponsor as follows: He was in acquired knowledge a walking library. He knew a great deal of many and a little of all subjects. His knowledge was derived from books that few people read and that many people never heard of. From these he extracted a great deal of rare and uncommon knowledge. He was an excellent companion and his conversation overflowed with wit, humour and instructive anecdotes. Unhappily he was like Doctor South, of a querulous disposition and more disposed to find fault than to praise. His usefulness to society was by no means proportional to his uncommon abilities and extensive knowledge. He rather resembled a fountain which poured forth streams in a royal garden for the amusement of spectators than a rich and copious stream that fertilised in its course an extensive country.[1]

That Nisbet was as much of a scholar as Witherspoon is quite true, yet he was of too splenetic a disposition and in too uncongenial surroundings to accomplish as much as the president of Princeton. As at home he had advocated the colonial cause in such a way as to make his position uncomfortable, so here, in the trying times after the Revolution, he imperilled his position by what a biographer calls a wit seldom equalled. In some letters to the old country he complains that there is nothing in this country like Scotland, except that the people do not walk with feet uppermost; we have no men of learning nor taste and everything is on a dead level and there is no distinction except wealth; learning is

---

[1] Benjamin Rush, *Memoir*, p. 179.

unknown and consequently not in request; the rulers of the people are either ignoramuses or smatterers; our lawyers are truly ignorant and read only a few reports and a few infidel books. So I live like a pelican in the wilderness and have few opportunities of serving the public outside of reading lectures to a few young men on the elements of morals. I have delivered to them already three hundred and seventy-five lectures on the first twenty-nine chapters of the Westminster Confession of Faith and I hope they will stay with me till I get through it. You may suppose that I do not live an idle life when I've been obliged to compose five and often six divinity lectures a week for these two years past and the three former years I spent in composing my lectures in philosophy.[1]

The lectures last mentioned have remained in manuscript until the present day.[2] Consisting of three courses on metaphysics, morals and logic, they amount to the grand total of thirteen hundred and fifty questions and answers in the Socratic form. Considering the difficulties under which they were composed, they truly exhibit the memory all but prodigious which their author was reputed to possess. Nisbet was an old school Calvinist, a member of the orthodox and not of the moderate party in the church, yet here he shows an unusual fairness in his discussion of schools other than the Scotch. In his metaphysics his primary assumptions are realistic, but in his morals his attitude is eclectic. Assuming the chief end of metaphysics to be the laying down of indubitable axioms which may agree to all our ideas, he somewhat indefinitely defines an idea as that which is immediately perceived by the mind when any particular object is presented to it. That these objects have a real existence is shown from our acquiring the idea of power from the changes we observe in things that are without us as well as those in ourselves. In a word, all human knowledge must be at an end unless our idea of power be allowed to be a real one; it is no contradiction of our idea of power that we see only the changes that follow on certain actions, for Mr.

[1] Letters to Charles Wallace, Edinburgh, Sept. 2, 1790; Aug. 17, 1791, in *Bulletin of the New York Public Library*, Vol. 1, pp. 116-120, 180-183.
[2] In the Ridgway Branch of the Philadelphia Public Library.

Hume, who resolves all our ideas of power to our having often observed that the cause produces the effect, confesses that he was not able to believe his doctrine in company.[1]

In his ethical lectures Nisbet gives a brief historical summary, beginning with the *summum bonum* of the Greeks and ending with an extended criticism of Hutcheson. He explains that the Stoics placed the chief good in honour, the Peripatetics in profit, and the Epicureans in pleasure; among the moderns, Hobbes, in the last account, supposed our morality, as well as our religion, to depend on the will of the strongest and that we ought to obey God merely because we cannot resist him; Lord Shaftesbury imagined that virtue was its own only reward; Rousseau endeavoured to introduce a sentimental philosophy founded on disinterested friendship without regard to speculative doctrines or a future state; Clarke that morality is founded upon the external relation of the fitness of things; Wollaston that it consisted in speaking and acting according to the truth; Hume, that it consisted in utility; Hutcheson, that it was founded on conscience or the moral faculty, that such conduct as is for our own interest is truly praiseworthy and that vice is only hurting ourselves.[2] Now while none of these authors, continues the expositor, are wide of the mark, and while they have fairly divided the truth among themselves, which is found by uniting their several systems, yet the last of them needs further explanation and criticism. As given in the dialogue form Nisbet's presentation is as follows:

Q. What is the System of Dr. Hutcheson on this question?
A. He makes moral obligation depend on conscience, or the moral sense, which appears to be the joint effect of all the physical laws of the mind, and our guide in distinguishing moral objects; as our external Senses are our guides in things that relate to them. This faculty implies an inward and instinctive, as well as instant approbation of moral good, and disapprobation of moral evil, prior to any reasoning whatever, and independent of both of them.

Q. Has not this faculty a greater extent and jurisdiction than any other yet mentioned? *A.* Yes: of all the single principles that

[1] Ridgway MS., *Metaphysics*, Qs. 56-60.
[2] *Ib., Morals,* Qs. 8, 42, 43, 59.

have been mentioned as the foundation of morals it is the strongest and the greatest in effect. It does not require long Study, is fit to be applied on sudden emergencies and its actings constitute the happiness, or misery of every individual.

Q. What is the defect of this principle considered as a standard of morals? *A.* The absolute need it has of knowledge and information and its being liable to superstition, bigotry, and enthusiasm, which pervert its judgment, and render it pernicious in proportion as it ought to have been useful: Men must follow it whether it is enlightened or not. It is capable of being blinded by ignorance, obscured by prejudice, and perverted by superstition. It requires a true knowledge of cases, and circumstances, and of perfect laws and rules of morals. But if it is mistaken in the fact, or in the law, which may often be the case, its judgment must be erroneous, and like an ignorant Magistrate in a state—may be the occasion of unspeakable evil.[1]

Nisbet's strictures on the moral sense theory form an effective counterpoise to the similar theory of his rival, Witherspoon; his strictures on materialism have the same relation to Joseph Priestley in the neighbouring town of Northumberland, and to the latter's mouthpiece, Thomas Cooper, who shortly after this taught in Dickinson College itself. So on this living problem, on which all conservative Scottish-Americans must needs have their say, Nisbet proceeds at some length:

Q. Is the union betwixt the mind and body capable of clear explication or solution? *A.* No: *causa latet, sed res est notissima.*

Q. Is not every volition of the mind accompanied with a certain motion of the body? *A.* Yes: but the cause of muscular motion is, notwithstanding, unknown.

Q. What theories have been formed to account for muscular motion in conformity to the volitions of the mind? *A.* Two chiefly: the system of the *fluor per nervus* or animal spirits; and the pre-established harmony of Mr. Leibnitz.

Q. How may muscular motion be accounted for on the supposition of animal spirits? *A.* The supporters of this hypothesis suppose that the human brain is a gland, which separates the finest parts of the blood from the rest, which it transmits to the

---

[1] *Morals,* Qs. 305-307.

nerves, and that this fluid being inconceivably fine, volatile and elastic, is capable of being put into motion by the mind, which is supposed to reside near the origination of the nerves; and that the motions excited in these animal spirits, are the cause of muscular motion.

Q. Have we any evidence of a nervous fluid, or animal spirits? *A.* So far from that, that not even the best microscopes can discover any hollowness or perforation, even in the nerves of Oxen or Elephants.

Q. Must not this theory then be considered as a mere hypothesis? *A.* Certainly; for tho' experiments have traced the cause of muscular motion as far as the nerves, they have not been able to trace it further; and if they are immediate instruments of muscular motion, it must be in some other manner than by means of a liquor.

Q. What is the System of Mr. Leibnitz? *Q.* He supposes that the soul performs its volitions independent of the body, and the body its motions independent of the soul; but that every mind is framed so as to form a certain number of volitions in a certain order, and every body is contrived to perform a certain number of motions and that the deity unites these souls and bodies, whose volitions and motions agree together by this pre-established harmony.

Q. Do any appearances in nature favour this hypothesis? *A.* No: it is only removing the difficulty by calling in the Deity, but it neither proves nor explains anything.

Q. What other opinions take place among Moderns on this head? *A.* Mr. Collins of the last century, and Dr. Priestley at present, have revived the System of Epicurus, by supposing the soul to be only a quality resulting from matter organised in a particular manner.

Q. What is the tendency of this hypothesis? *A.* As the other removed the difficulty by calling in the Deity; this denies it altogether, by supposing the whole nature of man to consist of one homogeneous substance.

Q. But when the consequences of this opinion are considered, does not the difficulty appear greater than ever? *A.* Certainly:

as those who embrace this system are obliged to explain all the Phenomena of thought and volition from the common laws of matter and motion.

Q. What is the main difficulty of this question? *A.* To explain how two substances so heterogeneous and diverse as body and mind can be united together, and mutually affect and be affected by each other.

Q. Does experience add or contribute any thing to the solution of this question? *A.* No: the mind of the greatest philosopher knows no more of the manner in which the motions are produced by his own volition, than the mind of the new born child, which possesses the power of self motion as perfectly as those that are in an adult state.[1]

Hitherto Nisbet's literary remains have appeared to be but the *disjecta membra* of a lost body of metaphysics, but with the recent recovery of a close copy of the original lectures,[2] his system may be articulated nearly in its entirety. Here metaphysics is divided into ontology and pneumatology; the former dealing with the most abstract terms as the universal or transcendental predicate called being; the latter dealing with spirits or those immaterial beings endued with understanding and will.[3] Without entering into the further scholastic definitions of the two grand divisions of his subject, it may be said that Nisbet took, in both of them, a thoroughly realistic point of view. He made the chief end of ontology to be the discovery of indubitable axioms to assist us in the discovery of truth; and the most useful part of the science of the mind to be the knowledge of ourselves by the immediate faculty of consciousness and without the intervention of any ideas. Against some modern writers who hold that we can have no knowledge of substances, but can only form ideas of modes or attributes belonging to these, Nisbet holds that as it is only in this way, *i. e.,* by ideas of their attributes, that we can know substances, and identify the known qualities with the substances to which they belong.[4]

[1] *Morals, Metaphysics,* Qs. 232-244.

[2] As taken down by Felix Hayward Gilbert, 1793, and now in the possession of Dr. Thomas R. Boggs, Johns Hopkins Hospital.

[3] Gilbert MS., p. 130.   [4] *Ib.,* pp. 1-4.

This epistemological identification of subjective and objective is dogmatically based upon the assumption that every being to be metaphysically true must be truly intelligible and capable of being the object of true knowledge, in which sense truth is called real. Hence the permanent beings that are the subjects of these modes possess their identification by retaining their essential properties at different times and places,—the Supreme Being by his eternity and immutability, other beings by their perpetual diversity.[1] Thus in the latter case a river is said to be specifically the same which runs nearly over the same place, although the water in it, at any point of time or space, is not the same with the water which was in it in another, for it is a saying as old as Heracleitus that a man cannot go twice into the same river. This last principle may have a difficulty in it, when applied to human beings, yet even the animal body, like the ship of Theseus, preserves its identity of form though not a remnant of its original matter remain.[2] So, too, in the mental life: every person may be said to have a certain relative measure of that which is peculiar to himself and suited to his own feelings, so that a lecture in philosophy may seem as long as a game of cards, though the latter be actually three times longer. Nevertheless, when we are attentive to our own thoughts we discover a sort of pomp or procession of ideas which succeed another in our minds with a regular pace or march, and this regularity could not exist unless we had a common measure without ourselves, a means whereby mankind can agree with each other with respect to the length of determinate things.[3]

If the idea of time is not merely a subjective principle, but an objective reality, so is the idea of power; our notion of the latter being derived from real changes both in ourselves and in outside things. The late Mr. Hume, indeed, considered this the weakest and darkest part of metaphysical theory; but certainly if we have no idea of power, or if the idea which we have of it is only an imaginary one, then all the events of nature without exception would be perfectly loose, vague, simple, unmeaning and unintelligible, so that nothing would remain in the world except a number of ideas and impressions without any order, connection or relation among themselves. This is the keystone of human knowledge,

[1] *Gilbert* MS., p. 11. [2] *Ib.*, pp. 18, 19. [3] *Ib.*, pp. 37, 41, 42.

which, being taken away, the whole edifice of human knowledge falls to pieces. To deny the idea of power not only denies all creation but all actual existence, because no being can be supposed to exist, if power is not supposable. Hence like the tyrant Caligula, who wished that the Roman people had but one neck that he might be able to destroy them at one stroke, Hume imagined that he had found out the neck or vital part of human knowledge, yet he was unable to effect his malevolent wish of taking away all knowledge and actual existence, for he could not believe his own doctrine. In fact, he would have taken it as a great affront if anyone had alleged that he had not the power of writing his *History* or his *Essay on Miracles*.[1]

Having by these keen thrusts of satire disposed of his sceptical compatriot, Nisbet turns from pyrrhonism to realism and asserts that our idea of power, so far from being an imaginary one, is not only natural but likewise involuntary in the same manner as those perceptions that we have of visible objects. By the principles of common sense we discern and receive all those primary truths on which all philosophical reasonings are founded. For as reason is that faculty by which we infer one truth from another, it necessarily supposes that primary truths are already discovered by some other means, because until these are discovered, the reason cannot enter upon its operations by means of which alone it discovers other truths. Besides, if we were to admit that the human soul is a *tabula rasa,* as Mr. Locke would have us to believe, this would entirely annihilate the judgment or discerning faculty, as the mind in that case would be like a looking-glass and would receive with equal ease and entire indifference any idea whatever that should be presented to it, in the same manner as a looking-glass receives the image of every object. Now it is only by the natural propensity or original determination of the soul, to admit primary truths rather than their contraries, that it is capable of discerning moral distinctions as well as conceiving a love of order and truth in general.[2]

Nisbet's epistemology leads directly to his pneumatology. When we inquire what we ourselves are, we are conscious of certain feelings which we discover by internal consciousness without rea-

[1] *Gilbert* MS., pp. 66, 68, 69.   [2] *Logic,* pp. 136, 137.

soning or the intervention of any idea. In a word the mind is immediately conscious of its own existence and operates and knows its substance to be the power of thinking, because thinking, as an accident, could not exist by itself.[1] But this does not mean that the soul always thinks, else it would 'follow that the waking man and sleeping man were two different persons, because the waking man is conscious of all that he does or thinks while he is awake, but has no more knowledge of what he thought in sound sleep than if it had been thought by another person; so that this wild hypothesis of Descartes out of every simple man would make two different individuals, who had not the least knowledge of the thought or actions of each other.[2] And the same thing is to be said of the rhetorical fiction which personifies the different faculties of the mind and speaks of them as of separate beings, although all of them belong to the same nature, for it is the same mind by whatever name it is designated, that both understands, assents and judges.[3]

By the same process of simplification which reduces the mind to a single entity, and reality to that which is directly known, the realist next comes to the defence of natural principles or propensities. Considering these historically, as presented under the form of innate ideas, Plato, he says, made these to be common notions prior to instruction and therefore relics of a pre-existent state; Descartes considered them to be stamped by the hand of Divinity in the mind of every man, in order that building upon them and reasoning from them, they might arrive at a knowledge of all other necessary truths.[4] Locke, on the other hand, who had a great zeal against the Cartesian philosophy, probably because it was not made in England, endeavoured with all his might, to demonstrate that mankind has no such common notions or ideas. But against his arguments in the first books of the *Essay* we may resolve the question as follows: (1) that it is one thing to say that men have by nature the knowledge of certain things and another to say that they have a propensity to receive it when proposed. (2) Although natural propensities may be obscured, checked and

---

[1] *Metaphysics,* pp. 131-139.   [2] *Ib.,* p. 146.
[3] *Ib.,* p. 157.   [4] *Ib.,* pp. 242, 243.

concealed for a long time by means of superstition, or tyranny, or want, yet this does not prove that there are no such principles. (3) That the beliefs and judgments of men are not always to be inferred from their actions, because many of the actions of men are theatrical or feigned and others are produced by impulse or passion against their judgments. (4) That when we are investigating the principles of human nature, barbarous nations and those that live under tyranny and oppression ought not to be taken into the account; far less ought they to be made an example to others. (5) That many travellers, who have pretended to give us accounts of barbarous nations, were unfit to give us a true account by not being acquainted with their language and wanting an opportunity of learning their notions of religion. (6) That if there are no innate principles, then it must follow that reason is not natural to man because it cannot be exercised antecedent to sensation or reflection.[1]

By the help of these compendious principles, Nisbet goes on to examine the celebrated arguments in the *Essay on the Human Understanding*. Thus, he says, by taking hold of the loose expression, innate ideas, Locke had it easily in his power to represent these as absurd and inconceivable; and after having succeeded in this, he proceeds to innate principles where he changes his method of attack, although he never loses sight of children and idiots on whose ignorance of innate principles he enlarges with an air of triumph. Besides, he gives no proof that men may attain knowledge of speculative principles by the use of their faculties, except that men are obliged to learn language and to be acquainted with those terms by which they express their opinions, before they could have a distinct idea of the propositions that express these natural principles; so that if a man had not heard of that famous axiom—It is impossible that a thing should be and not be at the same time—till he had read it in Leibniz, Mr. Locke would not allow that he had any previous propensity to admit this axiom, rather than its contrary, because he had never heard of it nor read it before.[1] But while Mr. Locke is so eager to confute what was never asserted, he takes no notice of what lay directly before him, viz., the original propensities and dispositions of our nature. These

---

[1] *Metaphysics*, pp. 249-251.   [2] *Ib.*, pp. 258-259.

he implicitly denies and explains away to nothing, leaving mankind entirely to accident with respect to what principles they should adopt. For, if there be no innate propensities in human nature, there can be no principle of agreement among men, nor can they be capable of reasoning with one another. Mr. Locke does not question that mankind have always lived in society. Now, in order to this, certain principles are necessary to be agreed on, as society could not subsist if contrary speculative principles were natural to different persons. But if nature has not given men a propensity to receive these principles, how comes it to pass that they are to be found, as he says, among barbarous people; or if the human mind is a *tabula rasa,* how comes it to pass that we do not find any nations in which ingratitude is accounted honourable, or the whole is reckoned less than a part?[1] But by far the strangest of Mr. Locke's arguments is that no moral rule can be proposed of which we may not justly demand a reason, and consequently that there are no moral axioms. Now, if we may justly demand a reason for any assertion whatever, it was certainly incumbent on such a universal sceptic to give us some reason why he was determined to demand a reason for everything without end. But further, if mankind have no natural conviction of any moral rules, or if they know of no rule of which they may not demand the reason, then, they could never form any judgment at all on their own conduct, because a judgment implies the comparing two ideas, and, if man had no moral maxims, either from nature or institution, to which he might compare his own conduct, it would be impossible for the greatest part of mankind to have any conscience at all.[2] Hence we conclude that there is no reason back of infallible moral principles, because conscience has a relation to some rule too evident to need any reason. Thus there is a natural sense of justice which all men feel at least when they suffer injustice. In fact, it is no invalidation of such innate principles because nobody has yet been able to give us an exact list of them; they may exist, although they be neither exact in their working, nor possess those precise qualities of priority, independence, universality and certainty demanded by Lord Herbert. We may, therefore, call such innate principles, inclinations or propensities in the mind to admit certain principles

[1] *Metaphysics,* pp. 259-262.   [2] *Ib.,* pp. 266-272.

when proposed rather than their contraries, and to perform certain activities as soon as an opportunity offers, just as a child born in darkness would, if its eyes were sound, have a faculty of sight, though without the least knowledge or experience, of the faculty. In fine, Mr. Locke himself, when out of the heat of dispute and on cool second thought, owns intuitive knowledge, which implies innate principles and tendencies in accordance with reason and common sense.[1]

Nisbet's defence of innate principles is not a defence of innate ideas, for he believes that there are no ideas, properly speaking, distinct from perceptions of the mind. Ideas, he holds, are either the immediate objects of our understanding or else certain images representing objects and supposed to be impressed on the brain and by this means presented to the mind. But the latter supposition is both figurative and false: when we say we receive ideas of things we only use a figure borrowed from corporeal objects, such as seeing a picture of anything placed before our eyes. The doctrine of representative perception is likewise false, and for two reasons: when we consider the nature of matter we may be easily convinced that it has no power of action, and consequently cannot produce either an image of itself or of anything else. On the other hand, it would be strange to suppose that the mind itself forms those images of objects we called ideas, without having consciousness or exerting any volition to that purpose; as we find by experience that when any objects present themselves to us steadily, before we have thought of them, nay, often against our will, we immediately form ideas of them which cannot be supposed to be produced by the actions of our own minds. For all these reasons, while we are obliged to reject innate ideas, we may put in their place innate habits and principles in the frame and constitution of the mind previous to the occasion which draws them forth.[2]

As in respect to the original ideas Nisbet was a common sense realist, so in respect to the relation between mind and body, he is a common sense dualist. Between these two substances he sees no affinity in common qualities. The mind is not corporeal, because the faculty of thinking is not corporeal. This disposes of the theory

[1] *Metaphysics*, pp. 273-284. [2] *Ib.*, pp. 286-304.

of Epicurus that the mind is a quality of the body resulting from
its organisation, of the theory of Locke that bodies may be endowed
with a power of thinking, and of the theory of Priestley that two
different collections of properties may belong to the same subject.
In brief, the wonderful conjunction of mind and body is a mystery
which has not yet been explained by philosophy. Aristotle says
that the body is moved by the mind by means of desire or choice,
or any change in the senses and imagination. But the question is,
in what manner all this is accomplished. Descartes imagined that
the deity moves the body in a manner corresponding to the volition,
in the same manner as an indulgent nurse carries a child the very
way to which it points; Leibniz imagined a *harmonia praestabilita,*
a perfect conformity of motions and volitions determined by the
original frame of those minds and bodies betwixt which it took
place; many moderns following the mediæval physiologists imagined that the animal spirits which they conceive to be of a middle
nature betwixt body and spirit constitute the copula or nexus betwixt these discordant substances; the most recent theorists have
endeavoured to account for muscular motion by means of the electric fluid, which is as likely to be of as much use to them as occult
qualities and substantial forms were to the Schoolmen, or attraction to Sir Isaac Newton. In fine, from the Cartesians to the elec-
tricians, the theories seeking to explain the constant regularity of
thoughts and motions are only ingenious hypotheses, invented for
explaining the phenomena, but giving us no light with respect to
the modes of the wonderful union that subsists between substances
of so different natures as the soul and body. Therefore a candid
confession of our ignorance in this matter is the conclusion to which
the most acute philosophers find themselves obliged at last to come,
after a number of disappointments and conjectures.[1]

This agnostic conclusion of Nisbet is based on his further examination of the various hypotheses as to the organisation of the body
and the origin of the soul. First, he rejects the ancient theory of
the soul as a plastic principle modelling and contriving its own
wonderful habitation, because if the soul itself were the agent
in this case it would certainly be conscious of its own agency.
Again, he rejects the scholastic theory of the soul as made up of

[1] *Metaphysics,* pp. 310-325.

sensitive, vegetative, intuitive species, because this would no more remove difficulties than the supposition of the eastern magi that each star was controlled and kept in its orbit by its proper intelligence. Finally, he rejects the modern revival of the Epicurean theory of traduction, because it would make the soul a corporeal thing and propagated like the body. This last theory, which Locke favoured and Priestley and the French materialists openly professed, is based on incomplete information and false analogy. When these men affirm that the soul is corporeal and dependent on the body for its existence, they affirm a thing of which they cannot be certain, because the properties of mind and body are so different from each other, that we cannot ever conceive them as belonging to the same substance, nor discover the least affinity betwixt them. Besides, they bring no arguments to prove that the soul is corporeal and propagated with the body except one from analogy, namely, that plants and brute animals are propagated by seed and that all their properties, according to their kinds, are derived from the progenitors by means of the seeds. But analogical reasoning at best implies only a slight probability, as they have no evidence that this is actually the case; for those resemblances to their immediate and remote progenitors, which are observed in some men, may be easily accounted for, without supposing that the soul is corporeal and derived, inasmuch as they may be justly attributed to education, imitation, or to a similar configuration of the bodily organs.[1]

After his attack on the modern materialism, in which he inadvertently touches on the evolutionary principles of environment, Nisbet finished his extant lectures with a discussion of the immortality of the soul.[2] Although the arguments are trite and futile, they are significant as presenting the Scottish-American's obstinate realistic point of view. This belief in the future of the soul is so agreeable to the common sense of mankind that it has been uniformly found among all nations; it is so suitable to the innate propensities of men, that the supposition of the contrary appears to be shocking. Indeed, it is so natural, that it is easy to make children believe it. If we do not stay to answer their little impertinent questions, but deliver to them a system of sound principles without

[1] *Metaphysics,* pp. 330-342.   [2] *Ib.,* pp. 359-372.

any arguments whatever, a great deal of light breaks into their minds at once. This is because the intuitive faculty and innate habits are prior to reason, and because we are capable of discovering the evidence of primary truths before their lustre has been darkened by reasoning. In fine, this belief, like the other sound doctrines of the immortality of the soul, depends on the general sense and belief of the generality of mankind.[1]

Thomas Law (1759-1834), was a member of the English family signalised in Galton's *Heredity and Genius*.[2] Son of Edmund, bishop of Carlisle, Law entered the service of the East India Company, became Governor of the province of Bahar, and was associated with Lord Cornwallis in a successful scheme for the fixed settlement of the landed revenues of Bengal. Coming to the United States in 1793, not so much, as has been reported, out of admiration for American institutions, but, as he himself says, for his disapproval of the impolitic and exhausting war which England was then carrying on against France, Law became connected, by marriage, with the family of General Washington, and further distinguished himself by his efforts to establish a national currency, to construct a Chesapeake and Ohio Canal, and to develop and build up the National Capital. For such projects Law has received little credit, but for this he has himself largely to blame. As a publicist, he dissipated his talents because of the multiplicity of his interests. So did he as an intellectual. His linguistic accomplishments are proof of this. He knew French, and, as Talleyrand, his fellow traveller, described him, was 'toujours instructif et toujours intéressant'; but he failed to master the French philosophers such as La Harpe on irresistible instincts, and Helvétius on the moral infancy of the race. He knew Hindustani and Persian, but he used his eastern lore not so much to adorn his moral philosophy as to enliven what he referred to as his 'poetical ludibria.' In short, Law was a brilliant but erratic genius, a veritable multiple personality, if one consider the dramatic rapidity of those mental changes intimated in his literary remains. As a schoolboy at Ely he appears to have incurred his aversion to the dogmas of Calvin, 'that disciple of the denaturalised monster,

[1] *Metaphysics*, p. 373.   [2] New York, 1884, p. 95.

Saint Augustine'; as a student at Oxford he evidently gained his inclination for materialism, for then he heard Joseph Priestley, although he was half fearful of the censure of prejudice of listening to the great chartist; as a traveller in France he recollected the shocking scenes produced by the Godwinian doctrine of universal philanthropy among those deluded wretches whose patriotic zeal for public utility smothered all affection, pity, and sympathy; [1] lastly, as a Crown officer in India, where his pre-eminent position gave him an insight into the religious as well as the civil opinions of society, he noticed that the Hindoos, when they relinquish their belief in metempsychosis and the plurality of gods, deny our trinitarian doctrine and settle into unitarianism, or more distinctly, deism. [2] To this last phase of thought Law was himself strongly inclined, for he wrote in his maturity: ' It is impossible for a man who studies the book of nature and who examines himself not to be sensible of the First Great Cause in this book; all is reconcilable to our natural feeling, all is consistent, all harmonious; no controversies about different interpretations, no persecutions about heresies can arise from tracing nature up to nature's god. [3]

While the intellectual beliefs of the son of the English Church dignitary varied from the orthodoxy of a sheltered childhood to the vulgar deism of Thomas Paine, there was one persistent phase into which his philosophical personality resolved itself. This was the natural realism expounded in his published writings. To these writings there is a kind of imaginative introduction in the form of a dream, a description of which Law claims to have penned immediately on awakening. In this dream he entered a temple dedicated to Truth, and there heard a venerable high-priest ask to receive from the people an account of their discovery by an investigation of their instinctive movements, impulses, and feelings, in order that we may ascertain whether there is a perfect system given to all the human race, a universal language, not like words, so arbitrary and variable, but one which no difference of tribe, no diversity of tongue could render doubtful. [4]

[1] *Second Thoughts*, pp. 6, 30, 58.   [2] MS. Note. Oct. 14, 1826.
[3] *Memoranda of a Journey to Bedford*, August, 1816.
[4] *Moral System*, p. 28.

Law's temple of truth, to judge from this literary fragment, was built upon a Scotch foundation. In his *Thoughts on Instinctive Impulses,* he shows as much by an attack upon English philosophy. Locke, he begins, is reputed to have proved that a child has not any innate ideas, and that a man's mind is like a blank sheet of paper or a piece of wax; but how is the mind excited, how is it operated upon, how does it obtain knowledge? Is it from corporeal pleasure and pain, our five senses, or from our instinctive emotions?[1] Most of our metaphysical writers state that our knowledge is obtained by the senses, overlooking the emotions and impulses created by and through them. But it is much more profound to look upon instinct as upon the principle of gravitation in bodies, which is not to be explained by any known qualities, but is an immediate impression produced by the First Mover, and is the divine energy acting in his own creatures.[2] But not only are the empiricists of England wrong, but the materialists and the associationalists. If man were a mere inert, material being, without pleasures and pains and instinctive impulses, what could operate upon us but force?[3] To talk of the association of ideas producing sensations, without admitting that there must be, first, a separation of ideas and feelings, were to speak of shadows without substances, or of echoes without sound. A thing pleases because, by the constitution of our nature, pleasant sensations arise from its colour and form every object giving us an agreeable or disagreeable sensation.[4]

In his *First Thoughts on Instinctive Impulses,* Law merely cleared the ground, but in his *Second Thoughts* on the same subject he attempts to erect the structure; yet in this he was hardly more successful than in his building operations in the City of Washington. During the three years that elapsed between the two essays he says that he waited in vain for someone to develop a theory of moral sensations into a regular science founded on primordial, universal, and invariable principles; but now in support of the doctrine which he at the first thought a rather novel one, he has found very great authorities.[5] Here he picks and chooses. He resents the Baroness de Staël's objections to Adam

[1] *Instinctive Impulses,* p. 12.
[3] *Ib.,* p. 18.
[4] *Ib.,* p. 79.
[2] *Ib.,* p. 15.
[5] *Second Thoughts,* p. 3.

Smith's theory of the 'sympathetic sentiments,' which place us in the situation of another; he also dislikes Rochefoucauld's vilification of human nature which attributes man's best acts to selfish motives, and prefers Hutcheson's doctrine that virtue is founded upon instinct and affection. So, too, in accordance with Reid and Stewart, he considers that to think is but to feel, and that the mind is but a consciousness of sensations. Hence the sensorium represents to consciousness every object with the accuracy of a mirror, accompanied with proper likings and dislikings, or of impulses to seek or avoid.[1] In the next attempt to define and classify these instinctive impulses, Law is forced out of a rank realism into a ranker utilitarianism. Taking those desires and aversions which arise from man's sensual feelings as an individual, he describes them as that sympathy and antipathy which are implanted in man, who, as a social being, is attracted by a kind of magnetic influence to some of his fellow creatures and is repulsed by those who evince dissocial passions.[2]

In defining instinctive impulses by means of analogies derived from sympathetic medicine and animal magnetism, Law adopted French notions of the baser sort; but in classifying these impulses he goes to higher sources. This is evident from his specific reference to Charles Bonnet's *Essai analytique sur les facultés de l'âme,* with its scheme of knowledge derived from sensations, sensations from vibrations, and vibrations from the actions of outward objects. By taking this scheme in reverse order, Law gives to it a sort of genetic appearance. Instead of working from ultimate psychic relations back to the original sense data, he works from sense data to psychic relations. Briefly summarised, his elaborate table amounts to the following series of phenomena: Given (1) as the initial cause of the corporeal feelings outward objects of the senses, we have (2) an impression, when an object being presented to the senses an emotion is excited in the proper nerve; (3) the sensation, when the nervous fluid flying like an electric to the brain excites what we call a sense of beauty or ugliness, of melody or discord; (4) the emotion, when the vibration affecting the brain and evoking sensations causes liking or aversion; (5) the impulses,

[1] *Second Thoughts,* pp. 33, 42.   [2] *Ib.,* p. 24.

when the nervous emotion calls out an instinctive desire to possess
what pleases or to get rid of what displeases; (6) the will, when
the power given to man to command both body and mind follows
immediately and instinctively upon the experience; (7) the action,
when man's limbs obey his will and his thoughts are directed to
an agreeable or away from a disagreeable train; (8) the consequences, when a desire to repeat a pleasure or an aversion to neglect a pain gives rise to another train of motives, sensations, etc.[1]

Taken in connection with his opinion that the brain is acted
upon automatically by internal sensations, Law's table might be
said to have adumbrated the modern doctrine of the circular reaction, where there is a brain state due to stimulus, muscular reaction which reproduces the stimulus, the same brain state again
due to the same stimulus, and so on;[2] but unfortunately by the
intrusion, into its very midst, of his familiar instinctive moral impulses, he has destroyed the continuity of a real cyclic process, or
circular activity on the bodily side.   Nevertheless he had a purpose
in thus emphasising his central principles, and that was his conviction that these instinctive impulses are the foundation of the ideas
of morality, and that morality is the end to which the whole process moved.   So he expresses his surprise that a work has not yet
appeared, showing how our corporeal sensations first operate by
hunger and digestion, then how our perception is occupied, and
then our intellectual faculties, and lastly our moral emotions, sensations, and impulses.[3]   To such a work Law addressed himself,
but old age coming on, it remained but another of his unfinished
schemes.   As he himself confessed, like a painter who begins late
in life, he can draw tolerably, but he cannot properly blend his
colours and cast light and shade to form a complete picture.

Although the *Thoughts on the Moral System* did not appear
until 1833, the year before the author's death, yet his favourite
doctrine was already known to his friends.   One of them writes
that despite his experiences in a political campaign of Jacksonian
vulgarity, and against the doctrine that the moral sense is wholly

---

[1] *Second Thoughts,* p. 22.
[2] J. Mark Baldwin, *Fragments in Philosophy and Science,* New York,
1902, p. 168.
[3] *Thoughts on the Moral System,* p. 13.

acquired, he maintains Law's doctrine that the moral sense is instinctive, since he conceives it to be an original faculty of the mind. We come into existence with certain susceptibilities of emotion. By these original tendencies it is not meant to suggest that the mind resembles a machine which is so constructed that it will of itself gradually develop certain experiences, but that every created human mind exhibits in certain circumstances certain phenomena. Conscience is then an internal monitor, implanted in us by the Supreme Being, and dictating to us on all occasions what is right or wrong, and not merely our own judgment on the moral rectitude or turpitude of our actions.[1] Law's ethical principles are perhaps better summarised by his correspondent than by himself, for his system as he acknowledged was written by fits and starts and spoiled by digressions and want of connection. And yet in these more friendly hints and fragments there is considerable interest, for as Law's original temple of truth was built out of a variety of materials, so his own mind was a kind of asylum for stray ideas. Hence the moralist's intellectual hospitality is as great as his social, for his doors are open to English as well as Scotch and French philosophers. From Locke he takes the suggestion that morality is capable of demonstration as well as mathematics; from Combe that moral qualities are hereditary; from Darwin that the knowledge of the beautiful commences in infancy. And yet with these new guests he has some differences, since the last fails to draw a sharp line of distinction between the spirituality and corporeality of man; the second in declaring man to be virtuous or the reverse according to the bumps in his skull goes too far; and the first does not go far enough, for as the author himself believes propositions in ethics may be examined with the same exactitude as in mathematics. In the latter we appeal to facts which are ascertained only by the conscious sensations and established by the immutability of natural laws. In the former we appeal to similar criteria, tests or standards; for example, when it is to be demonstrated that the violation of another's right is impious, it will be shown that every man has painful emotions and

[1] Holograph letter from John Browne Cutting, August 29, 1824.

sensations in receiving an injury, and consequently that it is self-evident that he ought not to cause pain to another.[1] Law had previously assumed that the All-wise, All-good Creator had implanted in man primary principles for morality as in water for hydraulics, in matter for mechanics and in the universe for order; now he goes even further and declares that the moral sense is a sacred law, a divine revelation, a mysterious spiritual excitement of the moral sentiments, the peculiar gift of God, an emanation from the Supreme.[2]

Here ends Law's moral system; beginning under the apprehension of being called an infidel and sceptic, he concludes with an outburst of mystic rapture and the dogmatism of a defender of the faith. Instead of resolving morality into a science mathematical in its exactitude, he reduces it into a system well-nigh mystical. Despite this abrupt conclusion, he performed a logical service, for he inadvertently proved that the appeal to common sense was essentially irrational, and that instead of being based upon the common principles of reason it was an appeal to an ineffable trust in inexplicable principles.

James Ogilvie (1760-1820), was one of the lesser realists of the South who was an interesting, if not an intimate, connection with the early Scottish philosophers. A presumable graduate of King's College, Aberdeen,[3] in the very year in which Beattie's *Elements of Moral Science* appeared, he was also an unsuccessful claimant to the lapsed earldom of Findlater, to whose last representative Reid dedicated his *Inquiry into the Human Mind*. Coming to America at the age of eighteen, Ogilvie became a literal peripatetic philosopher, teaching school near Monticello, where he enjoyed the friendship of President Jefferson;

[1] *Second Thoughts*, p. 45.   [2] *Ib.*, p. 4.
[3] This is a mere conjecture, according to the *Dictionary of National Biography* (Vol. 42, p. 18), but the *Southern Literary Messenger* (Vol. 14) gives the *Recollections of a Pupil* who cites Ogilvie's references to Old-Aberdeen University; while Ogilvie himself speaks of knowing William Ogilvie, Professor of Humanity in King's College, Old-Aberdeen. (Compare Ogilvie's *Supplementary Narrative*, p. xliv., to his *Philosophical Essays*, Philadelphia, 1816.)

speaking from the rostrum in Philadelphia, where he was repri-
manded by Dr. Rush for his doubtful orthodoxy in espousing
the doctrines of Godwin,[1] and finally becoming a lecturer on
rhetoric in the College of South Carolina some three of four
years before the coming of Thomas Cooper to that institution.   Except for his arguments against miracles, which like
Thomas Ewell of Virginia he sought to counteract by the works
of Campbell of Aberdeen, Ogilvie was a devoted admirer of Hume.
For this reason, in contrast to Thomas Law, who carried the
principles of the intuitional philosophy to the extreme of mystic
incomprehensibility, he was led off into another direction, reaching
like Hamilton, but without reference to him, a rationalistic doctrine of the relativity of knowledge.   Considering the phenomena
of the natural world as infinite and capable of being presented to
the senses progressively and associated in the mind of man in an
order that approaches nearer and nearer to the original order,
Ogilvie defines knowledge as being not a perfect coincidence but a
continual asymptotical approximation betwixt the order in which
the phenomena of the material universe really succeed each other
with that in which the ideas respecting these phenomena are arranged and associated.[2]

This passage, which contains in a striking figure of speech the
finest epistemological definition in the early speculative literature
of the country, is found in the chapter on the Nature, Extent
and Limits of Human Knowledge, which follows a preliminary
chapter on the Study of the Mathematical Sciences. While the
latter furnished the clue to his epistemological definition, the former contains the grounds on which it is based.   Taking the initial
standpoint of inner experience, Ogilvie builds his doctrine of relativity upon the Humean principle of necessary connection.[3]
Against Beattie's *Essay on the Nature and Immutability of Truth,*
his probable hearer contends that we are indebted to the sagacity
of Hume for the first satisfactory elucidation of the fact that our

[1] In his *Philosophical Essay* (p. 135) Ogilvie quotes from a letter of
Godwin to the author soon after the *Political Justice* began to circulate in
Virginia.

[2] *Philosophical Essays,* pp. 96-98.   [3] *Ib.,* p. 96.

knowledge of cause and effect embraces nothing more than a perception and belief of the uniform antecedence of one event and the sequence of another. The writer consequently endeavours to expose the fallacy of the plausible objections by which Reid and his disciples have tried to controvert this principle. They resolve our belief that the succession of events in time future will be similar to their succession in time past into instinct; he himself, on the other hand, resolves the principle of certainty into experience—into a habit gradually formed of correcting our ideas in the order in which the phenomena by which they are excited have invariably succeeded each other in the past, this habit being strengthened by the concurring recollections of our contemporaries, of history, and of tradition. If human belief in this recurrence were instinctive, a child would distinguish immediately betwixt those successions of events that are casual and separable and those that are indissoluble, or, as Dr. Johnson would express it, betwixt what is collateral and what is consecutive.[1]

In his resolution of our belief in cause and effect into custom and habit, Ogilvie is at variance with Reid, who would make it a part of our constitution; but in basing this belief on general human experience he comes perilously near the common-sense criterion of universality. This is the first inconsistency in his criticism of the earlier realism; the next arrives in what he calls the full doctrine of aitiology, which takes up the problem of knowledge not only in so far as it is founded in the relation of cause and effect, but also as it concerns mind and matter. As regards these latter entities, Ogilvie apparently inclines to a sheer phenomenalism. Following the Humean principle that we observe a constant conjunction between certain events, he claims that external phenomena are not originally and spontaneously presented to our senses according to the relation of cause and effect, but merely reflect, *veluti in speculo,* the truth of things.[2] By this simile the author evidently means that we see the external world but darkly, apprehend the succession of outward occurrences but imperfectly. But he goes further and extends his doctrine of phenomenality to inner as well as outer. So his former conclusion has as its correl-

---

[1] *Philosophical Essays,* pp. 43, 47-49.   [2] *Ib.,* p. 79.

ate the statement that the subject of consciousness, the mind itself, is an unknowable thing; of the substance of mind we can know nothing, for otherwise we would put both among the *omnia scibilia* of transcendental ontology. But this would be scholastic metaphysics and not metaphysics in the correct sense of an analysis of the proper subjects and impassable boundaries of human knowledge; for to resolve the question whether mind is single or compound, extended or inextended, material or immaterial; whether the substance of matter is passive or active, possesses inherent or derivative properties, essential qualities or accidents,— speculations of this sort might serve as a kind of mental gymnasium, but they would contribute nothing to the stock of human knowledge.[1]

About to be forced into the gulf of agnosticism, as the result of a strict construction of the Humean phenomenalism, Ogilvie abruptly turns his back on the British sceptic and returns to the British empiricist. Taking the two Lockean inlets of knowledge to extricate himself from his double difficulty, he holds that mind and its energies are the objects of reflection, matter and its properties the objects of sensation, provided reflection be defined as a concentration of consciousness on whatever excites peculiar interest, and provided sensation be defined as the medium of impressions made upon our organs of sense.[2] If one were to apply the principles of his favourite science of rhetoric this passage of Ogilvie might be called a pure anti-climax, for he has suddenly dropped from the heights of idealism to the common level of realism. Here two things made him lose his hold upon his doctrine of relativity: one, his conviction that we have a distinct and direct knowledge of reflection as of any other mental faculty; the other, that, although we can never perceive any constructive principles among phenomena, internal or external, moral or natural, yet we are irresistibly led to believe that a constructive principle exists, the word efficiency, or some other term of similar import, being as necessary for the ordinary as well as for the philosophical purposes of language.[3]

[1] *Philosophical Essays*, pp. 52, 57, 59.
[2] *Ib.*, pp. 33, 66.   [3] *Ib.*, p. 89.

But whence comes this efficiency, this binding principle whereby we gain the idea of substance to express mental qualities in a state of permanent combination? It is by marking and recording the irreversible succession of phenomena as it is spontaneously and progressively presented to our view.[1] Here is another reversion of judgment which brings Ogilvie to the conclusion of his final approach to realism. Starting with the postulate that the mind begins with phenomena instead of things, he has come back to a belief in the stable cosmic order of events. At the first by his advocacy of Hume he leaned toward a doctrine of subjective idealism, the doctrine that the mind creates its own object, but now, by his mathematical studies, he confessed himself irresistibly led to infer that the order in which the phenomena of the mental universe succeed each other has been so established and appointed that, although the human mind can never reach absolute certainty, yet its faculties are so admirable that it can attain such a continual asymptotical approximation between the external order and the internal ideas that it amounts to a knowledge of the relation of cause and effect sufficient for the purposes both of speculation and action.[2]

Ogilvie's *Essay on the Nature, Extent and Limits of Human Knowledge* ends with a note of practical realism, in close accord to Reid's definition of common sense as consisting of certain principles which the constitution of our nature leads us to believe and which we are under necessity to take for granted in the common concerns of life.[3] A similar agreement is to be found in the writings of the Northern representatives of the Scottish school from its official exponents in the colleges of the first order to the lesser realists who held that Reid had said the last safe word in philosophy and that Kant opened up the abysses of scepticism. All this may carry investigation over into the later nineteenth century realism, with which transcendentalism had a life and death struggle, yet it is necessary, in treating of the early schools, to give a comparative estimate of these two systems in order to determine how

[1] *Philosophical Essays*, p. 80.   [2] *Ib.*, p. 96.
[3] *Inquiry*, Vol. 2, p. 791 (Hamilton Ed.).

far the one or the other was destined to be the coming American philosophy.

In regard to natural realism, it may be said that as it was foreign in its origin, so it remained an exotic in its characteristics, lacking those qualities on which the men of the new world prided themselves. First, it was unprogressive, being rightly accused of failure to advance; thus the two principal definitions of the movement, although seventy years apart, were in substance essentially the same. Again, it was illiberal towards unrestrained inquiry; being opposed to the speculative ferment of Hume and the free critical methods of Kant, it was rationalistic but only within the limits fixed by respectability. Lastly, it was intolerant of other systems; as it fought the European forms of deism, idealism, and naturalism of the eighteenth century, so it came to look askance upon the French positivism, the German idealism and the British evolutionary doctrines of the nineteenth. These are the shortcomings of realism, but inasmuch as its aim was to be a safe and sound philosophy, they are to be considered not as fundamental deficiencies but only as the defects of its qualities. In marked contrast, however, to the Scottish realism was the New England transcendentalism, whose characteristics were the direct opposite of its chief rival. Instead of being a foreign importation brought over in the original form, it was essentially a native growth deeply rooted in its age and surroundings. Historic forces were visible in it, but these had been so assimilated that they appeared not so much initial impulses as remote resultants. Hence transcendentalism possessed the typical marks of the receptive American mind. First it was progressive; starting with the Platonism latent in Puritanism, it drew nourishment in turn from the Berkeleian, Kantian, and Hegelian idealism. Again it was liberal; instead of opposing the spirit of free inquiry, it exhibited a generous interest in regard to other systems, translating not merely the philosophical classics of France and Germany but, as in the case of Emerson, seeking inspiration from the sacred books of the East. This lenient attitude towards an unrestricted immigration of foreign thought brought about the last and most obvious characteristic of transcendentalism, its utter tolerance of other systems. Thus it took from the puritans their individualism, from the deists their arguments for design, from the idealists their phenomenalism, from the materialists their dynamic conception of the universe, from the realists their doctrine of immediate intuitions. This may be considered such an extreme eclecticism as not to deserve the name of a system; it may nevertheless be said in conclusion that whether or not transcendentalism was the coming philosophy of America, it at least furnished a native epitome of American philosophy as it was developed in its early schools.

APPENDIX

NOTES

BOOK I.—PURITANISM

CHAPTER I.—PURITANISM

Additional references: *American Journal of Theology*, Vol. 1, p. 699; *History of Puritan Theology of New England; The Awakening of New England*, by Francis H. Underwood in *Contemporary Review*, August, 1888; J. A. Doyle, *The English in America*, Vol. 5, New York, 1907.

CHAPTER II.—ANTI-PURITANISM

Reason the only Oracle of Man, or a Compenduous System of Natural Religion. Alternately Adorned with Confutations of a Variety of Doctrines Incompatible to It; Deduced from the most exalted Ideas which we are able to form of Divine and Human Characters, and from the Universe in General. By Ethan Allen, Esq., Bennington, State of Vermont, 1784.

Other editions of this work appeared in New York, 1849, and Boston, 1854. Cf. Duyckinck, *Cyclopædia of American Literature*, Philadelphia, 1881, 1, 217 note; *A Narrative of the Captivity of Colonel Ethan Allen*, Albany, N. Y., 1814; Hugh Moore, *Memoir of Ethan Allen*, Plattsburgh, N. Y., 1834; *Vermont Historical Society Proceedings*, 1901-2, pp. 65-86.

BOOK II.—IDEALISM

CHAPTER II.—SAMUEL JOHNSON

Johnson's works include the hitherto unpublished MS. of Johnson's *Cyclopædia of Learning* from a bound volume labelled *Sermons* in the Library of Columbia University. Beardsley (*Life*, p. 123 note) says that at the end of what must have been the original draft of the first edition of the *Introduction to Philosophy*, Johnson made a note: 'This system did not please me well and I drew another.' In contrast to his later dichotomous scheme Johnson here prefixed the following more complicated trichotomous scheme:

PHILOSOPHY is the Love & Study of Truth & Wisdom; i.e. of the Objects & Rules conducive to our True Happiness.

& it consists of 3 parts	Rational which cultivates our Rational powers for enabling us to find out & communicate the Truth in	*Logic,* the Art of reasoning *Grammar* of Speaking *Rhetoric* of Persuading *History* of Narration *Poetry* of Description
	Natural which teaches the Truth of Things, i. e. their true Natures that we may know how to conduct our selves & all Nature consists of	1. Ideas, certain Combinations whereof we call Bodies The nature of is taught in *Mathematics* of Numbers & Measure *Physics,* of the phenomena & Laws of motion & Gravitation &c., &c. Knowledge of earth & its Inhabitants *Astronomy* of the System of the Universe 2. *Spirits* the Nature of is taught in *Metaphysics & Theology*
	Moral which consists in the application of that knowledge to practice	In *Ethics* of our Duty to God our neibour & our Selves. But with respect to Theology & Ethics God has given a particular supernatural Revelation of his Mind & will for our Direction

In an autograph copy of the *Elementa Philosophica*, Philadelphia, 1752, Johnson gives a more accurate ' Table for the Partition of the Sciences' than that of page 14, which began 'Learning is the Knowledge of Everything.' This more accurate table is repeated in Johnson's *English and Hebrew Grammar*, London, 1767, Appendix, *A General Scheme for the Partition of the Sciences* . . . or a Synopsis of All Parts of Learning.

An Introduction to the Study of Philosophy, exhibiting a General View of All the Arts and Sciences, for the Use of Pupils, with a Catalogue of some of the most valuable Authors necessary to be read in order to instruct them in a thorough Knowledge of each of them. By a gentleman Educated at Yale College. . . . The second edition enlarged; the first having been published at London in the Republic of Letters for May, in the year 1731. Art. xxxvii. N. London. Printed and sold by T. Greene, 1743.
Ethica Elementa, or the First Principles of Moral Philosophy . . . by Aristocles, Boston, 1746.

This is included in Johnson's last published work, with its first and second titles.

Elementa Philosophica: Containing chiefly Noetica, or Things relating to the Mind or Understanding: and Ethica, or Things relating to the Moral Behaviour. Philadelphia: Printed by B. Franklin and D. Hall, at the New-Printing-Office, near the Market, 1752.
Noetica: or the First Principles of Human Knowledge. Being a Logick, Including both Metaphysics and Dialectic, or the Art of Reasoning. With a brief Pathology, and an account of the gradual Progress of the Human Mind, from the first Dawnings of Sense to the highest Perfection, both Intellectual and Moral, of which it is capable. To which is prefixed a short Introduction to the Study of the Sciences.
No trace is to be found of Johnson's reputed *American Annotations on Bishop Berkeley's Treatise on the Principles of Human Knowledge* reported in T. H. Montgomery's *History of the University of Pennsylvania,* p. 7. Cf. *Passages from the Memoirs of Dr. Samuel Johnson relating to King's College,* copied from the original MS. by Anne J. Johnson, 1846.

CHAPTER III.—JONATHAN EDWARDS

No complete bibliography of Edwards has been compiled, but partial lists may be found in the following works: A. V. G. Allen, *Jonathan Edwards,* New York, 1889, pp. 391-393; A. L. Jones, *Early American Philosophers,* New York, 1898, p. 79-80; Benjamin Rand in J. Mark Baldwin's *Dictionary of Philosophy and Psychology,* Vol. 3, Part 1, pp. 188-189. Cf. also J. Ridderbos, *De Theologie van Jonathan Edwards,* Amsterdam, 1907. § 15 on the *Mind* leaves Edwards' relations to Berkeley and Malebranche an unsolved riddle.

BOOK III.—DEISM
CHAPTER II.—HARVARD COLLEGE

For information on the early philosophical courses at Harvard I am indebted to an unpublished paper of Dr. Benjamin Rand. Some information is to be gathered also from William Brattle, *Compendium Logicæ Secundum Principia. D. Renati Cartesii,* Boston, 1758, to which there are added such notes as these: Descarte's followers, Tillotson, Stillingfleet and More, were opposed by Locke, who claimed that the Cartesian ontological proof was a mere paralogism (note, p. 6).

CHAPTER III.—YALE COLLEGE

This Chapter is reprinted from the *American Journal of Theology,* 1905, pp. 474-493.
Addison, D. D., *The Clergy in American Life and Letters,* New York, 1900.
Baldwin, Ezra, *Annals of Yale College,* New Haven, 1838.
Clap, Thomas, *The Religiou· Constitution of Colleges, Especially of Yale College,* New London, 1754.
Dexter, F. B., *Yale Biographies and Annals,* New York, 1885; *The Literary Diary of Ezra Stiles,* New York, 1901.

CHAPTER IV.—KING'S COLLEGE AND PRINCETON

Samuel Johnson: Cf. *American Journal of Education,* 7, 461 ff., ·27, 448 ff; *American Medical and Philosophical Register,* 3, 137 ff.; *Columbia University Quarterly,* Dec., 1898, March, 1899.

Johnson's successor, Myles Cooper of Oxford University, left no philosophical remains. For his character, see Stiles' *Diary*, Vol. 2, p. 339; and Miller's *Retrospect*, 2. 369, note.

Johnson speaks of a 'Dutch professor of divinity' being wanted in King's College. In this connection note the following selections from Johan Daniel Gros' *Natural Principles of Rectitude for the conduct of man in all states and situations of life; demonstrated and explained in a systematic treatise on Moral Philosophy, comprehending The Law of Nature, Ethics, Natural Jurisprudence, General Economy, Politics, and the Law of Nations*. New York, 1795.

Soul is defined to be a power susceptible and capable of representations. The different modes in which that power exerts itself are termed *faculties*.

The faculties of the human soul distinguish themselves into the *cognoscitive* and *appetitive*, both of which must be furthermore distinguished into the *inferior* and *superior*.

Sch.—The inferior we have in common with brutes; by the superior we are elevated to the ranks of spirits.

The *inferior* cognoscitive faculty is that power of the human soul by which we have representations of *material* objects. It comprehends sensation, imagination and fancy.

Sensation is that faculty by which we have representations of material objects *present*.

Sch.—Present here signifies any object that strikes our sensory organs; thus a fixed star, and a distant sound which is heard, are present.

Imagination is that faculty by which we have representations of material objects *absent*, but which have once been *wholly* present.

Sch.—We see a friend, and remember the city, with other circumstances, where and under which we saw him.

Fancy is that faculty by which we form representations of such absent material objects as have once been present *in part*.

Sch.—We fancy a golden mountain, having had partial ideas of gold and of mountains. Hence the fictions of centaurs, nymphs, etc.

CHAPTER V.—PHILADELPHIA AND FRANKLIN

On the subject of the Pennsylvania Pietists I have received valuable information from Profs. M. G. Brumbaugh and M. D. Learned of the University of Pennsylvania. Cf. Oswald Seidensticker, *Bilder aus die Deutsch-pennsylvanischen Geschichte*, New York, 1886, chapter 10; *Die Mystik in Ephrata;* also *The First Century of German Printing in America*, 1728-1830, Philadelphia, 1893. The ramifications of the Pennsylvania mysticism is a topic that calls for further investigation. That a perverted form of this cabalistic pantheism had an influence upon the esoteric doctrines of the Mormons, or Latter-day Saints, I have suggested in an article on Joseph Smith, Jr., in the forthcoming Scotch *Encyclopædia of Religion and Ethics*, T. and T. Clark, Edinburgh.

For the speculations of the Quaker mystics see in the *Friends' Library*, John Fothergill (13, 429), Richard Jordan (13, 292), William Savery (1, 369), Thomas Scattergood (8, 7). On American Quakerism I have derived valuable suggestions from Professor Rufus M. Jones of Haverford College, and Principal Joseph S. Walton of George School, Pennsylvania, who writes me as follows:

'In reference to Mysticism among Friends, it seems to trace back to the writings of Isaac Pennington, and is noticeable in Woolman's works and a number of speakers among Friends during the century of Quaker Quietism in America. It was during this period that translations and selections from the works of Fénelon were circulated quite largely among American Friends; much more so, I imagine, than among English Friends —also traces of the works of Juan Valdes, which were translated into the English church in the days of old Isaac Walton, are noticeable among the teachers of a certain class of American Friends who read little other than English religious works during a certain period of the American history of Quakerism.'

For Franklin's fostering of French literature in America, cf. P. L. Ford, *Franklin Bibliography. A List of Books written by, or relating to, Benjamin Franklin*, Brooklyn, 1889. In the library of the American Philosophical Society there is a copy of J. P. Brissot de Warville, *De la Vérité*, Neuchatel, 1782, evidently annotated by the author; also a copy of Cabanis, *Rapports du physique et du moral de l'homme*, Paris, 1805, presented by Destutt de Tracy. In the *American Review* (3, 472) *there* was a proposal for an American edition of Charles Bonnet, *Philosophical Inquiries concerning the Christian Religion.*

For the reputed unpublished letters of Jean Jaques Rousseau to Stephen Girard, I am informed by Professor Pierre François Giroud that they are not to be found in the Girard College library. (Cf. Lewis Rosenthal, *Rousseau in Philadelphia, Magazine of American History*, Vol. 12, p. 46.)

As an example of Franklin's early philosophizing, there is here reprinted:

A DISSERTATION ON LIBERTY AND NECESSITY, ETC.

TO MR. J. R.[1]

SIR: I have here, according to your Request, given you my *present* Thoughts of the *general State of Things* in the Universe. Such as they are, you have them, and are welcome to 'em; and if they yield you any Pleasure or Satisfaction, I shall think my trouble sufficiently compensated. I know my Scheme will be liable to many Objections from a less discerning Reader than yourself; but it is not design'd for those who can't understand it. I need not give you any Caution to distinguish hypothetical Parts of the Argument from the conclusive. You will easily perceive what I design for Demonstration, and what for Probability only. The whole I leave entirely to you, and shall value myself more or less on this account, in proportion to your Esteem and Approbation.

SECTION I.—OF LIBERTY AND NECESSITY.

I. *There is said to be a First Mover, who is called God, Maker of the Universe.*

II. *He is said to be all-wise, all-good, all-powerful.*

These two Propositions being allow'd and asserted by People of almost every Sect and Opinion; I have here suppos'd them granted, and laid them down as the Foundation of my Argument. What follows then, being a Chain of Consequences truly drawn from them, will stand or fall as they are true or false.

[1] Reprinted from James Parton, *Life and Times of Benjamin Franklin*, Boston, 1834, Vol. 1 Appendix III.

III. *If He is all-good, whatsoever He doth must be good.*

IV. *If He is all-wise, whatsoever He doth must be wise.*

The Truth of these Propositions, with relation to the two first, I think may be justly call'd evident; since, either that infinite Goodness will act what is ill, or infinite Wisdom what is not wise, is too glaring a Contradiction not to be perceiv'd by any Man of common sense, and deney'd as soon as understood.

V. *If He is all-powerful, there can be nothing either existing or acting under the Universe against or without his Consent; and what He consents to must be good, because He is good, therefore Evil doth not exist.*

Unde Malum? has been long a Question, and many of the Learned have perplex'd themselves and Readers to little Purpose in Answer to it. That there are both Things and Actions to which we give the Name of *Evil*, is not to be deny'd, *as Pain, Sickness, Want, Theft, Murder*, &c., but that these and the like are not in reality *Evils, Ills*, or *Defects* in the Order of the Universe, is demonstrated in the next Section, as well as by this and the following Proposition. Indeed, to suppose any Thing to exist or to be done, *contrary* to the Will of the Almighty, is to suppose him not Almighty; or that Something (the Cause of *Evil*) is more mighty than the Almighty; an Inconsistence that I think no one will defend; And to deny any Thing or Action, which he consents to the existence of, to be good, is entirely to destroy his two Attributes of *Wisdom* and *Goodness*.

There is nothing done in the Universe, say the Philosophers, *but what God either does, or permits to be done.* This, as He is Almighty, is certainly true. But what need of this Distinction between *doing* and *permitting?* Why, first they take it for granted that many Things in the Universe exist in such a Manner as is not for the best, and that many Actions are done which ought not to be done, or would be better undone; these Things or Actions they cannot ascribe to God as His, because they have already attributed to Him infinite Wisdom and Goodness; Here then is the Use of the Word *Permit;* He *permits* them to be done, *say they.* But we will reason thus: If God permits an Action to be done, it is because He wants either *Power* or *Inclination* to hinder it; in saying He wants *Power*, we deny Him to be *Almighty;* and if we say He wants *Inclination* or *Will*, it must be either because He is not Good, or the Action is not *evil*, (for all Evil is contrary to the Essence of infinite *Goodness*). The former is inconsistent with his before-given Attribute of Goodness, therefore the latter must be true.

It will be said, perhaps, that *God permits evil Actions to be done, for* wise *Ends and Purposes.* But this objection destroys itself; for whatever an infinitely good God hath wise ends in suffering to *be* must be good, is thereby made good, and cannot be otherwise.

VI. *If a Creature is made by God, it must depend upon God, and receive all its Power from him; with which power the Creature can do nothing contrary to the will of God, because God is Almighty; what is not contrary to His will, must be agreeable to it, must be good, because He is Good; therefore a creature can do nothing but what is good.*

This proposition is much to the same purpose with the former, but more particular; and its conclusion is as just and evident. Tho' a creature may do many Actions which by his Fellow Creatures will be nam'd *Evil,* and which will naturally and necessarily cause or bring upon the *Doer,* certain *Pains* (which will likewise be call'd *Punishments*), yet this proposition proves, that he cannot act what will be in itself Ill or displeasing to God. And that the painful consequences of his evil Actions (so call'd) are not as indeed they ought not to be, *Punishments* or Unhappinesses will be shewn hereafter.

Nevertheless, the late learned Author of The Religion of Nature (which I send you herewith) has given a rule or Scheme, whereby to discover which of our Actions ought to be esteemed and denominated good, and which *Evil:* It is in short this, 'Every action which is done according to 'Truth is good; and every Action contrary to Truth is evil. To act ac-'cording to truth is to use and esteem everything as what it is, &c. Thus 'if *A* steals a Horse from *B* and rides away upon him, he uses him not as 'what he is in Truth, viz., the Property of another, but as his own, which 'is contrary to Truth, and therefore *Evil.*' But as this Gentleman himself says, (Sect. I., Prop. VI.): 'In order to judge rightly what any Thing 'is, it must be considered, not only what it is in one Respect, but also 'what it may be in any other Respect; and the whole Description of the 'Thing ought to be taken in.' So in this case it ought to be considered that *A* is naturally a *covetous* Being, feeling an Uneasiness in the want of *B's* Horse, which produces an Inclination for stealing him, stronger than his Fear of Punishment for so doing. This is *Truth* likewise, and *A* acts acording to it when he steals the Horse. Besides, if it is prov'd to be a *Truth,* that *A* has not Power over his own Actions, it will be indisputable that he acts according to Truth, and impossible he should do otherwise.

I would not be understood by this to encourage or defend Theft; 'tis only for the sake of the Argument, and will certainly have no *ill Effect.* The Order and Course of Things will not be affected by Reasoning of this Kind; and 'tis as just and necessary, and as much according to Truth, for *B* to dislike and punish the Theft of his Horse, as it is for *A* to steal him.

VII. *If the Creature is thus limited in his Actions, being able to do only such Things as God would have him do, and not being able to refuse doing what God would have done; then he can have no such Thing as Liberty, Free-will or Power to do or refrain an Action.*

By *Liberty* is sometimes understood the Absence of Opposition; and in this sense, indeed, all our Actions may be said to be the Effects of our Liberty. But it is a Liberty of the same Nature, with the Fall of a heavy Body to the Ground; it has Liberty to fall, that is, it meets with nothing to hinder its fall, but at the same time it is necessitated to fall, and has no Power or Liberty to remain suspended.

But let us take the Argument in another view, and suppose ourselves to be, in the common sense of the word, *Free Agents.* As Man is a Part of this great Machine, the Universe, his regular Acting is requisite to the regular moving of the whole. Among the many things which lie before him to be done, he may, as he is at Liberty and his Choice influenced by nothing, (for so it must be, or he is not at Liberty) chuse any one, and refuse the rest. Now there is every Moment something *best* to be done, which alone is *good,* and with respect to which, every Thing else is at that Time *evil.* In order to Know which is best to be done, and which not, it is requisite that we should have at one view all the intricate Consequences of every Action with respect to the general Order and Scheme of the Universe, both present and future; but they are innumerable and incomprehensible by anything but Omniscience. As we cannot know these, we have but one chance to ten thousand, to hit on the right Action; we should then be perpetually blundering about in the Dark, and putting the Scheme in Disorder; for every wrong Action of a Part, is a Defect or Blemish in the Order of the Whole. Is it not necessary then, that our Actions should be overrul'd and govern'd by an all-wise Providence? How exact and regular is everything in the *natural* World! How wisely is every Part contriv'd. We cannot find here the least Defect! Those who have study'd the mere animal and vegetable Creation, demonstrate that nothing can be more harmonious and beautiful! All the heavenly Bodies, the Stars and Planets are regulated with the utmost wisdom! And can we suppose less Care to be taken in the Order of the *moral* than in the *natural* system? It is as if an ingenious Artificer, having formed a curious Machine or Clock, and put its many intricate Wheels and Powers in such a Dependence on one another, that the whole might move in the most exact Order and Regularity, had nevertheless placed in it several other Wheels endu'd with an independent *Self-Motion*, but ignorant of the general Interest of the Clock; and these would every now and then be moving wrong, disordering the true Movement, and making Continual Work for the Mender; which might be prevented by depriving them of that Power of Self-Motion, and placing them in a Dependence on the regular Part of the Clock.

VIII. *If there is no such thing as Free-Will in Creatures, there can be neither Merit nor Demerit in Creatures.*

IX. *And therefore every Creature must be equally esteem'd by the Creator.*

These Propositions appear to be the necessary Consequences of the former. And Certainly no Reason can be given, why the Creator should prefer in His Esteem one Part of His Works to another, if with equal wisdom and Goodness He design'd and created them all, since all Ill or Defect, as contrary to His Nature, is excluded by His Power. We will sum up the Argument thus, When the Creator first design'd the Universe, either it was His Will and intention that all Things should exist and be in the Manner they are at this Time; or it was His Will they should be otherwise, *i. e.,* in a different Manner: To say it was His Will Things should be otherwise than they are, is to say Somewhat hath contradicted His Will, and broken His Measures, which is impossible because inconsistent with His Power; therefore we must allow that all Things exist now in a Manner agreeable to His Will, and in consequence of that are all equally Good, and therefore equally esteem'd by Him.

I proceed now to shew, that as all the Works of the Creator are equally esteem'd by Him, so they are, in Justice they ought to be, equally us'd.

SECTION II.—OF PLEASURE AND PAIN.

I. *When a Creature is form'd and endu'd with Life, 'tis supposed to receive a Capacity of the Sensation* of Uneasiness *or* Pain.

It is this distinguishes Life and Consciousness from unactive unconscious Matter. To Know or be sensible of suffering or being acted upon it *to live;* and whatsoever is not so, among created Things is properly and truly *dead*.

All Pain and Uneasiness proceeds at first from, and is caused by somewhat without and distinct from the Mind itself. The Soul must first be acted upon before it can re-act. In the Beginning of Infancy it is as if it were not; it is not conscious of its own Existence, till it has receiv'd the first Sensation of *Pain;* then and not before, it begins to feel itself, is roused and put into Action; then it discovers its Powers and Faculties, and exerts them to expel the Uneasiness. Thus is the Machine set on work; this is Life. We are first mov'd by *Pain,* and the whole succeeding Course of our Lives is but one continu'd Series of Action with a View to be freed from it. As fast as we have excluded one Uneasiness another appears, otherwise the Motion would cease. If a continual weight is not apply'd the clock will stop. And as soon as the Avenues of Uneasiness to the Soul are choak'd up or cut off, we are dead, we think and act no more.

II. *This Uneasiness, whenever felt, produces Desire to be freed from it, great in exact proportion to the Uneasiness.*

Thus is *Uneasiness* the first Spring and Cause of All Action; for till we are uneasy in Rest, we can have no Desire of moving, there can be no voluntary Motion. The Experience of every Man who has observ'd his own Actions will evince the Truth of this; and I think nothing need be said to prove that the *Desire* will be equal to the *Uneasiness,* for the very Thing implies as much; It is not *Uneasiness* unless we desire to be freed from it nor a great *Uneasiness* unless the consequent Desire is great.

I might here observe how necessary a Thing in the Order and Design of the Universe this *Pain* or *Uneasiness* is, and how beautiful in its Place! Let us but suppose it just now banish'd the World entirely, and consider the Consequence of it: All the Animal Creation would immediately stand stock still, exactly in the Posture they were in the Moment Uneasiness departed; not a Limb, not a Finger would henceforth move; we should all be reduced to the condition of Statues, dull and unactive; Here I should continue to sit motionless with the Pen in my Hand thus—and neither leave my seat nor write one Letter more. This may appear odd at first view, but a little Consideration will make it evident; for 'tis impossible to assign any other Cause for the voluntary Motion of an Animal than its *uneasiness* in Rest. What a different Appearance then would the Face of Nature make, without it! How necessary is it! And how unlikely that the Inhabitants of the World ever were, or that the Creator ever designed they should be exempt from it!

I would likewise observe here, that the VIIIth Proposition in the preceding Section, viz: *That there is neither Merit nor Demerit,* &c., is here again demonstrated, as infallibly, tho' in another manner: For since *Freedom from Uneasiness* is the End of all our Actions, how is it possible for us to do any Thing disinterested? How can any Action be meritorious of Praise or Dispraise, Reward or Punishment, when the natural Principle of Self-Love is the only and the irresistible Motive to it?

III. *This Desire is always fulfill'd or satisfy'd.*

In the *Design* or *End* of it tho' not in the *Manner*. The first is requisite, the latter not. To exemplify this, let us make a Supposition: A person is confined in a House which appears to be in imminent danger of Falling, this, as soon as perceiv'd, creates a violent *Uneasiness*, and that instantly produces an equal strong *Desire*, the *End* of which is *freedom from the Uneasiness*, and the *Manner* or Way propos'd to gain this *End*, is *to get out of the House*. Now if he is convinc'd by any Means, that he is mistaken, and the House is not likely to fall, he is immediately freed from this *Uneasiness*, and the *End* of his Desire is attain'd as well as if it had been in the *Manner* desir'd, viz.: *leaving the House*.

All our different Desires and Passions proceed from and are reducible to this one Point, *Uneasiness*, tho' the Means we propose to ourselves for expelling of it are infinite. One proposes *Fame*, another *Wealth*, a third *Power*, &c. as the Means to gain this End; but tho' these are never attain'd if the Uneasiness be removed by some other Means, the Desire is satisfy'd. Now during the Course of Life we are ourselves continually removing successive uneasinesses as they arise, and the *last* we suffer is removed by the *sweet Sleep* of Death.

IV. *The fulfilling or satisfaction of this Desire, produces the sensation of pleasure, great or small in exact proportion to the Desire.*

Pleasure is that satisfaction which arises in the Mind upon, and is caus'd by, the accomplishment of our *Desires*, and by no other Means at all; and those Desires being above shewn to be caus'd by our *Pains* or *Uneasiness*, it follows that Pleasure is wholly caused by *Pain*, and by no other Thing at all.

V. *Therefore the Sensation of* Pleasure *is equal, or in exact proportion to, the Sensation of* Pain.

As the Desire of being freed from Uneasiness is equal to the *Uneasiness*, and the Pleasure of satisfying that Desire equal to the *Desire*, the *Pleasure* thereby produc'd must necessarily be equal to the *Uneasiness* or *Pain* which produces it. Of three Lines *A*, *B*, and *C*, if *A* is equal to *B*, and *B* to *C*, *C* must be equal to *A*. And as our *Uneasinesses* are always removed by some Means or other, it follows that *Pleasure* and *Pain* are in their Nature inseparable: So many Degrees as one Scale of the Ballance descends, so many exactly the other ascends; and one cannot rise or fall without the Fall or rise of the other. 'Tis impossible to taste of *Pleasure*, without feeling its preceding proportionate *Pain;* or to be sensible of *Pain*, without having its necessary Consequent *Pleasure*. The *highest Pleasure* is only Consciousness of Freedom from the deepest *Pain*, and *Pain* is not Pain to us unless we ourselves are sensible of it. They go Hand in Hand; they cannot be divided.

You have a view of the whole argument in a few familiar Examples. The Pain of Abstinence from Food, as it is greater or less, produces a greater or less *Desire* of Eating, the Accomplishment of this *Desire* produces a greater or less Pleasure proportionate to it. The *Pain* of Confinement causes a *Desire* of Liberty which accomplish'd yields a *Pleasure* equal to the Pain of Confinement. The Pain of Labor and Fatigue causes the *Pleasure* of Rest, equal to that *Pain*. The *Pain* of Absence from Friends, produces the *Pleasure* of Meeting in exact proportion, &c.

This is the *first Nature* of Pleasure and Pain, and will always be found to be so by those who examine it.

One of the most common Arguments for the future Existence of Soul, is taken from the generally supposed Inequality of Pain and Pleasure in the present; and this, notwithstanding the Difficulty by outward Appearances to make a Judgment of another's Happiness, has been look'd upon as almost unanswerable; but since *Pain* naturally and infallibly produces a *Pleasure* in proportion to it, every individual creature must, in any State of *Life*, have an equal Quantity of each, so that there is not, on that Account, any occasion for a future Adjustment.

Thus are all the Works of the Creation *equally* us'd by him; And no Condition of Life of Being is in itself better or preferable to another: The Monarch is not more happy than the Slave, nor the Beggar more miserable than *Croesus*. Suppose *A, B,* and *C* three distinct Beings; *A* and *B* animate, capable of *Pleasure* and *Pain*, *C* an inanimate Piece of Matter, insensible of either. *A* receives ten Degrees of *Pain*, which are necessarily succeeded by ten Degrees of *Pleasure; B* receives fifteen of *Pain*, and the consequent equal Number of *Pleasure: C* all the while lies unconcern'd, and as he has not suffered the former, has no right to the latter. What can be more equal and just than this? When the Accounts come to be adjusted, *A* has no Reason to complain that his Portion of *Pleasure* was five Degrees less than that of *B*, for his Portion of *Pain* was five Degrees less likewise: Nor has *B* any reason to boast that his *Pleasure* was five Degrees greater than that of *A*, for his *Pain* was proportionate. They are then both on the same foot with *C*, that is, they are neither Gainers nor Losers.

It will possibly be objected here, that even common Experience shews us, there is not in Fact this Equality: 'Some we see hearty, brisk and cheer-'ful perpetually, while others are constantly burden'd with a heavy Load 'of Maladies and Misfortunes, remaining for Years perhaps in Poverty, 'Disgrace, or Pain, and die at last without any Appearance of Recompence.' Now tho' 'tis not necessary, when a Proposition is demonstrated to be a general Truth, to show in what Manner it agrees with the particular Circumstances of Persons, and indeed ought not to be required; yet, as this is a common Objection, some Notice may be taken of it; And here let it be observed, that we cannot be proper Judges of the good or bad Fortune of Others; we are apt to imagine, that what would give us a great uneasiness or a great Satisfaction, has the same Effect upon others; we think, for Instance, those unhappy, who must depend upon Charity for a mean Subsistence, who go in Rags, fare hardly, and are despis'd and scorn'd by all; not considering that Custom renders all these Things easy, familiar, and even pleasant. When we see Riches, Grandeur, and a chearful Countenance, we easily imagine Happiness accompanies them, when often times 'tis quite otherwise: Nor is a constantly sorrowful Look, attended with continual Com-plaints, an infallible Indication of Unhappiness. In short, we can judge by nothing but Appearances, and they are very apt to deceive us. Some put on a gay, cheerful Outside, and appear to the World perfectly at ease, tho' even some inward Sting, some secret Pain imbitters all their Joys, and makes the Ballance even: Others appear continually dejected and full of Sorrow; but even grief itself is sometimes *pleasant*, and Tears are not always without their sweetness: Besides, some take a Satisfaction in being thought unhappy, (as others take a Pride in being thought humble,) these will paint their Misfortunes to others in the strongest Colours, and leave no Means unus'd to make you think them thoroughly miserable; so great a *Pleasure* it is to them *to be pitied;* Others retain the form and outside Shew of Sorrow, long after the thing itself, with its Cause, is removed from the Mind; it is a habit they have acquir'd and cannot leave. These, with many others that might be given, are Reasons why we cannot make a true Estimate of the *Equality* of the Happiness and Unhappiness of others; and unless we could, Matter of fact cannot be opposed to this Hypothesis. Indeed, we are sometimes apt to think, that the uneasiness we ourselves have had, outweigh our Pleasures; but the Reason is this, the Mind takes no Account of the latter, they slip away un-remark'd, when the former leave more lasting impressions on the Memory. But suppose we pass the greatest Part of Life in Pain and Sorrow, suppose we die by Torments, and *think no more,* 'Tis no Diminution to the Truth of what is here advanc'd; for the *Pain,* tho' exquisite, is not so to the *last* Moments of Life, the Senses are soon benumb'd, and rendered incapable of transmitting it so sharply to the Soul as at first; She perceives it cannot hold long, and 'tis an *exquisite Pleasure* to behold the immediate Approaches of Rest. This makes an Equivalent tho' annihilation should follow: For the Quantity of *Pleasure* and *Pain* is not to be measur'd by its Duration, any more than the Quantity of matter by its extensions, and as one cubic Inch may be made to contain, by Condensation, as much Matter as would fill ten thousand Cubic Feet, being more expanded, so one single moment of *Pleasure* may outweigh and compensate an Age of *Pain.*

It is owing to their Ignorance of the Nature of Pleasure and Pain that the Ancient Heathens believ'd the idle Fable of their Elisium, that State of uninterrupted Ease and Happiness! The Thing is entirely impossible in Nature! Are not the Pleasures of the Spring made such by the disagreeableness of the Winter? Is not the Pleasure of fair Weather owing to the unpleasantness of foul? Certainly. Were it then always Spring, were the Fields always green and flourishing, and the weather constantly serene and fair, the Pleasure would pall and die upon our hands; it would cease to be Pleasure to us, when it is not usher'd in by Uneasiness. Could the Philosopher visit, in reality every Star and Planet with as much Ease and Swiftness as he can now visit their Ideas, and pass from one to another of them in the Imagination; it would be a *Pleasure* I grant; but it would be only in proportion to the *Desire* of accomplishing it, and that would be no greater than the *Uneasiness* suffered in the want of it. The Accomplishment of a long and difficult Journey yields a great *Pleasure;* but if we could take a Trip to the Moon and back again, as frequently and with as much Ease as we can go and come from Market, the Satisfaction would be just the same.

The Immateriality of the Soul has been frequently made use of as an Argument for its *Immortality;* but let us consider, that tho' it should be allow'd to be immaterial, and consequently its Parts incapable of Separation or Destruction by any Thing material, yet by Experience we find, that it is not incapable of Cessation of Thought, which is its Action. When the Body is but a little indisposed it has an evident Effect upon the Mind; and a right Disposition of the Organs is requisite to a right Manner of Thinking. In a sound Sleep sometimes, or in a Swoon, we cease to think at all; tho' the Soul is not therefore then annihilated, but *exists* all the while tho' it does not *act;* and may not this be the Case properly after Death? All our ideas are first admitted by the Senses and imprinted on the Brain, increasing in Number by Observation and Experience; there they become the subjects of the Soul's Action. The Soul is a mere Power or Faculty of contemplating on, and *comparing* those Ideas when it has them; hence springs Reason. But as it can *think* on nothing but Ideas, it must have them before it can *think* at all. Therefore as it may exist before it has receiv'd any Ideas, it may exist before it *thinks.* To remember a Thing, is to have the Idea of it still plainly imprinted on the Brain, which the Soul can turn to and contemplate on Occasion. To forget a Thing, is to have the Idea of it defac'd and destroyed by some Accident, or the crowding in and imprinting of great variety of other

Ideas upon it, so that the Soul cannot find out its Traces and distinguish it. When we have thus lost the Ideas of any one Thing, we can *think* no more, or *cease* to *think* on that Thing; and as we can loose the Idea of one Thing, so we may of ten, twenty, a hundred, &c., and even of all Things, because they are not in their Nature permanent; and often during Life we see that some men, (by an Accident or Distemper affecting the Brain,) lose the greatest Part of their Ideas, and remember very little of their past Actions and Circumstances. Now upon *Death,* and the Destruction of the Body, the Ideas contain'd in the Brain, (which are alone the Subjects of the Soul's Action) being likewise necessarily destroy'd, the Soul, tho' incapable of Destruction itself, must then necessarily *cease* to *think* or *act,* having nothing left to think or act upon. It is reduc'd to its first inconscious State before it receiv'd any Ideas. And to cease to *think* is but little different from *ceasing to be.*

Nevertheless, 'tis not impossible that this same *Faculty* of contemplating Ideas may be hereafter united to a new Body, and receive a new Set of Ideas; but that will no way concern us who are now living; for the Identity will be lost; it is no longer the same *Self* but a new Being.

I shall here subjoin a short Recapitulation of the Whole, that it may with all its Parts be comprehended at one View.

1. *It is supposed that God the Maker and Governour of the Universe, is infinitely wise, good and powerful.*

2. *In consequence of His Infinite Wisdom and Goodness, it is asserted, that whatever He doth must be infinitely wise and good.*

3. *Unless He be interrupted, and His Measures broken by some other Being, which is impossible because He is Almighty.*

4. *In consequence of His Infinite Power, it is asserted, that nothing can exist or be done in the Universe which is not agreeable to His Will, and therefore good.*

5. *Evil is hereby excluded, with all Merit and Demerit; and likewise all preference in the Esteem of God, of one Part of the Creation to another.*

This is the summary of the first Part.

Now our common Notions of Justice will tell us, that if all created Things are equally esteem'd by the Creator, they ought to be equally us'd by Him; and that they are therefore equally us'd, we might embrace for Truth upon the Credit, and as the true Consequence of the foregoing Argument. Nevertheless we proceed to confirm it, by shewing how they are equally us'd, and that in the following Manner.

1. *A Creature when endu'd with Life or Consciousness, is made capable of Uneasiness or Pain.*

2. *This Pain produces Desire to be freed from it, in exact proportion to itself.*

3. *The Accomplishment of this Desire produces an equal Pleasure.*

4. *Pleasure is consequently equal to Pain.*

From these Propositions it is observ'd

1. *That every Creature hath as much Pleasure as Pain.*

2. *That Life is not preferable to insensibility, for Pleasure and Pain destroy one another: That Being which has ten Degrees of Pain subtracted from ten of Pleasure, has nothing remaining, and is upon an equality with that Being which is insensible of both.*

3. *As the first Part proves that all Things must be equally us'd by the Creator because equally esteem'd, so this second Part demonstrates that they are equally esteem'd because equally us'd.*

4. *Since every Action is the Effect of Self-Uneasiness, the Distinction of Virtue and Vice is excluded; and* Prop. VIII. *in* Sect. I. *again demonstrated.*

5. No State of Life can be happier than the present, because Pleasure and Pain are inseparable.
Thus both Parts of this Argument agree with and confirm one another, and the D⸻nstration is reciprocal.
I am sensible that the Doctrine here advanc'd, if it were to be publish'd would meet with an indifferent Reception. Mankind naturally and generally love to be flatter'd: Whatever sooths our Pride, and tends to exalt our Species above the rest of the Creation, we are pleas'd with and easily believe, when ungrateful Truths shall be with the utmost Indignation rejected. "What! bring ourselves down to an Equality with the Beasts of the Field; with the *meanest* part of Creation! 'Tis insufferable!" But, (to use a Piece of *common* Sense) our *Geese* are but *Geese* tho' we may think 'em *Swans;* and Truth will be Truth tho' it sometimes prove mortifying and distasteful.

CHAPTER VI.—VIRGINIA AND JEFFERSON

References marked (W) are to the *Writings of Thomas Jefferson,* 9 vols, Washington, 1853; those marked (F) to the edition of P. L. Ford, 10 vols., New York, 1892-99; unmarked references are to the edition of Lipscomb and Bergh, 20 vols., Washington, 1904. Cf. also J. P. Foley, *The Jeffersonian Cyclopedia,* New York, 1900; H. B. Tompkins, *Bibliotheca Jeffersoniana,* 1887.
As to the Jefferson *Bible,* a copy of the original *Syllabus* was sent to Francis Adrian Van der Kemp (cf. *Life,* by K. L. Fairchild, New York, 1903), and then published through the latter in the *London Monthly Repository of Theological and General Literature,* LXXX., Vol. 2, Oct., 1816, pp. 573-576. Was the latter the same as the autograph copy of the *Syllabus* now in the possession of the Buffalo Historical Society? Writing to Van der Kemp (March 16, 1817) Jefferson says: 'I learn that the editor of the *Theological Repository* possesses the name of the author of the *Syllabus.*'

BOOK IV—MATERIALISM

CHAPTER II.—CADWALLADER COLDEN

There are two early American lists of Colden's writings: Wm. Allen, *American Biographical and Historical Dictionary,* Cambridge, 1809, gives: —1. A new edition of the Principles of Action. 2. An Inquiry into the Operation of Intellect in Animals. 3. The Essential Properties of Light, interspersed with Observations on Electricity, Heat, Matter, etc. 4. An Introduction to the Study of Physics, in the form of instruction to one of his grandsons. 5. An Essay on Vital Motion. *The American Medical and Philosophical Register,* New York, 1811, Vol. 1, p. 301, gives:—1. An Introduction to the Study of Philosophy. 2. An Introduction to a translation of Cicero's Letters. 3. An Inquiry into the Principles of Vital Motion. 4. A corrected and augmented copy of the Principles of Action in Matter. 5. A Treatise on Electricity, etc. 6. Correspondence with Benjamin Franklin, 1747-1751, and with Peter Collinson, 1740-1764. The list given in the *Dictionary of National Biography,* Vol. 11, p. 260, is incomplete.
Cf. also James Thacher, *American Medical Biography,* Boston, 1828, p. 237; Alice M. Keys, *Cadwallader Colden: A Representative Eighteenth Century Official,* New York, 1906, especially Chapter I., *A Colonial Savant.*

The external history of Colden's printed treatises appears to be as follows: A few copies of the first two chapters of the *First Causes* were published in New York in 1745, but the London edition of 1746 was without the author's sanction (Preface to *First Principles*). In an undated memorandum (N. Y. H. S.), Colden adds that, as the words *First Causes* was liable to be misunderstood, he had changed them into *First Principles*, but that the former was translated into High Dutch at Leipsic by two professors there, with remarks on it by Prof. Kastner. It is also said that Jefferson wrote to Francis Hopkinson that Colden sent a copy of 'a small pamphlet on the subjects of attraction and impulsion' to Buffon, who wished to translate it. (Joseph Sabin, *Catalogue of William Menzies*, New York, 1875, p. 86.) Another version of this is that the *Principles of Action* was so rapidly taken up that in 1788 Buffon, having lost his copy, applied to Jefferson, who wrote to Francis Hopkinson about it. (Verplanck, quoted in J. G. Shea's edition of the *Five Indian Nations*, New York, 1866, p. xxxiv.)

CHAPTER III.—JOSEPH BUCHANAN

H. Collins, *History of Kentucky*, 1847, Appendix on *Science and Literature in Kentucky*, contains sketch of Dr. Buchanan by his son, J. R. Buchanan of Cincinnati. Cf. the same, 1874, Vol. 2, p. 218. R. Peter, *History of the Medical Department of Transylvania University*, Louisville, 1905, p. 14. Information from Col. R. T. Durrett of Louisville, through Prof. B. B. Warfield of Princeton Theological Seminary. Cf. Appleton's *Cyclopædia of American Biography*, Vol. 7, p. 39. Buchanan's apparent successor as professor of medicine in Transylvania University was James Fishback, who published *The Philosophy of the Mind in respect to Religion*, 1813; *Essays on the Powers and Susceptibilities of the Human Mind to Religion*, 1834.

CHAPTER IV.—JOSEPH PRIESTLEY

Cf. Henry Brougham, *Lives of Men of Letters and Science*, London, 1845, pp. 421 ff.; C. C. Everett, *The Old Unitarianism and the New*, Philadelphia, 1889; Thomas Huxley, *Science and Education*, New York, 1844; James Martineau, *Miscellanies*, 1852, pp. 1-52; *Proceedings of the Massachusetts Historical Society*, June, 1886.

CHAPTER V.—THOMAS COOPER

Cooper's translation of F. G. V. Broussais' *On Irritation and Insanity*, Columbia, S. C., 1831, contains in the appendix: *The Scripture Doctrine of Materialism; View of the Metaphysical and Physiological Arguments in favour of Materialism; Outline of the Doctrine of the Association of Ideas.* Cf. M. La Borde, *History of South Carolina College*, Charleston, 1874, pp. 162-166.

CHAPTER VI.—BENJAMIN RUSH

Printed Works.—*Medical Inquiries and Observations*, 1797; *Essays, Literary, Moral, and Philosophical*, 1798; *Lectures upon the Pleasures of the Senses, etc.*, 1805; *Lectures upon Animal Life, etc.*, 1811; *Diseases of the Mind*, 1812; *A Memorial of Dr. Benjamin Rush*, written by himself, ed. N. A. Biddle, 1905 (all Philadelphia), MSS. *Synoptical Compend of Metaphysics*, July 5, 1760, drawn by the Rev. Dr. Samuel Davies; (in the Ridgway Branch of the Philadelphia Library Company) ; *Extracts from Letters and thoughts* (*ibid.*) *Notes of Rush's Lectures* taken by [John?] Purnell [Maryland?] (Medical and Chirurgical Faculty Library, Baltimore.) General Sources. *American Medical and Philosphical Register,* July, 1813; *Delaplaine's Repository,* 1815. pp. 27-44; *David Hosack, Essays,* New York, 1824, No. IV; S. D. Gross, *Lives of Eminent American Physicians,* Philadelphia, 1861, pp. 17-85; B. W. Richardson, *Disciples of Aesculapius,* Vol. 1, p. 62, London, 1900.

CHAPTER VII.—THE MINOR MATERIALISTS

Cf. also Thomas Ewell, *The Properties of Matter, containing the Elements or Principles of Modern Chemistry,* New York, 1806; George Shattuck, *An Essay on the Influence of Air upon Animal Bodies,* Boston, 1808; Athanasius Fenwick, *On Volition and Pleasure,* Philadelphia, 1818.

BOOK V—REALISM

CHAPTER II.—THE PRINCETON SCHOOL

President Samuel Davies' *Synoptical Compend of Metaphysics,* as copied by Benjamin Rush, July 5, 1760 (Ridgway Library MS., Philadelphia), in entitled *Ontologia or Scientia de ente in genere ejusque attributis generalissimis.* The first section is as follows:

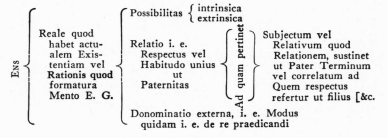

CHAPTER III.—JOHN WITHERSPOON

Lectures on Moral Philosophy and Eloquence, 3d edition, Philadelphia, 1810, pp. 314.
The introduction says that in justice to the memory of the Author, it ought to be stated that he did not intend these lectures for the press, they being merely a compend of class-room notes. A comparison of these notebooks, preserved in the collection of Princetoniana, shows no material departure from the printed editions.

CHAPTER IV.—SAMUEL STANHOPE SMITH

Essay on the Causes of the Variety of Complexion and Figure in the Human Species, 2d edition, New Brunswick, N. J., 1810.
The substance of this Essay was given as an anniversary address before

the American Philosophical Society, 27 Feb., 1787; it was published in book form in Philadelphia in 1787, and appeared also in *Carey's American Museum*, beginning July, 1789. For critical reviews of the American and English editions, cf. *ib.* Sept., 1789; *Port Folio*, 1814, pp. 8, 429; 1820, p. 153; *American Reviews*, Vol. 2, pp. 128, 166.

For the diatribe against materialism at the end of this chapter, compare Samuel Miller, *Retrospect*, Vol. 2, pp. 453-4, New York, 1802: 'The same ingenious and learned friend who contributed the notes on Edwards, communicated the following [above] remarks on materialism.' For the conjecture that this friend was Stanhope Smith, I am indebted to Professor John DeWitt of Princeton, who would exclude as possible authors these three colleagues of Miller's: *Ashbel Green* (1762-1843), A. B. 1783; professor of mathematics and natural philosophy, 1785-7; president of the college and founder of the seminary, 1812; author of polemical works, but of nothing philosophical except his edition of Witherspoon's *Works*, 1802. *Henry Kollock*, A. B. 1794; tutor *in absentia*, 1802; professor of theology, 1803; 'An Ornate and Vehement Orator' (S. D. Alexander, p. 275), published *Sermons*, Savannah, 1822. *Walter Minton* (1753-1796), a graduate of Edinburgh University; professor of mathematics at Princeton; published *Inaugural Oration on the Progress and Importance of the Mathematical Sciences*, Trenton, 1788; this says, p. 35: 'The mathematical sciences are not hurtful to religion and morality.'

CHAPTER V.—SAMUEL MILLER

A Brief Retrospect of the Eighteenth Century . . . containing a Sketch of the Revolutions and Improvements in Science, Arts, and Literature, During that Period. 2 vols., New York, 1803; 3 vol. ed., London, 1805, contains an index; *Letters from a Father to His Sons in College*, Philadelphia, 1852, pp. 159, 161; *Life of Dr. Samuel Miller*, by Samuel Miller, Jr., Philadelphia, 1864; *The Intellectual Life of Samuel Miller*, by John DeWitt, *Princeton Theological Review*, January, 1906; *Bibliography of the Works of Samuel Miller*, now being compiled by Miss Miller of Princeton.

CHAPTER VI.—FREDERICK BEASLEY

A Search of Truth in the Science of the Human Mind, Part I., Philadelphia, 1822, pp. vii. and 561. Beasley evidently drew his title from the *Recherche de la Vérité* of Malebranche.

Alexander (*Princeton College*, p. 298), says Beasley left in manuscript Part II. complete. No trace of this is to be found in either Princeton or Philadelphia, and it seems likely that it was never written. At the end of Part I., Beasley speaks of writing on a future occasion on the powers of abstraction, the moral faculties, etc., but his subsequent published writings include only the following pamphlets: *Review of Brown's Philosophy of the Human Mind*, Philadelphia, 1825; *A Vindication of the Argument, a Priori, in proof of the Being and Attributes of God, from the Objections of Dr. Waterland*, Philadelphia, 1825.

CHAPTER VII.—THE LESSER REALISTS

Charles Nisbet.

Dr. Thomas R. Boggs of Johns Hopkins Hospital has in his possession two volumes in MS., the one on page 395 says: *End of the I. Volume of Metaphysics, and V. of Nisbet's Lectures Delivered at Carlisle;* the other is entitled *Lectures on Logic, Vol. III., Delivered by the Reverend Charles Nisbet, D.D., P.D.C., and written by Felix H. Gilbert, A.D. 1793.* This volume begins with lecture 83, which is continued from Vol. II.; page 402 contains the note, *Lecture 128, the last, I hope and trust.* Cf. Miller, *Retrospect,* vol. 2, p. 382; *Memoir of Nisbet,* New York, 1840; Sprague, *Annals,* Vol. 3, p. 450; J. P. Wickersham, *A History of Education in Pennsylvania,* Lancaster, 1886, p. 395.

Thomas Law, *First Thoughts on Instinctive Impulses,* Philadelphia, 1810; *Second Thoughts on Instinctive Impulses,* Philadelphia, 1813; *Thoughts on the Moral System,* 1833; cf. G. W. Parke Custis, *Recollections,* pp. 21, 53, 56; A. C. Clark, *Thomas Law, a Biographical Sketch,* Washington, 1900; documents and correspondence in the possession of Mrs. Kirby Flower Smith, née Charlotte Rogers, great-granddaughter of Thomas Law.

James Ogilvie, cf. *Blackwood's Magazine,* Vol. 17, p. 198; *North American Review,* Vol. 3, p. 378; William Allen, *American Biographical Dictionary,* Boston, 1857.

INDEX

INDEX

587